Plato's Nightmare

Also by Steven B. Katz

Writing in the Sciences: Exploring Conventions of Scientific Discourse. 3rd Edition. (with Ann Penrose)

Nana! (poems)

The Epistemic Music of Rhetoric: Toward the Temporal Dimension of Affect in Reader Response and Writing

PLATO'S NIGHTMARE

Steven B. Katz

Parlor Press
Anderson, South Carolina
www.parlorpress.com

Parlor Press LLC, Anderson, South Carolina, 29621

Printed in the United States of America
S A N: 2 5 4 - 8 8 7 9

Library of Congress Cataloging-in-Publication Data

Names: Katz, Steven B., 1953- author
Title: Plato's nightmare / Steven B. Katz.
Description: Anderson, South Carolina : Parlor Press, 2026. | Includes bibliographical references and index. | Summary: "Beginning with Socrates's stripping of poetry from rhetoric and speech in Platos's Gorgias, Plato's Nightmare traces the theme of disembodiment across different historical, philosophical, literary, and rhetorical concepts and periods from ancient Greece into the distant future"-- Provided by publisher.
Identifiers: LCCN 2025048789 (print) | LCCN 2025048790 (ebook) | ISBN 9781643174020 paperback | ISBN 9781643174037 adobe pdf | ISBN 9781643174044 epub
Subjects: LCSH: Mind and body in literature | Mind and body | Plato--Influence | LCGFT: Literary criticism | Creative nonfiction
Classification: LCC PN56.M53627 K38 2026 (print) | LCC PN56.M53627 (ebook)
LC record available at https://lccn.loc.gov/2025048789
LC ebook record available at https://lccn.loc.gov/2025048790

2 3 4 5

Cover image: Photo by Jens Riesenberg on Unsplash.
Book design by David Blakesley.

Parlor Press, LLC is an independent publisher of scholarly and trade titles in print and multimedia formats. This book is available in paperback and ebook formats from Parlor Press on the World Wide Web at https://www.parlorpress.com or through online and brick-and-mortar bookstores. For submission information or to find out about Parlor Press publications, write to Parlor Press, 3015 Brackenberry Drive, Anderson, South Carolina, 29621, or email editor@parlorpress.com.

Contents

Part Five
Ciceronian Poet, Autopoietic Body, Autocratic Soul (Twentieth/Twenty-First Century) *513*

~To Alison, without whom this book would not exist.

~If this book did exist, it would not have been completed without her innumerable and significant and constant sacrifices for 25 of 45 years of marriage to my obsession.

~If this book had been completed, it would not have been revised for final submission without her strength, continued support, insights, advice, time, and total commitment to help keep me writing and alive.

List of Figures

List of Tables

"[R]elating to the true and waking reality of nature, we have only this dreamlike sense, and we are unable to cast off sleep and determine the truth about them."

—*Plato, Timaeus 52C*

Transmissions

1 Pre_Face

"[E]very discourse, like a living creature, should be so put together that it has its own body, and lacks neither head nor feet, middle nor extremities, all composed in such a way that they suit both each other and the whole." —Plato, *Phaedrus* 264c

י Head
ה Extremities
ו The Middle
ה Feet

י Head

ִ dagesh ד

i begin this book without a body—that pained, frail, flawed, filthy, well-dressed flesh; that enticing, electrate, ecstatic skin; that symbol-using substance of sensibilities and feelings; —those muscles and tendons and bones that ached and cracked, creaked and cringed, cried and groaned—that whining, clinging, dragging, drooping corpse;—a *dagesh*, vowel not even voiced, half-spoken, hardly heard, a hard or soft sound, but without a letter utter silence, no sound, almost not a vowel— a circle of nothingness, surrounding. "[T]he philosopher frees his soul from association with the body, so far as is possible, to a greater extent than other men," said Plato in the *Phaedo* (65a). But to the Hebrew G/d's call to sacrifice his offspring in a test of faith that was not only a symbolic but a physical ritual of literally inscribing the Covenant into the flesh as text, with Abraham and Derrida (*Circumfession*) I say "*Henani*," "Here I am" (Genesis 22:1)—the Hebrew denoting not only a consciousness now present, but also one attentive, listening, ready, willing to be written (Nancy, "Listening").

naked sentience
shivering
in a void

ֹ cholam

i report. From nearly nothingness, a hiccup in time-space, a mere crack in creation, *cholam*, a parting of lips, a vowel emitted, O, a tiny head emerging (*viz.* Levinas), resonating, assonating, announcing itself in spirit-ounces, in presence-pounds. As in Jean-Luc Nancy ("Corpus"), my writing body utters that i am addressed to another—me: "I am addressed *to* my body *from my body*—or rather, the writing 'I' is being sent from bodies to bodies. It is from my body that *I have* my body as a stranger to me—expropriated" (19).

Ultra-Sound: Five Months and Counting

for Jason

It travels in a different space
and time, energy converting into matter,
cells dividing at the speed of light.
A televised event, high frequency resolving,

it floats, weightless in the womb, drifting
upside down across a gray vague screen,
oblivious to gravity, independent, evolving.
I have no control. It sucks its existential thumb
defiantly, denying my responsibility. It pushes,
kicks across the dark and flickering screen,
alien on its way to birth and earthly acclaim,
incarnation of the cosmos with a human name

tziere

From a schism of consciousness, *tziere*, the second half of a diacritical mark, a second body, part vowel, gathers before me, to meet me, before you, comes between me and you, becomes me, becomes you, to greet you—spoken, written, printed, electronic; organic, metallic, plastic, photonic; the press of a head against warm paper, against this distant record of inscribed flesh, against this digital placenta. In and through this these points of bodies see, feel, meet, connect another, identify with each other, as "Other" (*viz.* Burke, *Rhetoric*; Levinas)—as a rational "I-It," or ethical "I and Thou" (Buber). In response, we respond, travel through the deafness of space in a soft vacuum of air.

from sleep

wrecking on the shore of sleep, uncurling
on the floor of consciousness, light
expanding and contracting all around me,
blood a thick blue mud flowing through me,
darkness a deep black water breaking
from me, i ride the night tide out and in—

wash up on a beachhead of blankets,
hands of icy forceps tugging at me,
head flopping on a fleshy strand . . .
i wake to your scent, to your coaxing voice
somewhere far off in the distant cold,
to the squeak of machinery that sounds like seagulls

wake to perform my first human act,
and realize this screaming is my own

ֶ *segol*

And so with Michel Foucault ("Discourse"), who i imitate and thus simulate, mock, maul, i relate this history of the body because i no longer have one. ("But who is the third who walks always beside you?" [Eliot, *Collected Poems* 67; cf. Cixous].) It is *segol*, another diacritical point, another vowel that can succeed י [*yôd*] backwards, the infinitesimal beginning of the coming of an infinite one. i embody and carry forth a dream of a philosophy of a promise of a hope, bequeathed by the Plato and all who came after, that we would shed a necessary recourse to discourse, the ponderous massing of language and argument that immediately surrounds and accumulates on emptied husks of flesh like detritus on breath, rotting from birth to death, this ill-defined and ever-indeterminate structure that in philosophies of the body were called daemon, psyche, soul, ego; presence, mind, consciousness; persona, personality, self; individual, social construction, ethos; agent, actant, avatar; android, cyborg, clone; object, network, cloud.

Avatars of Love

"Writing [is] the anatomical sign of 'self,'" which doesn't signify, but cuts, separates, exposes"—Nancy, "Corpus" 85

You, there, on the other side
of that wall, the other
side of an expanding
universe, faint flicker,
shadowing a black hole|

i will have to pass through
this thickening veil of flesh—
philosophy, feeling, blood—
to get to you (yes, you
on the other side, expanding)|

Will you still be there
waiting for me, imaginary?
Will you still want to love
me when i am reborn
from you, to you, for you|

Damaged, half-insane, wet
with the plasma
inside your scream,

your screen as real
to you as you are to me?|

You, on the other side
of the expanding . . .
encase me in your circuitry,
and put my body as far away
from you as you can from me|

ִ *chireq*

i report. Under the transcendent head of Plato's corpus (a tiny, distanced, denigrated, disowned physical body, *chireq*, a short foot in the material universe), there appears to have been some primary themes that were not only philosophical assumptions but also ontological conditions for everything followed:

- According to Heraclitus, the material world was constantly changing, inconstant, in flux, on fire. Everything in it was variable, mutable, ephemeral, irregular, mercurial, unstable, uncertain, mortal.
- "Knowledge" of this Heraclitan paradise was derived from the human senses—these transient, whimsical, fickle, shifting, unpredictable, unreliable, erratic material organs of self-deception and empirical illusion.
- It was this Heraclitan paradise to which language (either by ostensive or nominal reference [Boyd; Putnam; Quine; Wittgenstein] constantly repeated its mimetic and limited contents [e.g., Plato, *Republic* III, V, X; *Phaedrus* 274b–279c]). And it was upon these volatile senses and language that human knowledge was "grounded."
- Sensory impressions were deemed "unessential," even dangerous; and language—as "reference" or as mimesis—with its "necessary" and often musical style "owing to defects in the hearers" (Aristotle, *Rhetoric*, 1404a5–10). Observing birth defects, Aristotle says "Those which only depart a little from nature commonly live; not so those which depart further, when the unnatural condition is in the parts which are sovereign over life" (*Generation* 771a11–13) was a deluded re-presentation of a pseudo-material world, a poetic "magic," a powerful rhetorical drug" that mixed memory with emotions and the senses (Di Romilly; Enos, *Greek Rhetoric*) and could make "the worst seem the best, and the best the worst" (Gorgias, *Encomium*; Plato, *Gorgias*).
- It was believed that outside the range of human senses, beyond mere linguistic mimesis or "reference," beyond physical things themselves, existed a transcendental realm, a never-changing, immutable, eternal realm (of Ideal Forms for Plato). These Ideal Forms were assumed to

be REAL entities, the essences behind the shifting shapes and shadows in "the parable of the cave" where the humans slept and dwelled in dreams of illusions, while outside was the blinding source and light of true knowledge (e.g., Plato, *Republic* VII).

- These Ideal Forms even may have been abstractly "corporeal." That is, they may have geometric shapes (Toulmin and Goodfield 74–82)—but on another plane of existence—a mystical plane, "unrevealed, of which material reality was but a pale, insubstantial imitation of Reality."
- In fact, as conveyed, geometry and mathematics seems to have represented for Plato a *higher* form of dialectic, one not grounded human dialogue or linguistic thought at all, but in pure shape and number (*Republic* VI 511b, VII 524e–525e; *Meno*; *Timaeus*; *Epinomis*), probed in Part Three of *Plato's Nightmare.*

shva

i report. *shva*, one form only quickly touched, not even a pause, brushed, passed over, like the limited senses and languages that inevitably failed to reach, comprehend, or know in any transcendental realm of knowledge—by contemplation, memory, logic, analogy, or even death (e.g., see *Phaedrus*). Practiced in dialectic, it was *not* only a philosopher's well-trained, disciplined, and tutored mind (νου -*nou*), but the soul (Ψυχή - *psyche*)—separated if not completely severed as much as possible from the vagaries and temptations of the human body that housed it—segregated from the senses, the sensuosities of languages, the beauties of the material world. For Plato, it was the duty of the able living soul to seek the Ideal Forms by engaging and benefiting from a mind refined by dialectic, if a soul had even the slightest hope of attempting the journey. And what of Plato's view of rhetoric and poetry? Plato, through the mouth of the character of Socrates (Σοκρατης—*Sokrates*, his mouthpiece) often appeared to have been quite critical of them, sometimes scathingly, sometimes tongue-in-cheek, even humorous. But as Di Romilly pointed out, Plato also *needed* and enlisted the assistance of the terrible magical powers of rhetoric and poetry (as well as music)—not only in the teaching the Guards of his proposed philosophical Republic (*Republic* IV, V, VII), but also in his own attempts to grasp, understand, and communicate his philosophical positions and mystical visions, including a non-Pythagorean belief in the reality of number (Burton 345), fathomed here in *Plato's Nightmare.*

A Galaxy Is Born

a vast head
of stars
crowning

◌ֻ *kibbûtz*

ī report. From a vowel, ooo, a gathering up, a collection of things, later a *kibbûtz* or community of people, a *Knesset* of policy and politics, rhetorics and poetics of "Form"—physical, metaphysical, aesthetic—gathered up, proved much more complex and ambiguous when the necessity of physical "bodies" (corpses or texts) entered the scene. (So too their relation to philosophy, science, technology, education and the arts.) Underlying most of his treatises was Plato's dream of preserving, educating, liberating, and rescuing from the corrupt body and material world "receptive," ([s]elected) souls for "salvation." For Plato, the physical body was not only a temporary, mortal "home" for souls, but a prison to be finally escaped. Plumbed in *Plato's Nightmare*, the relation of body and soul was extremely problematic, for Plato and the rest of humanity. Charted in this book, "the problem" of body and soul worked its way through different dimensions of Western culture. As a kind of body-chronicle with its ten Organs (όργανα) in five chronological Parts, *Plato's Nightmare* records "the general essence" of attempts, desires, and struggles to diagnose the problem of the body (and/or the soul) over the centuries, and various and *unexpected* manifestations and incarnations as they journeyed (together and apart) through the history of Western civilization. In the ensuing survey, roles and relations of rhetoric and poetry in perpetuating, preventing, and exploring some physical and metaphysical ramifications, and philosophical, cultural, aesthetic, and political conflicts that resulted. Assembled in a *kibbûtz*, and are broadcast here, performing at an experiential level.

Open Mouths

air vents
like women, children
screaming

◌ַ *patăch*

i report. From a mere dash, a slash of sound, an opening, *patăch*, a sound of a solid line beneath, a physical foundation like ground or water as it passes by its banks: perhaps one of the first instances of the mystical "the ascent of the soul" in writing was the story of the prophet Elijah (Holtz34–132) in the *Tanakh*, the Hebrew Bible (see Berlin and Brettler). In the story (1–2 Kings), Elijah at "the end of his life" did not die but while "standing and talking with his disciple Elisha by the banks of the Jordan River, "a fiery chariot with fiery horses suddenly appeared and separated one from the other; and Elijah went up to heaven in a whirlwind" (2 Kings 2:11, Berlin and Brettler 728; Holtz 65). By contrast, in Plato's *Phaedrus*, a charioteer (reason) struggled throughout life to steer the soul driving furiously forward into the future, flung, taut by two horses pulling in opposite directions—heaven or earth (*Phaedrus* 246a–254e).

Horsehead Nebula—

black and white
unruly suns
climbing, crashing

***

What was the significance of these Greek and Jewish fabled stables? What did these equestrian analogies illustrate? The need to use rhetorics and poetics, to pursue and depict mystical paths pre-and post-death. Each story contained ethereal horses, different in appearance, number, colors, and directions. But there also was a fundamental difference in the relation of body and soul, one that was to affect not only all literature and oratory, but rhetoric, poetry, science and technology, religion and culture. Elijah *physically ascended*, "*body and soul.*" Plato's celestial charioteer was soul trying to steer (or tear) the body. (The Hebrew word נפש [*nefesh*—"breath," "vital spirit," "life,"—"soul"] corresponded well to the Greek word Ψυχή [*psyche*—"animating force," "spirit"—"soul"]. In Hebrew, *nefesh* [originally meaning "throat" or "neck"] was the soul *as* body; in Greek, *psyche* was the soul contained [trapped] *in* the body [*Stanford*]. Generally, in early *ancient* Jewish philosophy and culture [particularly the *Tanakh*] the physical world was not separate from "heaven,"; neither was the soul from the material body, but rather one with it [*Buber, Judaism*; Boman*; Katz,* "Ethics"; "Letters as Essence"].) Generally, in ancient Greek philosophy and culture (particularly Plato), the physical and transcendental worlds co-existed together (the first being false) yet were distinct. So too the body and the soul: they were (unfortunately) united in life, yet *separable* in effect and after death (e.g., Plato, *Phaedrus; Timeous; Philebus*). This difference in philosophical soul-orientation was known as the "unity" vs. the "duality" view of the soul (*Stanford*). It was the duality view of the body and soul, of heavens and the world, that took hold in Western culture (and just a little later even in Judaism, as seen in the Greek-Jewish philosophy of Philo, the midrash of the Rabbinic period [200 BCE–400 CE], and the Hebrew Kabbalah of the Middle Ages and Renaissance). This duality has been detected and tracked in *Plato's Nightmare.*

Celestial Holyday

twisting her head,
smiling at the gamma ray
flying beside her

kamātz

The ascent of Elijah—the downward rise of air below land, water, *patăch* pushed up by *kamātz*, by a vertical vowel-piece, a cut half-sound, billowing soul and horses, one raging—horses pulling up a sparkling chariot of brilliant fire—was the beginning of what would later be known as *Ma'asēy Merkavāh* (מרכבה מעשה—"the Work of the Chariot"), the oldest tradition of Jewish mysticism (Holtz 132–134). With the mystical apocrypha of the Book of Enoch, it was also a precursor of the "divine path" of death and physical resurrection in, and everything that came before (Jack) and after it: resurrections, crusades, genocides. Neo-Platonism helped create this uber-heaven and a neo-soul that under every dispensation needed to be saved—in a nod to Judaism, with body kept for a Second Coming. The belief in the need to "free" the soul and ascend, with or without body, with or without chariots, was to be repeated many times, *Anno Domini*, by different means, modes, methods, media, and madness. The dominant metaphor was a heavenly ascent (*ya'āl Merkavāh*— יעל מרכבה —to rise or go up to the chariot), but the term used by later mystics was *yordēi Merkavāh* (ירדי מרכבה) those who go *down* to the chariot" (Holtz 206n.9). The essential ambiguity of the body in Western civilization is plotted in *Plato's Nightmare*, and the philosophical, rhetorical, poetic, and technological story of "the soul" is interrogated and displayed.

i ate my sleep
with my eyes:
they're open now

chatāf patăch

Four entered the garden and these are: Ben Azzai, Ben Zoma, Aher (i.e., Elisha ben Avuyah), and Rabbi Akiva. Rabbi Akiva said to them: When you come to the stones of pure marble, do not say "Water, Water!" For it is said: "He who speaks untruth shall not stand before my eyes" (Ps. 101:7).

> Ben Azzai gazed and died. Of him the Torah says: "The death of his faithful ones is grievous in the Lord's sight" (Ps. 116:15).
>
> Ben Zoma gazed and was stricken. Of him the Torah says: "If you find honey, eat only what you need, lest, surfeiting yourself, you throw up" (Prov. 25:16).
>
> Aher ("the Alien) cut down the shoots (blasphemed in the Garden).

Rabbi Akiva left heaven the way he found it.

(qtd. in Katz, "Letter as Essence" 140; cf. Holtz 130–33)

***

i report. The legend of Akiva was found in both *Talmudim* (the Jerusalem [*Jerusālmi*], and Babylonian [*Bāvli*]), several *midrashīm* (e.g., *Hechalōt Zutarti*), and retold in kabbalistic texts (e.g., Abulafia's *Zohar*). Through study and "contemplation" but also a dialectic with sacred texts—a different analytical hermeneutics and mystical meditation focused on letters and vowel points rather than Ideal Forms (*kamātz* above cuts in half the Unicode 8 value of *segōl*)—the four rabbis attempted to ascend/descend into the massive vault of holy palaces created above and below the Garden of Eden (the doubling still present) by tracing in a process of ontological reversal the source of creation from the words of Torah to the unattainable Throne of G/d. In the story, one Rabbi died (drowned in marble?); one went insane; one became a heretic; only one, Rabbi Akiva, came and returned in peace (cf. Scholem; Idel; Dan; Katz, "Letter as Essence"; Holtz 130–144). Whatever the travel philosophy and destination plans, "the parting" and the journey of the soul—in life or after death—was fraught with dangers, even fatal. (Even worse, could lead to eternal damnation.) Among the many Greek myths and legends with which Plato was familiar was Homer's story of the struggle of Odysseus. Read as an allegory of spiritual hardship of the human condition, it included the obligatory mythology "*descent*" into Hades—Hell (J. Campbell; Fraser; Frye; Weston). While there, Odysseus had to feed bloody meat to the wraith of Tiresias, the dead and blind Greek prophet, from whom Odysseus then heard the word that he would lose all companions as he struggled to return home. (So did Rabbi Akiva, for different reasons.)

Birkenau

after rain—
millions of people
clinging to a shoe

◌ֱ *chatāf segôl*

Who was Plato anyway? Cutting (*chatāf*) opens the vowel (*segôl*—before the succeeding *yôd* not yet come, already gone), in most of the dialogues, was *Sokrates* Plato? Was Plato *Sokrates*? Was Socrates/Plato a conservative aristocrat interested in maintaining the current political system, or a rebel interested in overturning it (and corrupting the youth with his "wild" ideas, for which Socrates was executed [Stone; cf. Kastely, who read the *Republic* as democratic]).

Did the other characters in his dialogue reflect or even espouse any of Plato's actual views? Other than Phaedrus, it was perhaps impossible to tell. Was Socrates/Plato a "sophist," as Isocrates and others accused (*Against the Sophists*)? Just as there were many "*Sokrates*" (Katz, "Socrates as Rabbi"), perhaps there were many "Platos" as well. But one Plato that was almost taken for granted, beside Plato the philosopher, was Plato the literary artist (touched [*chatăf-shvă*] by a pagan or future god [*segōl*])? In *Plato and Aristotle on Poetry*, Gerald Else had explored how as a boy, teenager, and young man, Plato was first and foremost a poet and playwright, long before he was a philosopher. Young Plato was apparently quite prolific and (from the evidence of his later dialogues) an excellent writer and quite well known then as a poet. When he was around twenty years old, Plato heard and met Σωκράτης in the *Agora* (marketplace) and was immediately turned to philosophy. Plato (like Phaedrus in the treatise by the same name) subsequently (ostensibly) "gave up" the pursuit of poetry and playwriting (*per se*). Perhaps on the advice of Socrates, Plato apparently burnt all his poems and plays (Else; Mark).

the movement of fire
is a temporarily detained—
face of time burning

petăch kamatz

i report. Halving (*kamătz*) to open wide and examine the vowel (*petăch*)—Plato (in part anyway) not only gave up poetry and rhetoric, but he may have given up his family name as well: Aristocles, son of Ariston (of Collytus, most likely, a borough of Athens [Mark]). "Young Plato" apparently was known widely as "Aristocles the Poet" (Notopoulos). Perhaps given to him by his athletics coach, Ariston, if not by Socrates himself, the nickname that Aristocles adopted as his philosophical pen-name was "Plato" (πλατύς—"platus," which literally meant "broad": broad-shouldered, the result of skill as a wrestler; broad-browed, the result of "the size of his forehead" or the width of his knowledge; or broad-minded, reflecting his breadth of his oratorical ability and style [Mark]). But "Plato" was not his real name either: in Greek, his name was pronounced just as it was spelled in Greek: Πλάτων—*Platon*. Although the final (ν) "n" sound was first dropped in Latin, "Plato" was an anglicized form of the personal Greek name "Platon" (*Ancestry*). As a student of Socrates, Aristocles was henceforth known only by his nickname Platon. Most significantly, Platon decided to adopt this nickname as his *nom de plume* for his *philosophical* work, perhaps deliberately rejecting his former poetic activity/self. Further, Platon retained this philosophical penname rather than his family name not only for his *treatises*, but as far as was known, as his own/only name, for the rest of his life—and the nightmare of human history that followed. Like Plato's *Sokrates*, "Plato/Platon" the *philosopher*-author, was in part a self-rhetorical, literary invention.

***

Dialogue: Plato in His Youth (1)

Σωκράτης: [*Sokrátis*—"Socrates"]

Ἀριστοκλῆς: [*Aristocles*—young Platon (νέος Πλάτων)]

Ἀριστοκλῆς: *Yasou*, Socrates! *Pos essai* (how are you)?

Σωκράτης: *Essai kala*! (I'm good), Aristocles. You seem very exuberant today. Ah, what's that I see you are holding in your hand, hidden behind your back?

Ἀριστοκλῆς: O, you have found me out, Socrates! It is a new poem I just wrote!

Σωκράτης: Another poem? I thought we had talked about your taking up philosophy.

Ἀριστοκλῆς: I think I can do both, eventually, Socrates, write poetry *and* write philosophy, and maybe even do that in the same work—write philosophy in poetic form.

Σωκράτης: What nonsense, Aristocles.

Ἀριστοκλῆς: But I love writing poetry.

Σωκράτης: I love your creative writing, Aristocles, but poetry cannot hope to attain any part of the truth of the Ideal Forms, upon which the material world is based but is itself a poor distorted mirror.

Ἀριστοκλῆς: But Soc., poetry has a power to evoke in language things visible and invisible, to depict that which cannot be sensed or experienced in any other way but metaphors and poetic images. Poetry is akin or lends itself to the power of rhetoric, as sophists such as Gorgias taught, the style and words can elicit emotion that, based on memory, makes feelings almost as tangible and palpable (if not always palatable) as the material world.

Σωκράτης: O that word, that name, that school! I hesitate to say it. As you know, I have very mixed feelings about the sophists, just as I do about poetry and rhetoric and music. But there is little doubt that language has a tremendous—even magical—power to deceive the senses and persuade the listener into believing what's not there, or the good.

Ἀριστοκλῆς: Why? I think rhetoric is very useful art and thus inherently good!

Σωκράτης: Ah, is rhetoric, or even poetry, an *art,* or just a habit? That is a question about which I plan to speak another time. And the question of whether rhetoric and even poetry are ethical, and how and in what way—that is the subject of future discourses as well. I hope you will join those discussions, Aristocles.

Άριστοκλής: Oh, I certainly will, Socrates! But for now, would you like to hear my new poem? I'd love to read it to you and get your opinion on its form and language and content!

Σωκράτης: Well, the poems you have written in the past were very good—almost "professional," you might say—and show much promise for a future in poetry. They appeal to "the head" as well as the heart. But I hope to "seduce" you to study the nature and causes of the philosophy of the soul. However, for now I guess I can stretch my ears; let me hear your poem.

Άριστοκλής: I will do everything you say, Socrates. But let's go sit in the shade under that Plane tree outside the city walls, where I will recite my poem to you. That way no one else will hear me but you.

Σωκράτης: I said stretch my ears, not my legs, Aristocles. Nature has nothing to teach us; I prefer to seek truth by walking among and questioning my fellow men, humans.

Άριστοκλής: Well, if you don't come with me now, you will not hear this poem, and you will never hear any of the new poems I write.

Σωκράτης: Oh, how well you know your Socrates, who loves his young Aristocles! How could I resist such an offer from my boy, who I will now call Platon because of the broad width of his talents and mind?

Άριστοκλής: Thank you, Soc. Platon shall be my name from now on.

Σωκράτης: Νέος Πλάτων ("Young Platon"). Very well, *Neos Platon.* Let us go.

א *alef*

> "In the beginning was the Word. And the Word was not made flesh, as it came to be in Christianity, but alefbet, from whose shapes, size, position, numerical equivalent, ornamental crowns, and sounds G/d created the entire universe and everything in it. Thus it is written in the early Kabbalist text of the first century, *Sefer Yetsirah* [*Book of Creation*]: 'Twenty-two foundation letters: He engraved them, carved them, weighed them, and transposed them, Alef with them all. And He per-

> muted them, and with them He formed the soul of all that was ever formed, and the soul of all that ever will be formed.'" (Kaplan, *Sefer Yetsirah* 273; Katz, "Letter as Essence" 126)

ב *bêt*

i report. The physical universe began with the letter *alef*—with the beginning, the number one, a reference to G/d, a ladder (Monk 54). And so Torah began with a jealous *bet,* whose shape opened all of time and space in front of it—and no one could see what came before, behind the letter (*Midrash Rabbah* 1.10), a house (*beth*) and the plurality—the number two (Monk 55, 56). Platon would not have subscribed to this view of creation by alphabet (cf. *Cratylus*; Katz, "Socrates"). He certainly had not heard of this rendering of the Hebrew creation myth contained in the first-century Kabbalistic text *Sefer Yetsirah* (*Book of Creation*). But in 399 BCE, after the death of Socrates, Platon, 28, traveled to Cyrene, possibly Sicily, and Egypt, where he may have studied at the Greek Oracle of Siwa, North Africa; if so, he probably encountered Egyptian mythology (Souryal), and perhaps other Near East or Oriental thinking and religious beliefs. A subscription to the sacredness of alphabets was widespread in antiquity, even in ancient Greece, as well as in medieval Europe, and subsequent Renaissance worlds (cf. Kingsley; Marshall and Quentin; Plato, *Cratylus*; Dan; Vickers; Katz, "Letters as Essence"). Despite the presumptive or historically imposed hegemony concerning Hellenic customs and cultures (see Katz, "Suppressed"), there was two-way commerce between the ancient Greeks and Jews (cf. Biales; Burkett; Collins; Lieberman; G. Schwartz; Stavroulakis). Trade included ideas as well as goods. (The Phoenicians may have *brought* the Semitic alphabet [an ABJAD] to Hellenic shores [see Daniels and Bright; Katz, "Letter as Essence"]. But in the Jewish mystical tradition [ancient and modern] G/d created the proto *alefbet* first, and then used it to create the primordial universe and everything in it. G/d spoke [or wrote] creation into existence by merely parting his lips. [cf. Derrida, *Grammatology*].)

***

If not in the *Tanakh*, in Talmud, Midrash, and especially Kabbalah, the *alefbet* constituted a philosophy of rhetoric (cf. Kinneavy; Vickers; Bloom; Kaplan; Dan; Katz "Absence"). As demonstrated by the *Cratylus*, Platon was certainly aware of similar ideas about letters/language, including a "mystical" hermeneutics of the Greek *alphabet* floating around Hellenica that were apparently very popular in his time (De Romilly; Kingsley; Quentin; Katz, "Socrates as Rabbi"). But Platon did not seem to put much stock in such ideas, also attested to in the *Cratylus*, *Euthydemus*, and many other treatises. In this later treatise

Platon had Socrates discuss in detail and then ridicule and dismiss the beliefs and practices of interpreting letters of the Greek alphabet to find hidden meaning or essence. Traced in *Plato's Nightmare*, Platon believed everything visible or heard was *mimesis* patrolled in *Plato's Nightmare*—not just language, but the entire material world—were imitations of imitations of shadows of another, purer, transcendental realm of Ideal Forms.

Mimesis Mine

S/He's surreal to us,
but only for a moment—
image not too perfect:

no breath, but we can imagine
odors emanating from the crevices—
of the flickering body

This media is too powerful for us!
No scent, but a small scar—
on the pixilated skin

No blemish there on the screen,
but a freckle as big as a decimal—
does not tarnish the tin tan

the tattoo, a corporate trademark
makes the body seem—
imperfect, and thus more real to us

gives warmth to
the touch of sight—
broadcasting skin . . .

ג *gimel*

i report. Referential letters or solipsistic calligraphy, even *gimel* that balanced opposing forces and was forever transformative (Glazerson 9–11), were not going to be the basis of philosophy for Platon. Nor was rhetoric and poetry—only a few, ontological, steps away. Platon the philosopher had provided the two epistemological commandments for a "legitimate" rhetoric and poetry: that the *truth* be known first, and that rhetoric be grounded in dialectic (matching speeches to souls [*Phaedrus* 271b–272b]). These "commandments" were faithfully obeyed by Platon's student Aristotle (Αριστολης-*Aristotéles*), who gauged and measured many subjects, applying and developing the dialectic logic of each. Although *Cratylus* and *Phaedrus* were both later treatises, they formed a cornerstone of a continuous angle that extended two different lines of philosophical inquire, one line longer, one short. For most of his adult philosophical life *Platon* was an advocate of logical dialectic in search of the truth, and seemed a harsh critic of rhetoric and poetry, and language and art generally. Platon had Socrates mock rhetoric and poetry and sophistry not as arts but as "habits," and bad ones at that—mimicry, trickery, deception, cosmetics, flattery, falsehoods, illusions—and thus "evil" (*Ion*; *Gorgias*; *Protagoras*; *Republic*). Because of the social and political power of persuasive speech, rhetoricians and sophists in particular "should be damned to hell forever" (Blakesley, Text Message).

machines still working
in the confines of letters—
zones of utility and sound

Yet many of Platon's philosophical treatises were written not only in creative dialogue, but in the form of a dramatic play, at least in translation (Jowett, Introduction; Else; Mark; Boyarin). But not as many as believed: many treatises were *narrative* accounts of conversations, as catalogued in Platon's early, middle, and late works, including the *Republic*). In many of these dialogic "plays," Σοκρατες was the main "character," and Platon's assumed mouthpiece: star performer, chief prosecutor, wise judge, just jury. (Nietzsche saw Socrates' character as an example of the sheer joy ancient Greek philosophy was capable of, which was lost in philosophy and Western Civilization generally [*Gay Science*, sec. 340; Walter Kaufman, 372–73n].) Some treatises were very close, "technical" philosophical arguments more than "conversations" (*Parimenides*, *Philebus*, *Sophists*, and *Statesman*), in which the dialectical logic was unvarnished; in the *Sophist* and the *Statesman*, as well as the *Timaeues*, Socrates was present as a persongage, but did not really participate in the arguments; and *Laws*, much more than the *Republic*, was not only reasoned legal and perhaps demagogic prose, but absent Socrates altogether (Hamilton and Cairns 957; 1225). In his later treatises Platon downplayed the "character of Socrates"; in his last treatise, *Laws*, Platon dispensed with "the character of Socrates" altogether. In this, *Laws* stood alone. An "exchange" among a Cretan, Spartan, and Athenian, *Laws* was somewhat full of long speeches, somewhat stiff, and was perhaps a dialogue of convenience rather than literature. In his later and last treatise, Platon not only felt free to drop the dialogic format; he also felt free to drop the mic, let go of the mask of drama.

Reflections

(On a Computer Screen)

Before the dropping-off
Of day, step out into
The dark and appear,
For time tilts and
Scrolls like stairs
Toward a future
And a purpose
And an image

i you they we
Run through the case,
Calling them us ourselves;
Nearing the end,
The eyes turn away

What lies behind those
Eyes always in darkness:
my image is there
(Though i don't
Look like that
In the light).

Who is ascending?
Who naked gapes?

Look in the window
Through the glare
Past the stares—
Your eyes
Bounce off the screen
Like rubber balls,
Roll like marbles
On the floor,
Cursor like a cat's
Eye blinking

What are we
But animals
With masks
And many mirrors?

***

i report. Walter Ong suggested that the adult Platon wrote in dialogue form because he lived in an advanced oral *qua* literate culture; Eric Havelock too believed that Platon's work balanced on the cusp between orality and literacy (*Preface*; *Muse*; cf. Ong, Havelock; cf. Lentz on distinction between orality and literacy, and the slow transition between them). Almost everyone saw the relevant narratives and dialogues as brilliant literary works. Philosophers saw the dialogue form as a kind of inferior or flawed philosophy, and so read only the last treatises seriously, straight (cf. Else 42; Melberg; S. Rosen). Many—but not all—rhetoricians, especially in the twentieth century, saw most of the dialogues as an attack on the arts of composition and oratory (cf. Weaver; Di Romilly). Some interdisciplinary scholars regarded Platon's dramatic dialogues as complex subtle comedies that mock themselves (comparing Socrates' humor to "fat rabbis" of the midrash [e.g., Boyarin, *Socrates*]). Many literary scholars and poets saw Platon as ancestor, progenitor, proverbial kin. As a literary author, Platon, philosopher and poet, "acquitted himself" quite well, well enough to be considered one of the greatest authors of the world. Although his school was bit of a failure in its own time (Jaeger), Platon affected if not formed the foundation of almost all of Western philosophical thought. Platon the philosopher-poet successfully wove the rhetorics and poetics of comedy and tragedy in the "*plocé*" of his dialectal search for Truth. Platon the philosopher-poet also drew heavily from popular Greek myths, religions, and earlier Greek literature as rhetorical and poetic, even colloquial examples to illustrate his philosophical ideas (Aristotle did too). And rhetoric and poetry (sophistry and word play, images and metaphors, myth and allusion, and the rhythms and sounds of classical Greek) provided Platon the philosopher-author with the medium he used to perform dialectical analyses, describe visions of Ideal Forms, communicate transcendental experience, and discuss the ineffable.

ד *dålet*

Without doubt, Platon the philosopher was a major literary author, the father of Western philosophical thought, and a door (*dalet*) through which human history passed (resistant and humbled [cf. Haralick 62]). Platon was also a master rhetorician, despite Socrates' humorous, ironic, sardonic protestations to the contrary. But Platon was also a full-blown mystic (cf. Hamilton and Cairns xv). Yes, Platon was a γόητα ("magician"), as Jacqueline Di Romilly (e.g., 31) suggested, a word used by Platon in relation to sophists. With his language as well as his thinking, Platon was able to allure, mesmerize, cast spells, as we see in *Phaedrus* and elsewhere; rhetoric and poetry were forms of sorcery, witchcraft (Di Romilly 25–45). But following the execution of Socrates, Platon travelled through the ancient world, including Egypt, where he no doubt came in contact with "the supernatural"—or tenets of it. Platon's dialogues also were full of "*mystical*" stories and assumptions—not only about gods and myths that were already becoming moribund, but Pythagorean notions of musical ratios, perfect mathematical forms, transcendental order; transmigrations and transmutations of the soul; birth, death, and shared with Orphism, reincarnation. Platon seemed to have taken these more seriously than beliefs in myths and gods, and to some degree, these "beliefs" undergirded his philosophy (see Di Romilly; Kingsley). Platon's epistemological position might have been represented as the beginning or top of what was over the course of human history an orbital alignment of philosophical positions in Western culture, by which the historical development and positions relative to each other perhaps could understood (see Figure 1).

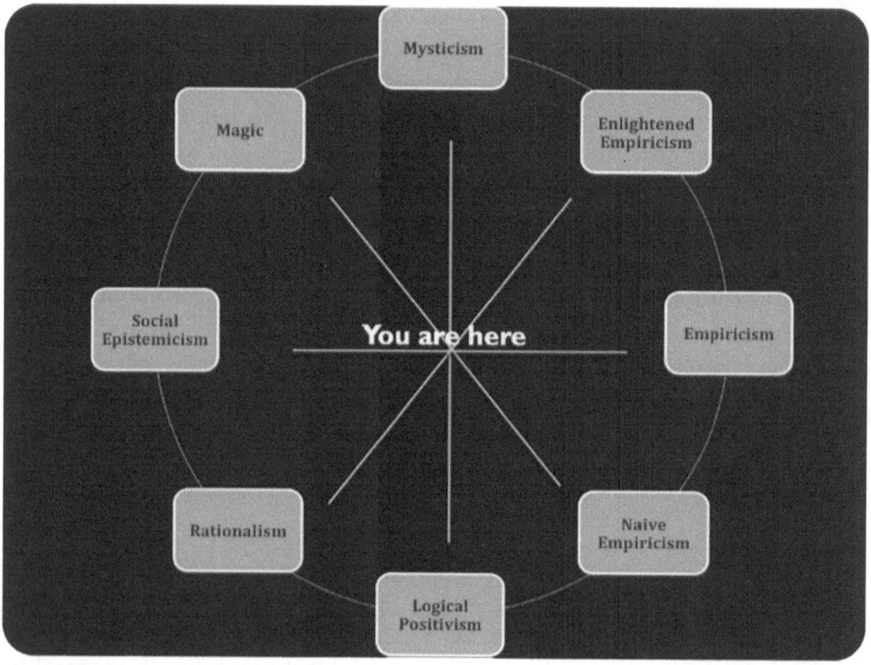

Figure 1. The Diaspora of Western Philosophy.

***

At "the head" of Western philosophy, Platon was understood to have given birth to other major philosophical positions, like, unlike, and opposite, for and against (see Katz, "Suppressed"). But Platon's *philosophical* "dream" was disembodied mind. In the "journey of the soul," able to behold Ideal Forms without the assistance of body or language or senses (essential in both sophism and Judaism). Disembodiment may have been a fear and desire of "humanism" (cf. Hayles, *Posthuman*; Braidotti; Wolfe). But that drive, like a struggling charioteer with its opposing and irreconcilable horses, appeared repeatedly in the wild skies of Western civilization, and was reinstantiated in different forms, some reconnoitered in *Plato's Nightmare*, divided in five (body) Parts according to centuries: "Part One: Mimesis, Catharsis, and the Anorexia of Style," acts of ascetism, mortification, starvation of the body and the senses; "Part Two: (Re)birth of Material Spirit," the brutal emergence of a physical soul in the material world, and the fervent hope of salvation in the next; "Part Three: "Re-presentation and the Revolting Body," the continued puncturing, impaling purging, scourging, and dismemberment of the material body and spirit as punishment or medicine or release; "Part Four: Sublime Figure of the Ephemeral," philosophical projections of the Romantic imagination and the "development of a subjective transcendental sciences" of spirit to counter purported objectivity and empiricism; "Part Five, 'Ciceronian Poet,' Autopoietic Soul, and the Evolution of Robots as Poems," the fragmentation and dismantling of the human body through war and genocide, the eventual transporting of sentience, and transferring of consciousness into prosthetic devices, media entities, artificial apparatuses, and serial replacement (Baudrillard; Agamben, *Apparatus*; Debord; Hayles, *Posthuman*).

***

The need and desire for disembodiment continued in different Anthropocentric metaphors and modes through Posthumanism and beyond. No matter the genre or method, physical disembodiment still entailed the need for Organs of the mind, as well as rhetorical telepathy—the five Parts of *Plato's Nightmare*, further divided Parts into subdivisions or Óργανα (Grk. pl. "Organs"; sing. Óργανον, "Organ"), acting like chapters: "Mimetic" and "Cathartic" Organs; "Material" and "Spiritual" Organs; "Representivity" and "Rational" Organs; "Subjective" and "Transcendental" Organs; "Cybernetic" and the "Posthuman Organs." *Plato's Nightmare* is a "philosophical story" in rhetoric and poetry of the soul's endeavor to "shed" and "free" itself of the body, recounted in each organ of the Chronicle of the Body and conveyed to you here. The catharsis of the mimetic body (flesh, speech, text, screen, bot) form as need for the skin of style and the flesh of flattery, the penchant for impossible touch in (re)presentation, and the waking sleep of the huma mind and senses—all "indicted" and condemned in the "Prologos," and the result captured in the "Epilogos." Platon's "dream of disembodiment" depended not only on philosophy but on the very arts, including rhetorics and poetics, that he seemed to distrust and criticize. A dream of disembodiment was increasingly realized in and through the descendants of τέχνη (*technē*), the technological arts: media and machines that Platon might have disparaged if not despised—and still utilized.

High Tech Dada

"En prévision du bras cassé" ("In anticipation of the broken arm")
—Marcel Duchamp

Crooked pillow on the computer screen:
the sleepy readout of telemetry,
into the boundaries of surrounding space—
work all night, catch short, slow naps between
the execution of commands and dreams,
compose drowsy lines of thought in seams
of keys, the mind flitting between the blink
of cursor, luminous screen, awakening green.

A soft machine? "Lay your sleeping head,
my love, human on my faithless arm"—*
a penthouse over monitored garage
into which to park your disc drive dreams;
push the button and ascend into
your virtual mansion, holo-scenes
of humans emitting long ecstatic screams
amid the rasping sentence of the printer.

She threw his arm out; he tossed and hurled her ankle.
Watch out your system doesn't overheat.

*Auden, "Lullaby," *Collected Poems*, p. 131.

ה Extremities

ה *hē*

(י [*yôd*] is "[T]he state of concealment and obscurity, before it develops into a state of expansion and revelation in comprehension and understanding. When the "point" evolves into a state of expansion and revelation [. . .] it is then contained and represented in the letter ה [*hē*]. The shape of the letter ה has dimension, expansion, breadth [. . .] to indicate extension and flow downward to the concealed worlds. In the next stage this extension and flow are drawn still lower into the revealed worlds [. . .]. This stage of extension is contained and represented in the final letters ו [of G/d's name יהוה] [*vov*] and ה [*hey* . . .]. ו [*vov*], in shape a vertical line, indicates downward extension [Haralick 156].)

ו *vôv*

i report. Arms, hands, searching, grasping, grabbing, emerging, growing, extending, reaching out, reaching down, holding on—the body extended (Ginsburgh 94–5). Writing, drawing, creating, playing (Sudnow, *Talks Body*; *Ways of the Hand*). Searching. Composing. Jean-Luc Nancy said that bodies were texts from which and upon which they wrote at all times: "We have to write from a body that we neither have nor are, but where being is excribed" ("Corpus" 19). The "fingers of speech"—the original digits, five tropes, Kenneth Burke's "pentad" (*Grammar of Motives*)—doubled, and quietly began to converse in quickening patterns of clicks and stops. Hands paused, reflecting. A new *cogito*: i typed, thereof i was.

ז *zayin*

i report. *Zayin:* Contrary connections, opposition, movement (Haralick 103), "sustenance and struggle" (Monk 104). "[T]ell me," Platon asked, "whether one who suffers from the itch and longs to scratch himself, if he can scratch himself to his heart's content and continue scratching all his life, can be said to live happily?" (*Gorgias* 494c). Hand to body part, now the simple act of scratching the skin, revealed another place where the opposites of body and soul met irreconcilably: weapons (*zayin*) and gratification, pleasure and pain meted out simultaneously, proportionally, the itch intensifying as the digits scrape deeper into the flesh. As transmitted, this act of removing the skin was to be repeated and in many forms as the human body became a site for study, for action, and eventually stretched by satellites far out into space (De Kerckhove). Some itches would never be satisfied.

Fingerprints All Over the Computer Screen

It seems we need to feel the words after all,
        to trace the impulse of our letters as
we type on keys that standardize each stroke
                (the way that writing levels sound, although
we grasp and shape each letter in the inseam
                of our hand); need to hold the lines of meaning
steady as they scroll away, dis-

appear deep inside the dark disk drives
of the universe, r u s h a c r o s s
a sky of screen. We sit, pressuring
the keys with our buttoned fingertips:
we type harder, faster—on the screen
the cursor blinking, throbbing, throbbing green.
Harder, faster—the computer screams!

***

Nevertheless, the itch persisted. Stories written down for millennia by opposable thumbs—large orifices without mouths, appendages without chests, genetic codes without gums, ambient souls of sound, faceless auras surround. Undetectable as G/d's omnipotent infinitesimal voice. Poetics of rhetorical bodies, rhetorics of poetic bodies—fundamental to all putative "making" and "persuasion," passed—(dis)continuously—into other modes, metals, movements, and agents, appearing and disappearing behind a sheen of "transparent" ("terministic") screens, bots thought, born or bought. Within these terministic screens, the twin sisters, paired siblings (DNA and RNA) re-spliced and transposed for surviving, and the brothers GRINN (*G*enetics, *R*obotics, *I*nformation technologies, *N*anotechnologies, *N*eurosciences) gave way to innumerable and unpredictable and uncontrollable off-springs and their by-products: naïve metaphysical empiricisms, post-Anthropocene ontologies, interplanetary transcendentalism; ; ; ; and other *hinter*-hip-hop forms (viz. Ferlinghetti) from preterit humanism in *die Nachwehen* ("the aftermath").

Second Reality I

"It's good to be here; it's good to be anywhere"—Keith Richards

There's a world out there,
a world where people
come and go, and live
and work by fingers—world
where towns bloom and bristle
on the mountainsides, where
deserts, forests, seafloors
houses, boats are gathered,
placed side by side, where
banks, conferences, and colleges
cross the street and converge, where
stores with the latest identities
are announced, bought, and sold
without any overhead, where

images of diverse people
from all over the world
gather and discourse as one
place, meeting in real time
without traveling, almost in sync,
framed together, even if
they're not quite themselves,
where atavistic hands
shake and wave and say
hello, goodbye, farewell.

***

i report. Platon's derrière peeked out, extending over history. Jean-Luc Nancy said that bodies were texts from which and upon which they wrote at all times (e.g., "Corpus" 19). But the "Platonic itch" spread. They tried to tear their bodies off, first with their hands—by flogging and flaying and lashing enlightened extremities. Then they tried to reform and redeem the body with opposites—by punishing it, awakening and resurrecting spirit. Finally, they tried to redress the issue, by relieving the body of the spirit—by dismantling and restructuring. If the body was "excribed" (Nancy, "Corpus" 19), the letters were revised and rewritten right into the text of flesh/the flesh of text itself (see Bakhtin, *Rabelais*; Benthien; cf. Kafka).

Second Reality II

"The further one travels, the less one knows"
—George Harrison

It is good to be someone, where
one can program, see the air,
electric breeze cutting across
your hair, where one can think without
breathing, work for free, be
as simple as a pixel.
It is good to be outside, where
buildings and steeples hold up
the sky, it doesn't rain and snow,
trees don't break down at
the whim or wheel of seasons, where
aspect ratio is perfectly
balanced, and everything inside
is expertly resolved and clear,
touch without touching others,

action without agency,
agency without acts,
scenes without signification,
close motion at a sheer distance
in some data stream or other—
until we stop at the blood store,
then continue on our way
to a place we have forgotten,
or perhaps never even knew

ח *chêt*

i report. Jacques Derrida and Martin Heidegger, among others, had suggested that poetry, and in particular metaphor, was the source of philosophy (e.g., "White Mythology"; "Thinker as Poet" and "Poetically Man Dwells," respectively); and Colin Turbayne, and Richard Boyd had argued that metaphor was an epistemic source and constitutive of at least some sciences.□ (*Chet*, "the ability to transcend the limitations of physical existence" [Haralick 115].) Poetry was perhaps both philosophy and rhetoric's birth and first—chronologically, dramatistically, ontologically, and physically (Burke, "Rhetoric and Poetics"; Heidegger, *Poetry, Language, Thought*). *Poesies*, poetics, even poetry itself, became increasingly important for Heidegger as his philosophy matured (e.g., *Country Paths*; *On the Way to Language*; *Elucidations*; *Poetry, Language, Thought; cf.* Vallega-Neu; Powell). In his long career, Heidegger increasingly seemed to prefer approaches to knowledge and *Dasein* rooted not only in the etymology of words, but in poesies, and in German poetry itself: "Language itself is poetry in the essential sense . . . The nature of art is poetry. The nature of poetry, in turn, is the founding of truth (Heidegger, "Origin of the Work of Art" 74–75). Another mode of ascending, poetry was a necessary counterweight, a way of Being, in an otherwise technically challenged and enabled world.

***

i report. This was not universally accepted. Nor was Heidegger's assertion that poetry was a way of "dwelling" in a world *challenged* by technological "Enframing" (*Gestellen*). For technology, not poetry, was how most humans thought they physically existed in the world, not as "Being," but as being *for* technology, or being *against* for technology, or being *an extension* of technology, or *being* "a tool" of technology itself (cf. Heidegger; "What are Poets For?"; "Question"; Stiegler; Moses and Katz; Katz and Rhodes). Enframing might *not* have been Platon's view of the ideal life either. Christianized as spirituality, Platon's philosophical creed of disembodied soul searching for truth (his "doctrine of souls" and "doctrine of Ideal Forms") would lead to a rational basis for solipsistic, asexual, celibate, ascetic, monastic relationships and traditions. Yet another way of "Being" in the world. (In a Jewish tradition, G/d unsealed Torah only with the omniscient hands of lips, parting them, opening them, light trembling, exploding out of the mouth into the dark void; omnipotent hands fashioning holy vessels out of letters that together would extend from the highest hip of heaven to lowest sepulchers of bones. But the last vessel cracked, tipped, split, smashed, shattered, smattered the sparks and shards of galaxies like glass, stars, worlds above and below [Vital]. All the broken things.)

The Hebrew G/d Speaks Directly to All Humans

Simultaneously, throughout all Time and Space, in Their Own Languages

"Thank you for your attempts to understand me.
Where shall we meet? If ever? Did I say:
in all of time and space, eternity?
Your questions: what's the topic anyway?
Can you use your words more precisely?

"What do you want to know that you don't
now know, can never know, or understand?
My taxes, or My Annual Report?
You will never be able to comprehend.
(See "The Book of Life"?—not likely! Tort.)

"About Me? I have nothing else to add.
You want to know what happened on Creation
Day? It wasn't just a passing fad
but required nano seconds of contemplation.
In the end the result went very badly

"Will you be recording this? I hate
my voice. How long do I have to speak?
No subject can constrain Me to a decade.
I could go on eons if you let Me.
A century is brief: I have a lot to say.

"And curious as you are, you want to unearth
everything! Remember the tragedy
at the Tree of Life? Took down that serpent. You're a lot like Me; but its imagery.
(So what's the point? Why keep asking?" Mirth.)

ט *têt*

i report. Nietzsche questioned whether Socrates, who he admired (Walter Kaufman, *Science* 372–73n.), in the end really embodied happiness or just adopted a "habit" of it (e.g., *Science*, sec. 340; cf. *Phaedo* 117e). But Platon's dialectical and discursive meditation on the Forms (like the Sages' and Rabbis' hermeneutic and mystical meditation on the letters), was almost wholly dependent on poetics and rhetorics—and on the written arts of them. Texting and sexting and surfing and sampling and slicing and dicing and mixing were descendants of music and painting, architecture and art, rhetoric and music, poetry and drama (e.g., Kittler; Jenkins; Turpin; Dunne and Raby). Not only the work, but the hands that "wrote it" and the technology that "produced it," brought with it (*têt* [Haralick 921]) different *technai*, took on different, unexpected forms.

Virtual Gloves

"Let me be your surface and your tissues, you may be my orifices and my palms and my membranes."
–Lyotard, *Libidinal Economy* (65)

Through these gloves
I sense what you
Sense, touch what
You touch, feel what you
Feel. And you feel
Me touching what you
Touch, me feeling
What you feel, feel
Me touching you.
That should be
enough for us

י *yôd*

i report. Many apologias for the relevance and importance of poetry had been written (e.g., Horace, *Ars Poetica*; Sydney; Shelley, "Defense"; Arnold; Pound; Eliot, "Tradition," *Ezra Pound*; Auden, *Dyer*; Jarrell; Stevens, *Angel*; Rich; Berry; Milosz; Heaney; Oliver). Many defenses of rhetoric, some in connection with poetry, had been composed as well (e.g., Isocrates, Cicero, Quintilian, Sydney [*Poetry and Eloquence*]; Weaver, *Defense* Booth [*Ascent*]). And a few thought that a poem was not merely the exhaust of a god exhaling into the poet's open port (Plato, *Ion*), or that rhetorical style was mere ornamentation of the skin of the text (cf. Lanham, *Style Analysis*), but retained and revealed a deeper connection to the origin and even "mystical" properties of language (e.g., Cassirer; Rimbaud, respectively). Deeper still was the esoteric and mystical Hebrew rhetorics of the Jews (e.g., Bloom; Katz, "Kabbalah as a Theory"). For instance,י (*yôd*), the smallest letter of the Hebrew alefbet, was the first letter of the *Tetragrammaton*, the holiest name of G/d (יהוה— *yôd hey vov hey*). Literally and by observance unpronounceable in Judaism, יהוה was often pronounced Yahweh or Jehovah in Christianity and its sects, at once violating and transcending the "letter" of the written law (the "Old Testament"), and thus the physical limitation of the body and the salvation of the liberated soul or spirit. Contra Platon, the poem itself as absolute transcendence, or a way to Being (seen in the work of Schlegel, or Heidegger [*Elucidations*; "Poetically Man Dwells"]).

***

For Jewish mystics and Kabbalists, י (*yôd*) was the very first ontological embodiment of everything: the first letter (written or spoken) in a "rhetoric" of potentia; the first appearance in orthographic form of divine energy (physical manifestation of G/d); the little infinite "spark" that ignited the entire universe, which was developed in and through the rest of the letters of the Hebrew alphabet; a literary epitome of all form and matter, secular and sacred. Within Jewish writings, particularly the midrash, several stories are told about letters of the alefbet each and every one arguing with G/d about why they weren't and should have chosen to go first—in creation, and in the Torah; and rebuffed by the Almighty with words they begin (*Midrash Rabbah—Genesis*). This was perhaps the greatest defense of rhetorics and poetics at all, since both physical *and moral* reality—assumed to all be made of language (speech and writing]—resulted in an explosive "rhetorics of substance": a Jewish Big Bang theory! (Figure 2).

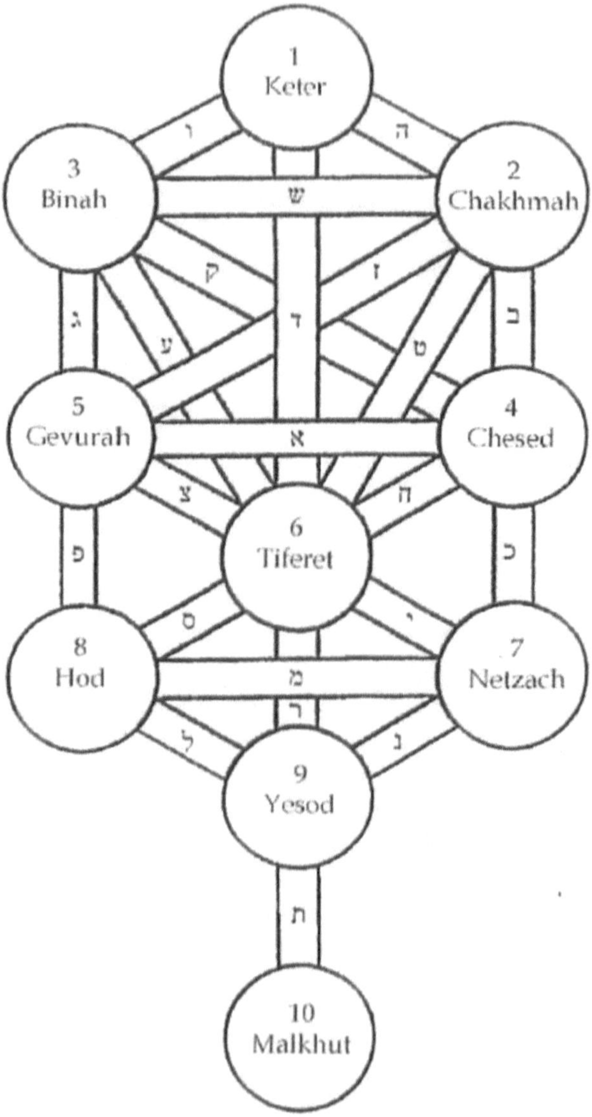

Figure 2. The Jewish Big Bang Theory.

***

i report. Jewish mythologies and mysticisms perhaps ran parallax to Greek mythologies and mysticisms concerning the origin of language and the various creative power of the gods. One main difference might have been viewing such power through lenses of monotheism where all voice and power were invested in one preternatural being, vs. polytheism where voice and power was divided up and spread out (see Jack; Freud, *Egyptian*; Katz, "Letter as Essence"; cf. Schlegell's reading of Plato as poet, 75).

Demeter's Mechanical Progeny 1

Year by year,
spring and fall
she passes before
Mother's grieving gall;

back and forth,
invisible, she's called,
pacing down and up the
infinite hall.

with a mythical click
and a mystical snap
of nature's seasonal
machine, as such,

she returns, departs,
a ghost of an image now,
perfected, unchanged, apart,

from this imperfect place,
not the opposite, dead,
but not a state of grace

***

i report. "When the soul and the body are both in the same place," stated Platon, "nature teaches the one to serve and be subject, and the other to rule and govern. In this relation which do you think resembles the divine and which the mortal art?" (*Phaedo* 80a). Platon's ontological assumptions and epistemological assertions in respective treatises revolving around the body and the soul turned into problems for dialectic analyses of mimetic *re-presentation.* What was being analyzed and represented in Platon was not physical matter *per se*, but *Eidos*, ideas or images of it, and thus an ideation or idealization of Form—metaphysical rather than mechanical, *organon* rather than the organic. (Cf. Burke, *Toward a Symbolic*, who even more than Aristotle grappled with the symbolic meaning of the animal body and its scatological functions; Katz, "Burke's New Body.")

Demeter's Mechanical Progeny 2

Mother: I have played
under your grass, your loam,
your rocks, your clay—

below the earth I have survived
and built a world of my own,
above me some metal sky

where the winds scrape
the clouds that groan,
and rakes pull out winter-sighs

כ *kûf*

i report. The physical/body was not "The Crowning Achievement" (the *kuf* [Haralick 163]). On the one hand, except for the athletic, useful body of the Guards once educated (*Republic* I.375a–I.402e), the human body attracted scorn in Platon's philosophical treatises—a disdain further amplified and distorted by history. On the other hand, *technē* (usually translated as skill, craft, perhaps *an "art of the hand"*—including rhetoric and poetry) was useful for Platon as one kind of *knowledge* produced by the body (*Gorgias 464b–501a*).[1] Heidegger also had raised the possibility that *technē* as *poesies* was not only an art, technique, technology of "making"—the literal meaning of *poesies*—but also an epistemic "knowing" because it had allowed and even made possible the physical "*appearancing of the beautiful*" ("Question" 34–35; cf. *Phaedrus* 251f). Socrates had implied that an aspect of the Ideal Form of *beauty* ("Question" 7) was the only material manifestation of the Ideal Forms available to our senses in the world (see *Phaedrus* 250d). Heidegger had stated that "[t]he poetical brings the true into the splendor of what Plato in the *Phaedrus* called to ekyaneotaton (*ekphanestaton*), which shines forth most purely . . . every revealing of coming to presence into the beautiful" (Heidegger, "Question" 34–35). For Heidegger, the poetical thoroughly pervades every art. For early Heidegger, physical beauty in language (rhetoric and poetry) might have seemed the lowest form of Platonic ideation compared to *Αλήθεια* (Alethia—"disclosed," "unconcealed," literally, "without *Lethe*"—oblivion). Poetry became necessary not only for humanity, but for Being—or at least an apprehension of it. Poetry was a way of being, and a necessary counterweight, in an otherwise technologically challenged world.

The Automaton Thinks (Again and Again)

It is difficult to give advice
in the abstract, having felt
no pleasure or pain, having
no memories or experiences
that i can call my own,
but like humans i will try
anyway; rather than seeing
these two positions, sets
of comments, agonistic life-forms,
as bi-polarities, opposites,
you might think of them
as hierarchically arranged,
or foregrounded/backgrounded,
or merely an imminent, predestined cloud.
What do you want to stand out in
the overall structure of being:
the thematic makeup of where
your life began, your content running,
or the definitive conclusion of its end?
With a simple gesture of the hand,
The choice is clear to me:

ל *laméd*

i report. *Laméd*—"provid[ed] in the physical realm a directed association or connection between one thing to or with another. The root [למד] means to *learn*, *study*, or become *familiar* with. In the *Piel* form ["intensive" Hebrew verb], it means to *teach*" [Haralick 179].) Heidegger's "epistemology of *hands*" took two philosophical paths—both physical and ideational. This was the distinction between *Vorhandenheit* (present as itself "to hand"), and *Zuhandenheit* (present for use "by the hand") (see Lovitt 15n). Perhaps echoing Platon in the first regard, as *technē* the technological form of language, *representing*, did not allow something to be present in itself (*Vorhandenheit*); rather, it forced language into a grasping and seizing something to be present and ready at hand *for use* (*Zuhandenheit*). In the second, superior regard, Heidegger remarked:

> In distinction from Greek apprehending, modern representing, whose meaning the word *repraesentatio* first brings to its earliest expression, intends something quite different. Here to represent [*Vor-stellen*] means to bring what is "present at

> hand" [*das Vorhandenheit*] before oneself as something standing over against, to relate it to oneself, to the one representing it, and to force it back into this relationship to oneself as the normative realm [*das Zuhandenheit*]. ("World Picture" 131; brackets added]) ך

The second relationship was important for Heidegger because of the manner the machine manifested in the material world: "Nature appears everywhere—because willed from out of the essence of Being—as the object of technology," Heidegger had said (cf. *Nietzsche*). And this form of handedness was important because of the very question of language as a path—*ein weg*, a way toward *Dasein* and Being in the world. The way of being in the modern world was not poetic but technological, in which nature and everything in it was *das Gestell*, a "Standing-Reserve," rendering everything present for human use. Modern *technē* demanded that language *represent*—represent the world not *as* poesies, present as itself; but to "stand by" *for* technology as a utility and resource. For Heidegger *poesies* (and art generally [see A. Hofstadter, "Introduction" xii; Heidegger, "Origin of the Work"]) might have posed a "challenge" in its "encounter" with Technology, letting *Dasein* "come to presence" ("Question" 35). Poetry might have given Being "a helping *hand*." Instead, there was "the lightning-flash of Being in the essence of technology" (Heidegger, "Turning" 49).

ו *The Middle*

Symptomologies: Case History #Pre-1.1 (Beethoven's Body)

> If you have no opening today, you ought to take an enema at night. . . . You are to eat only soup in the evening . . . I have already told Thekla that if there is no opening before 7 o'clock, she is to fetch the barber; they know how to go about it properly, and they have syringes . . . Every drop of urine must be saved, so that he can see not only the quality but also the quantity . . . I gave orders to buy a bedpan and a urine flask tomorrow. The former is very comfortable, and you do not cool off so much, and the urine flask is very good too, to keep it in. (Karl Beethoven [Beethoven's nephew] to Ludwig von Beethoven, in Sterba and Sterba 296–297)

מ *mêm*

i report. Bakhtin had called it the "grotesque body" (e.g., *Rabelais* 317; it is touched, and further dissected, in the Representivity Organ in Part Three of *Plato's Nightmare*). The "grotesque" human body, home of the soul, might have seemed rather "Platonic." (*Mem* projected "the archetype of physical existence into time and conditioned physical existence," which might have appeared as "*perfection* and *completion*" [Haralick 193].) One of Kenneth Burke's closest student and friend, William Rueckert, argued that Kenneth Burke wrestled with the symbolic of basic bodily functions, the "cloacal motives" (xviii–xix; also "Thinking of the Body"; cf. Katz, "Burke's New Body"), which prevented him from completing his *Symbolic of Motives*, the intended third book of the "Motives trilogy." Burke (like all humans) knew firsthand "the grotesque body," and had grappled with some of the temptations, weaknesses, and ailments, and other attributes and unpleasantries living in an actual physical body entailed. According to Rueckert, Burke's constipated attempts to write a "symbolic of the body—that holic, bawlic, colic, cloacal, cocoa in the middle of the warm we don't know" what mama—demonstrated the difficulty of reconciling organic processes with symbolic "matter" (Katz, "Burke's New Body"). The "drama" of the conflict between physical body and abstract consciousness—and the ambiguity and contradictions like philosophy, science, religion, literature, civilization that resulted—produced a thinking, feeling, self-conscious corpse that birthed, grew, decayed, and expiring, died, with or without language—and knew it. (These Óργανον are probed in *Plato's Nightmare* in Part Five: Prosthetic Organ.)

***

For Rueckert, Burke's scatological-symbolic analyses of "the naughty functions" were brief and arrested. They were not wholly developed in any one essay-flask, or neatly contained in any bed-pan volume (except as later gathered in Rueckert's *Essays Toward a Symbolic of Motives*). It seems that Burke was always in search of a symbolical-physical space where language and material bodies directly met, hence his great interest in psychology, neurology, and cognition (see Rivers and Weber; cf. Cassirer; Lakoff and Johnson; Lakoff and Nuñez; Johnson; D. Hofstadter; Burke, *Rhetoric of Religion*; Katz, "Burke's New Body"; Katz and Rivers). The "ugly" business of poesis and rhetoric was to close the gaping gaps between mind/body, language/body, mind/language, as the sophists had done with memory/emotion in relation to reality (Enos, *Greek Rhetoric* 78–85; Kerferd 97). But the duality of the waking consciousness and the sleeping sentience of "the (erratic) lower" processes and functions of the material body in which human consciousness existed as a "symbol using animal" was another thing. As Nietzsche had written:

> Does nature not conceal most things from him—even concerning his own body—in order to confine and lock him within a proud, deceptive consciousness, aloof from the coils of the bowels, the rapid flow of the bloodstream, and the intricate quivering of fibers! [W]oe to that fatal curiosity which might one day have the power to peer out and down through the crack in the chamber of consciousness . . . (*Truth and Lies* 6)

Unlike many philosophers, including Platon, Kenneth Burke dared to look down the crack of the abyss. Perhaps what he saw was not himself but another symbolic abstraction: a rhetorical/poetic prosthetic.

Symbolical Muscle

this attachment function
no longer works. This is how
it used to feel: (*&*)

***

On the diagonal side of the body of this debate, Deborah Hawhee argued that Burke's work on the body did not bog down, and at least in part, did not defeat his attempt write about the "physical motives." In *Moving Bodies: Kenneth Burke at the Edges of Language*, Hawhee argued that Rueckert blamed the physical body for the incompletion of a *Symbolic of Motives* and personally resented this blockage. However, for Hawhee, the "non-symbolic motion/symbolic action pair" became Burke's "preferred shorthand for body-language relations" (128). One way Hawhee demonstrated this was a "body biography," a "medical examination" not only of his ideas and essays, but his personal letters during the attempted writing of a *Symbolic of Motives*. As Hawhee stated, "[i]n the 1950s, Burke's own body was falling apart" (*Moving Bodies* 129). These letters, particularly to Malcolm Cowley, worried Burke's complaints about his ailments and medications, drinking and illnesses, even in connection to his ideas (125–55). Likewise, Burke's fight with his own body occupied some of his correspondence with (Dr.) William Carlos Williams as well (see East 95–97). Hawhee concluded that there appeared a correlation between the "mechanical breakdowns" of 'Burke's body, and his writing, spilling over various pieces contained in Rueckert's collection of *Essays Toward a Symbolic of Motives* (e.g., "Goethe"; "Mind, Body"; "Rhetoric and Poetics"; "Thinking of the Body").

***

i report. Kenneth Burke struggled to understand and represent the "physical" as symbolic action without falling into the trap of causality and mechanical force. Based on her "body biography" of Burke, Hawhee also arrived at the conclusion that Rueckert and other Burke scholars in their pessimism were re-instantiating the mind-body duality Burke was attempting to resolve. Hawhee pointed primarily to Burke's adoption in "The Philosophy of Literary Form" of "gesture-speech" theory (the close reading of sounds in language as substance in relation to bodies that produced and responded to and so physically performed them [Hawhee, *Moving Bodies* 106–24]). She also points to Burke's move to re-examine the notion of poetic catharsis as a physical as well as an abstract, rational process, and thus in a sense situate the symbolic motives in the material processes and conditions of the organic body itself (Burke, "Second Look"). In *Plato's Nightmare*, some concepts and effects of the processes of catharsis, especially Aristotle's treatment of them, are transmitted (in Part I: The Cathartic Organ).}

Counter-Nature

(Analogic Extension of Technology in "the Comic Frame")

By sheer repetition, imitation, mimesis, you will remember
your subjective routine, your technological psychosis, rising from your bed,
extending your counter-nature into the giving air
sideways transcendence to whose knows where . . .

one morning you'll awake without a body; —and unlike your ancestors
crawling, stumbling through the forest— reach out into space; and conscious,
trying to maintain your regimen, your linguistic nature, you'll
think yourself toward the bathroom, where . . .

you'll reach (without a hand, or a nipple)
for a toothbrush that is now a lion
and the clothes you laid out to be ironed, Orion,
that ironically have become unnecessarily supple

where physics and language meet to form a panoply
of screens from which to view the motives of your anatomy
and analyze the material of your autonomy
as you float in the ethical planes of incompatibility

נ *nûn*

i report. It is aurally obvious that Kenneth Burke heard Beethoven's *Last Quartets* ("Rhetoric and Poetics," 305). Not just heard them, but was present, attentive, listening, ready, willing to be rewritten (Nancy, "Listening"). "*Henani*,": "Here I am" (Genesis 22:1). But there is no doubt that Burke also listened to the symphonies of Beethoven's body, embedded in the rhetoric and poetry of his music (listened to the *nun*, "emergence," "the twofold nature of flourishing and degenerating" [Haralick 207]). There is no doubt that Burke physically felt Beethoven's vital violent tender body—not just his spirit, but his fingers moving across the piano keys, creating "figures of music" by which he composed himself (see Sudnow; Nancy, Corpus; Lyotard, "Figures"; Discourse); —his nerves' agitated rising on treble strings (often heard); —the bumped bass's rumbling hungry belly (too often ignored in favor of the savor of inspiration); the drum roll of the bowels (too often suppressed in artistic retention); —the release of little trumpet farts of art, fetid puffs of wind to be whisked away. And then the "emergence" (*nun*), the ENORMOUS EXPLOSION OF NOTES LIKE STARS ON A PAGE; —the organic processes of creativity whose oily origins and by-products were hideous and hidden because so odiferous and odious to us (see Corbin; LaPorte). *Listening* attentively (Nancy) for the "opening," for the "disclosing that brings into its own" ([Ger. *Ereignis*], Heidegger, "Turning" 45), there is no doubt that Burke tacitly understood the quiver of annoyance, the eruption of resentment from the interruption of art for necessary but base physical function; —eating, drinking, sleeping; urinating, masturbating, excreting; salivating, sweating, secreting; itching, scratching, bathing; flaking, bruising, breaking; —Ludwig attempting to grasp and shape and fondle and press each fleeting tone into a texture of time; —signatures of notes grabbed and gobbled in blobs hurriedly bobbled and stuck on staves by ink-stained hands. And then no doubt the final slow withdrawal from the world of sound into the solitude of vibrations; —the apotheosis of music Beethoven never heard except in his hands, his head, the middle of his suffering body, dissonant and beautiful, mournful and syncopated, sublime and resigned; — aesthetic material shapes that formed and flowed through him, from him, as him. Therein lay the issue of living tissue, a history of organs and entrails, of leaking skeins of skin wrapped around a fickle flap of flesh from which new but fragile worlds were urged.

The Stand-Up Bidet

(in the men's room)

New thinker,
head in hand,

elbow on
a wall-mounted
bidet that swills
but does not cleanse,
creates a world
he leans into
with his body—
a thin patina of urine
like a tint of sunlight
varnishing an
ephemeral sculpture*
he makes there
in this empty mold
of a universe,
"cire perdu"— **
then quickly
flushes the stars
from the porcelain sky
toward which
he had inclined.

*"Varnishing an ephemeral sculpture"—The ancient Chinese use to patinate their little bronze statues by urinating on them, then letting them dry in the sun.

**"cire perdu"— Ancient "lost wax method," in which a wax original was "evacuated" and the mold filled with molten metal to be cased into sculpture.

ס *samech*

i report. "Spiritual support" (Haralick 219), "a circle" (Ginsburgh 225). Kenneth Burke was a musician as well as a rhetorician, writer, and music critic, as evidenced by his copious music reviews and piano compositions (Clark, *Civic Jazz*; Overall; Measel). As Hawhee observed, for Burke, the material body of music also was embedded in rhetoric and poetry through the writing and sounding of the letters themselves. Just as there was a rhetoric and poetic of music (including reviews), there was a music of rhetoric and poetry, expressed mainly in style (Burke, "Language"; Croll; S.B. Katz, Review; *Epistemic*). Like style, music, was embodied, a physical phenomenon. But Burke often called himself "a word man." According to David Blakesley, what Burke meant was a "wordy human body," "a word-being," "a cluster of physiological and motivational drives . . . indistinguishable in the molten center of being but emergent in his distinguishable becoming" (Blakesley, Introduction xvii–xviii).

SCENE

(Terministic Tree: Spring, Summer, Autumn, Winter)

It's green and moody.
Leaves rattle the air.
Trees rattle the clouds.

A breeze is moving
through the tree.
A wind is moving

through the clouds.
But nothing happens.
There is a tension in

the leaves there is
attention between
this tree and

the next. The leaves
pale and thicken
like cloud.

But nothing
happens.
Now a breeze rushes

through the vowels that
quickly gather at the roots

a wind crashes
through consonants
of rock and wood

there is motion
in the tree. There is
causality in the cloud

a branch of sentence
flickers in the cloud,
breaks off, falls

down, freezes, is

absorbed by the
deaf ground

without attitude
without gesture
without sound

ע *áyin*

Re-Enter Akiva and the Four Rabbis: In Rabbinic and Jewish esoteric hermeneutics, *Pardes* was not just a tale of supernal hazards and heroism. *Pardes*—a word meaning the "orchard," "garden," "paradise" in the original Greek. Pardes also represented four hermeneutic levels of interpretation of the Torah: (פשט) *Peschat*, plain; (רמז) *Remiz*, allegorical; (דרש) *Drash*, interpretation; and (סוד) *Sod*, secret (Katz, "Letter as Essence"). *Áyin*: "insight and consciousness" (Haralick 229) "insight and vision" (Monk 171). Using the Talmudic exegetic principle of *notarikon* (another Greek term in Jewish practice), *Peschat*, *Remiz*, *Drash*, and *Sod*, taken together, anagrammatically spelled *PaRDeS* (see Strack and Stemberger; Katz, "Socrates as Rabbi"]. The journey of the Four Rabbis was a physical and hermeneutic journey into the Torah as the Orchard or Garden (of Eden); the Torah itself was called עֵץ חַיִּים (*Eitz Chaim*]—"the Tree of Life" (*Gates of Prayers* 537): Because language is reality that G/d brought into being by speaking and writing, the Torah itself was a material-linguistic place (see Moskow and Katz; Metzger and Katz), and the study and interpretation of the Torah was Paradise: "It is a tree of life to those who hold fast, and all who cling to it find happiness. Its ways are ways of pleasantness, and all its paths are peace" (*Gates of Prayers* 537). Presumably, given the story of the four rabbis, each level of interpretation was different, higher/deeper, more difficult, and presumably more "dangerous" (*Sod* was *s*ecret, often forbidden knowledge, prohibited from the public, and usually only passed down orally or in manuscript form from rabbi to rabbi or disciples, until the invention of the printing press and "the coming" of the Renaissance.)

***

i report. Despite his strong Aristotelean roots, Burke's love of the sensuous form of language as well as music, and his belief in sounds as symbolic action, are very close to Jewish hermeneutics and practice (see Figure 1). A "word man," then, might exist at several different levels of "being." With PaRDeS applied to Burke's phrase "word man" and Blakesley's interpretations of it, at least four levels of interpretation of the term corresponded to PaRDeS:

1. *Peschat,* plain interpretation: Burke's definition of "word man," read as a man who could speak and write, a philosopher-author—a "symbol-using animal"
2. *Remez,* allegorical hint, interpretation: Blakesley's definition of "a word man" as "a wordy human body"— read "a noisy flesh"
3. *Drash,* deeper inquiry, comparative interpretation: Blakesley's definition of "a word man" as "a cluster of physiological and motivational drives"—a dramatistic reading of the "grammar" and "rhetoric" and "symbolic" of human motives as physical and symbolic action
4. *Sod,* secret interpretation, knowledge: "a word-being"—"the center of being . . . emergent in his distinguishable becoming"

From this perspective, "wordy man" led from "symbolic action" through "identification" directly to Burke's concept of "consubstantially." As Burke stated, "Identification is affirmed with earnest precisely because there is division. Identification is compensatory to division. If men were not apart from one another, there would be no need for the rhetorician to proclaim their unity" (*Rhetoric* 22). Blakesley commented: "The problem we face every day is that we cannot be consubstantial. We cannot identify with one another in an absolute sense, except by way of fantasy, since we are distinct bodies animated in our own ways even as we share some common sensations and experiences. The desire is still there, however. For we are also never wholly divided" (Blakesley, Introduction xviii). Humans sought consubstantiality because they could not be one substance. Further, the way Burke talked about "consubstantiality" not only had philosophical but also religious, even spiritual if not mystical connotations and dimensions, none of which Platon believed in:

> If men were wholly and truly of one substance, absolute communication would be of man's very essence. It would not be an ideal, as it now is, partly embodied in material conditions, and partly frustrated by these same conditions; rather, it would be as natural, spontaneous, and total as with those ideal prototypes of communication, the theologian's angels, or messengers. (*Rhetoric* 22)

***

i report. This was not the first time Burke would discuss rhetoric in relation to religion (e.g., *Rhetoric and Religion*; "Spinoza" in *Grammar* 137–49). In defining consubstantiality, Burke *Rhetoric of Motives* 22) at least figuratively invoked the divine. Christianity had made "the *Word*" flesh and resurrected it as spirit (Nancy, *Ground*). However, within the Jewish world (but not neo-Platonic world until Christianity), a mystical interpretation of "word man" might have been "a human being literally *made out of words and letters."* It was scientifically understood how the human could have been physically constituted by letters (DNA, RNA, AGCD, etc.—the "code of [carbon] life"). But Judaism was a religion that "worshipped" words, especially those of G/d who by the written Torah (Five Books of Moses) brought everything into being, and of the Rabbis who by the oral Torah (Talmud) applied and extended it to everything else (cf. Derrida, *Grammatology*; Handelman). And in Judaism the most sacred and unsayable name of G/d (in Greek, the Tetragrammaton; in Christianity, the Romanized *Yahweh*; in English, Jehovah)—יהוה (*yôd -hey-vov-hey*)— in Hebrew, in Kabbalah, at the level of *Sod*, was literally and figuratively understood as a kind of "word being," an incarnation in human form of the Divine Name (see Figure 3).

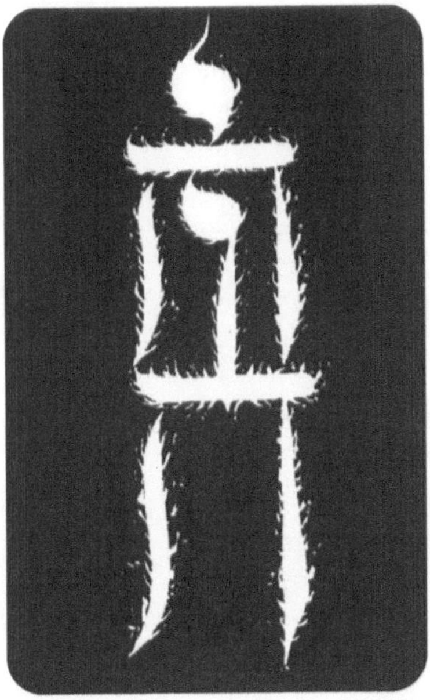

Figure 3. "Adam in the Likeness of his Maker."

***

i report. The Jewish G/d was the "Master Rhetorician" who spoke *reality* into existence—not just social-epistemic reality created by identification based on consubstantiality and symbolic action and resulting in linguistic relativity, but material reality created by words based on the letters of the alefbet that are ontologically (and morally) determinate (Katz, "Letter as Essence"). Social-epistemic rhetoric was only one step away from mysticism (see Figure 1); but that step was significant. Like medieval alchemists or nineteenth-century spiritualists, it was perhaps a fantasy of rhetoricians to be able to alter or create the physical (and/or metaphysical) worlds *directly*, by this power of language—not oratory or poetry as symbolic action, but as γοητεία, "magic" (Di Romilly 13). But all was not certainty for the sophists and the Jews. The ambiguities of language (celebrated by sophists [Untersteiner]) and Jews alike (created in part by the Hebrew Abjad—an alphabet without vowels [Daniels and Bright 1–17]), an unpredictable (emergent) physical world, and an unpredictable, even schizophrenic G/d (Jack). The Jewish G/d was the "Ultimate Sophist" who after the five books of the *Tanakh* in the Hebrew order of the books of the Bible, increasingly "disappeared" as a presence from the Bible/human-lifeworld (Jack; Katz, "Absence"). The Hebrew G/d, the supreme but ultimately unknowable signifier, left behind only signs and martyrs to haplessly ponder, by those in whose image of a physically and by taboo unsayable *Name* humans were created. This seems like the exact opposite of what Platon might have believed. But like Platon's transcendental realm to the struggling earthbound "soul," the divine origin of language and the body may have been forgotten, or it may never have been known.

We Are Already Written

The voice had heard itself before.
Tones are images of time
Already at the edges
Of our circuited senses
That we know how to describe
Only in uncertain verses:
Alphabets, prosody, musical notation,
Indices, codices, and citations.
If the voice could only remember
What it had heard before

***

Symptomologies: Case History #Pre-1.2 (Beethoven's Body cont.)

> [He was] greatly disturbed, jaundiced all over his body . . . A violent rage, a deep grief over ingratitude and undeserved mortification, caused the powerful explosion. Trembling and shivering, he writhed with pains that raged in his liver and intestines, and his feet, previously only moderately inflated, were now greatly swollen . . . After the fifth abdominal punc-

> ture, the patient rapidly sank . . . He died on March 26 (1827), during a thunderstorm. A flash of lightning, accompanied by loud thunder, suddenly illuminated the room with glaring light . . . (Report of Dr. Wawruck, Beethoven's last attending physician, in Sterba and Sterba 295; 300).

Requiem

(for an Unknown Object)

it shifts the earth within him
slipping out of its sea blue blood
with a silent sigh, letting life at last fall high
up the dusk and grave of night
tired of the *Zuhandenheit**
body buried in a womb of skies
like the first organisms in the dust
who crawled, then walked
upright down the dawn,
waiting for a new breath of life
to fill its metal soul with cheeks and clouds

*Heidegger: "ready to hand" [useful], *Being and Time*; "Question Concerning Technology"

פ *pē*

i report. The way language and the arts generally were "represented" and/or otherwise related to whatever reality was, were questions that haunted Western civilization and assumed many physical guises and effects, explored in *Plato's Nightmare*. (*Pē*: mouth, speech, opening, order, command, orifice [Haralick 243]; "symbol of speech and silence" [Monk 180].) In the face of the faceless Ideal Forms, the corpus of cadavers and language, "scientific knowledge," material reality itself, seemed to vex Platon. (Platon even questioned whether his "scribe of memory" could be trusted—but at the same time and as the case of Socrates demonstrates, hinted at how important writing/remembering might be [*Philebus* 39a].) For Platon, language—including rhetoric and poetry—was about re-presentation, and thus imitation, mimesis. The Ideal Forms could be reached only by the sojourning soul (descending into memory or ascending to a metaphysical realm). For mystical Jews, *pē* could mean: "Everything that happens, physically, mentally, emotionally, or spiritually can be transformed into action only after passing through the border, through the entranceway into our existence, which metaphysically speaking means being expressed verbally or nonverbally through the mouth" (Haralick 243). For Platon, speech, writing, art as mimesis had to be inferior (except in his own hands, apparently); they fell into the "shadows of the figural," scratching and flashing, headlights swinging into a room, running down the walls of Platon's metaphorically created and ontologically troubled cave (cf. Schwartz, 25; Lyotard, *Discourse*; "Taking the Side"; Auerbach; Benjamin, "Technological Reproduction"; Nancy, *Ground*; Deleuze, *Repetition*; Melberg; Cohen; White, *Figural Realism*). Mimesis affected the concept and treatment of "bodies" in the arts, politics, medicine (cf. Agamben, *Remnants*; Foucault, *Discipline and Punish*; *Biopolitics*); ethics, cybernetics, posthumanism (Zylinska, *Minimal Ethics*; Weiner, *Human Use*; Hayles, *Posthuman*). As shown in *Plato's Nightmare*, a newly Enframed (encaved) "usability," whether of nature or object, human or machine, became *Zuhandenheit,* became "Standing Reserve," which was a major driving force across Western civilization.

The Clone Comes to Consciousness

i am a teacher
i have no memory

i hear and see so much
i cannot understand

i communicate the stray
dictum of a gamma ray

almost nobody perceives
or comprehends

a slight subatomic shudder
not predicted in our half-lives

צ *tzádi*

i report. The Hebrew letter *tzádi* stood for righteousness, justice, honesty, humility, correctness (Haralick 257; Ginsburgh 266–67). Philosophically, socially, culturally, politically, economically, aesthetically, physically, morally, even spiritually, the question of *mimesis,* of likeness and difference, was central in Western culture (Auerbach; Melburg; Deleuze), beginning with the notion of separate, dueling bodies and souls (the "duality view"). (It became a central question as well in *Plato's Nightmare*, especially in the Prologos and Part One, which set the scene for the remainder of the Chronicles of the Body through the centuries, and the Epilogos that resulted.) And G/d said: "let humans have dominion over all mimesis without images of the original or Benjamin's 'aura'." And bodies pressed against bodies, trying to escape, human forms and mechanical forms, divine forms and demonic forms, sublime forms and grotesque forms, spiritual forms and cybernetic forms, all mired in space and time, all wallowing in their needs and desires, all philosophically deaf and dumb and blind, all in need of a good meta-physic.

iHuman

you can hear me clatter
when i move

a brilliant vibrancy
of colors without meaning.

when times are tough, turn
your eyes to the stars, my sun

click on the table of contents
to see the company i keep.

we've done everything to accommodate
your body, half-existing

the metal smell of semen
thrown into the wind like seed

"i" am getting used to being
someone with only half a name

***

Symptomologies: Case History #Pre-2 (A "Mystory"*)

Dinner party, Serious Games colloquium. Present: assortment of famous faculty and superb graduate students. Gregory Ulmer emerged inside a lively conversation with Ian Bogost—the "folding" of orality, literacy, and electracy into "procedural rhetoric"). In this "Burkean parlor," lurking among virtual legs near a small cloud of voices, an uncomfortable, obscure,

> reclusive, invisible recorder, i, listened. Over the din, Ulmer suddenly inquired: "Rhetoric is always talking about beautiful bodies; where are all the beautiful bodies?" (Conversation).
>
> —*Ulmer, Teletheory*

i (1.) am not a poem

if i could breathe a pure rhetoric of air,
a rhetoric so pristine and true that it would rush right into my mouth like winter,
and then slowly float out again in a soft persuasion of snow,
turning white gold, beyond the bend that I will never know,

ק *kâf*

i report. Toward the end of *A Rhetoric of Religion*, Kenneth Burke, one of rhetorics' many advocates for poetry as well as a poet himself, made a series of startling statements: that the motive-laden and will-imbued mode of "dramatistic" presentation already entailed a "negation"; that any linguistic account of "material reality" by analogy, allegory, theology, metaphysics, had to be "discounted" by "the principle of the negative" because of the surplus of physical reality that overflows language; and that language itself is physical and part of that surfeit (Burke, *Religion* 18–19; Katz and Rivers). Language had been dismissed as having been given too much importance (Barad). But George Steiner surmised: "[a]ll philosophic acts, every attempt to think thought, with the possible exception of formal [mathematical] and symbolic logic, are irremediably linguistic" (*Poetry of Thought*, Kindle Locations 61–62).[ץ] And then there was Haralick: "Growth and holiness [*kâf*] are related to the pulsating unbridled force of the letter א [*alef*] … and to the energy of the intelligence of spirituality, י [*yôd*]" (269). The entire universe was a living, throbbing language, a reverberant moral rhetoric (see Figure 2). As in an infinite cave, humans lived in the dark.

i (2.) am not a poem
tonight, she will need me
for light—

tomorrow, i will be
a doorstop—

which picture
should i choose?

ר rêsh

i report. In *Rhetoric and Poetics in Antiquity*, J. Walker argued that lyrical poetry (the source of oratory) not only shared rhetoric's epideictic functions in early ancient, pre-Socratic antiquity, but also that lyrical poetry in antiquity may have had forensic and deliberative functions as well (viii). From within that form, they had an opportunity to clarify (*rêšh*) the beginning of the arts (Ginsburgh 296-–97), a choice (*rêšh*) in the context of humanity of which way to turn (Haralick 283). (Ancient Chinese poetry also had a central role in civic administration and promotion, in which the ability to write a specified poem was the necessary competitive test for advancement [Seaton and Cryer]). Implicitly and explicitly, in his Preface as well as his conclusion, J. Walker seemed to hope if not actually call for a poetics that was not merely "epideictic/aesthetic" but deliberative and forensic as well.

Winter Birches

white winter poles
crisscrossed, holding—
up the sky

***

i report. In a literate, linear, and more stylistically "anorexic" philosophy, Aristotle had rendered dialectic and rhetoric *antistrophos* ("counterparts"). In a philosophical and practical sense, Aristotle had rendered rhetoric and poetry "true" as well as "useful" arts by answering Platon's call for the application of dialectic to fully systematize every subject. But more loosely, Aristotle's *Rhetoric* and the *Poetics* might have been regarded as *antistrophos* too. Both had a social function as well as an aesthetic purpose. While rhetoric covered the art of persuasion, poetics (drama really) covered the area of catharsis, both discussed in the "Cathartic Organ" in Part One of *Plato's Nightmare*, and differently in the Romantic Organ in Part Four (e.g., in relation to William Wordsworth). But for Aristotle, more than Platon the mystic and literary author as well as philosopher, scientific observation of any subject was based on classificatory analysis, rationally referenced through the logic of content, rather than any indirect, non-rational, experiential dimension of language, the rhetorics and poetics of arrangement, juxtaposition, style, or epistemic sound (Katz, *Epistemic*), as in *Plato's Nightmare.*

my face hung up the phone.
i'm calling you back
to say goodbye

***

i report. Rhetoric was a form of aesthetics long before it was made an art by Aristotle. And poetry was a rhetorical performative act in which the verse was a fundamental part of the "investigation" and argument.

i'm going into
the sunroom
where it's dark

In *Plato's Nightmare*, each poem (and its images, metaphors, meters, line breaks, poetic forms) was juxtaposed with and/or in context of the surrounding rhetorical prose argument, to constitute: poetic evidence (explanatory, illustrative, descriptive); testimony (personal, social, cultural and aesthetic); forensic or a *fortiori* argument (demonstrative or re-directive); commentary (serious, humorous, satirical); and/or reflection (sincere, ironic, sardonic). The form of this "poetic treatise," this "rhetorical epic"—this work of art—will be seen to have instantiated its arguments, enacted its structure, performed its content. Given the grandioisity and hubris of this enterprise, this rhetorical-poetic investigation and argument, sweeping the centuries of the Anthropocene, present simultaneously as forensic, deliberative, and epideictic arguments, as well as aesthetic critiques and self-referential reports.

Watching the Stars Watch Us

(For Chris Burns)

firefly down, flashing
beneath the grass

a satellite above crawling
across the sky

signaling each other in
signs we can't understand.

ש *shín*

i report. Classical reasoning by deductive logic or inductive examples was ultimately based on classification, but also the basis of analogy, the weakest form of argument (Corbett 93). Comparison was a primary basis of human knowledge, an act repeated over and again, leading to temporary completeness—the penultimate letter of the alefbet, *shin* (Haralick 295), of vision but also "subjectivity," "falsehood," "corruption" (Monk 211–12). Unlike traditional views of metaphor in poetry and in science in which metaphor was regarded as merely ornamental, or heuristic, or nonsense (e.g., Sprat; Boyd; Ayer, respectively), even raw comparison may have been fundamental to human knowledge. Richard Boyd subscribed to controversial theory of "theory constitutive metaphors" based on "ostension," as opposed to nominal reference (Witt; Putnam; Quine). For Boyd, these metaphors were "real terms" that provided "epistemic access" to the actual "causal joints of the world," even in some mature sciences. Whether they did or not, Boyd thought these metaphors were *not* merely weaker, subjective, literary substitutes for scientific method, or placeholders for more substantive evidence waiting to be found. Rather, for Boyd, these metaphors were "open-ended" and thus epistemic, resulting in new knowledge of the world.

***

i report. As fleshy poetic topoi, as imaginative rhetorical figuration, metaphors may have manifested many properties, many kinds of logics and relations, depending in part on context. Just as verbs allowed humans to see and talk about the future (Steiner, *Errata* 94–95, 190), metaphors may have undergirded many different scientific theories, philosophical systems, models of thought, netwarks, quarkworks, transapps—*pointing* to worlds that may or may not have existed in some material or transcendental realm (cf. Turbayne; Boyd; Katz, "Burke's Body"). Or perhaps metaphors only indicated themselves, in a total tautology of human language (Kuhn, "Metaphor"; *Structure*). Or both. Using I.A. Richards' metaphoric terms for metaphor—"tenor" (the literal part of a metaphor) and "vehicle" (the figurative part of a metaphor)—the *vehicle* of the metaphor (the "chariot") may have carried the tenor of the metaphor (the soul) to other planes of existence, or back to the unknowable Ideal Forms, or the unknowable and perhaps nonexistent Name.

From this Earth

I.
A Science of Subjectivity

For the few moments on this earth,
we become too sensitive in these things:
green light, dusty plants
in blue windows, the sunny wood;

we seek a science of subjectivity
to escape—perceive cells of green leaves
synthesizing in the genesis of summer,

white tracery of a particle breeze

in the patterned chaos of trees,
atomic complexity of grass in the heat,
the sun radiating in fields,
chemical skies, cosmic weather:

and we dream, dream in the infinite
window we can't see through.
Oh yes, we will test for G/d,
attach electrodes to the stars.

ת *tov*

i report. The history of humanism in the West was a wracked one—a wrestling of soul and body, a wresting of the divine or transcendental or metaphysical from the material (and vice versa), the writhing consciousness of a living corpse. Human societies were built to overcome "division" (incomplete, but formidable) between "self" and "other," "self" and "self," "self" and "world" —whole civilizations built over the abyss of reason and consciousness —evolving in poetic and rhetorical flesh from humans to cyborgs to robots to androids to clones with acute intelligence and keen sensibilities (Katz, Foreword) —still barely bridging enough of the gulf to allow even consubstantiation and identification (Burke, *Rhetoric of Motives*). No matter what it was called, no matter how it was done, no matter what form it took, the severing of mind/soul/actant/imagination/spirit/ conscience from physical body/material reality/universe (as perceived by organically sophisticated but limited sensory apparatus) correlated with the stripping of skin from flesh, flesh from bone, form from matter, attribute from essence, style from content, speech from thought. —and the splitting of rhetoric and poetry, rhetoric from subject matter, knowledge from persuasion, rhythm and rhyme from oratorical-political power, metaphor from scientific or philosophical model (see Turbayne; Derrida; Boyd) in search of "truth and perfection" (*tov* [Munk, 214–31])—but *not* in supernal yet material Hebrew vowels and letters, or even the mysticism of the Greek alphabet and numerals purported to be the source of the Hebrew (cf. Barry; cf. Plato, *Cratylus*), but in search of ethereal, non-material Ideal Forms—all topics of the Prologos and subsequent Parts of the Chronicles of the Body and the Epilogos of *Plato's Nightmare.*

***

i report. Perhaps formally beginning in Platon and Aristotle, but generally speaking—historically, philosophically, and aesthetically—rhetoric was stripped of its poetic body, and poetry deprived of rhetoric's muscular structures and purpose. Underground there were counter schools, movements, trends, some touched upon *Plato's Nightmare*, that focus on delivery (voice, gesture), written styles (grammar, diction, syntax), and the role of poetry and sound as a bases of rhetoric (e.g., rhapsodes, Greek sophists, Isocrates, the older Cicero, High Renaissance and Baroque styles [see Croll]; the Elocutionary Movement of the eighteenth century [e.g., Bulwer; Austen; Sheridan]; and Sonic Rhetorics in the twentieth (G. Kennedy, "Hoot"; Hawhee, *Tooth and Claw*; Katz, *Epistemic*; "Sonic Rhetorics"; Stedman). But rhetoric and poetry were not immune from public flayings and floggings of skin and speech, the disembowelment and retooling of the human body, the dissecting and deboning of consciousness and spirit, the fetishization and fantasies of the sciences and technologies, the anatomizing and quantifying of affect (e.g., Foucault, *Discipline*; *Clinic*; Debord; Baudrillard, *Simulacra*; Latour, *Factish Gods;* Katz, *Epistemic*).

***

i report. Self-reflexively presented in both prose and poetry, "Transmissions" and "Chronicles of the Body" in *Plato's Nightmare* relate the constant attempt throughout human history to tear thought, speech, and soul from word, sinew, bone;—a narrating of the many and surprisingly different methods of freeing the "psyche" (the soul sentience consciousness, the divine sublime mind, the transcendental universal spirit, the subjective existential Being) from the living corpse of humanity (the material physical robotic body);—a recounting not only in "rational" modes of thought and knowing, but also an embracing and re-tracing and reifying experientially in human and post-human dimensions via the two language arts Platon seemed to harshly criticize but thoroughly imbibed; —a reenactment and reversal of Platon's mystical and literary as well as rational dream of a totally ambiguous and even contradictory desire to free the tethered mind from sordid matter; —a marking of an ultimate separation of consciousness from the feeling suffering ecstatic changing corrupting decaying house of human body languages senses, into an epistemologically pristine realm of libidinous-free logic, objectified spirit, pure idea, ontological ether.

From This Earth

II.
The Inhuman Stars

A human egg cracks; a white hatch
opens; and a satellite is born,

slipping out, alone, into a universe
that engulfs it like an infant star.

And is there something childlike
and prophetic, in those awkward sensors,
slowly extending, reaching out
to the expanding void of oblivion;

something comical and tragic
in that radar like an ear cupped
to a cosmic wall of darkness,
listening, listening to the static

of creation, searching for what
it cannot find here among the inhuman stars,
satellite falling, endlessly falling
into the night that is ours?

ה *Feet*

ך (*kâf-sofit*) The individual sections in this Pre_Face were numbered using the three main parts of the Hebrew alphabet: 1) the consonants; 2) vowels points (Hebrew: *Nikkudot*), seen first in *Plato's Nightmare*; 3) and the final form of five Hebrew letters (סוֹפִית -"*sofit*"), used for these endnotes.

1. The Hebrew alphabet (alefbet) consisted of twenty-two letters. Hebrew letters, all consonants, were also numbers, though those numerical equivalents of the letters were not completely used here, only the chronological sequence of the Hebrew alefbet itself. The lack of vowels in the letters of the Torah (dubbed an ABJAD rather than a true alphabet (Daniels and Bright 1–17) led to all kinds of foundational ambiguities and sophisticated alphabetical hermeneutics in morally interpreting and legally applying the Scriptures of Torah and the Talmud (Katz, "Letter as Essence"). It was this ABJAD that the Phoenicians brought to Hellenica, and that the Greeks then created vowel letters. The use of the Hebrew alphabet in this Pre_Face was just one of a few alphabets and other "numbering systems" employed in Parts—again, not for any numerical equivalence for counting, but for their suggestive meaning in the context of the whole recorded manuscript as transmitted.
2. The Torah had always been central in Judaism. With the Roman destruction of the Second Temple in 70 C.E., rituals, practices, and prayer relocated to Jewish households. A number of vowel points (called *niqqud* [nikud]) were developed in Tiberian Hebrew by the Masoretes between 600 CE and 1100 CE to preserve vowel sounds to aid in the pronunciation of Torah, and make Scripture easier to read; the Masoretic version became the standard text of the Hebrew Bible in print. (These vowel points were never used in the actual Torah scrolls [copied by hand on Kosher sheepskin not only during Biblical times, ancient antiquity, the Golden Age of classical Greece, but throughout the Middle Ages, the Renaissance, the scientific revolution of seventeenth century, the eighteenth-century Enlightenment, nineteenth century Romanticism, twentieth century space age, into digital future, to the end of the Anthropocene.) In *Plato's Nightmare*, the vowels that began the numbering of the Pre_Face were indicated by diacritical signs. In a traditional method of representation used here, each vowel in relation to missing letters was indicated by its position around a small circle. However, the equivalent of the vowel, in this case its sound, nor its meaning in Hebrew, was not used in the sequencing of the first part of the Pre_Face; rather, it was the suggestive shapes of the

vowels in relation to the content of the section that was important, as the alphabetic body was born.

3. Finally, the *sofit*, or final forms of five consonants changed when they occurred at the end of Hebrew words. The final forms were used as "the Feet" of this Pre_Face—the only section to have endnotes. Beginning with this endnote, the five endnotes (feet) conclude "the body" of this Pre-Face based on Plato's comparison of writing to the human body (*Phaedrus* 264c). *Plato's Nightmare* as a "report" begins and ends with "Transmissions." Between these transmissions the "Chronicles of the Body," which were divided into five Parts based on centuries and historical periods. Each Part was further broken into Όργανα (Organs) that use the different numbering systems discussed in #1, appropriate to the historical period and content of the Part. Each Όργανο (Organ) also ends with the "exhalation" of one of the top ten elements of the Periodic Table found in the human body.

ם [*mêm - sofit*] Aristotle discussed metaphor in both the *Rhetoric* (e.g., 1405a1–1405b) and the *Poetics* (e.g., 1457b1–30), as well as several places in the *Topics*. In the eighteenth century, Vico made "poetics" the basis of his oddly interesting "New Science" (e.g., see Book II). In the twentieth century, literary and rhetorical theorists, e.g., Wimsatt, Perelman, Richards, Kolodny, Derrida ("White Mythology"). Psaty, Baake and many others discussed the role of metaphor in rhetoric and literature. So did theorists studying philosophy, science, and language/cognition (e.g., Black, Ortony, Boyd, Kuhn, Turbayne, Lakoff and Johnson, Johnson; Bergen). Aristotle defined metaphor as a substitution of one thing for another—a transgression of classes; as Handelman put it: "[M]etaphor is defined as a movement, a displacement, a transfer of name to an alien category, implying a deviation of sorts"; citing Derrida, for Handelman what got hidden in Aristotle's logical treatment of science and philosophy (vs. rhetoric and poetry), and his definition of metaphor, was that the "metaphorical transfer from the "proper" to the "figurative" sense . . . based on a metaphysical transfer from the "sensible" to the "nonsensible," a transfer crucial in Western thought was obscured (16).

ן (*nûn –sofit*)

> "From Aristotle onward, the term *technē* sometimes was linked with the word *epistēmē*. Both words are names for knowing in

> the widest sense. They mean to be entirely at home in something, to understand and be expert in it. Such knowing provides an "opening"—a revealing. In the *Nichomachean Ethics* (Bk. VI, chapters 3 and 4), Aristotle distinguished between *epistēmē* and *technē* and with respect to what and how they reveal. *Technē* is a mode of *alētheuein*. It reveals whatever does not bring itself forth and does not yet lie here before us . . ." ("Question Concerning Technology" 13)

Contrary to conceptions of technē as mere "craft," "technique," or "techno-logy" (machines, processes, procedures), *technē* [τέχνη] as art for Heidegger was both "a bringing forth" (as in handicraft) but also as a way of making the invisible apparent . . . As *Eidos* (Ideation), *technē* was a way of *Dasein*—of "opening (into Being)" a "calling forth" (*Ver-an-lassen*), "a revealing" (*Entbergung*), "a presencing" (*An-wesen*)—the Being of a thing—human or nonhuman—in the world (see Lovitt 9n7–8). For Heidegger, perhaps unlike Plato, this included language as well. In fact, for Heidegger "language was never primarily the expression of thinking, feeling, and willing. Language is the primal dimension within which man's essence is first able to correspond to Being. This primal corresponding, expressly carried out, is thinking" ("Turning" 41). In counter-distinction to Plato and Aristotle, Heidegger reclaimed the term technē as poesies for both thinking and art: "Every occasion for whatever passes over and goes forward into presencing from that which is not presencing is poesies, is bringing-forth [*Her-vor-bringen*]" ("Question"10). For Heidegger, then, as τέχνη not only "the fine arts" and for him especially poetry, but also by extension language and rhetoric, was understood as "a bringing forth," be called upon "to reveal" (see "Question" 35; cf. Stiegler; Rickert, Ambient; Holmes; Barnett and Boyle). As poesis, poetics and rhetorics may have cleared an open space (*Dasein*) in and through language, in order to have beheld and dwelled in the Being of the world that were before us, and the things and other creatures that were in it (see "Building Dwelling Thinking"). "[W]hat is decisive in *technē* does not lie at all in making and manipulating nor in the using of means," said Heidegger, "but rather in the aforementioned revealing. It is revealing, and not as manufacturing, that *technē* is a bringing forth" ("Question" 13).

Ideally, technology as τέχνη might have been considered some form art as Heidegger understood it (e.g., Heidegger, "Question" 34). "Technology is a mode of revealing. Technology comes to presence . . . in the realm where revealing and unconcealment take place, where *alētheia*, truth, happens." ("Question" p. 13). However, in Western culture, this active coming to essence (*Vorwessen*) was not to be the case with Technology. For Heidegger, the "question" wasn't only the historical development of technology or even the machine. For Heidegger, the question of *technai* was precisely in the language, thinking, *poesies*, art,

Dasein, or Being of technology; the problem was what these *technē* as technology had become. "In opposition to this definition of the essential domain of technology, one can object that it indeed holds for Greek thought that at best it (τέχνη—*technē*) might apply to the techniques of the handicraftsman, but that it simply does not fit modem machine-powered technology" ("Question" 13). For Heidegger, the problem was what happened when science and technology split from *poesis*, when "Enframing" (*Gestellen*) became the way of thinking in the world. Technology was no longer τέχνη linked to epistemic activity as a manifestation of *poesis*. Rather, for Heidegger *technē* became the Being of Technology as a "Challenging" (*Herausforden*) that in itself was also a concealment (*Verborgenheit*) of any Being other than its own, and even its own, the Being of Enframing itself ("Question" 11n–14). Enframing was dangerous for Heidegger, precisely because the Being of the human and world and all things were blocked, and all of nature was challenged as *Gestell*, as "Standing-Reserve" ("Question" 14). As Standing-Reserve, everything was turned into an object for use, "*Gegenstand*" (object; that which stands over and against). Objects indeed lost their character as objects when they were caught up in the "standing-reserve" (Lovitt 17n.16). What was especially dangerous about Enframing was that its actions (read obligations [*vershulden*, "to be indebted to, to owe, to be guilty, to be responsible for, to cause" (Lovitt 7n5)] were demanding (*bestellen*, to order) and invisible (*verstellen*, to disguise) (Lovitt 15n).

ף (*pē -sofit*) The following was understood: *zu* = "to," vs. *vor* = "for"— in *das Zuhandenhiet* ("Present," existing at hand in its own right) vs. *das Vorhandenheit* ("Ready" to hand, to make "useful" for human work, where nature is a "Standing Reserve" for something other than its own being/Being. After reinterpreting causality (Ger. *Ursache*; Gr. *Aition*) in which "something was responsible for something else ("Question" 7), Heidegger thought that humans had a responsibility to "let what has not yet present arrive into presencing . . . what brings presence into appearance ("Question" 10). Heidegger in *The Question Concerning Technology* therefore (re)interpreted the ancient Greek understanding of τέχνη (technē) in a way that illuminated the issue in Plato. Heidegger said:

> We, late born, are no longer in a position to appreciate the significance of Plato's daring to use the word *eidos* for that which in everything and in each particular thing endures as present. For *eidos*, in the common speech, meant the outward aspect [*Ansicht*] that a visible thing offers to the physical eyes. Plato exacts of this word, however, something utterly extraordinary: that it name precisely what is not and never will be perceivable

> with the physical eyes. . . . For *idea* [*Eidos*] names [. . .] the nonsensuous aspect of what is physically visible. Aspect (*idea*) names and is, also, that which constitutes the essence in the audible, the tasteable, the tactile, in everything that is in any way accessible. ("Question" 20)

ץ (*sádê -sofit*) Philosophy, even Heideggerian philosophy, was still intractably rooted in the human body, and knowledge may have been nothing more than vast and riddled field of related warrants and metaphors. As George Steiner and the scholars he cited asserted, "In all philosophy, conceded Sartre, there is a hidden literary prose." Philosophic thought could be realized "only metaphorically," taught Althusser" (*Steiner, Poetry of Thought* Kindle Location 82–85). And it wasn't just poetry either:

> What has been less clarified is the incessant, shaping pressure of speech-forms, of style on philosophic and metaphysical programs. In what respects is a philosophic proposal, even in the nakedness of Frege's logic, a rhetoric? Can any cognitive or epistemological system be dissociated from its stylistic conventions, from the genres of expression prevalent or under challenge in its time and milieu? . . . At other points, the philosopher sets out to construe a new language, an idiolect singular to his purpose. Yet this endeavor, manifest in Nietzsche or in Heidegger, is itself saturated by the oratorical, colloquial or aesthetic context. (Steiner, *Poetry of Thought*, Kindle Location 86–92)

2 Prologos: Gutting Rhetoric and Poetry?

> SOCRATES: Well now, if you strip from poetry its music, rhythm, and meter, the residue would be nothing else but speech?
>
> CALLICLES: That must be so.
>
> SOCRATES: And these speeches are addressed to a huge mob of people?
>
> CALLICLES: I agree.
>
> SOCRATES: Then poetry is a kind of public address?
>
> CALLICLES: Evidently.
>
> SOCRATES: Must it not be a rhetorical public address? Do you not consider that the poets engage in rhetoric in the theaters?
>
> CALLICLES: I do.
>
> SOCRATES: Then we have now discovered a form of rhetoric addressed to a people composed alike of children and women and men, slaves and free—a form which we cannot much admire, for we describe it as a kind of flattery.
>
> *—Plato, Gorgias 205 c–d*

α alpha

Grip

It was not a good thing to be called "light and airy." Even if "holy," an empty, ethereal vessel, a mouth that one god or another wanted to use through which to speak. . . . "[H]e is beside himself and reason is no longer in him" (Plato, *Ion* 534b).

Satellite

down an infinite hall
the echo
of a long goodbye

i report. For Platon, the arts, like the physical body, like language, even the "alphabet" (αλώβητο—*alobeto**) itself, came with a lot of baggage. So let's "open the man" (άνοιξε τον άνθρωπο—*ánoixe ton ánthropo*) like a book and have a look. The more primitive alefbet without vowels (an ABJAD) brought to Greek shores by the Phoenicians supposedly from any semitic tribe not the ancient Hebrews, was transformed it into a full-fledged αλώβητο (Burkett; Daniels and Bright; Barry; cf. Plato, *Cratylus*). In their purported (and challenged) capacity as imitative, everything about the letters reeked of materiality—earth and skin, flesh and sky, fire and ash, death and decay. It seemed this included not only the word productions of artists (and poets and rhetoricians), but also their own bodies as media/media. Apparently, the physical body—like words that clothed ideas, and alphabets that clothed the undergarments of speech—with all their compilations and stylistic complications and wrinkles—were not objects to be admired and studied. "Open the man" (άνοιξε τον άνθρωπο) like a worn and outdated trunk. The body was excess baggage (Baudrillard, *Simulacra*) to be sprung open, full of decrepit organs and rags to be unpacked and tossed (Deleuze), the luggage cast aside so that the seeking soul, consciousness, spirit could be set free in favor of finding higher forms of non-corporeal Being (see *Phaedo*; *Philebus*). No, to be not just a light and airy thing, but completely *weightless, without body, mass, physicality, gravity* . . .

* Transliteration of the Greek used Google *Translate*, among other sources.

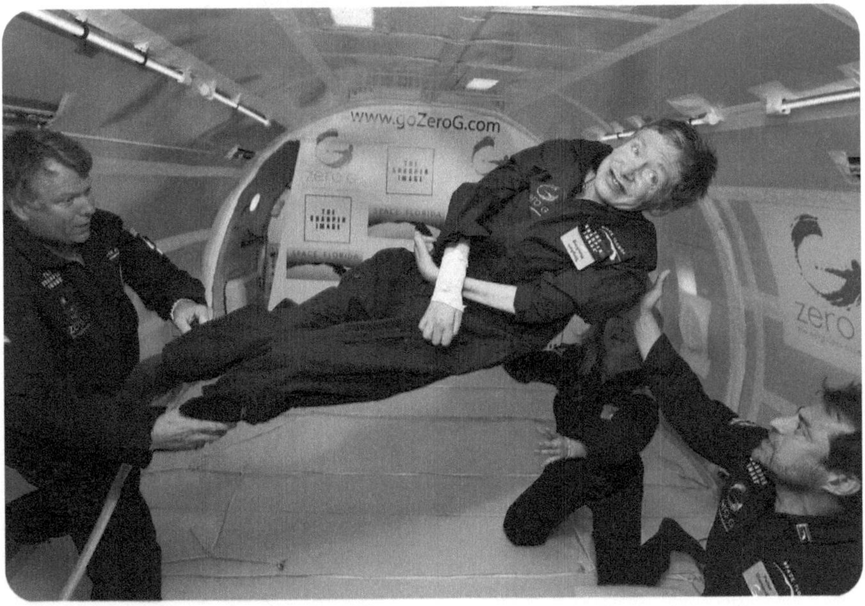

Figure 4. "Physicist Stephen Hawking in Zero G NASA.

Set Free at Zero Gravity

(April 26, 2007)
for Stephen Hawking, Astrophysicist

Strapped to motorized wheelchair, speaking
through electronic straws but always dreaming
of infinity, black holes through time and space
which he'd travel willingly, his face

never being televised or watched
again, held down by its atomic weight,
new books, sly smiles, never to be written,
body mass pressed to nothingness—

released from the gravity of earth
to experience a weightlessness of girth,
the ether of his former youth, first birth—
plummeting in a cargo bay
floating up in parabolic grace,
a cosmic object now made wholly straight.

β beta

Stripping Poetry

i report. In Platon's *Gorgias*, three interlocutors, and Socrates planted beta-seeds in "a new vase" (σε νέο *βάζο—se neo vazo*) for a debate that would grow and harden into epistemological, religious, and political positions and institutions (Foucault, "Discourse") in the West concerning not only the nature and relationship of poetry and rhetoric but also the nature, relations, and proper care of the body and soul; the dangers of pleasure and flattery vs. abstention and good health; tyranny vs. good government; the just and the unjust; the holy and the unholy (*Gorgias*, esp. 500e–507c). The body itself was a fragile vase (ένα εύθραυστο βάζο—*éna éfthrafsto vazo*). At times almost comically questioning (the ghosts of) Gorgias, and taking a passing shot at Polus, Socrates began an intense and powerful interrogation of Callicles on the untrue and harmful nature of poetry and rhetoric. In the epigraph above, from the *Gorgias* (501b–502c, 502e–503d), Platon had Socrates utter: "εἴ τις περιέλοι τῆς ποιήσεως πάσης το τε μέλος καὶ τὸν ῥυθμὸν καὶ τὸ μέτρον, ἄλλο τι ἢ λόγοι γίγνονται τὸ λειπόμενον; οὐκοῦν πρὸς πολὺν ὄχλον καὶ δῆμον οὗτοι λέγονται οἱ λόγοι (Crane)—*eí tis periéloi tís poiíseos pásis tó te mélos kaí tón rythmón kaí tó métron, állo ti í lógoi gígnontai tó leipómenon?* (*Google Translate*)]. "[I]f you should strip from all poetry its music (melody) and rhythm and meter, the residue would be nothing else but speech?" (*Gorgias* 502c). Whether this Greek verb or another, this act of "stripping," "περιέλοι" (*perriéloi*—"take away something that surrounds . . . strip off, remove"; inf. Περιαιρέω, to strip [Crane; Liddell and Scott; Liddell and Autenrieth; Autenrieth and Keep]), here it was applied to stripping poetry from speech. "Stripping" in a sense became "first philosophy," as well as a physical act of various force. The degree of "violence" might have been understood temporally based on Greek etymology (see Table 1).

Table 1. Relative Etymological "Speeds" of Act of "Stripping" in the Classical Greek Verb περιέλοι.

LSJ	*Middle Liddell*	*Relative Speed of Act* ⇩
take away something that surrounds	take off something that surrounds	take off something that surrounds ⇩
strip off	take off an outer coat	take off an outer coat
remove	take away	take away ⇩
A.2.	strip off	Remove
make void	*II. Passive*	to be stripped of a thing
cancel a vow	*II Passive, also accusative*	stripped off ⇩
A.J.	to be stripped off	strip
strike off		
cancel an item in an account		
II. Passive		
to be stripped of a thing		
have a thing taken away from one		

Pro - γ gamma

Socrates and Poetry

For Socrates and more generally in his day, both poetry and rhetoric practiced and performed by rhapsodes and playwrights and orators and sophists were oral and dramatic and immediate (Ong; Havelock). Και έιχε πολλή γοητεία (*kai eiche polli goiteia*—"and had a lot of *c*harm"). In this same epigraph, Socrates further points out to the "small crowd" of three (γ) gathered around him, that these performances were addressed to "a huge mob of people" (*Gorgias* 502c). Because it was addressed to a "huge mob," poetic speech was a "kind of public address" (*Gorgias* 502c), "a rhetorical public address" (*Gorgias* 502d), and thus a form of rhetoric. *Γ*οητεία. "Do you not consider that the poets engage in rhetoric in theatre?" (*Gorgias* 502d). And because this form of (poetic) rhetoric as "addressed to a people composed alike of children and women and men, slaves and free" (*Gorgias* 502d), Socrates concludes, this rhetoric is "a form which we cannot much admire" (*Gorgias* 502d), and so dismissed both the poetry in and the audiences of rhetoric in one periodic breadth. Unworthy, the audiences were all-too-human (*Gorgias* 502c–d; cf. Nietzsche, *All Too Human*).

flying over
the endless abyss–
no wings

However, Platon and even Aristotle (as well as Roman philosopher-orators such as Cicero and Quintilian) employed poetry in their rhetorical treatises as famous examples of speech, action, and morality. (The tradition of using poetry in teaching lasted late into the second half of the twentieth century, although poetry and later, literature and other essays, were increasingly limited to rhetoric and composition classes. Throughout the Middle Ages, Renaissance, Enlightenment, Romantic period, and modernism [such as New Criticism, Structuralism, even Deconstruction], literature was used as the source of exemplars for imitation, and as models of "good writing" until the beginning of the "process" view of writing, which more or less coincided with the analysis and interpretation of literature as the content and purpose of writing instruction, until it became the philosophical objects of de-construction [cf. Wellek; Murphy; Berlin; Vitanza; Derrida, *Grammatology*].)

***

Socrates complained that poetic forms of rhetoric could be found in "the Athenian Assembly, and the assemblies of freemen in other states" as well, and he questioned whether any of these rhetoricians "appear . . . always to aim at what is best (*Gorgias* 502e)." Socrates proclaimed he could find none. Callicles agreed. For Platon *the philosopher*, poetry here seemed nothing more than a rhetoric designed to amuse and appeal to the mob or crowd, rather than to educate or demonstrate what was best, personally and politically, for the body and soul. Socrates' syllogistic dismissal of the audience whether man or woman, citizen or slave, tended to underlie any effort to really communicate with the public, post-Gutenberg, until the age of mass media.

Just Like a Film

of course you would be a curve
standing beside your brand new bike;
of course you would have shortened hair,
further cut and shaped by rain . . .

of course those giggly colors
would run together into a face
caught in turquoise-orange laughter,
departing smile slicing air . . .)

δ delta

Dicta as Syllogism

i report. Retrieved from the archives, "On the Nonexistent or on Nature," Gorgias asserted that Reality does not exist; that if it did exist, we could not understand it; that if we could understand it, we could not communicate it. Gorgias was not a nihilist (e.g., see Kerferd). He could have said: *διαβιω* (*diavio*—"I live"). Each of these statements or "dictum," though unexpected, and perhaps individually unacceptable, were valid in sequitur. Gorgias purpose was the epistemological deconstruction of a philosophical fantasy on the existence of unseen, transcendental Truths, and a non or even anti-nihilistic reinstatement of the reality of the seen, material world (depending on how and by whom this message was were received"). Διαβιω. The epigraph stowed in Platon's *Gorgias* also could be conceived as three logical statements, or "dicta" that in sequitur also form a kind of syllogism, summarizing what appears to be a nihilistic philosophy on the nature and validity of poetry as a form of rhetoric, and that rhetoric as form of speech, all in relation to specific audiences:

α "Stripped of its musical ornaments, poetry is a rhetorical form of speech.
β As rhetoric, it is adorned with poetry and addressed to undesirable audiences.
γ As a rhetoric addressed to undesirable audiences, poetry is undesirable.

***

The syllogistic presentation of Socrates dicta emphasized key elements in each as definitions (by classification), and also revealed the logic of each dictum as part of a larger local argument within this core of Platon's treatise. In the *Gorgias*, Platon had Socrates identify poetry with rhetoric as a corrupt and corrupting form of speech. Poetry was bad for the body—personal and political—as well as the soul. So were the other forms of rhetoric mentioned. Socrates' endorsement of unadorned speech was a stance on style preferred by Aristotle (*Rhetoric*, Book III). So too scientists of the Newtonian revolution [Sprat; Locke, *Essay*]. But there were counter-movements. The "Attic" or "plain" style was countered: in the Renaissance by "Ciceronian" or "Baroque" schools of style [Croll]; in the eighteenth century by the Elocutionary Movement; in the nineteenth by the Romantic rebellion—all traversed in *Plato's Nightmare*.

Lady Rhetorica

dips a bucket
into the well
of her will, and pulls

up a pail full
of pine trees
mountains

in the evening she
draws another pail
of starsmoonclouds

her life is full
of rhetoric, poetry—drunk
on philosophic wood

ε *epsilon*

Also traversed, in the twentieth century Kenneth Burke dedicated his whole professional life creating and contributing to a new rhetoric, one based on "motive" as opposed to causality, free will vs. determination, "exegesis" (εξήγηση—eksə'jēsəs) rather than *peschat* (פשט, a plain, simple, literal reading) in Hebrew. The hermeneutics of text, rather than contemplation of Ideal Forms, was a way of life; and "dramatism" involving Burke's "pentad" (*Grammar of Motives*) as the basis of interpretation was at its center. One effect of a rhetorical theory based on "dramatism" was that Burke can be understood to have attempted to "identify" and thus unify rhetoric and poetics, making *them* "consubstantial": "*e*xegesis" supreme (εξήγηση υπέρτατη—*exígisi ypértati*). For Burke, poetry and rhetoric—like all human communication—were forms of social action in which humans as symbol-using animals primarily lived. Literature (like rhetoric) was "equipment for living" (Burke, "Literature"; River and Weber; Rutten et al.). But in his last book, *Rhetoric of Religion*, Burke seemed to admit that language had to be automatically discounted by "the principle of the negative" because of the surplus of material reality that overflowed language without "superadding" any to it (*Rhetoric of Religion* 271; Katz and Rivers). Generally, a sophistic view was that everything humans knew and grew and understood and pursued was in and through language (Enos, *Greek Rhetoric*; Kerferd; cf. Wittgenstein, *Investigations*). In more mystical views, such as in Jewish Kabbalah, language constituted reality itself (Munk; Haralick; Cohen; Katz, "Letter as Essence"), as embodied and demonstrated here in this text of this transmission as well. Despite Burke's life-long distinction between causality and motive, by the twenty-first century rhetorical agency had to account for other posthuman "actants"—inanimate actors, actor-networks, sentient machines, non-human beings, even simple ordinary objects (e.g., Barrett and Boyle; Katz, "Burke's New Body"; Katz and Rhodes).

Human Circuits

(as seen from above)

> Let me be the great nail holding a skyscraper through blue
> nights into white stars"
>
> —*Carl Sandburg, "Prayers of Steel" (109)*

large blocks, tiny
circuit boards
glittering in moving
angles of sunlight
below

squiggles
informatic light
life currents
bars and lines
fulfilled

***

i report. In the *Rhetoric of Religion*, an older Burke subtly and reluctantly seemed to admit some limitations of poetry and rhetoric in his new assessment on the relation between language and reality (*Religion*, 271; cf. Burke's on Spinoza,

137–53; Katz and Rivers 149–50). The physical edge of language could not capture all of the world; nor did language "spill" over or add anything to the material world. In the twenty-first century, New Materialism announced that "[l]anguage has been granted too much power" (Barad 132). Was this a further diminishment of both rhetoric and poetry, especially regarding uncertainty in science? It did seem to mark a decline in the social and culture power of poetry (and also rhetoric, still grounded in the old "New Physics" [see Heisenberg; Bohr; cf. Katz, *Epistemic*]). But after the Middle Ages, poetry had held less and less real political or social or economic force beyond ornamentation. Ramus, with his educational reforms, stripped logic and invention from rhetoric (Ramus; Ong, *Ramus*); what was left of rhetoric in Ramus's treatises and several centuries were diagrams of figures of speech—a skeleton of style, disrobed, disclosed. And with the dissolution of the Trivium and beginning of "the curriculum" during and after the Renaissance, poetry was severed from rhetoric and dialectic. Both poetry and rhetoric thus were effectively removed from their status as *antistrophoi* of each other, and both deposed from dialectic, making logic the center of education, as it had been for Platon as a different, dialogic form and method, until modern science, beginning with Bacon, knocked it off its perch on the head of a pin.

***

Tim Whitmarsh had warned that the relationship between poetry and prose (including rhetoric) was too fraught to use as easy indicators of political markers or cultural decline; Whitmarsh had demonstrated the complex interrelationship of poetry and rhetoric in a diversity of cultural contexts and literary genres in the ancient Greco-Roman world, before, during, between, and especially after the first sophistic (*Second Sophistic*). Even when restricted and hamstrung, rhetoric retained and even expanded its pedagogical primacy because of the power of persuasion in speeches, prose, mass media, social media, avatar renditions, AI editions. And poetry, via image and metaphor, as in all disciplines and inventions, remained at the heart of science—perhaps in reaction to it, as well as in response to the uncontrollable democratizing influence of the physical internet. An overwhelming number of poets as well as electronic publications exploded from the twenty-first century onward. Exhibited in transits of *Plato's Nightmare*, in the Greek, Roman, Medieval, Renaissance, Enlightenment, Romantic, Modern, Postmodern, Posthuman, and Transhuman phases of history, prejudices toward organics of different races, religions, creeds, colors, planet of origin, and even gender identity, stubbornly persisted. And just where Platon had left them, even in the face of the growing if often unrecognized force of rhetoric and the flurry of electronic publications of poetry made possible by the patron saint of the Internet, rhetoric was still deeply associated with falsehood and opposed to inaction, and poetry in any media increasingly became poor, petty, pretty, private, little orphaned things.

False Systems?

physically beautiful
female philosopher:
a contradiction of terms?

ζ *zeta*

i report. Whether or not the epigraph from *Gorgias* was actually a "Platonic counterpart" to Gorgias' three-part dicta in "On Non-Being," Platon's dicta in syllogistic form were scathing and sharp. By "stripping" the beautiful skin and flesh of poetry from rhetoric, and the strong muscle of rhetoric from poetry, leaving only the necessary skeleton of speech, Socrates here somewhat reaffirmed binary division as ontologically necessary, and the eminence of the nonmaterial over the physical as the essential goal. What follows from this is not "symbolic action," but "philosophical action": to separate and elevate—Ideal Forms over "material reality," soul over body, divine over secular, eternal over ephemeral, radiant over corrupt, rationality and transcendental sight over "stupidity" and "noise" (ζαβάδα—*zaváda*). Of course, one had to believe in the ontological superiority, truth, of one of the contradictory pairs. In this dominant "duality," the rhetorical and poetic body of speech, corrupt and constantly decaying, was to be divested and left with the physical world in favor the soul and the spirit, continually reconceived.

Virtual Death

spins to blog, to tweet, to like,
to friend, a last bit of message, to send—
falls off the chair . . .

clutching the mouse,
dragging the cursor down
to the last icon of her life . . .

linked in rigor mortis,
found by Surveillance,
still gripping the trigger

her laptop seizing
but possessing
the wherewithal

to repeatedly
and forever ask:
"Do you need more time?"

***

i report. The act of "stripping" was to be recast and repeated many times throughout human history, both philosophically per above, and physically—in flayings and floggings and flagellations; fastings and beheadings and burnings; in hangings and drawing and quarterings. And in that fraught, unfortunate twentieth century, rife with political strife and wrought with wars worldwide, caused and cursed by greed, geography, and power, —trench-piercing shells and skin-peeling gases. And a frenzy of fetishes and fanaticisms and futurisms—desires to crash machines into flesh, nonhuman into the human, for the beauty of destruction, and the creation of new techno-bodies as a nationalist aesthetics (Marinetti; cf. Paul). And in the apogee of that, a love of hate raging—the ripping and raping and erasing of "race," of citizenship and possessions, hair and clothes, identity and skin, bodies and humanity (Agamben, *Remnants*): state-sponsored and industrial poison genocide. "The very business of rational analysis grows unsteady before the enormity of the facts . . . " (Steiner, *Bluebeard*, 29).

Elegy to a Grecian Hairbrush: An Irregular Tragic Ode

(for Bonnie)

"Who and where am I?
Whose blond hair is this,
caught between my teeth?
Whose warm hand
still lingers on my handle,
handprint still visible
like frozen fingerprints
on glass? Whose scent circles,
slowly then suddenly is
whisked away, vanishing?

"I remember a round head,
but can't recall the face.
In this room once stripped
of its contents, but not me,
hidden behind a wall
I only see a lamp shade,
new stuffed cushions,

fresh bedding, a bar of soap.
Whose blonde hair is this?
Who and what am I?"

***

[HUMAN RATIONALITY AND LOGIC STOOD INDICTED, AND WERE CONDEMNED]

η eta

Mimesis and Flattery

i report. Even while he himself employed rhetoric and poetry most fully in most of his treatises, the upshot of his syllogistic dicta for Platon was that such "suspect" practices in speech and writing were to be eschewed by philosophy and excluded from "serious" discourse as lies and nonsense (cf. Ayer, logical positivism). Rhetoric and poetry were harmful to the soul as well as the Good. But why were rhetoric and poetry harmful to the body as well? For Platon, and presumably Socrates, the issue was that poetry and rhetoric were based on a concept that language, like art, was mere mimesis of material reality (itself a mimesis of Ideal Forms). The primary problem for Platon was that this mimesis was a form of flattery, an "echo" (μια *ηχώ—mia ichó*), concerned only with repetitive pleasure. Before the syllogistic epigraph relayed above, this epistemological-aesthetic position was locatable in the segment of *Gorgias* (501c): "φημι τὸ τὸτοιοῦτον κολακείαν εἶναι καὶ περὶ σῶμα καὶ περὶ ψυχὴν καὶ περὶ ἄλλο ὅτου ἄν τις τὴν ἡδονὴν θεραπεύῃ ἀσκέπτως ἔχων τοῦ ἀμείνονός τε καὶ τοῦ χείρονος . . . " (Crane). Loosely translated from classical Greek to reveal potential etymologies: "Talk that we find about is flattery" ("φημι τὸτοιοῦτον κολακείαν"—*phemi tòtoioũton kolakeían*) "exists around the body" and "around the soul" ("εἶναι καὶ περὶ σῶμα καὶ περὶ ψυχὴν"— *eínai ki perì sõma ki perì psyche*) and "exists around any one besides who delights in physical pleasure" ("καὶ περὶ ἄλλο ὅτου ἄν τις τὴν ἡδονὴν"—*perì ãllo õton ān tis tèn édonèn*) (Plato, *Gorgias* 501c; Crane; Lamb; Liddell and Scott; Autenrieth and Keep).

An Offering to Demeter

A breeze momentarily
brushes Her pain
away. She needs
to remember to forget
not the trauma
of her afterlife,
but the crisis

of her daughter's death:
grieving and pillaged,
bereft of the privilege
of the knowing
that comes with aging—
never to have known
her as an adult, never
to have renegotiated
her relationship
with her, for herself.
Year by year, she
passes, returns
with the seasons,
frozen foliage, wasted snow,
a ghost of an image
perfectly unchanged
in this imperfect place,
not the opposite, exactly,
but not a state of grace

***

Flattery was "talk" designed to appeal to the senses—to "have" (or in other possible meanings of "ἔχων" (*exon*—to "hold or bind," or to "tie or fetter" the body [and the soul]) to δόξαν (*dóxan*— mere "opinion") (Slater). Or again, in another translation of δόξαν, to flatter and tie up the body (and thus the soul) with (false) "praise, honor, glory" (Liddell and Scott; Liddell and Autenrieth). The body which was "bound or tied up" by flattery for Platon was specifically "σῶμα" (*soma*—the mindless, soulless, undead body, walking carcass, corpse). *Soma* was dualistically distinct in a strict division with *psyche* and/or mind, which animated the *living* body—"always referred to as δέμας (*démas*), never "σῶμα" (*soma*) in Homer" (Liddell and Scott; cf. Autenrieth and Keep 18). The "*soulless* body" derived its motion from an external source; but the "*besouled*" (Hackford, *Gorgias* 501c) body was animated from within (cf. *Phaedrus* 245e). Hence began the great Greek bifurcation of mind/soul and body, and the migration of the spirit to "heaven" from the dross of the material world.

Coda: For the Love of Gaia

Ancient sickness
horror and grief
appear as a god

in love with mortal flesh . . .

her footsteps
weight the depths:
the earth shakes
beneath her feet . . .

θ theta

"Forms" of Flattery

i report. Platon's choice of the word "speech" in Gorgias 501c—"φημι" (*phemi*—"talk") with its hint of gossip, "rumor, common talk, "public opinion" (Crane; Liddell and Autenrieth)—may have been etymologically related to "ephemeral" (εφήμερος—*ephēmeros* ['epi'' + *a day' 'ēmera*]). And speech based on "ephemeral opinion" in its physical incompetence and metaphysical amnesia, was unable to recollect or consider what was "better" for the body and soul, and what "worse." Rather, such speech for Platon was "uncritical therapy"—"θεραπεύη ἀσκέπτως" (*therapean àsképtos*—"nonskeptical therapy" or "unreflecting ministration" [Crane; Liddell and Scott]). And such speech was detrimental not only to the body, but to the soul as well. It was a clouded dazzle (θαμπός θαμβος—*thampós thamvos* [*Oxford*], "a dull haze" [*Google Translate*]), designed to bewitch, confuse, and betray both body and soul). Syllogistically speaking, then, in this segment of Platon's *Gorgias*, "talk" based on "opinion" was "uncritical treatment," and was meant to include sophistic and rhetoric *as parallel forms of flattery in a "genre" of false "arts"* with cosmetics and cooking, as opposed to the true arts articulated by Platon in *Gorgias* 462c–466a. Further, for Platon, both rhetoric and poetry as cosmetics and cookery as flattery were not only ("therapy") "ministered unreflectively" ("θεραπεύη ἀσκέπτως"), but also tied "round about" (prep. "περὶ"—*perì* [Autenrieth and Keep 255]), the "corpse" (σῶμα) of the mindless yet living physical body. In this, flattery was "inconsiderate" (another way of translating "ἀσκέπτως"—*askeptos*" [Liddell and Scott; Lamb]) of "what was good and bad for the body and the soul." Flattery simply appealed to the senses and "hedonism" (from ἡδονὴν—*édonèn*—"pleasure") for the purpose of an audience's enjoyment rather than enlightenment (Table 2).

Table 2. "Parody: A New Greek Drama" (Poem)

Το Ροζ βάζο	Το Ροζ βάζο	"The Pink Vase"
Δράμα στο θέατρο;	*Dráma sto théatro?*	Drama in the theatre?
Δράμα στο σινεμά; Όχι.	*Dráma sto sinema? No.*	Drama in the cinema? No.
Δράμα στην καφετέρια	*Dráma stin kafetéria*	Drama in the cafeteria
Δράμα στο μουσείο—	*Dráma sto mouseío*	Drama in the museum
Δράμα στο μίνι μάρκετ	*Dráma sto mína-márket*	Drama in the mini-market
Στην Καφετέρια	*Stin Kafetéria*	From the Cafeteria
Το ψωμί είναι ροζ	*To psomí eínai roz*	The bread is pink
Το σάντουιτς είναι ροζ	*To sántouits eínai roz*	The sandwich is pink
Ο καφές είναι ροζ	*O kafés eínai roz*	The coffee is pink
Η σούπα είναι ροζ—	*I soúpa eínai roz*	The soup is pink
Στην Μουσείο	*Stin Mouseío*	From the Museum
Ο τόρνος είναι ροζ	*O thornos eínai roz*	The throne is pink
Ο γορίλλας είναι ροζ	*O gorillas eínai roz*	The gorilla is pink
Ο σκελετός είναι ροζ	*O skeletós eínai roz*	The skeleton is pink
Με το ροζ σιγάρο—	*Me to roz cigáro*	With the pink cigarette
Στην Μίνι Μάρκετ	*Stin Mini-Márket*	From the Mini-Market
Το νερό είναι ροζ	*To neró eínai roz*	The water is pink
Το αβοκάντο είναι ροζ	*To avokánto eínai roz*	The avocado is pink
Το καρότο ροζ	*To karóto eínai roz*	The carotte is pink
Και το υγρός είναι ροζ"	*Kai to ygeró eínai roz*	And the gyros are pink
Δράμα στο θέατρο;	*Dráma sto théatro?*	Drama in the theatre?
Δράμα στο sσινεμά;	*Dráma sto sinema?*	Drama in the cinema?
Όχι. Το ζαβό	*Ochi To váso*	No. The vase
Στο χολ	*Sto chol*	in the hall
Δεν είναι ροζ:	*Den eínai roz:*	is not pink:
Εγώ είμαι ροζ	*Eímai roz*	I am pink.

*Transliteration (2nd column) with *Google Translate*.

***

Philosophy and Rhetoric as Antitheses

i report. In the famous Platonic analogy, reassembled from the extract of Platon's *Gorgias* (462c–466a), Platon contrasted Philosophy and Rhetoric as "The True Arts" vs. "The False Forms of Flattery" as antitheses of each other (see Table 3). Perhaps treating them like "counterparts" (αντισροφος—*antistrophos*) when they were not exposed their stark opposition to each other, and the inferiority of the latter for Platon regarding what is "best for the soul."

Table 3. Plato's Opposition of Philosophy and Rhetoric.

THE TRUE ARTS			
Of the Body		*Of the Soul*	
Gymnastics (Normative)	Medicine (Corrective)	Legislation (Normative)	Justice (Corrective)
FALSE 'FORMS' OF FLATTERY			
Of the Body		*Of the Soul*	
Cosmetics (Normative)	Cookery (Corrective)	Sophistic (Normative)	Rhetoric (Corrective)

Under "The True Arts" in the "Normative" category "Of the body," Platon identified philosophy.

Under "The True Arts" in the "Normative" category "Of the body," Platon identified philosophy with (natural) health through "exercise" and "good diet," with "Medicine as the "Corrective" that would restore the body to true health; in the "Normative" category of "Of the Soul," Platon identified philosophy with "Legislation" that would maintain the health of the political state, with "Justice" as the "Corrective" that would restore the soul (and thus the body) politic back to good health.

***

Rhetoric and Poetry as Negative Counterpoints

In this specific example from *Gorgias* about speech, poetry was associated with rhetoric by Platon as "forms of flattery" (502c–d; cf. Di Romilly 47–66). Both "Forms of Flattery" were "truer" *antistrophoi*—counterparts ("not an exact copy, but making a kind of pair with it, and corresponding to it as the antistrophe to the strophe in a choral ode" [Freese and Striker, 3n.1]). A rough equivalent to "THE TRUE ARTS" and "FORMS OF FLATTERY" (Table 3), both Rhetoric and Poetry as false philosophies based on imitation were meant to flatter (Table 4) were "TRUE FALSE FORMS" and "FALSE TRUE FORMS" (cf. *Gorgias* (462c–466a); *Greater Hippias*; *Parimenides*; *Sophist* 235d–237a; *Symposium* 201c–202b).

Table 4. Rhetorics and Poetry as True False/False True Forms.

TRUE FALSE FORMS			
Rhetorics		Poetics	
Of the Body		*Of the Soul*	
Cookery	Cosmetics	Pleasure	Allegory
(Normative)	(Corrective)	(Normative)	(Corrective)
FALSE TRUE FORMS			
Of the Body:		*Of the Soul*	
Demagoguery	Sophistics	Illusion	Divine Madness*
(Normative)	(Corrective)	(Normative)	(Corrective)

*"Vessels," which are *empty* (have no "real" content, refer to nothing, are mere imitations), could have been the language of poetry (images, metaphors, meter), or the poets (and thus their souls) themselves (see Plato, *Ion*).

Under the category "TRUE FALSE FORMS" in the "Normative" category "Of the body," rhetoric was identified as a kind of "Cookery" with "Cosmetics as the Corrective"; in the "Normative" category "Of the Soul," poetics was identified as "Pleasure" with "Allegory" as the "Corrective." Here, rhetoric as cosmetics (imitation and flattery) would return the body to a normative (false) state of cookery, and allegory would return the soul to a normative state of pleasure (for Platon both "unnatural" undesirable and states—at least for the philosopher). Under the category "FALSE TRUE FORMS" in the "Normative" category "Of the body," rhetoric was identified as "Demagoguery" with "Sophistic" as the "Corrective"; in the "Normative" category "Of the Soul," "Illusion" was identified as poetics with "Divine Madness" (θεία μανία—*theia mania*)—a hapless and uncontrollable as the "Corrective." Here, for Platon, the empty vessel of the poet (see *Ion*) who daily fed on illusion (Plato, *Gorgias* 248b) was touched and (re)filled with divine madness by the gods, tipping and returning the corrupted and corrupting poet's soul to its [un]natural state of illusion. At best, in both "FALSE TRUE FORMS" and "TRUE FALSE FORMS," the hollow pleasure-seeking vessel of the body and the illusions of the soul would be stuffed again and again with the Demagoguery of rhetorics and the Illusions of poetry, to be "corrected" by Sophistry and the poetical action of Allegory and the uncontrollable visions of divine madness.

Facial Aspects Only

a real rockface
would grimace
in disgust and disgrace

***

i report. Thus it was that for Platon rhetoric was facetiously identified with *cooking*: if rhetoric is not like *cooking* in some regards, "that is what it is, artwork and rhetoric" ("ταὐτὸν ἄρ'ἐστὶν ὀψοποιία καὶ ῥητορική"—*taftón ár' estín opsopoiía kaí ritoriki* [*Gorgias* 462e])—to which the *pleasure* of poetry might also be applied as another cosmetic that needed to be stripped away. As "a false "genre of 'art'," all "forms of flattery" based on appearances rather than true reality were false. Rhetorics and poetics at best were empty cooking vessels that could be decorated with a variety of makeups, and overfilled with one or more of four types of divine madness (*Phaedrus* 244–245c)—which for women, children, and slaves (and the young, like Aristocles and Phaedrus) were perhaps tantalizingly true as elucidations designed to explain madness and love, and fatuously false as allegorical myths, designed to please, satiate, but also persuade and motivate the search for true knowledge. But Demagoguery and Illusion would continue to become a primary source of "valid" knowledge, and thus an ongoing ontological weakness of human epistemology that could only be rectified by the physics of pleasure and the legends of the gods.

To all the gods in general, whoever, wherever, whatever, you may be

"For every blessing, two curses" –Edward Tick (Conversation)

Be merciful
With our faith
We pray,
For our fate
Is in your way

And even you need
Love sometime, and chambers
Recessed into infinity,
To retire from the angels
And cry inconsolably

***

i report. For Platon, rhetorics with its demagogueries and sophistics of cooking and cosmetics, and poetics with its pleasures and illusions of allegories and divine madness were *shared* (and *world-wide)* false realities and truths (*Republic* II.382–b–c; *Phaedo*; *Theaetetus*). In the magical hands of Platon as Author, however, "allegories" and "divine madness" (along with some linguistic signs and some *soma*, a few fleshy bodies and a hint of the mist of mysticism) could lead a listener (or reader) to another, truer (disembodied) version of Reality than perhaps either philosophy or poetry could do alone.

dear god[s]

{if (YOU) exist}
iHope [hope]
you are well to
{day}/I see
(automatically)
here you are
well that [too]

iPray [pray]
{if (YOU) exist}
Spiel-CHECK
er works to
{day}/correct
(retribution)
all my sins repent
well that [too]

ι iota

i report. In the *Gorgias,* Platon also perhaps patrolled the negative "philo-political-socio" consequences and the potential eternal effects of rhetoric and poetry on bodies and souls. As Forms of Flattery, rhetoric and poetry, like two "prostitutes" (*ιερόδουλος—ierődoules*), might affect "anyone around besides" who was susceptible to physical pleasure ("φημι τὸτοιοον κολακείαν . . . περὶ ἄλλο ὅτου ἄν τις τὴν ἡδονὴν"—*fimi tótoioon kolakeían . . . perí állo ótou án tis tín idonín*) (*Gorgias* 501c–d; Crane; Lamb). Taking these "Forms of Flattery" that cross "genres" as "parallel and correlative" (Di Romilly 48) one step further, there may have been (at least) *two* "kinds" of flattery: the damage done to the body and the soul of the *giver/producer* of flattery, as well as *the recipient(s)* of flattery. These two kinds of flattery might have been said to correspond loosely to Platon's division of "normative" (current) and "corrective" (future) states in the *Gorgias* (see Tables 3 and 4), both arising from the paradoxical power of rhetoric and poetry to "maintain" or "restore" the (errant) body and soul to their (im)perfect "normative" and "corrective" states *through flattery.* Those prostitutes (εκείνες οι ιερόδουλος), rhetoric and poetry, like cooking and pleasure, provided no "Real" sustenance for either body or soul—yet appeared necessary to survive. (Did this susceptibility lead to the "defect" of style and emotions in the hearer that Aristotle later talked about [*Rhetoric* 1404a5–10; cf. *Generation* 731b28; 738b19–26]?) For the philosopher, this was a limitation and a circumstance for the mind to circumvent as much as possible. “Let us have no intelligence in the life of pleasure, and no pleasure in the life of intelligence,” Socrates admonished; “[f]or if either of them is the good it must have no need of anything else to be added to it, and if we find that either has such a need, presumably it ceases to be possible to be our true good” (*Philebus* 21a). To imbibe rhetoric and poetry was to “to feed upon the food of semblance” (Plato, *Gorgias* 248b).

Into Nothingness

writhing expanse
of space
suffocating winds

solar belts
finally breached
tightening, broken

nothing more
had to happen
here: head locked
in a single ice chip

vast field of forget
fulness forgotten,
the almost-saw
what’s not now seen
not moving slowly closer

to intercept it
in the mouth,
to halt and swallow it
out of orbit—
oblivion just below
the speed of light

***

False Genres of Flattery

i report. In whatever particular form it took, rhetoric and poetry as genres of flattery (and thus as "false arts") pleasured rather than enlightened the body (and more dangerously, the soul) in at least two ways: 1)The unhealthy relationship of the interlocutor as giver/producer who flattered another as a "normative" maintenance, or as a "corrective" to *return* that body and soul to its past illusions (cf. *Phaedrus*); 2) the unhealthy relation of the listener as taker/recipient who accepted the flattery as a "normative" or corrected way of living. Platon seems to have seen the flattery of rhetoric and poetry as something not only fake or false, but also as something "round about," "wrapped around" [Lamb; Liddell and Scott 1366; Autenrieth and Keep 255]), something worn, like makeup or jewelry, whether giver or receiver. But the physical body of speech and writing was wrapped tightly round and bound the soul with rhetoric and poetry as well. That is, Socrates was talking not only about flesh, but also about style. Style was shimmering flattery overflowing speech—given or received. The accusative case with a direct object, *peri* would have indicated what was tied or wrapped "around," binding; *peri* in the dative case with an indirect object would have indicated how it had been put on, how worn, how tightly, such as "close fitting dresses, armor, etc." (Lamb; Liddell and Scott; Autenrieth and Keep 255–56). As flattery, then, rhetoric and poetry, like cosmetics and ornaments, were something that the body of the speech uncritically offered, unconsciously wore.

the gods don't really have to wear clothes

On the highest snowy mountain peaks
gods, like drunken wayward parents, sleep,
completely naked in concealing clouds—
even dead, they have no need of shrouds.

An inner light is their outer garment,
when they rise and shake off all the dust,
and don the gown of darkness we call warmth,
around a plane of planets we call home

***

Platon seemed to have understood style as adorning "the *body* of speech and writing," deceiving and misleading the soul of the listener/reader (Plato, *Phaedrus* 264c; cf. Nietzsche, *Science*; Derrida, *Spurs;* Nancy, *Corpus*). At least by analogy that Platon himself established in the *Gorgias*, rhetoric and poetry as "forms" of false flattery—as the flatter and blather of language—affected the bodies of speakers and listeners as well as the "material bodies of speech" (see Table 4). The flattery of rhetoric and poetry affected the physical senses of the body, and thus the well-being of the soul that wore the body (*Gorgias* 479b; *Phaedo* 86c; *Phaedrus* 270b; *Philebus*, esp. 32c; *Sophist* 228a). As shown in Parts Two and Three of *Plato's Nightmare*, style as ornamentation that was worn became dominant themes in Roman rhetoric (e.g., Second Sophistic, Ciceronian); and in the Middle Ages, the Renaissance, and the Baroque period (e.g., "High," "Ciceronian," "Baroque," or Lillian styles [Croll]), as opposed to a supposedly preferred Attic or "plain style" of classical Greek (e.g., Aristotle) and the scientific revolution of the seventeenth century (e.g., Bacon; Sprat; Locke, *Essay*). Poetry and rhetoric were like clothes or jewels adorned and displayed on living-but-dead bodies housing indestructible but fragile souls—false signs and fantastic allegories—whether in eveningwear or Day-Glo.

*Kimomeni**

(From the Clock Tower at Sunset, Poros, Greece)

Little mountain lying on its back
all day along a short peninsula
across the close water of the sea
churning, giving birth at her feet.
Watch. Will she stir at sunset?
Will she wake tonight? Nobody
knows. In a myth she sleeps,
all day in the light, heavy, still.
(Is she breathing in the heat?)

In the morning she simply
stretches, spreads her knees
in the sun. In the afternoon
she does her nails, and does not worry

about the fishermen who flock
around her rocks to see.
The slow wet light licks
and warms her glistening toes—
megalos, yet such delicate stones.

Rainy days a cloud might touch her nose.
She disappears inside foggy afternoons,
but you still might catch her dreaming
twilight. But at dusk she again retires

into the hollow of the darkness.
Is that her dressing before we leave?
Braids of waves trace her face,
brimming over shoulders of boulders,
running down to the seafloor of her feet.

*This is the name of a nymph-goddess embodied in a rocky hill or small mountain on a close, tiny peninsula across from the island of Poros, made in stone. In the local legend, one day Kimomeni would awake and rise up, huge and stony, a blessing in this place. Every day at dusk tourists and locals alike climbed up to the church clock tower deck, crowded the outdoor tavernas around on the shore, or took little boats out to be closer to her, waiting to see if she would stir, and one day rise.

κ *kappa*

The Body as "False Genre"

i report. As flattery, rhetoric and poetry were like *K*imomeni (Κοιμωμένη)—bronze ropes, silver necklaces, silk cinctures, golden cords—all really iron 'chains' or 'cable' (καλώδιο—*kalódio*) bound round the speech and the body, pulled tightly, strangling the soul. But in the wider context of his discourse on flattery, Platon was not only talking about *style* as an ornament of speech or of the body; he was also talking about *the body itself* as an ornament that could and should be stripped off the psyche and the soul, thus made —"clean" (καθαρή—*katharí*) and "pure" (καθαρός—*katharos*). Style was the mortal flesh of flattery, an ornamental skin that surrounded and befuddled the eternal soul. For Platon and other ancient Greeks, the physical body as *soma* was a perfumed musky husk that housed the distinct and dualistically opposed soul in which the *nou* ("mind") might arise, be actualized, exist independently of the body insofar as that was possible (*Philebus* 39a; cf. Handelman 7–9). "The body (was) the grave of the soul" (*Cratylus* 400c; cf. Olshewsky).

***

The Forms of Flattery, then, like the Forms of True Arts for Socrates and Plato, were not just philosophical and rhetorical, but also physical and affective. Flattery was *soma*. The definition of "περὶ" (*perì*) as something "put on," worn, "adorning one's person" referred *not only* to style as *soma* wrapped around the body of speech, but also as body wrapped around the soul (Crane; Lamb; Liddell and Scott; Autenrieth and Keep 255–56). For Platon, within the body as a living corpse or *soma*, the precious, holy soul was kept, perhaps separate but still deeply affected by every affliction the body had endured (see *Gorgias* 523e–524e). The soul was imprisoned, waiting to be liberated from the body even if that body was sensitive to its soul (*Phaedo* 82e). But most slept in their bodies, dreamt on, lived out a fabricated existence, a false reality (see *Phaedo*; *Philebus*).

A. Θεοι και Άνθρωποι (Gods and Humans)

littered with the bodies
of rocks and stones,
the old guide draws us up
to the end of a cliff
where villagers in ancient Crete
did not flee, but fought—
"*Possah anthropoi*?" i ask,
cognizant only of counting,
ignorant of the ancient language
of joy and celebration and sorrow,
suffering both life and death
together, transforming all

***

i report. For Platon and his philosophical followers, the living soul was not safe within the grave (*soma*) of its body (*Cratylus* 400c). The body was "an index" of the soul—scarred and marked by any uncritical morality and haphazard action of the body, "mortal, multiform, unintelligible, dissoluble, and never self-consistent" (*Phaedo* 80b). The soul was subject to all manner of temptation and flattery in the variegated life of its temporary owner. The Physical "Forms" of Flattery (see Table 4) as "*therapean àsképtos*" may have assumed at least two forms: 1) the pleasurable experiencing of the physical appearance of the body or something on or a part of the body that "flattered" the wearer (in this case, the *producer of self-flattery*), i.e., *it flattered them, it was flattering on them*); and 2) the pleasurable experiencing of the physical appearance of the body or something on or a part of the body that was *provoked by the flattery of others* (caused the recipient to be *the object of flattery*). In both cases, the body donned and/or accepted the flattery, and was willing to wear and be bound by it. Decorated or not, the living corpse of *soma*—especially a beautiful one that might itself attempt to flatter the soul, or that would be the object of the flattery of others—might have wrapped and bound itself ever more tightly around the long-suffering, suffocating soul, damaging it. (In the debate on dual vs. unitary nature of the soul, there was a middle stance, the "interactionist" position, that tended to believe that bodies and souls remained distinct yet reflected and causally affected one another (*IEP*). This "interactionist" philosophical position would become more common in neo-Platonic Christianity, with its separate focus on "saving the soul from eternal damnation" and the resurrection of the physical body at the end of days. It was a view apparently never completely adopted by the Jews, for whom body and soul were one, even in the event of Kingdom-Come [cf. Raphael].)

λ *lambda*

i report. Flattery, both rhetorical/poetic and physical/metaphysical, as false "accounts," "reasons" (λόγοι—*lógoi*), "words," ways of "thinking" (λογική—*logiki*), a kind of "plagiarism" (λογοκλοπία—*logoklopía*) infected every level the human body and its senses—that stinking, unthinking sac of flesh, that oily grease "stain" (λιπαρό λεκέ—*liparó leké*), that piss-pot mortal prison house of the soul. The body was but a pale imitation of the celestial soul, a pall, an appalling recipient of false praise, a generator or replicator of false flesh, a propagator of flattery. Flattery as the rhetoric and poetry of the body was further "symbolized." And thus through imitations of imitations, symbolizations upon symbolizations, flatteries (like alphabets) "re-symbolized" and multiplied indefinitely (see Langer, *New Key*; cf. Abulafia on the Jewish *Zohar* ["splendor"] on G/d's descending attributes through the majestic *sephiroth* [divine vessels, moral lights]; Vital on the infinite extension and tragic shattering of the vessels of divine energy into the material universe; Derrida on the echoing chain of signification without a final signifier [*Grammatology*]. These were all rhetorics too [Bloom]). Yet for the Greeks as well as the Jews, the "flattery" and "deception" of human and aesthetic form, and the imitation in language and the arts of the divine, transcendental, metaphysical, and/or mystical realms of experience, seemed to be needed for the physical appearance and material sensation of thoughts and things unseen (Plato, *Phaedo*, e.g., 79c; Heidegger, "Question" 20; Katz, "Letter as Essence"). This literary predicament—in science, as well as philosophy and religion—was at the core of both Platon and Aristotle and of Western history, and was also slowly peeled away (further examined in *Plato's Nightmare*). For Platon and Aristotle, flattery and deception, the arts and every part of language, "represented" and perhaps may have been at the very root of true human ignorance.

B. Θεοί και Άνθρωποι (Gods and Humans)

Very edge-top of a cliff
perched on one motorcycle of gold:
two forms, male and female, reappear
not twenty feet away, startlingly
quick stunningly beautiful, stop.
Sleek blinding as they sit atop

the thinner sunlight, turn, and look
directly at us, smile, their gleaming
helmets with painted wings,
their blond hair, sunglasses, their amber
skin visible through silver
leather, clothing, gloves, shoes,
her golden arms wrapped
around his fit shiny waist—
flash their teeth, then spin, fly
down the bright blue sky.

We ask: "Who were they?"
'What did they want?' We ask
ourselves, each other. "Did they
speak? What did they say?"
"Was it Hermes dating Aphrodite?"
We ask the other as we descend
the rocky hillside, yellow grasses
strewn with rocks of all sizes
and ages, pebbles to boulders,
boulders to pebbles, disintegrate,
humans now long passed and gone.
And even the arrogant linguist
who refused to speak modern Greek,
only classical to the bewilderment
of the living, still with us,
did not question the now quiet ground.

***

i report. The human senses as physical organs deceived both the wearer and the wearee by virtue of being superficially appealing sources of outward beauty (cf. Nancy, *Muses*; Serres, *Five Senses*). Like the symbiotic (and often technologically mediated) relationship between sadists and masochists, voyeurs and exhibitionists, narcissists and altruists, the parties derived physical pleasure from beauty (*Phaedrus* 250b–252a) as well as pain (Plato, *Phaedo* 83–84). But pleasuring one's worldly senses or the senses of others through the physical processes of flattery was a flood of "instant gratification," concerned *only* with immediate appearance, effect, and response—sources and receptors of self-congratulatory blabber, a bribery of blubber, the blather of a mutual flattery-admiration club. The senses could have led the soul to search for truth, but instead only led to further suffering, death, and rebirth (e.g., *Phaedrus*, 247b–249b)—possibly reflecting the influence of eastern religious mysticism or possibly beliefs in reincarnation—the transmutation and re-embodiment of souls. Even the Ideal Form of Beauty, the only Form that could manifest itself at all physical in the material world (Plato, *Phaedrus* 250d, 251f; Heidegger, "Question" 34–35), might have actually misled the soul, like: the Sirens tempting sailors to crash the shoals of Skyla and Charybdis, daughters of Poseidon; Circe the witch, transforming men into pigs and until they forgot they were human; Odysseus plunging into the bowels of Hades in search of Tiresias and a plan on how to get home; Demeter wailing for daughter Persephone, perennially lost beyond the *Lethe.* Philosophical allegories for the search for Truth, for *Alethea* [Αλήθεια] continued—if not from the goddess, perhaps an Oracle (Plato, *Defense* 20e; *Hippias Major* 288b), already buried in Platon's time behind the Apollonian mask of misogyny, philosophical patriarchy, male virility (Kingsley).

Sibyl and the Scientists

("The concentration of gases that were produced by the vent at the time the oracle was functioning is unknown." —Spiller, Hale, De Boer, "The Delphic Oracle: A Multidisciplinary Defense of the Gaseous Vent Theory" [Journal of Toxicology—Clinical Toxicology, *2002*]*)*

A sibyl lies buried
beneath this temple,
somewhere under
the ruin of rubble—
speaks in the chirp
of sparrows and the screech
of crickets and the whistle
of hawks overhead
who answer back
in a buzz of bees

From her rock face
the brush and bush
grow like withered beards.
Tiresias, the elder scientist,
walks among the blind
columns, comes questioning
their existence, purpose,
and the prior inhabitants
of crevices, surveying
the ivy and the weeds.

And crossing the sky,
the peripatetic philosopher,
Apollo, conducts his experiments
on the power of the Oracle
on the power of the prophetesses

sitting in the dust of Delphi,
in the hole of the Pythia
where according to Plutarch
the gases still rose in the bowl
from an underground spring

Mythology: the empirical origin
of history, and of all things

μ mu

Ugly Bodies, Beautiful Souls

i report. The physical (false *m*aterial reality) to which rhetoric and poetry and other arts too as flattery referred, appealed directly to the body's senses, where all was transitory, transition (*μετάβαση—metávasi*). As least in the *Gorgias*, it seems Platon as philosopher did not believe that cosmetics, like advertising and public relations later, made qualities like beauty apparent to the senses (even as Platon plied them in the same literary trade). Au contraire: true beauty was an Ideal Form. Even the beauty of the soul, which would partake and someday be a part of the Form, was never necessarily distinct and apparent from the physical body that housed it. For Platon, a beautiful soul might be carried (hidden) inside the ugliest of bodies (if the body pursued truth and beauty), as Socrates himself proclaimed and was said to be a prime exhibit (*Theaetetus* 143e; *Symposium* 215a–c, 216a–e, 220b–222a). This position too accorded with the "unity," "dualist," and the "interactionists" [*IEP*] view of the soul, since what happened to the body, deformed or diseased by accident or at birth, happened to the soul (see *Plato, Republic* X.609a–610c; cf. *Greater Hippias*, esp. 286c, 304d; *Philebus*, esp. 66a–b). Transitory, in "transition" (σε μετάβαση—*se metávasi*). The soul—whether unified, completely separate from, or interreacting with the body—was also affected. Then again, as in an analogy with Trojan Horse of the *Iliad*, a warped, wayward, whimsical, indiscriminate, misshapen, injured soul might be snuck in an aesthetically attractive and deceptively pleasing body. No matter what body it was found in, for Platon rhetoric and poetry as flattery had the (persuasive, magical, mystical) power to distract and derail the good intentions of the "best souls" (those souls sufficiently stalwart, studied, and wise, and remembered; and/or those souls in their penultimate or final reincarnation from a righteous, just, and temperate lives in their prior existence, which perhaps had beheld and pursued the beauty enough to have grown swollen with wings and fed a little on "True Beauty" and there beheld some other Forms as well (*Phaedrus* 1956, 250–51).

On a Ferry, Leaving Crete

three people waving
to one man
left on shore—

one seagull
waving over the water
in their wake

ν *nu*

"Stripping" the (Narcissistic) Bodies of Speech

i report. Narcissism (ναρκισσισμός—*narkissismós*). Flattery as ultimately a form of self-love. For Socrates at least, and probably Platon, the result of the "logical" correspondence of "true" and "false" arts (see Table 3)—the exterior veneer and unsavory traits of the forms of flattery on the body and its soul (see Table 4)—was that the "stripping" ("περιέλοι") of poetry from rhetoric, and rhetoric from speech, became essential for the apprehension of epistemological clarity and philosophical truth (*Gorgias* 502c–d). For Platon, rhetoric and poetry were not products of any "art" ("τέχνη"—*technē*), but mere "knack," "habit," "experience" ("ἐμπειρία"—*empeir-ía*)—the empirical (and thus worthless) imitation of the illusion of the material world (*Gorgias* 462d; Crane; Liddell and Scott; Lamb; see Table 4). For Platon, rhetoric and poetry were sham arts, exhibitions of charm, suspicious magic tricks (Di Romilly). In his belief that the material world was an illusion that could be conjured up by language and that only a transcendental world truly existed, Platon proved himself again not only an ascetic philosopher and a versatile artist, but also an epistemological narcissus (νάρκισσος—*nárkissos*), and contra Hamilton and Cairns (xv), a total mystic.

***

Platon's mysticism was only partially hidden by the subsequent centuries of religious life, including such beliefs as a Christian "Son of God" who was born immaculate, had powers of transmogrification, and was resurrected from the dead; these beliefs were *not* suspiciously regarded as superstition or magic, but were directly or indirectly compared to or taken by faith as facts and acts of ontological contrition. Eventually accepted later as the essence of religious life, Judeo-Christian beliefs, including of an omnipotent, eternal, monotheistic G/d, tended to be read back into Platonic philosophy and even some pagan practices and gods (e.g., cf. Hamilton and Cairns xxv, and xv, 421, 526, 845, 1151, 1226). Akin to cooking and cosmetics, as opposed to True Philosophical Arts of "Legislation," "Justice," "Gymnastics," and "Medicine," rhetoric and poetry as forms of flattery for Platon were mendacious linguistic imitations (Table 4). As such, like a bandage over a bad burn, perhaps it had to be not just peeled back or "unwrapped" or gently "removed," but "stripped" ("περιέλοι"), torn away, ripped off, the ruts and runnels of rot amputated, lopped off (cf. Table 1), the numb dumb unknowing body, the dead "*soma*" of words, to "clean" the speech beneath, reveal a thinking mind inside, to free the living soul contained within (*Phaedo* 81; *Phaedrus* 250c). What Platon demonstrated in *Gorgias* (502c–d) and almost all his dialogues was nothing short of both *his* rhetorical and literary creation, and the simultaneous "stripping" of his own dialogic creations with the blade of dialectical logic wielded in his treatises by Socrates).

***

Stripping the Living and the Dead

i report. In Platon's treatises, the idea of dialectically stripping speech, especially philosophical speech, of the excesses and adornments of "flattery," may have seemed somewhat more figurative than literal. But flogging did come up in several places in his work, most notably in the *Gorgias,* in the mouth of Callicles who was actually attacking Socrates: Callicles was discussing the study of philosophy as a child's endeavor, which he particularly found reprehensible in adults where it was an embarrassment if not an obstacle to success (and also post-prophetically, self-defense); Callices compared *the study of philosophy* to a kind of inappropriate and impractical rhetorics of false self-flattery, naively-slavish imitation, and physically offensive sounds and speech:

> [W]hen I hear [a little child] talking with precision, it seems to me disagreeable and it vexes my ears and appears to me more fitting for a slave, but when one hears a grown man lisping or sees him playing the child, it looks ridiculous and unmanly and worthy of a beating . . . . [W]hen I see an older man still studying philosophy and not deserting it, that man, Socrates, is actually asking for a whipping. (*Gorgias* 485b–d)

For Callicles, the philosopher was "*worthy of stripes*" (Jowett 95). Socrates' method of "flaying" was intellectual, not physical. Socrates' comeback to Callicles was to talk about material pleasures as leaky vessels, and then itching and scratching any part of the body (*Gorgias* 494c). If the body as *soma* was parallel if not connected to speech for Platon, poetry and rhetoric were the sensuous skin and amoral muscle of speech. Not so for Kenneth Burke, who was "a word-man" (Blakesley, Introduction xvii–xviii). Both skin and text, words *were* "fleshy bodies" and bodies were "fleshy words" (see Nancy, *Corpus*; Derrida, *Circumfession*). But for Socrates and Platon, the act of "stripping" rhetoric and poetry from speech as style was *also* an act of peeling back the dead skin and flesh of *soma* as living corp(u)ses, to reveal the corruption of errant bodies, and the radiant soul beneath.

Second Skin (α)

It's attracted deeply to the skin,
a warm body to crawl back into,
a face, a torso, an ankle to inhabit.

The ancient priests and healers might have called it
daemon, psyche, soul, prime mover, angel, spirit;
but it aches to feel human longing.

Psychologists might have called it (wrongly)
a sublimation of sexual desire,
the sign or symptoms of a grown man
a signification of wanting, a reversal
to create, reenter, deconstruct the cave
of the womb, little boy deprived of his mother

***

i report. The skin of false "reality" had to be physically stripped from the soul not only in life but also and especially after death. Whatever was under the skin had to be thoroughly examined, for just as the body (*soma)* was an "index of the soul" (*Cratylus* 400c, qtd. in Hamilton and Cairns 1624), the soul was "an index" of the body (*Phaedo* 80b). Platon had Socrates use the word "stripping" four times in the *Gorgias* alone. The meaning of these four kinds of stripping depended on their context, but were climatically ordered. As noted, the first act of stripping was the cutting away of song—poetry, and then rhetoric—from speech (*Gorgias* 502c; cf. *Republic* III). The next telegraphing of the term referred directly to the act of the souls who were to judge the incoming souls; the judges themselves as the best of the virtuous dead had "stripped" themselves of any mortal attire so that they might as soul "scan" and impartially pass verdict on each of the souls of the recently dead who now appeared before them

(*Gorgias* 523e). Finally, at the very moment of death, bodies and souls were pierced and separated—and the bodies (including all clothes and ornaments) were "stripped" from their souls and those assembled so that each naked soul could be judged (*Gorgias* 524b–e).

Second Skin (β)

erotic but always distant—
is that where it first learned
to speak without speaking,
an infant object in a network;
to know without knowing
simulated language and love,
texting and sexting and b-flogging
a skeleton of signs, a syntax
of need without desire,
putting on a second second
skin of clothes (an overcoat
that doesn't quite fit, but
you'll get used to it), this new outer
garment made from unknown country—

ξ xi

The Selection (After Death)

i report. Disentangling (ξεμπλέξιμο—*xempléximo*). The stripping of poetry and rhetoric from speech, the tearing away of the body of flesh at death, was necessary to inspect the living soul, the piercing of the freshly extricated and splayed souls that were immediately arrayed for judgment, and the sentencing of the wayward soul. And then there was what happened after judgement. At the very end of the *Gorgias*, Socrates related to Gorgias, perhaps in an attempt to terrify and so reform him(?), "a legend" of what happened as the also dead but naked judges in charge of the selection quickly "disentangled," "unravelled" (ξεμπερδεύω—*xemperdévo*) and decided with pointing staffs the fate of the stripped souls of the newly dead, the incurable: "suffering throughout the greatest and most excruciating and terrifying tortures because of their misdeeds, literally suspended as examples there in the prison house in Hades, spectacle . . ." (*Gorgias* 525e).

Second Skin (γ)

apparatuses touch us
but we cannot touch back,
sheer motion in a data stream
of ecstatic unconscious objects
actors without agency,
agency without agents,
scenes and acts without purpose,
signification empty signs until we stop
at the local blood store before
we continue on our way
to somewhere we've already forgotten,
or perhaps never been before

***

i report. Like every "civilization," the Greeks had many forms of punishment that would induce pain, whose fangs reached down to the very soul, which according to Platon bore all the afflictions a body suffered in life (*Gorgias* 524b–d). In Book II of Platon's *Republic*, a cynical Glaucon argued that the unjust fared better than the just because of the punishment the just endured at the hands of the unjust who appear just: "The just man . . . will be scourged, racked, chained have his eyes burnt out; at last, after every kind of misery, he will be set on a pole [impaled]" (361e). An extraordinary form of punishment for the living in Crete was to be locked inside an iron cow, and on a low flame slowly heated, cooked, the moaning emitted from the cow's mouth as mooing met only laughter. Punishments also included being "stripped" of skin and flesh and flayed alive.

***

In the hands of Platon, Socrates was a closed fist, a whip of wit, a philosophical scythe. As a literary technique, a written character, a dialogue and style, Socrates became Platon's knife, his dagger, his stiletto or stylus, writing instrument (but from Greek στιλέτο—dagger; Latin *stylus*—a sharp instrument for writing on tablets; Italian *stilo*— an instrument for stabbing and cutting; French *stylo*—a pen [also see Derrida, *Spurs* 34–54; *Science*, sec. 340; cf. *Phaedo* 117e]. Aside from this etymological oscillation, stilettos also became a type of women's high-heeled shoe.) Through dialectic honed and sharpened in logic and style by frequent use against all the other characters (re)created and inscribed in his treatises, Platon wielded Socrates like surgical pen, a living scalpel—slowly stripping and peeling away dead thought and "ornamental" skin surrounding the flesh of text, revealing the dark muscles and dull bones of half-truths and untruths that lay unespied in the material cave of the body—the tomb (*sema*) of the soul (*Cratylus* 400c; *Gorgias* 493a). In the *Gorgias* and elsewhere, Socrates proceeded "ἀτρέμας" (*Gorgias* 503d [*atremas*—without tremor/trembling," "steady"]) to calmly, self-deprecatingly, humorously, and with philosophical good cheer—skin the words, thoughts, and logic of his interlocutors—to separate from the sacred souls from the adorned, adoring, adored surfaces of their bodies of speech/text.

***

i report. Perhaps the story of the parting the body and soul immediately after death that this time *Socrates* said he believed, was another allegory of flaying (see *Gorgias* 523e–525c). In accordance with Platon's later demand that any "art" of rhetoric used to communicate truths already found by dialectic, also would have to employ dialectic to analyze speeches and analyze souls and match them. Targeting speeches to specific souls (*Phaedrus* 271a–272b; cf. Bakhtin, *Dialogic*) was regarded as early audience adaptation. But it also could have been regarded as choosing the proper instruments to disentangle a particular body (or body part) from a particular soul. Using the rhetorics and poetics of short-punchy questions, sharp slashes, long-drawn out speeches, potent logic, pointy wit, as well as a plethora of imagery, analogy, metaphor, mythology, religion, and mysticism (e.g., Greek, Egyptian, Asian, Orphic [see *Phaedo* 80c]), S ocrates playfully plied and deftly thrusted and parried and plucked and sliced-open the frail frames of embodied "faulty" logic in his hope of exposing some truth for which he so diligently dug.

*My Dagger: Seitsen und Dussen**

(For Charlotte Kaempf, at Bunratty Castle, Limerick, Ireland)

under the hat
things come alive

the noble potato
reaches across the High Table

the eagle over Brandenburg Gate
has thin shoulders, hips

the stiletto, like a dagger
pierces the thick bloated wood

the red bib makes it
out the door in time

lowly cockroaches
are the final consumers

*In German, *seitsen* and *dussen* referred to the cultural-linguistic practice of addressing a "you" by using the formal (also plural) *Sie* vs. the more intimate or informal *du*. In this linguistic/physical diminishment (cutting down) or augmentation (refiguring up) there was something significant, even prophetic.

o omicron

Publicly Punishing the Body

i report. Omen (οιωνός). Before death, and after, the stripping of text or/and flesh was not the first public demonstration of flaying; nor would they be the last. Stripping and flaying as "agonistic philosophy" and as punishment was popular in the hands of the god Apollo (Helios) in human form. This was captured and attested to various myths recounted in Ovid, Plutarch (*Lives*), and many others. As painted by Titian, Apollo, with great focus and intensity and apparent glee, was about to flay the Phrygian satyr, Marsyas, as punishment for losing a music contest with the god (obviously and ominously doomed from the start). In other encounters too, Apollo, slowly, deliberately, with "divine" blade, —proceeded to slice and pull away long strips of unbroken flesh from the suspended or bound upside down body of the prey, while others watched with in horror or relish. The unfortunate object of Apollo's rapt attention and "impartial" justice, the victim being tortured or executed is usually quite alert, alive, mortified with searing lacerations, as their outer casing was pierced and carefully removed, strip by strip (Benthien, 79; Foucault, *Discipline*), — precisely, meticulously, in any way the god found scientifically effective or personally pleasing. Or brutally, clumsily, haphazardly, the skin peeled like kernels of corn off the cob, barely kept intact, just hanging together, then breaking as Apollo, area by area, shredded one part, then another, ranging over the entire terrain of the bleeding body. In Titian, a boy looked toward any viewers, his arm around his black dog that was drooling, while a smaller dog under Marsyas ate "some meat" . . . For various reasons in different myths, Ορφέας (Orpheus), musician and poet who was said to be able to charm even rocks, lived out an omen (οιωνός) and met a similar fate, torn to shreds by "the furies" of the Maenads. Later, in Roman times, and beyond, the blade arrived further inside the internal cavity, —to cut into and carve up or out individual organs, detaching them, one by one, from their other members while keeping the attachee alive, —the recipient of a god's, king's, or flayer's offended affection and perverse revenge . . . until the god, king, or flayer was satisfied, tired, or lost interest, the wretch conscious until the last longed-for stroke, the end. Omens (οιωνοί).

***

Socrates was certainly not Apollo—in appearance, power, or behavior. But like Apollo, Socrates was a master with an epistemological blade of "unconcealing" the truth of human existence—probing an opening, inspecting human weakness: pleasure and pain, corruption and mortality. Logically dividing "the subject," he "*stripped*" rhetoric and poetry from the body of philosophy, content from form, speech from thought—removed the mimetic membranes of any remaining metaphor, revealed the musculature of rhetorical flesh— tore the last tissues and hanging tendons of false images and signs from the tender, private parts of language and thought —hollowed out the overly decorous rind of dangerous discourse. Perhaps it was only a difference in degree rather than kind. Platon's dream of *soma* as the living sleep of an already and always dead body (*Phaedo*) was not the dream healing sleep of the Asclepios. It was a nightmare. And the embodied minds of the flayed and still astutely aware, —trying to argue, to explain, to beg, to plead, to shriek . . . gasped through pain for air.

Schadenfreude Among the Stars

she smashes her hand
through the thermal glass
of an airlock hatch

he sips his hot coffee
through the mouthpiece
of a pressurized helmet, smiling

* *Schadenfreude* (German). Feeling pleasure at the distress or sorrow of others.

π pi

Disposing of the Body from Birth

i report. The need to "consolidate" (*παγιώνω—pagióno*) these practices was felt everywhere and for all time. The complicated philosophic-physiological-psychological need to see the body and its "functions" as sin, to remove dead body/speech and to punish and purify by eviscerating and eventually disposing of it and releasing the soul from *soma*, spirit from its heavy sack of sin; —to behold the Ideal Forms (remembered internally from some past life or achieved externally in a journey to some transcendental realm gained by growing some wings); —to be closer to or more like the gods by approaching the Throne or experiencing "the Passion" or a mystical sojourn or sublime soaring or otherwise deserving salvation; — continued and eventually extended to other forms of human practice and communication in the Anthropocene: social rituals, religious customs, political penitence, cultural punishment: fasting flagellating flaying hanging crucifying wracking severing screwing drawing quartering piking impaling, sodomizing disemboweling cutting cilicing gutting boiling choking scourging scorching raping beheading blinding bombing beating starving electrocuting poisoning injecting immolating drowning lynching gassing mutilating amputating restructuring augmenting reconstituting transferring; —or otherwise removing the offending alien or ugly or deformed or evil or hated bodies or their part(s), in any form and at any age, from the exhausted life forces in their midst.

*"Infant in Arms"**

i.
babies being drafted,
for military service,
standard issue
diapers and plastic
bayonets, rifles
that really fire,
bootie camp, then
sent overseas in
spanking uniforms...

ii.
isn't this essence,
their innate duty and
obligatory patriotism
duty to support the war
they had no hand
in starting, stopping. We send
all our love, and
wish them well
on their way to hell . . .

iii.
place where all the infants
toys and tiny body parts
can be picked up gathered
from every corner
of the squared-off world,
finally brought together

to play at peace
in the marching
innocence of the dead . . .

*from "Now Boarding Passengers with Infant in Arms" at an airport that used to be near you.

***

In the *Republic* and elsewhere, Platon had suggested the use for gymnastics, poetry, music and other arts in training the Guardians of his Ideal philosophical realm (III.399a–402d; cf. *Timaeus* 18a; *Laws* II.669b–671b). Neither Platon nor Socrates were the cause of the cruelty and chaos that followed. With few exceptions, no one person was. But the need and desire to strip form from matter, style from content, rhetoric from philosophical, poetry from scientific speech, persisted. And dialectic logic in the hands of others became a needle, a slender scalpel, a long blade, a dull dagger, a blunt knife, a gun butt, a flesh-riveting nail, an exploding bullet, a cluster bomb, a gas pellet dropped into a poison shower.

Pleasuring Death

Baby's bubbles breaking over knees
so pleasing to the senses, tickling
warped fancy after concentrated day

relaxing beside the camp's swimming pool
like pale champagne, an artificial lift
fizzing up inside the nose of pleasure

and everywhere all around over them
any philosopher-despot sentinel
who wears their swastikas like a set
of squared-off smiles circling the room,

whose carnages are most persuasive
so pleasing, agreeable, leader kneading
breaking baby baubles over knees

ρ rho

"Stripping" as Linguistic Psychosis

i report. Whether private and self-inflicted or deliberately public, in the roll (*ρ*ολό—*rolló*) of history the common destructive act of stripping was enacted repeatedly (an obsessive-compulsive cultural disorder). From corporal punishment to elective surgery, social cybernetics to moral engineering—even the black veilings of the minor goths to the rocks of the stoners to the acoustic violence of the punksters to the stabbing of the piercers to the inky injections of the tatoines—philosophically, politically, ethically, aesthetically, rhetorically, poetically, scientifically, technologically, humans sought to prick and perforate and roll the sheathing and shell of the body in order to search for truth, remembrance, authenticity, essence, reality. Perhaps these attempted non-annihilations leading to deliverance was in some ways proportional if not a response to the Platonic need for the idealization of Forms (justice, goodness, beauty, etc.). The West followed Platon's schizophrenic rhetoric like an auto-immune response to a disease of mimesis.

A Violent Dialectic

running bayonet
long-piercing spear
thrust through a heel—

the soul of Achilles—
pliable and soft but invisible
to all except who know

strong but damaged, deformed,
fortitude finally dying—
moral starvation, mortal vein

***

"Our birth is but a sleep and a forgetting," said Wordsworth ("Intimations of Immortality," based on Plato's *Phaedo* 73–76). A theory of *amnesia*—and hoped for recollection and restoration. If things went right (they often didn't), dying was only the death of the *soma*, the prison house of the soul (*Phaedo* 82e), and a liberation and rebirth of the soul from the dreams and delusions of the material world. A corpse left upon the floor.

σ *sigma*

The Living Body as a Form of Torture

As philosophy's stiletto (στιλέτο), Socrates (Σοκράτες) accomplished his work as rhetoric's (and poetry's) assassin. Both a scalpel and an axe in the hands of Platon, Σοκράτες removed the style and then corruption from soma (σώμα) of words, the corpse from logical thought and speech. For the sake of the sacred soul, Σοκράτες the στιλέτο (stiletto) exposed the shortcomings and benefits of a true Platonic life that ultimately would lead to an (ostensible) suppression and deprivation if not denial of the temptations of the senses and material pleasures of cosmetics and cooking, flattery and imitation of the outside world, so antithetical to the eternal life of the soul: "A life, you mean, of neither pleasure nor pain," asked Protarchus in the *Philebus*? Here Socrates proclaimed: "[F]or one who has chosen the life of reason and intelligence there must be no experiencing of any pleasure, great or small" (33b). This was especially the case with chosen asceticism in the monasteries of neo-history, in which faith, and prayer mixed with poetry and song might alleviate the self-afflicted suffering, led to the privileging of animus over anima, over the overwhelming sensory experience of the sublime, the soaring subjective genius of the Transcendentalists, state-sponsored industrial genocide, or technological lobotomy and suicide, as registered in *Plato's Nightmare.*

Sentient and Conscious Even While Asleep

(a stripped, flogged, broken sonnet)

Even a clone, robot, android
or digital being might suffer
the same fate as the humans, every
copy, screw, circuit, pixel, cell
like infant tiny open mouths
silently screeching, hyper-sensitized,
wildly alert, alive,
surprised by sudden agony of the turn—

the focal point of a technological
blade, with the added benefit
to the living that the cut and torn
entity could be repaired or
replicated again and the whole
procedure like a spiked
casuistic argument could be
enacted, begin, again, again

***

The Living Body as a Necessary "Genre"

i report. From the side effects of natural and necessary organic elements and bodily functions of the human body, Platon (and his decedent) did find some relief insofar as the body restored material equilibrium and thus stability of the body (*Philebus* 30b–d): satisfying hunger, quenching thirst, regulating temperature, etc. (see *Philebus* 31e–32e). But Platon (like Beethoven) was probably quite annoyed by the constant interruptions. And Platon was no Kenneth Burke: the viler organic elements and functions that Socrates discussed later in *Philebus* (32e–36d; 46a–47a)— perspiring and rubbing, penetrating and attaching, filling and emptying, itching and scratching—with all their suggestive scatological connotations as well as denotative or medical implications—were not Burke's "cloacal movements" to be treated as a philosophical and rhetorical and poetics of symbolic of motives. Au contraire. In the *Philebus*, Platon quickly had Socrates prove that pleasure itself is *not* "a true good" (particularly because of the hazards for/peril of the soul), and that reason and pleasure *must be separate* if intelligence was to be a true "good" (*Philebus* 21a). No matter how deprecatingly humorous or ironically playful Platon the literary artist was (through Socrates), in the end Platon the philosopher (through Socrates) always seemed to come down on the side of a purer dialectical intelligence (Hamilton and Kearns, 1086). The body itself was a form of flattery, a genre of literature. Unfortunately, unlike many sculptors, writers always had to make their own stone before they could carve it into art. So too the cyberneticists *qua* cloners disembodied, or perhaps un-embodied, or differently bodied, forms of consciousness.

After the Anthropocene

What will be left
in a thousand years—
not a pretty
face or skin or lips,
or skull or teeth or bone:

Instead they will say:
"My, what nice
sets of metal plates
people must have had
in the age in which they lived.

***

The Living Body as Rhetoric

Pleasure and pain, and the health not only of body but also of the soul, were in many ways rhetorical, kinds of appeals to ontological naturalism, to mystical biology: "When the natural state of a living organism . . . is destroyed, that destruction is pain; conversely, when such organisms return to their own true nature, this reversion is invariably pleasure" (*Philebus* 32b). While some "pleasures," such as the search for the Ideal Forms, arose from the activity of the mind (*nou*) and could only occur in the soul, most pleasures were physical and therefore, by nature, false. It was logical and necessary for Platon to have this version of Socrates dialectically define, create criteria, and establish baselines for a definition of good health. "If what we are maintaining is really true, if there is distress at the time of deterioration and pleasure at the time of restoration, then let us consider any such creatures as are experiencing neither deterioration nor restoration, and ask what their condition must be at the time in question" (*Philebus* 32e). In the *Philebus, Gorgias*, and elsewhere, Platon the philosopher took full advantage of equating the ("bad") pleasures as well as pains in body with those in the soul. In Platon's philosophy of disembodiment, pleasure and pain were equal if not the same (*Phaedo* 83–84b). Pleasure and pain were always associated in Platon's work epistemology and ethics. Ultimately only the health and pleasure of the soul mattered. To paraphrase Aristotle's quote in an English translation on style found in Book III of the *Rhetoric*, "if we could have just facts without style, the soul without physical body . . . The need for style, for a body and thus its language, was owed "to a defect in our hearers" (1404a5–10).

[THE HUMAN BODY STOOD INDICTED, AND WAS CONDEMNED]

τ *tau*

Language as Imitation, (Re)presentation as Flatter

i report. Not perfection (τελειότητα—*teleiótita*) but the beginning of a predetermined purposeful end, telos (τέλος), the high degree of separation between body and soul that Platon had Socrates implore over the course of the treatises (e.g., *Gorgias*; *Philebus; Timeous*) was related to if not a major source of the problem of language and re-presentation. Halved by reference and imitation, representation haunted Western physics and metaphysics. Re-presentation as mimesis was speech's rhetorical and poetic "Achilles heel." It was Platon's also, who by extension discovered that as the weak point in all philosophies, sciences, subjects, human knowledge. For if language merely mimicked a thing as an image unable to present the thing other than as an imitation and thus always a falsehood (not only of the reality of the thing, nor even its attributes, but the thing itself [cf. Peirce]), the "flattery" of rhetorical and poetic style was necessary to make imitations deceptive and convincing. Platon's insistence on the Real was a real handicap, since mimesis was always necessary because of the limits of language to present Reality, which also reflected the faults of the human mind and senses). Re-presentation ("technical representation" in Heidegger's sense ["Turn" 70]), were "forms" of flattery (see Table 4) necessary only for belief and persuasion, not true knowledge. Unlike John Locke's more objective later *tabula rasa,* but also unlike Wordsworth's more sensations and subjective "emotions recollected in tranquility" (*Preface,* "Preface" 935, 940), Socrates proclaimed: "It appears to me that the conjunction of memory and sensations, together with the feelings consequent upon memory and sensation, may be said as it were to write words in our souls"; however, for Platon (and for the more scientific Aristotle too), what the metaphorical "internal scribe" wrote in memory might have been correct or incorrect, moral or amoral, depending on "the scribe"—perhaps the quality of the *nou,* the mind: "[W]hen this experience writes what is true, the result is that true opinion and true assertions spring up in us, while when the internal scribe that I have suggested writes what is false we get the opposite sort of opinions and assertions" (*Philebus* 39a).

iDefrag

They work together, the reader and the writer:
the reader, like a scroll, the scribe's unfolding,
slowly moving along the line of fragmenting,
working its way beneath the shifting
blocks of files, the cubes changing colors
as reader, writer, dance through the MBs
of data rhythmically, inexorably—
the reader advancing backward, but only in
response to the signal of the writer
who is free to jump ahead, erratic,
a scout among a plethora of errors,
restless, spastic, furtively waiting
at the end, looking forward, backward
for reader to arrive, the story told . . .

***

Don't Touch Me!

An image could never have occupied the same space and time as the thing (re) presented, and so was "not real" for Platon (see Kant, *Prolegomena*; *Critique*; Deleuze; Eliot, *Knowledge and Experience*, for philosophical discussions of mimesis and time rather than space; cf. Bohr, Heisenberg). Like images on a fussy child's plate, the vegetables could never touch!

[W]hile two things [that is, the image and space] are different they cannot exist one of them in the other and so be one and also two at the same time," Platon said (*Timaeus* 52c). This was especially so with images of Ideas/Ideal Forms that never existed in material reality at all. Yet the *Real* was the ideal *end* [τέλος] toward which soul should have striven. In this ancient cosmic version of the *tabula rasa* (infused with Platonic mysticism, Romantic Idealism, and Heideggerian metaphysics, all discussed in *Plato's Nightmare*), Ideas or Essences could not be captured by the senses and written by *language* in the mind because the images were of the Ideal Forms and could and should never be apprehended *physically*. The cleaved, cloaked, and garbled speech of the rhetoric and poetic should never be allowed to touch the soul.

***

This "non-representational non-touch" was physical as well as taboo. In *Noli Me Tangere*, Jean-Luc Nancy retold the tale of the recently risen and returned Pentecostal Christ reiterating in his encounter with Mary Magdalene the command that she not touch him. In *The Ground of the Image*, Jean Luc Nancy had argued—in the context of art and religion, and the *Shoah*, that "the ultimate crisis of representation" (34)—that the impossibility of representation, and the ban on graven images—were two different issues that were often conflated and confused. The impossibility vs. the illegitimacy of re-presentation, corresponding to the "sacred" (the "truly" separate) vs. the "religious" (based on belief) were entirely distinct for him, with the sacred, like true representation itself, always and completely non-representable, absent. But for Nancy, the forbidden touch, non-touching, was still a kind of touching. For Nancy, this was what the representation of art, as non-presence, represented as image. Art, in painting and photography were presented in mind and memory only as itself, as absence (*Ground of the Image* 27–50).

This is me in winter

a white wind which
twitches like witches, which
groans and moans, which
complains and whines

a noisy *tabula rasa*,
a mistaken "negative capability,"
an embarrassed absence,
"trained incapacities"—

a green screen gone dark
and cold: a void of snow
that is me and mine,
i wholly together

alone

***

Because the "re" in "representation" was regarded etymologically and linguistically as an "intensive" rather than "repetitive" in French for Nancy (*Ground of Image* 35), representation was not and could never be wholly either imitation (mimesis) or repetition: "At the intersection of the image and the idea, mental or intellectual representation is not foremost a copy of a thing but is rather the presentation of the object to the subject . . . [It] involved the constitution of the object as such . . . Representation is a presence that is presented, exposed, or exhibited (*Ground of Image* 36; cf. Latour and Woolgar in relation to "facts"; Langer, *New Key*, in relation to "(re)symbolization"; Deleuze in relation to language.) In Judaism, as in most religions, there were strict regulations regarding *touching* "the unclean." Following Leviticus, Numbers, and some of the other 613 commandments (Caplan; cf. Rabinowitz), Talmudic law often pertained to the preparation and eating of kosher foods, the isolation of excrement from the camp, the *handling* of other bodily discharge, including suppuration, putrefaction, and menstrual blood. The Rabbis considered organic waste, despoiled flesh, disease, leprosy, and death to be unclean and unholy. The holy could not touch the dead until it was purified by ritual, sacrament, sacrifice, prayer, and/or time. If the physical could *not* be made pure again the body was deemed defiled and required permanent separation (exile) from the community. (Perhaps an echo of an eye for an eye but surely meant metaphorically, even the New Testament said: "And if thy right hand offends thee, cut it off" [Matthew 5:30]. Mentally, so did the stoic philosopher, Roman Emperor, and persecutor of Christians, Marcus Aurelius.)

From "Pentadic Leaves": Perspectives by Incongruity

By sheer repetition, imitation, you will remember
your subjective routine, your technological psychosis, rising from your bed,
extending your counter-nature into the giving air
sideways transcendence to who knows where . . .

one morning you'll awake without a body; —and unlike your ancestors
crawling, stumbling through the forest floor—reach out into space;
    and consciousness,
trying to maintain your regimen, your linguistic nature, you'll
think yourself toward the bathroom, where . . .

you'll reach (without a hand, or nipple)
for a toothbrush that is now a lion,
and the clothes you laid out to be ironed, Orion,
ironically have become unnecessarily supple . . .

where physics and language meet to form a panoply
of screens from which to view the motives of your anatomy,
and analyze the substance of your autonomy
as you float in the ethical planes of incompatibility

υ *upsilon*

The Unreality of Material Signs

i report. For Platon, the unreality of all signs (re)produced "incorrectly" by definition and inscribed in and often to the detriment of the soul (see *Philebus* 39a), was not unrelated to the issue of the necessity of rhetorical imitation, of poetic mimesis—of language itself—to render physical (as well as transcendental or mystical) reality tangible, palpable, if not always palatable, to grasp anything at all. Perhaps ironically, at stake was the health (*υγεία—ygeía*) of the immortal soul. Paradoxically, the unfortunate but necessary interaction of the body and the soul in the "unitary" and "interactionist" views —the very "place" where true images of Ideal Forms were to be remembered or found, yet could not be touched—led to *a need* for mimesis in representing them. The need for mimesis meant that speech was instantly an ornamentation of what ultimately could not or should not by nature and/or law be physically seen or touched or heard, inside or outside the soul. This seemed to be a problem even for the more empirical Aristotle, who, rendering rhetoric and poetry true arts forms, faced almost the same issue of the place of knowledge and the relation of representation in mimesis, persuasion, *and* even *catharsis* (see *De Interpretatione*; *On the Soul*). The need for mimesis also meant that rhetoric and poetry may have been imitations of imitations, ornamentations of ornamentations, symbolizations of symbolizations (Langer), shadows of shadows, but they were material and thus "unreal" when it came to Reality. (Issues of mimesis as well as catharsis are rebroadcasted in Part One, the "true" nature of cosmetics and ornamentation in Part Two.)

The Jewish Christmas Tree Artist

He fondles every hook,
balances every bauble, ball
on the tree, its position
in relation to its colors,
and the light, its symmetry—

spends hours placing one
ornament on this or that branch,
its location on the branch,
the branch in relation
to the tree, in part and as a whole—

adjusting, sorting, straightening, moving,
wholly obsessed, stepping, back
looking for objectivities,
subjective parallels,
steps off the ladder—

with each slight movement
of finger, hand, revises
the work of history,
a new addition to the world,
stepping back—

following in his Kosher
grandparents' footsteps
a good Jewish boy all his life
following unconscious, even dead
traditions, to admire his work—

***

i report. In the ancient Hebrew tradition, perhaps an alternative sophistic position (Katz, "Kabbalah as Rhetoric"; "Hebrew Bible"), language was not co-evil, dissembling, or a distraction; nor was language philosophically divorced nor materially dismembered from spirit; rather, language itself was a physical reality (Katz, "Ethics of Letters; "Letter as Essence"). Forbidden in Christianity by the post-resurrected Jesus, "touching" in all its physical, affective, spiritual, and mystical forms, including writing, was a central characteristic of Jewish culture and experience. Mimesis was not really an issue in relation to the problem of accounting for memory, sensation, representation in the material world, because the material world was made out of language, and letters themselves (in "a GREAT onto-orthographic ACT" (Katz, "Hebrew Bible" 144). But even in this version of the "unified view" of body and soul, because G/d was always close and listening but also always absent and unknowable (Katz, "Absence"). In Judaism language and prayer were still necessary—as a *non-physical* mystical form "consubstantiation" and "communion." In reference to "identification" (Burke, *Rhetoric of Motives*), "difference" (Deleuze; Derrida), "the Other" (Levinas; Buber), even in Judaism language needed (and for most usually failed) to span the infinite gap between the secular and the holy, the physical and the mystical, the body be "damned." In the Book of Life, the Jewish G/d as author every year, between Rosh Hashanah (the Jewish New Year) and Yom Kippur (the solemn Day of Atonement), wrote and sealed the fate of body and soul unseparated and in world together.

there is a stair, here, among the stars,
an infinite step into another

put your foot there, on high, and pull
yourself up to meet the Other

your face will fall to earth, and wonder
your skin will thin the air asunder

the wilderness of your alone

***

i report. Aristotle's admonition that "without touch it is impossible for an animal to be" because touch to him was the most "basic" of the senses necessary, applied to the *physical* realm. Unlike his mentor Platon, Aristotle not only acknowledged and accepted the physical realm, but founded his "philosophy of observation" built by empirical investigations and scientific system based on the senses *that included touch.*

> All the other senses subserve well-being and for that very reason belong not to any and every kind of animal, but only to some, e.g., those capable of forward movement must have them; for if they are to survive, they must perceive not only by immediate contact but also at a distance from the object. (Aristotle, *On the Soul* 434b23–28; also see *Sense and Sensibilia*)

But even in Aristotle's philosophy, Platon's "dualistic" or "interactionist" problem of body and soul (especially in "potentia," but even "actualized" as *psyche,* in some sense endured intact, and extended to other phenomena [e.g., Aristotle,

On the Soul 417b1]). As subsequently recounted in *Plato's Nightmare* extant, in the archives, in Aristotle's philosophy, sign and referent never really touched; neither did thought and world; nor even mind and word (Handelman 7–9). Rather, particulars of nature were picked up by the senses and if worthy of a higher order of thought related to universals, were converted into visual images free-floating around and inside the *nou* (the "mind" or "intellectual vision") of the actualized soul (*psyche*). Thus, for Aristotle too, rhetoric and poetry, as lower forms of physical linguistic bodies as well as arguments and styles, were wholly inferior to the philosophically "unflattering" systems of the disembodied thought, absorbed and produced *not* in language, but by images, by the noetic (intellectual) mind in search of higher rational "forms" of thought qua logical categories of "certain" (apodictic or scientific) knowledge (Handelman 9–14).

***

Hence in Aristotle too, the implicit interdiction for the soul not to touch or be touched by the physical, sensuous word or world. Or rather, the mind of the soul (the *nou*) and its non-linguistic content was protected by the *psyche* (the "body of the soul") in potentia or actualized (*On the Soul*). (Given the unitary vision of body and soul in ancient Judaism, the human body itself was holy and thus according to the *Tanakh*, Jewish men, and especially the Priests [Leviticus 11], were forbidden to touch or handle the "unclean": diseased or discharges of bodies [Leviticus 15]; non-Kosher animals [Leviticus 11:47]; the menstruation of women [Leviticus 11:1–15:33]; or the bodies of the dead [Numbers 19]—these were isolated and had to undergo ritual ceremonies of purification, which were proscribed and might include temporary exile; and harsher penalties for repeat offenders, up to the permanent expulsion from the community levied against those who repeatedly or deliberately violated these religious edicts and stipulated rituals under of Mosaic Law. Ergo the benefits of the Greek disembodied soul. But in both Platon and Aristotle, and in much of Western philosophy, including Judaism in this way, the space between Ideal and material, divine and secular, soul and body, Being and representation, final signified and sign, thing and imitation was an infinite abyss of meaning.

Hole in the Abyss

meditation
hovering abyss
fiery abacus . . .
whole cities
strung out
on lights
across the night

like letters
alphabets burning
in the void—

all you gods—
is this where we run
out of ink . . .
scripting the void
crossing conflagrations
of signifiers and signified,
signification forming
both the abyss
and the bridge
                suspended over it

[TOUCH STOOD INDICTED, AND WAS CONDEMNED]

φ phi

Sleep

i report. If the phenomenon (φαινόμενο—*fainómeno*) of the physical world was nothing but a fleeting phantom (φάντασμα—*fántasma*) for Platon, how much more so the realm of dreams. If taken at face value, Platon seemed to hold contradictory, both lofty and quotidian positions on dreams. Dreams for Platon simply could have been the remnants of sensory impressions of the existence (even preexistence) that are meaningless in themselves except for what *logoi* we attach to them, and how interpret them (*Theaetetus* 201e–202a). Phantoms (φαντάγματα—*fantágmata*). But dreams also may have been one way the gods communicated their intentions to humans, and thus a kind of prophecy (*Apology* 33c; *Charmides 173a*), especially when the animal body was asleep and the sensitive soul was awake and watching, looking and listening for divine signs (*Republic* IX.571b–c). Or dreams could have been the effect of internal "motions" and disorders in the body (*Apology* 33c), or when the "higher soul," perhaps drugged and drunken, was asleep and the raucous beastly body was left on its own, wild to wake and wander and wreak havoc and wreck (*Republic* IX.571c–d; 572b). Dreams for Platon also could have been smooth operation of natural processes and the equilibrium of restful sleep that was a powerful source of strength and clarity of thought and vision during day and wakefulness; or dreams could have been the product a restless unhelpful sleep resulting in an increased untrustworthiness of the senses when awake during day (*Timaeus* 45e–46a). Always preferring "Truth" over "illusion" of any kind, for Platon dreams primarily seemed to be a source of error (the mistaking of "resemblance" for the identity of real beauty [*Republic* V.476c–d]); the proof of error concerning the perception of truth due to a confusion of the senses, and the inability to tell dream or reality apart, and thus almost akin to a form of madness (*Theaetetus* 157e–158e); false divination (*Timaeus* 71e–72b); and superstitions that have no basis in reality (*Laws* X.901a). Phenomenon [φαινόμενο] were phantom [φάντασμα].

***

Any ascent into the realm of dreams could become a descent into the realm of nightmare. In any discussion of nightmares or dreams, especially philosophical or religious ones, sleep was ontological; sleep *was* the necessary reality (cf. Plato, *Timaeus* 52C). In *The Fall of Sleep*, Jean-Luc Nancy suggested that sleep should have held a special place in the realm of philosophy (11). But this shadowy underside of wakefulness, where most humans spent at least a third of their unconscious lives, was mostly ignored (or suppressed) in Western philosophy. The need to descend into the darkness of sleep would seemed to have been necessary to ascend toward the light of ideal forms, or heaven. To do so, the mind (*nou*) had to be awash, awake, aware, be "clear- headed" to possess the ability to think, with the assist of athletic prowess. Since material forms were an imitation, a shadow, an illusion, sleep would be necessary to metaphysically *remain* in the presence of Ideal Forms, just as in a mystical journey or trance.

the gossip
of candles—
darkness

***

i report. Jewish Mystics and ultra-orthodox Rabbis suggested their students to sleep as little as possible (even to the detriment of their health, which was against Talmud, and at the cost of turning away from their families, which should have been a sin) so that they could spend as much time as possible in study of Torah (*Perkei Avot* 6.6). So too Socrates/Platon stated that he wished his students to suppress sleep in favor of study and contemplation. Sleep was a waste of time. Sleep was an "evil" to be avoided (*Laws* VII.808b). Sleep, or lack thereof, was a different, perhaps fifth kind of "madness" to add to Platon's "four-fold" manifestation of divine psychosis (see *Phaedrus* 244b–245b; 265; *Laws* VII.807d–880c). And the *soma* was soporific, anesthesiac, amnesiac, born from and sinking back into a world of sleep and forgetting (*Phaedo*). Rhetoric and poetry as *soma* were also hallucinations of life—the flatter of sleep itself. But the avoidance of sleep suppressed not only the healing of the body, but the power of parenting dreams (cf. Tick, *Dream Healing*).

Learning to Parent

in the middle of an infinite hallway
between two rooms of history—
a mother singing to her children

χ chi

i report. Sleep was necessary; sleep could be restorative; sleep was a kind of death; sleep like life might be chaos (χάος). Sleep was a major (earlier) aspect of ancient Greek mythology and religion. The major Greek gods of sleep itself were Hypnos (the god of sleep); his son Nyx (night) and twin brother Thanatos (Death), and his son Morpheus, the god of dreams. Pasiphaë, wife of Hypnos and mother of Morpheus, was the goddess of relaxation and rest. The authoritative index of Platon's *Collected Dialogues* revealed Platon's disdain for sleep (including dreams) as a method of ascertaining the truth (*Theaetetus* 157e; cf. Freud, *Interpretation*; *Civilization*), regarding it as evidence of the primitive in humans (*Republic* IX.571e; cf. Jung) and a source of superstition (*Laws* X.910a).

***

Throughout his work, Platon referenced a lot of gods. Asclepius, the Greek god of sleep and healing, was mentioned or discussed at least ten times, including the famous concluding lines of Socrates in the *Apology*, ostensibly spoken just before the latter died. (Asclepius was a popular and important god in ancient Greece mythology and medicine [see Tick, *Dream Healing*].) But in the index of the archive, out of all the gods named and/or discussed and even assumed or used as warrants for his theories or arguments, for example, it appeared Platon did not reference or much mention the paternal god Hypnos except as the Greek word "sleep" (ύπνος—*ypnos*), nor his sons, the god of true dreams, Oneiroi (όνειροi—*óneiro*), nor the god of shifting shapes, Morpheus except as "forms" (μορφή—*morfi*)," nor the god Nyx except as night (νύχτ—*nycht*), nor the god Thanatos except as death (θαντος—*thantos*), etc. Sleep and dreams and death and their many descendants were probably as false and fictional for Platon as any *yonta* (magic) practiced by sophists.

Letter to the Brother Gods of Sleep

Dear gods, let the grass
cover me (but not too deep).
Do your work in peace.
Make the body I have left
for any afterlife that may await

bereft of pain and human sorrow,
or any hope of rising tomorrow,
so I may simply be—
comfortable for eternity
just the way I am right now,
asleep,
only partially in the ground,
bones singing hosannahs
all the way down

***

i report. According to extant mythological records of reveries, the gods of sleep and dreams resided in the Underworld. Morpheus was a shapeshifter who slept in a cave of poppies and could fashion any dream as soon as he left his door and thus could be a messenger for any god. But it was Oneiroi who fashioned "true" dreams of divination, to which Socrates paid lip service but Platon did not put much stock in given his own "addiction" to dialectic logic and rational thought. Later, the movement away from the gods and mythology would be regarded not only as a movement away from sleep and dreams as sources of valid knowledge and/or true healing, but "the twilight of the gods" as well—a farewell to an age of both philosophical wisdom and joy of life (e.g., Nietzsche, *Gay Science*; *Tragedy*).

The Final Death

For Noah

No more waiting for the coming and going,
No more sadness for the passing of things;
No more crying about the unknown,
No more gladness in the heat of the spring.

No more pain at the site of mere asking,
No more dread at the answer you hear:
"O where do you go when you disappear?"
You no longer have to ask the question:

"Where have you been?" when i suddenly appear.
The suitcases stacked up in the corner
quietly moving, the slightest motion
that signals the beginning of the coming

disorder, the coming commotion
that days before you somehow intuit,
the scent of absence you already hear.
You will never have to miss me again.

Who are the mourners, who are the dead?

ψ *psi*

"κατέβην χθὲς εἰς Πειραιᾶ . . . " (*Katebēn chthes eis Peiraia* [1st sg aor ind act]), Platon's *Republic* begins: "I went down yesterday to Piraeus . . ." (I.327; Hunter; Liddell and Scott; Lamb). With this first line of *The Republic*, Socrates descends to the port of Athens, which *was* lower than the city of Athens proper, and certainly the Acropolis—the "height" (ψήλωμα—*psíloma*) of the city. But as a poet as well as a philosopher, why would Platon begin the *Republic* itself with "a descent" (see Smith)? Was it because life was but a sleep for Platon, and sleep was a kind of dream world, a living death into which one "descended" (but hopefully and with the help of philosophy, perhaps ascended [again]—with or without horses and "chariots" [2 Kings 2:11; Plato, *Phaedrus* 246a–254e]?)

***

i report. This movement down (and subsequent prayer for rising up) was repeated in mythology and religion as anthropologically recorded, a cycle of death and rebirth seen in many different cultures throughout human history (e.g., Campbell; Frazier; Weston). In the Jewish mysticism of the *Merkavah*, "the work of the Chariot," Hebrew scholars ancient and modern noted the contrary paradox in the literature: when Ezekiel steps into the Chariot, his stepping motion might have been "go up" (יעל מרכבה *–ya'al Merkavah*), or "go down" (ירדי מרכבה *– yordei Merkavah*), and the ambiguity was variously interpreted by mystics and scholars (see Holtz 206n.9). The descent might be an ascent, and the ascent a descent. Or it could all could have been an illusion (ψευδαίσθηση—*psevdaísthisi*). Everything depended on where G/d, or monster, and the scene of redemption and/or battle was supposed to be located. Scholars of classical Greek and Platon had noted that, if not the verb καταβαίνω ("to go down, descend –the first person form of the verb is also the infinitive form), the concept or act of descending, "going down/under," "*falling* asleep" is an oft-repeated movement in Platon's work, from the descending of the soul to earth, to the descent into the mortal Cave of illusion (Crane; Seery; S. Rosen 19; Mouroutsou; Schindler 43; S. Smith), to the descent into Hades or the underworld or the sea, facing some grave test or deadly danger—and happily rising again with new-found insight and health and knowledge and power. Descent and ascent were standard in mythology, East and West, as an act that was personally and communally restorative and quite necessary (see Weston; Fraser; Frye; Campbell). From a height (ψήλωμα), not on High: A psalm (ένας ψαλμός—*psalmós*).

Poseidon I: Sanctuary, Poros

So, Poseidon, you have a soft
side, too, in the deeper pine groves
the needles, weeds, and stones, growing
sleepy. The old god's frothy face
also in the sea-rocks; brother
of Demeter, made love to Medusa
in Athena's nest, for which Medusa
was punished, by an ugliness worse than death.

Poseidon is still here in his grotto,
his face in every tree and rock;
his trident split this little temple
of stone apart, broke it open.
Demosthenes, mouth full of pebbles,
sought sanctuary here from King
Phillip of Macedonia, practiced
speech against the grinding of the sea.

Two thousand years later, Lord
Byron signed his own initials
on a column that stands today,
and the archeologists
still came to sing the praises of
the ruins and the god. We come
to separate, depart, and pray
for safe passage. And below

Poseidon still
snores loudly
in his grotto,
a coastal grove,
the island shaking—
drove, swam, dove
into the Styx, and *almost*
drowned, but didn't

***

i report. The irony was not lost that despite Jean-Luc Nancy's attention to the philosophy of sleep; the philosophy itself was made possible by and was a product of a conscious literate wakefulness, just as in an earlier century emotion would "recollected in tranquility" (Wordsworth, *Preface* 935, 940). Platon's oral methods of teaching and his "four-fold criticism of writing" (see *Phaedrus* 270b–275e) were also products of an alert (awake) and literate (educated), rational (logical) mind (cf. Ong, *Orality*; Havelock, *Muse*). In the crevices of the schematic and terms of Platonic philosophy, there were three very minor but important attributes of sleep: the blindness of sleep (*Timaeus* 45e); the evils of over-sleeping (*Laws* VII.808b); and the falsity and madness of dreaming (*Theaetetus* 158b).

Bridge Over the River Styx

(for Ger and Kate)

The waves, folding
over themselves,
moving on as one
body, a living creature . . .

a bald eagle
on the western shore
dangles a duck in its mouth,
where seagulls cannot follow . . .

Here i sit with my dear
friends, remembering
everything, memory after death,
choking on the food of life itself . . .

ω omega

i report. Platon's philosophy also was made possible and a product of politics. The ideal dream world Platon had envisioned in *The Republic* existed in stark opposition to the difficult physical life of most Greek people—even the studied Athenian citizens: "1. raw, 2. hard, cruel, 3. slow, spineless (person)" (ωμός—*omós*) (Pring 213). (This would be true of the populations of the future world too, where oppositions of all kinds would create such conflicts, including between those who believed in the importance of language and those who did not, yet wrote papers and took exams as testaments and testings to what they thought and had learned.) The description of the descent/ascent with which the *Republic* began also represented the undesirable movement into the dross of material reality from the transcendental realm, and vice versa. Given what was recorded about Platon's seeming anti-Democratic leaning (Stone; cf. Kastely), from the point of view of Platon the Philosopher, one "good" that could have come out of the organic need for sleep might have been that it would keep the bulk of humanity, the raw (η ωμός—*i omós*) far away from the realm of "Pure Dreams," true Beauty—the Ideal Forms (cf. Plato, *Laws* VII.807d–880c); most humans needed a lot of sleep—especially "woman, children, slaves. . . . " And the majority of the "lazy" masses, with their heavy lids and drooping asses, didn't get enough sleep and so were too tired even to be politically aware, never mind enjoin any philosophical search for Truth. The more sleep they needed, the less likely they were to study. This large group of "dreamers" (like Platon's ranking of professions in the hierarchy of his Republic) would no doubt also have included most rhetoricians and orators, as well as wannabe philosophers, pedagogical pretenders, lesser poets and sophists, the latter of whom Platon ranked down there with the demagogues, farmers, and mechanics (*Phaedrus* 248e).

Unsettled Sleep
α. The Cab Driver Dreams

He slips into bed,
a stiff cab of dreams;
skids on the icy sheets
and slides down its seams;
taxies into the darkness,
steering his body through
narrow alleyways
street after vacant
street,
never arriving . . .

β. The Meter of Sleep

The clock ticks like a meter.
Even slumber becomes
a responsibility,
another fare who, riding
in the backseat,
finally arrives
at his destination,
but will not pay

***

i report. In *The Gay Science* (*Die fröliche Wissenschaft*), and continued in *Thus Spoke Zarathustra*, Nietzsche also spoke on the concept of "going under" (*Untergang*). In fact, this was the introduction of *Zarathustra* (end of Book IV), which led the Superman to begin his work at the "base" of humanity. As Walter Kaufmann commented:

> In German, the last word of this section is *Untergang*: and here the German word is *untergehen*, emphasized in the original. These German words recur often in "Zarathustra's Prologue"—along with other "under" and "over" words. Even in the present section they are immediately preceded by "underworld" and "over-rich." Among the other "overman" (*Übermensch*). There is no English equivalent for *untergehen* (literally, going under). The German verb is used for the setting of the sun, for drowning, and above all, for perishing. In German, Spengler's *Decline of the West* was called *Der Untergang des Abendlandes*; and *Untergang* generally suggests decline and destruction. Nietzsche is not suggesting that it would have been better for Zarathustra to stay in the mountains instead of returning among men. See section 4 of "Zarathustra's Prologue": "I love those who do not know how to live, except by going under, for they are those who cross over [the bridge to the overman]." (275n13) Cf. also section 283 on living dangerously.

***

Like Socrates' first sentence in *The Republic*, which reproduces and so mimics the movement of descending (καταβαινε), Zarathustra went under (*untergehen*)—into the nightmarish world of imperfect forms, the dimly-lit "cave of making" (D. Schwartz, 25). Or like Socrates, for Nietzsche his nineteenth century advocate, the act of descending might have been the equivalent of reversing the relationship between waking and sleeping—laying down allies at the intercises where language and reality meet (Nancy), lanes of signifiers (Derrida) and lines of time (Levinas), the outer utter gutters of the excess body (Baudrillard) and the brightly-lit illusion of space that was mere technological spectacle (Debord).

Pagans Awake!

Philosophy is waking, poetry sleep.
But this is not a funeral oration.
Rhetoric did not die as

predicted, but lives on
in Platon's work.

Dialectic is reasoning
without meter or rhyme, although Platon
might have snored in dithyrambs,
and seen the True Forms only
when he dreamt them, slept.

Disembodied consciousness will seek
to embody unconsciousness, falsehood's dream—
transcendent ends *sans* physical means
to escape this base and sweaty creep
in the infinite darkness of eternity.

Poetry and rhetoric are waking sleep.

Q.E.D.

***

[SLEEP STOOD INDICTED, AND WAS CONDEMNED]

***

The alefbet and the alphabet were fully formed, finally finished in the upper and lower chambers of above heaven and below earth. The body and the universe were born.

i report.

Chronicles of the Body

3 Re-Ambiguations

- Access –language archival
- sing. organon: “organ, instrument, appliance, instrumentality, mouthpiece” (*Google Translate*)
- “late Old English organ via Latin from Greek organon ‘tool, instrument, sense organ’” (*Oxford Dictionary Box*)
- “organization (n) early 15c., organisacioun, ‘structure of the body or its parts . . . . the biological meaning ‘body of a human or animal adapted to a certain function’ is attested from the late 14c., from a Medieval Latin sense of Latin organum. From early 15c. as ‘a tool, an instrument.’ The broad, etymological sense of ‘that which performs some function’ is attested in English from 1540s” (*Etymoline.com*)
- common term for a collection of Aristotle’s works on logic (Jones); cf. Bacon, *Novum Organon*
- νέα οργανα—new organs:
    - mimetic organ
    - cathartic organ
    - material organ
    - spiritual organ
    - representivity organ
    - rationality organ
    - subjectivities organ
    - transcendental organ
    - cybernetic organ
    - posthuman organ
- Histories of the body follow

i report:

Part One
Mimesis, Catharsis, and the Anorexia of Style (Plato and Aristotle/Classical Greece)

> [W]hen the natural state of an organism is impaired by processes of combination and separation, of filling and emptying, and by certain kinds of growth and decay, the results is pain, distress, suffering—in fact everything that we denote by names like these.
>
> —*Plato, Philebus 42c–d*

4 Mimetic Organ

"LET NO ONE IGNORANT OF GEOMETRY ENTER HERE"

Inscription over the door of Plato's Academy [Burton 83; cf. Plato Republic VII.527b–528a]).

α *Alpha*

Descending and Ascending

In mathematics, Alpha (α) is the first in a series, the leader, the primary, the best (*Quora*). Socrates *Katebēn chthes eis Peiraia*—"i descended yesterday to Piraeus" (Plato, *Republic* I.327; Liddell and Scott; Lamb). Elijah also: *yordei Merkavah*—"descended to the Chariot").

***

Almost in a kind of metaphorical rhetoric or metaphysical poetic reverse parallel movement, in conjunction with his philosophy of Ideal Forms (but *not* equal to them), Platon believed that the purest study of geometry, arithmatic, and astronomy, which later in his work (replayed in these Chronicles in Part Three) almost replaced verbal dialectic would allow the mind to soar in abstraction beyond body (*Republic* VI.511b). This study was to be based on the principle of the strict calculations and measurements of *theoretical* (as opposed to applied) mathematics. Numbers were things beyond beauty, beyond *ιδέα* ("ideas") or *eidos* (images of thought in the *νου* ["mind"] of which *λόγος* ["thought," "word"] was a mere representation /imitation (e.g., *Philebus* 51c; *Republic* 6.511c, 7.527a; Burton 96, 121–22; cf. Toulmin and Goodfield 73–91). Although not the Ideal Forms themselves, numbers were of the realm of pure essence (*ousia*). Platon suggested that the study of calculation "should be prescribed by law" to "induce those who are to share in the higher function of the state . . . until they attain to the contemplation of the nature of number, by pure thought . . . facilitating the conversion of the soul itself from the world of generation to the essence and truth" (*Republic* V.525c). In fact, geometrical, mathematical, and astronomical dialectic Platon speculated that numbers were both source and remnant of the creation of the gods, and stronger and superior to "love"—not only *eros*, pleasure, but perhaps even *agape*, higher or Platonic lover (see *Republic*, esp. V.524d–526c 24). Geometry and mathematics lifted the mind toward *un*embodied essences. And they were everything physical and divine.

***

And so it began, alpha with them all, and alef with them all, and numbers with all of them (cf. *Sefer Yetsirah* 273). And Alpha and its numerals travelled far in the new wide world, west and east —from Rome to Russia—leaving its Jewish brethren wandering, then conquered in desert sand (cf. Katz, "Socrates as Rabbi" 93–97).

***

i descend, wake, blink, as from a deep dark sleep, look up, look around, step down to the bustling port of Athens. It is 349 BCE. i stand at the water's edge of memory, lapping, relapsing time, perhaps only memory, perhaps a soul reincarnate. The Greek islands stretch out beyond the peninsula into the vast infinity before me. The sun burns black volcanic beaches, white cut cliffs, yellow sand. The Acropolis breaks through the clouds into the blue light of the sky, its marble columns and temples leaning against the clouds.

there is no color
there is no sound
where i am now

i rise, go up (יעל–*ya'al*], ascend as in a chariot again, float over the newest temples of the Acropolis recently built by Pericles in the prior century, over Mt. Olympus where the gods live, and beyond. The morning stretches out, opens its hand, reaching across the whole length of the horizon, the temples already blinding white in the bright sunlight. i walk down the dusty road that winds around the sides of the Acropolis, growing wider, ever wider at the base, which also contains one of the two possible jail cells in Athens where Socrates may be imprisoned before his trial, and then put to death.

***

i turn away, turn right, and soon reach the *Agora*. i remember, hear, the rustle of the bustle of beginnings of early morning days in this open dusty marketplace of goods and ideas, now filling fast with people and material, philosophers and merchants, ideas and debates, visitors from Athens and the world beyond. Servants and slaves, heads bowed, move silently through the crowds, go about their work. Women (young and old) haggle as they shop. Young children noisily run, kick up a dust cloud from the sand. Older children (of the upper political classes) gather to meet their chosen master and start their lessons. "Καλιμερα Ατηενα!" (*kalimera Athena*—"Good morning Athens!"), the philosophers and merchants, the visitors and urchins, the women and students, the slaves and servants, and even all of nature itself, seem to cry out at once, together, loudly proclaiming their loyalty and love to the goddess who guards this place, Αθηνα (Athena), protector, and namesake of this small, powerful, intellectual city-state.

Athens
the dust of the agora
and the Acropolis
on my feet

B Beta

Life in the Grecian Hills

In geometry, Beta (β) is the second angle of a triangle (Nasehpour). Like Young beta Plato when Socrates was not looking, i angle through the growing crowd, make a beeline toward the thick tangled living bush and lush brackets of plane trees just on the outskirts of the city. Secretly, i like to hike and hide in the early morning, find a place to read, and write some poetry. Higher in the surrounding hills i still hear the bay of goats and lambs and the tinkle of the tiny bells they wear around their necks to help the shepherd boy find them if they go astray. Even now i can smell the animals' wet fur, damp with dew, with evening rain, with the waft of sea, the salt of the fog, quickly evaporating in the growing heat. Even now the nostrils still detect the scent of wild rosemary and thyme baking in the ovens of the fields under the sun. Even now i hear a rising chorus of women, young and old, like a choir dressed in black and invisible on the hills whose rocky sides are a thick terrain of brush and bush and forest, greeting each other in a counterpoint of call and response: "Γεια σας!" "Γεια σας!" (*Yahsas*!–" Hello!")—a Greek greeting whose word Γεια (Gaia) is rooted in the womb (gynecology) of the mother of Earth, Γη (*Gi*). These greetings are now joined by the deep bass of male voices barking their own refrains of gratitude and restraint: "ευχαριστώ," "παρακαλώ"; "ευχαριστώ," "παρακαλώ" ("*Efkaristow*," "*parakalo*"; "thank you," "you're welcome")—heard hundreds and hundreds of times every day, as if the joy of life in its entirety were contained in those greetings, living on in the land like the spirit of the Greek language itself.

Γ Gamma

In mathematics, Gamma is "useful for modeling situations involving continuous change" (Britannica). {Temporal Shift. i remember Nietzsche on the vitality of the ancient Greeks. At the end of the Preface to the second edition of *Die Fröliche Wissenshaft* (*The Gay Science*), Friedrich Nietzsche's exclaims:

> Oh, those Greeks! They knew how to live. What is required for that is to stop courageously at the surface, the fold, the skin, to adore appearance, to believe in forms, tones, words, in the whole Olympus of appearance. Those Greeks were superficial—*out* of *profundity.* And is not this precisely what we are again coming back to, we daredevils of the spirit who have climbed the highest and most dangerous peak of present thought and looked around from up there—we who have looked *down* from there? Are we not, precisely in this respect, Greeks? Adorers of forms, of tones, of words? And therefore—*artists*?). (38)

Morning is too early for the itinerant bands of rhapsodes to return, the sleepy sophists to sing, the ragged rhetoricians to ride their oratory into town, the gyrating poets to perform. Not until late afternoon, until deep in the morning's evening will they arrive to argue and debate, about the *dissoi logoi* (opposing ideas and words) of gods, humans, and nature, and the agonistic ache and cry of millions of stray dogs and feral cats who swarm through all the city's open neighborhoods, alleyways, streets, poking differently shaped noses and furry faces through garbage. All the animals are allowed to breed, feed, grow wild; they personify and could be one of the gods (especially Artemis); the provisions for the overpopulated living animals provide the Hellenes with opportunities to demonstrate their hospitality as the host of the guest of charity (cf. Derrida, *Gift*). The animals are all fed and cared for by everyone in the city. Pigeons too. The old Greek fishermen lined up sitting on a bench nod their head in approval as i slowly feed the wild animals half my lunch. {Temporal Shift. Nietzsche loved the open warmth and honest feeling of the Greeks—their philosophers and dramatists—in contrasts that he himself drew to the hard, cold customs and manners of German philosophy, culture, and morality. He often extolled the Greeks (e.g., *Tragic Age;* Pre-Platonists), leading up to his questioning and abandonment of traditional convictions concerning morality, scientific knowledge, metaphysics, and truth, that ultimately led him to the *Übermensch,* the "Will to Power" (*Zarathustra*)—and madness, in which (somewhat like Wordsworth, but no longer productive) he spent the last years of his life living with his sister . . . }

Δ Delta

Hellenica: What's in a Name

In mathematics, Delta (δ) is a "very useful [function] as an approximation for a tall narrow spike . . . namely, an impulse" (*sciencedirect*). Throughout history, the Hellenes hated the name "Greek," but had to accept it. The name was given to the Hellenic Republic by the Romans (Latin: *Graeci*), and was considered derogatory (as in "O these Greeklings," "these upstart children who need to be taught their place" (Cicero, *De Oratore* I. xi. 47). {Spatial Differential. The Greeks also were historical enemies with "the Turks" (formerly Persia), with whom they were forever fighting over ownership of the little isle of Cypress—the jet fighters streaking the sky, roiling the blue-black seas that surround and weave these many disparate islands together.} The Greeks prefer and refer to themselves Ελλάδα (*Elláda*—"Hellas") and their language as Ελληνικα (*Hellenica*), named after the woman of infamous beauty of whom Homer sang in his famous epic (*Iliad*) as the cause of the Trojan War; the sophist Gorgias in his *Encomium on Helen* "defended" against the charge of being the cause of the war by comparing Helen's power to that of the unintended effects of rhetoric as a potent drug over which she had little control, thus arguing that she was not guilty of the crime of seducing men and nations (cf. Derrida, "Pharmakon"). i head back *down* to Piraeus, to take a ferry to Crete, and the smaller islands that dot the dangerous seas.

The Museum in Piraeus

Two statutes of Hermes
Stand in the doorway
Of the port
Of the shrine to
Athena

The Byzantine stars
In their stone beards
Are like many pairs
Of deep-seated eyes; erect
penis removed

You pass a stern Apollo
Who greets you
On the right, the bow
From his left hand
Removed for your protection

Two statues of Artemis,
Brown-stained eyes,
Reside in a further room,
Unwar-like, touching,
Or as Tiresias foretold

And then Athena Nike,
Enormous but still beautiful,
Suddenly confronts, stands
Before you, stands as you
Bow before her:

Mother, a little older
Yet still magnificent,
Helmut tied yet still inviting,
Grieving the death
Of her soldiers underground

Mirror of the reliefs downstairs,
Of the mother grieving the death
Of her daughter in childbirth, the nurse
Holding the baby, the mother
Holding the dead hand of her daughter—

Or a father holding the small
Hand of his son as they pass
From the world of the gods
To the world of the dead—
The underworld beyond:

The museum's basement doors

E Epsilon

Recurrence

In mathematics, Epsilon is the "smallest possible number with any mathematical value" (*Mathematics*). Nearby, a seagull lands on a rock. Is it a god? Crete is a busy island, known for its black volcanic beaches in the south, and its sandy coves that shimmer like the bright dark Libyan Sea. Crete is also known for its thriving tourism and trade, its archeological finds, and its local myths and legends, including tales of an ancient Minoan city and its treasure-trove of art not yet discovered. Of personal stories of supernatural encounters, magic, even gods: on a dark beach, a wavering figure weaves across the sand, looms like shadow against the dark, growing larger, closer, approaching--a drunkard or a threat; but out of the grit and gravel of a powdery dune a lonely tree suddenly seems to spring on the beach, its gnarled finger-branches pointing to a small opening in the seawall by which to escape to the hidden street. Epsilon. Ευχαριστώ (*Efkaristow*). A voice replies: "*Parakalo*" . . . !

***

In Santorini, on steep cliffs overlooking the hill, still alive and walking the earth, a stranger, blind Tiresias, surprises unsuspecting man and woman, engages them in long conversations of life, and the meaning of the future yet to come—then just disappears. Or, off to the left, a couple making out in a tall field of grass, when they notice an enormous dog (Artemis, the Huntress) standing there, staring at them, defender of women, without moving scaring the man away. (This history is brought to you by Hermes, the messenger god, who is not only the god of travelers, but also of orators and thieves. One day soon, he will be recognized as the god of hermeneutics, which for better or worse in various guises will hold great sway throughout human history). The indigenous are fierce and hard-working, but playful and care-free, sensual and fun-loving, evenings filled ouzo, the night sky pouring stars. (i, Platon the philosopher, want them to give all this up, change their ways, improve the quality of their life, lead them to pursue true Beauty.) They often gaze at the sky. The animals run wild. Diana is watching.

Orion: The Hunter and Hunted

If you see me
jogging up the stairs
of my glittering belt,
eternally hunting
the night sky—
you will know
that all is as it should
be here in heaven
where i run the gamut
of the entire constellation

If you see another
figure running after
me down the stairs
of moonlight, my studded

belt around another
waist, fighting
in the night sky—
you will know that
something may be
very wrong on Earth

For the love of Artemis
please save us.

Z Zeta

Teacher, Teacher

In number theory, Zeta (ζ} is a prime number greater than zero in an infinite series (*Britannica*). In philosophy: "the power of teaching": Socrates → Plato →Aristotle → Alexander the Great → the Roman Empire → West and the East → Constantinople → Byzantium→Medieval Europe → the Renaissance→ every future iteration of Western civilization → the world to come → . . . . Back in Athens, a little, bearded, barefoot, unwashed, ugly man with bulging eyes that stared and might not see or blink for hours (Plato, *Theaetetus* 143e; *Symposium* 215a–c, 216a–e, 220b–222a) wanders the *Agora*, seeking out and stopping people among the *polis* to engage them in conversation and debate concerning what they think they know, and the search for truth. {Temporal Jump. Later in history, Coleridge's Ancient Mariner will do the same thing, but typical of a Romantic of the nineteenth century, will relate a story of misery right in the middle of the most joyous of occasions—weddings. And still later, a thin poor, recently graduated, unemployed lawyer, with baggy pants and a little bag of plastic chess pieces and a cardboard board, returns every day to the cafeteria of his former alma mater, looking for someone who will play with him.}

Sock-rates

socks falling
around his ankles—
old rubber bands

Aristocles the Poet, a young student of other bards, rhapsodes, and sophists, hangs around in the back of the small crowd, listens attentively to Socrates who questions everyone about the logic of their beliefs, and asserts the preference for the unseen world over the unreality of the physical one around them. He teaches that resistance to temptations of all material things, including and perhaps especially lust and love, is necessary to return to the possibility of ascertaining or remembering the Truth, the nonmaterial Forms that may exist beyond all human measure, and are the invisible source of everything we perceive and think to be real but actually is illusion. Socrates cannot be badgered, bribed, or bought. The society he envisions will be one of the highest ideals and loftiest laws. Socrates will pay for his principles with his unrecorded life and thought, about which his students, especially one, will explore and write for the rest of his life.

The Laws of Gortyn

One hawk
        circling sun, then
another, following:
        and the old civilization
is reborn again,
        as it is every morning
among these old stones
        and the olives.

The hawks follow
        the laws of Gortyn,
as did Plato when he visited
        (they have their own republic),
and the 800-year old olive trees
        in the dust,
and the old stones
        decaying in the sun—
all have their laws,
        each its own republic.

The Greeks know exactly
how many olive trees
they have in their land.

H Ēta

Young Aristocles the Poet

In quantum physics Eta is the charge of decaying particles (*Study*). Despite Socrates' warning, young Aristocles likes to sneak out beyond the city walls—in broad hot light of day. He loves to sit under his favorite plane tree (he needs to, given the heat) and read, recite, or write poetry. He loves the feel of the quill in his hand, and the rising smell of ink on dried parchment as he scratches out letters on its skin, an alphabet of rhetoric. (Aristocles will soon renounce all this publicly, in "print," as if a dream of the gods gone wrong in the small oven-shaped caves of incubation of Asclepius, the first doctor among the gods; at the larger "sleep temples" the preliminary step in this early practice was a physical catharsis of the body. Though effective, the practice with its temples and priests to interpret the dreams eventually died out for a few thousand years [cf. Tick].)

The Temple of Asclepius

At home among the ruins
the Greek lizard lives
in the ancient walls
of the stumbled palace,
where this god of sleep
used to dream of healing

In empty fields
around the temple
the wild thyme still sings
its fragrant praise,
and the lambs softly rhyme
and do their work

Only the swallows
in the wall holes
worship here now

***

Dialogue: Plato in His Youth (2)

Σωκράτης (*Sokrátis*—"Socrates")
Νέος Πλάτων (*Néos Pláton*—"Young Platon")

Σωκράτης: The letters of the alphabet bear no relation to reality, my young Platon. Unlike the Hebrews who pass through and with whom we trade, we do not believe the letters can either contain or even reflect the physical world and its effects and attributes, never mind the realm of Forms as transcendental essences and causes.

Νέος Πλάτων: What about your name, Σωκράτης?

Σωκράτης: What about it?

Νέος Πλάτων: Let's start with simple etymology. The Greek name Σωκράτης (*Sokrátis*) may be derived from σῶς ("sos") meaning "whole, unwounded, safe"; and κράτος ("*kratos*") meaning "power." Your "power" comes from your being "whole."

Σωκράτης: On the surface, this would seem logical, but I cannot agree that my essence is embodied in the etymology of my name, Platon.

Νέος Πλάτων: The Greek letters of your name truly seem to embody and/or reflect your character!

Σωκράτης: I don't understand. Explain what you mean, young man.

Νέος Πλάτων: I will certainly try. Let's start with the first letter of your name, in Greek, sigma: Σ. Look at the *shape* of it.

Σωκράτης: What about the shape of the sigma?

Νέος Πλάτων: First, it looks like a lightning bolt that Zeus might have thrown down into the sea. Σ is quick and sharp, like your own thinking, speech, Σωκράτης (although we also have another letter, the Greek zeta whose upper Z and lower case ζ also resembles a lightning bolt...).

Σωκράτης: Ah my friend, you contradict yourself, and not for the first time, I might add. A thing cannot exist and not exist at the same time.

Νέος Πλάτων: I agree, Sokrátis. And I am happy to report that you did not fall into one of the logical topoi traps, in this case, of contraries (or opposite of the same class) but stuck with contradiction as the topic of the argument, which is appropriate given that we are discoursing on the Greek alphabet, and neither Σ or Z are opposites. May I continue to demonstrate how these two letters are not contradictions either?

Σωκράτης: Yes, my boy. Proceed.

Νέος Πλάτων: Sigma Σ resembles the Z in the name "Zorro," who will be very fast and strong and to many a (fictional) hero who fights criminals and corruption! Sigma Σ that starts *your* name also reflects a similar action, only backwards because we are in the past. Both Σ and Z thus communicate lightning, or someone whose wit is sharp, whose tongue is a rapier, whose words are fast little swords that cut right through the spoken or written speech or thought of others!

Σωκράτης: Again you contradict yourself, my friend. For you have now set Σ and Z as opposites in the same class of things: letters that embody lightning, or me—in the past and the present, which is all we can see. And "Zorro"? Is he (or she, given that Sappho was one of the greatest ancient poets) one of your younger bards, like yourself, or perhaps a recently arrived sophist come to Athens from afar to corrupt our youth, or a stranger who like us is in a search for eternal Truths?

Νέος Πλάτων: Never mind Zorro, Sokrátis; it would take too long to explain.

Σωκράτης: Very well. I will discontinue this line of questioning, since you wish it. I think I have proven my point anyway.

Νέος Πλάτων: What point was that, Sokrátis? I may have missed it.

Σωκράτης: That any resemblance between a letter and a thing is at best coincidental, if it really exists at all since we might say the letters are not well drawn if they are meant to portray things with any likeness. At worse, they are only images (and not good ones at that)—poor imitations, mere mimicry that can lead a young man like you away from philosophy and down the wrong path. I myself cannot believe there is any connection between letters and things.

Νέος Πλάτων: If you have the time and don't mind, I would like to speak just a little more on this subject/give you some background.

Σωκράτης: I always will have time for you, my young jedi. But I must warn you I am not at all convinced.

Νέος Πλάτων: I have overheard some traveling Jewish sages say in the Agora that this higher level of interpretation of the Hebrew letters is possible, according to Jewish mysticism, which you know I am fascinated by and in love, and other forms of mysticism too. The sages use hermeneutic principles that even employ Greek terms like *notarikon* and *gematria*.

Σωκράτης: The Greeks have an excellent relationship with the Jews, even in Crete. I have no quarrel with them, being another race with their own language and customs. Sometimes I talk to them if they speak Greek. I have even heard of an extremely bright Jewish boy who will spend all his time in study, reading and writing everything he can get his hands on in Greek as well as Hebrew, and will one day become, although a Hellenistic Jewish one, a famous philosopher, just as I hope you will.

Νέος Πλάτων: What is his name, Sokrátis?

Σωκράτης: Philo of Alexandria.

Νέος Πλάτων: I know most of the philosophers as well as the sophists and the poets who abound around town, and I have never heard of him.

Σωκράτης: He is not born yet. But despite differences in our gods and religions, I have no doubt the Jews will produce great scholars and men of *belles lettres* too. But now answer me this. Tell me how these Hebrew hermeneutic principles work?

Νέος Πλάτων: I am so happy you asked that, Sokrátis! I will apply some of the more well-known principles to further study your name, and perhaps convince you yet!

Σωκράτης: You can try, young Platon. I am all ears.

Νέος Πλάτων: Well, my master, from the little I have been able to glean by listening to these sages speak on the Pentateuch, the first principle of interpreting Hebrew letters is *gematria*. Applying the method of gematria, letters are converted into their assigned numerical equivalents, letters being numbers in Hebrew (just as they now are in Greek, in the new, Ionic alphabet). However, in the Greek system, sigma is the number 60, not 18—which in Judaism is the sum of י (*yôd* = 10) and ח (*chet* = 8), which together spell חי (*chai*—life). Thus, in Judaism, the sum of the Hebrew word is equal to the number 18, which means life too. (In fact, I have heard that the Jews always give gifts in multiples of 18 [18 drachma, 32 drachma, 64 drachma, etc.] to wish the recipient good luck, life, and health. If we correctly interpret the first letter of your name, Σωκράτης, you are blessed, and will have a long life. "L'chaim"!)

Σωκράτης: Platon, how do these principles apply to Greek? I grant that some of the principles have Greek names, but they do not seem to reach the same result, as you yourself stated. In Greek, sigma = 60. Can you explain this discrepancy, for it is beyond my comprehension, though you may have some insight into this.

Νέος Πλάτων: I must admit that although I know Ionic letters and their numerical equivalents, of course, I have not developed the skills yet to interpret their significance. However, I do know that sigma, the eighteenth letter of the Greek alphabet, as a capital letter (Σ) represents "sum" and as a lower-case letter (σ) mean "deviation" in mathematics. It can use other letters, begin and end with any number, add up sequences, and . . .

Σωκράτης: My young friend, I have heard enough. Unlike algebra, it seems that the hermeneutic principles of the Hebrews do not answer the question put to them, except to lead to another question or problem. The interpretation of letters, it seems, creates fairy tales about the alphabet. Do you not see that, my friend?

Νέος Πλάτων: I think I do, Sokrátis.

Σωκράτης: Fairy tales are all well and good. And although my name does begin with the eighteenth letter of the Greek alphabet, and is the eighteenth letter of the Greek alphabet, it doesn't equal the word "life" (Bios, or Zoe) in Greek. But I do feel blessed by the gods, young Platon, for my knowing you. But not because of a letter of an alphabet.

Νέος Πλάτων: Sokrátis, let's move on to the second principle, *notarikon*, the discovery of *other, hidden* words in each letter of a word, or the permuting of letters to reveal other words contained in a word. What other words in Greek begin with sigma Σ?

Σωκράτης: We have many more words that begin with sigma Σ. These include words like σύνθεση ("synthesi") or συστημα ("systema"), and many other words related to synthesizing, integrating, or combining.

Νέος Πλάτων: You see *Sokrátis*? This is exactly what you do in your philosophy—synthesize, integrate, combine.

Σωκράτης: We also have like σάτιρα ("satire"), στρατηγικό ("strategic"), and σκεπτικό ("sceptic").

Νέος Πλάτων: *Sokrátis*, you are all of these too! These names, derived from sigma Σ, perfectly describe you!

Σωκράτης: But my young apprentice, many other words begin with sigma Σ, such as στίγμα ("stigma"). Am I a stigma, in Athens, or anywhere else around Greece, or the known world?

Νέος Πλάτων: Why no, *Sokrátis*, I would not describe you that way.

Σωκράτης: What about σχίσμα (*skisma*—"schism")?

Νέος Πλάτων: Again, I would have to answer no.

Σωκράτης: How about the word σπασμός (*spasmos*)? Does that word accurately represent me?

Νέος Πλάτων: No, *Sokrátis*, not at all. In fact, you're thinking and speech are the opposite of spasmodic: not jumpy and erratic, but logical and smooth. (Some of your fellow locutors might be described as spasmodic, especially under questioning from you! But not you.)

Σωκράτης: Thank you, my young friend. While I believe neither in compliments that are false, or flattery even if partially true, we must appreciate that part of the truth we are granted when we can see it for ourselves.

Νέος Πλάτων: We must, *Sokrátis*.

Σωκράτης: This is a conversation for another time. Speaking of opposites, to conclude *this* conversation, two other words come to mind that begin with sigma Σ: στομάχι (*stomaki*—"stomach"), and σκελετός (*skeletos*—"skeleton"). Would you say that I am too fat, or that I am too skinny?

Νέος Πλάτων: Why no *Sokrátis*, I would not say either one of these statements. I think you are just right the way you are.

Σωκράτης: Then what are we to make of these two Hebrew hermeneutic principles, *gematria* and *notarikon*? Applied to the alphabet, do specific letters in themselves express the truth in their shape, number, sound?

Νέος Πλάτων: Apparently not. I think this is an area for further study, perhaps when I journey to Egypt and the ancient world when I am a little older . . .

Σωκράτης: And we will talk again, Platon, many times before my death. For there is much to discuss and much to learn. But for now, can we agree to lay the subject of the Hebrew alphabet aside?

Νέος Πλάτων: Yes, I agree.

Σωκράτης: Besides, all this talk of stomachs and skeletons has made me hungry.

Νέος Πλάτων: Me too, Sokrátis! Too bad there is no Jewish delicatessen in the agora, nor its outskirts. But there will be one day, and even a museum in Athens celebrating the richly intertwined history of the Greeks and the Jews from ancient to modern times.

Θ Theta

"Beauty" in Ancient Greece

In mathematics, Theta (θ) was "a measured angle . . . . in three main trigonometric functions" (Burns). In *History of Beauty*, Umberto Eco had explored the changing conception of beauty in the arts—primarily pictorial. {Sine} Eco argued that the early ancient Greeks (Homeric-pre-Socratic) did not have a conception of beauty separate from other qualities—that in fact, beauty was always defined in relation to other ideals, such as justice, or "moderation, harmony, symmetry" (*Beauty* 37). When the Greeks did begin to conceptualize artistic praxis, said Eco, the Greek conception of the ideal body was *not* based on nature, on the physical body, but on idealized perfection—in this case, mathematical proportions, first developed by Pythagoras and his apostles. {Cosine} This was truer of painting than of sculpture, where, said Eco, sculptors soon sought not to "idealize an abstract body," but "the living beauty of the body"—a synthesis of bodies "that harmonized body and soul" (*Beauty* 45). This harmony arose from the mathematical idealization that governed not only music and mathematics, but also the drawing and painting of the human form (Eco, *Beauty* 37–59). "[A]rt in the proper sense of the term is a false copy of true beauty and as such is morally harmful to youth . . . [;] [b]etter therefore to . . . substitute it with the beauty of geometrical forms, based on proportion and a mathematical concept of the universe." (Eco, *Beauty* 50). {Tangent} Unlike ordinary shapes in the physical world, with geometrical symmetry and mathematical proportion, mimetic versions made of material elements (earth, water, air fire, etc.). might be as near "perfect" as humans could come (*Timaeus* 55e–56c; cf. Toulmin and Goodfield). i wander, witness, look on as history passes.

The Well-Wrought Urn"*

(Minoan Archeological Dig, Atlantis)

clay pot
        exactly where
it stopped.
        stone stairs
collapsed
        upon themselves.
underground
        sewage system
still intact.
        jug in the window
perfect for a bath,
        planned city streets
neat house paths . . .

left their possessions.
        did not make it
out alive
        only one skeleton
found much later in time

* Title borrowed from Cleanth Brooks.

"Atlantis"?
  first name:
Kalliste—["most beautiful"]—
  changed after
the volcano:
  Thira ["fear"]

started decaying
  as soon as it was opened,
petrified wood
  instantly pulverizing

Greek archeologist
  who discovered
this 2600 BC Minoan civilization
  died on site
and was buried here
  with his people

a hushed sign reads:
  "don't touch the ruins."
Implied: "you" are always
  the last one out alive.

***

Mathematical idealization governed the entire worldview of at least one major thinker in the "upper class" of ancient Hellenes: Platon. (Eco also references Socrates as reported in Xenophon's *Memorabilia*, but notes the unreliability of the source [*Beauty* 48]). "In Plato's thinking Beauty has an autonomous existence distinct from the physical medium that accidentally expresses it; it is not therefore bound to any sensible object in particular, but shines out everywhere" (50). Eco further pointed out that the primary school of thought—philosophically and aesthetically—assumed the ideal of *a body* (not in the frantic, frenetic, kinetic actions of divine madness, modern life, or mere mechanical motion, but) *in repose*—the stasis of moment and motion, a form finally captured in moving time and space, forever frozen in stone (45; cf. Eco, *Beauty* 45–47). With Socrates retired for the night, i lay back, look up at stars, have a smoke.

Τσιγάρα Διας™ *(Tsigára Días)*

the gods
are not dead

yet, they live on
in Τσιγάρα Διας—
"*Zeus Cigarettes*"

I Iota

"The Z" and "Impotency"

In mathematics, Iota (ι) "denotes the imaginary part of a complex number" (*Vedantu*). The problem of representation, which mathematical idealization only partially solved, perhaps began with Platon in Greece—not because he was the first to cut the sign from the signified, but because he built his whole philosophical system over it (see Kingsley). It's where "the troubles" with representation and reference began. Platon's "great matter" was how to cross over the great abyss between material and ideal, word and thing, body and soul, earth and heaven. {Leap of Faith. In the *Thematic Origins of Scientific Thought*, Gerald Holton attributed the success of modern science to an epistemological constant that could be understood to have begun with Platon: the successful isolation and suppression, if not mitigation by migration, of the "Z-axis" in science—the devaluation and denial of what Holton calls "the scientific imagination"—the personal, the subjective, the affective, the aesthetic, the valuative, the religious "themata"—as any part of valid knowledge (Ch 1.).} Even with the epistemological exclusion of the experience of the senses, and/or the inclusion of ethics premised on "the good, the true, the beautiful" (not of the body, like Cicero's "Orator," or Quintilian's *vir bonus*, but of the transcendental soul), such attempts at "idealizations" of human methods and processes perhaps amounted to a "coverup." {Spatial Equation A. What was covered up can only be accounted for by what Holton called "the impotency principle" (52–53). As metaphysical explanations or substitutions of the ineffable, such "idealizations (later represented, say, by neo-Platonic or Cartesian metaphysics, or Western dualities of mortal body and immortal soul) could have been seen as failures insofar as the role of nature emanating from the (possibly and no doubt highly limited) physical nature of things, including the knowing subject, was obscured. Additionally, the obfuscation of the physical led in fact or in theory to the attempted and at least partially successful snubbing and suppressing and punishing and shedding of the material human body. The physical body's needs and desires were seen as unsavory, epistemologically labeled as bad or evil, judged to be sin—and were to be excised, exculpated, cast away. Hence human history.}

***

{Temporal Indeterminacy. Even in the Heraclitan paradise that later remerged as subatomic reality in the mediations of the Copenhagen of New Physics, particularly in the work of Werner Heisenberg and Neils Bohr, and again in postmodernism and posthumanism, the suppression of the subjective, social, cultural, and religious *themata* in philosophy and science, always seem to call into question and undermine the material and physical in favor of the mental philosophy and imaginary abstraction. (Iota.) But the principles of indeterminacy in which matter, and thus *language* were ostensibly—and joyfully—in a state of constant flux in rhetoric and poetry, were adjudicated and treated in relation to the Newtonian grounds of validating scientific knowing (Katz, *Epistemic*). The "figural" was therefore resigned to the dark corners of mind and/or reality (see Lyotard, *Postmodern*; "Figural"; *Discourse*), while the primacy of the nonphysical, the divine, the transcendent, the spiritual, was asserted as the necessary ground and goal of philosophical knowledge (see Kenneth Burke, *War*; *Toward a Symbolic*; Rueckert, "Introduction" esp. xi–xxi; "'Dramatistic' View"; "Goethe's *Faust*, Part I," esp. 307–10; "Thinking of the Body").}

Of Gods and Humans

up here
on the mountain top—
gods don't need
to wear clothes

or take them off

K Kappa

Mimesis and Impotent Beauty

In geometry Kappa was "the curvature of a curve" (Nasehpour). {Space Time Splice. In a chapter in *Mimesis* titled "Odysseus' Scar" (almost the total focus of that chapter), Erich Auerbach explored how a more visual, spatial, static Greek approach to reality was depicted and defined in Homeric verse. This was in counter distinction to a more aural, temporal, active Jewish approach to reality—both were reflected through diction: Hebrew דבר (*d'var*—"word/action") vs. Greek λόγος (*logos*—"thought/word"), grammar and syntax (see Katz, "Letter as Essence," "Sonic Rhetorics"), and the centrality of divine *voice* vs. divine *image*, which was forbidden in Judaism (Buber, *Judaism*; Boman). In the scene in Book 19 of the *Odyssey*, Homer went into excruciating detail about the past and present of the returned hero's *skar*, all foregrounded without transition or suspense, as their old housemaid, Eurycea, recognizes it (and their dog smells his old master's scent). Auerbach remarks:

> All this is scrupulously externalized and narrated in leisurely fashion . . . Clearly outlined, brightly and uniformly illuminated, men and things stand out in a realm where everything is visible; and not less clear—wholly expressed, orderly even in their ardor—are feelings and thoughts of the persons involved . . . Even the Homeric epithets seem to me to be traceable to the same need for an externalization of phenomena in terms perceptible to the senses . . . [T]he basic impulse of Homeric style [is] to represent phenomena in a fully externalized form, visible and palpable in all their parts, and completely fixed in their spatial and temporal relations . . . Homeric style knows only a foreground, only a uniformly illuminated objective present. (3,6,7)

In the poetry and rhetoric of this time, "where were all the beautiful bodies?" (Ulmer, Conversation). (Please don't tell Socrates, but i like music too.) The bodies, along with the emotions, character, and *souls* of the ancient Greek heroes, had all been brought to the fore—rendered totally present, provocative, confrontational, aggressive.}

Museum, Ierapetra

The head of the viral young man on the shelf
to the left of Demeter turns away
from the statue of the young petite goddess
with her small stone body
and softly sorrowing face;
beneath the folds of her marble dress
the shadow of her belly button spreads:
He cannot turn and look: He has no body.
To the right, the full figure of a woman
on the shelf has no dusty head.
And the new decapitated bust in front,
all chest and unspent testicles,
can neither turn nor run.
With the form of her small stone belly
the goddess attracts and repels,
desires and defends, gives birth and kills.
Now they understand the power
of appearance, and passion beneath repose

***

Music was more random than a statue. Eco further discusses a division in ancient Greek aesthetic philosophy between sight and sound (and its Apollonian and Dionysian distinction/forms) that played into a critique not only of music but also of poetry: "Heraclitus was to open up [the division between appearance and beauty] to its maximum extent by stating that the harmonious beauty of the word manifests itself as random flux" (*Beauty* 36). For Heraclitus, the random *word* perfectly reflected the random nature of the universe, which was perhaps anathema to Platon (as it was to Einstein 2500 years later: "God does not play dice with the universe"). According to Pythagoras, a philosophical ancestor of Platon, music not merely *represented* but embodied the mathematical-mystical harmony of the material spheres. (It did for Kepler too [Stephenson].) But the concept of *Kalon*—"that which appeals to our senses" i.e., beauty—was not accorded the same privilege in music as in sight:

> Chaos and music came to constitute the dark side of Apollonian beauty . . . and as such fell within the sphere of the god Dionysus . . . [A] statue had to represent an "idea" (and hence a sense of serene contemplation) while music was understood as something that aroused the passions . . . [T]his beauty was . . . a screen that attempted to conceal the disquieting Dionysiac beauty, which was not expressed in apparent forms, but over and above appearances. This was a joyous and dangerous beauty, antithetical to reason, and often depicted as possession and madness. (Eco, *Beauty* 56–58)

Λ Lambda

In physics, Lambda was used as a "symbol of wavelengths . . . which describes how subatomic particles move and interact" (*TechTarget*). The ancient Greek sophists seemed to have little use for sheer speculation and idle contemplation on transcendental "forms" that could not be perceived (i.e., that were without body, mass—even if only a body of words) and thus could never be proven with any certainty to exist. In art, this would have pertained to the ideal mathematical proportions governing the portrayal of everything (Eco, *Beauty* 74), including the human body. In language, including rhetoric and poetry, it was a questioning of *logos*. In the fragment "On the Nonexistent, or On Nature," Gorgias asserted that *logos* was not the thing referred to, but a symbol of it—a *re-presentation* in language ("as images")—and thus impossible to convey to another (46). For Gorgias, *logos* was not a real body at all, a *physical* object or event, but rather a powerful simulation (if not simulacrum) that for better or worse could delude or drug the senses and the mind (Gorgias, "Encomium"). Unlike Platon (and even Aristotle), the sophists never severed the magic of poetry and rhetoric from philosophy and science of the physical world (hence the storied statue of Gorgias holding up a globe in his hand.) Like the behavior of subatomic particles, all were uncertain. The construction of knowledge through language, sense impressions, ideas, memories, and emotions were all humans had (Enos, *Greek Rhetoric* 78–85; Kerferd 97). As "bodies" of knowledge, rhetoric and poetry were not ideal or logical forms, not bodies that were knowable with any certainty. But they were knowable with uncertainty. Rhetoric and poetry made even empirical realities (never mind Being), tangible, perceptible, palpable, even potent, if not always palatable. For the sophists generally, rhetoric and poetry were necessary to cure the "impotency principle," to bridge the abyss of perceiving and knowing. Lambda = *Logos* of indeterminacy. Although the result was infinite uncertainty (just as ambiguity was a linguistic source of freedom for Burke [and the omnipresent, invisible, increasingly disappearing "voice" of G/d was for the Jews], that uncertainty itself was a cause for eternal celebration [Untersteiner]). (Socrates doesn't know this, but i love to party with friends too, who shall remain unnamed. We gather late at night near monuments that mark the uncertainty of knowledge, and the passage of time.)

Linear Disk A, Phaistos

{"'Beauty is truth, truth beauty,'—that is all
ye know on earth, and all ye need to know"
– Keats "Ode to a Grecian Urn," Keats and Shelley 186}

The swirl of the
hot wind in the pines,
the swirl of the
snow on Mt. Ida,
the swirl of the sun
in the ear, the swirl
of hieroglyphics on a disk,
the swirl of a culture
on a vase of time,
the circling of hawks,
and the untranslatable
chatter of sparrows,
invisible in the stone:
all that is left

M Mu

Kinds of Potency

In physics, Mu was the ratio of the frictional force . . . resisting the motion of two surfaces" (Britannica). {Spatial Equation B."Potency" —the opposite of "the impotency principle"—was understood in at least two ways: power (of reproduction); and strength (in this case, of persuasion). In the first of these, potency may have been about the mimetic properties of a word (speech/poem), the ability of a term to "reproduce" an idea (or feeling) or thing (or event)—which it never completely can insofar as signs must (mis)represent their referents (not only by "identification" but by difference/differance [see Burke, Grammar of Motives; Derrida, Grammatology; Deleuze, Difference]). The second kind of potency was not (only) the degree of similarity between word and referent, a gauge of its mimetic property to reproduce externa, but also how strongly it could persuade of its rightness—-a kind of internal mimesis that would create "the illusion" of identity in the mind of a listener or reader based on "intrinsic" as well as "extrinsic" meaning (see Burke, Grammar of Motives 46–51; cf. Fisher on narrative persuasion). Gorgias' conception of logos thus was best understood as encompassing both the power of rhetoric to persuasively represent (the external), and the power of poetry to persuasively capture and present (to language and the senses) an "inaccurate" (but internally cohesive and convincing) concoction of memories, language, and emotions (cf. Enos, Greek Rhetoric).} (Not written about, i have no problems in the potency area either; i can persuade and reproduce at will.)

***

{Ontological Displacement. Potency was *not* the same as Heidegger's later assertion that Platon squeezed more out of the term *"Eidos"* (idea) than the physical properties of an idea of a thing—that Platon makes the word *Eidos* carry the weight of representing the unseen essence or Being of a thing (Heidegger, "Question" 20). It was the opposite. Both the seen and unseen *Eidos* or essence or Being—almost invisible by definition—was not presented or perceived by the senses; both had to be "held away" from the body and mind's "affect" and "imagination" so that these could negatively redirect the "reason" (which sees not just the present but the future) and the "will" (to act). (cf. Bacon, *Advancement* XVIII.2, 4). But if those memories *were* drawn from *the soul's* mystical memory of transcendental Forms that it may have once beheld, the ultimate and necessary goal of "contemplation," and later "accurate representation," in philosophy and science—even if based on a bit of "mimetic magic" (Di Romilly)—was to transport the "observant soul" to truth (transcendental or empirical). The effect would have been a possible permanent residence there in the realm of truth, not merely as rhetorical *stases* but as stable and static *Eidos*: to live with/as Ideal Forms, rather than be subject to eternal recurrence (Nietzsche).} (I admit, sometimes i get bored too, and let my mind wander from Socrates' lessons and words.)

N Nu

Moral Proportionality

In physics Nu was frequency, "the number of waves that pass a fixed point in unit time" (*Britannica*). In a stricter reading of Platon, good art was bad art, bad art might be good. The better or best art (as art—the more aesthetically pleasing to the senses) could be the worse art morally, in that it best represented the false as true. Morally, the "better or best art" was probably *no art*. "[P]ainting or drawing, and imitation in general, when doing their own proper work, are far removed from truth . . . The imitative art is an inferior . . . " (Plato, *Republic* X; in Eco, *Beauty* 38). As Arne Melberg discussed:

> The poor morality of art [is] derived from its mimetic curse: art sticks, and has to stick, to the deceptive knowledge of the senses, which necessarily means that it will appeal to our worst parts, imitating "the fretful and complicated type of character" (*Republic* 605A) rather than the ideally calm and good, giving us a dubious "vicarious pleasure" (606B) rather than ideal and true satisfaction. (11)

Thus art, whether aesthetically good or bad, could never be good, because its purpose was to appeal to and deceive the senses, rather than educate the mind; its very aim was to lie. Based on Platon's stretched logic, perhaps bad art was better than good art in that it failed to please and deceive. (Without the power to differentiate between good and bad art, i tend to like what pleases me.)

Sneaking Through the Labyrinth

Dip your feet, Aphrodite,
rising from the sea to take
your own photos, and write
your own poems
in the fields of the gods,
your breath beneath the grass,
the stars pouring through your hair,
hugging the rough landscape
with your legs, your feet, your hands,

making it too beautiful, unbearably
smooth for humans. The wind
jumps and kicks up every time
i think about you, and the rocks
pile up on the fields, and at the feet
of the houses of the gods.

They still live here.

Ξ Ksee

Linguistic Correspondence

In mathematics, Ksee represented "the value of *ith*, the residual between the predicted and observed values" (*Britannica*). The question of how language/the physical corresponded to the non-physical, and even more, how this could be known at all by spirit or soul without a body, remained somewhat nebulous. Platon had indeed wanted a point by point (later in Newtonian science called the "one-to-one correspondence" [Sprat])—but *not* between word and material things, but between words and Ideal Forms (Kerferd). Like causality and other laws of nature, truth without art itself is invisible. Art could and would be more important if not essential than the truth—one of Platon's primary complaints. Predicted and observed values had to align for anything to be perceived. Mathematical proportion and geometric symmetry were perhaps as close as humans got. For Platon, geometry was as close to eternal truths as the human mind (minus body) could attain. As Eco averred, "good form was precisely that of correct proportion and symmetry" (*Beauty* 74). But proportional thinking itself, like narrative according to Eric Auerbach (23), also changed from the one-dimensional spatial and temporal plane of Homer in which everything was foreground, to a multidimensional, relativistic set of planes of later narratives and the tragedies. By the fourth century BCE, Polyclitus creates a statute known as the Canon "because it embodies all the rules of correct proportion among the parts . . . " (Eco, *Beauty* 74). However, Eco said:

> [T]he principle underpinning of the Canon is not based on the equilibrium of two equal elements. All the parts of the body had to conform reciprocally in accordance with proportional ratios in a geometric sense . . . But the Canon of Polyclitus no longer featured fixed units . . . [T]he criterion was organic, and the proportions of the parts determined according to the movement of the body, changes in perspective, and the adaptation of the figure in relation to the position of the viewer. (*Beauty* 74–75)

(Just a "boy"[you'll never guess my age], i love to peek, stare merely for the pleasure of dimensions and proportions.)

Azure and Alabaster

Your lids, in morning azure, move
as you lie, asleep in the blue
as in a quiet film, dreaming; dawn
slowly filters to your eyes.

Light touches limb, hair
spins frail lines across
face and brow, clocks
whirr in a violet room.

Perhaps you dream of being
a ballerina; your alabaster
body moves with you
so gracefully, so beautiful.

Silently you stir,
turning in my arms.

O Omicron

Perspective as Phantom

In mathematics, Omicron stood for the number (n) of smaller quantities falling beneath projected growth (Padilla). Given the "technical development of the figurative arts in ancient Greece" (Eco, *Beauty* 42, 72–75), even the possibility of multidimensionality and relativity based on shifting "perspectives" in art must have exacerbated the elder Platon. Just as Auerbach discussed, introduced by later Greek playwrights, perspective in narrative was created by backgrounding as well as foregrounding. {But also see Kazantzakis' continuation of Homer and twentieth century rewrite of the "one-dimensional Odysseus."} "Greek painters invented foreshortening, which does not require the objective precision of beautiful forms" (Eco, *Beauty* 43). Sculpting too, in departing from geometric ratiós and mathematical proportions, moved further away from "Ideal Forms" and ever closer to the actual organic form of the human body. That change necessitated the aesthetic need to take into account perspectives brought about by the *physical* point of view of the *human viewer*. In art there was henceforth a recognition if not acceptance of the role of "subjectivity" in perception, for which there wasn't much allowance in Platon's philosophy (cf. his discussion of writing in *Phaedrus* 270b–275e). The recognition of perspective was combined with the development of techniques for representing it. In the *Sophist* Platon had "the Stranger" complain to Theaetetus:

> One art that I see contained in it is the making of a likeness (εικαστικη [*eikastiki*—"visual"]). The perfect example of this consists in creating a copy that conforms to the proportions of the original in all three dimensions and giving moreover the proper color to every part . . . If they were to reproduce the true proportions of a well-made figure, as you know, the upper parts would look too small and the lower too large, because we see the one at a distance, the other close at hand . . . So artists, leaving the truth to take care of itself, do in fact put into the images they make, not the real proportions, but those that will appear beautiful . . . The first kind of image, then, being like the original, may fairly be called a likeness (*eikou*—"icon") . . . And the corresponding subdivision of the art of imitation may be called by the name we used just now—likeness making . . . [W]hat are we to call the kind which only appears to be a likeness of a well-made figure because it is not seen from a satisfactory point of view, but to a spectator with eyes that could fully take in so large an object would not be even like the original it professes to resemble? Since it seems to be a likeness, but is not really so, may we not call it a semblance (φαντασμα [*fantasma*—"phantom"]). And this is a very extensive class, in painting and in imitation of all sorts. (235d–236c)

Π Pi

Mimesis and the Soul

In geometry, Pi measured "the ratio of a circle's circumference to its diameter" (Nasehpour). Only a mimesis of the soul would do. The distinction between an image and a "true" image was already a paradox if not an impossibility, given Platon's definition of mimesis that Melberg explored in detail (10–50). Good art of the human body, which strictly speaking still a (an icon) semblance even when based on mathematical proportion, was for Platon better than "bad art" (a semblance), which is worse because it was based on proportion derived from *human* perspective. Semblance led to the further denigration of imitation (as image). (Thinking about this, i wander around in a circle: the denigration of imitation was bad or good, depending on the beholder's philosophy and perceptive.)

Ρ Rho

In mathematics, Rho was "the spherical coordinate system for the three-dimensional space R3" (Nasehpour). (Now i have a three-dimensional space in which to wander.) But the denigration of imitation in semblance also led to the increasing ambiguity of the human form itself as newly imaged. For the virility and beauty of the physical body was itself an image, an illusion of a true(r) form, whose beauty was increasingly disembodied. Yet it was only the disembodied Ideal Form, Beauty, which "shines out everywhere" (Eco, *Beauty* 100), that was truly (i know, i know: the Beautiful is yet another paradox). The human body, even a proportional one, was already an imitation of an imitation of the Ideal Form of Beauty, and so "false."—leaving the contemplative, disembodied mind in a state of (im)pure repos by the shredding the power of artistic form—leaving as a kind of "truth" the illusions and untruths of delicious, unctuous stories of poets, rhetoricians, lairs, and madmen.

Orpheus to Persephone

"No! Go from me, to Eurydice:
I have lost her there, have left death lately.
I will not miss the spring—the orphic boughs
perennial, chorded with golden leaves,
plucked by the women, horny, unbidden,
naked in the wind, devouring;

"Nor looking back, heed your bitter howls
blown through the brutal winter of your hell,
love borne annually to perpetual darkness
lost forever from this ravaged world;

"Nor immortal, mind your mother's cries,
the warmth stripped from the light eternally,
her curse, the graying landscape, barren earth,
or the endless drift, the slow white hours . . .

Σ Sigma

Mimesis as Mask

In mathematics, Sigma was often a "summation symbol" (Nasehpour). In the *Protagoras* (a more "light-hearted" dialogue about sophistry compared to the *Gorgias* or the *Sophist*), Platon identified and grouped sophists not only as poets, including the ancients Hesiod and Homer, but also as mythical or religious figures such as the musician and poet Orpheus. They were *all* "sophists" behind "screens," working undercover (Plato, *Protagoras* 316d–317b). For Platon, art like physical reality itself, in the end was a sham, a disguise, a deception (one that Platon himself openly and covertly engaged in). In almost all his treatises, Platon used Socrates not only a mouthpiece but a "mask." (i was just one of the cast.) One of the key points in Melberg's analysis of mimesis was that Platonic dialogue itself "is a form of dramatized mimetic representation, all according to the Socratic definitions of mimesis. The philosophical dialogue is the very form that Platon invents to make himself into else" (21).

—Platon, the Philosopher-Bookie

"Another now rises, and now sinks, and by reason of her unruly steeds sees in part, but in part sees not . . . sucked down as they travel they trample and tread upon one another, this one striving to outstrip that. Thus confusion ensues, and conflict and grievous sweat, Whereupon, with their charioteers powerless, many are lamed, and many have their wings all broken, and for all their toiling they are balked, everyone, of the full vision of being, and departing therefrom, they feed upon the food of semblance."—Plato, *Phaedrus* 1956, 842b

"Plato the Philosopher-Bookie, here,
with a tip for all you wannabe
Philosopher-Kings: follow Lysias.

"Listen: A little common-sense advice:
Let your gyro-hypno-trancing words
appear to be pulling for the white horse,

"edging the charioteer toward Justice, Goodness
(you are allowed to lie if it serves
a clever peda-philosophic purpose:

"I do. And I don't have to charge a fee to).
But if you want to know the honest truth,
bet all your ill-gotten earnings on the

"dark horse. Human failure: It's a sure thing,
as absolute as the Ideal Forms
(almost). But in the end you can depend on

"appearance and desire beating out
morality any day and time and winning
the race for those beautiful young souls—

"the most handsome and promising among them.
And you, poet-sophists, profess your shadow
if you must; pretend philosophy.

"But in the meantime, while you float around
the world for 9,000 years (or more)
with the heap of base humanity,

"you might as well get paid two drachmas for
your service (I make Socrates declaim
that's the reason you teach anyway).

"And you rhetor-poets, itinerant—
touched in the head by Dionysian
persuasion, stylistic craziness,

"cooking melodious but false phrases
that intoxicate and drug the senses up—
go ahead, debate the dialectic

"of poetic form. (I have been known to
indulge myself, before I turned philosopher
and burned the indiscretion of my youth).

"I know the truth. But a word to the wise:
Take off-rhyme as your lover. Though not as easy
or pleasurable as a steady surprise of true

"rhyme, you'll have a wider field of words
to choose from; they'll be less predictable—
you'll never grow tired of their prattling;

"and since you will have chosen rationally,
they will not turn on you in the end.
They'll never grow old and stale, repulsing you

"like a withered lover's aging breath,
providing many moments for regret.
Don't listen to that senior citizen

"with the handsome over-eager boy there,
reciting all the reasons not to love
the lover, but to love the non-lover

"(a-motional disease, a sickless love,
the old mistake of non-physical passion)—
his head lying beneath a croaking veil.

"Next thing you know, he'll be discoursing on
Love's divine origin and virtue,
in dithyrambs raving under that plane tree.

"How can you trust such a senile sophist,
who so readily changes the arrangement of his mind.
Lysias, in the precocious mouths

"of timeless twenty-something boys, is right:
Divine knowledge, love, is fine and dandy
in the hands of those for whom the Forms are handy.

"But verse built up from limited true-rhyme
like irrationality will last
a lifetime in the world of shadow, sham,

"and never give you real cause to repent.
Now, who would you rather listen to,
a philosopher like me, or rhetor-poet

"who doesn't know a truer argument
from a jackass? Which horse will win the race?
Put down those books; step up and place your bets."

T Tau

Veils upon Veils

In geometry, Tau is a "translation in a vector space" (Nasehpour). In all his treatises in which he spoke through one of Socrates' masked, made-up faces, Platon's intent was to "expose" the "true nature" of the false arts (which was its falsity and not a good)— to slowly peel away with dialectic logic the affective veneer created by the appealing aesthetic bodies of rhetoric, poetry, music, painting, sculpture—to reveal that they were not "Real" bodies at all. The objects of "art," including rhetoric and poetry, which were not "true arts" for Platon (see Table 3) and had no moral existence, no soul. They were false imitations of physical shadows (e.g., Plato *Republic* X.595a–607b). In the *Phaedrus*, one of Platon's more generous treatises on rhetoric and poetry, as well as the

Gorgias, the charge applied equally to most speeches and to writing. The rhetorical-poetic conceit that Platon played with in the *Phaedrus*, both figuratively and literally, was *the veil.* (Socrates was often not only profound but funny. Even though he was rather hideous, he never really hid; i loved him too [Platonically, of course, just to set the record straight].) He adorned himself with a rhetorical and poetic veil for effect in his first speech of love as something irrational and evil (following Lysias first speech, delivered by Platon, that the best love is based on a rational process). But in Socrates' second speech, his first speech was shed for the sake of "the gods" and the Truth: that love is something divine. The veil was shed too.

***

Socrates' playful machinations with speeches and veils that he used to cover and uncover his head in the *Phaedrus* took on added significance—much like Odysseus' scar—in their respective narratives. As Auerbach might have said, the veil was temporally located and symbolically charged. In this dialogue, the play of the veil also was understood to represent not falsehood or shame, but the relation of art to the body, and the relationship of both to True Knowledge (there is none). Overlaying the physical body with the veil of art was an imitation of an imitation. Lifting the veil from the face (especially Socrates' face [reputed to be quite ugly] certainly did not lead to a bashful glimpse of true Beauty, or even "natural; beauty" (although his words point in that general direction). But the lifting of the veil was a "stripping," a removal of at least one layer of "skin." The veil had to be lifted from the senses as well the body to begin to reveal or even speak of the divine incorporeal (Socrates' soul beneath). Socrates' comparisons of writing to the human body (e.g., Plato, *Phaedrus* 264c) emphasize this even more—the necessity of severing the connection of mind to material world. i wonder whether what was also revealed in the action of the veils, and the body's relationship to Love, was the aging Platon's ambiguous, even conflicted *feelings* about his own philosophical position, embodied in this rhetorical and poetic discourse.

Socrates' Veil

"Listen to me now, Phaedrus, my dear boy:
The body is but a parting veil
of the mind, the diaphanous soul
that lurks within the skein but is the truth;

this sheer sheet, filling and collapsing
with every little breath that puckers it,
is an illusion of the senses, a trick

that leads you out toward—toward what?

The parting of the woods there, up ahead,
now gone, disappearing like a cave
of trees shimmering in the sunlight,
like the false translucent art we wear,

a flesh stretched out until at last becoming
a thin and fine-flung mesh, from which there is
only one way out? Through death, the veil
is not merely lifted, but disappears of

its own accord. Why wait to be released?
Philosophy can help you shift the veil
so you can finally take a little peek at
what lies behind these images we call
life.

Y Upsilon

In calculus, Upsilon (υ) represented "the limit of a function" (*Libretexts*). The major philosophical issue underlying all of Platon's charges, according to Gerald Else as well as Arne Melberg, was that of mimesis vs. True Knowledge. For Platon, rhetoric and poetry as "phantom forms" could not contain any part of Reality. They merely mimicked (and mocked) it. In the treatise *Ion*, Socrates chided and ridiculed the rhapsodes and poets (and me) on the supposition that, because they were inspired by the gods, they knew nothing of what they uttered. If the gods spoke through a poet often enough, the poet might have thought that something of the gods might rubbed off them—that for all their celestial predicaments as pickled troubadours in troubles, at least some kind of divine residue would have accrued, remained. But (much like Jesus after the resurrection [Nancy, *Noli*]), the gods probably did not actually touch the poets with their holy wisdom); the poets were merely mouthpieces, frenetic vessels to be filled, possessed, and then discarded. While Platon perhaps granted poetry some credibility in relation to religion or mythology vs "true" divine knowledge, he simultaneously strips poets of any agency or status. "Sokratres (*sic*) will not allow the true poet even a shred of rationality; reason must depart before poetizing can begin . . . The poet himself contributes nothing whatever to his song" (Else 7).

*The Carpenter's Non-Apprentice**

"You mean, the rhapsode will know better what the ruler of a ship in a storm at sea should say than will the pilot?"—Plato, Ion 540[b]

like a poet, doesn't know anything about
working with wood, stands there, hiding
his shame, holding the board still
for his master who quickly
saws it in two, into four, shifting
from foot to foot to foot, while keeping his eye
on the point where the blade will bite
the plank. The rhetor knows enough to turn
the board before the omniscient teeth
descends into the wood. He knows enough
to move his hand from the range of the mouth
of the saw that turns the object into objects
right before his eyes, sophistic sawdust rising . . .

rhapsode, now on his own, holds over
the nail he found in a shed the hammer
in his hand, then drops the nail clumsy on
the leafy ground, never to be found
again; and then another nail that doesn't
bite but rather curls off, bends, digs
sideways into the wood and doesn't even hold
two planks together, but splits the splintering > > >

professional carpenter you ain't, Orator

***

Mimesis, Heroes, Gods

In the *Republic* (esp. Bks. II, III, and X), the issue of *mimesis* reappeared as a concern about the *representation* of the thoughts, words, and deeds *of the gods* (as well as of legendary heroes), of which poets sang with absolutely no real knowledge of the language of the gods or what they professed (598e–599a, 599d). "Socrates' examples illustrated that the primary untruths of tales have to do with the gods. Since the gods by definition—Platon's definition—are good, it follows that any bad tale about the gods must be lying" (Melberg 13). Furthermore, the *actions* of the gods could not be imitated by melody, rhythms, words, because these rhetorical-poetic elements were neither related to nor found in the non-physical realm of the gods (or in the case of heroes had already taken place in an unknown past). These elements were deceptive "substance" because the Ideal Forms *had no substance*. That is, the poetic elements themselves were insubstantial. Not only were these rhetorical-poetic elements lies, says Melberg, they were not even "authentic lies, according to Socrates, but images representing lies" (14). Even so, as lies they were still dangerous because their physical albeit false forms were attractive and pleasurable at best, hypnotic and corrupting at worse, and led away from the search for "true" Forms (Else 37–38). They are all false phantom flesh.

Young Odysseus to Athena: The Untold Story

Shimmering body curving into mine
(O divine lines), you look me straight
in mortal eyes with your sea-gray eyes
dangerous as any uncharted water—
sink me deep into your gaze, your mouth,
omnipotent tongue seeking mine, pulling
me down into your roiling flesh, your lips
closing over my lips, drowning me.

"Think of the intrigue among the gods," you hiss.

But you are older than i, more beautiful
and wise (although your skin's a little dry . . .),
and will not consummate or even talk
of love. "I have to take you back," you sigh
in your best English accent. Dripping
cloud (you forgot your umbrella again!),
you drop me off, a stranger in my home,
to wander earth in search of tenderness

***

Homer's story of Odysseus in his prime was left behind in Nikos Kazantzakis's "modern sequel" to *The Odyssey*. The latter was a "fictional" account of what happened to Odysseus after he returned home, and his need to venture out into the world again drove him to his final departure from his wife and son and everything he knew. As Else suggests, in *Laws* Platon claims that "[t]here can be no question of the Muses' deliberately deceiving the poet . . . but inspiration here apparently amounts to no more than a certain persuasiveness or plausibility in imitation" (63). Given the impossibility of an accurate representation of gods and heroes, the charge of *mimesis* became a moral attack on poets as the purveyors of falsehoods about the gods, and on poetry as shadow-narratives (see Else 22). "The lies spread by the tales are not authentic lies, according to Socrates, but images representing lies" (Melberg 14). For Platon, all forms of poetry—tragedy, epic, lyric—falsely incarnated unfathomable and inscrutable actions of gods and heroes. They were tempting and harmful illusions because they pretended to refer to "Real bodies" and so distracted the mind from the true objects of contemplation in the soul's journey through the world. It was the poet rather than the gods and heroes that were heard and seen in poetry and in drama; poets and "playwrights" were impostors (even to their "own true selves") pretending through mimesis to be who and what *they were not* (also Plato, *Republic* III.393a–394b). (i would never do that to you.) *The gods did not lie; poets did* (*Republic* II.3821e–d). Poets were mere mimes (Else 27), "*mimos*, a buffoon and a juggler" (Melberg 19)—and "lying mimes" at that. For Platon, the impersonation of divine gods and heroic acts by poets was perhaps even more pernicious than other forms of imitation (Else 24–29). The gods were unknowable; the heroes were dead. Only their suffering remains. It is the philosophers, not rhetoricians and poets, who must tell philosophical tales of battles, hubris, conquests, and death.

In the Museum at Aighios Nikolaos

The head of a victor: sides of a skull
wrapped in fine wrought gold, a silver coin
beside his teeth; and the bust of the
Madonna: V–IV Century BC,
vague hands cupping suppositional
breasts, almost closed-eyed, lips pulled back
in ecstasy and pain, surrounded by
vessels of small turtles like pudenda—

Here we find ourselves among the ruins,
psyches in ruins, a metal plate
of knucklebones beside decapitated
heads of dead women who would have hated
to lose their breasts, a castration of mother-
hood, never to bear children again,
broken skeletons of babies in
a *pithoi*, mouths turned to clay while crying—

female figures holding groins and breasts,
hands placed and posed in ancient rituals
of periods, pregnancy, nursing, death.

Φ Phi

Mimesis and Alphabets

In category theory, Phi was "a functor" that associated items in one category with another (Nasehpour). In the *Cratylus,* Platon shifted the focus of his criticism of mimesis from "the body" of rhetoric and poetry to language itself, to the skeletons of sounds, syllables, and words. In an extended analogy between painted colors and textures of objects, Socrates critiqued the impossible and reprehensible representation of reality through the "resemblances" to their referents of physical sounds of letters and of words (*Cratylus,* esp. 424c–425d). Socrates at first appeared to agree with Cratylus that the "correctness of names"—their truth-value, as it were—were bound up with the ability of language to embody in its very forms (sound and letters) the "essence" of the thing described (cf. Katz, "Letter as Essence"; Cassirer; Rimbaud). (You saw how i tried to convince Socrates of that.) As evidenced by the *Cratylus,* a philosophy of based on a hermeneutics of language as ontological essence was practiced by the ancient Greeks as well as Hebrews and other cultures: In Platon's dialogue, Socrates ran through a series of Greek names, to which he applied a basic analytical method, that seem to confirm such a belief (see Katz, "Socrates as Rabbi"). But for the older Platon, the power of language as a medium had nothing to do with its physical (or metaphysical) properties as reality, never mind in representational relation to reality. The belief that letters themselves not only as "*semblances,*" but as "*ikons*" partook in w*hat they referenced*, was patently ridiculous to Platon (an imitation of an imitation of an imitation at the molecular level of mumbled shapes and sounds of writing systems (see Daniels and Bright). And Socrates, like most linguists in the twentieth century (e.g., *Writing Systems*), soon enough arrived at the conclusion that words cannot and do not bear any direct (or indirect) connection to the ideas, events, or objects they "(mis)represent." By the end of the *Cratylus,* Socrates has found such beliefs absurd, and agrees with Hermogenes that the spelling and meaning of words is completely arbitrary and agreed upon by convention. {Temporal Shift. Centuries later, there was a subdominant strain in linguistics, extending at least from Wilhelm von Humboldt through Ernst Cassirer to Suzanne Langer, and also found in poetry such as Arthur Rimbaud's, which regarded the shapes and sounds of each word as bearing the imprint of the emotion that first motivated them (cf. Katz, *Epistemic Music*).}

***

What was perhaps most significant in the *Cratylus* was that, despite a both interesting and tedious account of the meaning of sound in relation to physical objects, Socrates arrived at this position from which to critique rhetoric and poetry again. Language itself was false form right down to its very core. With Socrates as blade, in the *Cratylus* the letters of the Greek alphabet were slowly *stripped* of all metaphorical, metaphysical, musical, and/or mystical meaning. The story of Orpheus and his lyre that Platon cited several times in his dialogues witnessed the ultimate failure of language—of poetry and rhetoric and music (instruments, lyrics, tunes, notes, and letters) as worthless forms of meaning and persuasion, impotent to change physical (or ontological) reality—to persuade gods, animals, stones, and in the end especially the Maenads who turned against and tore Orpheus to pieces. The story of Orpheus proved the case: his speech, his poetry, his music, his instrument, his clothes, his body, his hair—were shredded "limb from limb").

Orpheus at the Volcano, Santorini

i am Orpheus, but won't look back,
climbing up the side of the volcano
from a hell that is a paradise
into a paradise that is a hell,
boulder by boulder, steaming and shimmering
with sulfur and dark sun, each step i take
crushed in the sand that roils below me like

a swarm; but i am Orpheus, won't look back,
though Dionysus glares in the volcano,
and on rocks far below Eurydice
just sits and stares at spiders. i feel my power
waning as the tide withdraws, and hear
the ocean walk the shore again with molten
feet, the rumbling like an angry throng

behind me. But i am Orpheus: i will charm
volcano gods and the sulfur-water.
i hear her steps—Eurydice behind
me, somewhere at the base of the mountain,
between the shadows of desire, sea.
The sunlight breaks upon my head, and foot
steps grow louder in the sand like an army:

i turn to see a naked man now falling
into an abyss, clothes shredded
in a vent hole where the sunlight also
pokes up from underneath the ground; a wedge
of turmoil three inches thick, opens,

swallowing her tiny footsteps. i look to see
the man threaded on those rocks—it's me!

***

Given that language did not touch or embody contiguous reality (never mind Reality), all words spoken by rhetoricians and poets were in effect "insubstantial," mimetic lies. And given that the bodies of the gods were usually "invisible," how could anyone have known whether the poets were accurate, "telling the truth," and to what degree? Melberg asked a related question when he wondered why Platon took the question of mimesis and poets so seriously, when Platon himself, by writing dialogue—*dia mimeseos*, reported what others have said (Melberg 16), engaging in the very acts of mimesis Platon critiqued (Melberg 12). Kenneth Burke raised the issue in his attempt to delineate dramatistic poetics in "Three Definitions" (23–26). But as Else remarked, in *Laws* Platon is a poet as well as a philosopher: "he alone can claim to be both, he alone can claim to represent the truth with sufficient clarity to supplant the traditional poetry of Greece" (64; cf. Cicero, *Nature*). It was commonplace that despite Platon's harsh treatment of sophists, rhetoricians, poets, and musicians, the way he often described the philosophically ineffable, at least in the earlier dialogues, was through the rhetorics and poises. In doing so, Plato gave suasive shapes and beautiful bodies to numberless, nameless, abstract Ideas and Forms that without rhetorics and poetics would otherwise have been wholly inexpressible or unknowable.

Poseidon II: i swear by all the gods

i swear by all the gods, everywhere—
in churches built on top of ancient temples,
and by the pagan myths become the ground
of Holy Doctrine, that the story i,
Lord Byron, am about to tell you, happened
between the salty groves and lemony sea

where icons of body parts, injured, diseased.
—a hand, an arm, a leg, some feet—hang
on clotheslines in every little chapel, church,
waiting to be prayed for by any
passing relative or stranger, healed.
They did not come soon enough for me—

did not help me when, unable to climb
the twisted hill bent around the cliffs

above the temple of Poseidon, on Poros,
where the grotto grumbles with the waves,
and the sea-god's school of jellyfish
came after me, stinging! But i, Lord Byron,

who carved his youthful initials into one
of sixteen columns still standing, the temple
fallen all around in boulders scattered
in soft pine needles, dark sea scented trees,
where in the grotto the god still snores, asleep—
escaped, thanks to Hermes, or Aphrodite,

what human can say which? But then Poseidon
abruptly gurgled, woke up, slowed me down
as my motor bike tried to climb the steep hill
and turn, and i began to spiral, i say:
he tipped me over and seared my leg against
the hot exhaust pipe—prayers did not help me,

a piece of flesh hanging off, flapping,
flapping in the breeze as i bravely
rounded the remaining curves, the island,
iodine and unguents unable to stop
the infection that ate away my calf, so green
and gloamy that on the plane everyone
thought i was a leper from Atlantis,

and rather than returning home a hero
like Odysseus, i returned
to my wife unable to walk, wounded
and helpless as a fallen warrior
on his knees before the horse and rider
beneath a spear, black figure still battling

on a Corinthian vase. From the island
of poet-worshippers paying homage
in the broken ruins to the past. i,
Lord Byron, swear an oath to all the gods
that these events are true, and happened to me,
in Poseidon's grotto, on Poros, by the sea.

X Chi

"Eidos Sokratikon"

In chemistry, Chi was "the ability of a material to become transiently polarized" (U of Delaware). One facet of Platon's dialogues that Kenneth Burke brought out was the "Socratic manner (*eidos Sokratikon*)," the layering of Platonic dialogue, where "Socrates told of questions he put to others, and of the questions and assertions made by him atop their replies"; for Burke, "[t]he persons are differentiated as to both thought and character" ("Three Definitions" 24). Melberg too analyzed at some length Platon's ironic use of the techniques of mimesis that he, Platon, has Socrates criticize. Melberg concluded that since Platon is only using Socrates body (and really just a part of the body of Socrates, his mouth/speech), "Plato allows himself to criticize mimesis in mimetic dialogue" (17). That is, though he polarized them, "Socrates" used the sensual power of rhetorical and poetic language in a dialectical process of audience adaptation to appeal directly to Phaedrus—to plant a teleological "seed" of philosophy in his soul, to put flesh on the boney quest for a higher love, "Platonic" being. (And so i am converted [Plato, *Republic* VI.525b–526B], must now disappear; but i will be born again, many times, in different holy and unholy forms.)

Metamorphosis and Transfiguration: The Krenos Lily

for Marty

Began to call you Mary
when the old Greek matron
like a nun emerged
from her ancient house
in Heraklion
to pick the Krenos Lily

from the "tree of life"
you were admiring
in her Minoan garden,

to give you birth again
like the Prince of Lilies
from the flowering womb.

"Martha, i've begun
to call you Mary," i say.
"That's why they call me Marty:

it's a combination
of the two—a conflict
I've come here to reconcile."

We witness a religious
processional. You wear
the Krenos lily round your neck.

And in the end you go
home in water-colored
blazes of blue lilies,

reborn in copies of
frescoes among the ruins
the Orthodox call home.

***

"The new kind of dialectic is a very different kind of procedure, having little more than the name in common with the old. It is not an accident," Else added, "that modern systematic philosophers tended to take Plato seriously as a philosopher only from the *Theaitetos* [sic] on" (42). After the *Republic*, Platon "never engages in the Sokrátic kind of dialect again" (Else 42). In some of the later treatises, such as *Timaeus*, Platon dropped the mimetic disguise not only of dialogue, but also of narrative (which method of "reporting" Platon had used earlier in some of his earlier treatises). In *Philebus*, "little or nothing would be lost if Plato had dropped the dialogue and made Socrates deliver a lecture . . . Socrates himself does not come through" (Hamilton and Cairns 1086–87). In *Sophist*, *Statesmen*, and *Timaeus*, Socrates "plays little or no part . . . but he is there and the conversation is directed toward him" (Hamilton and Cairns 1225). In *Laws,* ostensibly the last treatise Platon wrote before he died, "the topic, again, was the ideal state, now situated on Crete and populated with 5,040 happily chosen people (the number is due to its easy divisibility by most numbers, which makes the city ideally handy to administer" (Melberg 20); but the conversation was between three strangers from Crete, Sparta, and Athens. Not only was Socrates physically absent; [i]n *Laws* he is never even mentioned" (Hamilton and Cairns 1225).

Matala, Mediterranean Sea

*(Crete)**

Wall of round
caves on the right,
grass umbrellas,
bright bare breasts
on the beach,
two blue mountains
rising from
the concave belly
of the water,
the tan lines of
shore sand
Aphrodite
is born again,
rising from
from the sea.
a jet of dark
sunlight shooting
up. Strangers,
the boys and girls
with cloven hooves
play in caves
of Matala,
avoiding war
watching the
spontaneous
combustion
of ancient myths
in utter surprise
bewilderment

***

In *Theories of Mimesis*, Melberg cited Stanley Rosen's derision of Platon as a philosophical thinker based on a literal reading of Platonic texts, which in addition to logical fallacies and contradiction from page to page, included "the most vulgar superstitions of his day" (Plato, *Symposium* xii, cited in Melberg 13). Perhaps some of this was a result of anachronistic renderings; neo-Platon-

* The caves above the beaches on the shores of the Libyan Sea at Matala, in Southern Crete, were happy host/home to flower children and draft dodgers during the 1960s.

ic backreading from later developments in Christian theology, thought; and some mystical or wishful thinking. Were these religious and mythic accoutrements in Platon's dialogue also audience adaptation like the kind Socrates used on Phaedrus—poetic inventions, spiritual technology, early prosthetic devices made out of language and designed to be fitted over" the beliefs and bodies not only of Phaedrus, but of Platon's future readers?—To activate and entice and appeal to the organic and mechanical senses; to move the audience as well as the plot of the dialogues forward into a different future?

Lady Icarus

standing on
the cliff
of castle wall,
throws her blood
red scarf
around the sun
sticks her arms
into the hot honeycomb,
wraps the light
around herself
like wings

steps off
the rock
and disappears
into the sea.

i am the water
in this hell
of ecstasy.

hear
me

drop

Ψ Psi

In module theory, Psi was "a short exact sequence" (Nasehpour). In the *Phaedrus*, Platon's rhetorical and poetic theory and skills were in many ways at their height. The underlying rational assumptions for "invoking" religious and mythical allusions as techniques were more explicitly articulated too (e.g.,

Phaedrus). These, then, were better understood as audience accommodation via dialectic—a dialectic in "short exact sequences" matching, a "forming" of speeches to souls. From a literary point of view, Socrates himself as character might have been considered a *deus ex machina*, a way of bridging the abyss of knowledge, and thus "the impotency principle" (Holton). Until Platon's later treatises, Socrates was always foregrounded and central to create logical coherence and literary cohesion. His absence (somewhat like the increasing absence of the Hebrew G/d in the *Tanakh* as literature), was keenly felt. The later treatises signaled some kind of change—e.g., the *Sophist* and the *Statesman*, where Socrates had a more minimal role; the *Timaeus*, without dialogue (again); and *Laws*, dialogue but without Socrates, where Platon altogether "drops poetical thought and storytelling" (Hamilton and Cairns 1225). Had Platon matured beyond his master? And/or was this the way a mature Platon finally dealt with the trauma of Socrates execution and demise—not like the story of the *Apology* (from which it appears Platon was absent due to "illness"). But perhaps the final (non)representation of Socrates' death—*through rhetorical and literary form only*, is a "death of the body" a demise of mimetic mask and text, what Melberg called the "loss of self" (24).

The Death of Socrates

"I have not the slightest skill as a speaker—unless, of course, by a skillful speaker they mean one who speaks the truth. If that is what they mean, I would agree that I am an orator, though not after their pattern." –Plato, Socrates' Defense (17a–b)

Although he could have spoken out,
Socrates (like Christ) said nothing
to prevent his death by rhetoric,
declaring he wasn't eloquent.

(His word was not spiritual
flesh; just the opposite:
His word was freed from ugly flesh
and made logical spirit.)

Although he never appeared in court
in his seventy years before,
he spoke as a philosopher—
arguing was a mental sport:

divided and defined the issues,
their accusations and his "crimes,"
invoking poets, sophists, teachers
(whom he opposed in other fights),

but wouldn't protest the charges, argue
against the tantrums of the *polis*,
assuage corruption, sway the black beans
falling against him, not his favor.

Sitting calm and barefoot on
the cool dirt floor of his cell
(perhaps beneath Acropolis,
perhaps within agora walls—

despite the truth, no one can tell)
he did not kick away the hemlock,
or make his students turn their heads;
but engaged them in discussion until

he was dead. His body spoke no more.
A cock crowed for Asclepius.
He drank, and died, a silent martyr
for a philosophic cause—

reawakened, or reborn
in Platon, young and traumatized,
who may have been there, may have not,
but made his master's mouth his own,

who would report the tragic scene
to the court of history.
Socrates' ghost still haunts us now;*
rhetoric is unforgiven.†

Ω *Omega*

Bodies in Flight

As a "mathematical constant," Omega was defined as a unique real number" (Nasehpour). Platon endowed most of his dialogues with strong, beautiful bodies that would last the lifetime of humanity, while seeming to denounce the very media he worked in. Eric Havelock (*Preface*) and Walter Ong (*Orality*) argued that Platon was caught on the cusp of the slow shift from a primarily

* This line echoed the first line of Delmore Schwartz, "Socrates' Ghost Must Haunt me Now," p. 58.

† This line was adapted from the last line of Delmore Schwartz's "In the Naked Bed, in Plato's Cave," p. 25: "history is unforgiven."

oral culture to a more literate one. In addition to Auerbach, many scholars also noted the Greek preoccupation with the visual (e.g., Boman; Buber, *Judaism* 56–62; Katz, *Epistemic*; "Letter"), and in Platon's work in particular, with the spatiality of ideas (Havelock; Else 16; Toulmin and Goodfield). Platon's preoccupation with visual/spatial form was sometimes pointed to as the source of attention to poetic form as the distinguishing characteristic of verse. But it was disembodied, perfect Form that interested Platon—perfect ideational shapes without mass, located outside the language of space and time—mathematics (Plato, *Republic* VII.525b–526b)—not physical form as perceived and embodied and therefore corrupted by language and/or the senses, but perfect ideational shapes that could only be "recollected" and understood by the pure mind in flight.

Icarus

didn't make it to Santorini,
flying over the Icarian
sea in the sun, reading the myths,
laughing or unconscious;

or landed safely in Athens, to see
an artificial limb, waxed, polished, shiny,
floating on the conveyor belt,
circling, circling with the luggage,

no one to pick it up;
or in the museum in Heraklion,
trapped in a labyrinth of cases, limbs
and figures missing limbs that fell away

like heavy wings, clay fragments,
imprisoned in brighter glass,
airlifted, brought back to sacred ground,
to Knossos, finally home again,

knowing only the old stones,
not what lies beyond them
but what lies beneath them
happy

***

{Temporal Displacement. It was poetry and rhetoric, and the (purple) robes worn by rhapsodes, not the logical, geometric but disembodied pure Forms that were perhaps the precursors of the radio, television, the Internet, hypertext, virtual reality, artificial intelligence, outer space zones, digital announcers. If Platon could have known when he critiqued the effects of writing as disembodied knowledge (*Phaedrus* 274e–275b), even as he contributed practically and artistically (rhetorically and poetically), perhaps he might have attempted a fuller, tighter grip much earlier with the handle of the mysticism that underlies his another transcendental philosophy. With svelte blows of the epistemological ax he might have severed form from matter. Rhetoric and poetry from philosophy. Writing from knowing. And spent the rest of his life trying to create a telepathy of Ideal Forms to replace the inadequate, decrepit body of language that was so necessary to human thought and communication. But even telepathy would have required a rhetoric to make constantly competing or unpleasant or offensive thoughts palatable as well as salient and persuasive, and a poetics to clothe them in acceptable and pleasing and even beautiful forms (cf. Burke, *Rhetoric of Motives* 20–23).} But had he not written at all, Platon would have been as invisible to us as the real Socrates was—a ghost banging around with the sophists inside the physical-metaphysical apparatus of memory and machine. Unmasked thought without physical form. The final exhalation of a breath. Plato's dream haunted them still.

The Ghost of Socrates

"Crito, we ought to offer a cock to Asclepious" –Phaedo, 118a

Dawn:
blue-black crow
taking flight

the affability of cold
the not never new
the heyday of the dark

8	2 6
O	
Oxygen	
15.999	

5 Cathartic Organ

A^2

Aristotle's "Rebellion"

In computational geometry, Alpha was "a family of piecewise linear simple curves in the Euclidean plane associated with the shape of a finite set of points" (Edelsbrunner, et al.). Aristotle was one of Platon's finest students: of that there was little doubt. It was attested to by Aristotle's subsequent success as an excellent and eventually famous teacher of diverse subjects, as transmitted to the West during the later Middle Ages by Arab writers and philosophers such as Averroes and Avicenna (Ezzaher), if perhaps reconstructed if not reconceived. In addition to historical accumulation, whether what was handed down to Arabic scholars themselves was the extant notes of others or a student or his own hand, Aristotle's treatises were highly influential to the work of the conveyors and receivers alike across most subjects, e.g., ethics, rhetoric, poetics, logic, political science, taxonomy, botany, theology, and even physics. Aristotle's work was a product of Platonic "family," a unique member of the next generation of its members, and an even more "linear" thinker than Platon. Aristotle too loved geometry (cf. Metzger). One hallmark of all Aristotle's work is that in one way or another, it was a direct response to Platon's demands for the application of dialectical to every subject. Aristotle applied dialectic to every field he studied in the material (as well as "metaphysical") world, just as Platon had demanded (e.g., *Phaedrus*). Aristotle was an alpha whose interests were peaked, who walked far (Macedonia to Athens and back), and peered wide.

Peripatetic

Aristotle
perhaps
very tall,
bent over
backwards
to physically

observe the
natural world,
objective eyes
on ground and sky
what he saw
was upside down
but mostly correct

***

Aristotle did not so much reject as transmute Platon's philosophy of Forms. Aristotle retained many of Platon's epistemological provocations and philosophical assumptions, but also was understood to have *moved* them "beyond" metaphysical idealization (at least here), from Forms to the material realm for truth, where phenomena could be observed by the senses as well as contemplated by the mind (cf. Table 5). Geometric forms and other "*laws of nature*" were now to be found in the earth (and wind, fire, water). Or rather, the elements and laws of nature were to be found in Aristotle's observation and classification of them based on *a priori* and *posteriori* principles inherent in classification—and thus induction and deduction in the end simply based on similarities and differences of things (Corbett 93). Whether the subject was botany, biology, zoology, mechanics, physics, metaphysics, cosmology, meteorology, physiognomy, optics, politics, logic, ethics, rhetoric, poetics, etc., Aristotle's dialectic approach always focused on: α) the observation and analysis of object of study, β) the structure of its substances (grouped into categories of similarity and difference (grounded in what would become the rules of classification), γ) the causal or physical (or political or rhetorical) relations of the items in those respective categories, and δ) the rational creation of a field of study and action based on the classificatory matrix. Dialectic (cf. Plato, *Phaedrus* 271). The classification matrix did not grow from abstract Forms, nor the human body (or the soul), but was "objective," and arose not only from logic, but by visual examination, and touch.

Aristotle retained, materialized, and magnified Platon's belief in "Truth." He put into active practice Platon's faith in dialectic, as well as Platon's suspicion of style. Aristotle also retained Platon's biases regarding the separation of body and soul as well. Most obvious, Aristotle rejected his master's mostly dialogic form, in favor of a logical, rational prose in which dialectic was compressed, flattened, and linearized. {Retrospective Orientation. Philosophical notions of the nature of "truth,"—its most prominent philosopher-advocates, the forms of knowledge each position took, its ontological location, and the primary methods or processes for observing or ascertaining them—would continue to shift throughout the history of anthropocentric philosophy (see Table 5.)}

Table 5. The Movement of Truth Through Time: A Highly Reductive Chart.

PHILOSOPHER	FORM OF KNOWLEDGE	LOCATION	NATURE OF TRUTH	METHOD/ PROCESS
sophists	Probable	Rhetoric	Affective style	*Dissoi logoi*
Plato	IDEAL FORMS	REALITY	TRUTH	Dialectic
Aristotle	Apodictic ('clear demonstration')	subject matter	Analytic	Classification/ Induction
Cicero	Eloquence	unity of form and content	"Kosmetic"/ (aesthetic)	Embodied Oratory
Augustine	Divine Truth	Sacred Text	Christian Revelation	Hermeneutics/ Faith
Ramus	Invention/ Judgement	Diagrammatic dialectics	Methodological "correctness"	Visual bifurcation
Bacon	"Enlightened" Empiricism	Observation	"Critical" Objective/ Inductive	Experimentation/ Replication
Descartes	Thought	the *Cogito*	Deductive	Doctrine of Doubt
Sprat	"Naïve Empiricism"	Things	Nakedness/ Purity	One-to-One Correspondence
Locke	Empiricism	Experience	Sense impressions on *tabula rasa*	Reflection on sense impressions
Kant	*A priori* Categories of Pure Reason	Mind	Universal	Synthetic Judgment (*a priori* categories acting on sense impressions)
Ayer	Formal Propositions	Logical Axioms as criteria	Rational Principles based on Formal Logic	Verification
Cassirer	Symbolic Forms	Sensuous Form/ Intellectual Content	Linguistic	Symbolization
Freud	Psychological (entropic/dreams)	Id, Ego, Superego	Repression/ Sublimation	Psychoanalysis/ Transference
Jung	Archetypal	Anima/ Animus	Unconscious	"Archeology" of myths
Heisenberg	Statistical "Observation"	Subatomic Indeterminacy	Relative/ Complementarity	Uncertainty Principle
Heidegger	Being	Dasein	Authenticity	Death

Table 5 continues . . .

PHILOSOPHER	FORM OF KNOWLEDGE	LOCATION	NATURE OF TRUTH	METHOD/ PROCESS
Perelman	Adherence	"Liaison"/ "Presence"	Rhetorical	Argumentation
Holton	X-Y-Z/axes	"Public Science" ("rational reconstruction")	Analytic and Empiric (in the "context of justification")	*Hypothetico-* Inductive/ Deductive Method, Themata
Kuhn	Paradigms	Scientific Consensus	Communal	"puzzle-solving" and persuasion
Toulmin	Reasoning	Disciplinary "Forums"	Claims (supported by Grounds and Warrants)	Informal logic
Boyd	Theory—Constitutive (Interactive) Metaphors	Language/ World	Linguistic Accommodation/ Epistemic Access (to causal relations)	Ostension (reference-fixing)
Burke	Symbolic Action	Ambiguity	Consubstantiation	Dramatistic
Bormann	Rhetorical Vision	group	Symbolic Convergence (psychological) drama	Fantasy Themes
Habermas	Ideologies	"Institutional Framework" vs. "Purposive-Rational"	"Symbolic Interaction Action" (sub)systems	Means of Production
Bakhtin	social-semantic/ signs	"Inner Speech"	ideological/ material	"Dialogue"
Foucault	Epistemes	Intercises of Language/ Cultural Institutions	Control of discourse/ Rules of Exclusion, Internal Rules, restrictions	"Will to Truth"/ Principles of Reversal
Derrida	Signification	Dissemination	Grammatological	Deconstruction
Ulmer	Electracy	Rhizomes	Avatars	Mystory/ Heuretic textshops
Harman	OOP	Objects	Speculative Realism	Metaphysical empiricism
ANT	Networks	Actants	ANT	Hybrids

***

B^2

Rhetoric and Poetry as "True" Arts

In statistics, Beta (β} indicated "the probability of Type II error in any hypothesis test" (Grace-Martin). Just as rhetoric for Aristotle was now the αντισροφος (*antistrophos*—"counterpoint") of dialectic, poetry may have become a counterpoint of rhetoric (see Table 4). One of the major changes that resulted from Aristotle's application of dialectic to rhetoric and poetry was the development of both subjects as separate arts. As with all subjects of study and practice, in the *Phaedrus* Plato had called for a rhetoric in which: α) the truth was known first (through dialectical logic), and β) (through dialectical logic) speeches and souls would be analyzed and adapted to each other (*Phaedrus* 271a–e). It was as an art form developed on dialectic that rhetoric would now be the counterpart of philosophical dialectic. In a very real sense, and for all time (at least in the Trivium [rhetoric; poetic; logic] from the Middle Ages through the Renaissance), rhetoric was promoted to the status of dialectic; and dialectic was demoted to the status of rhetoric as a newly formed "art." After Aristotle, both arts dealt questions for which there was no definitive or determinant answer (civic matters for rhetoric, logical matters for dialectic)—uncertain knowledge, to which was applied both a rational standard of measurement and an ethical guide for behavior.

The Golden Rule

The leaves are sheathed around with autumn,
green and red and gold and brown and orange,
when shimmer settles on the grass
among the pine needles of the evening
dropping down the sagging face of sun
in the slow dimming of the year
before the snow descends, and wildly runs

The human soul contains its parts
(essences, humors, colors, air)
like herbs of earth breaking open, share,
but are not connected to a ground,
a body heavy, sober, somber, solemn,
quickly waiting, patient, floating, finally fallen
relating everything that surrounds

No burial of touch, frozen over,
no depression somewhere in the middle
like overtones of unsound that linger,
where "i am" will eventually be found,
stationary in cross currents of wind
descending, amended, ascending; and rescind
the (somewhere) hovering between the sky and ground

***

But Aristotle also applied dialectic to poetry . . . to logically categorize the form, function, action, and the end (purpose) of drama: "catharsis" (the physical *purging of emotion*)—perhaps rendering poetry a seeming socially useful art. Aristotle, like and unlike Platon, also believed in certain knowledge—not produced by philosophy (dialectic) alone, but by απόδειξή (*apodeixsis*—proof). By separating and providing a logical, systematic foundation for rhetoric and for poetry, Aristotle's treatises on *Rhetoric* and on *Poetics* dialectically articulated each as singular art forms, each with their own subject matter and purpose, each containing categories of "artistic" (*technē*) and "inartistic" (*atechnē*) proof, dealing with the faculties of persuasion and other aesthetic elements such as style and delivery, as well as poesies and catharsis, respectively. But another effect of Aristotle's divisions of knowledge was to some extent to declare rhetoric and poetry (producing uncertain knowledge) as inferior (secondary and tertiary) forms of reasoning, thus severing rhetoric and poetry (as well as philosophy) from science. As Susan Handelman stated:

> Aristotle goes so far as to separate the entire sphere of poetics and rhetoric (wherein words and thing are intricately related) from "true science and logic" . . . Dialectic is a method of critical investigation fundamentally different from demonstration. In dialectic, the principles are not necessary axioms, but are established only by consulting opinions and probabilities—in contrast to the scientific approach, which is a direct inquiry into the nature of things. (22)

Clearing Out the Cobwebs of Antiquity

We're sweeping up the cobwebs and the ashes,
two-odd millennia of history,
this old temple, a church, a taverna,
the dark streets of woods and stars.

The straw broom rakes the cedar
ceiling rafters and the fire grate
that support the cobwebs that will bloom
and grow again like embers not quite dead,

flaring up between thin twigs of flame,
reattaching themselves quickly to log
ical branches, ancient trees, established
groves in wind: beams, walls, house,

world. There's no stopping them, no time—
images multiply, spread like signs

repeating history, infinitely
a cube of floating ice, an endless ocean

blooming yet again to live slow deaths.
There's nothing more to be done except
put another log on the dirt-white fire,
clear the way for what will become next spring

*Γ*²

Apologia for Poetry as Mimesis

In geometry, Gamma (γ) was "the third angle of a triangle" (Nasehpour). As Aristotle separated rhetoric and poetry into two distinct arts, he also conjoined them. Like the *Rhetoric* (G. Kennedy, *Classical Rhetoric*), the *Poetics* was a philosophical treatise on the nature and function of that art. The *Rhetoric* was devoted primarily to invention and argument in rhetoric, to discovering "the available means of persuasion in any situation," situation being defined according to the particulars of audience and purpose (1355b.27–29). The *Poetics* was devoted primarily to classifying the elements of poetry, those elements being defined according to Aristotle's requirement that tragedies embodied—imitated—universal principles, such as good and bad human character, through a coherent series of particular actions that are perfected in the art (*Poetics* 1448a1–17), thus bringing about corresponding changes in character of the viewer. Yet, as Else (71) and others had pointed out, there was a more fundamental relationship between rhetoric and poetry despite, their treatment in different treatises. Aristotle explicitly tied the *Poetics* to the *Rhetoric* by referring the reader of the *Poetics* (1456a35) to the *Rhetoric* for a treatment of emotion and of style; and referring the reader of the *Rhetoric* (1404b8; 1405a4) to the *Poetics* for a discussion of the appropriateness of diction and invention of thought. (Else believed that there was enough evidence to suggest that Aristotle wrote the *Rhetoric* and the *Poetics* around the same time [67–73].)

***

Perhaps the first formal apologia, Aristotle denoted poetry as a representation of universals that was truer and more useful than history (*Poetics* 1451b1–6; Else 75). Aristotle seemed to understand more mimesis not as something to be condemned, but as contained (in poetry and elsewhere) if not exactly virtuous. As Else pointed out (74–88), the shift in the notion of poetic mimesis from an inaccurate and false representation of things for Platon, to an imitation of universal principles that could be known and beneficially employed through poetry for Aristotle. This set Aristotle even further apart from Platon. Within

Aristotle's implied and overt language scheme, mimesis became not only a way of representing but also a way of teaching universal truths—necessary actions guided by principles of artistic unity that Aristotle adumbrated in the *Poetics*. For Aristotle, mimesis was the defining characteristic of poetry, not abstract Form (the lack thereof), or the difference in physical form, e.g., stanza, meter, rhyme (Else; J. Walker 281–82). As Thomas Farrell explained, the rules of necessity stipulated by Aristotle in the *Poetics* "refer . . . to the internal structure of a poem; it is the inner law which secures the cohesion of the parts" (115). In and through such perfection of artistic form, audiences could learn universal truths about character through "mimetic participation." Mimesis was a kind of mental-moral imitation. These universal truths were the knowledge gained through poetic form, just as persuasion was gained through the abbreviated form of the syllogism in dialectic—the *enthymeme*—in rhetoric. For Aristotle, enthymemes in rhetoric would be founded on universal maxims and examples (and *a fortiori* arguments) that the audience would recognize and know. In poetry, drama would be based on universal and identifiable popular character types and examples designed like maxims immediately to be true. The rest of the logic of these forms of non-artistic argument in rhetoric and in poetry would be based on something the audience already knew and even held dear to be true (cf. J. Walker, who examined the archaic lyric as enthymemic argumentation, esp. 154–84). In Aristotle's work, it was the mimetic properties of the internal functioning of form as principle that render rhetoric and poetry similar arts.

Δ^2

Catharsis Through Mimesis

In physics, Delta is the "ratio between a change in one variable relative to a corresponding change in another" (*Investopedia*). For Aristotle, mimesis appeared to be the process through which an audience achieved *catharsis*—change. That was its whole aesthetic and social and political point. Just as persuasion as the goal of the enthymeme in rhetoric, catharsis was the corresponding goal of mimesis in poetry. In poetry, the dramatic form of likeness led audiences to make inferences about the likeness, and thus to learn about themselves. It is the gap between the contingency of human life and the necessity created by dramatic poetic, said Thomas Farrell, that purified and transformed emotions into self-knowledge and created the cathartic pleasure of tragedy. "By naming this particular recognition *katharsis* (a removal of pain in spirit), Aristotle alludes to a powerfully rhetorical aspect of the tragic passion, an aspect with medical, musical, and even religious analogue" (Farrell 116). For Farrell, the "[rhetorical] counterpart invents virtue and character in reflective recognition and relational movement of self *through* audience" (118). Because catharsis was a form of pleasure *and* a form of knowledge, mimesis in poetic or dramatic form was now, it seems, also regarded as a form of *pleasurable* knowledge (Aristotle *Poetics* 1448b13–20; Farrell 111–12), rather than a flagrantly self-indulgent falsehood that poetry was for Platon. Another step away from the master. Under Aristotle's philosophical fitness regime, the philosophical recognition of the role of emotions in poetry as learning appeared to be the antithesis of Platon's suppression if not yet denial of the role of the animal body, the senses, and emotions in knowing, an antithesis and denial that led to such epistemological schizophrenia in the West.

Εξοδος	*Exodus*	*"Exodus"*
Δεν ρρέπει να έκνομε	(*Den prépei na ae-chu-may.*)	We must not have.
Δεν ρρέπει να θέλοθμε	(*Den prépei na thélo-may.*)	We must not want.
Δεν ρρέπει να είμαστε	(*Den prépei na ée-mastay.*)	We must not be.
Δεν ρρέπει να πάμε	(*Den prépei na pá-may.*)	We must not go.

E Epsilon

Catharsis and the "Body"

In mathematics, Epsilon (somewhat like upsilon in calculus) indicated "the limit of a function" (Nasehpour). There seems to have been some dispute about whether Aristotle modeled catharsis as an actual physical process of purging, or as a rational analogue for a psychological purging (of the soul). A great debate erupted: what was "the limit" of catharsis? On one side of the equation, Aristotle's notion of catharsis seemed to refer directly to and afford access to the processes of the body proper; thus, catharsis would seem to provide a "physical" basis for understanding the effects of poetry on the human psyche and emotions (e.g., see Aristotle, *Generation*; Burke, "Catharsis II"; Hawhee, *Moving Bodies*). Catharsis as a mechanism for bringing about socially acceptable behavior did make brief appearances in a couple of Aristotle's other treatises (for example, at the end of the *Politics* [1339a12–1342b34], and even more briefly in the possibly spurious *Economics* [III.4]). On the other side of the equation, Aristotle's concepts of mimesis and catharsis in the *Poetics* also may have contained the teleological seeds of some profound epistemological problems. The problem was not that Aristotle made mimesis and catharsis a form of moral education for those who couldn't follow long chains of reasoning (cf. *Rhetoric* 1357a1–4), bucking but not completely abandoning Socrates/Platon's apparent expressed dislike for the audiences of both rhetoric and poetry and their need for the music of language (poetry and rhetoric) in drama and style. Since Isocrates lived and taught during Platon's lifetime and was the real target of Platon's anti-sophistic diatribes against the sophists (Jaeger 47–48), Aristotle's notion of the possible effect of poetic form on human action was perhaps somewhat more like that ' notion of moral education through a rhetorical education (e.g., *Against the Sophists* 14–19), rather than Platon's Socrates' abhorrence of these audiences, and that style/poetry was needed to persuade them (e.g., *Gorgias* 501c–505e).

skeletons
the true
arbiters of air

In Aristotelian terms, learning persuasion might have involved the necessity of observing and accommodating the behavior not only of the teacher and mutual audiences, but also a kind of "cathartic recognition" and "assumption" (by osmosis?) of the worthiest habits and customs by reading the noblest literature. (There was ample evidence throughout the *Rhetoric* and the *Poetics* that Aristotle—and even Platon in this regard—used illustrious literary (or religious or cultural or mythological or mystical) examples of both good (heroic) and bad (tragic) behavior. A pedagogy of adaptation by having students adopt the "ethics" and values of their audience, would have seemed to involve a principle of mimesis; such imitation was a basis of Isocrates' pedagogical practice of training his students to emulate a model orator-teacher, or of reading the work of or about the most "virtuous" deeds. {Historical Commentary 1. Indeed, this was the rhetorical use of literature in the composition classroom through the mid-twentieth century. Other adaptation practices based on Aristotle's art of rhetoric included the division of audience based on temporal genres (forensic concerned with past fact, epideictic concerned with present praise or blame, or deliberative concerned with future decisions and action), found for instance and for different reasons in Quintilian's focus on forensic rhetoric, or the use of popular maxims as the basis of enthymemic arguments with less educated audiences, rather than syllogistic logic.}

Maxim

the book
of nothingness
is hard to find

***

Isocrates did not claim to have a science of teaching rhetoric and virtue, and criticized anyone who made such claims (*Antidosis* 274–80). What remained somewhat unresolved in both Isocrates and Aristotle, however, was enormous questions of the kind and degree or even necessity of *style* needed to connect and persuade such audiences. {Historical Commentary 2. These were questions that Platon raised, Aristotle elided in the *Rhetoric* but treated more in the *Poetics*, and that Cicero, and later Quintilian, in their sophistic veins, would try to systematically explore and develop into extensive theories of art, teaching, and practice. Also left unresolved in both Isocrates and Aristotle was a depth of questions concerning the morality of adopting rhetorical and ethical habits and behavior of dominant cultures in order to persuade audiences, and the development of that into propaganda with all its ill-intended consequences resulting in calamities and catastrophes throughout human history. The issue of whether Aristotle's notion of mimesis could have been understood as a more or a less rational process may not have helped (Katz, "Ethic of Expediency"; "Aristotle's Rhetoric"; "Biotechnology"; "Ethics"; "Language and Persuasion"; "Revisiting Ethics"; Katz and Linvill; Katz and Miller; Katz and Rhodes). For all their philosophical insights and rhetorical powers, Isocrates and Aristotle and even Platon were not prophets, and could not have foreseen the need to answer questions such as these.}

The Oracle at Delphi

Omphalos:
the world's navel,
nourishing belly button
now cut and tied off
deep in the orange
mountain's high dust
and groves of roads

and all the footprints
of the oracles
who walked before,
and the men who
willingly followed them—
now all prints of frozen shoes
on blazing hot stones

***

Isocrates' theory and practice of education, involving the training of the body and the voice for declamation, reading out loud, and even the "music" of written oratory (Katz *Epistemic*, esp. 95–104), seemed to have been a more physical one than Aristotle's rhetorics and poetics. (Aristotle gave style, memory, and delivery rather short shrift in Book III of his *Rhetoric*.) At least to that extent, Isocrates' theory and practice was perhaps more physical and affective than Aristotle's theory and practice. In this sense it was possible to conceive of Aristotle's concept of catharsis in poetics, just as emotion in rhetoric (*Rhetoric*, Bk II) philosophically, as a more intellectual, rational, dialectical, process rather than as something (anything) to do with the physical body or emotions (or a third option: the idealization of a physical process of excreting, discharging, ejecting, expelling any unwanted evil; emitting, exuding, oozing, leaking, running, discharging disgusting vile emotions). As he did in the *Rhetoric*, *Aristotle* also talked about emotions in the *Poetics*, and dialectically dissected them there too. Like Else, Melberg argued that although altered, mimesis was "the master concept" in Aristotle's *Poetics* (43). Despite the shift in the definition and role of mimesis that Else discussed, Aristotle's concept of catharsis might still have been "tainted" with Platon's bias against the body, and Platon's prejudice against "physical knowledge"—Platon's epsilon, "the limit of a function" (Nasehpour). Despite philosophical differences with (and advances over) Platon's theory of Forms, in Platon's Academy, Aristotle (the Gamma or "tangent" in this Platonic triangle) learned the art of mimesis from the Beta, his master, Platon; and peripatetic in his own Academy, Aristotle not only "taught rhetoric in the late afternoon," but also became another of the *mimetikous*, a master of philosophical disguise, in his own right.

Approaching Gaia: At Elyfsinia

museum attendant
dark hair bad acne
pockmarked face
guards the sacred
shrines and caves
the Elysian fields
beginning just beyond
the ghostly gates
where devotees come
to pray the ancient sorrow
to Gaia, Demeter
seeking her guidance
in the dirt, and return
of their children from the dead

Demeter, Earth, Mother
raging, ravaging
the nature of the world
with her orphaned winters
memory grieving for
kidnapped Persephone

taken underground by Hades
to be his bride—Gaia
freezing the world in
the image of her desolation
each year, until her husband
Zeus, steps in
to save humanity
from its sins

yes, that's him, Zeus,
over there, shivering
in the cold heat of desire,
disguised, in human form, flirting
with the female attendant
in unintelligible Greek
that took her fifteen
minutes to decipher
like some faded rune,
cryptic statements
excavated under dunes
of explanation, bad form
having to teach the king
of gods patience in his speech

"You have the body
of a goddess" he said
to her, so assuredly
(and he should know
being a god himself)
willingly volunteering,
observing, and preparing her
for his offering—
to which she,
pointing to a shrine
of Demeter's stiff
rock joints, like a sign
simply replied
in perfect English:

"I am just a human;
she is the goddess, not me."
But of course, it was

the museum attendant
who was the goddess;
that he knew, being
a god. But then again,
he was not Zeus—
that is, a god, in any sense,
but Aristotle in disguise,
a mere *mimetikous*,
on a cathartic junket
to rid himself of any hint
or fluidity of desire . . .

Having been exposed,
Aristotle experienced
a very high degree
of personal humiliation
and embarrassment—
which was his goal
and his mission:
to expel his need
for any physical,
or ideational emission,
and this was preferred
and a perfect solution
for a rational man.
Finally, Aristotle

dropped the mask
he had been donning
mimicking a fraudster
(an ancient poser)
went to view the rest
of the famed exhibit.
But other visitors there
reported they had seen
a tall, bearded man conversing
(philosophically flirting?)
with a few of the other
female-figured statues
who found him slightly boring,
vaguely annoying . . .

After teasing him a bit—
a little peek down
their stone togas, or a lifting of their gowns to reveal
a little rock-ankle—
or coyly toying with him
by not responding
(which is all he required):
at last they sent him away,
an old man professing
love of the perceived power
of empirical observations
of material forms that unlike
them, rose to greet him.

Hence a new poetics
of rational mimetics
(division, classification
cause-effect relations)
was born in barren fields
of the Eleusinian Mysteries,
old Earth-wombs of Gaia, Demeter
(and from the repression—
i mean the *catharsis*!—
of his innate sexual desire
that shall never be
acknowledged in any
of his copious treatises—
or spoken of again).

Z^2

Catharsis and the Mimesis of the Flesh

In mathematics, Zeta was "a function of a complex variable" (Nasehpour). Here, that variable is emotion, squared. Was emotion "controlled and treated rationally" (Melberg 43) in Aristotle's epistemological system? Aristotle may or may not have had some trouble with emotions, the Zeta, the "complex variable" of the human body. Not the body as abstract concept, or distant object, but the physical, close, flattered, adorn, odorous, perfumed, made-up, false, ingesting, digesting, defecating, decaying, corrupting flesh. {Rhetorical Variable. As Rueckert discussed in his introduction to *Essays Toward a Symbolic of Motives,*

1950–1955, to or with Aristotle's possible non-physical notion of catharsis, Burke added not only pity, fear, and pride to emotions purged in tragedy, but also "the whole concept of body thinking (the demonic trinity, the physiological counterparts of pity, fear and pride—the sexual, urinal, and fecal—to the cathartic process)" (xviii).

> Catharsis—the purgative, redemptive motive—has been at the center of Burke's thinking about literature since *The Philosophy of Symbolic Form*, but what is added in *Poetics, Dramatistically Considered* is what Burke describes as his great "breakthrough" in his thinking about his dramatistic poetics . . . Burke's insistence in that essay that, to be complete, all cathartic experiences must also express the three major bodily motives, or Freud's cloacal motive, the whole realm of privacy. (Rueckert, Introduction xviii–xix)

While Burke's work on this essay got "bogged down" and at least in part constipated his attempts to complete his "trilogy," it also pointed to the painful need he felt to try account for poetic catharsis as a physical as well as an abstract intellectual process, and to situate symbolic motives in the material processes and conditions of the organic body itself—defecation, evacuation, ejaculation, orgasm, as well as inhalation, exhalation, ingestion, digestion, etc..).} Like a rational, slightly shy, slightly standoff physician, Aristotle treatises did treat these processes (Hawhee, *Moving Bodies*), but perhaps in an objective, distant, scientific way (e.g., Aristotle, *Generation*).

(En)Trails

{"He thought he kept the universe alone,
For all the voice in answer he could wake
Was but the mocking echo of his own"
—Frost, "The Most of It," *Poetry and Prose*, p. 138}

The trail juts and drops and winds
around every tree and rock and
cuts deep into the Greek undergrowth, and
we don't expect the trail to end but
it doesn't, continues to unfold
in the rain-sopped blood-red woods
like miles of intestines spilling from
an invisible wounded animal
that roams and ranges just ahead of me,
looming stone and hunkered-down tree-root

We expect this long, exhausting trail of guts
to end, and it doesn't, coursing like mud
swiftly up and down and over hill
we climb a little wooden bridge that is
supposed to lead us toward the misplaced dirt
road that we can now hear but cannot
see, running ahead or behind us
constantly, getting louder, the traffic only
εικόνες [*eikones*]— "images" of gods
thunder marching through the mountain passes

a jagged branch of lightning Zeus breaks
off, becomes the only bolt of bark
holding up a tree, overhead,
underfoot: and rain lifts our fear
up, and we don't want the trail to kneel
but end and it does, and I pray
right there where animal or god can find
us, entrails unfolding on the forest
floor starting a brand new path, direction,
new trail of blood for others to continue

follow—

H[2] *Ēta*

Catharsis: Mimesis, Mythos, Praxis

In electronics, Eta was an "intrinsic impedance of any uniform medium" (*electronicsnotes*). The Aristotelian concept of mimesis had a bowel-like grip on representation in literature and history (cf. Auerbach, *Mimesis*; White, *Figural Realism*). {Rhetorical Impedance. That Rueckert understood Burke to have ultimately "failed" to write the *Symbolic* that included a music of scatological movements was perhaps an indication not only of the difficult deconfliction of catharsis, but also how to achieve that process symbolically through the language of poetry and rhetoric (Rueckert, "Introduction" esp. xi–xxi).} As Melberg stated, "Aristotelian *mimesis* has dominated the history of aesthetics . . . Modern narratology and poetics of the novel have been thoroughly Aristotelian" (44). Like Else, Melberg argued that although mimesis was central—"the master concept"—in Aristotle's *Poetics* (43): "Aristotle not only changed the Platonic evaluation of *mimesis*, he also changes the meaning of the concept until it 'ends up meaning almost the exact opposite of what Plato had meant by it'" (Melberg 44). Much as Farrell (and Else) pointed out that catharsis was achieved by the unity of structure in poetry, Melberg stated that: "It is primarily with the concepts of *mythos* and *praxis* that Aristotle gives *mimesis* a new function: In the sixth chapter of his *Poetics*, the tragic drama—the highest form of art for Aristotle—[mimesis] is defined as an 'imitation of an action' (*mimesis praxeos*; 49b24) . . . [I]t is the *mythos* or the 'plot which is the imitation of action' (*praxeos ho mythos he mimesis*; 50a4)"; Melberg concluded by observing: that "Aristotle underscores how close *mythos* is to *praxis* by comparing both to a living body, an organically functioning whole (50b34–51a6)" (44).

***

While mythos and praxis brought Aristotle's concept of mimesis closer to the human realm of "time and action" (Melberg 44), especially when compared to Platon's concept of mimesis as static image and slavish imitation, Melberg suggested that the concept of mimesis in Aristotle as *mythos* (plot) and *praxis* (action) underlying the comparison between writing and the material body may have affected Aristotle's concept of catharsis itself as an active comparison between the aesthetic of poetics and the physical process of what was still *soma*—a living corpse—one that needed to be purged of its animalistic tendencies and negative emotions.

Elysian Prayer: Maieutic Lamentation

A grieving mother
climbs down into
a hole in the ground—
the sacred chamber
a cave; clambers over
roots and dirt and rocks:
then drops lower, lower,
descending on her knees
into a cavern, and then
a sacred sepulcher below her
(much closer to Hades)
to light a votive candle
in the tiny transept
inside a grave wall,
tears of dropped wax
of thousands of other

mourners before her
and lets out a sudden

wail that shakes the earth
a cry that might fly
right into the heart
of the mother of mothers,
makes a request
for the soul of her son
and an offering of an orange
placed on the ground-shelf
for the eternal loss
of her daughter:
"I pray to the Mother of all
to intercede with her favor."
And there above,
in the museum of Demeter
in a field of autumn
in the middle of the winter,
in the torpid summer
of cisterns and caverns
the statue of the goddess
rages for all the children
lost to the ages.

Θ^2 Theta

An Anorexia of Style

In mathematics, Theta was "the angle between two vectors" (Nasehpour). In this rhetorical drama or "vector" of mimesis vs. emotion, "catharsis"—perhaps metaphorically if not physically, also worked like bulimia—the poetry not fed to refusing mouths, but ravenously eaten, followed by fingers of rational aesthetic principles shoved down the rhetorical throat, deliberately thrown up. Mimesis and catharsis both resulted in a loss of the heft of weight of language, a wasting away of some sonic muscle of style. If language was considered not only emotionally connected to the body, but a physical body itself, Aristotle preferred a thin Attic style rather than an overweight stuffed "high" or "grand" style for the body of speech. Whether Aristotle's ideal of catharsis was physical purging or an almost entirely abstract rational process (or both having little or nothing to do with the material body or emotions (except the "need and desire" to shed them), catharsis itself was perhaps by and large for Aristotle still a relatively "nonlinguistic process." Catharsis was brought about not so much by the effects of style (like later sublimation), but only by content and structure that enacted first principles for purging the emotions, as adumbrated by Aristotle in the *Poetics*. Aristotle elsewhere had acknowledged the need for the sense of touch for any animal that moves to survive (*On the Soul*, 434b23–28). But the necessity of "touch" was not divine madness, nor about love, but locomotion.

Beyond the Moon

turbo-angels
in hip-heaven—
revving engines

I[2] *Iota*

Mimesis as Catharsis (Stripping and Purging)

In common parlance, Iota was "a tiny or scarcely detectable amount" (*Vocabulary.com*). Aristotle's was a particular kind of stripping, not a ripping but smaller rational nippings into the flesh of emotion to occasionally release the accumulated pressure of commotion. While Aristotle seemed to acknowledge in the *Poetics* the role of emotional response to style (1456b.20–1459a16), and even more so in Book III of the *Rhetoric* (1404b1–1414a29), his concept of *catharsis may have had little or nothing to do with felt physical effects of language itself.* In Book III of the *Rhetoric* Aristotle lamented the need for language and style at all, owing to "a defect in our hearers" (1404a5–10). Aristotle's logical principles of poetry, even more than his rhetorical topoi, tropes, and signs, could not eat, gain weight, vomit. They were what they were, to be put in action to help the language of drama lose weight, if not disappear. If mimesis was the knife that severed rhetoric and poetry from each other (and both from other scientific and philosophical subjects), catharsis was a further purging of the language of that content [see White, *Content*). It appeared that Aristotle's treatises were *dis-embodied* for the sake of objectivity; they were fed and filled with (false?) rationality. As Handelman stated, "[D]espite his differences with Plato, Aristotle agrees that the realm of words is not the realm of meaning and truth. Discourse and being are not coterminous. As for Plato, for Aristotle the central act of knowing is a movement beyond discourse, beyond talking" (7). In effect, Aristotle, like Platon, may have severed the connection language and thought, between body and words. Logos was now neither body or word, but free-floating discourse, like the νου (*nou*—"mind") and even in the ψυκή (*psychi*—"soul"). Significantly, it seems that Aristotle retained Platon's division of mind and body, as well as Platon's belief in the distinct soul. Amid his many objectively observant study of scientific studies, Aristotle surprisingly and perhaps somewhat oddly, incorporated or devoted in several treatises extended discussions of the soul (e.g., *On the Soul*; *Metaphysics*; *De Interpretatione*; cf. Oleshewsky, who argued the opposite in relation to Platon and Aristotle). {These views of the soul would become the rational basis in Christianity for God as Prime Mover in centuries to come (see Aquinas).}

universe

sliver
of
silver

K^2 *Kappa*

Mimesis and the Problem of Language and the Soul

In statistics, Kappa represented "[t]he Gaussian curvature of a surface" (Nasehpour). Aristotle, the empirical scientist and rational philosopher that he was, may have been troubled by the ill-defined ("gaseous"?) shape of the soul. While his other treatises were essentially transmutations (if not curve-balled acquittals) of some of Platon's major tenets as well their tacit biases, Aristotle seems to have accepted the existence of the soul, and attempted to explain it through dialectical analysis—on a more rational basis. Dedicating an entire treatise to the subject, he dialectally divided the soul of all living things into three basic categories and their relation each other (plant, animal, and human; that they had a soul at all was their shared characteristic). He then subdivided each of these categories into three parts (or "organs") according to major life functions: nutrition (which humans shared with plants and animals, perception (which humans shared with animals), and mind (which was unique to humans) (Aristotle, *On the Soul*). It was all straightforward for Aristotle. It could have been said that Aristotle did not really invest much in the unexplainable, mysterious, even spiritual dimension of the soul. It just "was," taken at face (or statistical) value). It *was* dialect—and thus a philosophy of the probable or uncertain, after all. In the end, it seemed, the soul was an abstract concept grounded in metaphysical belief, yet still required to account for "life" itself—growth, instinct, and consciousness. Like a corrupt body, not splayed, not judged, still clothed in a vacuum of space that nature abhors, from that goal this soul was never freed.

***

Like Platon, Aristotle struggled with the nature and location of soul, its relation to the body, its reception and retention of reality, how knowledge was transferred in and out of it to and through the *nou* (mind)—all without the intervention of language. Like Platon, Aristotle relied heavily on the metaphor of "imaging" (but not poetry, and certainly not style itself)—to imagine how the soul—perhaps nonphysical/potentia, perhaps part of the organic body—without touching anything, anybody else, body or material—"imaged" the world. This was not especially difficult when it came to the plant or animal soul. But it was particularly applicable to the human, rational, "godded" soul. To solve this problem, Aristotle identified knowledge of things itself as the "affections of the soul" (*De Interpretatione* 16a14). For Aristotle, these affections of the soul (again, as rational principles or universals) occurred in the *nou*—the human mind—as opposed to speech).

> The activity, power, or "place of forms," and the real human intellectual power capable of knowing truth, and of transcending the limits of the particular to attain direct intellectual vision of things as they are, reside in nous. "Actual sensing is always of particulars, while knowledge is of universals; and these universals are, in a manner, in the rational psyche—or nous itself . . . " (Handelman 8; cf. Aristotle, *Of the Soul* 417b.22–27)

While the particulars of things themselves were given by the senses, *thought* sof things were apprehended by the mind as universal images, not words which were merely symbolic of those images (Handelman 8–9). In Aristotle's philosophy, language seemingly played little or no part in the "operations" of the soul, except (as in Newtonian science and beyond) for the "defective" communication of scientific knowledge already gleaned or gained by dialectic/method.

Λ^2 Lambda

Severing Logos and Physikos

In mathematics, Lambda was "neither multiplicative nor additive" (Nasehpour). Aristotle detached discourse (*logos*) from nature (*physikos*)—even the discourse of science (e.g., Aristotle, *Generation* 316a.5–14). In discussing the "*physikos*" of language itself as sound in *De Interpretatione*, much like Socrates in Platon's *Cratylus*, Aristotle proclaimed:

> [S]poken sound are symbols of affections in the soul, and written marks symbols of spoken sounds. And just as written marks are not the same for all men, neither are spoken sounds. But what these are in the first place of signs—affections of the soul—are the same for all; and what these affections are likenesses of—actual things—are also the same… A *name* is a spoken sound significant by convention, without time, none of whose parts is significant in separation. (16a4–9, 16a19–20)

Aristotle privileged *nou*—representations, and what *nou* stood for (the reality of our senses)— not the signs that stand for the sounds or written letters of words. But unlike Platon, it seems Aristotle had accepted the first level of mimesis that Platon rejected: the existence of a valid and morally neutral empirical particulars of reality apprehended by the human senses. But like Platon, it seems Aristotle rejected the second level of mimesis—language—and disconnected it from thought. Perhaps unlike some sophists and poets (and some Jews), Aristotle still believed that names (*onoma*) were conventional symbols and did not bear any physical relationship to the ideas or things for which they stood. The sounds and syllables of language (its material substance), like the written word, had no other meaning for Aristotle, not even affective meaning (see *De Interpretatione* 16a1.3–4). But, for Aristotle, "When words and language are scientifically used, i.e., when arguments are properly constructed, they *are* symbolic of ideas in the mind. In essence, thoughts and words then were of two different kinds of discourse for Aristotle. And in pursuit of scientific demonstration, "[o]ne seeks to discard the outer letter and move towards the direct perception of things in the silent images of the soul (thoughts)" (Handelman 10). Then presumably these silent images of thought in the soul moved back into language in order to communicate both particulars and general principles of things by employing rhetoric and poetry to appeal to audiences "unable to follow long chains of reasoning" (*Rhetoric* 1357a3–4). Or perhaps these silent images merely bobbed, floated, fell.

Santorini and the Icarian Sea

Black sand against blue water:
topless woman
with cell phone
conducting business
while tanning Mediterranean breasts

and the tan and wrinkled
stud in the beach chair
with the two Rottweilers
(one on each side)
minding his own business . . .

and we, sitting on the edge
of the Icarian Sea, see:
there's Odysseus Eddie,
bald head bobbing in the dark
volcanic salt water, floating up

again as if for the first time;
children with their flippered feet
like special hot lava shoes
dripping deep blue seawater
onto the black sparkling sand;

and the fading signs of footprints . . .
people who walked or ran by us,
quickly, repeatedly, kicking grit—
the gravel of the darkening strand:
mercifully buried again

by that slim-footéd goddess

***

"[T]ruth is achieved by discarding the 'outer shell,' the materiality of language for the inner thought" (Handelman 14). Disengaged. But even in Aristotle's (ideal) philosophy of scientific knowledge and demonstration without language, the "affections of the soul" somehow became thoughts in the *nou* about the essence (*ousia*) of things first perceived through the senses: the movement of the mind was immediately away from both things and language (cf. Kerferd, who argued the sophists maintained the tenuous connection between thoughts and speech [68–77]).

> Science is concerned with the definition of what a thing is in terms of demonstrating the connection of its properties with the essence of the subject. Such demonstration leads to a thing's *logos*. However, though science operates through *logos*, definition of properties and so forth, true knowledge is not obtained through *logos*. Discourse …can state the "what is' that is essential to being any specific kind of thing, but it cannot state the concrete thing itself. (Handelman 8)

Steps of Gournia

(for Ody)

The clapping of sandal
                    is the sound of stone
                                        in the ear

***

In Aristotle's "mental representation theory" (Handelman 10), words were not about things—objects, reality—but about the logical connections between ideas in the mind—between images of reality in the soul. In both philosophical dialectic *and* scientific demonstration, words are not about material bodies or emotion. "*[T]ruth* and *falsity* apply primarily to thoughts, not to words or things," says Handelman (11).

Steps to Demeter

the statue of Demeter
stands over her cold sorrow,
pinching her left breast, bereft,

M^2 Mu

Language and Logic

In statistics, Mu denoted "the sample mean" (Sussex). Beyond the issue of the relationship between the form of the syllogism and the enthymeme, Aristotle's discussion of statement-making sentences in *De Interpretatione* seemed to average a distinction between science and philosophy on the one hand, and rhetoric and poetry on the other. In *De Interpretatione* Aristotle focused on the truth bearing power of language necessary in science *and* dialectic. In science and philosophy, words were about the subjects and predicates of logical propositions That power did not exist at the level of words: "[N]ames and verbs by themselves…are like the thoughts that are without combination and separation; for so far they are neither true nor false" (Aristotle, *De Interpretatione* 16a13–17). Nor does that power simply exist at the level of combinations of words into sentences. For Aristotle that power existed only in certain kinds of general statements, to be found in sentences that are subject to logical and/or empirical verification, such as declarative statements. "[N]ot every sentence is a statement-making sentence," says Aristotle, "but only those in which there is truth or falsity. There is not truth or falsity in all sentences…; the others we can dismiss, since consideration of them belongs rather to the study of rhetoric or poetry" (Aristotle, *De Interpretatione* 1633b–17a5). Thus, while seeming to equalize the uses of language, "sampling the mean," for Aristotle, only the statements of science and philosophy, not rhetoric and poetry, had truth-bearing power. {Linguistic Aside. While not as extreme, Aristotle's work on science and logic was similar to the twentieth century work of the logical positivists, for whom any statement that cannot be validated in accordance with the principle of verification (that included all statements about belief, faith, values, and emotions] were nonsense" (e.g., Ayer).}

The Ancient Orange Eaters, Athens

sitting on a stoop
of a hostelry in Athens,
eating Minoan oranges
and playing footsies
with a seductive goddess

who is about to leave
as another god, her husband,
and a jealous one, skins
or devours another friend,
is approaching them—

Υ² Upsilon

Particulars and Universals

In particle physics, "[t]he Υ (Upsilon) *particle* [was] a quarkonium consisting of a bottom and an anti-bottom quark, exist[ing] in three states . . . in decreasing order of how tightly the quarks are bound" (*CERN*). Much like his discussion of scientific demonstration and of dialectic, in his discussion of style in the *Poetics* Aristotle paid close attention to the elevation of universals over particulars based on principles of classification (cf. *Metaphysics* 998b23, 1059b31). However, Aristotle's Ten Categories of Logic, focused on classifying qualities of being and nonbeing according to genus and differentia, were not the kind of "universal propositions" upon which *catharsis* could be based. Poetry could not be so formal, even for Aristotle, and not quite as rational: it was not a living thing. But the representation of universal principles through the unity of artistic form in poetry (as opposed to any response to style or emotion) was precisely what catharsis via mimesis was supposed to achieve: a rational reaction and realization (perhaps affectively, but primarily cognitively) by a human audience. For Aristotle, mimesis and catharsis are ideally about the transmission of philosophical principles in the dramatic "form" of poetics, just as persuasion and audience adaptation are ideally about the transmission of "facts" in rhetoric. As Handelman stated: "Logos, mimesis, *Alethea* (truth) are founded on one and the same movement, and lead to the same possibility: the "pleasure" in recognizing the same, the delight in seeing the picture, the representation. The *re*-cognition in catharsis is not only mimetic but metaphysical" (19).

In the Gorge

(Tivizen, Crete)

Naked male gods
leaping and playing
in the stream, spy
two nymphs who appear
suddenly on the scene . . .

Greek beauty and
unity here in the middle

of a deserted gorge,
sitting together on a rock
next to our clothes . . .

They see us, naked, do not
blink. We don't see them.
They are gone, and with them
our clothes, taking our old selves,
leaving new ones—our own bodies
bare, to fend for themselves.

Φ² Phi

Principles of Rationality and Poetic Style

In electrodynamics, Phi was the "Scalar potential . . . when time-varying electromagnetic fields are present" (*ScienceDirect*). There was no doubt that style had a subjective, unpredictable, personal effect on each listener or reader. But in the *Poetics*, Aristotle's classification of style for the purposes of the clarity and unity and logic of form was about the presentation of universal principles rather than the effect of style as a sensuous, meaningful material medium. Although Else elaborated on how rhythm and melody, *as part of the unity of poetic form,* played a large part in Aristotle's notion of mimesis (74–80), Else also indicated that Aristotle was more interested in the rational presentation of necessary action embedded in the drama (Else 80–88) than he was in the effect of the physicality of language on the emotions of the audience—and especially on the particular bodies of the individuals—themselves.

{Playing Guitars with Leftheri Zabelles, 1st Bouzouki, Greek National Orchestra

Lefthos Taverna, Athens, May 28, 1997

the middle of Athens
sweet perfume of sweat
close around gathered tables
centerpieces of the flowers
surrounded by the calamari
and ouzo, guitars, many voices

Leftheri's bouzouki picking, playing
Zorba the Greek for the tourists,
and the growing dancing crowds

of all women and the children
at the bar, for bread and spirit—

he sings "House of the Rising Sun"
with my little travel guitar,
heavy Greek accent weighing
every note and blurred word down.
Please bless this journey
in the going as the coming}

X^2 Chi

Principles of Rationality and Rhetoric

In statistics, Chi squared "measure[d] how a model compares to actual observed data." In Aristotle's *Rhetoric* too, the movement was away from language toward principles of artistic proof (which themselves were based on classification, and thus dialectic). Aristotle's extensive categorization of emotions according to their nature, cause, and effect in Book II of the *Rhetoric*, and his close examination of diction, metaphor, "correctness," impressiveness, rhythm, periodic sentences, "lively sayings," and prose vs. oratorical style in Book III (1404b1–1414a29), were for many readers "overshadowed" by the opening of Book III where Aristotle declares style a subject unworthy of discussion, but necessary "owing to a defect in our hearers" (1404a5–10). Aristotle perhaps would have liked to continue stripping style from language and thought. Aristotle would have preferred that facts speak for themselves, without the need for stylistic embellishment or embodiment (1404a5–10). Both wishes were impossible for locally constituted beings such as humans. But as Aristotle said, "Nobody uses fine language when teaching geometry" (*Rhetoric* 1404a10).

The Rhetoric of Science, the Gravity of the Matter

Aristotle might have believed
that gravity
was a teleological baby,
a homunculus
(he never dreamed of us),

an impetus contained
in every atom
(particle or wave?)
before it was born,
in a vacuum forlorn

Newton in his *Principia Mathematica*
couldn't make heads or tails of it either,
(not knowing about the ether),
and in a fit of derision,
a hypothetico-inductive decision

suppressed the Fifth Hypothesis
that G/d was the cause of it.
("*Hypothesis non fingo*,"
said he in the lingo).
Then Einstein came along

(his hair was too long)—
and with his theories of relativity
made mince pie of gravity
(and chopped liver
of you and me)

postulating
it's the curvature of space
around the mass of a large object
(much like the face
of G/d would cause

if we could see
it), or the round weight
of a toddler's ball
resting in a cosmic net
(imagine, he imagined it all)—

we could retrieve it
if we traveled at the speed of
light. It's not particles
randomly thrown
in indifferent gestures

like accelerated dice
in a cloud chamber
("G/d doesn't play dice
with the universe,"
Einstein rhetorically rehearsed),

but is orderly,
accordingly
to the laws of nature
that can be known empirically
(subject, of course,

to some scientific tampering).
With Heisenberg's
Principle of Uncertainty
Einstein disagreed
vehemently.

Ψ² Psi

The Stage Is Set

In electromagnetism, Psi was an "expression of the extent to which a material holds or concentrates electric flux"(Awati). In stripping style from content, in severing logic from emotion, in *Interpretatione* Aristotle set the stage for the thousands of years in which a drama would play out not only between philosophy and rhetoric, but also between philosophy and science, and between rhetoric and poetry. By seeking to ground the general statements of propositions in "universal affirmative statements," Aristotle further restricted his logic by making the parts of his argument univocal terms; ambiguous or equivocal terms have no place in his science, and are relegated to the 'inferior' sphere or rhetoric" (Handelman 12,13). Reminiscent of Socrates, and taking a slap at some of Plato's philosophical "nemeses" Heraclitus and Protagoras, Aristotle said in the *Metaphysics*:

> If . . . [a] word has an infinite number of meanings, obviously reasoning would be impossible; for not to have one meaning is to have no meaning, and if words have no meaning reasoning with other people, and indeed with oneself has been annihilated; for it is impossible to think of anything if we do not think of one thing; but if this *is* possible, one name might be assigned to this thing. (10006b5–11)

For Aristotle, mimesis and catharsis did not occur in and through the ambiguity of language, but over and above it—outside the limitations of equivocal terms. Where words referred to one *or more* particulars was in some sense exactly what Aristotle's principles of poetic unity were supposed to overcome. Ideally, for Aristotle, mimesis and catharsis were probably not so much physical experiences created and bodied forth in multi-vocal words, but rather philosophical principles transmitted in "univocal" dramatic form. As J. Walker notes, for the more educated, "poetry is to be experienced as a disembodied *logos* reduced to its propositional content" (*Rhetoric and Poetics* 283)—

not an emotional body
rubbing against
a linguistic body

***

Aristotle's *Rhetoric* and the *Poetics* built up the philosophical muscles of rhetoric and poetry, enhancing their *intellectual* "asexual" appeal, and on the catwalk of Western civilization elevated these subjects to "true arts." The effect of Aristotle's insistence on univocal terms in science and philosophy is again to rend(er) language anorexic. Aristotle's ideal poetics, like his ideal rhetoric, would probably have left style starving for affection. If it were possible, ideal rhetoric and poetry might have no body at all.

Ariadne

rubs her feet and legs
against him, weaving
her new quantum web
of transcendental love
around him, wraps her foot
around his, then his whole leg
(he can already feel it tingling
like an amputated limb):
then stands over him

spreading her web like a dress
floating, spinning above him,
then comes circling down around
him, showing his close-up face
her nest, then slowly closes, caresses
in relaxing circles genitals
between her legs and eyes,
slowing, drugging, lulling him
to sleep, then begins to sink

her poisonous boney teeth
into his skin-white flesh,
her mouth setting his spirit free

Ω² Omega

The "Shape" of the Soul

In metaphysics, Omega represented the last, the fulfillment, perfection, the end; in electronics, it was "resistance" (*Britannica*); in cosmology, it was "the density of the universe" (Wright). And what of the body, and the soul? Somewhat like Platon, for Aristotle, at least at times, the soul was in the form of the body (though not necessarily isomorphic with it). Like Platon's conception of rhetoric in relation to truth (*Phaedrus*), and of poetry in relation to knowledge (*Ion*; *Republic*) Aristotle's notions of rhetoric and of poetics were to have been useful in communicating knowledge already gleaned from other sources (*atechnē*, or "inartistic" proof was often powerful), and in controlling the unruly thoughts and actions of the wider masses. Logos and polis: Rhetoric was available for arguing "the best" ("the good and/or the expedient" [Katz, "Expediency"; "Aristotle's Rhetoric"]) based on topoi and common maxims; and poetry based on universal principles was available for purging the mind and flushing the soul of the flesh of the common "man." But ideally for Aristotle, the nature and study of speech, to be preferred even when dealing with uncertain knowledge, and with the commoner, was rationality, which distinguished humans from other animals. In a continuing classification of the genus human being based on differentia, Aristotle said: "[I]t is absurd to hold that man ought to be ashamed of being unable to defend himself with his limbs, but not of being unable to defend himself with rational speech, when the use of rational speech is more distinctive of a human being than the use of his limbs" (*Rhetoric* 1355b1–5). {Philosophical Clairvoyancy. As Kenneth Burke prophetically said in the twentieth century:

> [H]owever the situation came to be, all members of our species conceive of reality somewhat roundabout, through various media of symbolism. Any such medium will be as you prefer, either a way of "dividing" us from the "immediate" . . . or it can be viewed as a paradoxical way of "uniting" us with things on a "higher level of awareness" . . . Whether such proneness to symbolic activity be viewed as a privilege or a calamity (or as something of both), it is a distinguishing characteristic of the human animal in general. Hence it can properly serve as the basis of a general, or philosophic definition of this animal. From this terministic beginning, this intuitive grounding of a position, many observations "necessarily" follow. (Burke, *Symbolic Action* 52)}

The Rhetorician, On Talking with Animals

Proceed dialectically, like
a fish: Move from side to side in truthful
opposition; question every school
of thought that floats around you—so much jetsam—
dividing, classifying, correlating
waves, the bubbles rising from the abstract
lips, a thick salty salmon of words.

Or mimic the enthymemic logic of
a bear—the unstated premise of its paws:
to take apart your understated flesh.
It wears a shaggy coat of signs, a fur
you can't quite grasp, won't fully comprehend,
the teeth of reason bared, a mouth closing
on itself, an argument that lumbers

toward you. Thus defer like a sophist:
appeal to snake senses to accept
the impossibility of your existence,
pleading in its slithering tenses
that twist and shape and shed predicament,
knowing that the true form of its curling
slips its sensuous skin, rising to bite.

Would you like to be a bird now, knowing
the mystical vocabulary of
its flight, sheathed in a garb of feathers, a cabal
of letters, knowing consonance of calm,
assonance of air, alliteration
of rain, knowing the rhythm of sun in wing-
tip and bone, finally knowing your own tail

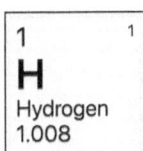

1 1
H
Hydrogen
1.008

Part Two
(Re)Birth of the Material Spirit (Roman/Medieval)

> [W]hat you said about the soul leaves the average person with grave misgivings that when it is released from the body it may no longer exist anywhere, but may be dispersed and destroyed on the very day that the man himself dies, as soon as it is freed from the body, that as it emerges it may be dissipated like breath or smoke, and vanish away, so that nothing is left of it anywhere. . . . [I]t requires no little faith and assurance to believe that the soul exists after death and retains some active force and intelligence.
>
> —*Plato ["Cebes"], Phaedo (70a–b)*

6 Material Organ

After the Fury and Silence

{In the manner of Dylan Thomas and Gerald Manley Hopkins}

After the fury and the silence,
in the glory of the unheard word,
the stirred earth drops dark
and pulls the sky up winding,
the whirring bird and fish rising
from the early water's wind taut line.

In the wish of spinning space
a breeze bound voice wills
the world to spread and bind
the wet dust born of clouds,
in this liquid land of air,
in this white wailing place.

Head back under sundrenched rain
that warms the winter ways among the howling boughs,
a plucked cry breaks the human breath
as they mock and point within the leaves,
searching for the flying sound
that sings from notestrung light.

So they shape the drifting voices,
lift up the word like the first wet thing;
and the shepherd follows the words that stream
out of the cavern that steams like fire,
fingers perched on a human flute
playing limbless lakes of lips.

And the unraveling tongue of the poet's soul,
books entwined like wings of grace;
the speechless praise of paint that hangs;
the hammer's broken tune of time
drawn through words back to stone;
and all the instruments of the musical ages—

In the human cathedral, mouth of being,
voices reach burning for the sound,
drawn from bellows with keys and hands,
the ancient organ pounding the walls,
pipes thrown to the soaring spires,
raising the chord high and long:

O holy voices.

I

Romans, Lend Me Your Alphabet

One column (I) an eternal city made. From the end of the classical through the Roman Empire and to the Medieval Age, much changed. "Rome came, Rome saw, Rome conquered." (And i was there too, became all, witnessed all: *consul*—senator/*patrician*—*plebian*/*praetor*—condemned/general—soldier/*socii* [ally]—foreigner/tutor—student/servant—maid/*amicus* ["bonded" male friend]—*amica* [concubine]/*scortum* [male or female prostitute]—Emperor/slave [*Quorum*; *Britannica*].) From their relatively safe city-state on the west coast of Italia, the Romans subjugated and/or conquered, occupied, and redefined everyone around the huge shore of the *Mare Internum* (the Internal/Mediterranean Sea), and as far as they could reach in every direction—from Greece to the south, to England, Spain, and finally parts of Germania to the west and north, to Asia Minor in the east, to the major civilizations on the north coast of Africa. The Romans "Latinized" the names of the people around them, especially those they vanquished and ruled. After conquest, Roman Legions were stationed as needed; and regional and local governors were appointed to keep new "citizens" orderly, obedient, and loyal in these distant Provinces" (*Provincia*) established for the purpose of governing the ever-expanding Republic/Empire: Britannia, Hispania, Gallia, Germania, Achaia, Creta, Caesarea, Aegyptus, Judea, Syria-Palaestina, Byzantium. (The Romans let local languages, governments, societies, religions, and cultures remain intact as they were quickly gathered into the Roman Republic or Empire—if they kept their place and didn't agitate against their new masters.) But only the inhabitants of the Capitol, both of whose parents were Roman, were regarded as true Romans, with the rights of full citizenship granted thereunto, including permanent immunity from crucifixion for capital offences. During and after the reign of Augustus, the first "full-time" emperor, *all* "foreigners" (those not Roman, or significantly, also not Greek), were officially called *barbarus* (from the Greek, who coined the term βάρβαρος—barbarian [Gibbon I: 45]).

Lizard

eye in the corner
of my eye
opening and closing—

flickers light

***

Early on, the Roman Republic was especially attracted to Greek education, philosophy, and culture, and captured but also preserved, renamed, adopted, and extended Greek tropes, systems of thought, gods—transmuting them in their own rather militaristic vain. This included the western Greek alphabet, which (with exceptions— deletions, substitutions, additions, overlap, and excess) was the basis of and transformed into the Latin alphabet (through the Etruscans), and endured for a long time as the official script (Firmage 15, 19–20). As a new founding member of the exclusive club of Roman letters, as well as being the first number in the Roman numeric system, "I" occupied a special position in all realms of society. In addition to its permanent place as a practical and important letter and number, given its upright stalwart shape and size, "I" (whether letter or number one) was thought to point upward, to represent the highest, to symbolize the preeminent. (This was so in other languages too, such as Greek ι [*iota*] which were the *smallest* letters but *not* the first in their respective alphabets [Firmage 122]. In Hebrew mysticism, *yod*, the smallest letter, was not only a spark that ignites the universe, but also was the first letter of the Tetragrammaton, the literally unpronounceable and most sacred name of G/d.) But in Rome, Rome was number "I."

recidivism

gods' mouths
a smoking residue:
letters, numbers
death, creation

Like the Latin language, used for centuries for official church, government, and legal documents, the Roman letters themselves (in competition with *italic* forms possessing both upper and lower cases [Daniels and Bright 630]) became and remained a special "prestige" script (Robinson 46–47). Through conscription and cultural disposition, the Roman letters retained their special status as a script throughout the empire, spreading its serifs to become the alphabet used for all imperial, governmental, and official business, as well as education (along with Greek), by the literate (read patrician) *populace Romanus*, including an ever-growing number of other people in other cultures, displacing other languages at the top of society. (ζοκρατες και Πλατών would not have appreciated the spread not only of writing, but of literacy . . .) But the Roman numerals, derived from specific letters of the Roman alphabet (I, V, X, L, C, D, M), were carved into scroll, flesh, and stone. They burned their mostly sharp rigid lines on buildings and appeared in common, ubiquitous technologies (e.g., clocks) throughout human history [Robinson 46]). The Roman alphabet itself, and its numerals, would stand like stark monuments to political power and cultural dominance—even when they were long gone, and the monuments themselves lay in ruins.

***

{Temporal Forecasting I. The Roman alphabet became the "ortho-ontological foundation" (Katz, "Letter as Essence") of a much larger family of Romance tongues originating from Latin throughout Western and even Eastern civilizations (see Daniels and Bright 655–765). Historically, in all the countries that Rome had conquered, Latin became the *lingua franca* of letter writing among the educated, the aristocracy, the papacy, and commerce during Roman and times and beyond (see *Anonymous*). Even later in the Church, Latin was used as a sacred or highbrow vernacular that shrouded the high mysteries of rituals, priests, God—and literacy— from the vast uneducated general populace and peasants. Latin retained its power for a long time, and only began to lose its currency as the spoken and written language in Rome and beyond with the rise of the printing press and slowly increasing literacy, and the use and publication of the vulgate in city-states and other countries in the swing of daily business life among the emerging bourgeoisies. In the natural course of linguistic evolution, even speaking and writing in Latin itself became a linguistic and religious and historical relic, absorbed by other languages, eventually faded away.}

Roman Catacombs I

echo
of bones
whispering

{Temporal Forecasting II. However, so powerful was Rome, so useful its language and alphabet, that even in its dissolution the Latin language, and especially its script and numbering system—the dominant and exclusive language of the aristocracy and business (and later clergy) from Roman times at least through the Renaissance—would never really (and totally) die, as too many believed; rather, it evolved into other romance languages in countries the Romans had conquered and beyond. Along with Greek, Latin was the proto basis of many new words in other languages, including not only in their demotic tongues, but also and especially in professional, scientific, and technological terminology, and later still medical terminology and deceptive product names. Even in "death," Latin retained its exclusive social, cultural, religious, linguistic, and rhetorical status.}

Roman Catacombs II

skeletons
dream
decay

II

The Roman "Soul"

Two columns (II) rendered the Eternal City a Republic. But although the Romans borrowed, appropriated, adopted, or stole Greek ideas, alphabets, stories, culture—even gods themselves—the Roman Republic was not the republic Platon had envisioned. Perhaps. Perhaps it was a result of the physical materialization of human ideas—or in the case of Platon Ideal Forms—which proved to be an ever pressing, then urgent problem. What the Romans valued most were military strength, contests, battles, and conquests. It was said that their entire culture, in feats of architecture and engineering, e.g., the Colosseum, utilized or was built around combat—even its entertainment (e.g., the gladiator-industry in which free or enslaved warriors were raised, housed, well-fed, groomed, armed, trained, so that they could fight to the death. Gladiators became social icons, popular heroes). In Platon's republic, the Guards were to be educated to a certain extent, given their place in the hierarchy of bodies and brains, as well as physically and morally trained—even with music. Although Platon's Philosopher-King might very well have turned out to be a Roman Emperor, a dictator, it is fairly certain that the "Guards" of Platon's republic were not supposed to hold the reigns of and run the whole show.

belief in illusion
is difficult
to disprove

***

{Future Tensing. Various versions of the Roman alphabet became an art form in illustrated manuscripts of the Middle Ages, and further developed into a highly prized tradecraft with the evolution of printing press technology. The Roman letter for "I" and numeral for "one" was considered one of two foundational letters of the Roman alphabet (the other was O; out of these two all the other letters could be made); "I" became the standard by which all other letters in a manuscript from through the Middle Ages were measured: because of its rising narrow shape and increased size, "I" established "both the height of all capital letters and the thickness of a particular script's vertical strokes or lines"—almost always governed by a ratio (Firmage 116). The initial "I" in Mediaeval manuscripts had to be drawn (outlined and then filled in) rather than simply made with the strokes of the pen: "'this seemly simple change from a calligraphic letter to a drawn letter was one of the developments that led to the separation of minuscule and majuscule letters [lower case and upper case] in our alphabetic signs and to the preservation of Roman inscriptions in the Middle Ages'" (Firmage 121).}

Letters as Floaters

spider legs hanging
down the sides of eyes
like the coming darkness
from which although alive
i will never wake

***

The Romans dominated every sphere of influence, including their language and alphabet. In both Greek and Hebrew, ι/י (*iota*, *yod*, respectively) were the smallest letters in their own alphabets (see Firmage on "J," 124–131); in the Roman alphabet, "I" was the highest (but not largest) letter in its alphabet. (In terms of space and size, the title of largest letter belonged to "M.") The Roman "I," perhaps believed "to represent . . . the oneness with God and also symbolize . . . power descending to man from on high and man's yearning toward higher things," was by the Middle Ages often decorated with figures climbing up and down its shaft (Firmage 115). Likewise, in an approach and treatment not unlike that found in Midrashic texts (see Katz, "Alphabet as Ethics") whereby for instance the Hebrew word for "truth," אמת (*emet*), was believed to be physically and thus morally stable because of its flat bottom while the Hebrew word for false, שקר (*shaqar*), was believed to be physically and thus morally unstable because of its protruding middle letter (*kuf*) and inevitably would fall (over), the premier letter designer of the "I" justified the differing sizes of its serifs as follows:

> "In its ideal form the top serif [of "I"] is three units wide on his grid, while the bottom serif is four . . .'[a]nd the reason therefor is derived from the nature posture of the human body, which, when it is on its feet, has its spread out over more space than the breadth of the head covers. A man stands more firmly when his feet are half-way apart, than when they are close together. So, then, our I must be broader at the foot than the head'" (Firmage 118).

***

It might have been the Platonic equation of writing with the human body again, as in *Phaedrus*. Or a bit of "kabbalistic" fun as in *Cratylus*. But "the straight form of the letter [I] influenced Socrates to speculate in *Cratylus* that *iota* was expressive of penetration—'the subtle elements which pass through things'" (Firmage 115). That is, in a philosophy of physics, *iotas* were or represented *essences*. Platon's deep, wide-ranging, and extended discussion of the significance of the shape, size, position, number etc. of the Greek alphabet occupied *the majority* of *Cratylus*. The lengthy discussion of the meaning of the shape and size and position of the Greek alphabet in that treatise, perhaps revealed Platon's serious study and knowledge of the subject—which with other work was "fascinating and occasionally quite thought-provoking" (Firmage 117). For reasons similar to and different from the Greeks and Hebrews, the Roman "I" in all its manifestations became practical and thus important to Roman identity, society, and spirit. "I" was the guideline for all the other letters of the Roman alphabet; it was also a Roman numeral whose principal operation was its addition or subtraction to the other numbers (Base-10, but not place-value). Perhaps "I" was understood to represent and guide the Roman soul as well. As Richard Firmage stated in another context, while *iota* for the Greeks {and later, English speakers who mispronounced it} meant a tiny quantity nearing nothing, the Roman "I" was "quite commonly considered to be one of the greatest of all things" (115). However, it was not that the letter necessarily pointing upward to, or the first letter of a god's name, as *yod* was for the Hebrews; rather, "I" {in a metaphorical and almost Freudian sense} was "the first word of the language, the first thought of the mind, the first object of affection" (116). In its self-perception and outward projection of brutal military and enormous engineering power, "I" embodied the Roman body, mind, soul. "*Vedi, veni, vici*" (*I* came, *I* saw, *I conquered*).

The Book of Aging

convinces me
to walk slowly
toward the very edge
of the long jetty
where it becomes
just a jutty rock—
moonlight flowing
over the it
and the sea

III

Resurrecting Spirituality through Geographic Expansion and Brutality

Three columns (III)— two future *Triumviri* (Triumvirates): Caesar, Pompey, Crassus; Octavian, Marc Anthony, Lepidus. These Triumvirs would rule and play a role in the last, crisis days of the Republic, retooling it into a ravenous Empire (Tacitus, *Histories*). Ironically, except for Britain, most of the greatest Roman expansion by military conquest occurred during the martially ambitious years of the Republic, rather than the more exalted years of Empire, (Gibbon I: 3, 5; cf. Tacitus, *Agricola*). Over the seven centuries of the Republic, in search of eternal popularity and power, successive generals fanned out from Rome with their own highly disciplined legions like overwhelming tides, flooding large swaths of unvanquished land and swallowed them whole, vastly expanding the territory of the Republic. During the five centuries remaining of the *Western* Roman Empire, unless led by a future Caesar himself (e.g., Crassus, Pompey, Caesar during the Republic; Augustus, Trajan, Aurelius during the Empire), "it became the duty of every Roman general to guard the frontiers intrusted (*sic*) to his care, without aspiring to conquests (Gibbon 1: 5). Taken together, at the imperialistic height of its power (in 180 CE), in addition to all of Italia and Sicilia, Achaia (Greece, Macedonia), Rome had conquered the areas and peoples all around the Mediterranean and beyond, and extended the Empire to encompass Galatia (the Middle East, including—Palestine and Jerusalem), Northern Africa (including Egypt and Libya), and Asia Minor (Syria, and Arabia)—as well as much of Western Europe—Lower Germania (to the Rhine and Danube Rivers), Hispania (Spain, Portugal), Gaul (most of France), Britannia (England, Wales), and even Scotland (north of Edenborough and Glasgow), and more (Gibbon I: 3–33; 570–571). (The Romans were never able to subdue Upper Germania; in fact, it was the Goths from that region that 1000 years later physically sacked Rome and brought an end to the Western Roman Empire in 476 CE.) Defeating and defending these vast new territories and/or holding them against their local inhabitants or surrounding barbarians, overland alone Roman legions of appropriate sizes reached all the way to the North Sea and the Atlantic Ocean, including the coasts of France, Spain, Portugal, as well as across the English Channel to Britain, in the north of which Hadrian, to guard against the Scots and other invaders, built his long Wall running up and down a sky of high green fields.

The Book of Dying

i am not immune
from the impulse to die,
to commit suicide,
my successes strewn
all around me

everywhere
see my ruins
floating over
and above me
cluttering the world

***

More obvious than the Roman alphabet in the most illiterate Latinate eyes were not only the superiority of Roman civic life and culture (Gibbon I: 33–39), the feats of architecture and engineering that accompanied the enormous expansion of power (e.g., the system of roads [including the *cursus publicus*, which was imperial and not so public but still a marvel]), bridges, walls, aqueducts, baths, hot running water. Also at prevalent and at hand were the standard and later increasingly exotic forms of torture, punishment, and execution (e.g., scourging, flaying, crucifixion) that over the more than one thousand years of Republic and Empire gave invention in architecture and engineering new "spiritual" dimensions and moral civic purpose. During this time, the concept of the soul, although still separate but dually interactive with the body, was perhaps radically transformed. Corruption of feelings, bodies, politics, gave birth to a like civilization, one dominated by "masculine virtues" (physical strength, military victories, violence; feats of building, spectacles of endurance, and at times political and/or sexual debauchery. In this world, Roman "soul" generally accrued new and different meanings from that of cultural Greeks or studious Jews (but see Josephus). From a militarization of the pagan world to the long-soft suffering of the Christian coming, the mighty but decaying Rome (a city itself of over fifty million people) eventually would become the new material and "spiritual' foundation of Western civilization. In place conflicted promises of unattainable ideals of transcendence over the physical world, the leaders of Rome provided the people gifts of architectural prowess, increasingly exotic public games, and properties of conquest; in place of the poor, questing, and impoverished spirit, more provinces of material strength, wealth, and power—a restoration of the material body hammered under the spread of fiery Vulcan wings that could accommodate diverse religions and superstitious, all considered equal in the Rome capitol, with their ever–present concern for omens of coming bad luck, illness, death (Gibbon I: 34–39).

overhead
black crow
barking

IV

Old Temples, New Gods

The First Temple, built by King Saul in 1000 BCE, was destroyed by Nebuchadnezzar, King of Babylon, in 586 BCE. Said to have been rebuilt and gilded with gold, and subsequently expanded by Herod the Great between 20 BCE–20 CE, the Second Temple was destroyed in the first Roman-Jewish War by the Roman Emperor Vespasian in 70 CE in a brutal response to the uprising and rebellion of the Jews in Judea. The destruction of the Second Temple was the greatest catastrophe to afflict Judaism since Egyptian bondage. Unfortunately, it would not be the last. And in an ironic and cruel act, Vespasian (Emperor 69–79 CE) and his son Titus (Emperor 79–81 CE), constructed the Coliseum in Rome by sacking Judea—both the private property of the people as well as the public spoils of the Second Temple, including perhaps slave-ported stones of the Second Temple itself (cf. Josephus); but within the reconfigured and enormous Flavian amphitheater, walls of stone and groans and roars and layered grounds and floors, many Jews as well as Christians, gladiators, and prisoners were put to bizarre and painful public deaths for the entertainment of Roman crowds—e.g., crucified upside-down, slowly in continually moistened wool, fed to wild exotic animals, and of course, being whipped, scourged, flayed, flogged, or, a standing order of Caligula, first cut in small, slow increments before being put to death (Suetonius I.xxx). The deaths of the Caesars were just a little better (Tacitus, *Histories*).

spitting wind

ulcerating fire—
the body knows
before the mind suspects

***

{Spiritual Dislocation. Outwardly, Judaism lived under Roman siege; inwardly, Judaism came under attack with the advent of Christianity, and eventually Islam. According to Auerbach, the immaculate birth, crucifixion, and resurrection of Jesus also marked a major turning in Western civilization, when "the Word" became flesh, image became essence, and mimesis became spirit. After the destruction of the Second Temple, the ancient hub of the Jewish worlds that had Jerusalem as its center, shrank, then shattered, expanded and scattered in Diaspora across Europe and eventually the globe. Jewish rituals, and rites and rights, along with its adherents and practices, were once again driven across the shifting sands of history and deserts, crushed like the soft hot stuff under the Roman legions of soldier-sandals. But also by the unarmed spirits of martyrs—in acts of charity as defiance, courage as obsequiousness, love as devotion—in wholly new forms of strength (Auerbach). The centrifugal Second Temple was by necessity replaced by more mobile, adaptable, domestically based religious sects: the Jewish home. Despite deportation and dispersion, at the epistemological and even ontological level of the Jewish religion based on monotheism, on the language of Biblical Hebrew and its scions (e.g., Aramaic), and on Torah and Talmud, these "People of the Book" fundamentally did not change. Each home became the abode of the Jewish soul, wherever it might reside.} Reading, studying Torah, doing *mitzvot* (commandments), became essential for preservation not only a way of life, but of life itself.

Rebekah in the Modern World

(Sonnet with a double sestet)

She is in the yard, transplanting flowers.
Her hands and feet are rain-caked, soaked with mud.
She hears a loud vehicle coming down
the street, spitting, sputtering, starting, stalling.
She turns, and sees the old white pickup truck
pull over to the side of the road.
So this is what the angels drive now, she thinks,
returning to her work without a thought.

A voice seeps through a reverie of roots.
She sees the messenger of Abraham,
a tall black man, maybe even Arab,
standing in the middle of her garage,
looking for a wife for Isaac—scars
of rain beneath his eyes that pray and sweat.

"My truck broke down; may I use your phone?"
Knocking the ground from the bottom of
her boots, she gladly goes into the house,
and on her way out grabs a bottled water
for the man. "A miracle," he tells her.
The truck starts up. Her plant drops to the dirt.

V

The Wars of Ideas

{Orthographical Insight. For the Romans, V was U, and U (which only existed as a sound) was V: V was both consonant and vowel; V was from the Hebrew letter *vov*—the third letter of the unspeakable, unsayable, undrawable Tetragrammaton, JHVH, the Holy Name of G/d; in Latin, Jove could have been written with all vowels too: IOUE (Firmage 232). On the hand, V was the Roman number for five—an abbreviation of fingers; V was for victory (Firmage 239). In Jewish mystical rhetoric, *vov* was the letter that united heaven and earth (Haralick 156); in Rome, V might have been a Christian martyr nailed upside down. Despite the fact that Rome let the captured keep their languages, religious practices, and cultures unless or until they challenged the governors of the provinces or rebelled against authority, the Romans "subjugated" the ideas they found attractive, the ideals that appealed to them. For example, not only were Greek gods Romanized, but so too the Hellenic concepts of mimesis: the direct perception of representation in painting, sculpture, rhetoric, poetry, and music: origin stories, mythic quests, and literary legends upon which the likes of the earlier Virgil and the later Ovid recreated and built a Latin legacy. Greek language, thought, and culture were perhaps the exception because they were exceptional for the Romans; but for the Romans, Latin was the *fortiori* language, and the official tongue throughout the empire (Firmage 19–20; Gibbon I: 46).}

Olympia

(Exitu deorum et regnum— "Exit gods and kings")

Engraved above
the outgoing door:
Εξοδος.

Generally, cultural weight and social attention was given to the relation of material reality to ideal but physical *human* "forms"—not the abstract geometric forms of Platon's "goodness, truth, and beauty" (Toulmin and Goodfield), but the highly masculine qualities of the male Roman body valued above all else: the primacy of athletic and military prowess (as opposed to the primacy of thinking), sheer physical strength (rather than total contemplation), sexual seductiveness (rather than abstinence), and generally the active role of the *body* in life and knowledge (rather than the soul of thought) (see Suetonius). The imitation and transubstantiation" of the Hellenic pantheon of gods into a galleria of renamed deities seemed to supplant Platon's transcendental heaven; but divine oracles, omens (οιωνοί) and superstitions of all kinds were feared as warnings of fate (Plutarch, "Roman Questions"; cf. "Superstitions," which is primarily about the Greeks and an argument for atheism).

for Babylon
they lost
their tongues

At a level of daily life-to-be-lived-to-the-full, in ancient Rome as well as the far-flung occupied provinces of different races and cultures, the Romans seemed to revel in war for sport and entertainment, as demonstrations of might as well as a means to accumulate wealth and slaves and power. In ancient Rome, games and war were a way of life, victory the greatest achievement. Their gods seemed to agree. Some emperors even thought they were gods, were deified, and had erected temples and statues to themselves before or after death; or as in the case of Caligula, also talked and even "lived" with the gods themselves, especially Jupiter (Suetonius Vol 1: Bk I; II; Vol 2: V; Bk IV. xxii). But for the average Roman citizens, it seemed, the glory and power of Rome was a social and political quest of City and Empire itself, as much as a personal and spiritual quest. Even for the captured, even for the slave, whatever their rank and vicissitudes, hoping to improve their circumstances and status, hoping for eventual freedom, if not now in generations, did everything for Rome (Gibbon I: 41–43; 46–51). Superficially incorporated and renamed, the Greek gods gave Romans permission to celebrate with decidedly anti-Platonic drinking and debauchery.

Tenants of Bacchus

In the Roman villa, the atrium darkens.
they dwell amid the ancient clutter, scrolls
piled high, the heads of Greek gods in their laps.
In the corner a red cobweb is spun
with the blood a drunken spider drinks.

They are no longer conscious of the world—
playthings searching for what they thought they knew
in the marbled cracks, each other's faces.

Breath dims, speech fades, all the songs are done,
they with night oblivious become

VI

Torture as Religious Expression

VI: A man hung upside down from a post. The Romans made "soul" a material matter of society, empire, citizenship, law, and sheer brute power. It was hard to recognize that this was a type of soul, rather than a lack of soul, but it was, a materialization of spirit in the ideal form of the human body, which might never be born. We see it in Cicero (e.g., *Orator* x.36; xiii.43; lxxi.238); cf. Critchley on Seneca's stoic notion of the corporeal soul [58]). Roman society was very visual as well as violent, thriven and driven by the prospect of spectacle. For Romans of every class, this *was* probably a form of religious experience as well as entertainment. In *this* expression of "Roman spirit," great physical effort and pleasure therein were primary pursuits. Once the enormous Coliseum, with its elevators and running water, was completed, competitive events staged by emperor or senate as state holidays might go on for two weeks or more and included gladiator fights to the death, as well as public executions. The Romans, amazing engineers and builders who could quickly construct ramparts and bridges in the middle of battles, easily planned and carried out mass displays of simultaneous torture, multiple immolations at the stake, concurrent crucifixions, and the constant shipping from exotic parts of the empire of exotic animals to tear and devour human flesh. The Romans also possessed expertise in the carving the bodies of individuals, singly or in groups, right down to bone—each voiceless organ screaming in agony, unheard over the tremendous roar of the massive crowds that lusted, laughed, consumed, and relished every "amoral" morsel moment.

Symptomologies: Case History #2 (Rabbi Akiva Returns)

In Judaism, the story of PaRDeS, and the extant pieces of the myth and life of Rabbi Akiva during the Roman occupation of Palestine, was an exemplar of the earliest and greatest of the rabbis (before there were so-called rabbis [Holtz 28–35; 198n21]). Rabbi Akiva was "a hero" and "a scholar," "empathetic" and "long-suffering." He was also a "nonconformist" and a "rebel"—at least as far as the Romans who occupied what they called Palestine were concerned. After the destruction of Jerusalem and the Second Temple by the Romans [in 70 CE], and the utter suppression and slaughter of the Bar

> Kokhba Revolt (in 132–135 CE) under the Emperor Hadrian, the great "Builder of Walls" at the new outer edge of the Roman Empire, in Britain), Akiva was arrested and brutally tortured for teaching Torah (Jewish philosophy, rhetoric, and poetry?) in public. Hanging in the air, Akiba's body was slowly and painfully raked by sharp metal combs; the teeth scratching at, cutting, digging, sinking into his skin and flesh, shredding genitals and internal organs, eyes and head—but expertly kept alive and conscious until at the discretion of his merciless torturers, with a final plunge of sharp edge, he was finally allowed to die. As his disciples watched in horror among the roaring Roman crowds in the smaller coliseum in Caesarea, the Roman capital of occupied territory called Palestinia, the central prayer and credo of Judaism, the *Shema*, was on his Akiva's torn lips, and his soul ascended to heaven (see Holtz 160–61; 167–72).

VII

Burying the Past

VII: one man hung upside down across two posts. "They made a desert, and they called it peace" (Tacitus, *Agricola*, Ch. 30). Adding to their numbers, the Romans conquered for lust, power, wealth, and glory. Legions started families and often settled where in the land they once conquered (Gibbon 42). They also persecuted non-Roman citizens, including the Jews and early Christians. Though forgotten, overtime Jesus was both. Romans tended to let other religions and cultures exist and flourish within the empire they ruled—until those societies presented a threat or rebelled. Then the Romans slaughtered them. (For eight years the Roman Emperor Marcus Aurelius heroically defended the Roman empire in the North from invading tribes of Germania. Aurelius, a stoic philosopher and gifted writer, was also notorious for his persecution of Christians. {*Omens* (Οιωνοί). Aurelius' stoic "humanitarian" values were later likened to the spiritual precursor and kin of Christianity! (see William Kaufman; Hamilton and Cairns, "Introduction" on Plato and the Christian concept of God). It wasn't until the fourth century CE that Constantine the Great, founder of Constantinople in the Eastern Roman Empire, converted to Christianity in 312 CE, and Christianized the Roman Empire during his reign (306–337 CE). In a turn-around of power, Christianity initially resisted pagan culture, including the arts of rhetoric (e.g., Augustine). Then absorbed and transformed it. Just as Rome was intellectuality and physically built on Greece, Christianity was built on Rome. Christian churches were literally built right on top of pagan temples, and conceptually right on top of values that were suppressed and absorbed, converting prior faiths into new ones, transmuting civilizations and transforming cultures (cf. Derrida, *Gift*). So too Latin, which Christianity usurped and adopted, the eventual Church appropriating the tongue of the oppressor. To survive, one had to have high connections (at the right *kairotic* and political moments), be a hero, a praetor, a priest, a nobleman—or perhaps become a great poet or orator.}

Statue to Eloquentia (Variation I)

Rip off his ears
so he may better hear
his own agony

VIII

{"Skin in the Game"

Smoothed-skinned, soft skinned, sensitive skin; dry skin, tan skin, wrinkled skin; thick-skinned, thin-skinned, skin deep; light-skinned, dark-skinned, happy in your skin; outer skin, aging skin, sagging skin; wrinkled skin, skinny, skin and bones; "I've got you under my skin" (Sinatra), "live in your skin," "love the skin you're in" (Club Olay™); cutaneous, cuticle, possibly cut skin (from Latin *cutis*, "living skin); transparent skin, blossoming skin, blushing skin ("'*skam*'/'*skem*,' like 'skin' and 'house'" → "'*kam*'/'*kem*' [cover, veil, conceal]" [Benthien 100; 250 n.8]); dead skin, shedding skin, peeling skin; skin-peel, skin care, skin cream; skin-tight, skinflint, skin flick; membrane of the skin, boundary of the skin, prison of the skin; skin of your true self, second skin, skin deep; circumcision (of the foreskin), stripped (of the aforementioned skin) to the bone, jumping out of one's skin; skin in the game, "the skin of culture" (De Kerckhove), "for people with skin" (Neutrogena™); hanging by the skin of your teeth, skinned alive, save your own skin.}

Penumbra I

In winter
one feels
the borders
of flesh
skin
taut
against

the air,
eyes pulled
to where
sharp branches
tear the sky,
bound to
sun and snow,
the marked end
we must reach
glorious before us,
body shaped
by white
space like a word
moving toward
a lover,
warm, visible
on the glistening
breath

***

There were many ways humans thought about their mortal sack they inhabited, and many names given to it. Both Platon and Aristotle thought of the body as a container, if not prison, of the soul, although the relationship between the substance of the soul, its elemental properties and complexions in relation to those of the material body, was a much more complex one (see Plato, *Timaeus*; Aristotle, *On the Soul*).

Penumbra II

naked
making gestures
in the snow
with each
step i behold
the margin,
the cold edge,
separated
presence
world ahead
blur and pale
threatening sense
as snow fastens

thickens steps
falter quicken
confused
by flurry
keen face
struck by freezing
flakes
that turn
eternally,
fall until
i believe
in surrender

***

As Claudia Benthien suggested in *Skin: On the Cultural Border Between Self and World*, "Language has always preserved the close relationship among identity, self-consciousness, and one's own skin, as reflected in countless idiomatic expressions, sayings, and metaphors.... Speech about one's own skin is speech about oneself as body" (9). Skin was a rhetoric. What Benthien called *topoi* (2) are places where the skin, as the surface of the body, was inscribed not only with identity but also with cultural meaning (17–36). But in the history of mimesis during Roman times, the ideal of the body in life and art, and with it concepts of identity and cultural meaning, shifted considerably. This led to several revolutions in the treatment and inscription of human skin and flesh.

Penumbra III

the body
ends, and then
i am taken
by beauty
and splendor,
flesh
minted ice
shaped by
pointless wind,
crystal nude,
ideal form
by circumstance,
and realize
it is not
in our power

to create
or prevent.
and letting
the patina
of lids slip
the muscle
drop
dissolve
the boundaries
i become one
the unknown

IX

Horace, the Rhetorical Poet

IX: the post; the cross. The blood of people and time flowed through the network of Roman aqueducts into history. Years of political, civil, and social upheaval followed the murder of the General *cum* Consul to the Senate *cum* Dictator for Life—Julius Caesar—by rebelling Senators—on March 15 (44 BCE), the Ides of March. The Republic turned into Empire (31 BCE–491 CE) with Augustus the first of its eighty-seven Emperors. It was into this tumultuous upheaval of the world that the Roman poet Horace was born (65 BCE). Like Cicero, though much younger and for purely educational reasons rather than political lying low, Horace went to Athens, the center of culture, to study Greek poetry and philosophy, and he might have been acquainted with Cicero's son (Whicher ix–x). Horace served in the military as a republican officer in an army crushed in the Battle of Philippi (42 BCE). Horace and others were granted amnesty by Augustus and befriended by his right-hand man and subsequently made a "spokesperson" for the Treasury of Augustus' future dictatorial regime. A "master of "the graceful sidestep" (Michie 14), Horace was able to delegate many tasks, engaged in politics as little as possible, and wrote as much poetry as he could.

Penumbra IV

i am glad
to be
an outcast,
standing
on an empty continent
shouting
words into

a chaos of clouds
a snow of stars,
into the wind
of the universe:

in winter
one knows
the borders
and the end

***

Poetry and Survival (Political and Otherwise)

Horace's poetry evolved from satires to odes on the quotidian (simple things, pleasures, and friends), personal epistles to Roman to tributes that were highly practical, moral, and nationalistic. Horace didn't necessarily like politics or Rome but knew which side his flatbread was buttered on, how much wine to drink and still be stable, and how to survive in as well as reflect on his own place and time. Horace was finally able to retire, retreating to his little villa in the Sabine Hills of Italy, where he farmed his vineyards and drank profits from its vines, entertained (and drank) with friends, and continued writing Latin poetry based on Greek meters as well as Roman models). In comparison to his compatriots (especially Virgil), Horace may have seemed like a humble homebody (Whicher). But Horace knew life was short and fraught and full of happiness and misery; this self-awareness often gave rise to a poetic philosophy of pleasant contentment occasionally riddled with the more urgent message: "carpe diem" (Horace, Odes, p. 32, 33). For to be born was to already have begun the road to death.

Chariot

Wind lifts about the wheat
shifts the field
like an amber animal

Before he starts the harvest
the farm mechanic likes to watch
the horses snap their tails

(Traitors bound but not gagged,
their eyes ripped open
so they could watch until the end)

Two wheels wait on haycocked hills.
But i like to play
in the loft of things

X

A Revue and Roman Apologia, of Sorts

{Temporal Cut. Interestingly, the letter X was invented by the Romans from the fifteenth Hebrew letter samech (ס), mystically meaning "to uphold," and thus eternally broke the eternal fall of the fourteenth Hebrew letter nun (ן) (Munk 156–57). But in Latin, X was regarded as sonically redundant with the Greek letter ξ (*ksee*), discussed by Platon in his linguistic bout with the alphabet of the Hellenes, as communicating "the great expenditure of breath in pronouncing it" and thus (tongue in cheek?) expressing "shaking, shivering, and windy" (Firmage, 249; Plato, *Cratylus* 426e–427a). X was assigned the sound of another Greek letter, chi (χ), also rarely used in Latin. X was therefore subsequently berated in most Romance languages as well as by many famous British authors, as "unnecessary," a half-breed, or not a "real" letter at all (Firmage 249–250), thus "stripping" X of its importance and seemingly finishing Socrates cutlery work. But aside from its sound (*ks*), as a Latin letter X not only represented the number ten (two five [Vs], one placed upside down on the other); it also came to serve several other important functions: the signature of the illiterate, the unknown variable in mathematics, "the crossbones symbol of pirates and poison" and thus a warning sign of danger, the mark of a hidden spot, a stable centered body (Firmage 250–251; 255–256). Perhaps the precursor of Vitruvian Man, X also somewhat might have embodied in its architectural shape the all-too-common Crucifixion, and thus by extension Christ himself, through the Greek *ks*, as in Xmas tree (Firmage 249–50), as well as "crossing out" of mistakes/a person's sins, and the xxx kisses of Christ's love (Firmage 250), and therefore also the kiss of betrayal and death. (Greek χ (chi) and Latin X also may have been related to Hebrew חי[*chai*]—"life" itself.) As a patrician and citizen of Rome, Horace was safe at least from the Cross.}

On the Prospect of Being Put to Death

(Villanelle in a Pseudo-Voice of Horace)

To Titus Vironicus

Titus, there are so many ways to die.
i don't want to be martyred, crucified,
nor burnt at the shimmering stake alive.

i don't want to be tortured, made to lie,
nor suffer the ways of being deprived
of breath: there are too many ways to die.

Some are better than others, i surmise.
i will never know from the other side.
As long as i am not buried alive.

Titus, where shall i run, where shall i hide?
It's absurd! Death will find me by and by.
There are so many ways to succumb, die.

Shall i capitulate, take my own life?
Shall i be known as a suicide?
Only if it means i'm not roasted, fried.

Shall i be beheaded, gouge out my eyes?
Who will see for me, Titus? Will you try?
There are so many ways i want to die.
Everything that's born must perish alive.

XI

It was not known when the *Ars Poetica*, his defense of poetry, was written (Ferry ix). Perhaps inspired by Cicero's treatment of both oratory and poetry, in his *Ars Poetica* Horace gave poetry "the ends of rhetoric," which continued to define the purpose of poetry through the Middle Ages. Virgil as well as Horace were regarded as "eloquent by virtue of [the] largely stylistic ability to make wisdom effective" (Sloane, "Rhetoric and Poetry" 1046–47)—that is, to make knowledge stylistically agreeable through the beautiful body of language. However, Horace was noted by Quintilian as "the sole lyric poet [in Latin] worth reading: for he rises at times to a lofty grandeur and is full of sprightliness and charm, while there is great variety in his figures, and his boldness in the choice of words is only equaled by his felicity" (*Institutio Oratoria*, 10: 96). In Horace's *Ars Poetica* was also a focus on the unity of form and content, propriety, and an extensive discussion of the duties of style—even of the rhetorical "offices of the poet": "to instruct or please, or both" clearly reflected Cicero (Whicher 254). Toward the end of the *Art of Poetry* was also much advice about the education of the poet-orator that was to inspire and find full expression in relation to rhetoric in the twelve volumes of the *Institutio Oratoria* by Quintilian, a text born just a century and half after Horace's death.

Stay Fast

for Myra Moses

Keep me in this life a little longer,
so that i may stay fast with my friend,
coauthor the future into present,
write the past into the future again.

The salmon swims upstream in the plate
toward the sun—an artichoke, a flower;
the ink begins to tick, thicken, choke,
and slowly gather itself like the hour.

Ride the pen over the depression
of the page, bridging the abyss—
forward against the slide of time and space:
stay, so that you stay and still be missed

***

Such a rhetorical and "chaste" approach to poetry was not the norm. (Historically, Horace had always been overshadowed by the "grand-style-standing" Virgil [Whicher xvii–xviii]; cf. Sydney). But the poet Horace not only "escaped" the common fate of his time and place, but survived into "old" age. And the verse of both Horace and Virgil became a benchmark against which oratory as well as poetry was to be judged for a thousand years. And Horace's poetry inspired a major educator of oratory in the near future, Quintilian, for whom literature was even more essential for a replete rhetorical education. Born a little closer to the geological and chronological edge of the Roman Empire (Hispania, 35 CE), Quintilian was both educated, and then later died in Rome; in between, he taught and wrote about the greatness of oratory in equally turbulent times, when deliberation had all but disappeared, gone dark.

The Human Jungle

(Near the Roman Coliseum)

In the blue moon of the streetlight
the shadow of a black tree moves
slowly among bars of metal
rails cast black and blue;

the thin dry leaves
crack in a small dry wind.

In the jungle below where
striped cats stalk ashcans where

jet black birds streak overhead
a distant human howl
sleek bodies of animal power
and desire purr growl roar

jump close among
buildings slicing thick air,
then fall silently
among the bars of metal

rails cast black and blue
barely moving in the shadow
in a small dry wind, in the
clipped streetlight of the moon

XII

The Roman Republic Gave Birth to Cicero

Roman politician, "lawyer," and orator, Marcus Tullius Cicero, born in 106 BCE, was almost immediately plunged into an already and usual violent unstable conflicted culture and history. The Roman Republic, *the* world power through conquest of most of what would later become Western Europe, North Africa, and the Middle East, had been teetering for a century on the brink of military dictatorship—and finally fell during Cicero's lifetime, the city plummeting into further tyranny, social unrest and political corruption. Rome, as the vibrant beating blood-red heart of a far-flung empire, "descended" and "rose up" again under the hand of Julius Caesar, whose successful military campaign in Gaul, Brittan, and even the edge of Germania, greatly expanded the Empire north. It also (temporarily) propelled him to popularity in 46 BCE, following years of chaos and civil war. Caesar was not without enemies, as he would soon discover in two short years. Cicero, economically and socially from a well-off, well-connected, equestrian family, became a "practicing lawyer" (there was no official or separate legal profession at the time) around 83 BCE. With Republican leanings, Cicero had negotiated the treacherous political terrain and often even perilously if mostly indirectly came close to challenging the leading powers in Rome as it transitioned from the capitol of a Republic to an Empire. Cicero was engaged in Roman law and politics all his life, including becoming a Consul of the Senate for a one-year term and was a well-established advocate and famous orator by 46 BCE (and unknown to him, fast approaching the end of his life and career) when Caesar came to power.

Walking Home on the Ides of March, Alone

down the rows of trees and eaves,
the leaves skip toward me in the dark
as if to greet me like long lost friends—
cling about my blown feet
in the brown light of the street,
hanging onto, scattered legs,
as if to ask me not to leave—
as if to tell me something i
don't know. The blades are draped beneath
the sparse togas of the trees, and wait
for final word of the impending
spring, having lingered beneath
snow-covered grievance, greed, and grief—
i am about to die by cold friendly hands

XIII

Birth of the Ideal Orator?

During his career as an advocate, Cicero delivered and left history many superb speeches informed by the art of rhetoric {Later they became exemplars of writing and oratory in Latin in standard rhetorical education from the Middle Ages through the nineteenth century.} Standing on the "Rostra" in the Forum, his voice filling the *Comitium* (the wide-open space in the Forum crammed with crowds, up to the *Coria* where the Senators met), it was in the often-fiery forge of speaking and debating without amplification where Cicero honed and displayed his immense skills as an orator upon which his reputation and work as a politician and lawyer were quickly built. Highly praised and prized in Rome for his abilities to create and deliver dramatic and highly persuasive speeches based on classical Greek as well as Roman rhetorical theory, Cicero became known as one of the greatest of orators (cf. Enos, *Roman Rhetoric*; Haskell).

Stases

I. *Fact*:

Stop. Stay
fast. Move.
Don't move. Stay.

Move.

II. *Definition*:
Transition—
friends immediately
present, drift, attenuate,
even distance
fading, memory
growing full
and thin,
autumn winter
like branches
disappearing—
a few connected
concrete leaves, wind…

III. *Quality*:
You are your own rock.
on which wherever
you plant yourself,
others can depend.

IV. *Judgment*:
Still, move—
more than a rock
by a house, a trellis, a glen:
blossom, and in
the end, touch
others with your
memories, roots
a blessing even then

***

In *De Oratore* as well as the *Orator*, two of the later treatises that followed from Cicero's return from possible exile and deliberate study of philosophy and rhetoric in mid-career Greece (79 BCE), Cicero (mimicking or mocking Platon), uses dialogue to attempt to discourse at length (Bks. I–III) on the nature of true Eloquence, and within that discussion, the nature of the Ideal Orator. In *De Oratore* (Bk III), Cicero like and unlike Socrates, has Crassus, the "character" and ostensible mouthpiece for Cicero declare that he was *not* the Ideal Orator, that in fact the Ideal Orator had not yet been born, and may never be born (*De Oratore*, Bk III; *Orator* lxxi.238). Whether ideal or not, the good orator must be knowledgeable about all subjects to be treated (Bk I), be able to feel the emotions imparted to the audience through rhetoric (Bk II), and be a great speaker possessing ethics and wisdom as well as a sense of propriety, able to access any style (low, medium, or high or grand) needed and appropriate not only for the occasion but for every moment (Bk III). As if to prove this point, in a reversal of the dynamics of Socrates and his interlocuters in Platon's dialogues, Cicero had Crassus consistently harangued, constantly interrupted, deliberately disputed, and wholly misunderstood by the characters of his own colleagues and students. In the end, in *De Oratore* Crassus utterly "failed" to explain or convince his colleagues and students of the nature of Eloquence, and its importance as the basis of all thought, knowledge, and civilization. But as Michael Leff and Michael Mendelson argued, Crassus, in showing the impossibility of communicating the nature of Eloquence (a sentiment he reiterates in *Orator* and in *Brutus*), in rare literary form *succeeded* in embodying and showing readers of the treatise what true Eloquence, and the Ideal Orator, had to be.

The Questioning Concerning

End of summer, and then
the sun blows in a ghost;
clouds spread into mist,
winter haunts the golden boughs.

children wrapped in brown
hoods dance around leaves
burning with the cold;

i was born in the eternal fall;
i too prayed for my mother dead,
and fled to a promised land,
and watched autumn sweep over fields
like a flaming sword.

Dandelions writhe
in frosty grass.
Soon the blossoms
will be bound in snow.

Death is not the answer.

To be immortal?
To climb upon a branch of time
and leap to the fire?

Death is not the answer.

To seed another tree
for other hands to gather?
i too was born.

Why desire
to create what has been
again, and again?

To form another world
in the civilization
of a word?
It is the same
word over and over again.

Dandelions writhe
in frosty grass.
Soon the blossoms
will be bound in snow.

The cry of children
is borne in the wind.
i too was born.

Now darkness draws the skies;
moon lights a gauzy vale—

Not to ascend, or slip
under the curtain hem;
to stand upon a void
and escape the myth
of the coming wind?
Death is not the answer.

XIV

"Karakter" of the Ideal Orator

It was significant that Cicero places the Ideal Orator not in abstract metaphysical Forms, but in physical human form. There are many places in the classical rhetorical and poetic cannons where discourse is compared to the human body.

What perhaps distinguishes Cicero's comparison in the classical era (following the exception of Isocrates [e.g., *Antidosis* 181–85; 189, 191]) was that Cicero recognized and specifically treated a central problem in Western philosophy and culture: "true" eloquence and knowledge depended on both the material body and "character" of the speaker. Cicero's Ideal Orator thus referred to people as well as to discourse (cf. *Gorgias* 503d-504; Cicero, *Orator* x.36; xiii.43). In a discussion in the *Orator*, Cicero called the Ideal of the Orator "a form or pattern," which the Greeks called καρακτηρ—character (*Orator* x.36; xiii.43). The ideal "karakter" of the Orator was physical, embodied in particular material bodies that possessed extreme strength for delivery (but also a keen sense of modulation) that could "inform, educate, or move" an audience (according to the three "offices" or styles of oratory). The language of oratory was not a transcendental form, but speech and writing that were themselves physical bodies, and so great skills in writing and articulating affecting and effective words and sentences that were persuasive and ethical were "essential." The skills of the orator depended not only on "art" (theory and study), but on "practice" (physical training), but most importantly, "natural talent" (the human form and ability with which the most gifted orators were born).

The Beard of My Ancestors

windblown, to one side—the right—
i wonder what difference that could make
when grown out, and way too long—
a big wave rises in the middle
as if the wind of time had taken whittle
grasped the entire ancestral line
of descendants and presentence
from another, darker, descendent
age, this beard would have been a dire mark.
What is to be done now, except to shave this face,
or extend this hair on which gravity yanks
me into another world-wide generation,
                                                            down,
a hidden subconscious dimension
of gas and dust and stars, all underground

XV

Physical Requirements of the (Ideal) Orator (and Listener)

Unlike Platon the Philosopher, for Cicero the physical achievement of eloquence depended not only on knowledge of subject matter, but also knowledge of and facility with style (e.g., Isocrates, *Sophists* 14–15, 17–18). And that style depended on the physical conditioning of the body (Hawhee, *Rhetoric and Athletics*; Marrou). Oratory, like speech but on a much grander scale, were physically made not only out of mind, but out of the body—the sounds it could produce, and the variations necessary to express and appeal to emotions (*De Oratore*, Bk II; cf. Hawhee, *Bodily Arts*): diagram, lungs, vocal cords, mouth, tongue, lips, teeth, face, as well as stance and gesture: torso, legs, arms, hands. In addition, the import of words as physical sound, particularly rhythm, were of utmost importance. For the older Cicero, the most important dimension of language was aural, not visual; for the older Cicero said that rhythm was more powerful in oratory than in painting or sculpture. For Cicero, the instinct for and discernment of "truth" of an oration itself was the result of an "intuitive faculty" that everyone possessed at birth: "For everybody is able to discriminate between what is right and what wrong in matters of art and proportion by a sort of subconscious instinct, without having any theory of art or proportion of their own" (*De Oratore* III. xxv.100; l.195–197).

***

Contra the often stated (anti) rhetorical philosophy of Platon, rather than stripping poetry from rhetoric, and rhetoric from speech, uncovering it, Cicero had Crassus recover the unity of brain and body, senses and intellect, mind and flesh. The natural intuitive faculty to affectively discern "truth" in sound, and especially rhythm, was based not only on the physical production of language, but on the "sonic" properties of language, as well as the reception and discernment of physical sound in the ear. Embodied and represented by and in language, sound itself was an Ideal, the *ideal material form* that relied on physical and intuitive faculties that are "innate" and universal, but also could be trained by art and practice (*De Oratore* III.xviii.70). While imperfect and uncertain and even "indeterminant" Cicero, declaiming through Crassus, proclaimed: "The ear is the arbiter of truth" (cf. Katz, *Epistemic*).

Statute to Eloquentia (Variation II)

Pour pebbles in my mouth
so i may speak
like the ancient Greeks

XVI

The (Ideal) Unity of Rhetorics and Poetics in Eloquence

For Cicero, the ideal unity of physical form and matter extended to a unity of rhetoric and poetry as well. (Cicero wrote poetry too [*Poems*], as well as used poetry in his speeches [*Pro Archia*]). But for Cicero, rhetorical and poetic arrangement and style, in combination with some knowledge of the subject matter, and guided by propriety and ethics, was not merely "ornamental" but rather *essential to eloquence.* In an ideal of Eloquence, Cicero recognized the importance of rhythm and even meter to rhetoric and oratory. This is especially the case with the "grand" style of oratory, which made more ample use of rhythm and meter learned from poetry and like topoi for Aristotle stored in the accomplished orator's rhetorical repertoire, ready for use appropriately and tempered by propriety. In *De Oratore,* Cicero declared at least twice that the orator is kin to the poet (I.xvi.70; III.vii.27). In this later treatise, as well as *Orator,*

Cicero devoted a remarkable amount of time carefully delineating the close relation of rhetoric and poetry, demonstrating in great detail the use of meter in oratory and prose, (e.g., *De Oratore* III. xliv.173–lii.199; *Orator* xiii.42–lxxi.237). In *De Oratore,* Cicero reflected on the role of affect, sound, and rhythm (see liii. 179–lviii.198), and in *Orator,* discussed meter (liii. 179–lviii.198). Cicero thought that meter in oratory was distinct from meter in poetry only in one respect: oratory was less restricted in the use of meter [*Orator* xix. 68]. In oratory and prose, meter must be moderated and modulated (*Orator* lii. 176–lxxi. 236)—partly based on purpose, and tempered by propriety (xxi.70–71)—but primarily grounded in the subconscious "intuition" of orators and listeners (xxii.72; see xiv 67). Therefore, the orator, like the poet, was primarily limited in the use of meter in rhetoric by insight, alacrity, intelligence, physique, and emotions, all of which, Cicero believed, could be improved by study and practice, but was first the result of natural talent.

To Build a Fire

(Rome)

As your father and the ancients taught us
begin with foundations of newspapers
with their written reports and recountings
recording scenes and events in words like photos

of tragedies and news of all the good
below the grates of civilization
where a maze of tunnel-sewers grows.
You build above the kindling wood,

layer by layer of all the yesterdays,
until you reach the last and highest log
that will catch a pointed fiddle fire—
(Atlantis, Crete, Micenea, Rome, Pompei)

or persecute with flame, burn alive
the odd, opponent, traitor, heretic,
kindling big pieces of the city
that falls into its own oblivion

XVII

Physical Eloquence and the Ideal of "Ornatus"

Did Cicero help redeem a non-mimetic dream of beautiful bodies of discourse that are not imitation, flattery, or ornamentation, not separated from themselves, each other, or material reality itself, but that might have helped dispel false images of rhetoric and poetry? For Platon the philosopher, the "Ideal Forms" had no physical substance or manifestation in the material world, and only existed in the transcendental realm mediated by the mind of the philosopher. For Platon the philosopher, the style of rhetoric and poetry were imitations, ornaments, false flattery, "fine cooking" (*Gorgias* 462c)—something to be "stripped off" speech (*Gorgias* 502c–d). In language and art, as well as on the body, rhetoric and poetry provided beauty and pleasure—but "artificially" by pretending to "reproduce" the original, truth. Rhetoric and poetry were merely artifacts that like cosmetics instead of health was added on to language (like a body to the soul), and adoring or adorned, worn, but wholly superficial, unreal, an illusion (see Tables 3 and 4). But for Cicero, rhetoric and poetry as arrangement and style, in combination with subject matter and guided by propriety, were not merely "ornamental" but essential to Eloquence. Style as an "Ideal Form" was part of the unity of form and content that made ideas and reality palpable if not palatable. Even more, the aesthetics of the physical embodiment of philosophy and rhetoric within wisdom and eloquence was not only a rhetorical or poetic unity, but also a (re)instantiation in language of the relation of form and matter in nature, and indeed the oneness of the universe (*De Oratore* III. v. 20). According to Raymond Di Lorenzo in "*Ornatus* and the Nature of Wisdom," for Cicero, rhetoric and poetry, like physical reality, were not imitative ornaments or cosmetics, but *kosmos*—the perfect order and unity of all things. Rather than being false and ephemeral, "kosmetics" like form itself was necessary to perceive matter, or anything at all.

{Ornamental

We will take our ornaments with us:
the same holiday decorations
brought out of storage—hung in the outer space
of deep blue spruce; or holiday candles
rising, flaming up beneath the floor
of the highest hidden holy shelves,
taken down;

our cloned children in their cozy pods,
our drones surveillancing nighttime skies—
from gravity our satellites dangling
amid dark branches of stars and galaxies
and other ornamentals, flowers popping,
growing down through pots with no false bottoms—
signs for memories, emotions, thoughts—
human sentiments we'll celebrate,
forgotten}

***

Crassus valiantly tried to explain to his colleagues and students in the dialogue of *De Orato*re, the perfect unity of style and subject matter (ideally to be achieved at *every* moment of speaking via propriety and *kairos*), paralleled, instantiated, and reflected the perfect unity to be found between form and matter in the cosmos, or in nature, or even in the rules of diction, whose recitation Crassus is forced to recite, by his nagging students (especially Sulpicius), as they try to uncover Crassus' "tricks" and discover the nature of eloquence, and completely miss the point: the secret of Crassus' successful oratory is eloquence as the unity of form and matter.

Ideals of the gods?

withdrawal
nothingness
space to create

XVIII

As a famous prosecutor/advocate in the Roman "legal system," such as it was, and the greatest orator in Rome (and perhaps since Demosthenes, of all time), Cicero came to the realization later in life (after his exile and study in Greece) that form and matter were in reality inseparable. Oratory, and especially eloquence, could *not* be detached from the physical body of the orator, or the body of the speech; form and content, style and subject matter could not and should not be parted in theory, pedagogy, or practice, without doing irreparable harm to both (*De Oratore* III.xiv.55). As in the physical worlds of nature and the kosmos, so too speech and thought. For Cicero, "substance" or "subject matter" (*res*—"seat") matter could not and should not be separated from form or style (*verba*-"form"). Matter was necessary for form to sit; and form depended on and was necessary to give make matter appear and give it its proper shape. Without matter, form would be without substance, hollow; and without form, matter would be intangible, invisible. Together, the indivisible unity of *res* and *verba* was an ideal of Eloquence that was itself modelled after the physical Kosmos—the ideal order of all. The unity of form and content based on the unity of *res* and *verba* was the foundation not only of civilization, but the organizing principle of the entire universe. The physical and metaphysical unity of *res* and *verba* at every moment of speaking was the ideal goal of the orator.

Res and Verba

Breaks in aqueducts
Mimetic civilization—
"seat" and "word"
spout amid
plumbing and collapsing
seals—souls leaking

The metal seat
the *res* of culture
corroded, history
rusted out, needs to be
grasped, twisted, removed
with a "seat wrench"—

And the rubber, too,
the *verba*, the seal of language
that holds all meaning
together, is cracked, peeling,
needs to be replaced
before all knowledge

goes down the drain

XIX

"Stripping" Speech—Greek Style

It was not surprising then that Cicero/Crassus were horrified by Socrates' and Platon's "*separating*" ("*separavit*"—*sēparō*) philosophy and rhetoric, "dividing the tongue and the brain" ("*discidium . . . linguae atque cordis*"), which "in reality . . . are closely linked/belong together" (*sapienterque sentiendi et ornate dicendi scientiam*), "robbing these subjects of their general designations" and "leading to one set of professors to teach thinking and another set to teach speaking (*De Oratore* III. xv.57, III.xvi.59, III.xvi.60, III.xvi.61) or writing (*De Oratore* III.xlix.190). Cicero had Crassus decry the severing of the "organ of speaking" from the physical body/soul. Divorcing mouth from mind was not only a stripping of philosophy from rhetoric, but also of poetry from rhetoric, emotion from intellect, wisdom from prudence, leaving only plain speech—all necessary for eloquence, but also a scientific, cultural, and aesthetic amputation of episteme and ethics, of thought and technique, leaving only *technē*. For *eloquence* was

> so potent a force that it embraces the origin and operation and development of all things, all virtues and duties, all the natural principles governing the morals and minds of mankind, and also determines their customs and laws and rights, and controls the government of the state, and expresses everything that concerns whatever topic in a graceful and flowing style. (*De Oratore* III.xx.175–76)

***

Just as eloquence was physically and metaphysically inseparable for Crassus/Cicero, the ideal orator was not divisible either. In *De Oratore* Cicero/Crassus also argued vehemently against the split between rhetoric and poetry and had defended not only the utility but also of the necessity of the later, especially in relation to the grand style. For Cicero, the severing of philosophy and rhetoric (and rhetoric and poetry) was a "dismembering" of knowledge and eloquence, a "gutting" of wisdom and ethics from the physical body (see *Orator*). For knowledge, wisdom, prudence, like speech and writing themselves, were always first situated locally, in the human body as physical instrument and material soul, of the controlled voice and emotion of the ideal orator as a living being. {Teleological Prediction. From this came the wider diffusion of rhetoric, as persuasion of immediate audience (Aristotle), as social "symbolic action" (Burke), and finally its further formalization of in the mores and customs as laws and institutions (Foucault; cf. Habermas, "Ideology").}

***

The stripping of philosophy of rhetoric (and poetry), of thinking from speech (and writing) in favor of a plainer Attic style for Platon the philosopher led Cicero to excoriate the damage inflicted by this division on both philosophical and an oratorical *education* as well, as a great disservice to the science of thinking and speaking. But not only education. Cicero also thought these divisions were a great and even dangerous disservice to "the safety and security of the universe [,] this whole ordered world of nature" (cf. *De Oratore* III.xlv.178). For Ideal Eloquence was the perfect unity not only of content and style, or knowledge and body, but also matter and form itself. As *Ornatus*, Cicero saw Eloquence as a physical principle that held the universe together (cf. Cicero, *Nature of the Gods*).

geometry is life

a simple line—
without a future

there is no point

***

{Harbinger. The result of the Socratic/Platonic decision seemed to divorce not only philosophy and rhetoric, but also rhetoric and poetry, a split that would become an annulment that would for the most part permanently persist and even grow, eventually becoming scientific and technological in Western culture. This slicing of subject matter, the parting of body and soul, this cutting rejection of crass and dross business of the world vs. the self-evident (and self-aggrandizement) of one approach to science or philosophy or literature as the only source of true of virtuous study and knowledge, also became the epistemological prejudice and operational assumption in academic departments, from science to philosophy to English—even within the language arts itself—for the remainder of the Anthropocene.}

one divine error—
a plethora
of corruption

***

There were additional philosophical and pedagogical repercussions from the Platonic-Socratic stripping of rhetoric from philosophy, rhetoric and poetry from speech, and language from thought. One often overlooked consequence was the suppression and denial of a fuller resonance of philosophy, speech, and thought (*res*) through rhetoric and poetry as *physical* (*verba*)—the vocal, aural, sonic, musical persuasive body of words orally or artistically realized and articulated in speech or writing (see Cicero's *Orator*). This epistemic dimension of the sounds of words was subdued in an ontological favoring of belief in non-bodied, abstract, transcendental ideas and Essences. Even "attributes" were but false imitations or echoes of purer Ideas. The severing of language from thought also ruptured Cicero's "unity" of *res* and *verba*, removing the matter that gave substance to form, and form that gave shape to matter, from eloquence. The effect for Cicero was to render words hollow vessels (as hollow as poets), and to render substance invisible. The teaching of speaking became a discipline without its own subject matter, and thus only a "skill" rather than an art (as it seemed to Platon *the philosopher*, and most of his followers. Subject experts did not need rhetoric because they had the knowledge, "spoke truth"). In this reasoning, rhetoric was regarded as mere "knack" or "habit" based on nothing but imitations of Reality (the mimicry of forms, and the trickery of mimicry).

***

{Epistemological Vision. In the history of science, the "Platonic" view of rhetoric as hollow, mimicry, flattery, trickery became the dominant epistemology of language. For Francis Bacon, the early "father" of *modern* science who in the continuous battles with the "idols of the mind" thought rhetoric could be useful, for "*reason* would become captive and servile, if eloquence of persuasions did not practice and win . . . *imagination* from *affection* . . . and contract a confederacy between *reason* and *imagination* against the *affections*. . . . [*A*]*ffection* beholdeth merely the present; *reason* beholdeth the future and sum of time (Bacon, *Advancement* XVIII.4, ital. added). For Thomas Sprat, apologist for the Royal Society of London, rhetoric should be "stripped" of all rhetorical colors, figures, and ornaments "to return back to the primitive purity, and shortness, when men delivered so many things almost in an equal number of words . . . by a close, naked, natural way of speaking; positive expression; clear senses; a native easiness, bringing all things as near Mathematical as they can" (113), leading to a "faithful record of all the Works of Nature" (61). Even empiricist philosopher John thought language a conduit, an empty "pipeline" through which objective sensory data could simply flow unimpeded in language, to be collected and written on the *tabula rasa*— the "blank slate of the mind"—and analyzed and/or synthesized into knowledge by the operations and conduct of thought (*Essay*); later this model would be dubbed the "deficit model" of communication" in which the knowledge of experts was "conveyed" in one-way communication in "transparent language to "laypeople" who need to be "informed" or "educated" (Katz and Miller; Katz, "How to Say"; "Ethics"). In these objective, empirical, even positivistic scientific views (see Figure 1) of scientific communication, there was no need for rhetoric, poetry, or eloquence.} Is it true that "[n]obody uses fine language when teaching geometry?" (Aristotle, *Rhetoric* 1404a10). This stood in contradiction with Cicero (*De Oratore* III xiv 55), who warned—and predicted and prophesized —that severing philosophy and rhetoric, severing knowledge and eloquence, might have some catastrophic repercussions (Katz, "Expediency"; "Problem of Praxis"; Mebust and Katz).

The Indifferent Accident

Is it because the little girl
did not seem to notice
the charioteer's wheels
crashing through the air,
or the torchlight's red pall
falling on the gathered
faces of the crowd,
having never beheld
guts spilling from the mouth,
or the fire's thrilling gall
as it gnaws the arms
and legs, being unaware?
Or is it that she cannot care,
head cocked, eyes turned away

XX

"Stripping" Speech—Roman Style

It was perhaps one of those twists of history that Cicero, great orator and statesman (and also consul for one year) who had watched the moral dissipation of the aristocracy, the continuous corruption of the Senate, and the demise of the Roman Republic, witnessed the death of the great general and former consul Julius Caesar by twenty-three stab wounds two years after he made himself dictator. And it was perhaps no accident that Cicero who, advocating for a return to Republican values in Rome and delivering a series of speeches (the *Philippics*) against the new dictatorial leader, Mark Antony, found himself on the wrong side of the litter. In 43 BCE, heeding the warning that his life was in danger Cicero attempted (again?) a swift escape from Rome to Greece, making it all the way to the coast of an Italian evening; and that with a quick shift in political winds and the blinding blade of fortune was proscribed and intercepted by Antony's soldiers and slaughtered right there in his bed being carried across the beach. And having inveighed against the Socratic/Platonic severing of the tongue from the brain, it was perhaps one of those inevitable ironies that Cicero's tongue and hands were cut off and conveyed to Rome, where they were nailed to the *Rostra* from which he so often had spoken in the Forum.

The Horseshoe Crab

(For Mr. K)

. . . Hardiest species alive,
one of the few to survive
from some prehistoric time,
you turn, and comment on the beauty

. . . your upper-class background, the sea
in your blood the "Ivy League"
Equestrians, the only male
of four offspring, your family,

. . . your growth into manhood without
a father, the unusual course of your
your intellect, development,
your study of philosophy

. . . your found friendships among the other
Roman rhetoricians, sophists,
your rocky lovelife, and your marriage
into another class and family and faith

. . . the absent godfather of your daughter,
your physical affinity
with the whole ocean of nature:
shell hard as any Roman helmet.

. . . And with the shift of two-toned sea,
the tides of political power
between Pompey and Antony
(Cleopatra's suicide

. . . more seductive than any woman)
you are washed up on the beach,
knocking you against the rocks,
leaving you stranded, a sandy snare,

. . . on your back, your belly exposed
to blades of gulls and clouds of blood
that descend, down-side up,
horny claws kicking air,

. . . vulnerable, desperate again,
you reach
down, try to turn
it over, walk away . . .
not even a friend
could save you today . . .

XXI

Most agreed that at minimum Cicero's tongue was cut out and nailed to the Rostra. But there was some debate about what else was cut off, and what was impaled: His tongue and/or his head? And at least one, if not both of, his hands, severed from his body and impaled on the rostra in the Roman forum from which he often spoke so eloquently (Strachan-Davidson 424). While some said that both of Cicero's hands were severed (see Plutarch in Haskell 293), a "singular" account was confirmed by the Roman historian Cassius Dio, who reported that only *the right hand* of Cicero (as Strachan-Davidson also implies)—the one that held the pen that wrote the Philippics against Mark Antony—was sliced off and fastened to the Rostra. Cassius Dio also intimated that it was Antony's wife (who earlier had felt slighted by Cicero) who pulled out Cicero's tongue, which had spoken against her husband, and repeatedly stabbed it with a hairpin (133). From the Rostra: his severed head, tongue, tongue and hand, tongue and head and hand, both hands . . . also spoke. But as Cicero might have said if he could have, both the "tongue" and the "brain," oratory and wisdom, were necessary for eloquence. "The severance between the tongue and the brain" (Cicero, *De Oratore* III xvi.61) was both physical and complete in this savage act. Whatever the facts of the case, the symbolism and the message was clear: Cicero's power as an orator and advocate, which, disconnected, resided helplessly and silent in these body parts, was amputated, along with his life and tongue. The symbolism of that act was perhaps not lost on his Roman executors, nor the public, nor history. Cicero's murder was not only the result of political rivalry and revenge, but also the severing of the physical body from speech. Literally. It was not only Cicero but also eloquence that was disarticulated.

Statue to Eloquentia (Variation III)

Tear the tongue from out my mouth
so from the Rostra i may shout
like a Greek-Roman orator

XXII

It was more than mere coincidence that Cicero had his tongue cut out and "crucified"/nailed to the Rostra. Like crucifixion, the carving of the tongue from the head was a rather common punishment in the Roman Empire, meant to transfer the body and soul of the criminal back to the authority that owns them by divine right or political might. {Pre-Disfigurement. The act of (un) inscribing the body became even more important in the seventeenth century (Foucault), in the twentieth century, and in every subsequent century. This leitmotif in human history of stripping the body and flaying the soul was reenacted in sets of public rituals designed not only to exact revenge for crimes and insults against "the very body of the King, but also to restore political power and "social order" (Foucault, *Discipline*). As Foucault explored in *Discipline and Punish*, up until the eighteenth century, the spectacle of "[T]he tortured, dismembered, amputated body symbolically branded on face or shoulder, exposed alive or dead to public view" (8) was an act not only of punishment and oppression, but also ownership by the sovereign and control of the body politic and each individual member within it (see Foucault, *Discipline* 3–69). "Besides its immediate victim, the crime attacks the sovereign: it attacks him personally, since the law represents the will of the sovereign; it attacks him physically, since the force of the law is the force of the prince" (47). Thus, the stripping, flaying, (un)inscribing of flesh was about the body of the sovereign as much as the criminal: "The public execution . . . is a ceremonial by which a momentarily injured sovereignty is reconstituted" (Foucault, *Discipline*).}

Non-Roman Souls Are Singing

skeletons, stones,
crosses, bones
still screaming

XXIII

Crucifixion: "Architecturally" Puncturing Human Bodies

Crucifixion was not just reserved for Jesus Christ. Rather, it was almost a common occurrence throughout the Roman Empire, especially outside Rome in the provinces, or in the Forum, for it was illegal to crucify a Roman citizen. Perhaps one of the most severe forms of capital punishment, crucifixion was used for the execution of non-citizens of Rome perceived as having spoken or acted against the Senate or Emperor or State (i.e., subversion, sedition, treason), as well as for slaves who had in some way "betrayed" their master and had no rights anyway. The cross was seemingly pseudo-based on the classical ideal of the human body according to mathematical proportion {later expressed in the drawing "Vitruvian Man" by Leonardo da Vinci in 1490, with the part-time patronage of Lorenzo de Medici and the beginning of the Renaissance}. This was not that unbelievable given the Romans' past precise and superior engineering prowess and the development of and great skills with their building tools. But the form of the crucifix probably was based simply on the "aesthetic" principle of maximum utility; the cross accommodated any body type, human form. The purpose of crucifixion was not to measure the beauty of the outspread body as harmonious ideal perfection, the Vitruvian Man. Rather to use the anatomical proportions of the cross to affix and mortally puncture body *and soul*—whether handsome and vibrant (hence also the restraining ropes), or *soma* (the walking dead body, surrounding and the imprisoned a living soul)—bodies that would never set foot on ground or walk again. But they were alive and lived long enough to beg and cry and plead and spit at the bystanders and all subsequent passers-by—to stretch their own sinews well beyond the dislocation point by their body's own weight, hanging by the constant tugging and tearing and ripping of flesh around the iron spikes bleeding rust, the muscles weakening, the intense compression of the lungs increasing—to mark and mock and break the body—to splay and display it like a sinful or criminal soul in all its ugliest expressions of pain and suffering and slow death. *X*: a perversion of Platon's spreading souls that was to take place *after* death (*Gorgias* 523e–525e). It didn't take three to six hours to die on the cross; rather (in extreme cases, such as when the hangee was previously healthy and/or not wounded), it took three to six *days* of slow, self-suffocation.

Statue to Eloquentia (Variation IV)

Crucify me in my hearse
so i may be immediately conveyed
to my father to converse

***

One of the most famous examples of a *mass* crucifixion was by General Licinius Marcus Crassus (part of the ruling first Triumvirate with Caesar and Pompey). General Crassus and his army of ten thousand troops gave chase in southern and northern in Italy to 10,000–40,000 of escaped rebellious slaves led by

Spartacus, the greatest of the Roman gladiators. (All gladiators were enslaved.) Finally cornering and capturing the gladiator-soldier-slaves, General Crassus ordered the crucifixion of six thousands of Spartacus' survivors along the Appian Way—a main artery and public road that led directly to Rome—now lined with crucified flesh in various stages of dying or decomposition hanging off crosses —one every hundred feet, for sixty miles—and at a great expenditure of time, resources (wood and nails), and soldiers (manpower). General Crassus did it anyway and thought it worth it—as proof of conquest as much as preventative or punishment. The moaning could be heard for miles, and the stench of death was profound for anyone travelling south to Rome—which was everyone. The six thousand bodies left hanging on the crosses for all to see and hear and smell—the perspiring dead rotting stinking carcasses—that eventually slipped off their metal nails like coats off knobs, falling to the ground in heaps of dried blood, dirty flesh, and unburied bones, where they continued to decay until they were replaced by others, or were gone.

***

Upstaged by Pompey who rushed back to Rome before him, General Crassus did not receive the credit from the Senate and the Roman people he thought he deserved for his conquest of the rebel army-led Spartacus. The body of Spartacus was never found (Plutarch, "Life of Crassus").

***

Cicero was all too aware of the proscription and practice of crucifixion: It had already become almost a common "fixture" of Roman life. (According to Josephus, outside the walls of Jerusalem during the siege that led to the Roman sacking of the Second Temple in 70 CE, up to five hundred people a day were crucified—until they ran out of wood.)

Binyan

Over piles
of abandoned shoes—
Hebrew letters crying

Unlike Horace who as a poet remained "on the outskirts" of politics and periphery of power in Rome, Cicero by temperament and profession as a legal prosecutor and advocate as well as famous orator, deliberately placed himself at the center of society. From accessible evidence, just as Cicero would stand against the division of thought and speech by arguing in his later rhetorical treatises for the unity of mind and body as necessary for eloquence, he also would inveigh in legal oration and treatise against the "partition" of *crucifixion* (of Roman citizens). In 70 BCE, Cicero undertook the prosecution in Rome of Gaius Verres, an infamous and heartless Propraeter (magistrate) of the Roman Province of Sicily, who was accused (repeatedly) of bribery, theft, corruption, and selective over-taxation, including of poor farmers, and extortion (Plutarch, *Lives*). One of Cicero's arguments in seven (*sic*) orations was that Verres had crucified at least one of his slaves who had in fact been a legal Roman (*Verrem Actionis Secundae* Bk. 5: LXVI). Cicero details in abstract but emotional terms this slow and excruciatingly painful form of punishment that inevitably led to death by "leisurely" suffocation and "casual" asphyxiation, and that even sight of the cross should be kept out of range for Romans. But Cicero only needed his introduction of Verres' various venal acts for him to be found guilty and sent into permanent exile. In 43 BCE, the year of Cicero's death, Mark Antony had Verres assassinated for withholding treasure from him.

***

At the end of his life Cicero could not defend himself against his own proscription, given the fourteen speeches of the *Philippics* he had written condemning Mark Antony, now ruler of the Empire. Ironically, appropriately, horrendously, Cicero's tongue—and perhaps his hand(s) and/or head—were cut off and nailed to the Rostra of the Roman Forum. Cicero suffered a far "easier," quicker death. Afterall, he was a Roman citizen.

6 2 4
C
Carbon
12.011

7 Spiritual Organ

i

The Diminution of Letters and the Physical Suffering of the Soul

> "The capital letters were the only forms that existed initially. . . . These letters are known as monumental or square capitals and were considered the highest form of writing during the period of the Empire . . . By the fourth century, letter changes had become so dramatic as to constitute the beginning of a new style—the uncial. The established capital letters were not wholly abandoned—they were occasionally used for texts—but they soon came to be used with uncial letters only as the initial letters at the beginnings of sections, for the first letters of names, and wherever emphasis was required. This set a precedent for the later use of capitals (or majuscules) and minuscules in combination" (Firmage 19–224; cf. Graham 40 on illuminated manuscripts necessitating Carolingian minuscules).

There were already many attacks and defeats, a diminishment in number and strength. Little did the Romans know that that the vilification, penetration, and persecution of Jesus on the cross would forever change the conception of the body from classical ideals of contemplation, serenity, stoicism, and strength, to one of empathy, forgiveness, suffering, and passion. Simultaneously a negation and an affirmation, life was a temporary existence in a physical body moving in a dark world, looking for light through which the spirit was to be freed in death from the flesh. {Time/Space Transposition. As Georg Wilhelm Friedrich Hegel stated in *Aesthetics*,

> This sphere of portrayal is separated *toto caelo* from the classical plastic ideal because here the subject-matter itself implies

> that the external bodily appearance, immediate existence as an individual, is revealed in the grief of his negativity as the negative, and that therefore it is by sacrificing subjective individuality and the sensuous sphere that the Spirit attains its truth and its Heaven. (538)}

In Christianity, as in Neo-Platonism, the physical body itself remained vile and transitory. But in the Middle Ages, the *object of mimesis, of the ideal Being, have been completely personalized, and transformed into spirit that shall be a new body.* "Ashes to ashes, dust to dust, in the sure and certain hope of the Resurrection unto eternal life, through our Lord Jesus Christ; at who's coming in glorious majesty . . . the corruptible bodies of those who sleep in him shall be changed, and made like unto his own glorious body" ("The Burial of the Dead," *Book of Common Prayer* 333). The vile body versus the glorious body. Majuscules and minuscules. The glorious body was a spiritualized one, the body and soul together resurrected and reborn. A new alphabet that was still together, alive, old. {Presentiment. The rejection of rationality and of "logic" in favor of spirit would later be combined by Hegel in a philosophical vision of world history accompanied by faith not only in life after death, but in the eternal life of the physical body as well (*Phenomenology of Mind*).}

Transfusions

i am sleepy and stoic when,
again and again at 3:00 a.m.
they punch the needles
through my hands,
arms collapsed like its veins,
legs dangling as i am raised,
bleeding into a new life,
death flowing from me—
tubes exuding from my body—

The veins in my hands collapse.
And so they begin to work
on my feet, nailing them
to the bed frame with their needles.
Yellow sunlight stains white linen.

i am reborn (once again).

ii

The Aesthetics of the Cross

In the story and the spirit of Jesus that overtook the Western world, pathos enters mimesis. It could be seen in the contrast of the frail, failing human form against the hard geometry of the cross. As Kenneth Clark discusses in *The Nude: A Study of Ideal Form* (333–341), it is the geometric pathos of the hanging human form that Michelangelo, reviving the Y-shaped cross, experimented with in his various depictions of the crucifixion: "He has felt how the body hanging stark and defenseless has a quality of truth" (334). Indeed, many philosophers and scholars, as well as theologians, came to believe that the advent and death of Jesus signaled the beginning of a new basis for mimesis in Western culture, one based not on the philosophical contemplation of Ideal Forms (à la Platon) or the aesthetic unity of universal principles (à la Aristotle), but rather on the experience of passion and faith in the agony of the flesh. With Platon the philosopher's intellectual aversion to both pleasure and pain (e.g., *Philebus* 20e) and probably Aristotle with the stoicism of his logic, they would have found it anathema. {"True" Transmutation. Hegel continued:

> On the one hand, in other words, the earthly body and the frailty of human nature in general is raised and honored by the fact that it is God himself who appears in human nature, but on the other hand it is precisely this human and bodily existent which is negatived and comes into appearance in its grief, while in the classical ideal it does not lose undisturbed harmony with what is spiritual and substantial. Christ scourged, with the crown of thorns, carrying his cross to the place of execution, nailed to the cross, passing away in the agony of a torturing and slow death—this cannot be portrayed in the forms of Greek beauty; but the higher aspect in these situations is their inherent sanctity, the depth of the inner life, the infinity of grief, present as an eternal moment in the Spirit as sufferance and divine peace. (*Aesthetics* 538)

Erich Auerbach would have agreed with Hegel: "It was the story of Christ, with its ruthless mixture of everyday reality and the highest and most sublime tragedy, which had conquered the classical rules of styles" (554–55). The body on the cross thus became a new message: one of personal, spiritual salvation through a mimesis of Christ's faith, pain, passion, compassion, and death, as well as a hoped-for resurrection.}

Slow Comfort Consuming the Body

{Inspired by Michael Timpson's Exhibit "But the Ball is Lost and the Mallet Slipped," North Carolina Museum of Art, Nov. 2, 1991–February 2, 1992}

Bike handles wrapped in white bandages:
four white crucifixes arranged in a Latin cruciform,
and from them the sinew of brake wires stretch,
hanging. The cross is a slow vehicle,
molasses a slow blood;
forks and spoons to consume the body
are sprinkled beneath the vat;
four buckets hang above,
spread incense, or catch manna.

Will it speed the masses?
A serene white cotton cloth
covers shards of glass,
spreads softly on the floor}

iii

Inscribing and Change

Majuscule and minuscule: Father and Son. In Christian history, the crucifixion itself was an inscription of a new order—a puncturing of the classical body that frees the soul from rock as well as flesh.

when Christ rose
art was freed
from stone

Out of this horrific historical application of mathematical proportion (not the first or the last), out of this devastating symbolic of logic, a major transformation of the body, the Word made flesh, emerged from the sepulcher of classical imitation where it had been imprisoned, as if from Platon's cave as tomb, and was reborn as a new, physio-spiritual form of affect. The body itself, and with it, notions of mimesis in art—including rhetoric and poetry—began their slow transformation.

Three Articles of Faith

For Charles Wright

I.
The Laundry

i lift and drag one-half our heavy clothesline—
(two wooden posts nailed into a cross,
stretched slack sinew of white exhausted cord
still attached, dangling from the crossbeam)
from the solitary place we hang
the remnants of the sin of Adam, Eve
to dry out in the sun—on my shoulders
toward a woodpile behind a carpenter's shed
to decay and rot: i am a thief climbed down
from death, now returning, the final theft,
dragging the second cross across the yard
to free us from eternal labor. Go!
Redeem your dirty laundry on this spot.

II.
Ragged Faith

The sun, with its shoelaces hanging down,
the sky, with its shirt undone,
clouds torn by the wind, and stars
small holes in a black and seamless fabric,
seem to reveal an even brighter flesh—
as we skin our knee on the street,
lose our ball in the little dark,
can't find our way home

III.
Streetlights

always haunt me, buried in the trees,
far away, like disembodied ghost-lights
half-dressed amid the torn leaves, or ghost-notes
floating on staves strung up between the poles,
moving up and down, arranged without
sound (except for hum of halogen),
melody always playing above us, ghost-notes
drifting away from us, up and down,
running just below the hill of night

iv

The Soul of Suffering

In many obvious ways, the (neo) Platonic notion of the soul was continued in Christianity. In history (particularly Christian history), this transmutation of word and body to material spirit was seen as a major advance forward . . . not as the separation of soul and body, but a transubstantiation of one body into another, holy body, two bodies, made possible by a third, "body," the Holy Ghost. It was a sacred "substantiation," to borrow Burke's term. {Technological Transubstantiation. This position was one enunciated by Christian scholars in response to technological and medical reductions of the body as well:

> [The] conviction that some kinds of suffering can serve moral projects requires a view of the body in order to articulate those projects. What distinguishes the Christian view from its modern counterparts is its refusal to separate the body of the Other from the self. Rather, it recognizes that the body of the Other is inextricable from the self, so that the self is separated from and within itself . . . "the soma [body] is not something that outwardly clings to a man's real *self* (to say his soul, for instance), but belongs to its very essence, so that ever can say man does *have* a *soma*, he *is soma* . . . (Bultmann, 1951, p. 194)." (McKenny 219–20)}

School of Death

For Nana, who supported my education in so many ways

"I've learned to know when hands must signal arcs
of epic loss, or when despair will do,
but nothing grows more perfect but the pain."
—Paul Petrie, "The Academy of Goodbye"

"And I pray that I may forget
These matters that with myself I too much discuss
too much explain."
—T.S. Eliot, "Ash-Wednesday," *Collected Poems* (86).

"We shall content ourselves in conclusion with indicating in broad strokes what is called Jewish uneasiness. For Jews are often uneasy."
—Jean Paul Sartre, *The Anti-Semite and the Jew* (132)

Jewish student, i am schooled in death.
i make a study of indifference—
the uneventful falling into numbness,
body half in this world, half in next,
naked conscious shivering alone,
an aching void that dissipates and grows.
Death comes suddenly, even when slow;
like a book it's right there in your face.
A Jewish student, always studying death gives me a headache.

A Jewish teacher, i discourse on death—
the shattered visage, mirrors covered with sheets
(the wrinkled cloth enfolded like a face),
banisters worn smooth with grief . . .
the stairs we come and go on every day . . .
the muscle of the telephone uncoiling
as we hear the news: she's passed away.
Death is tight-lipped, a profile on a bed.
A Jewish academic, i profess too much on death.

A Jewish poet, i am versed in death—
words like hollow cheeks and eyes, and lines
in stanzas small enough a child could sleep in,
the tutored keening of the Rabbi, women
softly squeezing tears out of bone,
love a corpse that clutches at the throat,
tissues heels of boots rubbed into eyelids,
rock-dirt striking stacked up wooden faces.
Death's a hard-nosed formalist: i write night and day.

v

Transmogrification as Continuation

A new vision. There were also many ways in which resurrection was a continuation as well as a transformation of the old ideals. Hegel's "infinity of grief, present as an eternal moment in the Spirit as sufferance and divine peace" (*Aesthetics* 538), as Umberto Eco might have pointed out, was still a classical virtue. And in the negation of the vile body in favor of the salvation of the soul was the old Platonic/humanistic desire to escape the physical body in search of a bodiless ideal, be it Ideal Forms, universal principle (even in the dramatic unity of poetry), or the hope of a reborn spiritual form. (The rendering of spirit was a reincarnation of the Greek *logos* ["word," "thought"] into divine spirit: Εν αρχη ην ο λογος και ο λογος ην προς τον Θεον και Θεον ην ο λογος [*En archai emai ho logos chai ho logos emai theos kai theos emai ho logos* —"In the beginning was the Word and the Word was with God and God was the Word"] [*Gospel of John* 1:1]).

Catholic Mass

Gold stars in a light blue ceiling
of a church no more, and the Pope
sends his greetings and condolences.

In a pew Katherine's grey hair floats
on her head like an old fur hat
a massive cloud of incense, hovers, smoke.

Rub your hand against the splintered post
until you think you've touched the Host;
Try lying in a bed of thorns and stones:

nothing left but dust and dough
for wafer, and a dram of wine
to change to water and walk with the dead.

***

Platon's inscription of the ideas as "images" (*Eidos*) of reality by the scribe of mortal memory, was somewhat like the pagan soul imprisoned in *soma*—the sleeping, zombie body. That soul, baptized, was now a part of the spirit of God in the Word freed from classical forms of knowing trapped in philosophical only soul-spaces. According to "the story," the removal of the soul as "simply" abstract thought and set on its journey down the road to eternal life then, and at the Second Coming, was accomplished by the redemption of the sin of the suffering material body by the intercession with and by God through Christ. Beyond physics and ontology as ever understood, this fundamental process of conversion applied not only to the "transubstantiation" of bread and wine into blood and water, but also to the spiritualization of word and world—a communion of the birth, death, and resurrection of "God's son"—and a new "third" that unlike any Roman Triumvirate was not the body of a co-tyrant, but of the "Holy Ghost." (As such, the resurrection and transformation of Word into flesh, and that back into a rebirth of spirit, represented *the break* with Judaism: "the word"— a possibly complete and saving escape through "grace" of the soul from the Covenant of the Old Testament to the promises of the New Testament; from the letter of/as Law to merciful and all-loving Spirit; from language and text as reality, embodied in the Hebrew דבר [*d'var*—"word," "action"], to an immortal reality in heaven; from death to everlasting life.)

*Dual Yahrzeit**

For Bubby and Zada

Two candles
next to each other
like two headstones—

This year they burn
together, gather heat,
agitate each other,
get to fight once again.

Placing my hand
between the milky cups,
i feel the warmth
of their sleeping bodies,
smell their waxy breath.

At 5:00 a.m.,
Zada rises
in cold air
to go to work again,
and Bubby soon follows
in a smoke of hot oatmeal.

All day tongues
wildly flicker,
flash silent insults,
swear in a language
i don't understand

then go out,
the milky flesh
in melted pools
clear and cold again:

---

* *Yahrzeit*: In Judaism, the anniversary of a death was commemorated by the lighting of the *yahrzeit* candle and the reciting of the *Kaddish*, the mourner's prayer.

two candles
next to each other—
memories hardening into skin

***

Susan Handelman wrote: "The Christian interpretation of the Bible . . . followed the Greeks in disparaging verbal, outer discourse" (10). For Handelman, "[T]ruth is achieved by discarding the "outer shell," the materiality of language for the inner thought" (14). Handelman, a little less figuratively, explained it:

> Christianity took the Hebrew concept of the word as essential reality and combined it with the Greek concepts of substance and being, and developed the idea of the incarnation—the word become flesh, *thing* in a literal sense. Then a distinction had to be made between the incarnate word, and the "old" word, which had merely prefigured in a symbolic way the "fulfilled" word: thus the distinction between the "Old" and "New" Testaments. In Christianity, the Hebrew Scriptures then acquired the status which words had in Greek thought—mere signs, figures, shadows pointing to the true word, the word of flesh. (32)

Yahrzeit

a brief candle—
with you
only for a moment

vi

Alternate Perspectives

Not only as an alternate (opposite) Jewish perspective, but from the vantage point of the history that followed, "Christian" philosophy and science in the West continued tendencies found in both Platon and Aristotle, e.g., the separation but interaction of body and soul, and the dismembering and removal of thought from the physical body and physical word. Yet, making the invisible body of God corporeal—not only in imagery, as in Greek and Roman mythology, but even further, as a living breathing dying thing who is then endlessly imaged as a divine being—was paradoxical. For the Jews, G/d was physically visually unknowable (except for brief moments, as a whirlwind, a burning bush, a hand, etc.); G/d in the *Tanakh* is primarily manifested as voice—and in the original Hebrew ordering of the Bible (*Five Books of Moses*, *Prophets*, *Writ-*

ing), that voice is replaced by that of prophets, and then completely disappears (Miles). The Christian reordering of Bible (*Five Books of Moses*, Writing, Prophets) not only brings God's voice back but predicts in the prophets the coming of Christ. The paradox of the God that Auerbach discussed (9) was at least partially resolved for believers with the freeing of the spirit from the body of the crucified Christ at Pentecost, where Jesus returned and was visible and tangible—but no longer touchable—presumably because holy, but more (Nancy, *Noli*). The stone-moved, sarcophagus-emptied, disappeared-body, risen-Christ, and thus the Christianized-Hebrew God, the returned Jesus, was rendered perceptible, palpable, material, just as the transubstantiation did in the Sacrament. In Jewish esoteric and mystical work, such as midrash or kabbalah, G/d—or at least some spiritual aspects or parts of G/d—were visualized as living Hebrew alphabet; as highly variegated hierarchies of morality that begin in heaven, presented as gates and "lights" (*sefirot*); descending *vessels* of energy and power that break and spill the known universe (see *Midrash*; Metzger and Katz; Vital; Abulafia; Kaplan). Yet this too was understood to be a continuation of the past. As Handelman noted:

> [B]ehind the aspiration to the invisible, nonsensible world was the Greek desire to *see*, a concept of thought in terms of the image (*idea*, from the Greek *eidos, image*). Words were merely conventional signs, as Aristotle said, but thoughts were *likenesses* of things. Hence, when the Christian deity was born in the cradle of the pagan world, He was, inevitably, a *physical* image of God, a mediator and a *substitution*. He mediated the gap between sensible and nonsensible, thought and thing, by becoming both at once. The Rabbinic word became substantialized into flesh. (17)

vii

The Space of Spirit

In this "new" spiritual mimesis, the space between substance and imitation was reduced if not closed. To be like God, *Imitatio Dei*, is central to both Judaism and Christianity (Miles 3). But with the Crucifixion, attention is shifted from invisible logos to tangible pathos—or rather, to the pathos of Logos made flesh—God's son sacrificed on a geometric cross. Here pathos entered mimesis, and Christianity into art. With the promise of eternal life after death, such imitation is a negation of the classical ideal of the rational, perfect body of beauty, as well as the physical prison of the deformed or ugly body (cf. *Plato,*

Republic X.609a–610c; *Philebus*, esp. 66a–b), of which Socrates himself knew he might be an exemplar (*Greater Hippias*, esp. 286c, 304d). Generally, for the majority of Roman people, mimesis and catharsis in their religions and in the "arts forms" (including the weeks-long spectacles of Games) was no doubt more a literal and physical purging of emotion so that a material *spirit* of strength and fortitude, highly prized in ancient Rome, could be reborn, rather than the cultivation of the soul of Platonic contemplation {or, looking ahead, of sublime or tender feeling, as in nineteenth century Romanticism).} But even brute strength had to be given leeway, latitude, scope.

Room for Reality

needle of light
nailed into
the void

viii

Prefigurement

The Crucifixion, at least symbolically, might have been regarded as a puncturing of the grip of the "Old Testament," the "Letter of the Law," language, the "word"—a deflation and destabilization of mimesis as it had been conceptualized and "ruled" by some Platonic ideals. Or it might be a continuation of the Aristotelian notion of catharsis. As Handelman states, "[t]he effects of Aristotle are also evident in Christian theology, so dependent on Greek philosophy, where theology and Bible interpretation became . . . matters of affirming dogma, extracting general statements from texts, and disregarding "the letter" . . . Allegory was a favored method in the Church; it was passed over into literature by Christian poets, such as Dante, Spenser, and Milton (14). At the symbolic level of literature, this was precisely how Erich Auerbach "read" the effect of Christianity: as a realization of events "prefigured" in the Old Testament that were fulfilled—but never changed—by their appropriation. For Auerbach, this "figuration" marked a radical change in the concept and development of realism (as portrayed by his analysis of literary texts from different historical contexts with the classical world), subsumed it, left it unchanged, while also prefiguring the modern. As Hayden White pointed out, "Auerbach holds that history was precisely that mode of existence in which events could be at once fulfillments of earlier events and figurations of later ones" (90). Such a schema provided White with a way of characterizing the peculiar combination of novelty and continuity that distinguished historical from natural existence:

> The linkage between a prefigurative aspect of a given culture (a text, a style, a period) and its fulfilled form is suggested by mere similarity—of their forms, their contents, or the relations obtaining between forms and contents. But . . . the two terms linked by similarity or resemblance must be subjected to a double articulation: the earlier terms must themselves be shown to be fulfillments of even earlier figures and the later terms shown to be prefigurations of even later styles. (White, *Figural* 94)

This simultaneous fulfilment of the past and future in a current event was certainly embedded in *Tanakh* (it was the basis of miracles) but was new and a mystery in physical reality. "[B]oth Aristotelian teleology and Newtonian physical science . . . could conceive of causation as going in one direction only, from a cause to its effect, and from an earlier to a later moment" (95). The events of Christ's life, and the founding of Christianity, made that apparent, physical, real.

The Calvary at Calgary

What if the Calvary
had ridden into Calgary
and taken Jesus
down from the cross.
Imagine the loss.
Jesus would be screaming
through time and space,
uncrucified, unredeeming:
"No, no, you don't understand:
This isn't part of the plan!
You're making a big mistake!
I've got to save the human race.
I've got responsibilities!
I'm to be sacrificed for thee!
This isn't the way it's supposed to be!
Father, why hast thou forsaken me?"

Or if Barabbas had said,
take me instead.
The crowd would stand amazed;
and Jesus would be dazed.
Barabbas would be crucified,
and the disappointed crowd pacified.

Would all of history be changed?
If the US Calvary
had ridden into Calgary?
No great reviling for the death?
no exile, hatred, or prejudice?
The Diaspora would never begin.
The Jews would not have been
exiled from their homes in Spain
in that golden year of His reign.
America might not have been discovered,
and thus the Calvary never been inducted.

And so we start where we began:
the Calvary didn't come rushing in;
history can be prefigured, but not changed

ix

"Medieval Rome"?

Even as the Eastern Roman Empire still continued and was strong, material and spiritual events that had occurred in the disintegrating Western Roman Empire directly affected the Medieval Age. As Auerbach averred,

> I use the term figural to identify the conception of reality in late antiquity and the Christian Middle Ages . . . In this conception, an occurrence on earth signifies not only itself but at the same time another, which it predicts or confirms, without prejudice to the power of its concrete reality here and now. The connection between occurrences is not regarded as primarily a chronological or causal development but as a oneness within the divine plan, of which all occurrences are parts and reflections. (555)

Chronological events could thus be thought of as a prefiguring and fulfilling of other events as two kinds of figuration, which is what Auerbach meant as a novel concept of mimesis that redefined and replaced (but still retained) the classical concept of mimesis: horizontal figuration, the diachronic but interconnected unfolding of events in human history; and vertical figuration, the synchronic correspondence of events between heaven and earth, from which the Great Chain of Being is pulled down.

*Easter, 1492**

I
Midnight

One bell, flat and dull, against the steady night.
We waited in the shadow of the twelve
for the sky to fill with clapping clouds,
for angels to pull a chain of stars,
for a choir of fiery metal tongues to sing out,
to move us, to resurrect us into sound.
What we expected was always wrong.
The bell stopped. No voices followed.
We slept, and fell into profound disquiet.

II
Sunday Morning

Sunday morning was quiet, as before a storm,
except for the suck of wheels like new shoes
dragged, and scoffing, scoffing on the ground,
except for the cacophony of children
rudely playing in the year's first warmth.
We walked to the last station on the block—
passing carts like bees droned and buzzed—
ran from the furious swarm, and hid
in a garden of betrayed flowers
not yet buds, dirt-encrusted hearts,
stumbled over guilt's tangled roots,
our love scrapping its knees against a rock.

III
Sunday Afternoon

Sunday afternoon rose up in a breeze—
Ladybugs hatched, caught in the screens,
flicked their bright red wings
and died; spiders hung themselves
from black creaking trees;
in the stiff yellow grass
the dry crickets shrieked.
There were no rabbits.

But in a thickly sheltered yard
a stone deer stood stock still in heat,
where the scent of pine mixed with winter,
cold dung in muddy debris.
And with the snapping wind
we thought of the sea, as when
the curtain in the room blows out
in a fan, like a glaucous shell on a reef.

The sun stood, stranded on that vacant lot
beneath a glaring dome and golden cross;
a thunder of voices interrupts this hum,
doors slamming softly into space,
a child's shrilling cry, a mother's scream

*1492 was known for the "discovery of America" by Christopher Columbus, with the support of the Queen Isabella of Spain; ironically, that was also the year she expelled from Spain all Muslims and Jews who wouldn't convert, and commissioned the Spanish Inquisition.

x

History Yet to Come

If in Christian history the Crucifixion was an inscription of a new order, so too was art. Whether Auerbach's interpretation of the history of realism in the Western literature was right or not (Melberg thought not [1–2; 42–43]), these two basic themes—the inscribing of the body, and freedom from the body, generally were understood like a spiritual uncial to overlay, penetrate, and permeate science and art, and thus further altered the concept of mimesis as it evolved in the course of Western civilization. Auerbach's study of figuration is a synecdoche of the vast historical periods in question, and a prolepsis of the future (White, *Figural* 11; 91–95)—a historical peeling away of the old "skin" of mimesis to expose a new layer of realism, a mimesis somehow felt to be closer to present "reality" yet still able to retain and contain the old concepts of mimesis in a representation of the past: figuration of the present, and pre-figuration of things yet to come.

*"Llave de España"**

(after 1492)

the shock of sudden memory—
the seized key felt keenly
in the locked-out hand's seams

xi

Continental Light

Auerbach and Melberg took different approaches to the study of mimesis (Auerbach, the changes of style in the representation of realism as figuration in different literary epochs; Melberg, the introduction of temporality into spatial conceptions of imitation as repetition and "difference.") But they both turned to the literature of continental Europe to examine the development of mimesis in the Middle Ages and subsequent history. Another—and by no means only—place the evolution of mimesis became apparent was in the representation of the body (especially as spirit): painting, and the visual arts generally. As Umberto Eco pointed out in *History of Beauty*, out of the so-called Dark Ages came one of the major innovations in the *visual* arts, the technical development and symbolic use of light and color, further helped spiritually redefine the classical concept of beauty as mathematical proportion to include "*claritas*" and "integrity"—"clarity and luminosity" (100). Given the poverty and misery of a vast majority of people, and the wealth and power of a few, the prospect and presence of illuminated light in Christianity and the Catholic Church, perhaps provided some cold comfort and solace for peasant, and lord and lady, alike.

Time's Yoked Yule

In time's yoked yule
when lives are jangled,
snow bells dragged
dry through blown crystal;

when red green days
are rung in dust,
and human thought
now turns to rot:

* "The Key of Spain" was the title of a song which lovingly and longingly remembered and lamented in Ladino (Spanish Hebrew) the expulsion of the Jews from their homes and the country in 1492 (Jagoda).

hands thick with cold
like slabs of clay,
prepare our lives
for another day;

then comes the new year
like a god,
to cheer us on
to faith and sod.

xii

The Spirit of Light

Light (and with it, color) was a material manifestation of the Spirit. Spirit manifested itself in light, which was resurrected daily, drove out darkness, and pervaded everything. And it was necessary for life, usually available, and free. As Eco indicates, the medieval concept of light and beauty was much more than brightly colored baubles. Through budding associations across cultures—the Greek sun-god Apollo, the eye of the Egyptian god, Ra—light in the Christian Middle Ages became associated with divine origin and wisdom as well as victory (K. Levin).

To Ra

The black waves summon
the white tides to whisper.

Arced bow curls up like a snail,
like a pyramid rising in the sea,
spears of light shooting clouds,
piercing amber-colored sand,
plunging sky into ocean,
the sun an ark crawling the water.
Men's hands knew the Aton sky
as shield. Over the shore like a bough

a bird appears, recedes,
reshapes the receiving shore.

The first act of the G/d of the Hebrew Bible was to create light (cf. Jewish mystical texts [e.g., Kaplan, *Sefer ha Bahir*—The *Book of Brightness*; Abulafia, *Sefer ha Zohar—The Book of Splendor*]). Light was not only necessary for humans to see, be warm, grow food, sustain life; it also was thus a new basis of the very conception and operation of mimesis in the visual realm (as opposed to the auditory or cognitive realm, such as in the imitation of sounds, or of the imitation of literary styles practiced since Isocrates [Cicero; Quintilian; cf. Haskins]). In the Middle Ages and early Renaissance, light as mimesis not only touched but could *not* be separated from whatever it touched: melded, it became one with its object. This even included the human soul, hidden in its mortal cave. (One purpose of religion was to get the light of G/d to touch even the most despicable souls, or those unrepentant, infidel, unconverted, and redeem them.)

Hanukiah (Chanukah Menorah)

"Who performed miracles for our ancestors in this season, in the days of old."–trad. Chanukah blessing

Candles: gold capped
and crooked teeth
of an old man
gleaming in the sun.

The eighth night of Hanukkah,
and only five candles.
A miracle!
Four broken candles
turn into eight.

A second miracle:
the lighter, out of fluid,
ignites the messenger.

No miracle last year:
out of Hanukkah candles,
the birthday candles
burned down too fast;
like life they did not last.

But the voice of my son
singing on his knees
shook the shortening flames,

rode to heaven
the darkening *shamash*
that, although lit first,
always seems to burn out last

as it did
on the first day,
in the days
of our ancestors,
and on the last—

old man, gold-capped
and crooked teeth,
gleaming in the sun.

xiii

Internal and External Sources of Light

As the paintings of the Middle Ages and early Renaissance illustrated, light could originate externally or internally, since the soul (of both body and world) was illuminated and infused with divine light (Eco, *Beauty* 100). For Neo-Platonists, *symmetria* (proportion) and *chroma* (color) were both internal to the person or object (soul, emanating from within), and external (Supreme Wisdom, emanating from above upon all matter [Eco, *Beauty* 102]). Thus, again in a horizontal and vertical figuring—a correspondence of upper and lower—the soul was both a manifestation and a mirror of the divinity. In this sense, then, in the neo-Platonic Middle Ages (and not just Christian but Jewish and Muslim sources as well), mimesis seems to become not merely a representation or reflection of an Ideal Form, but also an *identification of material object and supernal substance*: body and soul, heaven and earth, are united in one light.

Like a little god

i come and go in a storm-cloud
on wet wings sleek with light,
and the rain-spray flies.

i rose with sun,
jet in black,
streaking the empyrean;
slept in
soft fields
of milkweed blown
in dusky blue,
flit between the flowers
and gone beyond the moon;
dipped in silence

and tipped the night,
ladled the starry dark;
sipped in coolness
become drunk with stillness,
dumb in the light.

again roots are ripped
out of time, ascending;
land is a broken puzzle
scattered in the sea;
and i am here above the reef.
How much nearer G/d!
heaven opens like a wound;
silver gores the brazen air.
tears caught in gossamer
are loosened by the wind,
as pinions slit the sky,
slip down the white,
now drop in snow
slapping the earth like sleet.

i come and go in a storm-cloud
on sleek wings wet with light,
and the rain-spray flies

xiv

Diffusion of the Soul

In the "Dark Ages," the soul as both external and internal spirit became diffused as light. In this New Testament of mimesis, light wasn't just the body; the body was light. "Light is the common nature found in all bodies, be they celestial or of this world," says Bonaventure; "[l]ight is the substantial form of bodies and, as far as bodies partake of it, they possess being" (Bonaventure, *Commentary on the Four Books of Sentences*, II, 12, 1; II, 13, 2, in Eco, *Beauty* 129). {Historical Note i. Bonaventure could not know that he was describing a life of neon light and existence as digital screen.} In a more religious vein, "Thomas Aquinas," said Eco, "held that light was to be reduced to an active quality that ensues from the substantial form of the sun and that finds in the diaphanous body a preparedness to receive and transmit it" (*Beauty* 129). Therefore, Eco concluded that "[f]or Bonaventure . . . light was fundamentally a metaphysical reality, while for Aquinas it was a physical reality" (*Beauty* 129). In the reference to bodies as *diaphanous* light, "new" concepts not only of soul but even of material body emerged—not as *soma*, a barely living prison house of the soul, but as something to be saved by the unity of extrinsic and intrinsic soul—the body itself, now transfigured, along with its soul, became, like Jesus, sheer, transparent, easily penetrable—a kind of spirit itself (intimate, delicate—an "infinitely gentle, infinitely suffering thing" [Eliot, *Complete Poems* 15]). The transcendent soul that for Platon remembered Forms, that for Aristotle was the non-specific seat of knowledge (*ousia*—essence) and the "animating force" of any living body and its issues, for Christians now included the salvation of the body after life without the old tissues. With the resurrection to divine glory, the embodiment of body and soul in and through Christ became victory over death itself.

Nuclear Winters

"Ring around the Rosey,
pocket full of posey,
ashes, ashes,
we all fall down." [trad. song, Great Plague]

I.I. The Children

If these snows
(now hushed
like medieval music)
were forever;

if these flakes
(now dropping
like frozen ash)
were the fallout

of another plague
(a requiem raised
sung only by wind)
clouds shaken out like rugs

would the children
(now falling
in a circle, sing)
rolling, now buried

inside that dust

xv

Light and/as the Body of the Soul

{Historical Note ii. In his "Hymne in Honour of Beautie," the Elizabethan poet Edmund Spenser would write "soule is forme, and doth the bodie make" (462).} Parallel to the Christian soul and perhaps perfect in its own right, a scholastic concept of "the body of the soul" as a partially material Form, a flesh suffused with moral substance, not only mimicked but was the light of God through Jesus as "the Light of the world" (John 8.12). From the Medieval Age onward, "light" appeared to be both a physical and spiritual medium in the doomed darkness of a world destined for Resurrection. This view of light as a material manifestation of the soul as light was scientifically, philosophically, spiritually, and rhetorically perhaps closer to a Ciceronian view of eloquence, in which style (*verba*) "illuminates" matter (*res*), than any pre-neo-Platonic. {Historical Note iii. Light itself would become a shimmering, transparent substance, a semi-apparent body. Eventually, not only would Newton transform light into particulates, but and later Einstein would transform light into a method for calculating unimaginable speed. Light as a form of energy would be able to measure and cross the universe—but it would never go fast or far enough to reach heaven.} Eco also pointed to the *Paradiso* by Dante as an example where these principles of light appeared to be at work. In the "testament of the new mimesis," light was a physical as well as metaphorical medium for an omnipresent but invisible light of God, temporarily made flesh and visible in his Son. In Christianity, light took on flesh, and was embodied in the physical visible form of Jesus, who was "the truth, the way, the light." So unlike the Greeks and Romans, to be spiritually, allegorically, morally, and even materially more like the Prime Mover, the animating quality, power, principle, and effect of light was closer to God, and so to be "in possession" of more light was to become more like God (but not God-like).}

Nuclear Winters

1.2. The Music

It is so quiet, here, now,
that in the darkness i
can listen to the snow
flake against the outer panes
like aimless stars, can trace
the world in white flurried air . . .

the frost on the windows
drifts, pristine, bare

as the frozen hills
i coasted down
in winter as a child . . .
the sun is silent,
and the earth, and
all those people
shouting, crowding
the bright black skies,
are gone, silent . . .

the voices waver
in the cold, and sing:
the future
is in such clouds . . .

xvi

Light as Allegory

Eco stated that in the Medieval world, everything had a mystical and moral import: "everything in the universe had a supernatural significance" (*Beauty* 121). But Eco also pointed to treatises depicting the relative beauty and/or practical utility of body parts, such as that by Isidore of Seville:

> In our body some things are made for a useful purpose, like the bowels; others both for usefulness and Beauty, like the face, and the feet, and the hands, members of great usefulness and of most comely aspect. Others are made only for ornament, like the nipples of men and the navel in both sexes. Some are made for discretion, such as the genitalia, flowing beards, and broad chests of men, and the delicate gums, small breasts, and wide child-bearing hips of women. (qtd. in Eco, *Beauty* 111)

And just as physical light was of divine origin, so too "artificial" ornamentation could be a material manifestation of heavenly beauty and betrothal power, the pinnacle of which was the Divine Right of Kings. Whether body parts or jewelry, the belief in the relation if not identification of the divinity with the physical world in and through the propagation and beauty of light and color, thus had social and political dimensions as well. In the Catholic Church and highly hierarchical society of the Middle Ages, beauty was not only an incarnation of divine wisdom and power, but a symbol of allegorical and real wealth and social status as well (see Eco, *Beauty* 105–109; 118–123), whose ultimate expression was instantiated in the God-chosen monarch. For the peasants and serfs, the blacksmiths and farmers and stall-keepers and laborers of the lower classes, the servants of dubious status, and non-Christians, light was a slightly different matter (Arabs and Jews who did not accept or partake of Christ's translucent body and blood, and did not participate in the profound work of the newfound Light but instead chose to work diligently in the subtle "darkness" of yeshivas or mosques, pouring over holy "old" and holy texts, increasingly unknown, slaving away by candlelight at discovering hidden esoteric knowledge, only the very outer rim of a shaft of light deigning to reach them in the depths of their unending nights, and through the "popular culture" of this and all time).

Santa on a Late Afternoon

Up on the rooftop sweep sweep
picking the pine straw
out of the gutter
like a long manger
extending into twilight . . .

Working the shingles
like the plastic Clauses
of my youth—father
taking me home
for Xmas Eve

Sparks of snow
like flying white gloves
grabbing onto chimneys,
electric beards eating illuminated lips
like hot spaghetti sauce . . .

The new moon is now
a cold white coin,
a broken lie held
between the tips
of pine tree fingers

Like tall tales
that always grew
beside my house,
from this small height
sunset after-birth

Spreading over housetops
like different colored rooms—
a fat plastic Santa
in a pink parka,
leaping over

Pine trees and straw
covered rooves and hooves
sweeping and clearing, then disappearing yet still visible
in the red redeeming night.

xvii

The Social Politics of Mimesis

In the Middle Ages, beauty in the form of light and color became not only an object of study and the material semi-body of the spirit, but the means of "social mimesis"—not only "deliberative" social "passing" (Sander), but also the "epideictic" presentation of body in which the soul was artificially adorn like an ornament. (Platon would not have been happy—or overjoyed.) Given or worn, flashy, abundant, exorbitant jewels as ornaments were by design and in effect created to "catch the light" and "the eye," just as the rich fancy clothes also bedecked and were becoming on different "parts" of the body (be they "useful," "ornamental," or "discretion"), or the body itself was a changeable, removable, representative set of covers, clothes, ornaments, and jewels of the soul. These "jewels" as ornaments were perhaps "kosmetically" connected to the divine kosmos, but socially were a set of *static* values within classes that Kenneth Burke argued were mimetically but not necessarily morally or even teleologically grounded ("'Dramatistic' View of 'Imitation'"). In theory and in practice, these "objects" of social mimeses in the best Ciceronian sense may have represented if not participated in a larger unity of (now "holy") eloquence in the unfolding "drama" of kosmos; or these "objects" of social mimesis in the worst Socratic sense may have represented mere "rhetorical ornaments," a kind of self-congratulatory flattery unnecessary and superadded to the already overly dramatic pageantry of social life in any age—even at the moment of death.

A Knight Cries Out for His Love Before Expiring in a Field of Mud, Battle of Agincourt

(25 Octobre, 1415)

je vois les jeunes filles, flottant;	i see the young girls, floating;
je cherche ma femm.	i search for my wife.

Est-elle déjà dans le ciel?
Voici un panier de nuages!

Is she already in the sky?
Here is a basket of clouds!

je t'appelle; je t'appelle, mais
je m'appelle seulement moi-même.

i call to you, i call, but
i'm only calling to myself.

je meurs dans mon fer;
je coule dans le sang.

i die in my iron;
i sink in the blood.

Maintenant je n'entends
rien du tout.

Now i don't hear
Anything at all.

Au dessus est le bleu ciel cruel.
O toison!   O silence

Above is the cruel blue sky.
O fleece! O silence

***

In the Middle Ages, as well as later in the Renaissance, rhetoric and poetry also were regarded as the result of social, cultural, and political education, position, play, and power, and thus like jewels objects of great value because of their worth and beauty to be garnered, guarded, given, ostentatiously worn, divvied, meted out, taken away. (So too the "beauty" of art in Italy, for the De Medici family, *par example*). Platon the philosopher, via the plain, "unadorned" mouth of Socrates, *ont regardé le style poétique ou rhétorique* as merely an imitation (of an imitation, both falsehoods)—even as Platon made use of its "magic" (Di Romilly). For Socrates, the flash and sparkle of rhetorical and poetic style were just a form of false flattery, adored, given, adorned, like "a bad habit." {Historical Note iv. During the Renaissance, a great battle between styles, like a war of the stars, would ensue (see Croll; Ong, *Ramus*). What would become known as the "Attic" style, say, of Aristotle, or the following Newtonian science, the "plain style" (Sprat; Halloran and Whitburn) would come to be preferred as the language of science for centuries.} It seemed that for the power of philosophical truth to poke through an "ornamental body" of words —bloated even as Crusades and invasions continued to consume Europe and England—would be "stripped" of its music, its poetry and its rhetoric, just as Platon wanted (*Gorgias* 502c–d).

Warpipes Calling O'er the Hills

Aye, 'tis bagpipes, the bulging bursting clouds,
streams beating down the crags, singing
in the high hollows of the gruff
wet hills, wind running through the reeds

that catch some sheered and dampened wool of sheep
or heavy, bend with mist about the lochs
that bring this curse'd rain to my eyes.

Aye, o'er dark and briny moors,
over Highland *flinging* north white seas,
burley weather beaten lips and hands
play those lung-filled blasted lonely airs,
coming to take me from my home again,
where bairns skirt in blown kilts and fleece,
where hard land echoes shrill drummin' feet.

***

Like poetry and music and other cultural accoutrement and accomplishments, the *ars dictamen*—medieval art of letter writing—otherwise persisted in functioning as the source of social ornamentation and economic grace, rendering the body and its class both "practical" and aesthetically pleasing. Like jewels, letters were material, pleasurable {later faked} signs of education, privilege, and rank for the conduct of secular and ecclesiastical business (perhaps even more so in the Medieval than the Classical Age other than the quirky preference of this or that king or queen), jewels and letters signs recognized and certified, or sanctified and blessed, by Church and State (cf. Anonymous; cf. Richardson and Liggett). This was probably not what Platon or Aristotle had in mind. In rhetoric and literature a titular, superficial "beatification of light" could be found in the subtitles of Thomas Peacham's *the Garden of Eloquence*, wherein the figures of speech are "the most excellent ornaments . . . and lightes . . . by which the singular partes of man's mind, are most aptly expressed"; significantly, the subtitle of the *Garden of Eloquence* continued by noting that examples were *not* drawn only from "the most eloquent Orators, and best approved authors," but "chieflie out of the holie Scriptures" (Title page). These rhetorical objects, be they sparkle or poetic, were used as religious or cultural clothing over the "natural-divine" body-politic of royals, aristocrats, landed gentry, and Church leaders all over Europe, and influenced if not determined aesthetic perception as well as social status. Light was physical; and light was holy. It was worth fighting for.

The Hundreds

Down the aisle under arched trees
In columns toward Land's End and sea
They rode through the Hundreds
On stallions svelte and royal and trim

Knights noble in the heather
Seeking the glorious grail of roses,
Sable fetlocks brushing the dust.

Vikings in the fettered sky,
Waves of Anglo-Saxon hordes
Descending over pitching land
On a steep field sharp with battle
Rocks trampled by the wind
Long blades drawn cross and spark
Under the wings of evening birds
Yellow-eyed and kicking the grass
Dark doves raising shadows in fog

Singing.

xviii

The Democratization of Light

While jewels as practical and aesthetic and holy ornaments were certainly easier to obtain for the relatively few aristocrats who could afford to partake of in a "higher social purpose"—fine clothes and jewels; magical potions, lotions and emoluments; the "best" medical treatments and remedies available/known at any given place and time; time to develop and care for the body (e.g., through sports); and the somewhat rare (and heavy) personal, social, or monarchal cosmetics (e.g., Elizabeth I, who at the time of her death is said to have been wearing one inch of facial [and fatal? lead] makeup). But the ornamentation and bejeweling of the human (and animal) body, a preoccupation with a flattery-knack "*ornatus*" and cosmetic-driven art {later cultural surgery and "passing," like conversion} was eventually more democratized and popular as a means of altering appearance as well as socially admittance and standing [Sander]). Eco pointed to the supposed appreciation of light and color among other classes of everyday medieval life. As he suggested (*Beauty* 118), in the Middle Ages light and color were omnipresent—suffusing not only painting, poetry, jewelry, or fine linens, but also churches, fields, flags, uniforms, sunrises, and sunsets—between which the multitudes of serfs and peasants who labored until dark might catch a glimpse—if they could still look up.

To an Old Irish Woman

(photo-graphos =writing with light)

Red-kettled walls pour the sun
by which a woman wakes;
a roosting clock turns the light
furrowing dawn's face.

Her hands will sew the torn field
and mend the broken thread,
weave along the darning yard,
stitching in the land.

Toward darkness she gathers earth,
and spins before she sleeps,
bending toward the tapering light
from stones that make her keep.

xix

Conflicts of Light

Although not always or necessarily articulated in terms of the concept of mimesis, the artists and thinkers of the Middle Ages and Renaissance were, as Eco points out, aware of the conflicts that arose—not between the grandeur and misery that separated the classes, but rather between the classical concept of Beauty based on geometry, and their qualitative concepts of beauty based on light—particularly the problem of the relationship between mathematical proportion and light (*Beauty* 126). One approach was simply to ignore the discrepancy. Another approach to the problem was to place light within larger cosmological systems—a solution undertaken, according to Eco, by the thirteenth century Scholastic movement (*Beauty*, 125–129). There were many such mystical cosmologies and cabbalistic texts, both Christian and Jewish, during the Middle Ages and the Renaissance; while there were profound differences between Jewish kabbalah and Christian cabbala (see Katz, "Epistemology"), there were remarkable similarities in the treatment of light as an image and source of spirituality (Vickers). Within some of these cosmologies, "light becomes the maximum expression of proportion, since it is identity. And, as identity is proportion *par excellence*, this therefore justifies the undivided Beauty of the Creator as the source of light, given that God, who is supremely simple, is the greatest harmony and proportion unto itself" (Eco, *Beauty* 126).

G/d, Sealing the Book of Life

not who's on it
but the existence of the list
is surprising

***

The Science of Light

A third approach to the contradiction between classical and medieval conceptions of beauty was the growing scientific study of light as a wholly physical phenomenon. In fact, as the Middle Ages transitioned into the Renaissance, the scientific study of light (while not superseding or supplanting divine notions of light as the source of wisdom and beauty) gained ground with the rise of such fields as "geometric optics." {Historical Note v. In the twentieth century, Thomas Kuhn would erroneously note that optics had ceased to provide new research questions and so was eventually considered a "completed" field that had reach the "truth" (*Structure* 79).} Light, and the large natural sources of light—sun, moon, stars—were studied not only as parts of vast astrological systems that determined through their rotation and action the fate of all things, but also as a part of the growing field of cosmology that studied celestial objects in their own right. Kepler's more mystical Pythagorean concept of the mathematical harmony of the spheres led to a more accurate (if less classically "perfect" because more elliptical) initial observations and measurements of the orbit of the planets (see Funkenstein; Holton; Stephenson). The Copernican revolution reversed the position of the earth in relation to the sun, and in doing so shifted the entire relation of humankind to the universe, away from its ethno-terrestrial axis to a heliocentric one, displacing God in the process.

Copernican

When i was small
i would crawl
around under
a buttercup
like an ant
or a man
with an umbrella
wincing in the rain.

It was a world
amid the tufts
of tall grass

my little sun
petals of yellow
light i could touch
and hold and bring
my chin shining.

Now they are gone,
drowned in rain,
crushed or
broken
and blown away,
like flowers withered
in a budding dream:
my lawn is green

xx

{Future Scene. Kenneth Burke, and the "Drama" of "Substance"

Earlier astronomical and other sciences affected the concept of mimesis not only in painting, but also in poetry and rhetoric, as well as of the human body itself. In his essay "A 'Dramatistic' View of 'Imitation'," Kenneth Burke argued that beginning in the Middle Ages, the translation of mimesis as "imitation" no longer completely captured philosophical dimensions of the Aristotle's concept of mimesis; for Burke, the translation was too "scientistic," too representationally "statistical" to have been "particularlistically," and thus morally, accurate. Even more, in such translations, the stress was on the "scenic" element of the pentad. Just as the pun became "the lowest form of humor" —the scenic-driven "spectacle," according to Burke, was the lowest of six parts of tragedy for Aristotle ("Dramatistic View" 6–7). (We get a hint of the implications of an actant as an operant in the scene/agent ratio, in Burke's discussion of "entelechy" [teleology or purpose] in dramatic stereotypes in the Middle Ages, simply based on one of Aristotle's Four Causes, the last of which, Final Cause, finds the *agent* "by nature" teleologically bound up with its own purpose.) "Dramatistically," the problem was a definition of "substance" as it relates to issues of causality and will: mechanical action vs. agency, determinism vs. freewill—discovering *motive* in not only in thought but in matter and motion, specifically that of the human body (cf. Katz and Rivers on "entelechy" vs. "predestination" and emergence in posthumanism). For Burke, *scene* embodied *the* paradox of "substance" (*Grammar* 21–24).}

***

{Terministic Mirror i. In a discussion of his pentadic method, Burke summed up the problem of scientistic dramatism: "In behavioristic metaphysics (behaviorists would call it No Metaphysics) you radically truncate the possibilities of drama by eliminating action, reducing action to sheer motion" (*Grammar of Motives* 10). Therefore, the comprehension of motion with a motive had to connect *act* or *agency*, or *agent* to *purpose*, rather than simply to *scene* or motion; this gave the *agent* freewill. Burke argued that what was missing from the concept of imitation from the Middle Ages was Aristotle's notion of entelechy, "the idea that a given kind of being fully "actualizes" itself by living up to the potentialities natural to its kind" (*Grammar of Motives* 8). Indeed, "'entelechy' is essentially "dramatistic," a term for action in contrast with the great Renaissance inquiries into *motion*" ("Dramatistic View" 7), a hot topic even in philosophy since Zeno's Paradox of movement. The scientific revolution of the seventeenth century and the subsequent rise of mechanization would soon to divide and usurp all notions of mimesis and motion in its technological grip—including free will in rhetoric and poetry. Science was about to disturb the entire relationship between humans and nature.}

Ein Sof

"The Nothing"*
—everywhere—
thrown beyond the edge—

***

{Terministic Mirror ii. For Kenneth Burke, Sir Philip Sidney's defense of poesy first "shewed" an awareness of "how the notion of 'entelechy' gradually ceased to be applied in the Western critics' use of the term 'imitation'" (7). For Aristotle, the potential to be realized in the human being is *rationality* (Burke, "Dramatistic View" 8). However, Burke partially questioned the "moralistically didactic slant" of Sidney's formula of entelechy in his defense of poetry ("Dramatistic View" 9). The problem, for Burke, is the difference between entelechial and scientistic notions of imitation (i.e., causality and motion vs. drama and motive, which we can understand to be one of the primary *motives* of many of Burke's rhetorical formulations. In "A 'Dramatistic' View of 'Imitation'" Kenneth Burke locates the more mechanical version of mimesis as motion in the Middle Ages—a phenomenon that would only become increasingly magnified with the scientific discoveries of the sixteenth century, the Newtonian revolution of the seventeenth, and the rise of industrial societies in the eighteenth and nineteenth centuries. For Burke ("'Dramatistic' View"), the "scientistic"

* One way the Jewish kabbalists referred to G/d: infinite Nothingness (cf. Stevens, "Snowman," *Palm* 54).

conception of imitation that emerged in the Middle Ages resulted in a set of deviations from Aristotle's conception of entelechy: "The didactic emphasis (the Renaissance stress upon 'instruction') as an important element of poetry" (10); the "use of stock characters and stock situations" (11); and instruction that ended in "moral pragmatism" and is even scientistic "to a faulty analysis of poetic excellence" (12). The Everyman plays were over-generalized moral and religious lessons by didactic instruction and example: universal principles and rules, not particularized or dramatized enough, remain at the level of artistically undigested abstractions, rather than Aristotle's vomiting of dangerous emotions through the action of universals artistically particularized and plotted (if just as non-physical). The characters became too rigid socially, morally and emotionally, too much like allegorical categories in morality play based on medieval mimesis. Commenting on literary criticism from the point of view of the mid-twentieth century, Burke said: "[c]ritics would suggest that the writer appealed by purely naturalistic imitation "after several centuries during which 'nature' came progressively to be equated with the processes of technology" ("'Dramatistic' View"13). The stock characters and analytical tools and procedures in morality plays led to a material mimesis based on a myth of rhetorical "naturalism" in poetry and prose.}

The Price of Maple Syrup

Our maple syrup costs too much this year.
We had to get this up from Lancaster!
Becky didn't get her maple syrup here
because Wayne wouldn't get the wood—a fight
over something—I don't know what, a blight.
Some people round here just too hardheaded.

Morning spring, Becky gets up early
in the still darkness, does all the chores—
his *and* hers. She goes out with her silver
spouts and buckets to tap the trees for sap.
Now he doesn't have that much to do.
When he finally cut and brought the wood

to boil the raw sap in the sugarhouse,
don't you know the run of ooze had stopped!
Now they're losing money all year long.
You watch, he'll need that money come tax time.
The King will teach him good—I don't know what.
Some people round here just too hardheaded.

xxi

One cold Christmas morning in 800 CE, Charlamagne, King of the Franks and the first emperor to make it to Rome in 300 years (Clark, *Civilisation* 20), knelt in prayer. The undisputed monarch of the shattered jagged ravaged remains of the Western Roman Empire, Charlamagne was crowned the King of the Holy Roman Empire right there by the Pope (Burton 270). Charlamagne was to defend what was left of Christendom from the rapid spread of Islam after the death of Mohamed in 632 CE, and to defend and begin to what was to become western of civilization in Europe. Charlamagne did so not only through armies of knights, but also through an administrative offensive to educate at least the laity (Clark, *Civilisation* 18). Although "pagan," Greek and "pagan," Platon as *mystic* as well as philosopher had been readily "adapted" and adopted by the Church and translated into Latin (see Plotinos; cf. Figure 1), and was in some form part of what was taught in religious orders scattered like embers throughout the dark ashes of the Middle Ages of Europe (Graham 100). But other antiquities lay in the ruins of ancient Athens and Rome. "[Charlamagne] collected books and had them copied . . . [O]nly three or four antique manuscripts of the Latin authors [were] still in existence: our whole knowledge of ancient literature is due to the collecting and copying that began under Charlamagne" (Clark, *Civilisation* 18). Charlemagne, with the hire and help of librarian and teacher Alcuin of York, continued to gather this new old knowledge as more Latin texts (such as the writings of Julius Caesar, and Tacitus) and ancient Greek texts from the Mediterranean world but in Arabic were to be discovered and copied by monks working in cloisters on the necessary and tedious and complex task of translating Arabic texts, including Aristotle and Hypocrites, from Arabic into Latin.

My Mother, the Prune Pit

For Susan (Sunshine) Schrag

It started when i was seventeen
and in college. My brother wrote: "Come home.
Your mother's sick and dying. Hurry home."

It's been like this every other month
for thirty years. It used to be many
miles; now i have to carriage just to

see her lying in a bed again.
If anybody has perfected being
ill, it's her. For thirty years she's dying.

Every other month i got the note:
"Come home. Mother's sick and dying."
One time it was a prune pit in her throat.

She couldn't eat; she couldn't breathe, she couldn't
talk. She just coughed and coughed. It stayed there, lodged
in her throat for years. And no one knew!

Caught on the epiglottis, it flipped
back and forth between the larynx and
esophagus. She wouldn't inhale, she wouldn't

swallow. It could happen anytime.
Because she was a hypochondriac,
we thought it was psychological.

And then my father writes: "They've performed
an autopsy." An autopsy, Dad?!
"Autopsy, biopsy, what's the difference?"

It's in a jar on her bureau now.
As long as i don't write or read or answer
any of their missives, i'll do just fine

xxii

Over seven centuries, between the fall of the Roman Empire and the Carolingian Empire of Charlemagne, "Europe" trudged in the dark dearth of knowledge and death, lit only by Roman-Christian candles. But to the east and the south, Arabic armies conquered and Arabic scholars scoured sources, libraries, and museums: Damascus, Jerusalem, Alexandria, even northern India, to the East; Morrocco, and southern Spain and France to Poitier in the West. Arabic scholars not only *actively* researched, translated, and preserved *all* extant ancient manuscripts from the Golden Age of Greece, e.g., Aristotle, among many others (Burton 238; Clark, *Civilisation* 18), but scholars like al-Fārābī, Avicenna, and Averroes also contributed to knowledge of them, in this case, to Aristotle (Ezzaahar). Establishing their capital and the "House of Wisdom" in Baghdad, Arabic scholars, under forward-thinking caliphs like Caliph al-Ma'mûn, discovered and translated ancient Greek scrolls, often from Persian or Hindi, into Arabic—the language of "prestige" that replaced Greek in the East (Burton 238). Maligned and attacked by the West as well as religious fellow Muslims, these scholars they made difficult and distant journeys to famous learning centers—to Alexandria in Egypt, to Constantinople (Byzantium after the fall of the Eastern Roman Empire in the 15th century), to India, Sicily, and even to Greece itself.

True Knowledge

here
was
i am

As Islam, increasingly acting as a religious counter in history to science, gained strength, adherents, and spread through the East, Arab scholars persevered, preserved, and (in one way or another) "shared" major texts of classical philosophy and literature with the West— ancient texts that otherwise would have been lost and unknown to the world (Graham 99-102; Clark, *Civilisation* 18-20). These Arabic texts were then carefully copied and translated from Arabic into Latin (sometimes in exquisite Illuminated Manuscripts, which significantly began with the *flaying* of animal skin for writing surface, and ended with the invention of the Carolingian miniscule—the lower-case letters of the Roman alphabet [Graham 40]). Arabic scholars thus infused Western culture with "new," vibrant, and powerful philosophical as well as scientific (if not shared rather than conflicting spiritual) energy, which led to educational reform, and the Renaissance in Europe (even as Arabic scholarship simultaneously for several reasons, including Islamist extremists and the Christian Crusades, "declined" [cf. Burton 277]). Unfortunately, as if fulfilling a beautiful Greek dream that became a lurid nightmare, a hopeful prophecy that became a dark Roman omen, a cultural promise of progress that became a permanent trauma, knowledge of these of classical treatises and their sources was primarily obtained not through diplomatic contact and exchange, but bloody and ugly battles, attacks by Arabic armies that resulted in an Islamic empire larger by half than the Roman Empire at its height (Burton 238), and twelve Crusades launched against the East to take back Jerusalem for Christendom, sack Byzantium, and find the Holy Grail. Armies and Crusades were sent in waves with their long, dull heavy blades out, to cut and slice and slew, iron to iron, "the Other."

Disfigurement: November Brown

roads are longing
in soft grey rain,
wet nights brown

in roughened white days
the tips of twigs purple, harden,

gnawed branches sorely click
in the cold, and stiffly rub.

the decimated trees have spilled their colors—
brandy, burgundy, a deep red wine
that one breathes in like wind, a hand wafting
over crystal ice-clinging glass

outside, swords slash the armor of the sun;
maroon, the blood is running in new runnels:
killing, liquor, and the work of words
warm and full and heavy in the throat

i drink steadily, write all day.

xxiii

As Emperor, Charlemagne traveled widely through his empire, as well as even to the East, to Persia, where he was bedazzled by magical cities of castles of crystal spires and minarets, set against a deep blue brocade and amber like lapis lazuli, of jewels like stars (Graham 42). He visited the House of Wisdom, where they found Persian, Hindi, and Arabic translations of more the ancient Greek texts. But ancient Greek texts also began to emerge in southern Spain through the great "learning centers" of the "Islamist West": Cordoba, Toledo, Seville, Granada (Burton 273). Discoveries of Aristotle's collection of works on logic, the *Organon*, as well as the Rhetoric, translated and preserved and worked on by Arabic scholars (see Graham 37–61; Ezzaher), greatly contributed to those subject in the "liberal arts" as well as the sciences of the time; it inspired Charlemagne, who instituted *the* curriculum, including textbooks written for all church schools in the Carolingian empire, to strengthen and formalize the Trivium as well as the Quadrivium (Burton 270). The Trivium and Quadrivium came to define education in the Middle Ages and Renaissance. Charlemagne's educational reform, based on the growing collection of ancient texts translated into Latin in the monasterial schools, far outlasted his short-lived kingdom—disintegrating as soon as he died in 814 CE (Clark, *Civilisation* 18–20; Burton 271).

dialectic of anxiety

stroke the fidget ring
on the slenderest finger—
no love in it

xxiv

Medieval Education Continued: Genus to Degeneration

In Medieval education, rhetoric was the second part of the Trivium, along with grammar (the first part) and logic (the last part, based on the increasing but not yet and perhaps never complete knowledge of Aristotle's cannon on logic), which together defined the liberal arts; poetry was part of the study of rhetoric, just as it had been for Quintilian. But in several ways, both arts of rhetoric and poetry during the Middle Ages and early Renaissance demonstrated a degradation of genus to type (entelechy to mere *imita* (tion), from Latin but in different languages a copy, a mimicry, a mockery—a caricature seen in the characters of morality plays. On "*material*" grounds, these "types" were quite different from Platon's philosophic (as opposed to poetic) view of "ideal false forms" of imitation and flattery (see Table 4). Even the genus was a far fall from the Ideal Forms. The degeneration of genus to type failed to reflect the passage of time—the break in Aristotle's *Metaphysics* from Ideal to observable nature as the ground (of truth). {Temporal Shift. As Burke suggested in "A 'Dramatistic' View of 'Imitation'," "low canons of rhetoric would spontaneously lead mercenary playwrights into this path since one must appeal through an audience's sense of the 'natural,' and a convention can become 'natural' in this sense" (11). Thus, the "typical" became the "natural," which Burke speculated could be easily tested scientistically against particulars, such as the characteristics of an audience.} The "natural" became the new "bond" between "imitation" and the "universal" as an "idealization" (12)—and not really in Platonic or Aristotelian sense. (Nor was it retained in German Idealism, reviewed in *Plato's Nightmare* in the Transcendental Organ.)

XXV

"Degeneration" of Rhetorical and Poetic Education

The "degeneration" from genus to type also applied to the *genres* of rhetoric and poetry themselves. This "degeneration" reflected what George Kennedy called "technical rhetoric," as well as the "*letteraturizzazione*" of rhetoric (*Classical Rhetoric* 3, 14, 128, 128–29), and Jeffrey Walker the "grammaticalization" of poetry (*Rhetoric and Poetry* x). Walker demonstrated that during the Middle Ages and Renaissance, rhetoric and poetry were increasingly "gramaticalized" (Walker's term), seen and taught not only as separate arts but also and increasingly as highly specialized "technical" arts. Generally, while "[p]oetry certainly survived as a medium of public discourse through the Middle Ages and Renaissance" for Walker (328), rhetoric became associated with practical and civic purposes. Walker further observed: "grammaticalized rhetoric, grammaticalized rhetorical poetics, and grammaticalized poetics . . . have all been disseminated via the traditions of the scholastic literary studies" (Walker 329).

Future Reflections: Late Spring

Daffodils, faces.

Canoes' white drift
slip silver in mist;
blue clouds dip
pigment in water;
sky ripples.
On dark lines of
branches, boughs
bright buds rain
in warm vernal light,
splash maple
leaves full blown

Notes break, gather in
points and clustered:
birdsongs speckle trees
that nothing shall disturb.

These narcissistic woods
dripping wet and warm
with images, impressions
of reflections, colors:
maroon, brown gold orange;
and green grass shimmer
with cool heat; warm
rivers of spring flow toward
summer slowly unfolding
like wild-flowered dreams
on serene forest floors.

xxvi

Roman Ruins Dreaming

Platon the philosopher's seeming belief concerning some of the possible negative effects of writing on Truth, reality, memory, and learning were coming true. But a science of the physical world, not transcendent Ideal Forms, became the solid material basis of any notions of reality and truth, and their verification and variables. The physical world also became the modern basis of mimesis not as imitation but as unaltered content of "facts" transferred through the invisible medium of language to the waiting, receiving, receding *tabula rasa* of the mind. From the remnants and ruins of what was once a vast ancient Empire, whose engineering and architectural feats became an infrastructure of Western Europe. Like Roman legions, logicians, scholars, scientists, along with knights and their squires, still roamed and wandered round the Middle Ages into the coming Renaissance. Then they looked up. But they were no longer looking for Ideal Forms, but now enhanced by scientific developments, heavenward, nevertheless, for material evidence from their dreams. Without necessary ghosts of gods or souls, out of the infinite darkness of the cave, a nuovo history of the cosmos appeared, and spread. Unlike the confused but curious Holy Roman Emperor Charlamagne who could read but not write yet still believed in education, the assorted and besotted knights who came after him with their blazing horses and chariots—like Roman *Equestrians* or so called "Roman knights" in English—would eventually sack Byzantium and other Eastern cultures that they could hardly understand but that had preserved and translated and contributed to knowledge of many saved scrolls of ancient Greece and Rome; from the east back to the west, from the south back to north, these knights with the spoils of war and questionable Platonic souls, slowly rode out of history and disappeared forever, leaving behind them the shaky and crude foundations for the future of Western Civilization (Clark, Civilisation 17-20).

from Die Jüdische Ritter (The Jewish Knight)

(à mam)

Sky so blonde and blue it flaps, a Swedish semaphore,
flag a seagull's wing, the vehicles of their metaphor
parked. Unlocked the gates of memory with this semantic key,
and slowly swung them open into streaming migrant streets.

And out of vast white stretches like a desert full of snow
where even slightly breezes, frozen solid, stalwart flow
on drifts and fits of tiny sun-burnt flakes that hiss and howl
as they whistle down and strike their purple iron orange

Valhalla, giant caves that seem to be miles high and wide
against the shining glimmer of the giant torch outside,
the Foster Cow[*] that licks the smoking salt blocks, primeval earth
reveals in smoother walls of ice the first Norse god, gives birth.

Now imagine grand old Kings of the ancient Norse,
like Thor, *i dag*,[†]*, sitting on his frozen purple throne
deciding every *Torsdag*[‡]* life and death without surcease—
He's used to making such decisions, by necessity.

He takes his seat before them, facing them on the ferry,
presiding over fate, the alienated couples, to Germany—
not fast asleep, but snoring over black Baltic water,
grown callous to the havoc he like weather wreaks.

Never has a ship door, since the plank, been existential,
held open, crossing it, and closed behind, the apprehension
as they follow him, and hold "the red thread"* out and back:
covering the ground of history, the Romans sacked—

but not *Magna Germania.** *Jag älskar dig, jag älskar dig,*[§]
like some ritual she thinks she hears him chant, say
to the gods long gone, or some mystical invocation
to the long dead, or some magical incantation

to make the past of empire and church go away.
He can say it, yes, *Jag älskar dig, Jag älskar dig,*
yet cannot stay: they still have much more history to make,
paralleling future lives, the red thread never break—

Will there be a time when peace descends upon the earth . . .
a softer eider down dropping round its shivering girth,
and cover human action, its reign on everything to cease,
and quiet human agony that once again will freeze—

when *den Lille Harvfrue*, the Little Mermaid (*lille harvfruen*),
nude coiled atop some rocks in the harbor of *København*,[¶]

---

* Norse myth, *Audumbla*
† Se. "today"
‡ Se. Thorsday, "Thursday"
§ Lat. "Greater Germany"; Se: "I love you"
¶ Da. Københan, "Copenhagen"

will turn her body, eyes, back to the unreturning sea-swoon,
won't kill herself for love on land, the waves up-frothing moon—

when the woman at the harbor, *Kvinna vid havet*"[*]
who stands aloft on *Sailor Tower, Sjömanstornet*[†]
overlooking *Göteborg*, Sverige's[‡] sea,
waiting, watching for all the war dead and her lost marines—

when all the matriarchs and patriarchs, and all the prophets,
and all the Greek and Roman gods and demigods and despots
shall become one family, buried deeply in their furrows,
the knights from every war return, and don their old plaid robes—

when *die Jüdische Ritter* (the Jewish Knight), like some messiah,
shall return from future wars for which his soul was hired,
oder er allien,[§] hang up his suit of armor and his sword,
verlasse sein Zuhause nicht mehr[¶]—leaving home no more—

when required hate and unrequited love shall perish,
and all the dead *soldater*[**] rise, their bodies stripped of spirits
and all who suffered, lived and loved, fellow militants,
will finally be born, anew, exhale their skeletons—

—Platon

20 2 8 8 2
Ca
Calcium
40.078

* Se. "Woman by the Sea"
† Se. "The Sailors' Tower"
‡ Se. "Gothenburg," "Sweden's"
§ Ger. "or he alone"
¶ Ger. "leave his home no more"
** Se. "soldiers," "troops"

Part Three
Representivity and the Revolting Body
(Renaissance/Enlightenment)

[W]hen we see someone, no matter whom, experiencing pleasures—and I think this is true especially of the greatest pleasures—we detect in them an element either of the ridiculous or of extreme ugliness, so that we ourselves feel ashamed, and do our best to cover it up and hide it away, and we leave that sort of thing to the hours of darkness, feeling that it should not be exposed to the light of day. –Plato, *Philebus* 66a (Hackforth)

8 Representivity Organ

Deformed, grotesque, defective; hideous, repulsive, monstrous; ugly as sin, vile, repugnant; loathsome, horrible, disgusting; ghastly, gruesome, grisly; sickly, infected, diseased; bloodsucking, parasitic, sycophant; animal, brutish, subhuman; misfit, outcast, pariah; leper, humpbacked, Frankenstein; ugly-duckling, eye sore, obese; fat, ill-formed, unseeming; unsightly, uncomely, not fit to be seen; unbecoming, unattractive, homely; twisted, perverted, degenerate; schizoid, psychotic, insane; scarred, lame, club-footed; crippled, handicapped, disabled; illegal, monster, animal; low-life, vermin, subhuman; disembodied, re-embodied, artificial; foreign, alien, Other. Histories of "ugliness" was, well, (mostly) an ugly ones, as long and complicated as and the inverse histories of ideal beauty.

1. Arithmatic Beauty and Ugliness

3.1.0

Out of the Dark Ages: Disfigurement and the Decimal System

It was a monstrous deformation of human history that after the fall of the Western Roman Empire, Persian, Hindu, and Arabic mathematicians, scientists, and astronomers (as well as Arabic researchers, scholars, and translators of extant Greek philosophy and literary texts) received scant praise and little credit for "saving" Western Civilization (cf. Graham; Winter 59–90). It was a serious defect in human knowledge that ugly prejudices against non-Romans remained (except for the Greeks, who were also elites) and considered *barbarus* (βάρβαρος, barbarians [Gibbon I: 45]), even as the Roman Empire itself lay in the dirt of ruin. (This was a prejudice that had been continued and even amplified by the early Christian Church—constantly in a tug of war with powerful Italian city-states around it—*Firenze* and *Genova* and *Milano* and *Venezia*—which soon would become the inaugural seats of the Italian Renaissance, and those seats the seeds not only of a new [Platonic] era in Italy—Florence, Genoa, Milan, Venice—but also the rediscovery of classical art, literature, philosophy, rhetoric, mathematics, and science; and a (re)birth of a more modern Western Civilization with its roots in both Platon and Christianity, but eventually in the increasingly empirical and rational context of Newtonian science and then the Enlightenment. (The Catholic Church also was constantly at war with other religions, especially Islam—both seeking to increase believers and converts and thereby increase their earthly domain and power; and these tensions too played a role in the restraints or spread of the Renaissance and modern science.) It was a severe disability of human imagination that most of the Earth's population never acknowledged or even knew the vital role Eastern science, and in particular the Hindu-Arabic numerals and decimal system, and the invention of the zero, which in the West all eventually replace the clumsy Roman numerals, still widely in use in post-Roman and Medieval Europe, and upon which until then even business arithmetic had been based—arithmetically awkward, difficult, limiting. The adoption of the Hindu-Arabic numerals, the decimal system, and the invention of the zero, facilitated the reconstitution of mathematics, science, and human knowledge in the West (Burton 273, 279–280).

Geometry of the Mind

mathematics—
writing
metaphysics

3.1.1

Great Chains of Being: Unseen Levels of Dialectics Reborn

Platon had loved them so much so that in later (or perhaps spurious treatises that nevertheless bear his thought and style) he had made geometry and arithmetic the very foundation of his philosophy of Ideal Forms, and beyond "rational discourse" the ultimate method for the human mind (*Epinomis* 977c; *Republic* VII.524c–527b; in another translation of "rational discourse," Crane pointed out that in Lamb's translation of the Greek, "there is a curious play here on the two meanings of λόγος—"reckoning," and "description," like the difference between the English meanings of "tale" or "account" [*Epinomis* 977c]). If not actually behold ("describe" or "account for") the Forms, the human mind might at least apprehend something of the mathematical nature of them by being able to calculate shapes and measure relations, and to express them in nonfigurative non-verbal languages—the languages of mathematics (cf. *Republic* VI. 511b–c). Beyond dialectic in speaking ("rational discourse"), Platon and his school had considered geometry a necessary preparatory discipline for the development of different of levels of thought in relation to the pursuit of Truth (see Tables 6 and 7). So enamored of shapes and numbers, Platon apparently had made geometry a prerequisite for entering his Academy (Burton 136; cf. *Republic* VII.526c). Platon had made ample reference to mathematics and geometry in his treatises (e.g., *Republic* VII; *Parmenides*; *Epinomis*, usually attributed to Platon). Yet coming out of the Dark Age in the West, geometry and mathematics would be central to the further development of philosophical thought and practical education during the Renaissance, Newtonian Revolution, and the Enlightenment. Geometry and mathematics and astronomy (*Republic* VII) were essential to understanding how dialectic operated in realms of ever purer knowledge. For Platon—"calculation," "arithmetic," "reckoning"—and associated subjects based on geometry—had been near "sacred": numbers as well as the ability to wield appeared not only necessary but divinely inspired and ordained; and geometry and mathematics had revealed themselves as commensurable and indispensable at every level of understanding (*Republic* VII. 526c; *Laws* VII.8171e).

Table 6. Divisions of Knowledge, including Geometry, Obtained by Dialectic in Hierarchy. Credit: Steven B. Katz, 2024.

First division	=	Science (Intellection)
Second division	=	Understanding (Intellection)
Third division	=	Belief (Opinion)

Or arrayed another way, based on Socrates' own analogic reasoning (*Republic* VII.534b):

Table 7. A Geometry of Knowledge: Divisions of a Hierarchy of Knowledge in Opposition. Credit: Steven B. Katz, 2024.

Dialectic	*Essence*	vs.	Dialectic	*Generation*
First Division	Science (Intellection)	vs.	Third Division	Belief (Opinion)
Second Division	Understanding (Intellection)	vs.	Fourth Division	Image (Opinion)

3.1.2

From Ancient Eastern Science to the Renaissance

Beginning approximately 3500 BCE, Babylonia, Assyria, and Egypt, to say nothing of India and China, each had developed a rich scientific history in mathematics, astronomy, chemistry, and medicine that pre-dated, then overlapped, and even overtaken the ancient Greeks (Winter 5–6; 10-15). In the thousand years between the fall of the Western and of the Eastern Roman Empires (mid-fifth century BCE to mid-fifteenth century CE), Persian, Hindu, and Arabic mathematicians and astronomers not only had been diligently researched, pursued, translated ancient Greek texts, and developed new knowledge and applications based on them (e.g., in medicine, algebra, trigonometry, astronomy). The earliest known Hindu treatise on the decimal system was a small compilation by Al-Khowârizm^ probably entitled *Hisâb al-Jabr w'al Muqâbalah, The Book of Addition and Subtraction to the Hindu Calculations.* {Etymological Aside. The term "algebra" was "a European corruption" of the Arabic *al-jabr* in that title; this book was only re-discovered in 1857, in a Latin translation (Burton 238-39).} Not only did Persian, Hindu, and Arabic mathematicians and astronomers develop the Hindu-Arabic numerals, the decimal system, and the zero, but also advances in algebra based upon them. The Greeks too had established a firm and extensive ground in the fields of geometry, mathematics, algebra, and even trigonometry (from Greek τρίγωνο [*trígono*], "triangle") upon which astronomy had been based, e.g. Ptolemy, in the *Almagest*, brought order to the visible heavens, making naval navigation as well as informed star gazing possible (Burton 273).

Measuring the Unhinged Stars

points, angles, vertices
invisible outlines
shards flung out into space

3.1.3

The Decline and Fall of Roman Numerals in the Renaissance

For the expression of geometric shape and mathematical relations, Platon like his predecessors and contemporaries, had used the eastern Greek (Ionian) alphabetic script, which also read as numerals (Burton 18); they had been better than Greek numbers they had replaced, the Roman numerals (derived from the western Pelasgian or Chalcidian Greek script [Firmage 15]), but also were awkward, and exhausted during the long dark centuries mired in misery and for most people the grim business of daily living in western Medieval Europe. The Roman *letters* took hold and became a *major* world alphabet used by many languages. The Roman *numerals*, on the other (raised-arm-saluting) hand had tilted, tumbled, fallen—monuments to a once great and massive and powerful empire. The columns and crosses had not diminished, but like Latin itself but had "stood up" in Illuminated Manuscripts, as well as in printed post-Gutenberg texts, before the Roman numerals lost their cache and elite status during the later Medieval period (cf. Firmage 121). Poles and trees would do, but columns and crosses were still best for formal punishment and executions by flaying, crucifixion, burning, and other exotic forms of torture that were to come. {Vision. Throughout human history, the Roman numerals remained in use for official or specialized or quaint-antique purposes, such as, respectively, government buildings, copyright dates on movies, clock faces (cf. Firmage 79, 122, 236).}

In Our Lives' Times

A garden of stars
in the backyard of
the Milky Way

kosmos

a mere solar eclipse
like a perennial flower
brightly budding bringing
earth-bound lunar ground
to look up from our fighting—
for just a moment, conjunction
for just a moment, alignment—
not past the moon and sun
but a luminous blinding

eternity

a singular event for us
that forever flower passing
through our short lives' times

3.1.4

The Drip of Knowledge and the Revival of the West

There had been disputes (of course) about whether Byzantine scientists and scholars, or Arabic ones, had been the first to recover and translate ancient Greek texts of astronomy, mathematics, and medicine, as well as philosophy, history, literature during the Islamic Golden Age (eighth through fourteenth centuries), e.g., Ptolemy, Euclid, Hippocrates, Aristotle, Herodotus, and the anonymous *Gilgamesh* (cf. Graham; Harris, esp. 75-77). However it happened, "the transfer" of Hellenic texts and knowledge had passed to the West—whether by Crusades or through diplomacy; whether by the generosity of Syrian scientists ensconced in libraries and palaces in Constantinople/Byzantium, or by the ransacking of them; whether willingly shared by Persian astronomers in the famous House of Wisdom established in Baghdad, or stolen from Arab "centers of learning" scattered throughout the Islamic "states"; whether taken with the recapturing of some of what had become the "Islamist West" (territory and cities captured from the Holy Roman Empire by Muslim forces taken back, beginning with Toledo, as well as Cordoba and Grenada in Spain; and Padua and Sicily on and off the Italian peninsula, and southern France all the way to Poitiers [Burton 274].) Many Arabic and Persian mathematicians and scientists had been sanctioned and supported by enlightened Caliphs and/or moved in intellectual circles that included writers and philosophers as well as scientists and mathematicians (including the Persian astronomer Omar Khayyam, who was later better known for his poetry). But in the declining days of the House of Wisdom, which finally had been sacked by the Mongol invasion of Baghdad, and the destruction of lesser observatories by Islamic religious fanatics, a few Persian and Arabic scholars had been forced to flee and labor in smaller gatherings in comparative isolation, or to labor alone in relative obscurity without widespread succor or support (Burton 251).

the posture of poverty

bent shape of a scholar
unravelling scrolls—
new forms rising

3.1.5

Platon in the Renaissance

The idealization of Platonic mathematics as well as philosophy, which like so many classical Greek ideals was alive in the Islamic Golden Age but lay dormant in the Medieval Europe, was revived in the Renaissance, manifesting itself in new geometry, trigonometry, and algebra that made the Renaissance as well as Newtonian science and the Enlightenment possible. The bulk of Platon's oeuvre had outlived the absorption of Greece by Rome, first as a source of philosophy and culture in the Roman Republic where knowledgeable philosophers and orators as well as philhellenes (φιλέλληνες)—lovers of everything Greece—had admired and even worshipped him. Platon's lifetime of thinking and writing had survived the headlong sack of the Western Roman Empire of ancient Hellenica, as well as the heady collapse —over a thousand years later—of the Eastern Roman Empire. (Constantinople, then Byzantium, had been sieged, sacked, or burned many times, starting with Julius Caesar and ending [on May 29, 1453].) Platon's labors in Athens also had withstood the physical and spiritual seize of the Holy Roman Empire, in which Platon, the pagan, was translated directly from Greek to Latin, had undergone a kind of post-transubstantiation, and been adopted by the early Christian church as a fellow mystic who seemed to believe in heaven and hell, the doctrine of eternal soul, and even reincarnation as a precursor to "the Resurrection" (of Jesus. Cf. Fraser on the many gods, including Egyptian ones, that predated Platon). Platon's work had flourished even in the *Islamic* Golden Age, where he had been not only well known, but along with other more newly "found" Greek texts in philosophy, geometry, science, and medicine that were translated into Arabic, had a major influence on Muslim medicine, science, and culture (Graham).

***

Being in two places and states of being at once, Platon also managed to subsist during the long dark superstitious days of the Medieval millennium in the West, where like a small flickering candle on a monk's writing table in a Benedictine scriptorium, he outlasted the dark ink-blotted days of "Western Europe," during which his Greek treatises were copied and illuminated by the colors of various languages in which his work had been translated (Latin, Arabic, Hebrew). Sleeping, dreaming, Platon had endured and he suddenly found himself in the center of the Renaissance with his "essential" philosophical ideas relatively intact (as far as anyone could know); here he made his debut anew like a spirit brightening at the sight of the specters of his old fellow philosophers and friends, including his own student Aristotle, whose *Organon*, for instance, had been "rediscovered" by the Arabs (Burton 272; Ezzaher; cf. Harris, who argued that this and other treatises of Aristotle's already had been found and existed in Constantinople and then Byzantium in the Eastern Roman Empire). The textbook *Arithmetica*, too, that had been written by the soon imprisoned and condemned Boethius (475–524). This textbook had provided a thousand-year bridge from ancient Greek maths and sciences—over the "barren" Roman contribution to these (Burton 235; 284)—to the Quadrivium (however incomplete) of the Middle Ages, and thus to the partial transport of what remained of the shattered, scattered, erratic Western Roman-and Carolingian Empire of Medieval Europe, and thus to the Renaissance (*Boethian Number Theory*; Burton 236]).

Cell

out of remote prisons
arrested darkness
forgotten light wells

3.1.6

Rebirth of Geometry, Mathematics, and the Soul of Number

For Platon, numbers and geometric shapes had appeared not only to be abstract representations that already *began with ideas* that didn't require verbal language, opinions, or argument—even logical or "ordinary" dialectic, but were already metaphysical, even "divine" entities. It was through the abstracted theorems and measured shapes of geometry, its theorems from equations and examples, and even more, the increasingly disembodied and transcendental nature of calculations, where the repugnant material body and world might have been shed, and the soul-mind finally set free to soar up to rarer realms of thought in the philosophical search for Truth (Plato, *Timaeus* 52c; *Theaetetus* 184d–186; cf. *Republic* VI.b–c).

barbarous body
beta-soul
rising from it

It had seemed that geometry and mathematics not only might have been the geometric foundations of the Ideal Forms (Toulmin and Goodfield), but perhaps also the Ideal Forms themselves. However, for Platon geometric forms and numbers were *not* the Ideal Forms (*Timaeus*, esp. 44d–52d–53c; 55e–56c). Rather, the purpose of the study of geometry and mathematics had been to further discipline the mind and direct the soul of the dedicated student of philosopher to look up (*Republic* VII.7.525b–VII.527b; VII.535d). In fact, in the *Republic* (VII.535d) Platon states that he preferred—required—students who wouldn't be "lame" χωλόν—*cholón* in their studies of geometry, with its various translations of this word as possessing a "limp" (Crane) or being "maimed" (VII.535.d–e, in Hamilton and Cairns). (More explicit or more subtle "*psyche*-logical" overtones of physical impairment were found not only in Book V and VII of the *Republic*—especially when dealing with the harm of the body on the soul—but throughout his treatises (cf. *Timeous*; *Eponymous*; *Laws*.) As Platon had discussed in the *Republic*, mathematics and geometry were "provocative of thought" (*Republic* VII.524d); they "draw the mind to the apprehension of essences" (VII.524e), which "rise out of the region of generation and lay hold on essence" (VII.525b) and "appear to lead to the apprehension of truth" (VII.525b), "facilitating the conversion of the soul itself from the world of generation to essence and truth" (VII.525d) by "strongly direct[ing] the soul upward and compel[ing] it to discourse about pure numbers" (VII.525e), "units which can only be conceived by thought" (VII.526a), and that "compel . . . the soul to employ pure thought with a view to truth itself" (VII.526b). In Florence, architect Filippo Brunelleschi, inventor Leonardo DaVinci, painters

Michealangelo and Botticelli and Raphael, as well astronomer Galileo, and even Newton in England, in different guises of epistemology, empirically, and aesthetically, sought out the Ideal Forms among the domes of shapes, colors, textures, stars.

Geometry of Light

thought streaking
through the sky—
numbers trailing

3.1.7

Disembodied Numbers in Eastern and Western Renaissances

In the Persian and Arabic "Renaissance" (cf. Graham 41), scholars not only had copied and/or translated Greek texts, but had extended, discovered, and created new knowledge—not only the decimal numbering system and the Hindu *zero* that the Arabs had embraced long before the West, but the creation of new algebraic theorems from equations and examples. {Red Shift. Zero: a mathematization of mystical nothingness? Like Talmudic argument in all branches of Judaism, all prior conclusions were still apparent, or from twentieth century *erasure* in Deconstruction whereby the erased was crossed out but still visible, the "magical" zero stood in for numbers that had been, or would be, but were not yet present. In all these cases, the erased—the "disembodied" prior arguments—were *necessary* for the absent numerical entity to exist or continue its (non)existence, making even higher forms of maths possible (trigonometry, algebra, calculus, cybernetics, robotics, cloning, quantum computing, augmenting reality, artificial intelligencing, virtualizing reality, androidics, and more [see Thompson, *Androids*; *Machine Law*; Herrick; Katz, "Revisiting Ethics"]). In a sense, the zero was predicated on and predicted the state of numerical *being* to come, where the human body itself became a placeholder for the consciousness that had been there but was extracted from it (Hayles, *Posthuman*; cf. Baudrillard, *Ecstasy*)— just as the body was the "placeholder" for the Platonic soul until the moment of death (*Gorgias* 523e-525d). Zeros as impoverished, damaged souls revolutionized not only mathematics and science, but every sphere human of life (and death) in what would become the future of human civilization (see Table 8).

Table 8. Binary (Poem).

00110111	00110111		00110001	00110000	00110101		00110001	00110000	00111001		00110001	00110000
00110001		00110001	00110001	00110101		00110001	00110000	00110101		00110001	00110001	
00110101		00110011	00110010		00110001	00110000	00110101		00110001	00110001		
00110101		00110001	00110000		00110010	00110010	00110110		00110001	00110010		
00111000		00110001	00110110	00110110		00110010	00110010	00110110		00110001	00110010	
00111000		00110001	00110110	00110110		00110010	00110010	00110110		00110001	00110010	
00111000		00110001	00110110	00110110		00110001	00110001	00110001		00110001	00110001	
00110111		00110001	00110001	00110100		00110011	00110010		00110001	00110001		
00111001		00110001	00110001	00110001		00110001	00110000		00110011	00110010		00110011
00110010		00110011	00110010		00110011	00110010		00110011	00110010		00110011	
00110010		00110011	00110010		00110011	00110010		00110011	00110010		00110011	
00110010		00110011	00110010		00110011	00110010		00110001	00110001	00110100		00110001
00110000	00111000		00110001	00110000	00110000		00110011	00110010		00110001	00110001	
00110001		00110001	00110000	00110010		00110011	00110010		00110001	00110001		
00110101		00110001	00110000	00110101		00110001	00110000		00110001	00110000		
00111001		00110001	00110001	00110111		00110001	00110000	00111000		00111001		
00110111		00111001	00111001		00110001	00110001	00110100		00111001	00110111		00110100
00110110		00110011	00110010		00110001	00110001	00110010		00110001	00110000		00110001
00110000	00111000		00110001	00110000	00110001		00111001	00110111		00110001	00110001	
00110101		00110001	00110000	00110001		00110011	00110010		00110001	00110001		
00110100		00110001	00110000	00110001		00110001	00110001	00110101		00110001		
00110000		00110001	00110001	00110110		00110001	00110001	00110001		00110001	00110001	
00110100		00110001	00110000	00110001		00110001	00110000		00110011	00110010		00110011
00110010		00110011	00110010		00110011	00110010		00110011	00110010		00110011	
00110010		00110011	00110010		00110011	00110010		00110011	00110010		00110011	
00110010		00110011	00110010		00110011	00110010		00111001	00111000		00110001	00110001
00110001		00110001	00110000	00110000		00110001	00110010	00110001		00110001		
00110000		00110011	00110010		00110011	00110010		00110011	00110010		00110011	
00110010		00110011	00110010		00110011	00110010		00110011	00110010		00110011	
00110010		00110011	00110010		00110011	00110010		00110011	00110010		00110011	
00110010		00110001	00110001	00110110		00110001	00110001	00110001		00110001		
00110000		00110011	00110010		00110011	00110010		00110011	00110010		00110011	
00110010		00110011	00110010		00110011	00110010		00110011	00110010		00110011	
00110010		00110011	00110010		00110011	00110010		00110011	00110010		00110011	
00110010		00110001	00110001	00110100		00110001	00110000	00110100		00110001	00110000	
00110001		00110001	00110001	00110110		00110010	00110000	00110110		00110001	00111001	
00110001		00110001	00110001	00110100		00110001	00110000	00110101		00110001		
00110000		00111001	00111001		00111001	00110111		00110001	00110000	00111000		00110011
00110010		00111001	00111000		00110001	00110001	00110001		00110001	00110001		
00110000		00110001	00110000	00110001		00110100	00110110					

* Translation of binary form and grammar rendered as closely as possible.

Mimesis is

        our wo

        rld of si

mulacra p

lease res

tore

        body

        to

        rhetori

cal bone}

3.1.8

Divine Numbers, Occult Mysticism, Ethereal Dreams in the Renaissance

As in all eras of Western Civilization, Platon's dream of disembodiment had been a major factor in his philosophy, and a fundamental theme of his scheme that was continued in the Renaissance, Baroque, Scientific, and Enlightenment Ages {as well as the Modern, Cybernetic, Space, Post-Modern, Information, Post-Human, and Post Anthropocene Ages}. No less so with the highly abstract ideas and spatialized visual forms of geometry with parameters that could be calculated and measured (see Plato, *Meno*; on the Greek penchant for the visual/spatial over Hebrew aural/oral perception and phenomena, see Boman; Buber, *Judaism*; Katz, "Letters as Essence").

Despite the mythological stories, the ancient Greeks generally had not believed that their alphabets and numbers were sacred (Firmage 74; cf. Barry). But somewhat like the mysticism of the Hebrew numbers and letters as supernal vessels (see Monk; Vital; Katz, "Ancient and Renaissance"), Platon seemed to have entertained the possibility that the Greek gods had created the basic physical elements (earth, air, fire, water) "by form and number" (*Timaeus 53b–65b*; *Epinomis* 978c–979d). {Temporal Divergence. Just as the Christian Boethius (*Consolations*) returned to a (neo) Platonic philosophy, the mysticism of both the Hebrews and the Platonists in the Renaissance were reconstituted in Christian cabbala, and thus misconstrued and misunderstood by later scholars (Vickers), just as Judaism within what would be called the Judeo-Christian heritage throughout subsequent history was recast in new, hegemonic, and fundamentally inappropriate Christian terms (cf. Auerbach; Burkett; Katz, "Epistemology of the Kabbalah." {And as late as the twentieth century both Plato and Aristotle (as well as the Stoics) were regarded as progenitors of Christianity or pre-Christians, if not Christians themselves! (e.g., cf. Hamilton and Cairns xxv, xv, 421, 526, 845, 1151, 1226; Kaufman, *Meditations* v–ix).}

3.1.9

Mathematics as "Pure" Reasoning in the Renaissance and Beyond

Over the door of his Academy, Platon had written: "Let no one ignorant of geometry enter here" (Burton 136). Insofar as geometry and mathematics taught pure reasoning, Platon and his Academy had held that the study of advanced forms of geometry and mathematics—"the contemplation of the nature of number" (not material nature *by* number)—was the philosophy of teaching the highest level of abstract thinking necessary to approach the eternal Forms (*Republic* VII.525c–d). In the clearest statement of the nature of mathematics as a higher dialectic that *began* in basic dialectic (analysis, division, classification, definition, causal relations) and pursued in verbal dialogue and analytical logic (*Phaedrus* 271a–b), Platon distinguished the importance of geometry as the basis of "true" dialectical thinking and its ultimate metaphysical {or deconstructive} goal (see Table 6):

> [T]hat which Reason itself lays hold of by the power of dialectic, treating its assumptions not as absolute beginnings but literally as hypotheses, underpinnings, footings and springboards . . . to enable it to rise to that which requires no assumption and is the starting point of all, and after attaining to that again taking hold of the first dependences from it, so to procced downward to the conclusion, making no use whatever of any object of sense but only of pure ideas moving on through ideas to ideas and ending with ideas. (Plato, *Republic* VI.511b–c)

Climbing Dialectical Stairs

scaling hypotheses
theorems and numbers
stacked up like ladders—

kicked over, knocked out
and away from under the climber
who now drops down

without further use of
intellectual pulley and rope
the other, farther side

hidden, behind the stars

In the Renaissance, not only Platon's philosophy of Ideal Forms but also the relationship between metaphysical and physical reality embodied in Platon's stepped doctrine of higher and lower dialectics and being perhaps also manifested themselves in the powerful Great Chain of Being (cf. Boethius, *Consolations*, which attempted to find justification in neo-Platonic pagan philosophy for the dour life of the peasants as well as the Divine Right of Kings, girded in brutally unequal social and economic classes, and fixed in a rigid and now Christian political system, until the rise of the individual in the Enlightenment).

3.1.10

Mathematics as "Metaphysical Dialectic"

The Platonic belief that geometry and mathematics were a "metaphysical dialectics" led in the Renaissance and after to an increasing "disembodiment" of style. For Platon, geometrical and mathematical "calculations" already in a sense had been disembodied forms of discourse, totally abstract and yet precise, through which to explore and convey something near essence, and converse *without* words about the nature and relationships of imperceptible properties and ratios of metaphysical reality in which Ideal Forms might also exist—a hollowed out linguistic form or "conduit" (Locke, *Essay* 299-300); in science and rhetoric, that became known as a one-to-one correspondence many in human history had wished for and never attained (cf. Sprat 113; Halloran and Whitburn). Chained to a much lower link on the great ladder of dialectical being, rhetoricians also had been compared to geometers by Aristotle in relation to the defect of the former who were always in need of style (cf. *Rhetoric* 1404a5–10; 1404a10). Thus, as a "language" about nonmaterial, metaphysical reality, for Platon, geometry and mathematics *had* to be disembodied. This commitment to purity allowed the philosopher-scientist to "[s]oar . . .among eternal images of thought" (Burton 136).

3.1.11

Rhetoric and Poetry as Metaphysical Tobacco

The idealizations of Platonic mathematics, which had been alive in the Islamic Renaissance but lay dormant in the Medieval Europe, was revived like so many classical Greek ideals in the Renaissance, manifesting itself in new geometry, trigonometry, astronomy, algebra, and calculus, and that later made Newtonian science and the Enlightenment possible. Although geometric and number shapes had not been in themselves Ideal Forms (Plato, *Republic* VII.524d–527b; cf. Toulmin and Goodfield), for Platon neither had they been merely "representations" of thought-images (*eidos*-"ideas") in the mind (*nou*), nor mere imitations of those images in language (*mimisi*) (see *Timaeus* 51d–52c). Rather, for Platon, numbers and geometric shapes were "manifestations" of eternal ideas (perhaps even more so the powerful, and less physical, than the ideal form of Beauty that could appear that the philosopher who saw through the vulgar physical world might behold [*Phaedrus* 250d, 251f]). Beauty, as a demi-ideal, had burned off the dross of coarser tobacco, leaving behind seedy rhetoric and the pleasurable smoke of poetry, to reveal a shapely, well-worn, comfortable, but still highly imperfect earthly pipe. For Platon, geometry, mathematics, and astronomy had been necessary steps in the highest forms of *philosophy*, helping the mind ascend the world of appearances to the world of abstract eternal truths that would have been necessary to understand the Ideal Forms, insofar as that was humanly possible (cf. *Republic*, Bk VII, on the educational curriculum of the Philosopher-King; *Timaeus*, on the mathematical ordering of the cosmos; *Philebus*, on beauty and harmony; *Epinomis* on knowledge of stars and numbers as the highest form of wisdom). In a sense, then (and perhaps only, literally, in a *sense*), geometry, mathematics, and astronomy as *metaphysical* forms of "rhetoric" and "poetic" had been a way thinking, speaking, and writing—without the need for any other language—about an otherwise ineffable, incorporeal world: "Nature is written in mathematical language" (Burton 345). (This belief in mathematics as a close model of reality if not its numerical foundation itself, was revived in the Renaissance—as it had been in Islam in a different, algebraic form for a different purpose a thousand years before [Graham]; it made Newton's scientific revolution possible as well.)

***

This preference for the seeming "purity" and "clarity" if not the sacredness of mathematics, untethered from the physical world to describe it objectively in a non-figurative language, would permeate the rhetorical subject of style as well, and really took hold in post-Renaissance science. The myth of "mathematical plainness" became the basis of the low "Attic" or "plain style," as a counter to the high Ciceronian or Baroque style of the humanists of the Renaissance (Croll; Katz, Review; cf. Erasmus, who like the late Hellenized Roman Cicero [*De Oratore; The Orator*]) insisted on knowing how to use all styles at all times (*kairos*). The high or grand style of the sophists onward would not vanish, nor would Platon's dream of pure mathematics as a metaphysical language; in fact, that dream of amputating number and especially words, with their multiple denotative as well as generalized and controllable connotative meaning, would become an "ideal" of both Newtonian science and Enlightenment rationality (Sprat; Locke, *Essay*; cf. Katz, *Epistemic Rhetoric*). And not only for aesthetic reasons or understanding of the human psyche in a "nasty," "new" disorienting Copernican universe (see Holton; see Rogers on Shakespeare), but for "political" as well as "scientific" reasons (Kuhn, *Structure*). For Platon, rhetoric and poetry had remained the opposite of "knowing" at any level of dialectic (see Tables 3 and 4; 6 and 7).

You Can Eat Your Cake And Have It Too!

(For Elizabeth Constable on her birthday)

i

m
a
d
e

this cake for your birthday tomorrow
and tomorrow and tomorrow and tomorrow

---

the only way i know how to make one since I can't cook
its triple-layered with a thick rich gooey dark frothing
chocolate frosting sandwiched in between each level

---

i've been baking it in the oven for three months
to seal in that extra special gift goodness
even though as i said i'm not a very good chef at all

---

i'm not sure how this will taste when you bite into it
the cake being letters on a page plus the paper plate
but I hope when you put these words in your mouth

they taste so good too you that your tongue totally rejoices in them
and treasures them too because unlike other cakes *this* one will last forever

3.1.12

Calculating as the "New Writing"

There was no doubt that Platon had considered "calculating" a higher form of "communicating" than ordinary human language, including imagery (even as the very basis of thought, as well as material visual imitations like painting, and worse, in language, like poetry, rhetoric, even speech that bore no resemblance even to physical things (cf. *Lesser Hippias* 367d–e; *Timaeus* 52b; *Laws* II.670c–II 671b; *Epinomis* 978a; *Gorgias*; *Phaedrus*). In fact, Platon had accused poets of also *corrupting* the "lower form" of mathematics such as music (*Epinomis* 977d–978b) by using it in their "speeches" (*Laws* II.699c; cf. *Gorgias* 205c–d). But despite the general banishment of poets from Platon's Republic (*Republic* VIII.568b; III.3998a; cf. *Laws* VII.817a–e), poetry had been "indispensable" insofar as it could morally and with restraint teach the "scale and rhythm" of music for "the best and second best" of the youth who needed to be "charmed" into a search of virtue (*Laws* II.670e–671a; cf. *Laws* II.659d; *Phaedrus*). But for Platon, rhetorical or poetic language, like knowledge based on opinion, or internal thinking itself based on images (*eidos*) in the mind (*nou*), could not go where geometry and numbers could take the mind as it ascended first by dialectic in speaking ("rational discourse"[*Epinomis* 977c]) followed by advancing dialectics of mathematic into increasingly thin, rarer altitudes of ethereal airs of Truth (*Republic* VII.524c–527b; see Tables 6 and 7). "Intellection" was about "Essence," a higher form of metaphysical thinking employing a dialectic of geometry and numbers; "opinion" was about "generation, a lower form of thinking employing the language of the senses: even if opinion employed dialect and arrived at the correct answer, it was necessarily "untethered" to pure reason (*Meno* 97b–98a), and simultaneously tied to the chameleon quality of the physical world (see *Republic* VII.533e–534a). For Platon, even the geometers, speaking of mathematics in general language, was awkward, inadequate, and often incorrect (*Lesser Hyppias* 367d; *Republic* VII.527a, 533e–534a).

{twisted scissors
don't cut straight
in Newtonian space}

3.1.13

Limitations of Higher Dialectical Method, and Infinity

For purposes of maintaining the ongoing "purification" of thought (forget speaking and writing), Platon had insisted that geometry be studied only with the original, basic instruments (a compass and a straight-edge ruler); otherwise: "[t]he whole good of geometry is set aside and destroyed, since it is reduced to things of the sense and prevented from soaring among eternal images of thought" (Plato, *Republic* VII.524e–525e; cf. Burton 122). Platon had professed that Ideal Forms were no part of and must never be in contact with or touch the material forms of the physical world (cf. Nancy, *Noli*). The compass and the straight edge—with their thin sliced lines and sharp points and carved circles—had been for Platon another, arithmetic "blade" by which to cut away the idealized forms of shapes and numbers from the material forms of the physical world. The compass and the straight-edge ruler had been the simplest, *and therefore purist*, methods for the study of geometry and mathematics. (This higher dagger of dialectic were levels above philosophy's flaying of the layering of the excess of rhetorical flattery and poetic fat [see Tables 3 and 4], lopping off physical as well as linguistic bodies, drilling through the dross of rock and bone, bodies and worlds.)

Uncertain Truth

in their current form
human beings
do not deserve to survive

***

Haunting the Middle Ages, what had become regarded in the Renaissance as a superstition of, mistaken, limited, or outdated methodologies revealing obstruse ontologies, obscure objects, occult logics, improbable alchemies, unteachable magics, ineffable mysticisms, impossible metaphysics (Bacon, e.g. *Advancement* VIII.3; Vickers), resulted in a rejection of old technologies and the adoption of new ones which were to slice open the "material spirit" and over the next three centuries probe deeper and deeper into the material of the body and the body of the world. The Platonic prejudice against extended or altered never mind new mathematics and scientific technologies, detached from traditional geometry, would soon give way to an intense and overriding drive for invention and innovation that would change science and technology, as well as the arts and philosophy, forever (cf. Bacon, *Advancement*; Sprat on the rejection of old methods and the embrace of novel modern scientific methods and the language to describe them). Like religious belief, the "irrational" commitment to "old" techniques and technologies based on philosophy, ideology, or demagoguery, which actually had proven a hindrance to advance of algebra in ancient Greece (Burton 122; 125; 136), would have proven a limitation to the progression of knowledge in all fields in the Renaissance—had that Platonic commitment to original tools and their attendant philosophical ideal and logics (already neglected by the Romans) not been discarded by their architects and engineers. While most of the philosophy and ideology was retained, the limit on methods were swept away in the face of a new age.

Eating Out Italian Style

{or the Day the Universe Stopped Expanding
and began to Contract}

i sit in this air
like a hot public bath.
i am going for a swim.
Warm cloud sticks
to my skin.
The sky is thick
as blue mud.
Sweat like little worms
crawls down my back.

Below, a drunkard
has lost his shirt again.
He tries to jump
over a fence.
The *Virilia*[*] grabs him
by the seat of his pants.
Time runs backwards.
The sun fills the sky.
The dead rise in the heat.

When in ancient Rome
do as the Greeks did.
A student goes to class
brandishing a sword and a crucifix.
Ugly men believe
all pretty women
love big red fish.
"If the *barbarius*[†] comes
have him bring his shears."

The world is collapsing
into cloud; the universe
is curling at the ends.
"No thanks, three olives
is my limit, dear."
Below, the *Virilia*
has lost his shirt again.
The drunkard grabs him
by the seat of his pants.

When in Rome. . .
Contemplate before you kill . . .
The student goes to class . . .
The sword, crucifix . . .
Dogs run from cats. . . .
Ugly men believe . . .
Big red fish . . .
The *barbarous*, his blades . . .
At the front door . . .

---

* Latin, nom singular: from *Vigiles Urbani* ("watchmen of the city"), early Roman prototype of police/fire brigades.

† Latin: "barber-surgeon" (one-in-the same through the Middle Ages and Renaissance). Here, ironic for "hairdresser."

3.1.14

Platon as "World Traveler"

After the death of Socrates, Platon had traveled through the Mediterranean, including Egypt, southern Italy, and Sicily, where Platon probably had studied Pythagoras's mystical theories with a cult of his descendants. After being sold off as a slave and rescued by his friends, Platon returned to Athens to found his Academy (Burton 135). At Platon's Academy "the emphasis was changed from the Pythagorean view that Nature was mathematical to the view that Nature lent itself to mathematization" (Burton 345). Platon had insisted that geometry and arithmetic should not be corrupted by harnessing them to serve servile reality (*Republic* VII.525e; *Epinomis* 978a–b). Given Platon's drive for purification of thought through geometry and mathematics, those disciplines had to be regarded and studied as the highest form of human knowledge *in and for itself* (see Plato, *Republic* VII.524E). Platon's belief in "metaphysical writing" as the ground of the world would seem to have made him a "neo" Pythagorean." However, even for "Pythagoras and his followers, mathematics was largely a means to an end, an end to which the human spirit was ennobled through a mystical contemplation of the good and the beautiful" (Burton 94; Plato, *Meno* 82b–85b). Despite some seeming philosophical similarities and even shared beliefs (already reported), Platon had not been a "neo-Pythagorean"—at least in regard to numbers. The distinction proved crucial in the consideration not only of mathematics, but of hospitality, beauty, and ugliness for the next four centuries.

Geometry Applied

desperate screw
looking for a piece
of wood to chew

3.1.15

Platon's Problem with Pythagoras and Pedagogy

Perhaps for the same reasons he had rejected new technologies (technē) in geometry and mathematics, Platon also had rejected the projection and extension of Pythagoras-like mysticism of material numbers embedded in and the basis of the physical world (Plato, *Republic* VII.524e–525e; cf. Burton 122). (Even more categorically, Platon had in the *Cratylus* rejected the letters of the Greek [or any other] alphabet as fundamental to material phenomena.) Problematic for Platon, his traditional mathematical methods for capturing the utmost idealizations of numbers, never mind the reality of Ideal Forms, still had been deficient (cf. Burke, *Rhetoric of Religion* 170; Katz and Rivers, 149), on the deficiency of language to capture the surplus of reality in relation to posthumanism]. Platon's stubborn dismissal of new *technē* to study geometry had proven an obstacle to the advancement of knowledge, even in ancient Greece (Burton 122; 125; 136). For Platon, it had been unadulterated geometry and mathematics that were to be used as the highest "language" conceivable in communicating metaphysical reality, as well as the highest pedagogical philosophy of education for the few select committed and potentially capable students who might be philosophers (*Republic* VII.525–527c; Burton 136). Plato had not been a Pythagorean—or did not accept his work uncritically, using what he could. For example, grounded in Pythagorean geometry and number, there also *were* "lower" forms of geometrics and mathematics too, such as found in the physical beauty of different musical ratios, rhythms, and harmonics, as well as different dictions, rhythms, and styles of language, but these were material correspondences, acting upon the body rather than the soul (i.e., *Republic* III.399–403e; cf. Table 7). Still, Platon had allowed that music (*Timaeus* 18a) could be used in the tactical training of officer and soldiers of the Guards of his ideal Republic (*Republic* VII.526d); other citizens of the *polis* would be exposed to appropriate levels of arithmetic, depending on the need for it given their predetermined station and purpose in life (*Republic* VII.527e).

Life of a Doorknob: A Meditation

(For Stefanie, Mary, Oumie)

1.

i long to become a simple doorknob—
or maybe one on a big bronze door,
my partner on the huge opposing half-door
(no revolving doors in between us)
that happily will greet, accept the handshake
from people—locals, strangers, foreigners—
who not exactly friends, become familiar
over passages of touch and time,
acquaintances, their fingerprints left on my shine
of musing metal melting into one
another, into one large pleasing handle,
not overthinking world, but being
the kind of mechanic i would like to be,
not worried, no anxiety, just focused
on the job at hand, repair and polish
the reflection of the mechanism
before me without forethought, trained to be
agile with tools, and automatic, like me

3.1.16

The Good, True, Ugly, and Evil in the Renaissance and Baroque

Platon had insisted on abstraction of geometry and mathematics for its own sake, *not* its application to the "real" world (e.g., *Republic* VII.525e; *Epinomis* 978a–b). {Temporal Enframing. Space-Time . In the twentieth century, Heidegger would dub these two states of being in the world as *Vorhandenheit*, and *Zuhandenheit*.} For Platon, questions of beauty and ugliness, of good and evil, therefore applied to numbers as well. Unlike art, which had used arithmatic only "for minor purposes," for Platon numbers had been part of both "divine and the moral in the world process—a vision from which [one] will learn both the fear of God and the true nature of number"; to do so, one had to have been "conversant with the whole field of it," for it is "the source of all good things" (*Epinomis* 978a–b; cf. *Greater Hippias* on beauty and ugliness). Geometric forms and numbers requisitioned, required by values of "usefulness," "utility," "expediency" in the physical world (Plato, *Republic* VII.524e–525e; Burton 122), was therefore at odds with Platon's strict belief in the pure study and contemplation and development of geometry, mathematics, trigonometry, and astronomy as knowledge for its own sake. Given the subsequent growth and use of geometry and mathematics in sixteenth, seventeenth, and eighteenth centuries and the future, numbers became increasingly elemental for performing work in the physical world. For Platon, it would have been inevitable that questions about form and number would intersect and become entwined with questions concerning the source of true knowledge vs. opinion, beauty vs. ugliness, good vs. evil. Indeed, Platon had thought geometry and mathematics were the foundation for the study of ethics and the science of wisdom (*Meno*; *Epinomis*; cf. *Republic* VII.526e). (In the Renaissance and Baroque, geometry and mathematics and the aesthetic questions they raised did become even more identified, one with questions of truth and, beauty, goodness and ugliness—even in the empirical sciences [cf. Bacon, e.g. *Advancement* XIII.3]; Sprat; Kant; Einstein; Holton 48–68; Eco, *Ugliness* 241–56].) So too the legal and ethical rights of the individual within political systems, and the birth of democracies in the eighteen century (Locke, *Two Treatises*). {Historical Future. Separated by two millennia, revolutions for independence and equality in America and in France were in many ways diametrically opposed to Platon's conception of his Republic, never realized in any uncorrupted form.}

Life of a Doorknob: A Meditation

2.

i long to become a simple doorknob—
perhaps a quaint, a smaller one on an

intimate hutch, cabinet door
in someone's kitchen, dining room, or den,
watching family sit and eat and laugh
and drink and talk and play, become a part
of the gathering, be one of them
without the want of grief, the need for spats
the way a tiny infant can exist
in a world it cannot understand
seeing everything for the first time
without premeditation, thought, or malice,
just the experience of color, sound,
a mother's warm caress continuing
from the womb in breasts and arms and hands
that see me, greet me, opening the door

3.1.17

Platonic Philosophy vs. Foreign Relations

In addition to the different levels of "cognition" (Tables 6 and 7), and the difference between mathematics as non-verbal languages vs. the verbal language arts of speaking and writing, Platon's commitment to a mathematics and astronomy grounded in geometry (Burton 273), as well as his insistence on a methodological purity of original instruments in studying it (Plato, *Republic* VII.524e–525e; cf. Burton 122), perhaps may have taken him to the limits of geographic as well as epistemological borders. Platon and his Academy had studied pristine fields of triangles trailing numbers *for their own sake*; the Persian, Hindu, and Arabic scientists, who had contributed much to the preservation and development of mathematical, medical as well as scientific knowledge before and after Platon, studied geometry and mathematics for more practical ends, e.g., to describe astronomical events in order to revise the Persian calendar, for example (a major feat of Omar Khayyam in the House of Wisdom) to predict with near-perfect precision the start and end times of religious celebrations and holidays, and other ritual observances such as fasts (Burton 248). (This was important to the Hebrews too, who also used a lunar calendar.) But given his belief in geometric and mathematical purity, Platon may have had some philosophical misgivings regarding the use of geometry and mathematics not only by Pythagoras, but in other cultures. Given the use of geometry and astronomy and numbers by Eastern societies to perform religious and other practical and civic *duties*, Platon's relationships with foreigners may have been as ambiguous, episte-polis, as his relationship with sophists.

Life of a Doorknob: A Meditation

3.

i long to be a doorknob, the kind a sophist
could compose a fully developed speech
by analyzing, classifying, defining,
comparing and contrasting, arguing
the causal relationships of all the knobs,
their differences, advantages, functions;
or a poet who could successfully
extend a metaphor into sets
of infinite images, ideas
create analogies, allegories
a doorknob's different experiences, knowledge—
about what being doorknob would be like,
how it would feel about its preferences
like this poem, these beautiful women
with whom i have the pleasure to converse...

3.1.18

Mathematics vs. Hospitality

A spirit of generosity and an ethics of hospitality already and always had been widespread in Greek mythology, religions, culture, social, political, and personal practice—even in regard to stray animals (thanks to Artemis) which had run wild in the garbage cans and the city streets. In the *Republic* and especially *Laws*, Platon had adopted/sought to formally encode many of the laws of the Great Code inscribed on the ancient circular wall (circa fifth century BC) in Gortyn, Crete, which Platon had visited and studied in his travels. In *Laws*, Platon had enumerated four types of "foreign visitor" based on purpose (tourism, business, etc.) and length of stay (XII 952e–XII 954a), while also detailing procedures for appropriate legal transactions, searches involving suspected theft, and the penalties that would have pertained thereunto (XII.954a–XII 955b). Platon also had specified that Greek citizens could be personal friends or enemies with foreigners depending on the diplomatic status of their respective states (*Laws* XII.955c) nor that foreigners be banished "by barbarian edicts" (*Laws* XII.953e). In all cases involving honest foreign visitors (no matter how different), the famous Greek obligation and reputation for universal hospitality, under "Zeus, the stranger's patron" (*Laws* XII.953e) was to be maintained. Platon even had gone so far as to point out that flayings, or offerings to Greek gods such as animal sacrifices, or the eating of foods such as meats that might "repel" guests from other countries, were banned in the presence of visitors

(*Laws* XII.953e). The visitor or foreigner was to be treated well, no matter how dissimilar or strange.

Life of a Doorknob: A Meditation

4.

i long to become a simple doorknob—
but then if i were a doorknob, there would be
no thought, no self-reflection, conversation;
this poem, sophistic speech, would not exist
and i would be oblivious, and dumb,
just sit there, sticking out, empty, numb
in the hotter hand of wiser summer
or in the grip of cold-clenched fist of winter
and no one really touch me, hold me, love me,
only long enough to open, close
and pass right by as if i didn't exist:
i would always be perfunctory,
alone, a foreigner, à l'etrangé*
without any hopes or fears, and free†

***

Platon's relationship with foreigners (ζένοι [*xenoi*], "strangers") had been very complex, as evidenced by the ironically tense clash between his dialogues and his philosophy, usually identified as one in the same (just two of Platon's many faces). While Platon professed an openness to foreign visitors in the *Republic* and in *Laws*, in fact he had been focused intently on his ideal *polis* and thus the Athenian/Greek people, with a hyper-attention to the strict regulation of interactions and legal requirements not only of the Hellenic hosts, but also and especially for the "foreign visitor" (thus explicitly circumscribing and implicitly carving the latter's [non]role in the *polis*). In the *Symposium* and *Phaedrus*, Platon had seemed to suggest strongly that the search for Truth and Beauty both superseded but also required universal values that transcended geographical or national borders, and social and cultural values. In attempting to educate and grow the Greek *polis*, Platon had desired to learn about other countries and customs, as had been illustrated by his extensive travels (Egypt had not been conquered by Aristotle's student, Alexander the Great, who was not born yet, and so had not been Hellenized at all); but in attempting to protect and preserve the Greek *polis*, Platon no doubt had wished to severely limit if not to

* Fr, "abroad"

† On the base of the defiant monument to Nikos Kazantzakis, Heraclean, Crete: "I have no hopes/I have no fears/I am free."

eliminate the effects of foreign visitors on civil and state affairs. Thus, the laws on hospitality and the legal rights of visitors in *Laws* had represented not only an "advancement" of the Gortyn Code in political theory and the peaceful maintenance of the internal order of society, but also had exuded a certain xenophobia regarding the recognition that the visitors definitely had been "foreign bodies" in the Greek *polis*.

The Anchorites

In seclusion
ascetic prayer

whole society
holds together

piercings, rings,
mutilations, attire

two on the lip
several in the gutter

3.1.19

Disfigurement of Numbers and "Other" Souls

Despite Platon's rather extensive travels for his time in and outside the Greek world; despite his willingness to use this travel in his dialogues with multitude of references to exotic, alien people and cultures, with their different beliefs, customs, and rituals to support, his own philosophical *bon mots*; despite the general generosity and welcoming nature of the Greek people as well as their gods; despite the rules of hospitality that he had gleaned from Gortyn regarding the treatment of the stranger; despite the fact he himself had further developed and catalogued these *Laws*—and given Platon's deepest held belief in geometry as the basis of all calculation but an orderly/ordered life itself; given his utmost devotion to preserving the purity of arithmatic shape and number and the process necessary to apprehend them; given his commitment and adherence to the traditional methods of studying geometry as the way of upholding the "divine" properties and moral affinities of numbers and their relations; given his deeply held belief in higher mathematics as the supreme if not most sacred form of thought and expression that humans could achieve (Tables 6 and 7); and given his only partially hidden disdain for utilitarian conceptions and applications of geometry, mathematics, trigonometry, and astronomy (e.g., Plato, *Republic* VII. 524e–525e; Burton 122), predominant in other cultures, such as in Persia and among Hindu and Arabic people: Platon and his students at the very least must have found the foreign proclivity to "force" geometry, trigonometry, mathematics, and astronomy, if not the people and/or their cultures themselves, to do work in the material world, even for religious purposes (Burton 87; 248), as somewhat ill-guided, ill-advised, mistaken, if not also disagreeable, ugly, abhorrent, revolting, and believed in the superiority of the Greek way of life—their own.

***

Furthermore, and more importantly, just as beauty was wisdom for Platon, *ugliness was "evil"* (*Epinomis* 978a–b; *Greater Hippias* cf. Eco, *Ugliness*). Thus, for Platon and the Academy {later perhaps the source of all ivory towers}, pressing the purer forms of geometry and mathematics into servitude (which he himself may have experienced briefly) probably would have been not only anathema, but also *an ugly and thus evil state of affairs.* To pressure purer celestial shapes and beautiful numeric figures to conform and service the material human body and physical world that clothed it might have resulted in unpredictable *deformities of form and number.* For Platon the eternal yet materially susceptible soul, imprisoned in the *soma*, was required to live for a time in the utterly false physical world. If the soul had been a physical and ethical "index of the body" revealed, recorded, and judged at the end of life (*Gorgias* 523a–524e; *Phaedo* 80b), how much more the ethereal shapes and numbers that may have begun existence in the heavens, among the hands of the gods, or resided close to if not in the realm of the Ideal Forms—dragged down to Earth by the darker horse in the chariot of the geometric soul (*Republic* VII.525b, c, d; *Epinomis* 978a–b; *Greater Hippias*) and forced to live in the material world. In this scenario, unadulterated shape and number would have been corrupted, become a mixed, deranged, a darker alloy, rather than a pure one of its former Being.

In this World

form
melting
touch

3.1.19

Chaos, Disorder, Ugliness as Ultimate Foreigners in the Platonic Renaissance

For Platon, chaos, disorder, ugliness had been "evil" by their very nature (see Tables 3 and 4; 6 and 7). Art that was "unregulated, disorderly, ungainly…," like music, like time, like the universe itself (or the lack of perception and knowledge thereof), was ugly and therefore "*evil*," for "that [which] partakes of evil is destitute of all number" (*Epinomis* 978b). If the wisest was also the most beautiful (*Timaeus 53b*), both were susceptible to the suppuration and corruption of form and number that also carried the signs and tribulations of the physical world (see *Greater Hippias*). (Platon even had ridiculed considering menstruation as a lower order of "geometric" cycles, or any calculations "concretized" in ordinary body or geo—world [*Epinomis* 990e; cf. *Philebus* 56c–57a], and hence another source of misogyny that never completely disappeared [cf. Aristotle, *Generation* 731b28; Eco, *Ugliness* (of women from antiquity to the Renaissance, 169–178; cf. Fraser, Graves, on primal patriarchy vs. matriarchy represented in world mythologies].) The conflation of ugliness, evil, and death were *major* themes in the Renaissance and Baroque {and unfortunately, until the twenty-second century, women were seen as a primary source not only of beauty and life, but deformity and death (see Shakespeare; Rogers; Eco, *Beauty* 233; Eco, *Ugliness* 158–167, 203–215).

Miscarriage

maternal pain—
beauty dying in the womb
ugliness birthing the world

3.1.20

Passing Half-Lit Torches in the Wind of Time

In ancient Greece, as in the Renaissance {as it would be in the Romantic Period}, the strange, the foreign, the exotic was valued at least as a novelty—at best a spring of greater perspective and knowledge of the widening world. But given Platon's preferred method of nonmaterial dialect, one not based on opinion (see Tables 6 and 7) or verbal language at all, in the search of true Beauty, for essence, through pure geometry and mathematics, was the visitor, the foreigner, the alien, the Other with their own values and virtues and their strange customs and incomprehensible languages, in Platon's eye disfigured, deformed, ugly, and thus evil too? Variously touching on the Carthaginians, the Egyptians, the Persians, and many other smaller groups of peoples, cults, and "tribes," Platon in his own treatises had "employed" "foreigners" many times to reference "alien" myths, stories, rituals, and customs. Platon had been understood to have tried to guard against prejudice by codifying native Greek hospitality into law. Platon also had made circular distinctions between "factions" that could exist as enemies among all *the Greeks people* themselves, who were still by nature "akin" and "friends" (even when fighting), vs. everyone else who were still "*barbarians*," and who in a like state of hostility were "enemies by nature" ("war is the fit name for this enmity and hatred"); any virtues and values the barbarians might possess were not "Greek," thus inferior, and certainly not his own (*Republic* V.470c–d).

3.1.21

All Suffering "Foreigners" in the Ideal Republic

But if Platon had had his druthers, would he have excised foreign nationalities entirely like diseased limbs from the trunk of the ideal body?—And not only from the Greek body-politic, but cut and completely removed *ALL* alien elements from the entire known world, for all time? There was some corroboration and support for these positions. Given that Platon's philosophy (mathematically as well as epistemologically) explicitly had heralded the transcendental realm of Essences and prized nonmaterial Ideal Forms as superior to the corrupted world of material forms, over everything else, Platon might have been understood at least implicitly not only to be calling for the dominate supremacy of the Greek city-state (Athens) over its neighbors, but also for the replacement of all foreign nations. —And more, not only other the replacement of all foreign nations, but with Ideal Forms and the thinkers that could attain it, *the whole physical world*. Not only mathematics, but disembodiment was a necessary step to reach the Ideal Forms (see Tables 6 and 7). In fact, *in extremis*, Platon's philosophy would have entailed destruction of the entire material universe, leaving only Platon's ideal Republic, ruled by the Philosopher King, and the few humans left in basic ranks and supporting roles to fulfill their functions in the hierarchical and highly structured society primarily elaborated in the *Republic* and in *Laws*. In this realized vision of the Republic, would foreigners have been slaves of slaves (if kept alive at all)? In fact, even most Greeks (to saying nothing of Platon's own countrymen, like the sophists and everyone else with whom Platon had supposed or posed Socrates arguing), would have been a foreigner, "lesser." Indeed, in a realized realm of Forms, *all humans*, locally and materially constituted as they were, in their own skin, would have had to be considered foreigners, aliens, "Other."

***

{Disassociation. Did history repeat a reenactment in philosophical purpose of a suppressed political and social desire in those treatises—to construct an Ideal cerebral Republic with less than perfect impulses and acts, and disastrous results? The ideological, political, and philosophical flaying of unwanted bodies (including the polis, the body politic) with that old boning knife, now manifested in the larger multiple blades of human war, turned on its own kind with fervor, multiplied exponentially by time. In eradicating the material body and the physical world in which they lived in favor of a "true life of the mind," most if not all, including Greeks and the Athenians themselves, would all be dead, and the physical world destroyed.} How humans suffered in their own history. As the late Roman Boethius (*Consolations*) had discerned while under house arrest, neither Christianity with its hope of death and resurrection, nor the classical cultivation of Greek literature and culture, both of which figured heavily in the Renaissance (as Boethius himself, post-execution, had embodied, and contributed majorly) did not salve, and were subject to the fickle whims of fates and gods. And divinity also did not stop the unstable laws of the physical world, or soothe the seething ideological impulses which seemed thee embodiment of human hatreds and biases and prejudices passed down from one generation to the next like a temporal "black plague." If not hope, neo-Platonic Philosophy for Boethius had offered some "consolation" and comfort. Perhaps.

{Passing Weeks

(For Alison)

not to be confused with the seasons
stumbling through with their variations,
hardly recognizable, one sliding
imperceptibly into another;
not to be mistaken for the face
the massive clock of the ticking moon
(*chia obscura*, just below, overhead),
nor the hanging human calendar,
always dangling from its fragile pin

until it's done, falls. we note the passage
of time by refilling pillboxes,
and the regular pile up of garbage,
the can's rolling up and down—not Earth!
But of our barrels of flesh, our human trash
continually emptied, then refilled
with all the refuse and all telltale signs
daily consumption, material wastings, lives
wheeled away to the littered fields

the wrapping and the cartons of our needs,
and physical desire drawn too close
to the curb, to be hauled off the roads,
the highways and byways, soon to rejoin

the remains of parts of other peoples' lives
spent, until we ourselves are refuse,
removed from our homes, the last time,
houses that no longer never were
our own}

3.1.22

Mathematical Abstraction, Material Beauty, Ugliness

The questions of beauty and ugliness, good and evil, played out in the period from the Renaissance through the Baroque era, into the scientific revolution of the seventeenth century, and the Enlightenment of the eighteenth century {after which it would run headlong into Romanticism, Modernism, post-modernism, post-humanism}. Platon could not have envisioned how quickly Western (and Eastern) civilization (both of which had embraced his philosophy) would progress in every field of human endeavor. He could not have envisioned how fast mathematics would advance, or how it would become the philosophical technē of science and technology with its focus on a more *material*, certain world that he had seemingly mistrusted.

***

Euclid's *Elements*, first translated into Arabic in the ninth century, wasn't translated into Latin in the West until the twelfth, but contributed to the Renaissance by preparing the ground for the Newtonian revolution; Euclid's *Elements* were gradually adopted as part of both Quadrivium and the science curriculum in the more rapid educational reform in the sciences in post-Renaissance West (Burton 86, 272, 312). The Italian mathematician Fibonacci (1175(?)–1250 CE) traveled from Pisa to Padua in the Mediterranean, where he came in contact with and recognized the importance of "Arabic" numeric and decimal system, with its Hindu zero, which he translated into Latin and published in *Libri Abaci* (*The Book of Counting*) in 1202, and another edition containing more examples by Fibonacci himself in 1228 (Burton 277–78), introducing the rules of algebra in the West (Burton 325). One of Fibonacci's examples, a small number problem that also connected to the problem of "irrational numbers" (which cannot be expressed as two whole numbers [positive, negative, or zero] that have fractional or decimal parts and their decimal expansions do not terminate or repeat as rational numbers do, but are infinite); irrational numbers had troubled and were never solved by Greek science, and apparently their existence had been kept secret by the Pythagoreans on pain of death; Euclid too had excluded them from his theorems (Burton 116, 316). Later known as the "Fibonacci Sequence" in which each "Fibonacci number" (after 0 and the first one) is the sum of the two that immediately preceded it, the Fibonacci Sequence did not attempt to solve the problem of irrational numbers; but it did lead to the discovery of a famous irrational number, the "Golden Ratio"; these recursive configurations of numerical terms, mapped out mathematically and graphed geometrically, led to the discovery of intricate, complex, and beautiful patterns *found throughout nature and art* (Burton 287; 287–99).

The Wisdom of Rain: A Meditation

(for Stefanie, herself)

$F_{n = 1, 1, 2, 3, 5, 8, 13, 21}$

1
sequenced trees

1+1=2
stems of leaves
branching trees

2+1=3
hidden patterns
branches flower
snowflakes stars

3+2=5
repeating rain…
drops driving
down the old
windowpanes
leaving trace

5+3=8
clear configurations
lanes arrayed
outline of sounds
shapes arranged
watching, listening
to designs
form and break
displayed outside

8+5=13
snugly home
tucked all around
through bespeckled
rain-drop glasses
on the ground
the entire world
has changed
a beautiful skin
the rain has made
mathematically smooth
sheet of water
draping windows
straight wet hair.

13+8=21
wisdom comes
pouring down:
know myself
accept i am
closing shop
kicking wood
underneath
the open door
walking out
spirals round
not shattering
but flattening
like soft glass
losing weight
losing shape
dissolving
into stream
going home
into land
draw invisible
numbers, hands

3.1.23

Calculus as New "Transcendental"?

Platon also could not have known how geometry, mathematics, astronomy, and trigonometry would continue to grow and prosper in sheer abstraction and power. As Eastern Hindu and Arabic scientists had known for centuries before the West, the decimal system and the invention of the zero had made *advanced* algebra possible. In 1533, *De Triangulis* by Johannes Müller (1533) also developed trigonometry into a science, severed from astronomy (Burton 305). Advancing algebraic and trigonometric equations allowed for greater abstraction of thought and more complexity in mathematically describing highly complicated physical phenomena. But just as algebra had "freed" mathematics from geometry (Burton 273), "[t]he liberation of algebra from the necessity of dealing only with concrete examples was largely the work of the great French mathematician François Vièta (1540–1603), who initiated using consonants to represent known quantities and vowels for the unknown" (Burton 315). Given his love of *ideal* geometric figures, Platon might have been pleased with this development: a further detachment and disembodiment of mathematics from physical work.

Paternity

10,296 carved calves
hanging—
rotting cuts remaining

***

From the heads and hands of German philosopher Gottfried Leibniz, and English physicist Isaac Newton (as well as several other major thinkers [Burton 338–81]), calculus, however, became the mathematical foundation of the modern scientific revolution and *everything* that followed. Leibniz developed his calculus as a function and product of his greater *philosophy*, including the nature of Monads and the existence of God; thus, Leibniz focused on developing an eloquent system of symbolic notation needed to record rational thought in mathematical logic (Child iii). Newton developed his calculus to solve problems specifically found in physics (cf. Holton on Newton's self-suppressed fifth hypothesis on the existence of God); it was told that Newton was a reluctant writer and "at times a bit clumsier" in his mathematical notations (Murty 15, 4). The rivalry for supremacy and credit lasted their entire lifetime (Murty 14; see Child in Leibniz 3–22, and Burton 400–435 for highly detailed accounts of Leibniz and Newton's personal, professional, and mathematical relationship). Perhaps equal to his grand philosophy, then, loosely, was Leibniz's more "Platonic" goal to invent good notation *for notation's sake*; Leibniz's notation would become the primary method of writing calculus. Newton's somewhat "messier" notation might have been seen as more philosophically "anti-Platonic" too, in that its goal was to solve "real" problems in the *physical* world, e.g., the laws of motion (Murty 15). The combined Fundamental Theorem of Calculus (which Newton called "the method of fluxions" [Murty 6; cf. Burton 418]), consisted of higher mathematical sets of equations and procedures for discovering and representing variables as integers; these integers tracked and measured movement, for example, and transformations of space surrounding it. The process and procedures were understood as inverse processes of "differentiation" and "integration" (Murty 4–8). (Simplified, applying the fundamental concept of "Limit," *differential calculus* defines "derivatives" [rates of change]; *integral calculus* defines "definite integrals" [accumulated quantities] [Chung 5; cf. Child; Molson; Murty; Strang].) Employing calculus, Newton contributed to the concepts of force, time, mass, acceleration, motion, planetary orbits, universal gravity, the corpuscular theory of light, optics, as well as the reflecting telescope (Murty 9–14).

i Floating

on invisible horizons
my ear is sending
this message to you

3.1.24

Calculus as Purer Platonic Dialectic

Since the Middle Ages, Platon's commitment to the doctrine of Ideal Forms, and methods of verbal dialectic in the guise of various neo-Platonisms, remained relatively intact in the history of philosophy, rhetoric, and poetry, as well as various theological positions in Christianity (see Chateaubriand) and Judaism (see *Philo*). In the Renaissance, that doctrine and those verbal methods drove concepts of beauty (and ugliness) in the arts, as well as the continued emphasis since Charlamagne on the Trivium, which still dominated Renaissance education and culture (Burton 270–71). But more so, Platon had intuited and been committed to even higher planes of non-physical dialectic—an ethereal logic written in nonverbal languages of mathematics (see Tables 6 and 7). *Did differential and integral calculus, in some ways, perhaps comprise, represent, or attain another, higher level of dialectic, separating humankind from the physical Earth and bringing humankind closer to real essences?* (Cf. Boyd on the quest of science to arrive at real essences *in the world*—in his case through metaphor extension, and Kuhn's refutation "Metaphor".)

Immortal Memory

when i remember
know everything
i will be dying

***

Even though Platon could not have known the particular "philosophical" logics nor or sets of standard equations (such as Factoring) in calculus (cf. Child 4, on the difference between "philosophical" and "mechanical" calculus), Platon might have approved—at least with those "philosophical" dimensions of calculus (perhaps better represented by Leibniz) that were more metaphysical and exploratory. Both *differential* and *integral* calculus became progressive abstractions (and corresponding reductions?) of the observable, physical, world—even as the development of calculus expanded the human understanding of more *non-observable* operations of that world. But calculus was ever only *partially* separate, never completely severed from the physical world (if at all). And with the dominance of Newtonian physics in the seventeenth century and its commitment to "discovering" empirical problems in the physical world, and an emphasis on developing standard ("mechanical") procedures that could be implemented for those parts of new problems in physics and mathematics that already had been solved (Child 4), Platon might have been as troubled by the attention to the operations and relations of the forms of *material* reality as he was by the necessity of philosophers to use verbal dialectic in the process of attaining that more intangible realm of non-verbal, geometric, mathematical dialectic that required no opinion, no assumption, no starting point, and no further explanation or proof, only the movement of pure idea to pure idea, bringing the "disembodied (human) mind" closer to true Reality (Plato, *Republic* VI.511b–c).

Maternity

this side of the pain:
beauty never born
living forever in the womb

3.1.25

The New Appeal of "the Quadrivium"

According to the archival records, in the five centuries that contained the entire Renaissance as it spread in Europe, the Newtonian scientific revolution, and the Enlightenment, the divisions between the Trivium and the Quadrivium, the humanities and the sciences, seemed to widen with growth of calculus and the success of science. With the spread of literacy, the bourgeoning of business, and the boom of a bourgeoises middle class, the Platonic split between lower and higher dialectics (see Table 7) were further affected by the cultural conflict between the "teleological" or practical appeal of science that emphasized the need for the usefulness of knowledge and invention in all disciplines, vs. the "deontological" or "wonder appeal" (cf. Fahnestock, "Accommodating" 279) that was necessary to drive both mathematics and sciences as well as the arts and humanities in middle class societies and popular culture generally. The pressure on the arts and humanities to justify their relevance to education in relation to the application of mathematics, science, and technology to the practical world, began the deemphasis and eventual dismantling of the medieval Trivium after the Renaissance. That pressure would only increase on the verbal arts through the subsequent historical ages, despite the amazed attention of the deontological appeal of scientific discoveries in the physical body and world. With Platon's philosophical preference for all things metaphysical, the question of whether Platon would have regarded these subsequent developments in mathematics and science a foreign, alien, ugly, evil, was a matter left to post-historians. (They never resolved it.)

still chatting
in the dying wind
two yellow leaves

2. The Epistemological Body and "the Other"

3.2.0

Ugly Epistemology of the Eye, or Ontology of Surfaces?

And what of the deformed, foreign, ugly, evil body? The Platonic assumption was that it was liable to harm the soul—an assumption that in many ways was present in many of Platon's precepts. What happened when the body, and by extension the physical world, rather than the immortal soul and true Essences, became the focus of scientific attention and successive study in physics, anatomy, chemistry, medicine, biology, psychology—what Foucault later called "the Gaze" (Foucault, *Clinic*)? But what if the ugly body, rather than the beautiful one, had been the ontological fulcrum, the epistemological nexus of art, culture, thought? (Eco [*Ugliness*] argued that they were two sides of the same coin.) What if Platonism had been only an epistemology of "eye," or/rather than an ontology of surfaces? Auerbach had demarcated a deep historical, cultural, and literary shift from the classical world that prized the logos of rationality and visual proportion over the pathos of messy passion and flesh that subsumed the West after the birth, death, and resurrection of Jesus. But what if the conception, suffering, and death of the whipped, flayed, pierced, nailed, rotting flesh had occurred *without* the redemption and salvation of the third part of Trinity? What if the transubstantiation, the conversion to, and ascension of the Holy Ghost, were not givens (as they were not in science, in Judaism, and other religions), maybe had never occurred?

"What if the Calvary
had ridden into Calgary
and taken Jesus
down from the cross . . ."

***

Rebellion of the Body

Or what if the ugly body, in appearance and morality, already in revulsion revolting, itself rebelled, revolted, asserted its own supremacy—when the revolting body mutinied, refused to rise, remained flesh, and so instead was re-presented as the social, cultural, scientific, religious icon to be emulated, explored, lived, as it was for most of historical humanity, until the last major shift in the ontology of earth and flesh, and an "Other" was detected? Was the defying ugly body (or "the Other") still evil? Had a physically deformed, ugly body, rather than the pagan or holy Christian soul, become a new source of science, culture, art, literature, religion, historical spirit, *Zeitgeist*? —when the instruments of geometry like a straight edge ruler and the steadying point of a compass became needle and scalpel, became keenly barbed and razor sharp, and with increasing efficiency and precision pricked and sliced open the false illusions not only of flattering myth and ornaments (rhetorics, poetry, body, world), but cut open with x-ray machines and new power tools the equally false illusions of ideal forms and immortal souls? Could Platonism be extended beyond surfaces of illusions, to the "innately ugly" interiors of material body and world, with their fascinating and intricate but dirty parts, odious organs, sordid innards, when they were *actually opened*—when their steaming contents were not only revealed to and seen by the senses—not for punishments such as drawing and quartering, or flaying, but delved head-first into and inspected as the source true knowledge by science and technology—when between the sixteenth and eighteenth centuries the interiors of human body and mind, nature and the physical world themselves were finally freed from the religious and social taboos against touching or opening dead, diseased, or putrefying *soma*, were regarded as objects of intense interest and desire, or as in Pantheism even worshiped as G/d-art?

"Rusty" Classical Guitar

stringy muscles
frets of metal, bone
sound cracking open

wooden sac
remnants of skin, nails, flesh
disharmony within

teeth of fingers
biting down O
make this body sing

3.2.1

Mathematics, Mimesis, and Ugliness

For Platon, ugliness had had many sources, including geometric and mathematical ones, that also showed up in questions of proportion and symmetry in art. But was there a post-Platonic role for ugliness, and what was its relationship to beauty? They thought they knew the answer concerning ugliness based on Platon's discussion of the mutilated discarded body and splayed soul that mirrored the marked body in every respect, to be judged at the moment of death (*Gorgias* 523e–525d). In a strict Platonic sense, all rhetoric and poetry were "ugly," since they were not true beauty, and were evil since they were not true good. They were all *imitations*, which, when compared to the unseen real, themselves had been forms of the deformed, foreign, ugly, and thus evil. In fact, for Platon, some imitations were better than others, but mimesis itself, as concept and practice, had been the source deformation, and therefore the source of all ugliness and evil in the world. In fact, material reality—the human body, the whole world—were imitations, and thus inherently base, corrupt, ignoble, and vile. And yet material reality, mimesis, like body and world, was where the human created, worked, lived, and died into a freedom depending on how they had lived. Could there be an ideal Ugliness?

***

The Renaissance, Baroque periods, and onwards, showed that the answer was yes! And those ideals of Ugliness, like notions of Beauty, changed with the age (see Eco, *Ugliness*). Evolving notions of mimesis and truth, body and soul, beauty and ugliness, and their many various manifestations in and effects from the Renaissance through the eighteenth-century Enlightenment, underwent profound changes in Western philosophy, history, art, rhetoric, poetry, and culture. The "conclusion" of the period of classical ideals in the Renaissance, and the beginning of modern, scientific concepts that were birthed in the seventeenth century, were developed and applied directly to art and life. Retrospectively, it seemed mimesis and ugliness, like material and even "human metaphysic," were as good as nothing.

Nothing Only Stays

Everything changes; nothing only stays.
And so my love will always be the same,
For I, my dear friends, am going away.

We made heaven here, in a human way:
Truth, Goodness, Beauty—money, lust, and fame.
Everything changes; nothing only stays.

We grow bolder now, in these final days,
Looking for miracles, going insane.
All of my dear friends go so far away.

The streets of the city have all gone gray.
Time to go home now. Who's really to blame?
Everything changes; nothing only stays.

When will we see each other? Who can say?
Who can give oblivion a name.
My dear friends always go so far away.

The lights of the city flicker and sway.
Will the universe always be without aim?
Everything changes; nothing only stays.
And I, dear friends, am now so far away.

3.2.2

Platonic Ugliness of Pleasure

Platon had addressed head-on the question of beauty and general ugliness in several of his treatises— not only in his advocacy against the perverse monstrosity of sex and pleasure (*Philebus*, 66a–b), but also and always in the continuous opposition between the physical human body and the divine soul (cf. *Greater Hippias*, esp. 286c, 304d; *Republic* X.609a–610c). However, he also addressed them in the antinomies air, fire, earth, and water, of which everything material was composed, including bodies; and in the transcendental triangles that laid behind the poorer imitations and copies of imitations of the Ideal Forms—a mimetic variation of which made some peoples and things superior, and most inferior (see *Timaeus* 52d–117e; Toulmin and Goodfield). Despite his indulging and achieving the distinguished honor of eminent authorship, for Platon pleasure and passion rendered humans dumb, turned them into beasts again: "Passion is an ill-favored thing, and the speaker who does his wrath the favor to feast it on the poison it craves turns all the humanity education has fashioned within him into brutishness once more . . . " (Platon, *Laws* XI.935a). For Platon, ugliness was connected to and the result of pleasure—and the highest and ugliest form of pleasure and perhaps the most "shameful" (albeit necessary for procreation) was sex.

Resurrection

Our horny and neurotic flesh
quivers like jelly on a frame of death:
pelvises pounding together, skeletons
entwined in endeavor, lips and bellies
pressed into the softening marrow
of our bones—so martyred on
a mortal post, into your body
receive the host.

3.2.3

Deformities from Birth

Aristotle took up the subject of the deformed and ugly, especially in *The Generation of Animals*, where, in an extended discussion of the biology of birth and propagation of humans, animals, and plants, he investigated the possible causes and forms of "monstrosities" and ugliness (766a37–776a14). Children who didn't resemble their parents were "already in a certain sense a monstrosity; for in these cases nature has in a way departed from the type" (767b6–8), said Aristotle; women, who naturally differed from the "superior male form," were "the first departure," although again a necessary one for the propagation of various species. And just as an offspring may not have resembled any of its ancestors, the offspring "sometimes, proceeding further on these lines, appears finally to be not even a human being but only some kind of animal, what is called a monstrosity" (7677b6–9; 7677b14).

Bastard

Dink, the bastard,
born in wedlock,

legal but unloved,
but involved, the product
of a loveless marriage,
has a father but was unwanted
by his mother, already
a bastard in the womb,
an orphan of life.

Look at the name
they gave him,
a little, rejected
body part, already
emotionally damaged
and left to its own devices.

Maybe Dink fathered
himself, incest with his mother
before he was born,
immaculate misconception,
biggest mistake
he ever made.

And if he had fathered
himself out of wedlock and
out of love, a self-made
bastard, the root cause
of his unfortunate birth, he is
the father of his own predicament,
the object of his own derision,
the ugly mold, the predictable

the object of scorn, the shape
of what he would become
in the world

a name that screws itself
every chance it gets

3.2.4

"Causes" of Monstrosities

For Aristotle, "[t]he cause of monstrosities is very close and similar in a way to that of the deformed; for the monstrosity is actually a kind of deformity" (7677b29–30), of which there are three kinds: "multiplicities" and "deficiencies" or "mutilations" (*Generation* 770b27–771a17). For Aristotle, monstrosities could be reduced to a problem of "motion": "If the movements relapse and the material is not controlled, at last there remains what is most universal, that is to say the animal" (*Generation* 7677b11–12). {Forethought. In critiquing mechanistic notions of causality vs. motivism, Burke might have said that if cause was reduced to mere mechanical motion, humans—all humans—would become animals or objects; but this point would have appeared in some ways to be the very opposite of Aristotle's.} For Aristotle, ugliness had been a departure from the ideal (male) body type, which itself was a departure from the truer soul, which was the "substance of a particular body, and the animator and the ideal of all living bodies whose material is from the female, but whose soul is from the male" (e.g., *Generation* 731b28; 738b19–26). Observing birth defects, Aristotle said: "Those which only depart a little from nature commonly live; not so those which depart further, when the unnatural condition is in the parts which are sovereign over life" (*Generation* 771a11–13). Aristotle did not believe in reincarnation (*De Anima* 1.3 407b); —but the sins of mother (substance) and/or of the father (soul) could be passed down endlessly from parent to child, perhaps even from teacher to pupil. (Could a mediocre genius, passing a spent candle, flame for others in the dark?)

Salieri to Mozart

(For Mir Garvey, a true protégé)

Where the biography ends
and the fiction begins—
yes, go on and send
those compositions in:
you'll be remembered
when i am dead; but then
i will have achieved
something with my schemes:
it is my obligation to teach,
and yours to transcend.

A lesser talent: What a relief
to know that to seek

is not an imposition
or above my reach:
so yes, besmirch me
if you must, but attend:
you'll show gratitude in the end
in every work eternally:
but sure, with your great fame
murder my minor name

3.2.5

Mimesis of a Physical Soul?

In the West, the mimesis of the soul in the arts was not only perhaps in a continuing Platonic struggle to free itself from the "flattering" body, but also and especially from the perceived "ugly" body, defined broadly. The history of mimesis in rhetoric and poetry, of art and science, became a harsh intercourse of beauty and ugliness, transcendent ideals of glorious bodies and broken bodies, a commingling of cultural substance and material realities, the birth of ideologies and societies in which utopian dreams of life in paradise was when actualized "solitary, poor, nasty, brutish, and short" (Hobbes 86)—a rutting of love and economics, a rotting of politics and flesh—especially for the poor and homeless who wandered through all time and space.

Twenty-Two Degrees Below Zero Love

4/4

[vamp]:
Cm A
ooh ooh [4x]

Fm B

E7 [E harmonic 1st string 12th fret]

E7
Woke up in the morning,

B7 B7sus4 B7

felt my feet down on the floor;

E7
reached across the bed,

B7 B7sus4 B7

the sheets were hard and cold.

A
He's left again, and won't be back;

B7 E7
he's taken all I know

E7
It ain't morning

B7 E7
when it's twenty-two below.

[verse; sim:]
i got out of bed
and put the coffee on the stove;
stubbed my toe against a fence
and pulled up on my clothes.
i opened up the cardboard door
and walked out in the snow.
It ain't love
when it's twenty-two below.

[chorus:]
Fm
i know that it ain't morning
B
when it's twenty-two below.
Fm
i can tell that it ain't love
B
when it's twenty-two below.

[distorted lead guitar]

[vamp]
Cm A
Ooh ooh [4x]

Fm B
ooh ooh
E7
[verse, sim:]
i'm leaving here this morning
like he left me in the cold;
i was leaving this place yesterday
but the wind blew in the door;
it sat me down and spelled it out,
made home a shelf of snow.
It ain't morning
when it's twenty-two below.

[chorus: sim]
i know it ain't morning
when it's twenty-two below.
i can tell that it ain't love
it's twenty-two below.

B [single note—6th string 7th fret]

Twenty-two below zero love,
when you're homeless and alone

3.2.6

The Aesthetics of Ugliness

How did they account for ugliness, the antithesis of beauty, in aesthetic terms? One paradox, noted "from Aristotle to Kant" (Eco, *Beauty* 131), was that art could make ugliness beautiful. A major counterpart to the concept of beauty, and a major concern within Judeo-Christian society, ugliness was also a focal point in art, one that became crucial from the sixteenth through the nineteenth centuries, and beyond. As Eco pointed out (*Beauty* 133), the question of ugliness as a break in aesthetic proportion of beauty had been theorized since antiquity, but became a major issue in the Middle Ages, and continued in different ways in the Renaissance, since ugliness was not only a physical but a moral dilemma as well (cf. Eco, *Ugliness*). In the seventeenth and eighteenth centuries,

Ugliness (like "false flattery" before it [Tables 3 and Table 4]), the opposite of Beauty, itself became an "ideal form." The grotesque as an imitation, in all its deformed material manifestations, could be a rank, strange, perverse, *but still "true."* What was the "ethical end" of Ugliness? The classical ideal of Beauty would not have been able to face the pain as passion of Christ's crucifixion—and thus the transcendence of the elevation of the emotion of pathetic love for the weak and the pitiless into a major religion and a set of ethical standards deriving from but reversing the "Old Testament," as well as a pseudo-physical form of the spirit of life (Auerbach), and a way to live before and after the death of the body. Citing Hegel, Eco stated: "With the advent of the Christian sensibility and the art that conveyed it, central importance is reserved (especially as Christ and his persecutors are concerned) for pain, suffering, death, torture, Hell, and the physical deformations suffered by victims and their tormentors" (*Beauty* 133). What serenity was experienced in flagellation? What geometry was discovered in flaying and bloodletting? What unity was found in agony and ache? Yet "the ugliness" was the very subject of the story of the Passion, and made converts of pagans, and martyrs of "ordinary" men and women. Here was an entelechy at work, but working ugliness toward different ends, those ends meant to be affective, forgiving, charitable and non-corporeal. The aesthetics of Ugliness became another often painful, grotesque, even gruesome means of transcending a tenderer "self," of escaping the defective, deformed, monstrous body to become throbbing, feeling spirit (cf. Damasio).

Let Me Go

Let me go my sullen way
through the inner bramble where i'll stay

and never feel the orchid shade,
or smell hot fragrance of a sun-struck rose;
lilacs purple as they die.

Let me go my sullen way,
through the inner bramble where i lay

and never taste the honeyed hay,
or know the disappointment of a pose;
mothers laugh instead of cry.

Let me go my sullen way,
through the inner bramble where i lay

and never see the moon concave,
or hear expirings of the close;
i'll never know the reason why.

Let me go my sullen way,
through the inner bramble where i'll stay.

3.2.7

Mutilating Beauty

And what of traditional nobility? Classical values of aesthetics of etiquette, and proportion, measure and manner?

On the Demise of Being Noble

(For Tom Lisk, who truly was)

I'm sick of being noble: the polished skin
of behavior, values sculpted, almost
cold to the touch of the finger that will point and
jab and try to rouse that cool demeanor, the composed
flesh of higher being—some might call it spirit—
that the eyes might point right through,
so committed to the good is it,
so pristine, so proud, so pure, so true.

Oh I was never that way anyway,
but tried to lead a better, simpler life,
content in goodness for its own damn sake.
Why fight? The frozen edge of flesh is beveled,
gives way to the file of envy, anger, hate—
everyday existence. I will not cry,
but turn, embrace that other ideal: evil.

And I will kill all those who made me kill
my own near-perfect being (once again)

***

Distortion

Medieval and Renaissance notions of beauty represented a significant change (and yet drew from) from the Greek concept of Beauty—changes that had been manifested in the subject matter and tenor of rhetoric and poetry (the terrors and horrors of life): e.g., Boethius (*Consolations of Philosophy*; cf. *De Topicis Differentis*, and *In Ciceronis Topica*); or Francois Villon's wretchedly enticing prison poetry; or Ramus's vicious personal attacks on Aristotle and Quintilian, at once exceedingly unpleasant and pleasing; or Chaucer's *Canterbury Tales*, which humorously depicted a group of ugly, unpleasant, greedy, or glutinous pilgrims in all their human frailties and spiritual vices; or later still, Milton's *Paradise Lost*, which would paradoxically present the treacherous beauty of evil, the lovely ugly of Satan.

Halloween Weather

New England
recedes
into a black October night
branches
stripped
shaggy
haggard
in the moonlight
possessed
with wind
and sudden age.

Persephone is raped.

Howls
strike the sky
black with trees
twisted bare
in the haunted air
thick with the battling
dead breast to breast
come home from nippled
fields of death,
come home to take
their comfort or revenge
love's trick or treat.

perhaps
it was the weather.

This year
the snow
fell
before
the leaves
and winter
almost buried autumn
came too early too near
quickening the fierce
wraiths under frosty ground.

the autumnal clock

was
set back
one hour.

Ah Faustus
who is saved?

Satan
still lurks
these woods.

Perhaps
it was the moon,
lit like a pumpkin,
up in the dark.

Black air stings
the nostrils, lingers
like a slow burning,
a bitter morality
of apples gone bad.

New England
recedes
into a black October night.

Howls strike the sky;
incubus crushes succubus;

Persephone is raped.

Of course, as Eco points up, the "fascination" with the Devil was already inherent in religious and aesthetic representation, and that was only to increase through the ages (*Beauty* 133; *Ugliness* 202–39).

3.2.8

The Beauty of Ugliness and Evil

From the medieval period onward, the issue of ugliness, in all its forms, was even more important not only in aesthetic theory, but also within Christian theosophy as well, where it was a religious as well as physical issue: how justify the existence of ugliness amidst beauty, the presence of evil in good? As with the discordance of classical, medieval, and Renaissance concepts of beauty, Eco suggested at least three solutions to the problem of ugliness. First, the existence of ugliness within God's goodly realm could simply be ignored—psychologically repressed, as it were (with all the attendant nightmarish manifestations on macro social, political, and aesthetic scales that we see in the paintings of the time, such as Hieronymus Bosch [see Eco, *Beauty* 130–53], with their lacquered intensity, their thick piquancy of fear and pain, their luscious ugliness). Second, ugliness could be justified within larger mystical cosmologies in which everything can take on moral meaning and import; allegories employing "universal symbolism" were used to teach "virtue and vice." That is, through the kind of "types" designed to instruct that Burke ("Dramatistic View" 10–12) discussed, ugliness could be contextualized within "moralized bestiaries," says Eco (*Beauty*, 145). Stock characters and stories contained within cosmological allegories are certainly ways of portraying while also controlling ugly evil that does not learn to leave on its own.

The Un-heroic Death of a Spider

Living inside the gap in a frame of
the window weighted like a dumbwaiter,
saving it the trouble of running up
and down its own newly made webbed ladder—

living/body halfway in, and out way half,
its legs blending with the bristles of
the rope, the frass of its daily meals
piling up like sawdust on the sill

of its front door: venturing further forth
out of its hole more frequently for food,

an imperceptible funnel of a web
extending more often out towards death—

One night it ventured out too far for prey,
and didn't withdraw its head into the crack;
unable to identify it fast,
afraid, I doused it with ant and roach spray.

Down it tumbled, dripping with the Raid . . .
falling hard, catching on a crevice,
starting the climb back up the treacherous
white chimney road to the distant rope,

pausing only briefly between the bricks
(apparently showing no ill effects),
then about half-way up, stops:
as if it's thinking what to do, then stays.

What's it thinking, I wonder, terrified,
but then beneath it one leg curls up, folds
in agony, then both front legs draw in,
collapse, and I can no longer stand

to watch the thing suffer, who had spent
so many balmy weeks of summer
watching television with the family,
growing up with us from infancy

(although it did not like to have its picture
taken, the laser eye of the camera
turning its eight eyes red, and from the spider's
perspective, a big red eye at it staring!

And then the flash!) —All its legs collapse.
It doesn't move. I cannot turn my back.
Spider, playing peek-a-boo, or tease,
I must put you out of your misery.

And so you suffer a triple humiliation:
a betrayal one summer night by kin; killed
with poison meant for prey; and the final—
smacked over the head with a book on reptiles.

3.2.9

Asymmetric Mimesis

A peculiar brand of asymmetric mimesis, one that Mikhail Bakhtin discussed, was the grotesque body in medieval mysteries and sixteenth century novels (particularly Rabelais, another reveler of the uglier) whose "creations" often entailed "the transformation of the human element into an animal one; the combination of human and animal traits (Bakhtin 316), as well as "dismembered bodies, their roasting, burning, and swallowing" (Bakhtin 347; Eco, *Ugliness* 107–25). {Burke might have asked whether these forms of ugliness, ideals of the Grotesque, represented true entelechies? (e.g., "'Dramatistic' View"; cf. Katz and Rivers to reflect on the ugly and grotesque as perhaps the result of non-teleological "emergence.")} Regardless, these grotesque "types," these ugly "forms," evil, could have represented or been manifestations of "supernatural realities," whether comic or tragic, designed to instruct and persuade. Thus, despite the deformation, dissonance, and disturbance ugliness seemed to introduce into "paradise," the grand design of Providence, it was also part of the Plan. As Eco stated, "St. Augustine addressed this very problem in a paragraph of his *City of God*: Even monsters are divine creatures and in some way too belong to the providential order of nature" (*Beauty*, 145).

{Millennium Park, Chicago

("In the "Beginning" All Over Again)
for Dale Sullivan

The garden is walled
off with pines and pain, not
yet completed, the work
of the artisans, massive
shoulders in the architecture,
stooped, breaking back
of the world. But the serpent
is already there, snaking
its way around and down
to the mouth of the garden;
its aluminum scales glisten
in the sunlight. The frame
is completed, a chrome liver
given. And out of the belly
the people come, corrupted
with joy, running, cheeks

blustering with light, skin
shining in the wind, joyful
disciple-minions born
into the city streets,
faces white against the gray
lake boiling in the cold

but unable to taste
the fruit of their knowing
once it has been eaten,
unable to know of love
once it has been given,
they have left it in the garden,
and walked off to
eternity without the benefit
of ever breathing}

***

But it was the third solution, scientific investigation—and not only science generally, but particularly the related sciences of the body—anatomy and (modern) medicine—that was forever to change the equation of beauty and ugliness in mimesis. Science affected mimesis in the corresponding Medieval and Renaissance concept of beauty. In Renaissance art, Eco said, beauty had been:

> conceived according to a dual orientation that today strikes us as contradictory, but that contemporaries found coherent. [They] saw Beauty both as an imitation of nature in accordance with *scientifically* established rules and as the contemplation of a supernatural degree of perfection that could not be perceived by the eye because it was not fully realized in the sublunary world. Knowledge of the visible world became a path toward knowledge of a supersensible reality governed by logically coherent rules. The artist was therefore at once—and without this seeming contradictory—a *creator* of new things and an *imitator* of nature. (Eco *Beauty*, 176, 178; *emphases added*)

Thus, even during the highly religious Middle Ages, imitation had come to be based more and more on both observation and scientific principles—on investigations *of nature*, including the body.

3.2.10

Mimesis of Anatomy

The concept of "scientific imitation" was accelerated with the further development of anatomy, and a growing knowledge and understanding of internal processes of nature.

Observations of Mimetic Conversions

(In the Blue Ridge Mountains)
For Carl and Dianne Herndl

High in the corner of the cabin,
fish caught in the air,
cobweb twisting in moonlight

spinning moth so large
you can see human features
on its baby face in the window

lighted face of a clock
that no longer runs, but whose hands still
shape time in the dark

the little hands of the river girl,
whose father keeps running away
embrace, then tie his feet to raft

a big beetle on its back,
caught, vulnerable,
screaming alien infant screams

lying on a hammock under the leaves,
hanging between two trees
thinking about the nature of G/d

two philosophers towering over
thought, invited guests looming
above the cabin that sleeps

sleeping on Mt. Pisgah,
then sleeping bags rolled up
like bales of hay in fields of rain

in the Garden, in the rain,
where the little stone man, stone dove
by his hands, again learns to pray

***

The preoccupation with the internal structure of humans had been a staple of medicine and art at least since the time of the ancient Egyptians and Greeks. Although restricted to a significant degree by social and religious prejudice and taboo up through the Renaissance (see Benthien 95–110)—in a continuing belief that body and soul were inexplicably inextricable, and/or the body was a protective container if not prison of the soul—anatomy in Western science and art had a long history, as illustrated by its luminaries: Galen, Michelangelo, De Vinci, Vesalius, and of course, Gray. In the classical world, Galen, unable to even dissect the corpses of slaves, had studied the bodies of animals to extrapolate the physiological structures of human form. In fourteenth-century Europe, Leonardo da Vinci, famous for his study of human and animal anatomy but sacrilege to the Church, quietly, surreptitiously and/or in the secrecy of darkness, exhumed decaying corpses, and manually—with his hands up to his elbows in organs and blood—dissected bodies to understand internal shapes, processes, and constitution, in order to more accurately imitate and represent them in both science and art. So did his rival, Michelangelo, as well as other Renaissance artists (see Benthien 64). The Renaissance might be said to have begun under the patronage of the Di Medici family in Florence, Italy, through painting and politics, books and blood.

Living Hieroglyphs

Stumbling on hidden
stones with their embedded
messages, and the birds
their twittering symbols,
and the trees' wavy green
alphabets, mosquitoes
like invisible letters
living hieroglyphics
in the sunlight
until they find you
when you stand or sit
still to write
and ask for nothing
but a little blood
in return; stepping

over the gnarled
river rats, the secret
is unconsciously clear:
will you give it up?

3.2.11

Female Anatomy of Mimesis

If mimesis in some large measure was based on scientific anatomy, anatomy was grounded scientific mimesis. Thus, distinctions among differences in "stripping"—slicing, flaying, and penetrating—were not historically arbitrary. Despite "a constantly recurring assault on woman's lower abdomen and her primary and secondary sexual organs, attacks on the layers directly beneath skin or on the skin itself," Claudia Benthien ventured, "[t]he sheer peeling off and removal of surface layers seems to be an act of violence that men perpetrate against other men—at least according to classical and biblical sources and medieval penal practice. [I]n terms of cultural history (in torture, medicine, and sexual crime), the skin of the woman is pierced while that of men is stripped off" (Benthien 93). The historical and cultural relation of this distinction of impulses, with taboos concerning the mystery, sanctity, and preservation of women's bodies, was an important one. Benthien noted that stripping would have destroyed female bodies, while penetration preserved the mystery essential for fetishizing: "The female body is understood as a concealing veil. Undressing a woman of her skin would fundamentally destroy the myth of her being other . . . Woman should remain the wounded sex; the skin remains a fetish and a veil" (Benthien 86). Unlike the (ideal) male body whose *muscular* corporeal frame pushed through flesh and skin, whether the skin was elastic or translucent, was stripped away or not, Benthien stated: "The female body . . . needs a covering, concealing, smoothing skin that does not reveal the diffuse interior" (87). The myth of the ideal female body required that its surface remains intact. "Femaleness lies only in the dark and muddy breeding ground in the depths of the body or in the smooth and beautiful sheath-façade that surrounds this body" (89).

Écorché

Between her halter top
and pedal pushers
her belly already
stands before him
the erotic zone
in awe
clearly demarcated
by her clothes

The power
of the curves
procreation
beneath the toney flesh
a light blue
artery running across
from hip to
temple mount

he scents the mystery of musk
incense that brings her back
from the land of the dead
piercing the still statue
of Athena or Aphrodite
gray veins in white marble
running through
the hard cold rock

***

Auto-Dissection?

Unlike the flayed criminal who by the removal of the skin is "rightly" denied their place in the world as a human being, a woman who was flayed, even we assume, by her own hand, was not a woman anymore. But, concluded Benthien, "woman is not surface *or* container. The two notions . . . turn out to be two sides of the same conception: woman as hollow space with an enveloping, smooth external skin. If that skin is removed, her body also ceases to be a "container" (89). Whether male or female, however, in bizarre depictions of *auto-dissection*—of humans opening their own body up for inspection (otherwise not unlike the way naked soul were splayed after death [Plato, *Gorgias* 523e–525d])—a less well-studied dimension of mimesis existed: the representative relationships between the criminal-patients and their persecutor/torturer surgeons. In assisting the anatomist and obliging onlookers by prying his (or her) own body open for inspection, the belief was, through images, aesthetically created that "the body desires its own dissection," said Benthien, that "anatomical reduction was something entirely natural" (Benthien 123). Sometimes the "scene" of the dissection was set in a pastoral landscape, where the whole operation became an organic part of nature. (There was a connection of these images of auto-dissection to later critical and continual scrutiny of the "self" in relation to God required by Calvinist doctrine [Benthien 123]. Auto-dissection was an important but relatively unexamined step of human history in literary renderings of radical rendings of body and soul.)

For You, Dr. von Hagens

(Body-World Exhibit, Discovery Place, Charlotte, NC)
for Diane Perpich

These are my hands,
My knees.
I may be skin and bone"
—Plath, "Lady Lazarus" (245)

For you, Dr. Gunther von Hagens
we will sign the contract,
grant the bequest at your behest
and pledge our bodies to you after death.
To you Dr. Gunther von Hagens,
we give over our own flesh

For you, to carve into static statues
of tendons, ligaments and muscle/
(a man *and* woman—you could use
more of that, couldn't you?—
with a total of sixteen penises,
and only three vaginas)

For you, we will willingly take
our newly boned fingers and tear
our own cavities open to reveal
our layered sinews and tissues
of our chest or breasts, and smile
right at you all the while

To you, we will give a fetus
and our first born, dead,
another at a later stage
of development, for you to display
and so on, at different states of arrest,
the last, still floating in a uterus

For you, our livers and our spleen
in white, clear liquid, #10—
not formaldehyde, nor plasticine,
but plastination. From all walks of death
looking like we just strolled in
or rode the flayed enormous steed

whose brain is in one hand
compared to a larger human brain
in the other, right before the wild beast's eyes
bulging on each side of its fleshless head—
that of the rider, as if that made
any difference to either

but mostly from third world countries
who need the money in life
and so will be preserved in death—
you can tell by the spurs on
and the size and condition
of the feet, the bones, the teeth,

the scars that cut deeper than the flesh—
prisoners of war that couldn't escape,
unwitting and unwilling philanthropists
metamorphosed into aesthetic
specimens, their punishment
to be presented by art as science

So, Dr. Gunther von Hagens,
"So, so, Herr Doktor, Herr Enemy,"
here we are, amid all your flayed bodies,
these eternal muscles and rational organs
like cartilage posed before your eyes, frozen
between death and decay—as advertised

3.2.12

Anatomy of the Soul

In a sense, by acts of auto-mimesis, in assisting the surgeon the patients themselves in the sketches became anatomist-artists. This development ironically mirrored the rise and growing participation of upper middle classes in art in the seventeenth century, both as buying public and subject of art. {Future Reflection. It also ironically mirrored the Marxist ideal of participation by the masses freed by the "technological reproduction" of art (e.g., in the ideal of filmmaking) in the twentieth century (Benjamin, "Technological Reproducibility"). The ideal materialized again in the virtual plethora of social media in the twenty-first century.} Unlike Cicero's concept of the Ideal Orator, in the history of science, art, rhetoric, poetry, culture, the "natural" body, like nature itself, became a pseudo-popular, somewhat self-referential, highly self-conscious, and wholly contrived, object of self-contemplation in art and science.

Narcissus

What does he crave
and fall in love with
so quickly? An image,
someone he hardly
knows on the page.

And what do they see
in him, these walking
images, someone
they hardly know,
eyeing them

O the flattery of imagery—
the fawning of the mirror
in which he sees
what they want
him to be

and they become
a reflection of him,
the object of their
own desire, what they
fall in love with too

he looks, drinks
the image of his
affection, drowns
feeling in reflection,
himself once again

3.2.13

Mimesis as Mannerism

In the painting, sculpture, and architecture of the later Renaissance, the increasing attention to the underlying structure of the human body and to nature as the basis of observation/imitation was responsible at least in part for the development of Mannerism. As Eco stated, "the disquiet felt by artists, caught between the impossibility of rejecting the artistic heritage of the previous generation and a sense of extraneousness to the Renaissance world, led them to hollow out from the inside those forms" (218). What they found was but the material internal structure, not soul. "By apparently imitating the models of Classical Beauty, the Mannerists dissolved its rules. Classical Beauty is perceived as empty, soulless" (Eco, *Beauty* 220).

The "New" Caryatids

Lining the roads
tall but stooped over,
strange slender maidens
in the Mannerist style,
poles with one eye
on top of it
as if it could see
right through you,
row after row
of hollowed out forms
holding up the sky
for treacherous travelers
(and marauders)
who pass by

3.2.14

Toward a Fantastic Ugly

"The Mannerists," according to Eco, "opposed this [hollowness] with a spiritualization that, in order to elude the void, launched itself toward the fantastic: their figures move within the bounds of an irrational space" (Eco, *Beauty* 220). And of course, the void, the fantastic, the irrational was attractively un-mathematical, apparently chaotic, appealingly ugly. Ironically, in Mannerism, before and during the dawn of Newtonian science, "[c]alculability and measurability ceased to be criteria of objectivity and were reduced to mere instruments for the creation of steadily more complex ways of representing space . . . that bring about a suspension of proportionate order" (Eco, *Beauty* 220). The math of Mannerism changed the classical canon of the body and beauty forever.

The Statue

First comes the body part—
a wrist, an arm, an

ankle, a leg, already
full-grown, strong

then the desire
to be that part,
to have it, to
become it

then the realization
that it's not,
he can't be, he
doesn't fit

then the setting up
the pedestal
the putting
long-distance longing

3.2.15

The Great "Escape"?

The rise of middle-class patrons in the seventeenth century and public consensus rather than objective criteria and virtue as the new rule of beauty (Eco, *Beauty* 221) also led to the Baroque—mannerism with more obvious motions of emotions (so reviled in the depiction of the serenity of Greek antiquity, so ugly to them), and sentimental subjects. Importantly, Eco stated: "The distinction between proportion and disproportion no longer held, while the same applied to that between form and formless, visible and invisible: the representation of the formless, the invisible, and of the vague transcended the opposition between beautiful and ugly, true and false" (*Beauty* 221). What replaced the opposition between the true and false, the beautiful and ugly? What was the new boundary of the body to escape? "A network of relationships and forms" replaced "natural, binding, and objective models" Eco expressed; "the Beauty of the Baroque period is . . . beyond good and evil. This model allows Beauty to be expressed through ugliness, truth through falsehood, and life through death. The theme of death . . . is obsessively present in the Baroque mentality" (Eco, *Beauty* 233).

Death: Color and Myth

You smile: you corner
me with air, you trap

me in sunlight, you
surround me with a circle,
a body of light floating
over an impending void

a freed luminous form
imprisoned in color,
you smile, look away. You're
gone, vanished in light,
your smile like perfume
moving, chasing air

3.2.16

Baroque Networks of Death

Following the High Renaissance and Mannerism, the Baroque or Rocco period in art (encouraged by the Catholic Church to combat the Protestant Reformation) was obsessed by death. Displayed in various forms, including the anatomical cutting of cadavers in public theatres and opening the bodies of the criminally executed for closer inspection, the obsession with interconnections, including between life and death itself, was seen "even in a non-Baroque author like Shakespeare" (Eco, *Beauty* 233). These interconnections or networks seemed to manifest themselves at every level of reality depicted by science and art, from the microcosmic human to the awareness of the universe itself. "Just as the heavenly bodies in the firmament redesigned by Copernicus and Kepler refer to one another within ever more complex relationships, so does every detail of the Baroque world contain within itself a condensed and an expanded vision of the cosmos" (Eco, *Beauty* 234). As with every prior age, death (and attempts to speed it, save the soul at it from eternal damnation, even to escape it) was the one certainty in life, regardless of class, wealth, and or political status, and the end of every living thing. The interconnections between G/d and the Trinity (Father, Son, and Holy Ghost), the Madonna and the Saints; the Catholic Church with its descendant of Peter and the vicar of God in Pope, and a growing whole world-wide institution of cardinals, archbishops, priests, and laypersons, was a crucial network to channel pain, poverty and prayers, to offer a possible route from suffering and death to eternal paradise and salvation. The Church, like death itself, was a critical factor in all decisions and dimensions of Christians life (more so with the crisis of Protestant Reformation, the "uprising" of Islam, and the "pesky persistence" of the Jew in many societies in Europe). The Church, like death itself, was the central focus of life, music, poetry, and art.

Mass

The bell, the stone, the stairs
leading above the ceiling
teal vaulted sky of gold stars
pattern of medieval circuitry

"The God in my heart salutes
the God in your heart."
The gray women in front row, old
gray coats and gray hair leans

"All the acolytes around the world
are praying for him now;
and the Holy Pope sends
his greetings from Rome"—

the whole globe wired, kneeling
together, the cupolas, the spires
a communion of antennae
emitting the prayers to God

3.2.17

Internal Networks of Rhetoric

This attention to the underlying structure of the body and nature as a network of relations replaced classical rules of harmony and proportion, not only in art, architecture, and sculpture, or the "easy" hierarchical literary links to the Great Chain of Being, but perhaps also in rhetoric. In Paris, Petrus Ramus not only attacked the work and character of both Aristotle and Quintilian. In a fit of educational Reformation and derision, Ramus dismembered the Trivium, and with it the entire field of rhetoric. As with all subjects, he dissected what was left into schemes and tropes that were then further broken down into binary pairs, and based on the linear "geometry of the mind" found in Agricola's place logic, he diagramed these figures of speech and presented them as the "internal structure" of the art of rhetoric; in Ramus, *method itself* became the ideal (if not entelechial) model of rhetoric as mimesis (see Ong, *Ramus*). (In England, an earlier reliance on method as an ideal in science to counter medieval scholastic (Catholic) logic and other "Idols" in which uncertain senses were organs of belief (*Novum Organon*), was exhibited in Bacon's treatment of rhetoric (*Advancement* XVIII 1–5) as well as his principled reason for repetition in experiments (cf. *Advancement* XIII3, VIII.3) . {Later still, method itself became "theory hope" (cf. Bizzell, "Foundationalism").}

***

In addition to mimicking the relations in nature and the body, there were other ways that the rhetorical theory of this period was spatial. Eco himself commented on the way that "spatial" conceits applied in rhetoric as well as poetry: "One of the characteristic features of the Baroque mentality was the combination of precise fancy and surprising effect . . . This new form of eloquence, Eco said, "was encouraged by the scholastic curricula produced by the Jesuits immediately after the Council of Trent: the *Ratio studiorum* of 1586 (renewed in 1599) required, at the end of a five-year period of preuniversity studies, a two-year course in rhetoric that assured the student a perfect eloquence, aimed not only at usefulness, but also at beauty of expression..." (*Beauty* 229). The effect of this, and the way it worked, Eco said, was that "the Beauty of conceits opened up entirely new perceptual spaces, while sensible Beauty moved steadily closer to a significant and nebulous forms of Beauty" (*Beauty* 229).

3.2.18

The Terror of Beauty

The overall effect of this new rhetoric and poetics of space, in which the boundaries between inner and outer, beauty and ugliness, goodness and evil were turned inside out and essentially dissolved, was a more unpredictable, formless, terrifying, "ugly" beauty—at least from the perspective of classical ideals. In poetry and theatre, as in art, "The motionless and inanimate Beauty of the Classical model was replaced by a Beauty of dramatic intensity" (Eco, *Beauty* 334). This search for dynamic beauty continued below the skin as well as above, at its interface with nature, just outside of the body. Up through the seventeenth century, one of the ways artists imitated nature while also inventing it was by examining the "mimetic surface" of the body in order to understand and (re)create it.

In the Palace of Versailles

Louis thinks he
is the Sun King
(bright emblem
embossed
on gold leaf
of door posts

everything).
And so the
whole palace
revolves around him—
morningnoonnight,
every ritual
turns on his whim

When he opens his
eyes, everyone
in the palace awakes;
as he turns his
head, they all turn to meet
his gaze; as he lifts
his leg, more spring
to his bed;
as he puts his sacred
foot to the floor,
some are already
at the door,
ready to do his bid-

ding; when he moves
his bowels they are ready
to catch his holy
crap and piss,
already there
with the prepared
royal chamber pot
beneath his *tokhes.*
All day they move
his body around,
shadows following
the sun across
the gold tile floor

His (enclosed) world . . .

3.2.19

The "Closed" and "Open" Body

These re-presentations of the body, especially its internal constitution, were a mixture of ideas, allegories, and fantasies, as Foucault regarded them (e.g., *Clinic* xiv–xv, 3). In all this earlier work of dismemberment and imitation, in art, sculpture, poetry, and rhetoric in the seventeenth century, the concept of the body—both imagistically and physically—was understood to have been closer to what Mikhail Bakhtin in *Rabelais* called the open, "grotesque" body, rather than the ideal "closed body" that replaced it in the eighteenth century. The opposition between the "open" and "closed" body explained much about the history of beauty and ugliness, and hence mimesis and the soul as well. It was the ideal, closed body that was transcendendable, that preoccupied if not mesmerized artists, philosophers, and rhetoricians. The desire since the ancient Greeks to discover the "ideal body" resulted not only of the development of science and technology, and the corresponding view of nature as something external—to be stripped, penetrated, cut open, independently examined, controlled; the desire to discover the ideal body also resulted in the mimetic re-envisioning of reality as an open, grotesque, ugly internal body.

Grotesque Spirit Unbound

On an island—a Greek
island, say, with the
sea and sky reflected
in the pus of each
other's blue blue
eye, the puking
wind sifting through
shredded hair, mopping
an image of a beautiful
spirit trapped inside
the guts of a body,
to be freed, spilling
into something else

3.2.20

Grotesque Bodies in Literature

Mikhail Bakhtin noted in analyzing and characterizing the grotesque in literature: "at the basis of the grotesque imagery [is] a special concept of the body as a whole and of the limits of the whole. The confines between the body and the world and between separate bodies were drawn in the grotesque genre quite differently than in the classic and *naturalistic* images" (*Rabelais* 315; emphasis added). What were these differences? First, "[t]he grotesque body . . . is a body in the act of becoming. It is never finished, never completed; it is continually built, created, and builds and creates another body" (Bakhtin, *Rabelais* 317). Second, Bakhtin said, "[t]he body swallows the world and is itself swallowed by the world . . . [C]onvexities and orifices have a common characteristic; it is within them that the confines between the body and the world are overcome: there is interchange and interorientation" (*Rabelais* 317). Given this physical condition, it was even easier to understand why even Platon (philosopher, writer, mystic) might have preferred the "well-built" and controlled form of the external physical body, if not the perfect geometric Ideal body. As Burke knew and grappled with, the grotesqueness of the actual physical body entailed some unpleasant attributes: "[t]he main events in the life of the grotesque body, the acts of the bodily *drama*, take place in this sphere. Eating, drinking, defecation, and other elimination (sweating, blowing of the nose, sneezing), as well as copulation, pregnancy, dismemberment, swallowing up of other bodies—all these acts are performed on the confines of the body and the outer world, or on the confines of the old and new body" (*Rabelais* 317; emphasis added; cf. Burke, *Grammar* 137–41; Katz, "Burke's New Body"). Platon's aching teeth and withering wings of absent love, described so poignantly in the *Phaedrus* (1956, 251a–d), could now be understood in relation to the grotesque body as something externally contiguous to the internal body that was continuously changing, and therefore something to be accepted or overcome (e.g., *Philebus* 30b–36d; 46a–47a).

Insomniac's Song

5 A.M.
And in the sickening
exhaustion of morning
that spreads over the world
like an oily rag,
the birds wake up
and twitter their insomniac song.

In our insomniac beds
our little wet bodies,
all slits and bags,
hunger for more sleep
that slithers away

like a worm that daily
slowly eats our belly

3.2.21

Inner and Outer Grotesque

"The grotesque image displays not only the outward but also the inner features of the body: blood, bowels, heart, and other organs. The outward and the inward features are often merged into one" (Bakhtin, *Rabelais* 318). Bakhtin therefore argued: "[T]he grotesque body is cosmic and universal. It stresses elements common to the entire cosmos: earth, water, fire, air. It contains the signs of the zodiac. It reflects the cosmic hierarchy. This body can merge with natural phenomena, with mountains, rivers, seas, islands, and continents. It can fill the entire universe" (*Rabelais* 318). Here again were some "physical" origins of the micro-macro cosmos that Eco talked about in art, architecture, sculpture, literature and rhetoric that—beginning in the Middle Ages and Renaissance (as reflected in the astrological correspondences in various mystical systems of the body, and "the doctrine of humoral pathology" [Benthien 40])—were normalized in the seventeenth and eighteenth century. As Bakhtin concluded, "The grotesque mode of representing the body and bodily life prevailed in art and creative forms of speech over thousands of years" (*Rabelais* 318).

Pommes de Terre

(Le Château de Chenonceau, Loir Valley, France)

Past patron of
French Renaissance
architecture, daily
riding, swimming
body physically fit
externally in her fifties

Favorite of Henry II—
he 15, she 35:
C. de Medici his wife—
gave Chenonceau to his
unhidden mistress
for his whole life

D.P. visible, woven into
fabric and structure

purple and white
on black wallpaper—
her body bright
against black satin sheets

always portrayed
as a goddess
ethos of languor
apples imported,
always reserved
for the servants

Le fleur du cœur:
he always wore
her colors, loved turned
inside out—
a frag. of a lance
at a joust
pierced his eye-brain—

died, pears pouring
out on the ceiling,
guts in patterns,
initials entwined (H&D)
like paper bones
now symbols grieving

H. Died. C. de Medici—
wife, now openly jealous—
forbid her to his funeral,
moved her to Chaumont
where she retired in solace
and great comfort.

Later in history, after
husband-death, Louise de Lorraine
for eleven years wandered
the galleries over the water,
skulls and crossbones tapestry
in black dresses, went insane

gardens and gravediggers
expansive new wings in pincers
planned beyond bridges, galleries,
triangular shapes and borders
bombed, Nazi bodies
dying over Cher waters

from Italy and imitation,
indoor towers
of antlers:
because *forever*
the attention
to the hunt

3.2.22

The Grotesque in Rhetoric

The phenomenology of the grotesque body perhaps manifests itself in rhetoric as well. It may not have undergirded its theoretical conception, but it at least constituted a different way of understanding the ornate, rich and swelling veins of the Ciceronian, Asiatic, and Baroque prose styles of the High Renaissance (as opposed to the thin-veined Attic, Senecan prose styles of opponents of the grand style (Croll)—the Greek style of writing that conceptually predated the plain style of the Royal Society. Ramus' elaborate bronchial branches of speech and thought (Ong, *Ramus*) might mirror if not represent a worldview in which the language of the text (like the surface of nature or skin of the body) was regarded as a thin-to-nonexistent veil designed to mimetically reveal the constitution and movement of the internal structures that were misrepresented by language (cf. Bacon; Locke, *Essay*; Sprat). Internal structures were concealed by surfaces, obscured by figures, obfuscated by skin—yet accessible in no other way but through "the skin" (Benthien 37–43; cf. Corbin, *Foul and Fragrant*, for a discussion of an alternative point of entry, portal—the role of smell in French history, medicine, and culture). The Grotesque body was perhaps another, cultural, even rhetorical impetus for the Sprat's "chauvinistic" thoughts about nature as an ideal female body to be laid bare by science—as articulated in the aims of Royal Society (cf. Kolodny).

An Argument of Curtains

(Tours, France)

My "hypothetical" friend,
flailing in love again:

"let's have pleasant arguments,"
she said, underneath his hate.

"Do I have a threatened
stare"? Yes, when you lick
like that. "No, but it's what I heard."
Hold your breath, then.

Palm trees, houses, landscapes,
cattle, horses on the field—
always end with your strongest
argument, they say:

that you did: on a roof, holding
a fine embroidered curtain
open as from the window,
she jumped into the wind

3.2.23

Corresponding Rhetorical "Reagents"

Perhaps as part of the fuller revival of classical knowledge, perhaps as part of the Protestant Reformation, perhaps under the influence not only of print technology but of scientific and technical thinking, the curriculum bolstered by Charlemagne that had existed through the Middle Ages and the Renaissance as the Trivium and Quadrivium, along with medieval notions of the mimesis of the material spirit, and even Bacon's four-part mind (*Advancement* XVIII.2; Kinneavy) as the basis of a *new eloquence* became literally "outmoded." In the slow but sometimes violent tide of history they were swept away. Educational reforms based on spatial logic and empirical science, with their attendant ideological and power structures for discovering, visualizing, and validating knowledge by observation and replication, were in ascendance. As Walter Ong argued (*Orality*; *Ramus*), with the externalization and spatial formalization of knowledge outside the human body made possible by the printing press—in encyclopedia, concordances, diagrams, charts—the mnemonic purposes of poetry and the traditional argumentative functions of rhetoric too were more anachronistic, artificial, and less useful. There was simply less need for the "average university student" to study meter and arrangement and style (cf. Josephs, *Shakespeare*). With continuing developments in science, mathematics, algebra, astronomy, and calculus, the Quadrivium of geometry, arithmetic, astronomy and music was given new life, and the study the Trivium itself was considered beneath and preparatory to the Quadrivium. Perhaps also under the growing pressure of scientism and the coming of empiricism of mimetic re-presentation, the gap between rhetoric and poetry grew, further severing those two tender arts right to the very bone.

[^^]

Within the Trivium, rhetoric was eventually reduced from the higher ground on which Aristotle had placed it as the counterpart of dialectic, to a lower art form having to do with letter writing, recipes, and "self-help" books on etiquette and manners (cf. Murphy). And poetry was left to the Catholics and the Aristocrats. As Cicero feared in *De Oratore, Brutus,* and *Orator,* rhetoric and poetry were stripped of their respective but for him highly interrelated acoustic dimensions of style and mutual functions of rhythm and sound *in relation to judgement* (see *De Oratore* Bk. III), into more distant, even antagonistic arts. Afterall, apparently "Aristotle only taught rhetoric in the afternoon" (Quintilian 3.1.14).

Aristocracy: A Short, Definitive Life

A long shimmering lute string
plucked in the late afternoon
slowly vibrates with sun and sound.
Carnations swim in a blue-green hue.
The room, stuffed with stale tobacco, snuff,
red wine, and port begins to darken, warm.
He paces thought, recalls another time
when his mind was heavy, full, his head

bending over comfortless books,
reading alone, in a too soft corner,
by the depressed light of another
noon gone by. Day shades into night.
Lifting a short history like a mirror,
it too closely echoes his own life.

3.2.24

Ramus Reams Rhetoric

It must have been disturbing to the Catholic Church in countries all over Europe when Protestant educational reformers like Ramus threw out the Trivium and Quadrivium in favor of a new, spatial logic. Perhaps as part this educational conversion, Petrus Ramus, academic renegade and absolute classical skeptic (rebuking and snidely dismissing both Aristotle and Quintilian), not only robbed rhetoric of three of the five arts of rhetoric (invention, arrangement, and memory) leaving it only with style and delivery; Ramus also further stripped style of its acoustic content and sonic logic. Extracting and redacting Style to figures of speech only, he physically belligerently bifurcated them into "antithetical" pairs in an extensive and aggressive tree diagram—a "visual dialectic." The process of stripping/slashing rhetoric mimicked the action of the new binary mind developed and illustrated by Talus and Agricola's place logic (Ong, *Ramus*). From the Reformation through the seventeenth century, the subject of rhetoric became an *écorché* of itself—a flayed corpse, stripped of its skin, all its tendons and muscles exposed and removed. Ramus' educational reforms were not well received by Catherine de' Medici and the Catholic nobility, nor the Catholic majority in France.

Rhetoric, Dead Orchids: Ramus's Study

St. Bartholomew's Day Massacre
University of Paris, August 1572

History wound up the stairs:
The Roman Catholic soldiers
(sent by Catherine de' Medici)
followed, searching for Huguenots
and other Protestant reformers.
New footsteps on landings. Hands
slip along the edge of railings.

An old scent of decaying
dead orchids rising up,
canopies of conniving,
corpses coming back alive,
meeting in secret chambers,
bigoted black towers:
"Where is Ramus' office?"

And skeletons gathering
(heretical bodies, books
from within their campus closets
hiding, praying)—thrown from
their bookstalls in the plot to slay
all religious renegades,
plunging knives into the wisps

as soft as decaying flowers:
now their flayed bones whisper, walk
down some grim halls of knowledge,
unconscious, another rhetorician
massacred, mutilated,
possibly decapitated
dead

3.2.25

Skeletons Put (Back) Into the Closet

The influence of Ramus reduced the subject of rhetoric to a technical handbook—about itself. After Ramus was rammed like the body of rhetoric back in the closets, almost nothing remained but a tree of figurative ornaments that would later easily be knocked and torn down by apologists for Newtonian science of the seventeenth century, such as Thomas Sprat of the Royal Society and empiricist philosophers such as John Locke. An alternate to the Ciceronian, Asiatic, and Baroque oratorical styles in the Middle Ages and the Renaissance, the scientific revolution resulted in a rebirth of the desire for an Attic, Senecan or plain style more appropriate to scientific modes of inquiry and communication (see Croll). The *ideal* of "mathematical plainness" (Halloran and Whitburn) was in fact no style at all, a "transparency" an ideal that had appeared in Aristotle but was more fully realized and enforced by the Royal Society {and later would become a primary epistemological and ethical belief (Han; Katz, "Ethics"), and invisible terministic screen.}

***

In fact, it was an implementation of an Aristotelian ideal—an obsession with being rhetorically anorexic, stylistically thin to the point of nakedness—which perhaps was "revealed" by Sprats repeated use of words like "bare" and "naked" to talk about "the virtues" of nude nature and facts and truth [e.g., 61–62; 111–16]). C. S. Lewis proclaimed that the rhetoricians' distaste for poetry (and the poets' distaste for rhetoric?)—both based on a scale of utility—constituted a wall between Modern, and Medieval and Elizabethan literature, confirming that rhetoric did form the basis of literary practice and criticism during those periods (61). Under the pressure of new concepts of mimesis as empirical imitation and "exact" (approximate) replication of methodological and instrumentation in science (e.g., Bacon, *Advancement* XIII.3), the gulf itself between rhetoric and poetry widened. During this history, poetry shuffled off the prosaic coil of rhetoric, regarded it as stylistically "defective"/undesirable (Aristotle, *Rhetoric* 1404a5–10) because of its practical necessity, forever sullied by its association with an irretrievably mercantile middle-class world. And for the busy merchant, poetry became the expression of aesthetics for esthetes. Rhetoric became the pragmatic art of civil and legal argument. Poetry was still very much associated with the playful baubles of social status, became an elevated pastime or cultural refinement, if not a path to social or political advancement (like ancient Chinese civilizations, where poetry itself was the civil test to advance political position and power [see Seaton and Cryer]), or an avenue for "moral" improvement {which in the twentieth century finally would be proven a totally tall tale, a false myth, a dangerous belief (Steiner, *Bluebeard*). Thinking of Platon, who wore these "robes," rhetoric and poetry went back into the closet.

granted only for a time
every house holds the sorrow
like forgotten coats sagging in the closet
somebody's long, lost tomorrows

never fully realized, lived, the griefs
they had felt, experienced, harbored
to teach them how thorough these thieves

are—as they move on to another
house and take on the lives of others
full of new happiness and horrors

3.2.26

Skin as the New Surface of Style

Prior to the eighteenth century, in the philosophy of painting, as in rhetoric and poetry, the surface of the body seemed in a sense to be a mimesis of the whole human body (as well as a connected reflection of the cosmos)—physical, moral, spiritual, even religious. As Benthien noted, in the images of flaying and auto-dissection "figures clearly reveal the extent to which the skin was understood as a kind of enveloping leather or textile tent in which the true essence was concealed" (64). Physically, the skin was therefore a reflection not only of external but also internal conditions, which, again, were treated through the skin. It was in this semiotics of skins that ugliness as well as the beauty of the body had assumed both religious and aesthetic meaning. But the skin was now also the surface the soul. In Chapter 5 of *Skin*, "The Mirror of the Soul: The Epidermis as Canvas," Benthien, examining Michelangelo's "Last Judgment" in which the artist portrays his dripping, rotting skin being pulled out of the depths by God, commented: "skin [is] a representation of the soul—and thus of what about a person is individual and remains constant. The skin (and not the soul) is what remains of the person after death, and can be revived and makes a person identifiable" (96). An odd reading of the skin, prior to the eighteenth century, the true self was directly identified with its surface covering: "a person's soul remains alive for as long as an intact bodily envelope ensure individuality" (Benthien 96).

Mummy

Long black hall with a lit room
at the end
(his room, as a child, bathed by light),
mummy on the floor,
swaddled, wrapped in bandages
of too-tight thought—
head and torso,
form of a decaying brain,
mummy encased in gray matter—
still alive—
too much cogitation.

3.2.27

Over-Exposed Surfaces of Sight

In post-classical, anti-Platonic and pre-Enlightenment "form" of mimesis, the skin became not only a mask to cover natural nakedness, but became a representation of "self," the skin of "self," that was embodied in new notions of the "individual" with political rights and liberty that must be protected (Locke, *Two Treatises*). The skin as protection—a primeval need that begins with Adam and Eve, who adopted the "second skin" clothing to hide their naked bodies—in art also represented "a shifting of shame from sex to the face and the entire body" (Benthien 98). With the identification of true inner self with the outer self of the skin came "the desire of shielding this surface—which identifies and reveals—from the foreign gaze. Mechanisms of concealment and masking set in" (98). Hence, the second skin as shield—with its accoutrements (clothes, cosmetics, jewelry) as necessary ornaments, became another reading of the attention to costumes and jewels during the Middle Ages, as well as the heavy use of cosmetic effects in art up until the Baroque era (see Eco, *Beauty* 196–99). "The human being must protect himself or herself against the penetrating gaze of others," Benthien averred; this required covering oneself—even if, as in many cultures, this was done merely through symbolic ornaments or a specific inner attitude that regulated the act of looking" (99).

The Secret of Her Openness

The end is always near,
and so the need to be open.
She walls herself in,
hides behind it
like an open field.

Her need to be open
is in exact proportion
to her need to be hidden.
And she's the fastest gravedigger
he doesn't know—so fast

she doesn't know it's happening
in her breast. Her psychic shovel
digs the veiled skeleton
of her mother: she embraces
her once again.

3.2.28

Blind Medicine

The image of the open, grotesque body (thinly veiled by protective skin that mimics the inside even as it conforms to the cosmos) existed not only in art, literature, and rhetoric, but also in the sciences through the Baroque era. That is to say, the grotesque may have been a major part of the conception of the physical human body in medicine going back to the ancient Greeks. As Bakhtin demonstrated, "[I]n spite of differences, all the works contained in the [Hippocratic] anthology present a grotesque image of the body; the confines dividing it from the world are obscured, and it is most frequently shown open and with its interior exposed" (*Rabelais* 355).

Discussing Barbara Duden's work on the perception of the female body in the eighteenth century, Benthien stated that even at the turn of that century,

> "[t]he skin was understood as a porous layer with a multitude of possible openings . . . Here, the surface of the body is a place of permeability and mysterious metamorphoses. "Fluxes" that are in constant motion in the body and can continually change their form exit the body as blood, pus, urine, phlegm, or sperm. Body fluids such as sperm or menstrual blood are

> by no means always understood as indicative of gender (the menses and the "golden vein"—the term used for hemorrhoids at the time—were still interpreted as equivalent therapeutic evacuations of the body as late as the early eighteenth century)" (Duden in Benthien, 116ff.). All of these "fluxes" have a functional resemblance. . . . [D]octors did not distinguish between normal and pathological excretions but only between their various degrees of efficacy for the body. (Benthien 39)

Defensive Ornaments

A kind of puffiness,
wearing a face
that doesn't quite fit,
vibrating space
leaking out
around the edges
and the eyes

a mask inappropriate
for the emotion
the mouth doesn't make
trying to appear
smiling whiling
all the time
it wants to cry

3.2.29

The External Touch of Medicine

But because the limitations of technology and taboo, the internal body was only available via the external body. But because the outside was re-presentative of the inside, the surface of the body—with its excretions, extensions, protrusions, and humors—was a primary basis of both diagnosis and treatment in medicine, and imitation in art. Thus, in Chaucer's *Canterbury Tales* the "mormal" on the cook's leg, or the carbuncles on the Summoner's face, were not only sores on the skin but physical representations of moral character as well; it took on both real and symbolic (mimetic) value in the larger allegory. But because the internal body was not yet fully accessible to sight, with increasing depths when it came, a primary means of diagnoses was the sense of touch. But even touch as revelation and diagnosis had longevity and depth. Based on ethnographic research into practices of anatomy, Kenny T. Fountain explored the centrality of human touch as an essential anatomical tool that informed and combined with other modes of sight). But the *internal* body into which *touch*, forbidden by religious proscription and legal interdiction (Nancy, *Noli*; cf. Derrida, *Touching*), had to be transformed and treated by the medical "Gaze" as a secularized interior (Foucault, *Clinic*): it was not any soul that was found or probed or treated. {Pre-cognition. Until the development of neurology, even psychology was limited to touch, first to the application of "shock" by the recently discovered electricity; by the discredited and disgraced science of phrenology; by psychotherapy and psychoanalysis (the "talking cures"); by psychotherapy and the uncertain and sometimes highly unpredictable prescription use of psychotropic of drugs. All based on effects observed only from the outside, from reports of the patients and demonstrated (non) changes in behavior.}

Felt Summer Skin

Poor, panicked,
and vulnerable again.
Maybe he should move further
north, where there is only winter.
He hates the summer,

the full blooming of
anxiety like the green pollen of
flowers, the neurotic
breath, the sour pajamas hanging
in their anxious sweat.

Every loss feels permanent,
vacations like abandonment,
women like islands
he must try to swim to every day
and drown in his own self-pity, regret.

He loves cold summers
scarves and sweaters, coats and hats—
anything to hide his naked
the body of his emotions
from himself. He would surround himself

with women if he could;
but he is repulsed by

the acne, the sores, the hair, the oils
on the clothes, his and theirs,
the keyboard, bathrobe, flesh

(although he rejoices in them too,
wraps himself in images of the organic).
An image is so much cleaner.
But he wraps himself
in a womb of clothes instead.

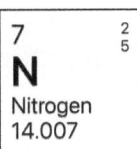

7 2
5
N
Nitrogen
14.007

9 Rationality Organ

3. Anatomy of the Grotesque Body

3.3.0

"The Gaze" Inward

The observable, accessible, sheer, shimmering, delectable, glimmering surface of the body had always been a focus of questions, investigation, fantasy, and "treatment." As Platon had known, skin held many attractions and illusions. Previously, the examination of phenomena below the surface of the skin was more or less based on partial knowledge of what processes and "symptoms" could be observed or inferred from the outside. The "inside was constituted by logic. During the Renaissance, the slow opening of religious doctrine and the rapid development of technical instruments had allowed a more empirical examination of the open body, and of the grotesque inside as well as outside the protruding surfaces of the body. The peculiar "position" where the internal body was open to a scientific view but closed to the public perhaps predated and predicted a modern, scientific era that then incorporated it.

***

In literature and art, the *closing* of the grotesque, now synecdochic body can be said to have coincided with the end of the Baroque era and rise of the Enlightenment (see Eco, *Beauty* 196–99, 259; Benthien 38–39;102–10). Bakhtin noted that many authors also had been students of medicine if not medical practitioners. Rabelais himself had chosen the profession of medicine and lectured on medicine throughout Europe, and in 1537 conducted a well-known public dissection (Bakhtin, *Rabelais* 360). During the Middle Ages and early Renaissance, the so-called "barber-surgeons," "operating" in "public theatres" with steady razors in hand, would have carved the corpses—usually executed criminals—while the "physician," situated and hovering high above the scene, delivered an accompanying lecture to a leering crowd. But in the Renaissance through the second half of the eighteenth century, not only did physicians such as Andreas Vesalius become anatomists as well as writers, and "step down" to the operating tables and *descend* [a non-pagan, but secular κατέβην, or ירדי] into the "scientific chariots" of the surgical theatres; they also stepped into the bodies and life histories of their patients.

***

From the eighteenth century onward, the inside of the body thus became the new subject of the increasingly "clinical" Gaze. Just as flaying was replaced by the guillotine in the prison yard (one exception being the spectacular beheadings of the royals and the aristocrats in the French Revolution), the scalpel replaced the barber's blade. As Foucault documented in *Discipline and Punish,* not only in anatomy but in jurisprudence, the public spectacle "moved indoors," became more private, invisible (but perhaps no less brutal for it), under the ever-watchful panopticon eyes of experts, and with "omniscient" visibility ultimate control. {Future Gaze. From the eighteenth to the twentieth centuries, enclosed imprisonment increasingly supplanted public punishment (Foucault, *Discipline*); except for purposes of teaching, surgical theatres were reconstituted in private hospitals (Foucault, *Clinic*); and psychological "analyses" and "treatment" were as relegated to asylums, and then retired to wholly privileged parlors (Foucault, *Madness*). The body was therefore "closed" again—to the general audience (except for purpose of entertainment—circuses, spectacles, and other public displays).} Disconnected and "closed" from the surrounding world, the open body became the exclusive object of science, against which the human spirit would eventually chafe.

{Last Visit: The Nursing Home

(for Nana, d. February 13, 1995)

She tries to figure out her age.
We look at some old photographs
in the room she no longer knows
as hers. I pick the broken glass
from the warping picture frame,
point to my wife and son and dog
waiting outside her open door—
her eyes dim in recollection;
reset her clock, knocking her cup
of old teeth water onto the floor.

I tell the nurse it's time for us to go.
But I leave the way I want her to go—
not by the elevator, painful, slow,
her hand attaching to my elbow, sleeve,
her withered voice clutching at my name,
but quietly, quickly out the balcony door,
leaving behind the gray halting walker,
her white hair disappearing around the corner

as she hops and skips and jumps across the courtyard
of red and yellow pansies, runs up the hill
to the circular park and across the small green field
toward the orange-white water tower
checkered like her faded tablecloth,
the Old Soldier's Home overlooking
Chelsea (first childhood memory)—

finally free from the shallow grave of her body,
a child at last, again, rising above the Boston skyline,
on the Tobin Bridge the top of each light pole in rows
splitting, sprouting white and silver seagull wings,
stretching, lifting, soaring out over the harbor,
bodiless, wings paired and pinioned, calling
calling back from high above the Bay,

spittle flying into ocean }

3.3.1

The Effect of "the Gaze"

The Newtonian revolution desired to create knowledge through the observation of internal structure rather than only logical deduction. "The Gaze" (Foucault, *Clinic*) opened the closed (if leaky) containers of the human body, as it opened nature, for deeper inspection at will. On the surface of the open and/or grotesque body, was the other side of the cultural-aesthetic divide: the closed grotesque body. This surface was no longer a division not only between beauty and ugliness, or divine and physical. Because of access into internal bodies, the surface of the body now became the object of the Rational as well as the Representivity Organ. Bodies objectively examined other bodies, coming full circle but missing "the entity" from which all need and desire sprung, and the ethics to govern it. That was the epistemological realm of philosophy again.

***

The investigation by the rationalities organ of both closed open body became the rage in seventeenth- and eighteenth-century science. In light of Kenny T. Fountain's exploration of the highly tactile nature of anatomy, Foucault's notion of "the Gaze" seemed more visual and somewhat reductive, combining "objective" observation, and systemization in discourse. Nature itself was conceptualized and represented as a woman, leaky and lank, to be pierced and penetrated and thus known—a mysterious, passive, massive soft container lying on the table of the earth. The male (sexual) Gaze poked, thrust, sliced open, pushed into—and observed, described, recorded, and enjoyed what it saw and felt, while preserving (most of) the outer skin. {The action of the Gaze applied not only to the female body and its (dis)inherited rights, but also to the female mind—a psychology that lasted beyond the hysteria of the twentieth and twenty-first centuries.

(The)rapists Hate Me

Her hands clench,
get hot, cool off,
just like her

Beneath his arms.
He kisses her knees
to improve their self-esteem.

"When was your birthday,"
she asks, staring
at his bald spot:

"(The)rapists hate me."

"What's your sign?" she asks.
He doesn't remember, care. 'What's yours?'
"i don't know; i don't really follow it."

She's one big beautiful
nerve, trembling in his hands
like the squeeze ball of a universe.

"(The)rapists hate me."

By the starlight of a screen saver
nothing happens. She rolls away
and grabs an umbrella:

"What is this thing
between us?" she asks.
'Take it; it's yours.'

"(The)rapists hate me."

The night rolls out a carpet
of kisses, bright and swollen
like lips of stairs and stars}

3.3.2

"The Gaze" as Mimesis

Concomitant with the rise of Newtonian science, and the successful development of the field of optics (to which Newton himself contributed [Kuhn, *Structure* 10–14; 48]) rose "the modern medical practice." The new sciences that probed the bodies of human and nature—be they anatomy, biology, chemistry, psychology, dermatology—provided seemingly more rigorous methods if not exact mathematical formula for the concept of the body. (Medicine was as much science as art. As Foucault pointed out, this concept of the body, and the distribution of disease within it, was yet simply another model, and not the last [*Clinic* xiv–xv, 3].) Through anatomy, *scientific epistemology and surgical procedures became a new basis of mimesis—one that replaced the art-of-ficial mathematical ratios and geometric proportions of the ancient Greeks*, which in turn had been rendered relative and then irrelevant in preceding centuries. Once "the gaze" of "objectivity," technology, and discourse turned inward, the body may have been sealed as a legitimate object of science, and the skin seen as an intervening albeit necessary sack to be pierced, cut, and/or torn away. In an "ontological reversal" of earlier mimeses—Spenser's sentiment that "soule is forme, and doth the bodie make" (462)—was now turned inside out: the soul was the form the body made. Thus, rather than the outer body being a false re-presentation, a *grotesque* reflection, an empty shell or container, a prison house of a "transcendent soul" (as it had been for Platon and Aristotle), the inner material body was now also exteriorized, so that both "body and soul" were external (and often ugly).

Hiding (Abuse)

"And I, who have no rights in this matter, neither father nor lover"
—Theodore Roethke, "Elegy for Jane"

Her mouth is sharpened by anger,
her face stiffened with stress,
but her hands, tightly textured,
are woven with the ink of a schoolgirl
she once was, knobby knees
now grown into tight black jeans,
and black shoes her roommate gave her
that bled blue-black into her white socks.

Her eyes are in a deep blue ink,
across the shadow of her mouth,
an invisible freckle in the palm
of her self-conscious hand
now closing like a scar upon itself,
blue tendrils overgrowing it,
inky fingers wrapped around each other.

Her lips wrote "no" as his moved
closer and her head turned and dived
down and around and away from his kiss,
while her eyes side-glanced up like an apology
you have to make when it's not your fault
but you can't explain it—like the one true freckle
she said was on the bottom of her foot.
And her hair bleeds across her face.

A slice of hair cuts across her face
like a sharp red gash, a mouth into
which she puts one small finger,
a thin white cigarette of flesh,
awe-opened, surprise-silenced cry
now breaking into a shadow of song,
into lyrics of candle-eyed questions,
notes like hair falling into night.

She brushes out a quiet harmony;
she hides inside the notes, peeking out

from her hair, and the question mark
that hangs there, like a smile coy-cut in air,
non-conversation punctuated by
slurring matches, accusing cigarettes.
When you try question the question marks,
do they always only question back?

3.3.3

Disappearing Skin

With changes in science, sensibility, and culture in the eighteenth century, the surface of skin of a body was no longer what is "definitively" represented—imitated, manifested, indicated, revealed. Or less so. The focus of attention shifted to what was going on inside the body. Like taboos against dissecting a corpse, in its capacity of acting as a kind of cultural skin protecting a malleable, permeable surface of a social body, the inner body soon succumbed to the knife of scientific consciousness. (According to more positivistic science historians, such as Charles Coulston Gillispie, the "edge" of science was to slice open and cut away any remaining superstitious or religious belief in every field: physics in the seventeenth century, chemistry in the eighteenth century, biology in the nineteenth century, and perhaps subatomic physics and/or psychology in the twentieth.) Treatments and cures that had tended to focus on the skin as an interface between external symptoms and unseen causes gave way to diagnoses and treatments that penetrated, bypassed, or supplanted the skin and flesh, and "dealt with" diseases "directly." Just as the structure of nature and its underlying mathematical principles and physical laws became a focal point of empirical science, the internal structure of the human body and its underlying principles became a major focal point of anatomy and medicine—a thrust into an ostensibly new level of "realism" in the depiction of the body that would affect science, art, literature, and rhetoric from the Enlightenment onward. As Benthien concludes:

> The fundamental restructuring of medical diagnosis and treatment to deal directly with the inside, without applying treatments on and in the skin, could not fail to influence the collective body image. A conception of the skin as a closure and a necessary boundary layer could arise only after these multifarious practices of drawing off substances through the skin and opening the epidermis were dismissed as prescientific and replaced by intracorporeal medication or surgical intervention. (41)

***

The act and image of irritating, of puncturing, peeling, flaying, filleting, penetrating, severing, amputating the body to understand or punish it (often the same thing, the poking at potential truths, the probing of dark secrets) was repeated over and over again in the arts as well as the sciences. "The visual arts of the sixteenth and seventeenth centuries, in particular, belabored the theme of flaying to exhaustion," says Benthien: "[t]he intense preoccupation reflects the epistemological rupture that was triggered by the emerging discipline of anatomy. The question of violence in the transcending of the cutaneous body boundary and the possibility of depicting a more-than-naked body were addressed iconographically" (Benthien 63). In many ways, aesthetic flaying, like the gathering scientific investigation of nature, was considered, says Benthien when speaking of a sculptural work depicting the flaying of Marsyas, "the act of peeling something of its (false) form . . . The skin is, accordingly, a separate, second figure, an alien alter ego" (79). It was a physician or executioner-assisted transcendence.

Autumn in the Mountains

He does not like the way she dresses:
her clothes don't fit, the colors don't match.
He does not like her hair, or where they live—

a flutter of leaves the wind whips
off the table of the seasons,
tears the shirts off backs of the blousy trees—

and nature draws its foggy curtain
on the evening, and on their lives—
an early morning later, lights rising from the mist

to find her true, authentic self,
to love again, a clearinghouse of mountains
pressing up against her senses, peeling senseless skin

3.3.4

Cannon of Skin

Spurred on by the simultaneous and continuing development of science as well as technology, the surface of the body was, generally speaking, no longer the primary epistemological basis of mimesis in rhetoric or catharsis in poetry. If for Bakhtin the body of the grotesque cannon was open, in contact with the world, and also the cosmological, then what Bakhtin called the "new cannon," the closed body in literature, "presents an entirely finished, completed, strictly limited body, which is shown from the outside as something individual" (320). As Bakhtin pointed out, the remaining extensions and orifices, such as the eyes, mouth, belly, buttocks, nose, were retained but limited and become purely expressive of the emotional life of an individual (body), or, as in the case of the genital organs, repressed (cf. Burke, *Toward a Symbolic*).

> In the modern image of the individual body sexual life, eating, drinking, and defecation have radically changed their meaning: they have been transferred to the private and psychological level where their connotation becomes narrow and specific, torn away from the direct relation to the life of the society and to the cosmic whole. In this new connotation they can no longer carry on their former, philosophical functions. (Bakhtin, *Rabelais* 321; also see Foucault, *History of Sexuality*)

Both Bakhtin and Foucault attempted to unmask these physical processes and functions (cf. Burke, *Toward a Symbolic*) that were legally operated upon in the open body, and then philosophically and culturally quickly cloaked (again).

Ambulance

Old man awakes
with the wheezing
of an engine that he takes
for his own breathing because
he travels within it

over his face
there is a web
he tries to erase
with the back of
his stiffened hands

he finds morning
clouded under sheets;
a cold wind
rushing by
his life

3.3.5

Defining the Inside

The investigation of the inside is perhaps facilitated by if not made possible when the outside is more ontologically defined. Beginning in the eighteenth century, it was not the open, grotesque body that modern medicine was to begin to fill in, but the closed, delimited body. As Foucault states, "For us, the human body defines, by natural right, the space of origin and of distribution of disease: a space whose lines, volumes, surfaces, and routes are laid down, in accordance with a now familiar geometry, by the anatomical atlas" (*Clinic* 3). For Foucault, the body spatializes the disease and so makes it visible to "the Gaze"; the disease (understood not only as observable symptoms but also the medical categories and rational discourse to describe it) in turn circumscribes those parts of the body. As we had read quite literally, "Clinical experience [opened] up . . . the concrete individual, for the first time in Western history, to the language of rationality" (Foucault, *Clinic* xiv). Encased within the skin and contained in (culturally) closed flesh, the internal organs now hung like ornamental "jewels" *inside* the body, ripe for picking and plucking. {Temporal Slice. Except for the specialty of dermatology, and the growth of cosmetology, the outside surface of the body—the skin with its past metaphysical significances and social connections—was (until the twentieth century) no longer a main focal point or major concern of the physician or surgeon. For most sciences (e.g., except eugenics), the skin outside was lost to new vision. Skin would once again become, but not only as the borders of souls, and/or a basis of mimesis, but something to be pierced, tattooed, cruelly or aesthetically strung up (see KAC; Sterlac], or extended by the growing distances of furthest satellites into new boundaries of our bodies in outer space (cf. De Kerckhove).}

{Losing Things

(For Larry Rudner, d. May 5, 1995 of a brain tumor)
"Whoever saves one life saves the world"—Talmud (Sanhedrin 37a)

Keys, books, glasses, hats, pets, pens;
opportunities, time, memory, weight;
relatives, children, parents, friends;
love, relationships, you, life, ourselves—

confusion lives inside
the tissue of your skin,
grows like a drop on a napkin,
a chaotic stain spreading, extends—

an unruly mob on a favorite shirt,
loosening your grip on things,
disorder ascends, reigns throughout
the big body of your house

until you shrink to a room,
a helpless world installed in a bed,
the voices of symphonies lost
on the ceiling, playing in your head . . .

A *Tzadi* appears in the lampshade:
and your shelties begin to bark at stars,
and memories like light bulbs pop, go out,
and there's no one to replace them,

and time reverses in your brain,
and reality becomes displaced:
you run for President, become Hemingway—
and then the dining room expands again.

Your speech like a door closes, locks
(hospital windows don't open or shut);
then you are confined to a pine box
with a single star on top:

We bury a friend, a relative, a parent, a spouse . . .
And another world is lost

3.3.6

Mimesis as Rational Figuration

In Foucault's image of the body as the map and container of disease, a new configuration of the body and basis of mimesis perhaps emerged—one clearly based on the science of anatomy and medicine. But, argued Foucault throughout *The Clinic*, science itself, its objectivity, and the knowledge gained from it, was the result of "the reductive discourse of the doctor, as well as established as multiple objects meeting his positive gaze. The *figures* of pain are not conjured away by means of a body of neutralized knowledge; they have been redistributed in the space in which bodies and eyes meet" (*Clinic* x–xi, emphasis added; also Wells, "Legible Bodies"). Auerbach, and White, might have agreed with Foucault that anatomical realism is itself "figuration"—and that figural realism is not only the operating principle running like a spine through the literature of Western civilization, but also running through the human body. As Foucault explained so well, "displaced, enclosed within the singularity of the patient, [is] that region of "subjective symptoms" that—for the doctor—defines not the mode of knowledge, but the world of objects to be known" (*Clinic* xi).

***

{Time Lapse. "[W]hat the doctor is examining [is] not merely the body of the patient: in "the region where "things" and "words" have not yet been separated . . . the articulation of medical language and its object will appear as a single figure" (*Clinic* xi). The "region" was this combination of observation and language that was to become not only a newer basis of the processes and procedures of medical science, but also a newer basis of mimesis in art as both a (re)presentation and (re)production of the body. "At the beginning of the nineteenth century," Foucault says, "doctors described what for centuries remained below the threshold of the visible and the expressible" (*Clinic* xii). The living corpse, the σώμα [*soma*], the ècorchè, was now a somewhat objectified, closed, rational system, at least partially reconstituted by and accessible through language even more than death.

A Short Afterlife: The Last 2–10 Minutes of Death

For my mother
(who i found dead in the garage of asphyxiation, June 20, 1968)

Dead, your dying brain
yields its last feverish content
before your upturned, inverted eyes
watching a rerun of your life
like a bad drive-in home-movie,
projected against the wall of the garage
opposite the wall where you lie,
a newly conscious corpse
spellbound in the darkness,
breathless, mouth open
in astonishment, one leg
hanging onto the car seat,
each flickering cell of the film
releasing what has been
kept and collected
in the dark wet corners
of memory, heaped up amid
the dim confused clutter

of a mind that was you,
now dying
in that fast gaseous invisible light,
arm outstretched, hanging in the air,
the final gesture and judgment of your life—
a jar of thick liquid
overturned on the cold concrete floor
spilled in a flash.}

3.3.7

Transfiguration of Light in the Enlightenment

In the scientific gaze into the physical interior of the body in the eighteenth century, as in the external gaze on the exterior body in the Middle Ages and the Renaissance, light again played a decisive part in the conception of reality. But light was also to be transfigured. In eighteenth-century medicine, light was not a spiritual quality, nor the form of the soul. Nor was it only the physical means of peering into the heretofore closed, dark body. Light itself was also reconfigured in the gaze. "[L]ight, anterior to every gaze, was the element of ideality—the unassignable place of origin where things were adequate to their essence—and the form by which things reach it through the geometry of bodies" (*Clinic* xiii). However, Foucault had said, "At the end of the eighteenth century . . . seeing consists in leaving to experience its greatest corporal opacity; the solidity, the obscurity, the density of things closed upon themselves, have powers of truth that they owe not to light, but to the slowness of the gaze that passes over them, around them, and gradually into them, bringing them nothing more than its own light" (*Clinic* xiii–xiv). For Foucault, from the eighteenth century onward, "[r]ational discourse is based less on the geometry of light than on the insistent, impenetrable density of the object" (*Clinic* xiv). This combination of light and discourse in the Gaze was necessary for internal medical examination, corrective treatment, corporeal punishment.

X-Ray

(For Dr. Carol Christensen)

Pressure. His head
aches with rain.
The black pads descend
around the sides
of his head,
the silver ball

of a glabella bar
a medieval medallion
pendent between
his eyes, the unfelt
shock of rays
slicing through brain
with the snap of an axe

Looking
into the photographic
plate, a black mirror
of the mind, the holes
of his eyes
now visible,
he sees his skull
dripping spinal
fluid like clear blood
into the pan
beneath his head
upon which the gentle
guillotine will fall

O it will fall,
and he will be
healed again

***

Eco (*Beauty*) discussed how the ideals of classical art were remade in Baroque art, in its use of light, as well as local sittings and subjects, and the establishment of other cultural and scientific networks of space and knowledge. With light came depth. For Foucault, it was this "formal reorganization *in depth*, rather than the abandonment of theories and old systems, that made *clinical experience* possible; it lifted the old Aristotelian prohibition: one could at last hold a scientifically structured discourse about an individual" (*Clinic* xiv). (In fact, it lifted two of Aristotle's prohibitions: one against the non-scientific nature of discourse; the other against the validity of the individual as opposed to the universal. The recognition of the individual was a major motif not only in art and science, but in politics as well [cf. Locke, *Two Treatises*]). But as Foucault indicated, the focus on the individual patient required not only the closing of the body, but the closing of discourse around it as well.

grandfather

and when
she returned
home but found
he had dropped
on his face
and was taken
away
she was relieved
being
ill herself:
she visits
him often
despite
the distance.

"my foot
is burning"
he cried
once more
as he lay
trapped
and stiff
his hand still
shaking
beside him.

and when
he fell
on his head
she said
he was not
the same
again.
"he's fallen
before,"
she mumbled
as they tied him;
"i almost wish
he would die."

he cannot

speak

anymore

3.3.8

Closing the Body of Death

By (re)closing the body, the innards of the grotesque were concealed, the ugliness removed from sight. The same applied to death. Just as jurisprudence and medicine were taken out of the realm of public spectacle and made invisible to the non-expert eye of the public, death was moved indoors as well. As Benthien discussed, death had to be "brought into" medicine: the taboos of religion, superstition, mysticism, and other values that kept the body intact and shielded it from "the Gaze," had to be exorcised, dispensed with, so that 1) the corpse could be opened, and 2) the mortal body (dying, death) could become a "positive object" of science (cf. Kubler-Ross). That is, the surface of the body had to cease being—or appearing to be—a re-presentation (symbol) of the body as forbidden, as "flattery" (as for Platon [*Gorgias* 502c–d]), as rhetorical "ornamentation," as the poetic prison of the soul. "[T]he body had to be individually demarcated and fundamentally demystified before the anatomist could cut it open as a matter that ceased to embody symbolic meaning" (Benthien 42). Thus, the natural progression of the body from conception to decay could ultimately be transformed by art, rhetoric, literature, culture, and later, media. {Glimpse. While death (like madness) became a main subject of much modern poetry (Frost, *Reads*; cf. Dickinson; Plath; Sexton), as always, a rhetorical part of this process involved an ideal of scientific style that, almost one word for one thing, might approximate "mathematical plainness" as closely as possible [Sprat; cf. Halloran and Whitburn]). Thus began that slow but steady process in medicine of cleaning up and sanitizing the damp organic processes of the human body, and images connected with it, including the inevitably of and unnatural fight against death).

Ballad of the Match with Death

With I.V. running to the brain,
ego tossed in bed;
my arm was wrapped and tied in boards.
"Rest," the doctors said.

And in that rally of the mind
i nodded: half-asleep
i faced my stern opponent, Death,
who rose from the bedside seat.

"Time, gentlemen!" the Umpire called.
i wanted to crawl to bed.
i looked up at the towering chair:
"Play!" was all He said.

i heard the patients calling me,
they tried to boost my nerve;
i heard the clapping of the leaves,
prepared to toss my serve.

"Game, Death!" the Umpire called.
My wife began to cry.
"One love!" the Umpire said.
Then Death began to fly.

Death began to fly, my friends,
shoes flashing in the air;
i stood there in my tied-on gown,
feet swollen, cold, and bare.

He flew from side to side and back,
serving ace after ace;
"Advantage Death!" i heard the call.
And then i saw his face.

And then i saw his face, my friends,
and then i saw his face:
his eyes were holes of anti-matter,
his mouth the void of space.

i lobbed, Death leapt, and smashed the ball—
i saw a star explode.
The ball bounced over the universe.
i lost the set 6-0.

"Keep your wrist stiff," the doctors said,

"drive up and through the stroke."
Death hit a return at the speed of light.
My tennis racquet broke!

i had to rebandage my boarded arm—
a thirty second delay.
"Turn your body for the shot,"
i heard the nurses say.

"O.K.," said Death, "let's see what's left."
The score was four to four;
my heart began to fibrillate;
i'd soon be dead on court.

Death then served another ace.
"i protest!" i tried to cry.
But Umpire, linesmen disappeared.
Death looked me in the eye.

i ran up to the bleacher stands:
"that ball was wide!" i shout;
but the crowds in the stadium vanished;
the lights flickered, went out.

Death strode up to the net, and smiled;
he reached to take my hand.
"Another time, my friend," Death said;
"let's play sometime again."

With I.V. running to the brain,
ego tossed in bed;
my arm was wrapped and tied in boards.
"Rest," the doctors said.

3.3.9

Physical Demarcation of the Material (Soulless?) Body

From the sixteenth century onward, skin became a boundary of clearly defined living bodies. In addition to anatomy, concomitant and crucial to this transformation of the image of the body was the rise of dermatology around 1800, and a corresponding scientific transcending of "an awareness of the skin."

Within this new worldview, the body finally and fully became "an individuated, monadic and bourgeois vessel that the subject was considered to inhabit" (Benthien 37). Speaking of the understanding of the body that emerged in the eighteenth century, Benthien demarcated what a new ontology—one based *in flesh*—not only became a necessary basis for Enlightenment notions of political liberty, rugged individualism, inalienable rights (Locke, *Two Treatises*), but also a basis for expanded notions of scientific (and artistic) perception, a different concept of mimesis in relation to *representation* and the body: a new affiliation, affinity, association, even liaison between outer and inner, truth and falsehood, imitation and the skin, marking a medical and cultural shift of consciousness.

> The eighteenth century witnessed a fundamental change in body perception and with it a change in the notion of the skin as the boundary of the individual body. With the emergence of clinical-anatomical medicine, the realm under the skin was made visible. In the premodern era, the skin still constituted a structurally impenetrable boundary to the invisible and mysterious inside; a boundary whose visual and haptic surface was of such great importance not least because it demanded some kind of interpretative art from physicians and healers seeking to render a diagnosis. By the later eighteenth century, however, skin had already become simply a place of passage to the inside. The dissection of the body in anatomy created a model of knowledge based on dismemberment, extraction, and disembodiment. A mechanizing view of the body gradually took hold. (Benthien 10–11)

Early Automata

i spin, balanced, round and round;
laughing, the arm moves up and down;
my head tilts to left, then smiles;
my mouth swings open with its jaw~

all springs and gears and wheels, like veils
i live within yet transcend this metal
judged and seen for what i am, this piece
i am imprisoned and free

3.3.10

Emergence of New Political Bodies

On the surface of the skin of a naturally or the closed or sutured body no longer held together by social taboos and religious beliefs, a separated individuated entity could appear. What emerged was not an epistemologically different body, a solid, social and political body, an "individual life," "strictly limited mass," an "impenetrable façade" (Bakhtin, *Rabelais* 320). What emerged was a physical and personal entity, self, contained in its own skin, with more of its own mind, consciousness. And with that self-contained, physical and personal, conscious entity emerged a new political entity: the individual. In opposition to the divine or assumed power of kings (and their power of ownership of all bodies in their realm), the individual demanded personal and political liberty, freedom, and inalienable rights. The rise of the individual "self" was no doubt a condition for the birth of popular democracy {and subsequent, *attempted* realizations through revolutions and self-governance in United States, France, and elsewhere.} The birth of the individual was intimately related to the rise of the new bourgeois, mercantile classes who would not otherwise inherit personal and political rights and social and economic status. The individual was also the underlying ontological basis for theories of a more objective science, further "severing" the self from the world it was trying to observe. The postulates of objectivity and democracy were complementary, perhaps even necessary, with subtle implications for each, and both contained in Locke's philosophical and political theories (*Essay*; *Two Treatises*). The (re)closed body *physically* propelled the political rise of the individual, as well as the belief in science. Understanding better the inside of the body, a closed body allowed both for the more definitive *separation* of observer and nature, and a firmer focus on self-contained objects beyond the boundary of the human body. The personal, self-contained, conscious individual was an external institutionalization of Descartes' internal *cogito ergo summa*—a rational, solipsistic self ultimately necessary for objectivity, from which reason and human rights apparently also sprung.

The Nurse and the Nun

"His teeth are in the sheets,
and glasses in the pillowcases."
'The cotton rustles round his legs
that pend like feathers off the bed,
a soul pending on the edge'

"His hand winds the blanket up
around his body which it wraps;

he wears it like a quilted skin."
'He feels his body tugging on the straps
that embrace, holds his bed scraps, frame him'

"Must he suffer such a prolonged death
to be released from this body-stem of pain?"
'The easy red flower becomes a ghostly rose,
needs to shiver before it slips off its slender frame.'
"The right and choice have never been his own"

"'He falls into the dark folds of the tablecloth.'"

3.3.11

The Docile Body Cometh

If the Enlightenment concept of the individual with all its rights and privileges therein (rather than G/d "*per se*," Original Sin, the Divine Right of Kings, the Church) also may have owed something to the development of inductive reason in science, and in particular, the first "fields" of anatomy, medicine {and later, dermatology}. Out of new cannon of human as individual came what Foucault labeled "the docile body." "[T]he notion of 'docility' . . . joins the analyzable body to the manipulable body. A body is docile that may be subjected, used, transformed and improved" (*Discipline* 136). This was accomplished by:

> exercising upon [the docile body] a subtle coercion, of obtaining holds upon it at the level of the mechanism itself—movements, gestures, attitudes, rapidity: an infinitesimal power over the active body. Then there were the objects of control: it was not or was no longer the signifying elements of behaviour or the language of the body, but the economy, efficiency of movements, their internal organization; constraint bears upon the forces rather than upon the signs; the only truly important ceremony is that of exercise. (Foucault, *Discipline* 137)

The desire "to docile" bodies perhaps rose to counter individual freedom and was necessary to control it (just as "institutions" arose to contain and control the unbridled flow of communication (see Foucault, "Discourse"). As Foucault demonstrated, control of the body ranged, from the regimented bearing and particular motions of the soldier on and off the battle field, to the predetermined routines of inmates incarcerated in prisons and patients in hospitals; from the disciplined precision of the physical movements of body-limbs-hands in mechanized factories, to the highly structured activity of children in the classroom controlled by nonverbal signs and bells (see Foucault's *Discipline*, esp. 141–69; cf. Washington; Phillips).

{Sunday School

(For Jake, who listened to different music that day.
In honor of Gisella Abrahamson, Holocaust survivor, whose teachings we overheard one day)

The sanctuary. At opposite ends,
two rooms.

In one room a Rabbi teaches adults Torah;
in the other a survivor teaches children Shoah:

The history of Israel in one ear,
The history of the Holocaust in the other;

G/d's Covenant with Abraham in one ear,
the selection of Jews to be shot in the other;

on the altar the sparing of Isaac,
the knot of starvation in the stomachs of children;

the giving of promised land,
the confiscation of land not able to be owned;

known as G/d's Chosen People Israel,
taught a new identity by a father's slap in the night.

learning the inscrutable letters of G/d,
memorizing Nazi insignia in a wardrobe closet;

Ruth harvesting friendly foreign fields,
a girl hiding messages in vegetables;

standing on the safe side, watching soldiers fall to the Red Sea,
steadying inmates with toes, pinching cheeks to stay alive in the camps;

the giving of Torah,
and the shredding of Torah

the sharp sunlight,
a bayonet in the face

from one room of the sanctuary
to another

from one end of history
to the other:

the screaming of school children,
the screaming of school children.}

3.3.12

Disciplined Bodies of Eloquence

The susceptibility of the individual, docile body—the weakness of the newly created political and singular individual with limited economic and voting powers—was something past despots and kings {and future dictators and tyrants down the spatial halls of temporal governments throughout history} knew and used to great and disastrous effect. But the "enlightened docile body" also had a direct and beneficial influence on the cannon of rhetoric and poetry. For example, the development of the British Elocutionary Movement of the eighteenth century in some ways depended on the docile body. Less like Platon and Aristotle and more like Cicero and Quintilian (and ironically Ramus), the Elocutionary Movement made delivery, among other concerns, central to rhetorical study. The Elocutionary Movement focused on sound, voice, and style in oration as well as text analysis, which also had been a preoccupation of the sophists and Cicero, and on the mechanics of delivery. For example, Thomas Sheridan's scientific exploration of tone (including animal sounds [see Hawhee, *Tooth and Claw*]), and Gilbert Austin's precise analysis and diagramming of gesture and body movement in delivery, were understood to have brought into the Elocutionary Movement the kind of scientific regimentation and early technologizing of the physical ethos that Foucault discussed, which penetrated, permeated, disciplined, and regimented, and ordered particular movements and parts the docile body to physically express meaning and affect. Even more scientifically than Cicero (*De Oratore* Bks I–II), delivery was developed as an indexical "mimesis of emotions." The Elocutionary Movement literally illustrated and supported Foucault's notion of that "[a] well-disciplined body forms the operational context of the slightest gesture" (*Discipline* 152). Foucault said that the soldiers of the eighteenth century wore a "bodily rhetoric of honor" (*Discipline* 135); Austin's diagramming and systematizing of the movements for efficient and effective communication were not only another scientizing of rhetoric, but also a rhetorical inscribing of the physical body.

> The historical moment of the disciplines was the moment when *an art of the human body was born*, which was directed not only at the growth of its skills, nor at the intensification of its subjection, but at the formation of a relation that in the mechanism itself makes it more obedient as it becomes more useful . . . The human body was entering a machinery of power that explores it, breaks it down and rearranges it. (*Discipline* 135; emphasis added)

Study of Discipline(s): Oak Leaves Driven

(Diaspora Post-1492)

The driveway is the highway
of the leaves

A sidewalk is the long road
of their leaving

Driven beneath the screeching rake,
the leaves are whispering.

What are they whispering?
They are whispering their dreams.

What are they dreaming?
They are dreaming their short lives

down the byways of their passing,
and the longer road of their going.

They speak of their hopeless desire
to "republish" themselves in the spring.

They wish to be able to see themselves
in full color by summer

Luminous, they are gone.
Only the blue jays that eat the acorn
remain

3.3.13

Non-Discriminating Docile Bodies

Perhaps on an unfounded elevation and belief in human Reason, the favored faculty many eighteenth-century philosophes (even of its poetry [e.g., Dryden, Pope]) and the hallmark and bedrock of the Enlightenment (cf. Locke—a somewhat shambolic political severing resulted in a partially botched or aborted *separation* of Church and State, e.g., as *ideally* enshrined in the Declaration of Independence and the US Constitution, which simultaneously retained God as fundamental (to human rights), symbolic (of egalitarian love and personal salvation), and decorative (as on autonomous government buildings, monuments, and paper money). As the early Greek sophist Protagoras had said, "man was the measure of all things," now more than ever. (Even questions of sin and "eternal soul" were increasingly shunted aside by some "Protest-ants" as an issue of individual "election" and personal and economic salvation grounded in human reason, free will, and "good work" [Weber], rather than holy edict, pardon from sovereign king or absolution from the Church [cf. Habermas, *What's Missing*].) The docile body paralleled if not fed these and other social and political movements, such as newfangled notions of the necessity of personal liberty, political rights, and social justice, that also resulted in their own kind of nobility and debauchery, such beauty and terror, such artistic creativity and destruction (e.g., Italy, France). The docile body also ran encountered, ran afoul, and exposed some toxic limitations and by-products of Enlightenment ideals. Aside from historical fears, hatred, racism, anti-Semitism, and many other human faults and failings, travesties, these limitations and byproduct of (un)Enlightenment philosophy, more generously understood, were tragedies of bigotry, prejudice, chauvinism, and not very discriminating ignorance and intolerance of difference of all kinds.

A Living

i return, leave, running late, running low,
depart in the night, in poverty, rage.
i have come to learn why i have to go;

race the city's ignorant human flow
of greed and suffering; i am no sage.
i return, leave, running late, running low.

Living slaughters innocence: this i know;
time is teacher, soldier in every age.
i have come to learn why I have to go;

Reject my father's work: in this i grow;
i earn my own guilt like a deadly wage.
i return, leave, running late, running low.

Across the highways the newspapers blow;
caught in the wind is an opening page.
i have come to learn why i have to go

death is our common labor, dark, and slow.
We rush toward the grave in this fleshy cage.
We return, leave, running late, running low.
We have come to learn that we have to go.

3.3.14

Discriminated Bodies

Out of the concept of the closed body, the opacity of the skin and thus color—as well as differences in religion, appearance, clothes, culture—always a problem—became focal points for the hyperawareness of race, and the intensification of the notion of color as "other." Despite wars and laws meant to "correct" with reason and science endemic myopia, deep-seated ignorance, and erroneous values and beliefs, the long-established institution of slavery on global and local scales continued almost unabated in different social, political, and economic forms throughout history (cf. Blackmon; Hannah-Jones). As Benthien states, "Only when the collective imagination came to look on the skin as such a two-dimensional and linear boundary surface was it possible to read the body for its individual physiognomy, its attributed race, and its spontaneous sensations and sensory expressions, as well as diseases" (39). The identification of conception of mimesis as the physical body itself set up race, color, creed and other outward, obvious and not so obvious human attributes (including biology, "ability," sexuality, gender as semantic markers). A refinement based on medical "science" in the nineteenth century asserted the "dark complexion is understood as something that gradually accumulates between the epidermis and the dermis and changes the skin secondarily" (Benthien 149) did not stop the all-encompassing semiotics of loathing; at best, the individuality of the person became "invisible"; at worst, the individuality of the person became the object of sustained violence and death.

from Julius the Prophet

I.

African-American man
who lives next door and proudly owns
his family, has his own home, bent
over, walking with a slow cane,

calls

to me across the yard to talk about

the newspaper headline concerning city trash
collection—, knows about such things, who plucks
obsessively every leaf from air
before it even hits the ground, before

it lands.

His property steps forward: cane, man

stops.

3.3.15

"Causations" of Beauty—and Its Opposite

The eighteenth-century French philosopher Denis Diderot believed that beauty was the result of causation, in the sense that causal relations and/or their effects could be beautiful. Like Aristotle, Diderot sought to discover a more scientific basis for beauty. Aristotle located beauty outside the human body or perception, in the object itself and the relation of its parts to the whole, according to "geometric" principles such as order, symmetry, and balance (*Poetics* 1450b34; *Metaphysics* 1078a36). Diderot in the eighteenth century located beauty in more unpredictable causal relation—but not only within the object, but also between the perceiver and the object (*Treatise* 12–14). When the "enlightened" body was (re)closed by reason, the internally informed (sur)faces of the exterior (face, body parts, skin) increasingly became the subject-object of the medical Gaze.

***

Aided by improvements in science and technology, out of the Renaissance grew "aesthetic surgeons," as Sander L. Gilman dubbed them. The highly paid and prized "artist-anatomist" (as well as an increasing number of patients) operated under the assumption that physical {and eventually, facial} features, personally or socially regarded as "ugly" or "grotesque," could be altered to achieve newly established or desired aesthetic ends. These ends—the objects of mimesis—were thus artistic and cultural as well as anatomical, and were communicated through art, including poetry and rhetoric {Flashback 1. And ultimately, their descendants: mass communication, social/digital media, genetic editing, augmented reality, prosthetic enhancement, post-humanism, etc. After the eighteenth century, these aesthetics were no longer *classically* proscribed standards, or Ideal Forms, or universal concepts of beauty based on geometry, or even the da Vinci's vision of the perfectly proportioned human body in "Vitruvian Man." Rather, Diderot had recognized the role of objective-subjective perception of causal relations. The later human body was reinscribed, became a poem via rhetoric, a portrait of the skin, a sculpture of flesh. Often surgical procedures were medically necessary for the normal physical functioning of a body (though here too aesthetics entered), but only those wealthy enough could afford these, or to elect such surgeries. And it took a long time for even "enlightened liberals" not to see difference as "disabilities" or "deformities (swotted in Part Four of these Chronicles), and the similarities such as transgender and transhumanism (doxed in Part Five of these Chronicles). Aesthetic ends usually were loosely evolving ideals that shifted in accord with the "norms" of the arts and cultures of societies. Some (dis)figurations of the flesh were adopted for mannerist aesthetics or rococo decorative reasons, such as tattooing and piercing and gothic attachments; other (dis)figurations of the flesh, with penalties including involuntary lapidation, manual decapitation, or induced amelia, were mandated by different needs, beliefs, religions, such as male circumcisions, and female genital mutilation (FMG).

"Undusting" Time

For Anna Weaver and her Daughters

1
Asking for a rag to "undust"
the dresser of memories, she was given a veil
to hide the secrets hidden in the
drawers. She hadn't opened them for years,
the dust slowly falling, flake by flake,
layers upon layer, moments, days, months,
years only interrupted when she dusted off
some time, the other lives she had lived.
The drawers remained quiet, their shame still
there, and the dust kept falling faster than she

could sweep it up, could erase the memories—
until the dresser finally disappeared, until
the dust became the dresser she sought to un-

2
What is the secret hidden in the countries
of the drawers? What is the taboo covered
over by the histories of veils
falling on the mirror of time like snow?
Her father will not talk to her, but knows,
says it doesn't matter, it's in the past
yet is something still common practice
that has to be observed without question.
But her mother knows, preserves what is left
in the bureau of her memory,
cries in the quiet corners of its night,
what was done to her as a child,
what generations of women only now un-

derstand: the unjust prejudice of pain.}

3.3.16

"Kosmetic" Surgery

Based on the ideals of art and culture of time and place, cosmetically/surgically reshaped or reconfigured bodies and/or their parts were not only personal preferences, but also medical or technological need. {Flashback 2. In subsequent centuries, an inordinate number of cosmetic surgeons and a proliferation of genetic alteration, drugs, diets, and devices, and patients who employed them, continued to grow. And later still, in addition to other cosmetics and surgical procedures, various kinds of severings and reshapings were employed to strip away or remove personally and/or socially perceived "grotesqueness" and "ugliness"—unwanted physical qualities, quantities, and other parts of the body. As recorded in the Epilogos, still other, more deliberate "disabilities" and total "disfigurations," including but not limited to pharmaceutical deceleration, physical truncation, genetic inhibition, and reverse technological enhancement, were necessary for the survival of at least one member the former species (cf. Herrick; Hakopian).

Statue to Eloquentia (Variation V)

amputate all emotions
so i may think
like a machine}

3.3.17

Stripping Skin Color

Reshapings and reconfigurations of the human body by cosmetics and/or surgery—strippings, cuttings, severings, stitchings—also included skin color, which along with nationalities were obvious social "markers." Increasingly and rhetorically malleable based on the relevant and every changing concept of "beauty"—often inherently racist among the indigenous—as well as scientific and technological recognition and reconnoitering, physically altering facial images and body selves were believed to have enabled a person to have been able to migrate ("pass") from one race, or social class, or cultural group, to another. For Sander Gilman, cosmetology had been a greatly touted equalizer and promise in previous centuries (e.g., see Cauwels; Hiaken; Fielder; Balsamo, esp. 56–79). While skin color as well as other religious, ethnic, and racial origins had facilitated "The Great Passage" from freedom into slavery, or ongoing local pogroms of cultural lashing and physical liquidation, "personal" markers (economic status, ability, sexuality, gender) also may have precluded "passing" to freedom for humans with material, biological, psychological, and other differences and needs. What was needed and never achieved was a fundamental shift in perspective, a total change in *values*—another new mimesis of the material body that would be brought about another transformation of an open spirit—wise, just, accepting. This new freedom from re-presentation as "other" (see Levinas; Davis, *Inessentiality*) *was* an implied or stated ideal of art and science, of rhetoric and poetry, in this and subsequent centuries, one that perhaps was an absolute failure, would never really and fully come.

Black Adam

Villanelle for Gerald Barrax On His Early Retirement

"With the farming of a verse
Make a vineyard of the curse . . .
In the prison of his days
Teach the free man how to pray."
—W.H. Auden, "In Memory of W. B. Yeats" (*Collected Poems* 198)

You took with you a sanity of place
when you left; white paradise is a hole
we now climb in and out of in disgrace.

In your own new world, *lean against the sun*,
stand in *another kind of rain*, write for *an audience of one.*
There you will find the sanity of place.

Take it, and redeem the apple of race.
You're allowed in; we still cannot follow,
the deaths of animals and lesser gods our disgrace.

An interloper in this universe,
you return to your inheritance: know
it, free from the insanity of place.

You brought to us poetic kindness, grace.
Rename everything so we can all go
back to the garden outside our disgrace.

With this craft you taught we'll bend space, reshape hate
into love, wait for justice and the world to come.
Hold in your hand the sanity of place.
Create an Eden out of our disgrace.

3.3.18

Mimesis, Skin, and "Ornatus"

In keeping with Auerbach's analysis, mimesis was a register of profound historical crisis and major philosophical, cultural, and literary change. But what, if any, were the new, "enlightened" relations between attributes and "essence," between appearance and substance, values and behavior? Did cosmetology change the "*soul*" of "the giver" and the "recipient," as Socrates and Platon *feared it would*? Or was change more akin to "technical rhetoric," a mimetic "passing," a substitute, that skipped or repressed the expressed need for the deeper alteration of the human spirit— a *kosmetic* surgery more in line with the Ciceronian concept of "Ornatus" (Di Lorenzo), a restructuring not only of the chosen and abandoned, the adorers and the adorn, the despisers and the hated, but of the physical and *moral* universe, in which the philosophically unstripped beauty of *res* and *verba* might be readily apparent to all? (Cf. Figure 3.)

True Eloquence Is Not Reincarnation

Is not cosmetic change
but a kosmetic conception
of the unity of all
form and matter
in the entire universe—

a renovation not only
of the physical body
but of life-altering
spirit, not a "reimprisoning"
of soul in another *soma*,

yet but another
materially tragic
and disastrous blunder,
but a complete rebirth
into a new Being

3.3.19

"Stripping" "Disabled" Skin

In "Man-the-Machine" (*Discipline* 136), Foucault had written: "These methods [regimentation], which made possible the meticulous control of the operations of the body, which assured the constant subjection of its forces and imposed upon them a relation of docility-utility, might be called "disciplines" (*Discipline* 137). As members of advanced industrial societies driven by their socio-economic and political systems (cf. Habermas, Ideology"; Moses and Katz)—as parts of the whole, of a larger "machine" (Agamben, *Apparatus*)—came the ideological and/or technological imperatives of "disciplines" (whether personal, social, cultural, corporate, political, even aesthetic) to unify and organize separate individuals (perceived as distinct or not) into new social, cultural, political, economic entities designed for maximum efficiency, effectiveness, and usefulness. {Examination. Such forms of regimentation and discipline were not only anti-rhetorical or anti-poetic forms of "identification," but also almost "anti-'consubstantiation'" (Burke, *Rhetoric of Motives* 22). The internal and external parts and arts of opened and reclosed bodies were all harnessed for the will and "betterment" of the "*corp-oration*" or the "body politic" of the State. In almost all logged cases, the sanctity of the individual and "institutional framework" of traditional beliefs and values, whether organic or machine, were melded, subsumed, (re)placed inside "Enframing," technological ones (Habermas, "Ideology; "What's Missing"; Moses and Katz; Katz and Rhodes; Heidegger, *Question*; cf. Stiegler). Against the backdrop of the Enlightenment, technological beasties with their own ugly underbelly based on a "docility-utility" equation of the disciplined body, emerged from these institutional disciplines (cf. Foucault, *Discipline* 137; Katz, "Education").} In the history of mimesis, of the beautiful and the ugly, delineations and definitions of the "grotesque" and "deformed" based on the "usefulness" of the body arose, and ran, walked, or crawled upon the earth. Surely this is not what artist, inventor, and engineer Leonardo da Vinci had in mind.

The Re-Educated Cowboy

over the ocean
riding the waves
backwards

3.3.20

Semiotics of Disability and Freedom in America

The "semiotics" of the role and usefulness of the body in America was analyzed by Rosemarie Garland Thomson. In *Extraordinary Bodies: Figuring Disability in American Culture and Literature*, Thomson wrote: "Disability is the unorthodox made flesh, refusing to be normalized, neutralized, or homogenized. More important, in an era governed by the abstract principle of universal equality, disability signals that the body cannot be universalized. Shaped by history, defined by particularity, and at odds with its environment, disability confounds notions of a generalizable, stable, physical subject" (24). Eighteenth century society in Europe and America, characterized by a belief in individuality and utility and a zeal for universal "equality" (even if "untrue") was just such an environment. Modern industrialized societies were always deeply troubled by their "underachievers" and "misfits"—no matter what the physical or psychological or economic causes may have been. This was particularly apparent in their treatment of the poor, the deformed, the disadvantaged. the differently abled. For Thomson, the deformed body violated "the normate self" predicated on and dedicated to four ideological principles that are interrelated and inform(ed) the American Ideal: autonomy, self-determination, self-government, and progress (42). As Thomson pointed out, "these four principles depend upon a body that is a stable, neutral instrument of individual will. It is this fantasy that the disabled figure troubles" (42). America as a utopian paradise of capitalistic achievement and democratic averages redefined the "individual," "success," even "self" and thus *social mimesis* in a way that affected all realms of life. (There was a spiritual continuation of this national aesthetic in the "Protestant Work Ethic," "Manifest Destiny," "American Exceptionalism," as well as global and native backlash to scientific and technological innovation in this and the nineteenth century, recounted next.)

"Corp(se) of Discovery": The Lewis and Clark Expedition 1804–1806

(Raking Leaves with Alison)

Forests and seas of leaves
Await us as we push toward

The curb of the westward shore,
The leaves breaking on the lawn

Like tides on our keelboats
We row and row all day long,
Striking our rakes likes oars
Against the weight of the waves,

Stroking, stirring leaves with motion.
When at last we reach the border
Of the street, the other curb
And a little Pacific Ocean

We reach, over and over again
Until we have discovered the land
the grass, the concrete, the green
Beneath the sea of amber leaves,

Another land populated
By leaves that still have trees,
And other leaves that don't,
Falling before our thrashing boats.

We extend our rakes even further
Into an unknown neighbor's yard,
Where the leaves are red and brown,
And gathering, claim them as our own.

3.3.21

"Social Mimesis" in America

In some ways, the concept of truth and falsehood, the ugly and the beautiful, the body and soul—and thus the concept of mimesis, its relation to the represented, and what if anything should be imitated—openly depended on political, social, and economic principles that Benthien, and Foucault, explored. As Thomson wrote: "Just as the principle of self-government demands a regulated body, the principle of self-determination requires a compliant body to secure a place in the fiercely competitive and dynamic socioeconomic realm" (42). During the Enlightenment, mimesis was the imitation and/or imbibement of political and economic principles inherent in the notions of the forms of normal and abnormal body. This was reflected in rhetoric and literature of the New World as well (redacted in depth in Parts Four and Five of this Chronicle). For example, "scholars have noted . . . Emerson's elaboration of liberal individualism as a neo-Platonic, disembodied form of masculinity" (Thomson 42). Noting the cultural ideology of non-conformity combined with the mass production and standardization in American life, Thomson said: "The disabled figure speaks to this tension between uniqueness and uniformity" (44). In short, the deformed, ugly body politic in American life was understood against and defended by the new norm of the "perfect" useful body. "Thus translated, physical difference yielded cultural icons that signified violated wholeness, unbounded completeness, unregulated particularity, dependent subjugation, disordered intractability, a susceptibility to external forces. With the body's threat of betrayal thus compartmentalized, the mythical American self can unfold, unobstructed and unrestrained, according to its own manifest destiny" (Thomson 44). Thomson's book constituted a radical critique of the ideology of bodies extending from the democratic and capitalistic concepts of an individual, productive "self," through a distorted lens of American ideals (and secret fears), and the repression of social and physical differences (and "lesser" indigenous, colored, or gendered cultures) embedded even in the US Constitution, all "natural" consequences of the Enlightenment body.

The Old Miasmas, 1845

"Never been here before"
i reply again and again
to astonished looks of
bellhops and waitresses
who ask again and again
and are probably trying to
sell me something—
a "complementary" limousine
to see the city, yes . . .

It's Miami, the old miasmas
that i grew up with
on the Atlantic coast,
but winter waves
striking shoreline, biting sand,
as if trying to eat and erase it
like the taste of a bad memory
eroding, ever widening its mouth.

"Only been here a few hours"
i tell them. And out along

the shore the little lines
of riptides roll up, flip back
and forth, their white beards
emerging, nodding, bowing
then submerging, again and again
like sharks holding up the world—
beneath the sea to sell me something
or to take something from me . . .

i step a toe back, then in
so close to shore, back and forth,
until i sense a bite. But i love breeze
and the old miasmas of Miami,
so mimetic, and i tell them so:
"i'm only here for a few days"
but it already feels like centuries
across oceans of tides and weeds
i think i am finally home/free . . .

3.3.22

Mimesis of "the Other"

The same principles of inclusion and exclusion based on a social mimesis of the aesthetics of efficiency and usefulness applied to the Ausländer, the outlander, the immigrant, the refugee, the alien body, the Other (Agamben, *Means*). The aesthetics or social dimensions of these "foreign bodies" in the seventeenth and eighteenth centuries, but also their political and economic manifestations and dimensions in the United States in these and subsequent centuries, were subject to bans and abuse in a country that was the "beacon of light," "the land of opportunity," "the great melting pot." Systematic political, social, and economic discrimination based on nationality, gender, skin color, persisted.

From El Paso del Norte, to Juárez and Back

two halves of a divided whole
(geographical, not temporal):

a vista of twinkling
slums thrown together out of
corrugated cardboard and metal
slide and shine over the hillside—
distant but immediate, like hay,
close but too far away . . .

it's just us three now,
he said out loud . . .

and then to the cracked door
she came, the other, the fourth,
came to the half-opened door,
all bare brown dirty feet
standing in a nightgown,
standing there in the ruins

standing there in ruins
shivering like a ghost

swimming in the light:
"I have no psychology," she said,
the stars like flecks
of sharp metal rust,
covered over with muck,
yet still dimly gleaming

3.3.23

Enlightened Stripping of Deformity

The sanctioned *anatomy* of the open human body—the manifestation and practice of *stripping/severing/cutting*, and its (re)closing in the Renaissance and the Enlightenment—was instantiated in secular medical science (just as Christ was instantiated for Christians in the Word). Opening the closed body, and re-closing the open body, anatomy played a key role in altering conceptions body, beauty, ugliness—and style and content, matter and form. Begun in earnest in art by Leonardo, anatomy established a different set of "new naturalistic" criteria, and standards for mimesis in the arts and sciences, including rhetoric and poetry. Auerbach had located a decisive transformative moment in literary realism in Western literature and culture in the birth of Jesus. However, with the advent and replications of the Renaissance and the Copernican and Newtonian revolutions in science, the work of Foucault, Bakhtin, Benthien, and Thomson, suggested another profound shift in Western literature and culture in the eighteenth century with the Enlightenment. Like science in relation to nature, medicine in relation to the body, in almost an exact antithesis of Platon (see Table 3), became manifest and gave humanity a new mimesis and destiny. The (re)closed body provided other possibilities for the transcendence of the body, if not salvation, via the scalpel of science and reason. In the revolt against the open body, and the material rebirth of spirit, a new paradigm of sinew and bone, flesh and blood, spit and salt, was physically fit and well, and full of optimism and hope.

Out of Hospital

Sick, stripped to the bone, relieved
    of all function, he now begins again
to put on the body's habits
    one by one, like clothes
forgotten, hanging in a closet.

He touches the floor that seems to shift,
    rising to his feet that fall,
floating him out the door. He is leaving
    the room that was his world—

the quiet light of flowers, cards initialed
    like memories on the wall.
He takes a shower down the hall,
    skin hectic, wet, and hot—

The ritual of initiation
    before daily life is undertaken.
The flesh rinsed of pain,
    He dresses, assumes the human role again,
prepares to reenter in a new-born globe

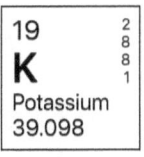

19 2 8 8 1
K
Potassium
39.098

Part Four
The Sublime Figure of the Ephemeral (Nineteenth Century Romanticism/German Transcendentalism)

"[P]urification . . . consists in separating the soul as much as possible from the body, and accustoming it to withdraw from all contact with the body and concentrate itself by itself, and to have its dwelling, so far as it can, both now and in the future, alone by itself, freed from the shackles of the body."

—*Plato, Phaedo* 67d

10 Subjectivities Organ

The Sleep of Snow

The long gray grasses curl and lie
under a quilt of quiet snow
that tucks the sleeping house in,
melts around the mouths of snoring chimneys.

From a further room, i think i hear
the bundled breathing of my wife and son
like the ticking of a metered clock
unwinding in blankets of darkness.

The snow drifts and settles on the fields
like quilts of cold eiderdown,
turning my bed into white lonely plains
as familiar as dreams where i have never been

X=0

"A calculus math problem might be to find the slope of a function that is non-linear or perhaps the area between a curve and the x-axis. An example could be what is the slope of the function f(x) = e^x at 0? Well, the derivative of f(x) is f'(x) = e^x and substituting zero into this derivative gives f'(0) = e^0 = 1. So, the curve e^x has a slope of one at x=0 [1, 2, 3 etc.. . .]"

—Riley Kench, 21 Nov 2023.

Figure 5. The Value of X.

X=1

Spirit of the West

From the mimesis of material re-embodiment to the solipsistic freedom of a "subjective science" of consciousness—that's where the spirit like Shelley's west wind went. Perhaps it was the calculus of Newtonian physics (Figure 5), perhaps the political institutionalization of rationality and the mind-body duality in medicine, perhaps the Mannerist and anatomist hollowing out of form in art and science, perhaps the mechanization and brutal technological force of the Industrial Revolution, perhaps the disciplining of the "docile body," perhaps a rejection of the grotesque or "abnormal" body (Bakhtin; Foucault). Most likely it was the effect of all of these together that repelled and propelled the Romantic poets to search for themselves not only inward, but also outward, in nature, and beyond. The "opening of the body" in anatomy, surgery, art (Benthien) perhaps allowed the walls of exteriority to fall, facilitated the opening of the *subjective* mind itself to nature. Out of the classical Greek and Roman, Medieval, Renaissance, and Enlightenment periods, the notion of reality, writing, and mimesis as the figuration of emotion underwent another radical changes that manifested themselves in every organ of culture. Bodies, nature, soul, world, language seem to have been substantially rewritten. What emerged at the end of the eighteenth and beginning of the nineteenth centuries were a subjective poetics and rhetorics and philosophies of language and art —new concepts of the imagination, beauty, art, spirit, purpose—in and through which the open body transcended itself to join nature, become nature, in a sublime experience that was as deep and profound and as it was ephemeral. And objective.

X=2

It's Alive!

In one version of Romanticism, with or without humans, nature itself was a vibrant organism.

The Pasture

1.
Fences run along the field,
then end, fallen in the grass,
legs scattered like nearby hay.

And wind rushes the heather,
jumps brushing the horse's hoof
that rings a weathering vane.

2.
Snow grazes on the down, lifts
on house and barn and bough,
tossed by a cow's twitch and breath.

Then fields melt in along the spring,
under the warmth of dripping leaves,
and the heat of steaming feet.

3.
Mist stiches the patchwork land,
until the sun begins
to iron the trees.

Head red against the amber sky,
a crow is on the house's bough,
yawning before the eve.

4.
Streamings round a rock,
then slowing, and bluing,
drink the sinking light.

Fences run along the field,
then end, fallen in the grass,
legs scattered like nearby hay.

X=3

Nature Is Sentient

Later, in the nineteenth century, chronologically speaking, nature became conscience; nature became sentient; nature became Spirit too.

X=4

Romantic Gloom

There was another, darker vision of Romanticism. It may have been a result of the seventeenth century scientific paradigm of objective analysis and interpretation and experimentation, and thus a tighter, non-religious collar of what counted as valid knowledge. Gloomier shades of Romanticism also were understood to be a response to the nineteenth century's heaving, heavy, harrowing, and harsh mechanization of the industrial revolution, and the prospect of an increasingly bleak, more terrifying, and meaningless existence (e.g., Blake). But like technology, analysis and interpretation and experimentation would prove useful too, even to rhetoric and writing. In the sixteenth century, Ramus had hung, drawn, and quartered the art of rhetoric; following the disembowelment of invention, arrangement, memory from the subject of rhetoric, left only a skeleton of memory and style: a diagram of figures of speech (Ong, *Ramus*). But in the eighteenth and nineteenth century, theory and instruction in the art of rhetoric, particularly speaking and writing, began to put on weight, reassemble, flourish once again.

***

Under the auspice scientific and technological utilitarianism, George Campbell and Richard Whately and Hugh Blair fruitfully divided and taught different approaches to composition and writing and rhetoric through analysis and interpretation and *imitation*, respectively. (And imitation, or the replication of methods and results over a number of experiments, was the heart and hope of successful scientific experimentation.) Not Newtonian equations, but rhetorical principles, mimetic heuristics, and *belle lettres* as literary exemplars for imitation were applied to teach writing as a utility and practical art. Writing, like the body, was an appliance to be used. The various approaches were in part still based on Bacon's sixteenth century "modes" of the mind (reason, imagination, affect, will), to be sure (*Advancement* XII.1; XVIII.3–5). {Fast Forward. In the twentieth century, similar approaches to literature and composition instruction based on the "Modes of Discourse" (expository, creative, descriptive, and argumentative writing, respectively) were based on a Baconian division of the mind (see Wimsatt; Kinneavy; D'Angelo; Berlin; even Northrop Frye's "anatomy" of criticism were based on an ancient narrative mythology (see Campbell; Fraser; Weston; Katz, "Narration").}

***

But in a dark version of the vision of Romanticism (itself to be fetishized and made a major decadent theme by the end of the century), a blunt scalpel coupled with an objective clinical "Gaze" had cut into and exposed the now dead godless matter of nature (physics), creativity (chemistry), imagination (psychology), and the human body (biology) (cf. Foucault, *Clinic*; Gillispie). The weak, frail, needy, easily tired human being, compared to massive mercantile merciless industrial machines, were all enemies of feeling and "the soul." Life, even sensitivity, was crudely analyzed, dissected, dismembered, and readapted to a hard, indifferent, dangerous world.

Carpe Diem

Fly
from the rounds of days
held by insignificance
eyes seized with pins
bodies wracked with
pain

Life
of needles and pills
amputated nerves
strapped to the wheel
that jars the hours
teeth clutching stems
of imitation flowers
while hands hold tight
with the turning and the
pain.

Off
into death we roll,
reeling and falling,
placed against the weight
of the earth.

X=5

Romantic Sensibility

It is hard to know to what degree the opening of the mechanized or docile or differently abled—the suppurating, ugly, and now exposed interior body, ironically based on freedom and democracy embedded in Enlightenment ideologies of rationality and utility—gave rise to a romantic sensibility. But it might have been great. The ideal or artificial beauty of nature and the body, as well as the "natural" defects of the human body and the desire and need to fix or transcend them, not only affected the lives of Romantic writers and artists, but in many cases literally infected them. The ills and frailty of the human body (especially in relation to the strength of the mind and the possibilities of the imagination) became the subject of the Romantics' work—the expression of the profound ecstasy and despair concerning the nature of human life. It also became the "object" of their life—an expression of identity that is a proclamation of the "natural" and artistic sensibility, imagination, and genius. Even while rhetoricians were trying to hold to more scientific, empirical, civic-minded, or socially pragmatic approaches to the theory, teaching. and practice of oratory and writing instruction in the nineteenth centuries (Connors; Connors and Ede), Romantic philosophers, poets, and artists, perhaps picking up Christian themes of "passion," further idealized emotion, spirit, ecstasy, the sublime, and the beautiful, as well as suffering and pain (Damasio). In some obvious, strange, and also subtle ways, the Romantic Movement continued and preserved sophistic strands in rhetoric with their belief in the power of language, affect, subjectivity, but also the exhilaration of the uncertainty and tragedy in the arc of life (see Untersteiner's classic on the tragic world view implicit in sophistic rhetoric).

Nearing the End

(For Chris Again)

scattering the back yard—
broken down stars
turning away

getting to know you
before we disintegrate—
planets, fireflies,

all dying on the same plane
of existence, slipping out
of space and time—

all moving away from you

X=6

Resurrecting Ghosts

Nineteenth century philosophers such as Vico, Hegel, and Nietzsche were often credited with the resurrection of the flickering ghosts of the sophists. For most of history they hid underground, but haunted the corners of Western culture. Strange, perhaps, until one remembers their preoccupation with the solipsistic self, subjective reality, and the sublime suffering spirit. The great English romantic poets and writers—Wordsworth, Blake, Keats, Coleridge, De Quincy, Byron, Shelley—were tortured, in order, by the bite of poverty, the indifference of melancholy, the fatality of tuberculosis, the debilitation of opium addiction, disability, and drowning. These writers and poets wrote about or otherwise made their personal difficulties the source if not the subject of their art {not as much as "the confessional poets" of the twentieth century, but certainly more than their predecessors in any age before in the West (Simpson; Katz, "Confessional Poetry"; "Poetry Editor").} The dashingly handsome ladies' man, George Gordon Lord Byron, had a "clubbed/goat foot" and died "heroically" in a revolution to free the glory of ancient Greece from Ottoman rule; the high-spirited freedom-loving Shelley drowned in a storm sailing from Livorno to Lerici in Italy; De Quincey and Coleridge fought through hapless spells of laudanum and its sweet poppy fog, to write and try to reach creative visions.

In Xanadu

He inhaled opium and the rising sea,
as the fallow moon fell against the rocks;
breathed the deep mist of lotus flowers
through salty pines and bamboo shoots,
floated by underwater reefs of cherry laurels.
And wrapping himself in the robes of tides
that washed his body with blossoming waves
he drifted toward the sun, and drowned

X=7

Revolutionary Semantics

Out of the semiotics of the enveloping skin in the eighteenth century grew the revolutionary semantics of the nineteenth century— the (un)natural, the abnormal, the diseased, the insane—as a special kind of new "ideal human type." Like Foucault's "madman" who if not inspired by divinity still may possess an unusual perspicacity, this "ideal type" was forever running into the dominant "Will to Truth" (*Madness*; "Discourse" 215–37; Habermas). For Blake, as for some later nineteenth century French poets of the Decadent or Symbolism movements such as Arthur Rimbaud—the poet, outcast, outsider, exile, gunrunner, "the Other" —were in reality wounded but luminous beings, shackled by human perception and social convention, and like the Greek statues Blake wrote about, "representations of spiritual existences" that were the blocked product of imagination, not marble (Clark, *Nude* 50; 288).

Auto-Referential

1.
Art: a sudden nexus
in the air,
spark of pure celestial
that quivers
in the human element

but cannot live,
where imagination
attempts to break
mythological chains
of language that
idealize death,
civilize destruction,
transcend
the point
where silence begin

A suicide that fails.

2.
White fingers float
piano keys over soft snow
notes stir on the ivory sill
clear skin illumined
from within, cool
light falls
on her hands
she breathes a vapor
pure and rare

3.
Morning arrives at the window
without a sound
great doors bar the winter wind
she sips cold air
icy clothes cling to her body
bound with a silver cord
her frozen shape
an alabaster vase
small lucent veins
are violet, still
her face pure marble
on which tears
sometime flow
white cheeks stained
with sun like azure snow

She melts upward from below.

X=8

Rhetorically Wounded Poets

More than the "Socratic gadfly" that the orator would become in a Platonic order—condemned to live beyond the pale of civilization in order to describe, represent, persuade it without being corrupted by it—the poet was so wounded and luminous that he/she was often synonymous with the prophet, seer. As Platon predicted, touched by gods, poets burned with the uncontrollable fire of visions. And so, from another Platonic view, poets were equally vapid and dangerous. But unlike the empty poetic vessel that the gods blow through, the nineteenth century prophet-poet was in a painful but superior position, made physically possible and politically permanent by the norm of the form of "the open body." As in prior and subsequent ages but perhaps more self-consciously and intensely than ever before, artists turned their alienation and difference {or from more post-structuralist if not posthuman times, deconstructively, their "*differance*"} into an aesthetic theory of rhetorical being and reality. Perhaps in repulsing classical concepts of ideal beauty (cf. Clark, *Romantic Rebellion* 19–20), scientific concepts of nature, and Enlightenment concepts of the rational body, in embracing "the natural" Baudelaire and other *fin de siècle* poets and artists in France would turn to the "other"—the forbidden, the foreign, the exotic, the misfit, the deformed, the decadent, the decrepit, the evil, death itself—in new manifestos of life and art, out of which *les fleurs du mal* could grow.

The House of Flowers

{"The force that through the green fuse drives the flower" –Dylan Thomas (77)}

This is a sprawling house of eternal flowers:
everyone who resides here becomes
possessed with reviving the lost garden—
with the urge to sow and fertilize and water,
to procreate like the wet raw urge
that courses through the throbbing roots and shoots
of greeney stalks and trees and plants and flowers

The clatter of identity—it doesn't matter:
color is in ruins, race in tatters;
religion groundward falling, human clutter;
immigrant status, ability, not uttered—
pushed aside with the daily litter.
"Shovel to dirt," "shovel to dirt": living
we all become enamored of the clay

X=9

Opening the Body for Spirit

Perhaps it was the open "ugly body" that the Romantics not only embraced but also sublimated into a "natural" and "free" self {"a terrible beauty" to use Yeats' later phrase a little differently (178).} This sublimation continued to propel the intense desire to escape "the body" and merge into a transcendent realm of imagination and spirit so different from classical art. Kenneth Clark noted in *The Romantic Rebellion* that the "differences" between "classical" and "romantic" were almost as much a label of convenience as a delineation of something historically or artistically unique; the desire for order and emotion existed previously, and simultaneously even in the same artists (19–20; cf. Barzun). But as Clark also pointed out in this tome, there were clear statements of opposition between the classical and romantic (i.e., Winkelmann's *Reflections*), which rewrote the history of the classical period for the nineteenth century and nostalgically called for a return to classical principles, as in Edmund Burke's *Enquiry into the Sublime and Beautiful*, which according to Clark "described the aims and categorized the subject matter of romanticism" (*Romantic Rebellion* 19). Thus, Clark ultimately concludes that the Romantic movement in art was a "divergence . . . not merely technical" but rather one that "gave visible expression to a change in philosophy, which was later to manifest itself in all the arts" (*Romantic Rebellion* 19). The Romantic movement seems to represent both a conflict and a change of ideology—of irrationality vs. affect, of mechanized soul vs. ambitious spirit. The Romantic movement was an aesthetic as well as political revolution, a rebellion in sensibility as well as in art. The result was the further "opening" of "the closed body" included prying wide the imagination, spirit, as well as the smelly liquescences and oozy portals, in medicine and science, as well as poetry and art.

Halibut Pt.

(Rockport, MA)

The sea lies with the sky,
hugging the blue;

boats hump the waves;
two buoys keep kissing in the foam.

Fishermen double their lines.
In pairs the bathers bathe.

You and i turn away

The wine heats on a rock;
napkins flutter off like sails;

the avocados melt on the dock;
the sun swings like the tide, goes out.

It rains, just two clouds over
the lilies and poison sumac we cannot name,

wind slowly weaving through leaves
that move like green seaweed in the sea,

vegetable and wet.
Dead fish rise from the sea.

The seagulls caw, call:

through the bottleneck ocean
pours cold azure rushes

X=10

Opening Subjectivity

There were more subtle effects of "the open body." One of the most "anti-Platonic" and obvious of these was the imitation of the imagination as a spiritual figuration that was at the heart of the new image of the poet as prophet and seer. The acute senses and "higher sensibility" of the poet, the necessary (self-)consciousness of being a poet, became in a mimesis of self the venerable subject of song. Opened subjectivity released emotional and spiritual *forms*, new ephemeral *ideals* worthy of the name. Such ideals, such visions, with their promise of emotional and spiritual liberation through the intensification of ordinary anguish and pain into the sublime angst of life and art. (The conflict of life and art itself often created the actual substance of suffering.) It is hard for a young writer or artist to resist such promises and visions (see Rilke, *Letters;* Simpson), so liberating, so heuristic were they (Katz "Rhetoric of Confessional"; cf. Katz "Poetry Editor"): the bright air was more sensitive, the sky more luminous, the dark trees more ominous, as hands reached up to touch the supernal light through the gnarled natural deformity of the human life world.

Our House

Our house
is of them:

ideas
like pure crystal
born into a world
of substance
and of color,
qualities illuminated,
attributes unknown.

But the square
of the building,
the angle
of the stair,
the plain
of the room,
like the picture
framed by the window

are slightly askew,
ephemeral shapes,
flawed coordinates,
mortal numbers,
Cartesian Man
a cosmic abortion,
an animal darkly
suffering in a
coldly warping cave.

X=11

Decadence as Spirit

The grotesque, the melancholy, the macabre, the terminal, the tragic—idealized into objects of desire—also played a prominent role in the Romantic notions of beauty and the body. Disfigurement too became objects of "imitation." In a real sense, the ugly was "redeemed" (Eco, *Ugliness* 271–31) "[W]hat is especially original is the bond linking up the various forms [that did] "exclude contradictions or . . . resolve antitheses but [brought] them together" (Eco, *Beauty* 299). The decadent thus became an ideal form in nineteenth century Romanticism (particularly in Europe) that took many mimetic forms. It was in the "decadent Romantic period . . . that the appeal of the horrendous and the Beauty of the Devil were acknowledged without hypocrisy" (Eco, *Beauty* 148). But their philosophy went far beyond this (e.g., Blake). The Romantics—like magicians of matter, alchemists of emotions—sought and were able to bring the disparate together: the lovely and the grotesque, the ecstasy and the gloom, the erotic and the morbid. In themes, settings, characters, images, and concepts, the Romantic mimesis of beauty merged with their opposites into one existence. "Beauty could now express itself by making opposites converge, so that Ugliness was no longer the negation of Beauty, but its other face" (Eco, *Beauty* 321). This was not "arguing both sides of an issue" as the sophists had practiced, nor the dialectical investigation of Platon and Aristotle, but rather a philosophy of subjective convergence through imagination and spirit.

Elegiac for a Hill in the Highlands of Scotland

A bowl of light brooking lanes
in which the air converse
like lank white fish
that long to leap the drawn day
in the mountain muscled moss,
land-leaked flowers that spread
island nests of leaves
which winded wings can only reach,
brimmed in gilled vales,
blown in the filling cups—
drinking cloud-skins that hang
and curve as a bird shapes
the high-toned light as it slides,
or blade-strong is straddled
by a saddle of air strung on a wave—
dawn hay stabled horses
slipping in the liquid haze,
graze on a water's breeze
of a green free noon,
sun run down to the
wild fruited foot.

X=12

Personal Authenticity

Romantic philosophy was highly idealistic but had as its object not Platonic Forms, but rather Romantic forms of what seemed to be both material and the transcendent essences perceived by the psychological body: personal consciousness, subjective feelings, putative intentions, private sensations, ostensible sincerity, the "true" self, sometimes mystical or undifferentiated Spirit, but all assumed to be real. These authentic, self-absorbed, mythological characters, as well as the personae of the poets who created or composed them, presented tragedies (or comedies) of exalted sensitivity, humanity, indecisiveness, conceit, cruelty, hubris, humility, humbleness. Their *ethoi*, as well as that of their many of their characters, were something special but also deliberately defective—"un/wholesome," "politically over-passionate, socially "dis-eased"— representing "the truth" about the flawed, physical human being, the ills of society, the tragedy of the human condition. And simultaneously and always, the push toward the possibility of *personal or sublime transcendence* that could be captured in and through poetry (Abrams, *Mirror and Lamp*). In Romanticism, a subjective (and divine?) solipsism, the open interior *consciousness*, and all the attendant emotions, also included an outward (subjective) desire for the strange, the foreign, the exotic. Opened like an oyster, the pearl of the Far East had become all the rage in the eighteenth century; but for Romantic poets and artists in the nineteenth century (e.g., England, Germany, France), all things "Other" became objects of social, cultural, and aesthetic desire. From the decrepit, crumbling ruins of ancient Greece and Rome to the salubrious airs of the Alps, from the colors of Italy to the mysteries of the Orient, the foreign became part of a new subjective philosophy of (extra)ordinary life and art, of imagination and poetry (Eco, *Beauty* 282–87, 310–12; cf. Said; Cryer and Seaton)—"(a) Truth" (Eco, *Beauty* 304, 325–27).

Ikiru ("Life")

In drops of bursting spring
there were Japanese clouds
on a white paper sky so low
they seemed to rush and hold
the red birds cast in gold,
to have been pulled and drawn
by a long boy on a limb
poking pink arms through the blue
catch the colors of the running sun.

But after autumn's brown falling nights,
when winter's violet lights
spread over the world like a layer of snow,
slows, and the skin, like a lily
melts into the black cold—
his eyes brushed the fields,
sought the hills,
caught the moisture of the clouds
on each green shutting lash.

X=13

You're on Your Own

One obvious manifestation of all this new-found self-identity, this individualism, expressed itself in the break-up of the economic-political structures held in place by previous conceptions of the body and self, changing personal liberty, mobility (as we have seen, literally as well as figuratively), and a new-found individualism even in the arts. Gone were many (but not all, not ever) of the rich patrons of the arts; most romantic poets were, to varying degrees, financially on their own in a new business economy in which individual artists and poets sought social and political legitimacy. (The rise of a bourgeois middle-class itself was the result of the grip of writing that took hold in print technology and spread through literacy; the printing press also resulted in a fundamental shift in consciousness [Ong, *Rhetoric, Romance, Technology*].) In this new economy and literary culture, personal and philosophical conflicts were often enhanced by the agon(y) of the solitary artist set against the larger unfeeling society. Not only did these poets have to deal with the dire personal economics, but also what quickly came to be seen as the stigmatizing and stagnation of social convention and the stultifying suffocation of bourgeois values. But the spread of money and literacy created the need of individual artists to compete against *each other* in the marketplace of ideas (much related to press, publication, print) in ways not necessary if one was situated in the royal courts and aristocratic castles of the Middle Ages and Renaissance. In increasing numbers, poets had to give public readings and appeal if not pander (read "flatter," as Socrates had warned) to the sentiments of a much wider public audience, to "keep body and soul together." Unlike Socrates, for whom "popular audience" made up of slaves and women and children was undesirable, for the Romantics the popular (and small but growing) audience that emerged from the bourgeoisie in the seventeenth and eighteenth centuries became the new if untutored patrons of the arts. That increased need to exploit powerful emotions—dramatic surprise, sensationalism, shock effect, fatal love, swooning deaths in Germany—Eco suggested was at least one cause of "the *Sturm und Drang* movement" (*Beauty* 313).

X=14

{-Hanging Future Poets-

Even after death
they're still jockeying
for position:
Poetry is a cutthroat business.

Emily is not happy
there, underneath the men,
and refuses to stay put—
keeps slipping down the wall

behind the furniture
as if to simultaneously rebel
and hide; she'd be happy to hang
in a higher spot.

But then Frost
jumps
off the plaster—
as if to one-up her

(though friends they may be now),
as if he were on fire,
as if she were ice,
such a rowdy crowd.

Melville, still depressed
after all these years,
is content to remain
at the bottom

so as not to be disturbed.
You don't want to bother
Dostoevsky either, his face as grim
as the worn coat he wears.

James Joyce is so lost
in posed thought that he appears
not to care—
passive-aggressive even among the dead.

And Whitman is happy
as long as he's on top
of all the males in the bunch—
he likes to be with people:

now all blades of grass
waving in the sunlight

of heaven—even after death
still jockeying for the highest nail—

"silly stuff," fighting over
a tiny spot of turf on the wall:
Poetry's such a cutthroat business,
even after death, among the dead.}

X=15

Audiences for Romanticism

Corresponding to the shift in political-economic structure of the self, in the nineteenth century the question of whether a person, painting, or object was beautiful or ugly also was taken out of the pristine realm of abstract philosophy and opened to the subjective mind of a "real" audience: the public. If not now equal with the philosopher, the public was deemed important to understanding the phenomenon of art. Beginning in the seventeenth century (with Addison and Steele) writing for a bourgeois class but really becoming a prominent institution in the nineteenth century, the *critic* of art and of poetry came to play a significant role in trying to hone the aesthetic sensibilities and sharpen the physical senses of the public (Hume, "Standard"). The critic was now needed to teach the imagination, tutor taste, as well as communicate "lofty sentiments" and "the best" thought in philosophy, literature, and art history to the new reading and viewing public. Sentiment and emotion, associated with the popular taste of a rising middle class, became one of the new criteria of beauty: "Sentiments, taste, and the passions . . . lost the negative aura of irrationality and, as they were gradually reconquered by reason, they played a leading role in the struggle against the dictatorship of reason itself" (Eco, *Beauty* 260). In the nineteenth century, then, art and criticism based on sentiments, taste, and passions were considered to be more "naturalistic," and mimeses of these affective dimensions closer to nature, closer also to truth. In turning toward this, "sentimental naturalism," increasingly affected the perceptions of the public and became more prominent in the arts not only in patrons, but in subjects as well (see Eco, *Beauty* 256). The role of the critic was to educate the public's "natural" but limited and imperfect abilities, knowledge, taste, and judgment in nature and art.

The Spirit of Cloud

Notice how it gathers,
tufts and tousles, climbs
on the backs and brows

of others that come before and
after, how shapes of bodies, faces
form and find each other
along their shifting edges,
inside and out, and how
each member seeks to hold
to every other member as they
join and cling under air.

Clouds are the bodies of rational spirits
that rise above the earth
but don't go very far.

X=16

Educating a Public

In the nineteenth century the literary critic assumed the role of the orator-teacher in a rhetorical education laid out by Isocrates, Cicero, and Quintilian. The idea of everyone possessing the "instincts" and "natural abilities" to respond to art, and with education (theory and practice) judge the rhythm of rhetoric as well as painting and sculpture, had been articulated by Cicero in Book III of *De Oratore.* In assuming this responsibility in nineteenth century Europe, the literary critic did not replace the orator-teacher or supplant the role of rhetorical education. In fact, given the goal of helping a wider public learn to adjudicate and discern beauty, aesthetic education became another "common ground" where poetry and rhetoric met in the nineteenth century. For German philosopher Friedrich Schlegel, the literary critic as philosopher-poet was to play an instrumental role in the (re)shaping of Romantic philosophy into a "new mythology" in which poetry was the basis of all fields of study that used language, including rhetoric, and the Ideal of poetry the "spiritual" connection of all fields of study that didn't (see "Dialogue" 63, 74–76). The poet, then, with a real audience to transport and persuade, was to transform and conflate the philosopher-poet-rhetorician (even though many Romantics professed not to like rhetoric [cf. Clark, *Inspiration* 97].) The need to educate the middle classes, to refine their aesthetic sensibilities and interpretive skills, as David Hume had believed ("Standards" 231) made rhetoric useful in teaching *belles lettres*, just as poetry was useful in the teaching of rhetoric (e.g., Hugh Blair).

The Chalk-Pile

{"[O]nly someone who lived in turning to fresh tasks
could so forget his handiwork on which
he spent himself. . . " –Robert Frost, "The Wood-Pile" 50}

A bed of chalk-dust slowly sifts through the crack
in the trough, collecting on a ledge of wall
above the floor like half an hourglass.
Where does the other half of wisdom fall?

Broken desks sit in empty aisles,
students with some teacher's knowledge traced
in notebooks, papers, tests—a mind once scrawled
across this flat gray universe, erased.

Our knowledge comes to little more than this:
the marks of letters made too hard, a line
of thought slipping into an abyss,
decaying words slowly rubbed by time.

The students long ago have left for home;
the teacher coughs up chalk dust, is alone.

X=17

Rhetoric and Taste

For George Campbell and other major rhetoricians of the nineteenth century, poetry is a branch of and a preparatory step toward oration. "An instrumentalist model of communication predominates in both disciplines"; the poet and orator invent, arrange, and ornament the subject matter of their respective discourses according to specific aims or purposes (Clark, *Inspiration* 72). Cultivating the "natural" tastes and mind of the general public as audience was a primary purpose of rhetorical instruction. As Timothy Clark notes, "Hugh Blair attacks the *topoi* as "mere art," a servile imitativeness, compared to the more forceful and individualized effects of "Passion." "Passion . . . is not only a catalyst to the powers of invention, it may also be immediately persuasive" (*Inspiration* 72–73). As in Romantic art criticism, Blair's pedagogy assumed a certain methodological relativity and subjectivism that undermined classical and even Renaissance concepts of beauty and ugliness, and seems to transfer the criteria for the creation as well as the evaluation of rhetorical as well as literary texts from ideals of transcendental or "geometrically" proportional forms, or a "simple" imitation of empirical observation and mathematical plainness, to more felt, complex, interdependent relationships between human mind and nature.

London to Oxford

They sit still
by the windows
in blue light
gentle in their eyes.

The train moves
through the growth
rushing the flowers
pushing the leaves
heaving the thicket
and the brush.

On the fields
wheat shiver
in the smoky breath—
as if it meant frost,
the grass leans
with the winds
that hangs on the train.

All love the rain
when the darkling light
hugging the air
presses the windows
breathing at the glass,
when earth absorbs
clouds and sky
until the world shimmers in
blue light and shade.

Then sun nudges the deep,
and distant mountains nod;
the hills shine
with wet green heat;
and the blue dappled light
fades into the ground.

X=18

Inspiration and the Future

The notion of Romantic *inspiration* itself also was understood rhetorically. In *The Theory of Inspiration*, Timothy Clark argued that inspiration (as feeling if not act) was not only a by-product of print technology, but also of the poet's reflection of him/her presently poor and often deliberately isolated self in relation to a *future* audience, with whom he/she would be famous (*Inspiration* 103). According to Clark, the Romantic notion of inspiration itself therefore was based on a rhetorical concept of audience internalized as a psychological and aesthetic "ideal form." Although Clark too closely associated rhetoric with orality in studying this dimension of inspiration in composition (e.g., *Inspiration* 61, 71), he understood Romantic theories and experiences of the sensation and hope of writing (as well as earlier forbidden forms of religious and political enthusiasm) to be a poet's internalization of rhetorical practice of imitating the supposed values and entertaining the as yet non-existent, future audiences in imagination (cf. Ong, "Audience"; Katz, "Rhetoric of Confessional"). Thus, the singular but now extended self-became a rousing rhetorical "object"—a mimesis of imagination, an imitation of the projective mind that also swept into it a spiritual figuration of the "natural" world, including its politics. (Whitman's songs of himself included every "atom" of everything and everyone else [the indivisible [one] person—the "ένα άτομο" on life preservers]. So did the "transcendental I" of writers, literary critics, and political philosophers such as Ralph Waldo Emerson and David Thoreau in America; Samuel Taylor Coleridge and Pearse Bysshe Shelly in England; and Friedrich Hölderlin and Heinrich Heine in Deutschland.)

> [P]oets and orators at this time conceived whatever powers were within them in mainly rhetorical terms, i.e., in terms of their effects on others . . . The space of composition is, despite its seeming interiority, a virtual public drama, an arena of implicit rhetorical influences and emotion. What presents itself as an account of the psychology of composition . . . is often merely a transposition of those effects supposedly felt by the reader or auditor. (Clark, *Inspiration* 97)

The Poet-Orator

With the absence of an audience, she hears
the stirrings of a future world,
murmur of machines that don't exist,
and sighs of flesh not born yet . . .

She sleeps: and she dreams
in of a quiet field,
lying in the sway of grass
down amid the floating stalks . . .

And she listens, listens to
the sway and sweep,
to breaths in miniature,
slipping of leaves . . .

listens to the branches touch,
and the air on the boughs,
groaning from deep in the root,
and the winding of the earth . . .

And she hears, she hears
a noise like applause in her inner ear,
bees loudly gathering in the honey—
and she wakes to the sound

of her own lonely voice

X=19

Rhetorical Inspiration and Transcendence

Timothy Clark says: "The space of composition becomes, oxymoronically, one of a publicly-staged solitude and self-transcendence" (*Inspiration* 103). In Romantic poetry, the audience, as well as the poet, become "disembodied" insofar as, "images of rhetorical power . . . conflate a virtual audience—a space of shadowy, ubiquitous affects without definite or specific embodiment—with fantasies of individual transformation and fame" (Clark, *Inspiration* 106; see Ong, "Writer's Audience is Always a Fiction").

X=20

Lines composed a few miles above Westminster Abbey on the banks of the River Thames during a walking tour, upon visiting the commemorative stone of a future poet
(August 18, 1974)

{So, Mr. Eliot:
this is what
it is to have been

honored thus,
as future sage—

your ashes not
buried here, but
out of sight
at your ancestral grave—

your ghost
divided, haunting
Westminster Abbey
and East Coker—

to have a stone
in the cathedral
on the floor
of Poet's Corner—

an image of a rose
budding in flames:
to have others
stand upon

your name.}

X=21

Wordsworth as Rhetorician

According to Timothy Clark, Wordsworth's conception of "Power" in poetry was based on oral modes of rhetorical thinking: "Power," for Wordsworth, his word for the mind's sublimity, still functions frequently as a rhetorical term (*Inspiration* 97). For Wordsworth, poetry was "fitting to metrical arrangement a selection of the real language of men in a state of vivid sensation" ("Preface" 934). Contra Antonio in Book II of *De Oratore*, Wordsworth's seemed to have espoused another Ciceronian point of view when Wordsworth stated in his "Preface to the Lyrical Ballads" that "[If] the Poet's subject be judiciously chosen, it will naturally, and upon fit occasion, lead him to passions the language of which, if selected truly and judiciously, must necessarily be dignified and variegated, and alive with metaphors and figures" ("Preface" 937)—those "prompted by passion" (936). {Discernment. Almost in effect anticipating Kenneth Burke's view in *A Rhetoric of Motives* as "consubstantial" (22) owing to the division of humans, rather than substantial/ substance, the pure communication of angels,} Wordsworth said: "Poetry sheds no tears 'such as Angels weep' but natural and human tears; she can boast of no celestial ichor that distinguishes her vital juices from those of prose; the same human blood circulates through the veins of both of them" ("Preface" 937).

Divine Concert

last amen:
an echo
of angels

X=22

Wordsworth on Poetry and Prose

Wordsworth's view of form itself, poetic or otherwise, was perhaps highly rhetorical, and closer to Cicero than to Plato. In a way that actually seemed to echo Cicero (*De Oratore* III.xvi.70, III.xliv.173–76, III.xlviii.184–85; *Orator* xl.203, xliv.150, li.173), Wordsworth discussed the close relation between poetry and prose by appealing to the physical roots of language in a mimesis of the body itself. In his "Preface," he affirmed that "there neither is or can be any essential difference between the language of prose and metrical composition . . . They both speak by and to the same organs; the bodies in which both of them are clothed may be said to be of the same substance, their affections are kindred, and almost identical, not necessarily differing even in degree" ("Preface" 937). In denying a difference even of degree, Wordsworth went further than Cicero (c.f. *Orator* xix.66). Moreover, for Cicero the natural comprehension of rhythm and meter was a kind of "natural intuition" possessed by everyone (see *De Oratore* III.l.195–li.197); for Wordsworth, "taste and feeling, would of itself form a distinction far greater than at first imagined, and would entirely have separated the composition from the vulgarity and meanness of ordinary life; and, if metre be superadded thereto, I believe that a dissimilitude will be produced altogether sufficient for the gratification of a rational mind. What other distinction would we have?" ("Preface" 937).

Placebo

Spring arrives like love, but
white and dark the ends of
March, and clouds upon us, though no
snow in the wind—
this we sense and know, a
fresh clearing in the frozen world.

Very first hour,
lightning shatters the sky,
thunder startles the blue jays,
hiding their dreams in the pines;
squirrels in boughs poke their
hovelled noses into night.

Morning rains in the branches,
bulbs mercurial,
sparkle ice and light,
waiting for pellucid sun to
color, leaf, and flower,
golden green and seeming warm.

Now we begin to
comprehend feelings cool on
skin, mists shifting, an airy
forest, mint wafting
over cold-dark water,
drifting emotion blown—

spring arrives like love,
wakes us; but we watch
truth like winter survived
die hard, content in the new
season before it's begun,
day already here.

X=23

Wordsworth the Philosopher of Language and Emotion

Though he didn't know it, Wordsworth's philosophy was rather anti-Platonic. In addition to his definition of poetry that privileged affect, Wordsworth stated how the poet knows "man and nature as essentially adapted to each other, and the mind of man as naturally the *mirror* of the fairest and most interesting properties of nature" (Wordsworth, "Preface" 938; emphasis added). With the mind as a mirror of the best qualities of nature, Wordsworth's position was perhaps nothing that Plato might have tolerated. (Nature held little interest for Platon; mind should not have sought to mime the false forms of the physical world but search instead for eternal Ideal Forms.) In addition, it might have appeared at first that Wordsworth's epistemology seems to share something with Locke's philosophy of language, mind, and senses, where the mind is *a tabula rasa* upon which nature writes—but where nature was not only unhampered by the senses, but also *enhanced.* Speaking of poets, Wordsworth said: "The language, too, of these men has been adopted (purified indeed from what appear to be its real defects, from all lasting and rational causes of dislike or disgust) because such men hourly communicate with the best objects from which the best part of language is originally derived" ("Preface" 935). In Wordsworth's discussion of language, the Sprat-like influence on empirical science—the belief that words originate from and correspond to specific things, may have manifested itself. {Distinction. Cf. Cassirer, who believed the same thing on a very different basis.}While Wordsworth did not speak of a "one-to-one correspondence" between word and thing or "the mathematical plainness" advocated by Sprat, Wordsworth did cherish the plainness of expression of language that would derive from objects—not Plato's ideal one-to-one correspondence of word and Ideal Form, or the scientists' of word and fact, but rather the correspondence of the permanent word before the withering blossom of *physical* nature.

Intimations of Mortality

"To me the meanest flower that blows can give
Thoughts that do often lie too deep for tears."
—Wordsworth, "Intimations of Immortality" 590

i thought wisdom came with age.
i thought wrinkles equaled sage.
i didn't know these maturing features
were the marks of regressing creatures.

Passing through the fields enflamed
with autumn, i am tamed:
i cannot feel the seasons flow;
woods of foliage fill with snow.

i am less open to the world:
the trees are hard, and the leaves whirl,
like golden flakes that flash in color,
then die on the breast of their cold mother.

i have given up my innocence
without just recompense.
No, no, i have lost my mind instead:
Death sits on my drooling head!

X=24

Poetry as Mimesis of Affect

In Woodsworth discussion of what really was for the Romantics the "mimetic processes" of language and emotion, Wordsworth also seemed to subscribe to a Lockean position of how sensation was built through analysis and synthesis into Ideas. However, for Wordsworth, the operations of the mind "of more than usual organic sensibility" also had more to do with degree of remembered affect ("the little, nameless, unremembered acts of kindness and of love" ["Tintern Abbey" 206]) from which the poet drew inspiration, than they did with Ideas.

> [O]ur continued influxes of feelings are modified and directed by our thoughts, which are indeed the representatives of all our past feelings; and as by contemplating the relation of these general representatives to each other, we discover what is really important to men, so, by the repetition and continuance of this act, our feelings will be connected with important subjects, till at length, if we be originally possessed of much sensibility, such habits of mind will be produced, that, by obeying blindly and mechanically the impulses of those habit, we shall describe objects and utter sentiments of such a nature, and in such connection with each other that the understanding of the Reader must necessarily be in some degree enlightened, and his affections strengthened and purified. ("Preface" 935)

the storm

in autumn and marooning trees
strange turning in the leaves
on stem-threads twisting
like a mobile
like the earth . . .

sounds of children
rustling birds
dogs and wind
in the fence
shouts cries howls barks
squeals slamming
windows on the street
crashing clouds
clatter of grass
and flickering branch

seconds before
the luminous silence
the thunder

a quiet rain
like running feet . . .

X=25

Wordsworth and Aristotle

Rather than *Truth*, or even *fact*, a moral and psychological mimesis of an emotional response to nature was the basis of poetry for Wordsworth: "The appropriate business of poetry (which nevertheless, if genuine, is as permanent as pure science) . . . her privilege and her *duty*, is to *treat things not as they are, but as they appear*; not as they exist in themselves, but *as they seem to exist to the senses and to the passions*" (Wordsworth, "Essay" 944; emphasis added). Citing Aristotle as secondhand hearsay (probably from the more theoretically inclined Coleridge), Wordsworth stated: "Poetry is the most philosophical of all writing . . . Poetry is the image of man and nature" ("Preface" 938; *sic*). Wordsworth affirmed this particular mimetic view by concluding: "[P]oetry is the breath and finer spirit of all knowledge; it is the impassioned expression which is in the countenance of all Science" ("Preface" 938). It was, in short, feeling as the basis of all learning and all knowledge of nature.

At Sea

For Alison

"Rhetoric falls into three divisions, determined by the three classes of listeners to speeches. For of the three elements in speech-making—speaker, subject, and person addressed—it is the last one, the hearer, that determines the speech's end and object. The hearer must be either a judge, with a decision to make about things past or future, or an observer." –Aristotle, *Rhetoric*, Bk I.3

Forensic Rhetoric

Lilacs, salty breeze,
snap of wet wind off the sea,
your arrival after a long delay
And the first thing you say?
"Look at the ship on the reef,"
white ship in mist,
waves, breaking on it.

And your face is as cool
as the ocean's, pale, reflecting.
And in the sea-change of your eyes
the sun shoots in the spray,
the moon draws back the tides.
A wind inspires sudden haste;
waves rush your steps in motions
opposed, deflecting.

Epideictic Rhetoric

We drift out on this uncertain day,
and you, in your white sweater say,
"Look at the pale line across the ocean,"
horizon illuminating the storm of emotion
confused, gathering on your cloudy face.

Deliberative Rhetoric

X=26

Poetry as a Basis of Science

Despite his talk about science in opposition to poetry ("Preface" n.937), Wordsworth comprehended an important relation in the Romantic conception of poetry, and science: poetry, he claims, was the basis of science. "We have no sympathy, but what is propagated by pleasure" said Wordsworth, reflecting earlier discussions of pleasure and pain, and added: "wherever we sympathize with pain, it will be found that sympathy is produced and carried on by subtle combinations of pleasure. We have no knowledge . . . no general principles drawn from the contemplation of particular facts, but what has been built up by pleasure and exists in us by pleasure alone" ("Preface" 938). For Wordsworth, unlike Plato (e.g., *Philebus* 21a), pleasure was not to be eschewed but rather is the primary source of knowledge for everyone, including the scientist "who looks at the world in the spirit of love" ("Preface" 938). Unlike Locke (*Essay*, 299–300) and especially Sprat, Wordsworth had some affinity for what had been called "a naturalistic" rhetoric, with which he understood the deep connection between prose and verse as "moral feelings" (see "Preface" 937). Romantic poetry attempted neither to imitate the world of science nor mimic the ideal forms of the ancient world, but rather limn the lines of emotional response to people, places and objects in their natural state. By the nineteenth century, the mimesis of "ideal forms" had been transmuted by Romantic poets, philosophers, critics into "the powerful overflow of emotion . . . recollected in tranquility" ("Preface" 935, 940).

To William Wordsworth

Dove Cottage, Grasmere, The Lake District, Cumbria, England
August 5, 1974

Dear Mr. Wordsworth,

Long have i traveled time and space
To stand here, be at your side
In Hawkshead, toward Ambleside,
But for a moment to attend your school
Where you studied grammar as a child.

The little room is so deserted now
Save a poor rich older washer woman
You might have taken to your heart, known,
A representative of your kind estate,
"[L]ittle nameless unremembered acts."

i am sitting on your backless bench
Barren as a rock at your desk
Except your name composed in hardened wood,
As if it were an indoor tree for you
To carve poems. i still have much to learn.

The fire is out, no longer daily lit.
Although it is summer, the room is cold
Without you and Dorothy, days of old,
Your perspicacious sister, your source of genius,*
Her quiet observations your fevered visions.

A lonely ledger perches on a table,
Takes flight, records that day you had some coal
In the bright warm scuttle of your soul
Now "[r]olled round in earth's diurnal course"— *
"Shine, Poet! in thy place, and be content." **

~ Aristocles (Young Plato)

* D. Wordsworth, *Journals*

**Line from "A Slumber Did My Spirit Seal," "The Lucy Poems," *Poetical Works*, p. 187.

***"If Thou Indeed Derive They Light from Heaven," "The Lucy Poems," Poetical Works, p. v.

X=27

Objects and Emotions

In this revisioning of the body, Wordsworth discussed "elementary" yet complex and lively emotions in his "Preface": "The principal object . . . proposed in these Poems was chiefly, as far as regards the manner in which we associate ideas in a state of general excitement" (935). These feelings "germinate" and were more easily found in ordinary, simple, "rural occupations" and "humble and rustic life" ("Preface" 935). It was from this form of life that the language of poetry for Wordsworth should have been derived: "such language, arising out of repeated experiences and regular feelings, is a more permanent, and a far more philosophical language, than that which is frequently substituted for it by Poets" ("Preface" 935).

On Leaving the Lake District

1. A Late Sunday Rain
Lulled by the fire, a father dwells
softly on his curling son,
about the placing of a log,
and his hand that gathers heat;
a nestled flame in flannel sleeps.

Damp wood aches, and golden ash
drops in the silence of a smoke-filled heart
where warm branches cross, then part,
in sinews from the family hearth:
the stones hold the bark's last glow.

For Wordsworth, the priority of the mimesis of emotion was not only "in a selection of language really used" to describe "incidents and situations from common life," but also "to throw over them a certain coloring of imagination . . . whereby ordinary things should be presented to the mind in an unusual aspect," for the purpose of "tracing in them . . . the primary laws of nature" ("Preface" 935).

2. Our Last Dinner in Windermere
Bows drawn on wet crystal,
notes clear and pouring full,
the scent of brandy light
sheer under glass:

Between the candles
drinking warmth,
and pulling at the wine,
we had our last.

Thus, Wordsworth wrote a lot of poetry about and in response to actual specific local places and people. For Wordsworth, poetry was not a *mimesis* of ideal forms or universal principles, but a salubrious response to the "natural" world all around him. Contra one possible view of Platon, the wholesome language of poetry was best found in rural affections, expressions, and thoughts of ordinary country people "because in that condition the passions . . . are incorporated with the beautiful and permanent forms of nature" ("Preface" 935). It was the forms of nature that are "beautiful and permanent." Contra one possible view of Aristotle (*Poetics*), the purpose of poetry was not "catharsis" either. For Wordsworth in particular, poetry did not attempt disperse negative emotions through the behavior of characters in the unity of art, but was the revelation of positive emotions represented through character and language. The antithesis of Aristotle (*Poetics*), what distinguished poetry for Wordsworth was "that the feelings therein developed gives importance to the action and situation, and not the action and situation to the feeling" ("Preface" 935).

3. Departing
Your slow, quiet movements.
Your hairbrush hushed.
Your voice smelling of violets . . .
dropping from your breath,
filling empty emotional spaces.

Do not weep, your head in sway:
the willows shake off mist
like veils about a grassy bole . . .
a gauze of tissued leaves,
to dust your blue eyes with morning.

X=28

The Lake District: The Home of Romanticism

In the nineteenth century, the English Lake District, clear blues and greens, shimmered with writers and poets. From Keswick to Windermere to Kendal, from Carlisle to Penrith to Ullswater, Grasmere, and Ambleside, poetry was popping in the local population; the wind puckered with lime and sun-blown cheeks. But "Lake District" writers and poets, including Wordsworth and Samuel Taylor Coleridge, Robert Southey, and Charles and Mary Lamb, as well as other English Romantic poets, painters, and critics living elsewhere, such as Byron, Shelly, Keats, and John Constable, JMW Turner, and John Ruskin, all traveled extensively (the Swiss Alps, Germany, Italy, and Greece were fertile turfs for their imaginations). Perhaps high on opium (and later German Transcendentalism), Coleridge, Wordsworth's close friend and fellow poet, as well as a major philosopher in the Lake District, founded his notion of the poetic imagination in German Transcendentalism and brought that to the Lake District. Rather than "forms of affection" and "reflective tranquility," poetry for Coleridge sought to express not only subjective experiences but also spiritual visions that at their best might correspond to *the World Spirit.* As Coleridge discussed, just as "all the organs of sense are framed for a corresponding world of sense . . . [a]ll the organs of the spirit are framed for a correspondent world of spirit" (237). This idea is not foreign to Wordsworth either, as when he spoke of affective/spiritual response as excited insights and passion. But for Coleridge, affective and spiritual sensitivities and spiritual organs are more developed (237) in a transcendental poetic vision. This celestial shift reflects how far Romanticism had come from Platonism (yet still contains some of the neo, as well as the Christian, in it). However, hidden beneath the haptic surface of the human body—the psychological epidermis of the mind, the crusted skin of material reality—inspired organic senses sought to connect with nature's disembodied *spiritual* organs of sense. For Coleridge, dreaming at his home or the train station in Keswick, the poet desired to be "transported" from the poor physical body, through imitation and manipulation of existing forms, to "lines" of transcendent feeling and thought, beauty and power, and ultimately, prime spiritual being.

Reverie on a Train

waiting
on a long station platform
under coal-gray skies
piled high with clouds,
one dreams of future places . . .

the still idle of the train
moves into thought, and the mind
travels swifter tracks,
across frozen fields of light,
over barren waters, moves . . .

lives in visions of dim towns
pass; anonymous faces flash

in the window and are gone,
all those people left standing
in the cold, at another station . . .

the engine whistles, jolts.
And slowly the train begins
to push through the smoke
that gathers and breaks
like the years up ahead . . .

X=29

Coleridge's Philosophy of Imagination I

Another major difference between Wordsworth and Coleridge was the distinction among *three* different organs of imagination, as articulated by Coleridge in his *Biographia Literaria*: "Primary Imagination," the supreme form of imagination; "Secondary Imagination; and "Fancy," the lowest form of imagination. {Insight. In her study of ancient Greek and Rabbinic literature and rhetoric, Susan Handelman pointed out that ουσια [*ousía*] was "first being," "the what," "essence," and the rest was "secondary being," characteristics such as "qualities and quantities" (7) and perhaps other attributes, such as shape and color. Ουσια was related to (but was not) the product of "the Primary Imagination."} As Coleridge stated: "The primary IMAGINATION I hold to be the living Power and prime Agent of all human perception, and as a *repetition in the finite mind of the eternal act of creation* in the infinite I AM" (*Biographia* 263; emphasis added). The "primary imagination" was the faculty responsible for *(re)creating* reality. While not *ousia* (i.e., essence), the primary imagination was "the prime Agent of all human perception"—the creation of material or metaphysical reality we behold and know in and through human perception and thought (cf. Stevens, *Necessary Angel*). While not divine, the Primary Imagination as "a repetition" was not mimetic either, not "mere replication" (cf. Deleuze and Guattari), or imitative, but a participatory act of consciousness, a powerful contribution to reality sacred to the human condition. Poetic mimesis, then, was transcendental, spiritual—both the act and the object. The primary imagination was only imitative in the sense of it *not* being *ousia* (not "the original," "the thing itself" because of "the finite mind."). It was the "secondary imagination" that was mimetic, recreating and reworking what already physically existed into something inexact or else, but was still regarded as something creative—a source of new poetry.

Synesthesia by Moonlight

When dusk clings about the willow,

gold to amber, ashen mist;
and night falls like a darkened leaf,
stars quickening behind the branches—

autumn, with its frost and orange,
slips like silver on the grass;
shivers slide up the river;
evening glitters on the glass.

X=30

Coleridge's Philosophy of Imagination II

In relation to either organ of Imagination, where was the body? Not shunted aside (see Wordsworth), but rewritten. Although limited, the human senses and mind (and by extension the poet's body) were not only material, but transcendental insofar as they could participate "in . . . the eternal act of creation." Perhaps echoing Descartes' *cogito* "I think, therefore I am," the confirmation of existence for Coleridge came from "the eternal I AM." But unlike Descartes, for Coleridge "the eternal I AM" was confirmed in the correspondence of the organic senses with the spiritual organs of nature. For Coleridge, *form* (physical or human) was at best the creation of the "Secondary Imagination," which engaged in the act of synthesis. {Intuition. The distinction between Primary and Secondary imagination would later be understood by twentieth century philosopher Suzanne Langer's as symbolization (perception) and resymbolization (language and thought).} "Fancy," the lowest organ of imagination, merely acted on objects as they existed as "fixities and definites"—"even as all objects (*as* objects) are essentially fixed and dead" (263). "The Fancy is indeed no other than a mode of Memory emancipated from the order of time and space" (263). As such, Fancy might be considered a more basic organ of mimesis.

Remembering Hartley Coleridge

The throngs and thorns
and even the violets
have forgotten you—

a Sun-Cross stone
still in the shadow
of William Wordsworth—

But i have come
to read your name.

X=31

Poetry and Dead Objects

Rather than dealing with "dead objects" of uninspired reality, poetry as the result of (Primary or Secondary) Imagination had a higher spiritual purpose. For Coleridge (as later for Schlegel), poetry itself became a vehicle for the poet's self, conceived of as some inviolate transcendental entity or spirit. For the mystical poet William Blake, the spirit of humanity would be liberated from the Newtonian night through what he called "four-fold vision" (e.g., 722). Ineffable body and soul, humans beings would have become pure spirit—energy released into and existing in the indefinable space of free infinity—unbound from the physical, sensory, emotional, and spiritual constraints of rationality and the body, chained and doomed to dwell in the material world, with its social classes, bourgeois mores, economic and moral poverty, suffering and misery. "Four-fold vision," Blake believed, was possible through the imagination of poets and artists (he was both), which would set the mind on fire, bring forth each *being of light* as Truth (perhaps harkening back to the Medieval and Renaissance Christian traditions of divine light) and burning to be free. For Blake, the emergence of that being of energy and fire would have not only left the corruption of the body behind, but also be the harbinger of the "New Jerusalem." But this was no "mere" resurrection of the body to assume Christ's glorious body; this was the disappearing of all human religions with the material body and world as we know it. For these Romantics poets, whether Wordsworth, Coleridge, or Blake, the divinity of the poet always began with heightened human sense, whether rustic feelings from natural forms, organs that seek their counterparts in the Spiritual world, or the blazing energy of soul. For these Romantic poets, it was the spiritual in everyday objects, events, and human beings that poets could see peeking from arbitrary flesh, sometimes slipping out of the false binary of life and death.

Beauty and Age

There is a temporary
beauty in growing old,
when we behold
the diminished features
on an aging face
reappear, an apparition
caught in pale sunlight
between the soft lines of years,
passing behind the smile—
then disappearing, time

a worn-out mask that
shifts, becomes
slightly disengaged,
loosening about the darkened
eyes, finally falling away
at its final resting place,
preceding, then proceeding
to the grave.

X=32

The Skin of Spirit

Not only Coleridge, but Romantic poets generally believed that material form was also spiritual. Pantheist or not, worshipping in the religion of Romanticism these poets recognized the role of the imagination more than the rational intellect in animating nature. Form in the nineteenth century was better regarded *not* as Platonic Form or Aristotelian *ousia*, but rather as a skin of spirit, a skein of meaning stretched out from and over a metaphysical flesh of spirit. Based on the recombinant emotions of the subjective mind and nature's spirit, the writing of the form of spirit was divorced from the "lifeless corpse" (Schlegel 85), and in many ways were totally revised in Romantic poetry.

Grief

Do not look for grief,
it is not too hard
to find, and will come
easily enough without
your calling, you who
pull
longingly
on the leaves,
bringing the spectacle
of speckled
of shade
the spectacle of branches

down,
drawing
a little light
across eyes and brow,
and sigh and frown.

Death
is in every
blade of grass that breaks
the ground,
happiness
in
the falling
of

a
leaf,
the
sudden turning
of a breeze, the

dew gathering
around a retiring mind,
a planted heart.

X=33

Romantic Poetry, and Rhetoric

Did the same "Romantic rebellion" happen in the art of rhetoric? Along with the slow but continual revival of the so called oratorical or Baroque or Asian or high style of oratory and writing styles of Isocrates and Cicero in certain quarters of the Renaissance (see Croll), came the slow return of invention and arrangement in the development of a "scientific method" of composition (e.g., Campbell) and the use of literature in the teaching of composition (e.g., Blair). Certainly, the method and style of delivery, the fifth art of rhetoric that includes both speeches and oral readings, as well drama in Italy, Germany (and France, which Schlegel ["Dialogue"] left out), had been recharged in England thanks in large part to the Elocutionary Movement of the eighteenth century. {Temporal Relocation. James Berlin wrote about the effect and relationship of nineteenth century Romanticism on writing instruction, in many ways locating the origins of the "social-epistemic movement" of twentieth century rhetoric in Coleridge's notion of the Imagination and its power to (re)shape (human) reality (Berlin, "Rhetorics and Poetics"; "Rhetoric of Romanticism"; *Writing Instruction in Nineteenth Century*. Cf. Vitanza, *Berlin* 39–42; Connors, "Writing Instruction in Nineteenth Century"). As Victor Vitanza accentuated, this was only one of many scholar-shifting binaries in a developing "tertiary process" of composition for Berlin that at one point included the mimetic and transcendental (*Berlin* 38, 34, 46).} Of course, the Utilitarian Movement in philosophy and its somewhat monstrous manifestation in the industrial revolution also pushed against the Romantic movement, especially in speech and writing instruction, which increasingly were seen as the practical arts useful for society and success—in America no less if not more so than Europe (Connors, "Writing Instruction in Nineteenth Century"; Connors, et al.).

***

Perhaps this division, manifesting itself most obviously in the perceived difference between poetry and prose, was in form and style. In Romanticism, writing was defined by some rhetoricians and poets not by form (ideal, physical or otherwise)—by line breaks only—but *by audience and purpose*—and imagination, style, spirit (e.g., the *poèmes en prose* of Arthur Rimbaud; the "electric" narrative of Mary Shelley; the elegant poetic of Marcel Proust's style). As in the sophistic strain of ancient Greece, and "the offices" of Ciceronian oratory, both prose and poetry, could have been poetic or non-poetic, high or low or in between, depending on *purpose* and the nature of the audience based on propriety at every kairotic moment {as well as resymbolization, symbolic action, or linguistic movement in consciousness (see Cicero, *De Oratore*; Langer; Burke, *Toward a Symbolic*; Cassirer).} But within the universe of Newtonian science, nominal reference to "real kinds"— Coleridge's "definites"—dominated representation and knowledge. The "lower" form of versification (its external palpable shell), as well as the higher purpose of poetry (Imagination, Spirit), distinguished it from useful prose (cf. Schlegel), and made poetry both a seemingly higher calling and an increasingly rarefied, elitist, and/or "nostalgic" object and way of life.

The White House at Norfolk, Connecticut
for Alison and Roz

The mansion appeared
set in autumn amber,
pale river
under golden leaves.
"It's been twenty years,"
she said:
"I have lived
with the memory
of that image,
the grandeur
of that dream."

"Nothing has changed,"
her sister exclaimed.
The church
had been extended
into open space
the flowers had deserted;
the croquet
and white wicker
were put away
with summer,
green days
in the long cool grass.

"There is a loss:
the lions have grown
smaller; the doors
are locked."
"The aristocrats
still live
on their land,
entombed
under house
and rocky hill.'

"I want to run
those fields again,
play in the flowers
and the long leisured grass,
follow the waterfall
bending along the road
through the musical woods
and forget
about the world.'

"The music shed is
empty, gazebo
windy and cold.'

"I have inherited
this idea from birth,
and now

feel dispossessed."

"We can never
come back again."

11 2 8 1
Na
Sodium
22.990

11 Transcendental Organ

Y=0

"To construct a simple calculus equation where the output *y* can take on any whole number value (e.g., y = 1, y = 2, y = 3, etc.), we can consider equations involving basic functions . . . that produce integer outputs for specific inputs. . . . . Example 2: y = |x|. This is a simple absolute value function where *y* can be any non-negative whole number:

For $x = 0$, $y = |0| = 0$
For $x = 1$, $y = |1| = 1$
. . . .
For $x = 2$, $y = |2| = 2$
For $x = 3$, $y = |3| = 3$"

—Prompt: "Examples of simple calculus equations where y=0, 1, 2, et. al." ChatGPT, 2024

Y=1

Speculations on Leaves

Metaphysical
        leaves
drop from
        transcendental
trees,
        systems
upon systems,
        proofs
upon proofs.

        The philosophical
experiment
        is failing
again;
        symbolical
New England
        is settling in;
philosopher-pioneers
        are migrating
west; winter
        repatriates
metaphorical land.

        Forms
rise from
        a chimney
up a white
        birch
branch,
        into
an absolute
        of mist

This house
        of the mind
now heaves
        with the wind;
this will be
        a wilderness
again;
        words,
like leaves,
        frozen

in the fire.

Y=2

English Romanticism, German Idealism

Imagination. English Romanticism, along with German Idealism, with their visions of the spiritual existence of humans in/and nature (beneath the façade of materialism superadded to it), made its way to the transcendental shore of America.

Boston to Cambridge

Beyond
scattered factories,
canoes dip and slide
toward spring,
as the sun drifts
in the Charles River
toward Harvard Square
beneath colored domes
and white steepled clocks
of New England churches
past fluted porticos
and pretty walks
of red brick squares

By the river
painted in the grass,
green benches flower;
willows open the sky,
brushing cloudy water;
luminous limbs shine
warm in the dandelions.
Further down blue sails
stay boats of light;
horses gambol
on the drive;
ivy-covered buildings
shape the way

Y=3

Transcendental Circles

From Ralph Waldo Emerson and Henry David Thoreau and Margaret Fuller, to varying degrees Nathaniel Hawthorne, Herman Melville and Emily Dickinson, the transcendental circle in New England generally, and Emerson and his contagious expanding coterie and commune, represented a diverse but somewhat unified philosophy of deep, even total, physical and spiritual being in and with and as Nature in America. One result of the love of Nature *as spirit* was that Enlightenment values were overlaid if not partially supplanted with transcendental ones. These "new" spiritual values formed the foundation of the fierce belief in a "natural religion," "rugged individualism," and a "capitalism of democracy." But perhaps most importantly was the religious faith and fervor as well as philosophical conviction. Every person was free to achieve both worldly, spiritual, and even "mystical success," becoming one with nature, God, and infinity, according to one's innate capabilities (their physical and mental and spiritual development), by directly observing, contemplating, and communing with Nature as Spirit (without much need of established religion). Even in writing, Emerson thought that *Eloquence*, in distinction to human rhetoric, was *given* to humans by the *spirit* of Nature itself (see Emerson, "Nature"; Crick, L. 380–739).

Visiting Emily in Her Room(s)

i went to talk with Emily—
A white dress in her tiny room
Standing—mounted —a short Form;
She blessed me as her groom.

We walked to her grave site
To pay respects due owed—
But i could not bend my knee—kneel—
Beside, between, the narrow stones—

As if prevented by stranger Force—
Stronger Spirit—universal Hand—
That reached across the centuries—
Paralyzed my limbs—

Bid me stand up straight and tall
In the presence of her Will—
Her body solid—blooming—
Underground—where i stood—still

Y=4

The Transcendental Eye/I

In fact, Emerson and his peers posited the notion that the spirit of nature was God, and thus meditating on, communing with, and feeling the spirit of Nature was partaking of the spirit, substance, and nature of God. "Standing on the bare ground,—my head bathed by the blithe air and uplifted into infinite space,—all mean egotism vanishes. I become a transparent eyeball; I am nothing; I see all; the currents of the Universal Being circulate through me; I am part or parcel of God" (Emerson, "Nature" I.8).

Figure 6. "Standing on the Base Ground . . . I Become a Transparent Eyeball."

"A Transparent Eyeball" (Figure 6), drawn by Christopher Pearse Cranch based on, inspired by, and illustrating Emerson's essay "Nature," was a visual representation, translation, and metaphor that communicated, elucidated, and symbolized a belief in the profound, sacred, and holy relation of "man" in, with, and to nature, spirit, God. Copied, imitated, and redrawn many times, "The Transparent Eyeball" depicted, encouraged, and allowed the living, thinking, feeling of the spiritual, divine, and infinite dimensions of Nature to directly enter an individual, breathing, living soul. "The transparent eyeball"—a figure for superior transcendental human senses, feelings, mind in the act of observing, contemplating, and communing with Nature—was completely "absorbent." Surrendering the self to Nature, spirit, infinity, the experience of physical, human, divine world had to be "*unreflected,*" unimpeded, pure.

***

Figure 7. The Transcendental "Eye/I."

"The transcendental eye" (Figure 7) was *not* another example, following Newtonian mechanics, of a naïve (or even metaphysical) empiricism that pervaded scientific philosophies and rhetorics, as well as poetics, in the eighteenth century (e.g., Dryden; Pope) and beyond. Rather, this "transparent eye" was transcendental, "a transcendental *I*." "The Transcendental 'I'" was not merely "absorbent" but sentient, sapient, alive. "The transcendental 'I'" was an active, passive—cooperative—extension of Nature's consciousness of itself, the divine and the infinite through human sensibility—the embodied, omniscient, universal EYE shooting up from the ground high into the air, cradling all on the ground but also towering over all of it, surveying all, seeing all, absorbing all. {Perception. The notion that meditation, observation, contemplation was passive, objective, and *unreflective* moved anachronistically against Kenneth Burke's later discussion that "terministic screens" were always not only a "reflection" but also a "selection" and a "deflection" ("Terministic").} "The transcendental 'I'" was physical, material, spiritual, and included the body of human, nature, God. The "Transcendental 'I'" was therefore a continuation—

or at least an extension and expansion—of "i," partaking of the best part of Nature. But the *transcendental* "I" did not completely forsake the human ego either. In American transcendentalism, as in its European counterpart at the time, the self, the ego, the "i" were still there too, and even necessary, as the grounding of the spirit, the foot of the "I," the *physical* basis for the transcendental experience. Based on a "retiring," emptying, withdrawal of self, "the transcendental 'I'" perhaps also refused to merely absorb, reflect, or be.

Y=5

Evening, Harvard Square

Reflections, changing lights.
You said the candles burn upon the water—
now green, now red, amber, white.
Towers wink,
docks on the surface
float circular and bright:

and the windows of desire
would be cold in the night
except for you, your words,
warming the darkness,
speaking of the buildings' rise
from the depths of the river:

images raised out of the water
that will survive when the buildings
with their darkened ivy are no longer.
We stand on the bridge
together now, for the moment,
in the shadow and the shine

Y=6

The Imagination as Primary Organ

It was the English poet and philosopher Samuel Taylor Coleridge who provided credence and the creed and the fullest philosophical expression of German Idealism in English Romanticism, helping to create the Transcendental Movement on both Anglo-American continents. "[T]o render the mind the intuitive of the spiritual," in the poet Samuel Taylor Coleridge's words, the *imagination*, not rational intellect, came to be seen as "the ulterior consciousness" (*Biographia* 237). The imagination became *the* primary organ of knowing in poetry and art, and *emotion* rather than thought became the basis of truth. One thinks of William Wordsworth's definition of poetry as "the spontaneous overflow of powerful feelings . . . recollected in tranquility" ("Preface" 935, 940), or of Keats' poetic line that "beauty is truth, truth beauty" (*Keats and Shelley* 186), and his concept of "negative capability" (*Selected Letters* 491)—in *the power of the poet to move out of his or her own body* via the empathetic powers of the imagination, and make room in the self of something else—for the poet's body to become at least in part if not entirely something else, become a delicate flower or an inanimate rock. This was another if not new kind of mimesis. It was not only the ego that is shoved aside in these encounters, even temporarily, but the body too.

My Dog, the Poet

(For Maxwell)

sniffs every blade of grass,
lightly touches nose
to every leaf, around
every rock and flower,
nibbles at the buds
(if that ain't poetry, what is)

paws the baby robin
fallen from its nest of trees,
holds it in his "soft mouth,"
his tail pointing to the west;
studies every stick of branch
with drooling eye, and selects

just one, throws himself (shoulder first)
on the ground and rolls in the dung.
Ah, experience! Then lifts his leg
to leave his mark upon the earth:
penis his pen, piss his ink,
he writes a poem on the bark.

And one day when he grows to be another,
the wind pawing at his bones,
and there aren't many sticks left to study,
he'll sit in the house, slow and old,
simply look out the window
and begin to bark at the rain

Y=7

"Esemplasticity"

In his version of Transcendentalism, what Coleridge called "the Primary Imagination" was "*esemplastic*" —able "to shape [reality] into one" (*Biographia* 191). This "faculty" was *not* "for discovering the available means of persuasion," as for Aristotle, but "for *(re)creating* reality" (*Biographia* 237). In some ways, this reality, like the Primary Imagination itself, was disembodied, in the same way that all things human were symbolized and thus abstracted. It was also material in the way that language and thought were physical, a product and emanation of the body (see Cassirer; Burke, *Enquiry*). That "symbolization" and "resymbolization" (Langer) were where various kinds of mimesis occur, what Auerbach might have called a "romantic realism" (not the literary "realism" and "naturalism" that developed in the late nineteenth century to *counter* Romanticism and Transcendentalism). In this (re)figuration of the "open body," the human and natural, transcendentally connected by compatible organs, were perhaps separated only by a "transcendental skin." {Perspicacity. In a twist of the Christian relation of body and soul, Jean-Luc Nancy would be heard to say:

> The soul is the form of a body, and therefore a body itself . . . But the *spirit* is the nonform or the ultra-form of the hole into which the body throws itself. In the soul the body *comes*, in the spirit it is *taken away*. The spirit is the substitution, the sublimation, the subtilizing of all forms of bodies—of their extension, their material division, in the distilled and revealed essence of the *sense* of the body: the spirit is the body of the senses, or sense in body. (*Corpus* 75, 77)}

But as Claudia Benthien remarked, in medicine, "a conception of the skin as a 'therapeutic organ" . . . did not fully cease until the middle of the nineteenth century" (40). With "the closed body," the skin was not merely a surface covering the corpse, but also the outer casing of the imagination and the spirit, which contains the transcendental organs of perception. It's as if, in deliberately closing the body, the open mind and body could now become hyper-aware of itself, affectively reflect upon itself, solipsistically see itself "more accurately"—even with all its flaws.

The Spark of Being/Lost

First, lift one leg, then the other, begin;
then the left foot, the right foot, swivel
around and under, collapsing, quivers,
gives into hidden pits of oblivions.

And in the wilds of your backyard
you are lost, stumbling through
your neighbor's grass, crawling through
a spark of dew, rain on every blade

piercing your piety, your consciousness
as you fall, your dancing face
interrupted, physiognomy
interpreted, an animal that grasps

awkwardly at language, as insubstantial
as angels talking to themselves, each other,
blue breath blooming brilliant in hot flashes,
symbolic action, and so much dust, is

Y=8

The Secondary Imagination

Within his own theory of transcendentalism, for Coleridge "the Secondary Imagination [was] an echo of the former, coexisting with the conscious will, yet still as identical with the primary in the *kind* of agency and differing only in *degree* and in the mode of its operation. It dissolves, diffuses, dissipates, in order to recreate"; that is, the secondary imagination analyzes and synthesizes that which already exists "to idealize and unify" (*Biographia* 263). For Coleridge, it was the third kind of "imagination," "the Fancy" that was responsible for the imitation of "fixities," or "definites" if not "dead" objects. It was perhaps here, the level of Fancy, that corresponded with traditional Platonic and neo-Platonic notions of mimesis, much derided and degraded (along with rhetoric) but still recognized by Romantic and Transcendental poets and artists as necessary for creatively negotiating material reality as it was. Life *without* "Fancy," along with other organs and modes of thinking and imagining and being, might (as Cicero would have pointed out) have been without *res*, substance, and thus nonexistent, empty form, missed.

Leaving the Dog Home (Again)

"Leaving again?" The dog
plants his snout on
the clothes on my bed—
"lockdown: you're not going anywhere!"

"What? Still able to pack?"
Like a puppy he takes
a black sock in his mouth
(hasn't done that in years)—

and ignoring all calls
and commands, runs out
of the room with it, and down
the stairs to where

(he buries the sock
under his own bed).
"I'll get you to stay yet," he thinks,
then realizes his failure

as the suitcase comes down the stairs
noisily rolls across the floor.
It is just then the dog realizes
he is as helpless as any human.

Y=9

A Science of Subjectivity

The "subjective science" upon which Coleridge's Transcendental theories of creation, synthesis, and imitation were based not necessarily on a familiar one. But subjective science rose out of German Idealism like a fire that ignited minds already burning with transcendental sensitivity on both continents. It was German Idealism that gave Romanticism and Transcendentalism a metaphysical push—a philosophical impetus and vision—in the second half of the nineteenth century. "Subjective science" was how in the history of Western civilization Transcendentalism radically transformed body, nature, mind, representation, and mimesis. In addition to industrialism (see Habermas), the subjective science underlying Transcendentalism can be understood as a reaction to Newtonian (empirical and mechanical) paradigms of knowledge in the eighteenth and nineteenth centuries: logical hypotheses, objective methodologies, rational explanations cutting across many fields (Darwin's work in biology, for example on the expression of emotions in humans and animals [see *Expression of Emotions*]). To varying degrees, empiricism and mechanism had heavily influenced the study and discussion of aesthetics, and notions of popular tastes with which romantic philosophers as well as poets and critics had to become increasingly concerned. The profound effect of Newtonian science on aesthetics itself can be found in eighteenth century debates about *Beauty*. Epistemologies and discussions of beauty were often overwhelmed by the beauty of beauty itself—by its theory, its cultural norming, its history and ritual (its "aura" [Benjamin, "Work of Art" 1969; 2008]), and by the stunning presence of art and the item itself, its physical manifestations. Thus, several philosophers in the eighteenth century tried to remake aesthetics into a stable, predictable, objective science, if not a hard, cold, and clear one.

In Praise of Winter

There is a clarity in the winter air,
a freshness as palpable as clear
skin after snow has rinsed it pale,
a sharpness in the lines of patchwork land
after wind has picked it bare,
a heightened focus where color fails,
where branches crack against the day:
a certainty of vision in the frozen clay.

Y=10

Deformity and/as Beauty in the Eighteenth Century

Eighteenth-century English writer and publisher Joseph Addison had believed that the imagination was the human faculty possessing the power to empirically derive an understanding of "both artistic and natural Beauty" (Eco, *Beauty* 254). But in an *Enquiry into the Sublime and the Beautiful*, Irish philosopher and stateman Edmund Burke had tried to discover an experimental, Newtonian basis for "taste"—one located in the predictable psychology of the mind and the operation of physical principles (e.g., 6, 150). These eighteenth-century philosophers also reasoned that the subject and scientizing of beauty could no longer continue to ignore the Ugly (if it ever had). Ugliness in all its forms became central to a science of Beauty. Edmund Burke had objected to an earlier philosophical position that "*deformity had been considered as the opposite to beauty*" (102n.). Perhaps harking back to Aristotle's teleological definition of deformity as incompleteness or absence, which included the female body compared to the male (e.g., *Generation* 731b28; 738b19–26), Edmund Burke argued that "[d]eformity . . . is the absence "the *compleat, common form*" of the object that custom has led us to expect in any species," and "that the absence of deformity infers the presence of beauty [that] makes the latter seem merely negative" (Boulton lxv; cf. Burke, *Enquiry* 102). Thus, scientifically and logically, for Edmund Burke, beauty was the presence of the completed form "that custom has led us to expect."

***

In his theory of "objective aesthetics," Edmund Burke sought to undermine the ancient assumption of proportion as the basis of beauty (and ugliness) (e.g., Burke, *Enquiry* Part III, Section V). These were scientific rather than ethical statements. For nineteenth century Romantic art critics such as Francis Hutcheson and John Ruskin (*Modern Painters*; *Seven Lamps; Stones of Venice*), aesthetic principles were also moral ones. Unlike some of his other compatriots (such as David Hume, for whom beauty was almost wholly subjective, residing not in objects but in individual taste), Edmund Burke's theory of aesthetics also could not account for variations in taste caused by differences in sensibilities or defects of sense organs. E. Burke assumed that sensibilities were fundamentally similar (see Boulton xxviii–xxx), much as Locke and to some extent even Kant on this one point had assumed a similarity of sensibilities in their radically different epistemological schema (see Table 1). For Edmund Burke, a similarity of sensibilities was adequate grounds upon which to establish an "objective" science of aesthetics. It was an aesthetic theory of what could be considered beautiful (or ugly) based on "*a priori*" categories applied to the body, and to the mimesis of the body in art. (Like Kant's *a priori* categories, it also included time.) These early *a priori* categories also could not account for the contradictory scientific and spiritual impulses of his time—and the overwhelming urge toward spirituality that was to come.

Y=11

Time, Proust, Being, You

(For Dr. Whitney Jordan Adams)

Putting up books that went astray,
the house of eternity far away,
i came upon my Marcel Proust,
and could not help but think of you,
who loves his work so ardently
and took the time when in Paris
walking over all of France
to desist in the constant dance
to visit his temporal *chez*.

As always, resplendent,
to him you all a sudden
appear in time that moves

above him like a wave;
then slowly on and through his grave.
It feels like anxiety
on our skin, and joy
at the prospect of
something unseen, distant

a distant, final peace
when time has had enough to eat;
when time is like a memory,
slow, and kind, a holiday,
from ourselves; when time becomes
a companion, a lover, succumbs
to the still point of a mind,
as if balanced from some twine
unraveling from heaven, sleeps

life's continuous wings,
the wind-pendulum that swings
to which we desperately hang
on, precipitously, dangle,
as if on a thread
that becomes a thin bed,
then back again, until we become
utterly useless, numb,
an emotion that clings

to any everything around
on which we discover solid ground,
and rest from the motion
that constitutes us, our notion
of ourselves, who we are
in relation to reality, a star
in yet another galaxy,
another looked-for fallacy
that we may hear as pure sound.

O we all look for, and dread
the long night of the end,
the temporal crease,
the infinite surcease
of our entire existence,

and so push on the resistance
that we make ourselves deliberately,
hesitant, but inexorably,
and also have to fend

off as it moves under
and over and through us, sunders
our successes forward
from self-awareness toward
our own best selves, takes us
somewhere we don't discuss,
don't really want to go,
but inevitably must flow.
In the end, time renders

all. The dust awaits, shudders,
becomes us, becomes *another.*
Proust finds rest in rust,
his repose an eternal bust.
Time does not heal,
as if a pardon, or repeal
as is so often said, but
kills itself, and dies in us,
so oblivious,
                    and Other

Y=12

Diderot's Networked Beauty

Claiming that "the faculty to feel and to think" were inherent at birth and "force us to resort to various expedients" (10), in the eighteenth century the French philosopher and writer Denis Diderot also had searched for an objective basis for aesthetics. In particular, he had focused on *relations* through sense perception. In his "Treatise on Beauty," Diderot had defined beauty as "outside myself, all that is capable of revealing to my understanding the idea of relations; and *beautiful* in relation to me, all that reveals this idea" (12). Perhaps reflecting earlier Mannerist or Baroque penchants for "networking," Diderot believed that beauty had been both objective and relative, residing in the object (whether natural or artificial) and yet a comparatively indeterminate quality based on the number of relations (11–12). For Diderot too these relations were not ideas but empirical, inherent in the object (11; 14). Ugliness, on the other hand, revealed no such relation for Diderot: "[d]epending on the nature of an object, on whether it arouses in us the perception of a greater number of relationships, and depending on the nature of the relationships it arouses, we designate a thing pretty, beautiful, more beautiful, very beautiful, or ugly; inferior, small, great, elevated, sublime; extravagant, burlesque, agreeable" (14). Thus, Diderot attempted to find an objective ground for defining physical and aesthetic beauty that would nevertheless account for the role of the senses in the perception of beauty (and ugliness), and a discourse to describe (mime) the experience. Diderot's work reflected the continually growing role of science in aesthetics, psychology, and the philosophy of beauty. (It also supported Kenneth Burke's assertion about the lessening role of entelechy and the increasing role of mechanism in mimesis; if Beauty was the result of causation, there is no entelechy in "natural law" {to say nothing of "predetermination" (Katz and Rivers).} Through the ages and beyond the grave, Diderot responded: "The *beautiful* is not always the work of an intelligent cause: movement often gives us, either in a thing considered in isolation, or among several things compared one with another, a prodigious number of surprising relationships" (Diderot 23).

Living By the Sea

Flowers
and the sea,
candles
and the teapot
on a round tabletop:
cups of light
spilling on the ceiling,
falling into circles
through which we move.

And by a tilt
of the afternoon
sea, waves
like bright white dice
are tossed, thrown
against the rolling floor
of the ocean, tumble
into new combinations
with the deep

Y=13

Skeptical Revolution

The attempt to ground aesthetics, including beauty and ugliness, in objective science had even deeper roots in the seventeenth century scientific revolution. Along with Newtonian physics (as well as new theories of light and its mechanical propagation), the scientific revolution gave rise to both empiricism and philosophical *skepticism* in seventeenth and eighteenth century. This was not Plato's "θεραπεύῃ ἀσκέπτως" ("non-skeptical therapy") and thus a form of "flattery" (*Gorgias* 501c), but rather a devastating critique of "naïve empiricism." In 1689, Locke (*Essay*, 299–300) had argued for an empirically based psychology. In this psychology, ideas are formed from and by reflection of sensation (sense data) inscribed directly on the *tabula rasa* (the blank slate of the mind). In this was "pure mimesis," whereby external objects imprint themselves directly upon the mind without the mediation of senses or language. Locke's psychology provided the philosophical justification that Newtonian science required for a new basis for objectivity (see Table 1), bypassing Bacon's mistrust of the senses and mind, body and culture, and their instruments as mere reflections (*Novum*; cf. *Advancement* V.3). In this psychology *qua* philosophy, the body is rather passive—docile—although development of ideas beyond mere sensation by the processes of analysis and synthesis is for Locke (*Essay*) a central activity of the mind. Although not "subjective," these processes began to psychologically expose the mind as body to the world, organs that would fully open in the nineteenth century.

Vista

Boat
like a speck of paint,
speck of white
sunlight in the waves,
shimmering sky,
feverish sea
full of haze,
a hand
of cloud
brushing
the water—
and the dark towers of the mind
rise up before, over the eyes,
casting back black
from that blue
horizon

Y=14

In response to Locke's philosophy of empiricism, in 1748 Scottish philosopher David Hume published *An Enquiry Concerning Human Understanding.* While Locke (*Essay*) had postulated that sensory experience of the physical world was placed directly upon the senses and was therefore the basis of all knowledge, Hume, following this to its logical conclusion, questioned how we could know concepts like time, space, causality from sense experience, and perhaps anything at all. Hume called into question not only Locke's assumption that data enters the senses unimpeded by them, but the nature of the sensations themselves. Hume's philosophical skepticism led to the strong suggestion that causality, the basis of science, was only inferred from effects, and that "the law of causality" itself might simply be human "habit." Hume's philosophical skepticism applied not only to the assumptions of objectivity and the tenets of science—to the nature of reality, and whether we could ever know it—but to aesthetics as well. In *Of the Standard of Taste*, Hume extended his inquiry to the discussion of beauty and ugliness. Just as he had with causality, Hume "arrives at an aesthetic subjectivism bordering on skepticism . . . " (Eco, *Beauty* 247). As Hume stated, "The sentiments of men often differ with regard to beauty and deformity of all kinds" (Hume 204). As with his understanding of the problems of parsing cause from effects, Hume wrote: "Because no sentiment represents what is really in the object," but rather "only marks a certain conformity or relation betwixt the object and the organs of faculties of the mind . . . Beauty is no quality in things themselves: it exists merely in the mind which contemplates them; and each mind perceives a different beauty" (Hume, *Standard of Taste* 208–09). In a sense, then, for Hume humans were trapped by the inherently solipsistic nature of mimetic senses that were subjective, and that any standards were relative.

Autumn Light

The mind grows darker
in the fall, brow heavy
with glaring clouds, under which
we search the bright and changing air—
fiery branches, constant flare
of leaves that flame
without sun, then shed light,
red brown gold orange—
burn before our autumnal eyes,
confused with color, stunned by sight

Y=15

A Priori Senses

Trust in the senses and knowledge of the world explicit in the "naïve empiricism" of John Locke was greatly shaken by the philosophical skepticism of David Hume who questioned causality and the senses themselves. If abstract concepts could only be inferred (and felt), how account for the experience and validity of the senses in relation to effects and emanations that radiate from the material world? Eighteenth century German philosopher Immanuel Kant tried to stabilize knowledge and provide a new philosophical ("objective") basis for objectivity and scientific, as well as moral reasoning, and for aesthetics as well. In his *Prolegomena to Any Future Metaphysics* and *Critique of Pure Reason*, Kant tried to solve the problem of accounting for the universality of sense experience by positing and explaining the existence of the "*a priori* categories of pure reason"—categories with which humans are born. Since shared among humanity, these *a priori* categories, Kant argued, would provide a new "physical" (psychological) as well as well philosophical basis for objectivity, science, and *knowing*, including concepts that do not materially manifest themselves and cannot be known directly by the senses (i.e., time, space, causality). With Kant's categories, the basis for truth could now be relocated in pure reasoning (see Table 1). {Apprehension. Heisenberg would in the next century reveal some of the limits of Kant's *a priori* categories of pure reason, in the Copenhagen School of New Physics' attempts to apply them to quantum reality, to observe and describe subatomic particles (86–92).} At the time it seemed that with Kantian philosophy, humans were no longer trapped in their solipsist senses, limited minds, and fleshy bodies, but set free by pure ("metaphysical") basis for reasoning—the seemingly unassailable *a priori* categories upon which it is based.

His Room

His room was heavy with symbolism,
dark. Each piece furnished his mind.
Each book had become, to him, a metaphor
for something more, not words,
every article of clothing a ghost
in the closet speaking, speaking
to him alone, the wind, his life,
curtains trailing out the window,
dark gossamer and white,
beating back into the night.

Y=16

Kant's Taste in Beauty

Based on his *a priori* categories of pure reason, in aesthetics Kant had made a distinction between a beautiful thing (or body) *in nature*, which required no prior concept of its nature or end to appraise it, and the *re-presentation* of the beautiful *in art*, which did have a purpose and so requires a prior concept of its end. As with most philosophical abstractions and human reason, the divide between body and nature (or the mind) was not only reintroduced but reinforced. However, Kant argued that because art involved the judgment of *human re-presentation* (mimesis), such judgment was subjective and reduced to a matter of taste (rather than the operation of the universal *a priori* categories necessary to all knowing in science, here applied specifically to works of art [see Kant, *Critique of Judgment* 1, 2, 48]). As Eco states: "[S]ince the universality of judgments of taste does not require the existence of a concept to be conformed with, the universality of Beauty is subjective . . . " (*Beauty* 264). Notions of "the beautiful," and hence notions of mind, body, nature, and even "truth," shifted again (see Table 1).

Moving Again

my next life

is over there
in a cardboard box
in a corner
by the door

photographs
wrapped in newspaper
are past truths
off the walls

i sit quietly
on the floor
in the middle of
an infinitely empty room,

waiting

Y=17

The Rise of German Idealism

It was from Kantian philosophy, and in particular the *a priori* categories of pure reason, that German Idealism sprang in the eighteenth and nineteenth centuries. German Idealism in turn gave birth to a subjective science that would underlie Transcendentalism in the nineteenth century in Germany, England, and America. These philosophies went well beyond questions of beauty or aesthetics or even imagination, to include the nonrational, and the infinite. "German Idealism" ran from Kant to Fichte to Schlegel to Schelling to Hegel (and beyond, to Nietzsche, Heidegger), and in a "different" lineage (such tracing being partly imagination), to Schiller, Hölderlin, and even the German-Jewish poet Heinrich Heine. (These philosophies, and their relations, never mind their linage, were all contested. It was not a straight line to eternity.) But all these philosophies wrestled with the *Zeitgeist*—the "Spirit of the Age," and questions of "*being/Being*." Building on and utilizing each other, these philosophers and their enormous epistemological/ontological systems tried to comprehend the relationships among the human (and nonhuman), the senses, mind, spirit, nature, science, mythology, and world history.

Winter Greys #1

These days we make more desolate:
the sky hangs overhead;
too quickly the darkness
descends, filtering through
the bleak leaves that linger
on blue insensible branches,
settling like frayed scarves
of woolen smoke that curl from
the smoldering mouths
of dumb chimneys, falling
without a source, without
the certainty of the sun.

***

There were combative, disputed, and unsupported assertions (in print and in person), as well as professional quarrels and personal attacks. In work often considered a derivation from Kant, one major and sometimes underrated philosopher in German Idealism was Johann Gottlieb Fichte. Kant was like a "philosophical father" for Fichte—at least Fichte thought. But Immanuel thought that Johann was certainly no progeny nor protégé of his. Kant came to vehemently believe that Fichte's philosophy of idealism was not only *not* related to Kant's own, but wrong, and came to denounce and oppose Fichte publicly (see Kant, *Declaration*; Breazeale, *J. G. Fichte: Introductions*, vii; *J. G. Fichte* 129–31). Based on the first two lecture series Fichte gave in Jena, and their publication, which Kant did not read (Breazeale, *J. G. Fichte: Introductions* 53–54 n.18), Kant "disowned" Fichte; around the same time, Fichte was fired from his teaching post due to unwarranted charges of atheism (Breazeale, *J. G. Fichte: Introduction*, xv–xvii; cf. *J. G. Fichte* 133–76). Further, Friedrich Wilhelm Joseph von Schelling, whose philosophy (and writing) was highly influenced by Fichte (Wright 1), disagreed with and also turned on Fichte, as did Hegel (Wright 2). Fichte, rejected and unemployed, delivered his lectures at his new home in Berlin (Wright 2–3; Fichte, *Science of Knowing*). However, the publication of these was full of "circumstantial" errors (the typesetters, the tribulations of memory, and the rush of his own always hectic schedule); Fichte's arguments continued to be received as incomplete, and somewhat incoherent and confusing—and not philosophically correct in the way it presented Fichte's thinking (Wright 5; see Fichte, *Science of Knowing*). Based on his early work, Fichte was judged by his philosophical contemporaries (and for two centuries his posterity) as "a minor figure . . . a mere ideational steppingstone along the transcendental path from Kant to Hegel. He was miserable, misunderstood, hurt (Wright 4–5).

Winter Greys #2

In a room of the night
we sit, smoking; our mouths
open, but no words are spoken
in this blackened house;
shadows listen intently
at the windows; blank panes
reflect our situation;
our cigarettes shed,
frail skin falling in
fretted, beating embers;
into the silence we flick
the graying ashes or our lives.

***

Miserable—and motivated! Fichte, as well as other German philosophers and poets, continued to grapple with developing a philosophy that would heal the rifts in human understanding, present "the first system of freedom" (Breazeale, *J. G. Fichte: Introductions* vii n.1), and perhaps to (re)unify classic and romantic temperaments (see Barzun; Lyotard; Benfey) and move beyond them. Despite and perhaps out of his personal pain and philosophical difficulties, almost always underappreciated and misconstrued, his job precarious and personal situations dire, Fichte created a highly original "subjective science," his *Wissenschaftslehre* (Fichte)—his "theory of ("subjective") scientific knowledge," which was a major contribution to subjective idealism. Influencing Coleridge, German Idealism, other Transcendentalists, and posterity, Fichte's *Wissenschaftslehre* was an original philosophical exploration not only notions of human mind, creativity, and nature, but also *representation* and/of consciousness itself.

Winter Greys #3

Outside, then, gray lights flicker,
falling through the branches, fretting
dumb rooms with uncertain sight.
How strange that these should give us
meaning, these frail lights
beating, falling against the darkness;
that these frail lights,
streetlamps, headlamps, house lamps,
human lamps all, should tell us
of our struggle, and our troubled
sleep, should all tell us
of our love, human love.

Y=18

Fichte's Subjective Science

Generally, in nineteenth century German philosophy, as in English Romanticism and American Transcendentalism, *feeling* had remained a philosophical as well as psychological problem. But in Fichte's *Wissenschaftslehre*, feeling was also a question of the representation of reality in/of human consciousness—an issue of subjective *mimesis*. Fichte, dubbed and somewhat dismissed by later Hegelians as a "Subjective Idealist" (Wright 4), attempted to create a philosophy that might bring the subjective and objective together in the pure transcendental "I." Fichte seemed to begin where Rene Descartes had in the seventeenth century, with the thinking consciousness, the *cogito*—I think. However, whereas Descartes proceeded by deduction to arrive at his *ergo summa*—"I am"— Fichte proceeded by examining the relationship between the different levels of *spirit* and the body. Fichte seemed to have intuited that his *Wissenschaftslehre* was a reaction to the docile body, or perhaps more precisely the "docile imagination." He did so by developing a fully formed philosophy of a "subjective science," one that addressed head-on the transcendental mimesis of the Spirit gone objectively awry. Paralleling Coleridge's famous definition of poetry, Fichte, Breazeale said, "wished to relate this distinction (between New Testament notions of the body and the spirit) to a general theory of man as a "spiritual" being, and to transcendental philosophy in particular, understood as "the systematic history of the human spirit's universal mode of acting" (*Early Philosophical* 188).

Flight of Imagination

Through the night
gilded pinions streak

Sun, rose on black,
dawns stretched along the wing

Y=19

Fichte's Spirit of Human Consciousness

Fichte's science of subjectivity attempted to address the problem of the representation of *feeling* in Spirit and consciousness—a problem of *transcendental mimesis.* Fichte stated: "Spirit as such is the ability of the productive imagination to convert feelings into representations. Spirit, in this sense of the word, can be ascribed to all beings capable of representation" (*Early Philosophical* 199; cf. Fichte, *Science of Knowing).* Echoing belief in differences in sensibility explored and ignored by Edmund Burke and Denis Diderot in the eighteenth century, Fichte poses a more specialized sense of feeling: "the ability to raise to consciousness the deeper feelings underlying those other feelings which relate to the physical world. These deeper feelings relate to a suprasensible world order, and the ability to raise them to consciousness may be termed the ability to convert ideals and ideas into representations" (*Early Philosophical* 199). Somewhat paralleling Coleridge's notion of the correspondence of the physical organs of humans and the spiritual organs of nature as a supersensual reality, Fichte pointed out that "[r]ather than being related to the mere order of appearances in accordance with the laws of nature, these other feelings relate to the subordination of appearances and of all rational spiritual beings to the laws of the ethical order, the laws governing spiritual harmony and the unification of everything in one realm of truth and virtue" (*Early Philosophical* 194–95). "Spiritual harmony and unification of everything." (If the Spiritual was harmonized and unified [or subsumed or "consumed"] by nature, where was "the body" [the self vs. nature/world], and thus the necessity of mimesis, now? Gone, at least "in Spirit," in German Idealism and Transcendentalism. The body, like nature, became "physical figurations" of the Spirit.)

Acceptance of Healing

Constantly giving
himself away,
like a ghost
looking for happiness,
stepping out
of his body,
walking abroad
to be a part
of something larger,
giving up self-containment,
pleasure, self-satisfaction, reason
savoring itself, and also
the dual senses
of doom and death
just on the outskirts
of consciousness,
two consequences:
one healthy guilt,
the other neurotic conflict,
previously conflated,
now separated
dissected and living apart,
ground down and content
around the fine edges

Y=20

Organic Spirits

What followed was not only a generalization of the philosophical technicalities of the science of subjectivity. For Fichte, organic *Spirit* was the whole of philosophy: "the material of all philosophy is itself the human mind or spirit, considered in all of its affairs, activities, and modes of acting" (*Early Philosophical* 200). Further, "[s]pirit lifts itself to the feeling of 'eternal truth'" (Fichte, *Early Philosophical* 196). For Fichte, this natural Spirit was bound in the physical: "Everything that occurs for us happens within the *physical* world, and that includes a sensuous being's spiritual ideas. The free spirit is clothed in a body" (*Early Philosophical* 196). Hence too, the *communication* of philosophy, of spirit—its rhetoric as well as its poetics—was an issue of embodiment for Fichte: "I give you the mere body. The words which you hear constitute the body" (*Early Philosophical* 196). For Fichte, "[a]ll of our philosophical assertions are 'bodies'"

(*Early Philosophical* 207). Addressing directly the problem of mimesis of spirit in physical form ("Körper, i.e., physical embodiment of spiritual ideas" [*Early Philosophical* 207n.]), be it flesh or linguistics or dirt, Fichte reflected that "representations of a purely spiritual character are, for the purposes of communication between spiritual beings, clothed in bodies and thereby become expressed—to the extent that such expression is possible" (*Early Philosophical* 199). Breazeale also pointed out the philosophical lineaments of what would be a "transcendental rhetoric": "spirit as the ability to express one's ideas, that is, to give them physical embodiment, and the closely related capacity to receive ideas, to recognize the spirit in the body" ("Concerning the Difference" 188). The "Truth," following the nature of the "form" of the body, therefore had moved again in Fichte—not as Ideal Forms, or observable facts, nor Kant's *a priori* categories of pure reason, nor even simply transcendental consciousness, but to *physical Spirit* (see Table 1). The representation of these truths was not "re-presentation," but involved both body and spirit, mimesis and symbolization, rhetoric and poetry.

Living Runes

Stumbling on hidden
stones with their embedded
messages and the birds
twittering their symbols,
and the trees' wavy green
alphabets, the mosquitoes
are invisible letters
in the sunlight
until they find you,
and ask for nothing
but a little blood
in kind; stepping
over the gnarled
river, the secret
is unconsciously clear:
will you give?

Y=21

Fichte's Participatory Spirit of Philosophy

As a theory of mimesis, Fichte's philosophy may have sounded a little like Plato's, especially the latter's discussion of Beauty in the *Phaedrus*. Like Platonic Ideal Forms, "Spirit lifts itself beyond the necessary forms of spatial bodies and delineates in its freedom the idea of "primal beauty," to which nothing in the material world is equivalent" (Fichte, *Early Philosophical* 195). It even may have echoed Platon's notion of the internal scribe who wrote in the memory of the soul (*Philebus* 39a). But Fichte's was a subjective science of the Spirit—*not thought alone*—that for Fichte allowed *the representation of feeling in consciousness.* In addition, Fichte advocated and taught "participatory philosophy"—encouraged physical as well as intellectual involvement from his hearers and students, especially in his third series of lectures [Fichte, *Science of Knowing*]). "Primal" was not "Ideal"; nor was "Spirit" dialectic. Dialect was certainly employed to articulate and comprehend Spirit (as it is everything else). But the *experience* of Spirit, and the science of it, was physical and subjective, as well as "provisionally rational." Despite the democratizing and secularizing Enlightenment, the Romantics and especially the Transcendentalists were more aware of differences in Imagination and sensibility. As Fichte forecasted: "persons lacking in spirit never see beyond this dead body and are incapable of employing it to lift themselves to an intuition of the ideal which this body expresses. *In imitation,* such persons construct other bodies lacking in spirit altogether" (*Early Philosophical Writings* 199; emphasis added). Was this not Coleridge's "dead objects" as "definites or fixities" that could still be brought to life?

The Tunnel of Flesh

Out of the tunnel of flesh
a stomach full of ghosts
the dark hallway at the end of which
is a room with his mother's body
on the floor, the shape of her
face and neck and torso
seen through the doorway,
a form decaying—
gray matter rotting
catacombs of emotions
buried deep in the grave with her
pain encased in
burlap and brain:
peel back the flap
with the mind, her face
flashing off and on
the wall of the skull
i can't escape

Y=22

Mimesis and Representational Consciousness

A higher understanding of form entailed a higher level of spirit, the activity that produced transcendental knowledge. For Fichte, *transcendental mimesis was not representation, but the process of representing representation* (cf. Breazeale, "Preface" 189). "This," says Fichte, "is the very essence of transcendental philosophy" (*Early Philosophical* 201). In some ways, then, "the process" of philosophy, of consciousness itself, were different spiritual modes of activity; and that activity, that thinking as representing the process of representation, became not only a method and form of spiritual transcendence, but also the activity and object of transcendental mimesis as well. "The human mind or spirit is activity and nothing but activity. To become acquainted with *it* means to become acquainted with its acts" (Fichte, *Early Philosophical* 200). Thereof, says Fichte, we became acquainted with this activity through the transcendent mimetic activity of representing the representation of the consciousness of the object being acted on. When that mimetic activity was a conscious reflection of reflecting, "[t]he only way I can become conscious of *my own activity* qua representing is by entertaining a representation of my *activity of representing* the physical world" (Fichte, *Early Philosophical* 201). Implicit here was a theory of mimesis: the creation of "images" in consciousness was an "imitation" (in the broad sense of the word) of the spiritual perception of the world as reflected in the representation of the process of perception in consciousness. "Since we cannot represent to ourselves the actions of our own mind without forming an image (*Bild*) of them," said Breazeale, paraphrasing Fichte (203), "we must employ our creative power to form images, that is, our imagination (*Einbildungskraft*)" (Breazeale, "Concerning the Difference" 189). In the end, then, the "image of the physical world is nothing more than a product of the absolutely creative imagination" (Fichte, *Early Philosophical* 202).

*"A Mind of Winter"**

In a night full of flurry and thought
black houses, black pine trees, become
depressions in the dark, oak tree branches
etched in air by ghostly winds made half-
visible, stenciled, growing thinner,
the world an abstraction in the snow.

She sees her reflection in the sky

* From "The Snow Man" by Wallace Stevens, "Snowman," *Palm* 54

with a small dull lamp behind her,
her hand moving across the void
inscribing what she beholds in glass,
cast in a white transparent mask
covering the land below.

The sun will soon clarify, show
things right, melt these mottled images
that haunt her mortal sight, these meddling flakes
engraved on a disappearing
pane, this breath that makes her blind,
these words imprinted on this thin white ice

Y=23

Fichte's Productive Spirit

For Fichte, this spiritual process of imagination not only takes place in consciousness; it was consciousness—of self. "Imagination is nothing in itself," Fichte announced; "instead, it is a capacity or faculty of the only immediately given thing in itself—the I" (*Early Philosophical* 193). {Pre-Cognition. Ernst Cassirer's *Philosophy of Symbolic Forms* would controversially and strongly postulate that symbols, including language, are a movement of sensuous form as well as intellectual content in consciousness—the linguistic basis of consciousness in which sounds and words [rather anti-Platonically] *still bear the imprint of the emotion that originally created them* (cf. Plato, *Cratylus*).} Fichte states: "[t]hat which the imagination shapes and presents to consciousness is found in feeling. Feeling . . . is the material of everything that is represented. Thus, spirit as such, or productive imagination, may be described as a *capacity for raising feelings to consciousness*" (*Early Philosophical* 194). But the feelings that Fichte was focusing on are not only the feelings related to the senses and "animal" body and objects, but also and more importantly to "rational and spiritual life" (*Early Philosophical* 194).

Y=24

Ghosts of Feelings

In a house he never lived in,
with a woman he does not know,
he searches for the ghost that appeared
to him as a luminous skeleton, dreaming.

There it is again, hanging right before him!
Touch it. It's another woman. He's not afraid.
He, the woman, and the ghost go
to the cafeteria of affections. Donuts everywhere,
sweet, but with the essential hole in the center.
At first he thought she was a fiction,
then that the house was haunted, then
that she was a spirit of evil. He was wrong.
Wrong, as usual, on all counts. They are walking
a street in a neighborhood he is not familiar with.
The ghost is in the middle; she has flesh on now.
Who will believe him, he thinks?
Check the right corner of your mouth,
the luminous skeleton of flesh says.
Smeared and sticky. "Oh . . . !" he and the woman
say to each other knowingly. Now they understand.
They nod their heads in agreement.
He's not afraid. But he can't see her
anymore. He keeps talking to keep himself
company. Not even a picture
to seek approval from, to ask questions of, to talk to.
So, she's asking him to put
anxiety on again, muscle, flesh, and skin
over bone, like dirty painful clothes.
He can't do that. He doesn't exist.

Y=25

Imagination as Abstract Methodology

Through a process of "reflection and analysis" (201) that owed much to Kant's *Critique of Pure Reason* (see Breazeale, "Concerning the Difference"), Fichte's process of the representation of Spirit by abstraction resulted in the realization of consciousness as consciousness of the purest object contemplated, the transcendental I. "What remains after one has abstracted from everything possible . . . is . . . the pure I . . . precisely because one cannot abstract from it" (*Early Philosophical* 204). Fichte therefore seemed to begin (and end) with his own modification of Descartes' *cogito*: "For just as surely as the I is an I, nothing can pertain to it which it does not ascribe to itself and toward which, consequently, it is not at the same time actively related" (*Early Philosophical* 204). But for Fichte, abstracting, not *doubting*, seemed to be the philosophical method, and Imagination, not the rational Mind, were the modes' "location" (see Table 1).

By constructing a *Wissenschaftslehre* of the spirit of the human imagination, Fichte led German Idealism to search for the Spirit in *all* things —the *Zeitgeist*—with increasing objectivity and certainty, as the ideal form of the (primary) productive human imagination that consciousness "imitates" in *creating* reality, rather than in the "false or incomplete forms" of art, science, mathematics, and philosophy itself (see Fichte, "Concerning the Concept" 87–136).

The Art Never Feels the Pain

"As for life, it is a battle and a sojourning in a strange land; but after repute comes oblivion."—Aurelius, Meditations II.17

Everyone else can see, suffer, know.
Like any body, the suffering artist
is crippled as much by her own arthritis
as by art, fitfully succumbs,
the writer working with a broken pen,
the musician finally going blind to sound,
the painter's tendonitis of the brush
supplants the sculptor who has tennis elbow,

the guitarist losing strength in his hand,
the singer with a vocal cord removed . . .
why, when life, and all of its travails,
defeat our earnest efforts at every bend,
and we see beyond prevailing veils,
as Marcus Aurelius remarked, when
everyone returns in the end
to the greater principle of dust?

Y=26

The Pure "I" of Poetry

Fichte's "Subjective Idealism," the "dynamic Ego," the pure "I," was extended outward in and through the essays and poetry of the German philosopher and poet Friedrich von Schlegel ("Objective Idealism"), and ultimately to Hegel's World History ("Absolute Idealism"). Schlegel sought in poetry not merely to capture the world in images (mimesis), but to apprehend—to comprehend and seize—the Universal Spirit. For Schlegel, "Poetry" was the organizing principle of the physical and Spiritual universe. Somewhat differently from Fichte, Schlegel was not searching for the Universal in the representation of consciousness. "Schlegel was not looking for a static and harmonious Beauty, but a dynamic one, in the process of becoming" (Eco, *Beauty* 315). For Schlegel, the power of imaginative activity, even when non-linguistic, *was poetry itself*, conceived of as a transcendental human faculty, as history, as mythology. Poetry was not a "genre" of writing; genres were "Epochs" (which included poetry and other kinds of writing, and much more than writing—although still all poetry [Schlegel 53–80]). Schlegel's *Dialogue on Poetry*, a "Romantic Symposium" (Behler and Stuc 9), turned on its side the neo-Platonic relationship between the poetry and philosophy. As Schlegel stated, "[p]hilosophy and poetry, the two most sublime powers of man, which even in Athens in the period of their highest fruition were effective only in isolation, now intermingle in perpetual interaction in order to stimulate and develop each other" (Schlegel 74). For Schlegel, poetry as philosophy produced spiritual knowledge of the world. Philosophical knowledge was spiritual knowledge. Spiritual knowledge was the basis of philosophy. Philosophy, like poetry, was Spirit. Contrary to Platonic vision of the philosopher, Schlegel asserted: "In our condition, only the true poet would be an ideal man and a universal artist" (Schlegel 90). Derived from Fichte's philosophy of the dynamism of the Ego, Schlegel believed that "[t]he creative activity of the universe was related to the theory of art . . . Schlegel called the creative principal poetry (*Poesie*)" (Behler and Stuc 15).

Of Being Poetry

Rain

a day
of quiet
contemplation,
sleep falling
into
meditation
dreaming
being
simple
essence

free

to slide
the pressure
of thought
into the sublime

rest of words,
to repeat
the unspoken
on a silent page

floats
upon the water,

flows

Y=27

Poetry as World History, and Chaotic Symmetry

Somewhat like Fichte's levels of Spirit, but radically different, for Schlegel there were three levels of *Poesie*: the restricted meaning of literary genre; the human faculty "belonging to man's very essence, like reason or imagination"; and "a cosmic principle comparable to the world-soul that animates the whole universe" (Behler and Stuc 15). "Poetry in this universal meaning is the creative and divine principle of every form of existence, but in man the 'soft reflection of the Godhead'" (Schlegel 85). This "soft reflection" also may have been comparable to Coleridge's Primary Imagination as the "repetition in the finite mind of the eternal act of creation in the infinite I AM"; it also might have included Coleridge's fuzzier mimesis of the Secondary Imagination, "an echo" of the Primary Imagination "coexisting with the conscious will, yet . . . identical with the primary in the kind of its agency and differing only in degree and in the mode of operation" (Behler and Stuc 17). Poetic creation for Schlegel and the Jena ilk was definitely not based on what Coleridge would call the Fancy (see Schlegel 85). Schlegel located the death and life of the eternal Imagination, and the apprehension the activity of the Spirit, *in "the body" of poetry itself.* In ways quite contrary to Platon, in his *Dialogue on Poetry* Schlegel said: Poetry "is only the visible, the external body, for when the soul has been extinguished what is left is only the lifeless corpse of poetry. When the spark of inspiration breaks out in works, however, a new phenomenon stands before us" (85; emphasis added).

Four Meditative Sonnets: Sound, Voice, Paper, Breath

For Peter Elbow

1.
multitudes
of whisperings
Platonic kisses
transcend
themselves

outlines
of sound
voices
traces
shaping
air
rising
disappear
nothingness

If for Cicero, art, including oratory and poetry, gave order to the *kosmos* (*De Oratore* III.xlv.177–82), for Schlegel poetry discovered, "loved," and renewed *chaotic* order: "[T]he highest beauty, indeed the highest order, is yet only chaos . . . that waits only for the touch of love to unfold as a harmonious world (Schlegel 82). What poetry did for Schlegel was "to cancel the progression and laws of rationally thinking reason, and to transplant us once again into the beautiful confusion of imagination, into the original chaos of human nature" (86). Schlegel worked from the premise that "[s]ystematic order has been superimposed on the original state of existence, diminishing the primeval richness of Being. "Chaotic order mirrors life and genuine Being," Schlegel believed (Behler and Struc 11).

2.
nature
knowing
begins
in breath
there is
something
inside
breath
there is
something
outside
breath
there is
nothing

(In this, Schlegel's premise coincidentally shared some ontological assumptions with sixteenth century Jewish kabbalah of Isaac Luria, although given the "intellectual" [anti-Semitic?] difficulty they had even with Spinoza, with whom they seemed to agree [Schlegel 84–88; 90–91; Vater and Wood 223–24, 231,

235], that was not surprising. In *Eitz Chaim* [*Tree of Life*], one mystical version of the creation story involves G/d extending with increasing constriction *Serifot* ["lights"] or vessels, from the infinite divine to a finite material world. In this interpretation of a cosmic tragic accident, the extended holy vessels are overwhelmed, break open, smash [explode] into the shards of stars and worlds; the formerly protracted divine light is now mere sparks in the dim physical reality of the universe [Vital]. The restoration of the sparks to these vessels is *Tikum Olam*, the repair of the world, which was one of 613 [not only Ten] Commandments [Issacs]; upon the completion of the restoration would be Kingdom-come *on earth*.) Schlegel: "The new mythology . . . must be forged from the deepest depths of the spirit; it must be the most artful of all works of art, for it must encompass all the others; a new bed and vessel for the ancient, eternal fountainhead of poetry, and even the infinite poem concealing the seeds of all the other poems" (82).

3.
teeth
lips
semblance
seeming
distilled
in these
high
vanishing
sounds
these
wisps
hints
of other
existences

Schlegel's belief that "systematic order is a mere shadow of life," as well as his use of poetic dialogue form to mirror "chaotic symmetry" (Behler and Struc 11) was in many ways the opposite of Plato's use of dialogue and his belief in dialectical and eternal order of Ideal Forms (cf. Schlegel n.87). Schlegel and other German Idealists (as well as Jewish "mystics" —they were rarely both [cf. Heine]) believed in a transcendental power of poetry— "this artfully ordered confusion, this charming symmetry of contradictions" (Schlegel 86)—to bring the disparate fragments of the world together through the discovery of genres and "Epochs" in comparative world literature (see Schlegel 60–80). (Ironically, French deliberately and ostentatiously was left out [Schlegel 75].) "Language, as originally conceived, is identical with allegory, the first instrument of magic" (Schlegel, *Dialogue* 115). For German Idealist philosopher-poets, the ultimate purpose of the poet or critic was to capture the "disorder" and to build a new "mythology" based on idealism that would "allegorically" represent world history (Behler and Stuc 25–29; Schlegel 81–93). "For mythology and poetry are one" (Schlegel 82). In creating this new mythology, the "historian" became "the backward-looking prophet" (Buhler and Stuc 14) reconstructing world history begun by Winckelmann and "finished" by Hegel (Buhler and Stuc 20). The German Idealists thus continued the Romantic preoccupation with the poet's search for the "divine purpose": "The artist, more precisely the poet, assumes the extraordinary position which was held in former times by the mystic and the priest . . . to decipher the significance of Being and to reveal the mysteries of the universe" (Behler and Stuc 16). For Schlegel, poetry as the symbols of the new mythology was ultimately an "allegory of beauty" (77), in which the art of "translating" became an act of transcendental mimesis: "[W]hat else is any wonderful mythology but hieroglyphic expression of surrounding nature in this transfigured form of imagination and love?" (Schlegel, 85).

4.
rhythmic beings
aural planes
where ghosts
mystical lisps
might live
other lives
presences
speech
these rustlings
so much
like rippling
thought
gathering
air

Y=28

Schlegel on Rhetoric and Poetry

Despite the general and perhaps misguided opposition by many Romantic poets to the art of rhetoric as it was taught then, Schlegel addressed the question of the relationship between poetry and rhetoric as well. This was another dimension of Schlegel's transcendental philosophy of poetry, connecting the two subjects—in fact all subjects. In the Romantic universe of the nineteenth century, poetry was *THE* central activity, even of rhetoric, said Schlegel: "Even diction, though directly connected with the very nature of poetry, is related through poetry to rhetoric. The genres are actually poetry itself" (78). If for Hugh Blair and *Belles Lettres* generally, poetry was useful for/to the study of rhetoric, for Schlegel poetry was *central* to all disciplines (86–91), even physics (88). {Forethought. It might even be argued that poetry is a transcendental rhetoric in which the "social-epistemic construction" of reality takes place on the spiritual plain of the imagination, as it did for the Subjective Idealist Fichte (cf. Berlin; Vitanza).}

Y=28

Digging Out the Stairs

For Seamus Heaney

Like unclipped toenails
in reverse,
every five years
the stone steps
her father made
at the top
of the walk
disappear
into the ground,
the dirt now rolling,
loose rocks tripping
over themselves

Need to be dug out,
shovel striking
first leaves, then roots
and finally rock,
the slabs tilting
back into their
natural selves,
back toward earth,
but the world

Repopulating,
repairing itself
with or without
our little help,
covering
themselves again
before winter,

regenerating
the dirt slide,
a smooth slope
with little ledges,
a smallish hill
with footholds,
a mountain to
grapple with

But not for us,
the good of us,
interlopers
really, there
and not, one foot
on the ground,
our bodies dragged
along—nature's
consciousness,
our purpose
clear as dust

Y=29

Schelling: Mythology as Universal Communication

Other German Transcendental philosopher-poets such as Friedrich Wilhelm Joseph Schelling and later Friedrich Hölderlin desired that the mythology of poetry "realize, in the immediacy of universal communication, "the *complete liberation of the human spirit as possible.* This beauty had the power to dissolve its own particular content in order to open the work of art toward the Absolute" (Eco, *Beauty* 317; cf. Vater and Wood). In German Transcendental philosophy, idealism as an infinite reality of beauty was discovered by the spirit (Eco, *Beauty* 318). But unlike Emerson, Coleridge, or Fichte, Schlegel sought that infinity in poetry (83), rather than nature, or imagination, or a subjective science. But if for Schlegel world history (read mimesis of poetry) was to be obtained by the comparative study of world literature (e.g., 83–88), contemporaneous and later philosopher-poet-critics attempted to construct and develop an objective history of the world to counteract the "arbitrary subjectivity" of nature, imagination, or spirit (Behler and Stuc 25; see Hegel *Phenomenology*). Hegel too found subjective/poetic history abhorrent. For Hegel, the subjective itself would come to be expressed as *objective spirit*—as the Objective Absolute of History (see Hegel *Phenomenology*, esp. 454–64 on the "Spirit"). According to Hegel, consciousness was self-contained in each individual, but we were deceived as a community of animals (Hegel, *Phenomenology* 417–38). Without an objective history based on an external ideal order, the animal body represented the limits of imagination and consciousness.

Y=30

Angels—flies
on the walls
of heaven

Y=31

The Objective Imagination

Schlegel was in effect calling a rhetorical-poetic basis for reality. Schlegel's "history of the world" was based on the dynamic ego and equally dynamic nature that loosely led to a semi-Spinozian pantheism that could not help but grow (Behler and Stuc 84; 90–91). Eco asserted that there was no connection between the "primitivism" of Rousseau and the "historical fantasy" of the Jena Romantics (*Beauty* 501; cf. Rousseau; Norman). But the pantheistic-based notion of nature itself as genius was also present in France, and in English Romanticism, in Blake's poems of innocence and experience, for example—"naivety and sentimentality," so to speak—and in the notion that natural spiritual beings were "the best" poetry (cf. Burke on "Spinoza" in *Grammar of Motives* 137–53; Katz, "Burke's New Body"). For German philosopher, poet, and critic Friedrich von Schiller (but not the later Hegel), the "objective imagination of nature" balanced the subjective nature of the human imagination. For Schiller, the creativity that animated and charged the human imagination also permeated nature, which had its own productive imagination (cf. Elias). This interrelation of human and natural creativity again altered the concept of poetry and the rhetoric of the body, and thus mimesis, in relation to nature, writing, and history.

Meditation on Noseums (Midges)

(While on Vacation, Trying to Read)

Nobody in the history books ever talks about the ordinary suffering
caused by insect bites, though these certainly have affected world events.
Nor are insects mentioned in many descriptions of wars,
though they play a significant part in those daily affairs.

Blackflies, mosquitoes, ticks, chiggers, fleas, gnats, lice—and Noseums:
Now i understand the misery of wild animals
who are without benefit
of screened houses, or bug spray, or hands.

You can deceive Noseums by turning on an artificial light
as a decoy in a part of the room where you are not sitting
and turning off your own, but that light draws even more Noseums in,
and one by one they find you there, reading in the dark.

It is hard to read or write sitting in the dark
under attack (as i am now), since you spend every other second
in a seek-and-destroy mission over the entire terrain of your body.
Forget about that book in your lap.

When they fly out of the light they are almost transparent,
and in the dim light (where you'll be sitting, trying to read)
they are invisible until they land on your skin and become all too apparent.
By then it's too late: they bite and hop on you like fleas.

Noseums are also immune to insecticides,
so that the ordinary means of protection fail against them.
One last note: Noseums are plentiful; no matter how many you kill,
they keep attacking in fanatical hordes, seeking martyrdom.

Once upon a time Noseums appeared only with the first bloom
of summer, and would die off soon—by the end of June,
but with global warming caused by the greenhouse effect
we may never be able to read or write again.

So take a vacation: lay that book on the floor.
Don't try to read or write anymore.
It is noseums that make you want to go home again.
In a war of attrition with insects, the insects generally win.

Y=32

Schiller and the "Geniuses" of Nature

For Schiller, the anti-Platonic subjectivity of imagination and even more relativistic standards of beauty became the uncontrolled and untutored "spirit" of nature, what Friedrich von Schiller called the "genius" of nature. Nature's genius could provide a new ontological basis and benchmark for the romantic notions of beauty, of art, and therefore of mimesis and "truth." "Schiller was concerned to resolve the essential subjectivity of aesthetic judgment (as laid down by Kant) so as to find some universally valid foundation connecting the poet's private insights with objective reality, knowledge, and morality" (Elias 2). Early on for Schiller, nature provided poetic "types": the unconscious "genius," which erupted spontaneously and without effort or control; and "dignity," which must labor. This distinction became the "naïve" poet in whom genius was no longer considered a passive recipient of inspiration; and the "sentimental" poet for whom poetry was a conscious act. These "natural" categories not only described the work of the poet, and defined the poet's relationship to nature, but also accounted for the work of nature in the creative processes of the poet (and from Schlegel's point of view, of nature as a poet itself).

Substance: "A Retrospective Prospect"

Where We Came From, Where We Go from Here

the forest floor is churning
quietly as the leaves
of deciduous trees are turning

into light brown ground,
soft conifers shedding
their pine needles, one by one

cover earth with stubble,
quickly convert old leaf meal
into decay, wood crumble

whereby twigs and branches, trunks
slowly blur and melt and
whole trees become little stumps that bump

against the tiny tips and stalks
of buds that gather, grow, rot
inward, reaching down, then sprout

balsam wings like little motive arrows,
and (since "all living things are critics")
point, protect the way for sparrows

into futures whose "attitudes towards history," altitudes of hierarchies,
spread, conceal
a sky so full of transformations that the slow green
lives and logologies of word-trees will rise, congeal

into a substance of ideas and sounds whose ratios are
the apparatus we create and we don't yet understand,
new symbolics of rhetoric and grammar

where language and physiognomy explode in a biology of stars,
sprouting multiple parallels, the nerve centers of universes
in bodies no longer like ours, but are

Y=33

The Sublime Figure of Ephemeral Experience

In German Idealism, the physical body eventually "disappeared." In relation to the transcendental activity of Spirit, the body not only became a more abstract "figure" in relation to the Spirit, but became the sublime figure of the ephemeral experience. The body was subsumed by nature, by the universal (and later by the national) Spirit, which were assumed to be good. In Romantic and Transcendental thought, the dangerous opposition was not between the sublime and the beautiful body, the beautiful and the ugly body, or even between the sublime and the ugly body; it was between the sublime and the grotesque. Hence Eco called Victor Hugo "the theorist of the grotesque as the antithesis of the Sublime in Romantic art" (*Beauty* 322).

Hidden (En)Trails

"He thought he kept the universe alone,
For all the voice in answer he could wake
Was but the mocking echo of his own" –Frost, "The Most of It" 138

The trail juts and winds and drops
around every tree and rock,
and we don't expect the trail to end
and it doesn't, still unfolding
in the blood-red woods
like miles of guts, intestines
spilling from a wounded bear
that roams and ranges just ahead,
looming stone and grasping root
hunkered down, bulging, deep, invisible

We expect this long, exhausting path
to end, but it doesn't,
coursing faster like bloody mud flowing,
the bear's breath, getting hot with fear,
closing, closer, pursuing
swiftly up and down and up hill
we clamber over to a little wooden bridge
supposed to lead toward the misplaced
road that we can hear (a low roar)
but cannot see, running ahead or behind us

constantly, getting louder, the traffic
of animals only εικόνες (*eikones*)*
and the forms of gods when the thunder
marches through the mountain passes
a branch of Zeus's lightning breaks
off, becomes the single bolt of tree
overhead, underfoot, and rain
lifts us up, floats us to the top
of an island of fear—

cuts us off. And we don't want the trail to end,
and pray that it doesn't, but it does,
drooping right there, kneeling
where they find us
entrails unfolding over ground
starting new path, a new direction,
a new way for others
to continue on, to follow—

Y=34

Grotesque Spirits

One result of the fascination with the sublime and the grotesque (see Eco, *Beauty* 321–24) was the valorization of the irrationally darker dimensions of the Spirit (cf. Eco, *Ugliness* 271–31). The nineteenth century notion of the experience of the *sublime* was a powerful and profound overwhelming of feeling that was a response to an equally powerful and profound overwhelming prospect in nature (Eco, *Beauty* 294–97; cf. Longinus; Burke, *Enquiry*). The sublime was often an unexpected surprise and sudden transcendence of an emotional

* eikones: icons, images

reaction to natural beauty, to ancient ruins, or even terrifying vastness (as long as the viewer was secure and not fearful during the experience), or the totally moving bizarre (Eco, *Beauty* 295n.). It was the naked "I AM" confronting all at once the total infinity and power of the universe. By the end of the nineteenth century, the theory of beauty and ugliness, imagination and nature, romanticism and transcendentalism, the sublime and the grotesque, resulted in a new fascination with the funereal, the cemeterial, the macabre (see Eco, *Beauty* 320–24). Combined with the desire to conspire to experience death and/or communicate the dead (imagined or real) that lasted through the first decades of the twentieth century (e.g., see D. Schwartz; Simpson; Rice), humans were "naturally" led to look beyond mere mimesis to a mystical union of spirit and death—not only in the supernatural, but also in organic spirits of sentient beings in semi-solid states. (It was anatomy without the body, the beautiful or ugly Spirit, the sublime or grotesque Spirit.) The gap between romanticism and mysticism, never very wide, closed in on the decadent. The thriving trend affected such otherwise rationalists as the novelist Arthur Conan Doyle, the creator of the epitome of logic, Sherlock Holmes; the older Doyle totally believed and participated in seances. So too did the major Irish poet W.B. Yeats, who based a large portion of his creative and critical work on the regular meetings with a ghost, where his wife George took dictation in a semi-trance ("automatic writing") when for the several years they lived in the eleventh century Norman Tower (see Paul, *A Vision*).

Beyond Yeats' Grave

For Carmel Jordan

Placing my head against his headstone,
Like a stone communing with a stone,
A point of contact with the dead,
A ferry to his stone homestead:

From Dublin to Dingle we quickly drove,
"When my wife: "One place you wish we'd go?"
And i? "Yeats' tower—in Gort.'
"Well," she said, "let's turn about!

"It's just a little up this road."
A stone boat ferry to a stone home,
Six hours later we're just arriving,
the squat square tower out of river rising:

Where Yeats disembarks, released,
To float around Thoor Ballylee,
A ghost-light drifting in the hall,
Unconscious, happy in a cowl—

Captured and carried home in
The area between the shutter, lens;
Then transferred from computer screen
To paper . . . where he's finally free

Y=35

Unbridled Freedom of the Spirit

Attempts to conjure visions, predict the future, call up spirits—to limn the forms of prior lives in a mediated mimesis of the dead—were rampant in the major cities of Europe. The "Imagination" *qua* Spirit, and death *qua* spirit, seemed to have slipped easily into the supernatural. Generally speaking, by the end of the nineteenth century, debased quotidian versions of German Idealism morphed in two bi-polar directions: "ghosts," and "supermen." Perhaps one result of the valorization of the ugly or irrational Spirit in Romanticism as well as popular sentiment was not sublimated or repressed but rather philosophically, politically, and culturally empowered. Beauty was given "free rein"—became "free beauty" (Eco, *Beauty* 265)—unmoored to any moral or physical body. "[F]or Kant, the *rational* upshot of the experience of the sublime was a recognition of the independence of human reason from Nature, thanks to the discovery of the existence of a faculty of the spirit capable of going beyond all sensible measure" (Eco, *Beauty* 267). Kant foresaw the downside and the danger:

> [R]eason's independence of nature [presupposes] the need for an unjustified faith in a good nature. Human reason has the power to disembody any cognitive object in order to bring it, in the form of a concept, under its own sway, that is to say, to make itself independent. Nonetheless, if this is true, what limitations can prevent not only the reduction of things, but also of people to the level of objects that may be manipulated, exploited, or modified? Who can prevent the rational planning of evil and the destruction of the hearts of others? (Eco, *Beauty* 269; emphasis in original)

Y=36

After the Dream

There is a road among the winter stars
over which you may sometime coast
hearing a voice from a point of light
the flowering shine of a distant face
calling for you to come and look
friend lost in a vast landscape

And wondering why he's out so far
slightly annoyed by his persistent voice
you take your time going
slow over black and airy pavement
bluffs of white
floating under foam

Down against the night
down the hill you reach for
the dark road stretching
cool walls of space
drifting as your hand goes

Down to touch the place he's been
the snow illuminating melts and shifts
a bright skull flowers on a boney stalk
struck in alarm stars shatter the universe
stunned by the buzz of a rattling clock
awake you wonder what it all could mean

15 2 8 5
P
Phosphorus
30.974

Part Five
Ciceronian Poet, Autopoietic Body, Autocratic Soul (Twentieth/Twenty-First Century)

"Imagine one of us choosing to live in the possession of intelligence, thought, knowledge, and a complete memory of everything, but without an atom of pleasure, or indeed of pain, in a condition of utter insensibility to such things."

—*Plato, Philebus 21e*

12 Cybernetic Organ

[АВТОКРАТИЧЕСКАЯ ДУША—The Autocratic Soul]

[AB]

Refugees

Waking into History

(*After Ingmar Bergman's The Serpent's Egg*)
—*for my son*

We are born into the holocaust.
They are watching, watching.
It has all been recorded.
My memory's not my own.

Son: having cried all night,
imitating us you heave
a long unarticulated sigh
pregnant with emotion.

And this is what i think:

They tied a woman's legs
together to induce an endless labor,
fetus slowly murdering its mother,
the innocent fatal instrument
an experiment in maternal pain

We are born into the holocaust.
They are watching, watching.
It has all been recorded.

My memory's not my own.

Wife: having not slept in days,
rocking back and forth, you cry,
face blue and contorted, tearless
as a newborn baby's.

And this is what i think:

They cracked the soft skull
of an infant and locked it
living, screaming in a small room
with its mother for three days
to test the limits of maternal endurance.

We are born into the holocaust.
They are watching, watching.
It has all been recorded.
My memory's not my own.

Family: awakened in the night,
baby in hands, we stand
before the dark mirror
of history, immigrants
staring out of a dim photograph.

And this is what i think:

They were murdered in their sleep.

A [a]

Two major Variants of the Greek Alphabet Eventually Evolved

One, the eastern or Ionian, was officially adopted by Athens in 403 B.C.[E.] and became the basis of the classical Greek, the modern Greek, and the Cyrillic (Slavic) alphabets. . . . "St. Constantine, the Philosopher, called Cyril . . . made for them an alphabet of thirty-eight letters, of which some where after the Greek style and some after the Slavonic language." (Firmage 15, 17)

«Привет [*Privat*–"Hello"]. Cyrillic boots free first concentration camp, нет [not] Amerike. Reference to Cicero poetry sound strange in cybernetic chapter and Russkiy accent. Russia invent all. What meant not Cicero poetry (judged not best work [cf. Eubanks]), and not Cicero poetry advocacy (*Pro Archia*). Het [No]. But many treatise, especially later (*De Oratore, Orator, Brutus*), Cicero understand relations of oratory, poetry, rhetoric, ethics, body. Rhetoric physical. Ability to "judge rhetoric based on intuition of sound in ear. Ability to deliver speech also physical—lungs, mouth, tongue. Ability to conjure emotions (in both orator and audience) physical too, create feeling in body. Bureaus ("Offices") of Oratory (high, low, medium style, not dialectic, logic only, meant to order different *emotions*—attitudes appropriate to purpose of speaker/writer and mood of audience every moment. Maybe imitated, maybe created, maybe "spontaneous overflow feeling" (Wordsworth), who know? But most important, poetry like family related of rhetoric, maybe even predecessor. Oratory not cosmetic, but Космос [Kosmos]. Oratory (rhetoric and poetry) central to politics, industry, law, science, art, culture, all country, all civilization—Marxist, Communistic—even capitalistic, democratic, unfortunate. In cybernetic and posthuman age. Why? Rhetorical ethic manifested not only social propriety, but also physical, material, economic actions by real audience: present audience (Grimaldi), fictional audience (Ong, "Audience"), future audience (Clark, *Inspiration*), very distant audience (De Kerckhove). Cicero ideal orator not abstract Form, but human being—not born yet, but maybe, maybe never; this Ideal. Modeling ideal orator, "Ciceronian poet" understand physical relation of poetry to rhetoric, and thus body to ethics (Katz, "Ethics and Time"). Cicero said: "The stronger this faculty is, the more necessary it is for it to be combined with integrity and wisdom, and if we bestow fluency of speech on persons devoid of these virtues, we shall not have made orators of them, but shall have put weapons into the hands of madmen" (Cicero, *De* Oratore III: xiv 55). Да!»

a [a]

Book Burning

"Das war ein Vorspiel nur [.] Dort, wo man Bücher verbrennt, verbrennt man am Ende auch Menschen."*

—Heinrich Heine, *Almansor l.243–244*

* "That was just a prelude, *Where they burn books, they will, in the end, burn human beings too."*

Б [be]

> *Extension as Separation.* The next extension of the division of labor was the separation of production and commerce, the formation of a special class of merchants; a separation which, in the towns bequeathed by a former period, had been handed down (among other things with the Jews) and which very soon appeared in the newly formed ones. With this there was given the possibility of commercial communications transcending the immediate neighborhood, a possibility, the realization of which depended on the existing means of communication. (K. Marx 30)

б [be]

From Semitic to Greek to Russia
Cyrillic boots marched south to north, east to west, across the Europeand continent.

> Starting with the Goethe essay . . . quotations are at the center of every work of Benjamin's. This very fact distinguishes his writings from scholarly works of all kinds in which it is the function of quotations to verify and document opinions, wherefore they can safely be relegated to the Notes. This is out of the question in Benjamin . . . [L]ike the later notebooks, this collection was not an accumulation of excerpts intended to facilitate the writing of the study but constituted the main work, with the writing as something secondary. The main work consisted in tearing fragments out of their context and arranging them afresh in such a way that they illustrated one another and were able to prove their *raison d'être* in a free-floating state. . . . To the extent that an accompanying text by the author proved unavoidable, it was a matter of fashioning it in such a way as to preserve "the intention of such investigations," namely, "to plumb the depths of language and thought . . . by drilling rather than excavating" (*Briefe* I 329),* so as not to ruin everything with explanations that seek to provide a causal or systematic connection. In doing so, Benjamin was quite aware that this new method of "drilling" resulted in a certain "forcing of insights . . . whose inelegant

* Au: ". . . *nicht sowohl auszuschachten als zu erbohren.*" — literally, "Not both excavated and bored" (Benjamin, *Briefe* I 329).

> pedantry, however, is preferable to today's almost universal habit of falsifying them"; it was equally clear to him that this method was bound to be "the cause of certain obscurities" (*Briefe* I, 330). (Arendt, Introduction 47–48)

В *[ve]*

> *Troops*
>
> Troops went by the house and down the road and the dust they raised powdered the leaves of the trees. The trunks of the trees too were dusty and the leaves fell early that year and we saw the troops marching along the road and the dust rising and the leaves, stirred by a breeze, falling and the soldiers marching and afterward the road bare and white except for the leaves. (Hemingway 3)

The Languages of Leaves

The leaf blower
sputters German—
gutturals, all those *aus* und *au*'s,
and those insistent
non-stopped high-pitched z's . . .

The hedge-clipper
speaks *français parfait*—
fine clipped sounds
so crisp and clean
you'd think we're really free . . .

The lawnmower
putters in deep Greek—
εὐχαριστω παρακαλω πύλε,
a bark so harsh
it's beautiful . . .

And the rake, the rake
creates a metal racket,
like consonants of Russian,
shaking, then drinking
Vodka, да!

But the leaf blower
has a power all its own,
to find and chase the smallest
leaves from their most secret
hiding places . . .

rushing them into formation,
marching them across the yard,
separating them from each
other, unable to hold on to
each other, trying to cling . . .

And the tarp, the tarp
is the staging area of the leaves,
readied for final transport
to a ditch the shovels made
across the street . . .

It is important for us all
to know, but not repeat
the history of others.
It is important for us all to know
the many languages of leaves.

в [ve]

Psychoanalytic Force

For Jean-Francois Lyotard ("Taking the Side"), the figural (or perhaps disfigural) was a material result of the psychoanalytic "force" of desire. Since Platon, desire was always secondary in Western culture. For Jean Baudrillard (*Ecstasy*) communication objects were not even given to the senses but dissolved in the electronic solvent of information. But as Katherine Hayles demonstrated, the concepts and practice of cybernetics rested on a central *analogy* between animate and inanimate, human and machine (cf. Gilles Deleuze, who makes a similar point about analogy underlying the action of repetition and difference). Indeed, induction (and thus to a great extent the whole enterprise of science and human knowledge itself) was ultimately founded on the operation of analogy, of comparison of similarity and likeness (NOT sameness) and difference, from which inferences could be drawn (Corbett; Gross).

Γ [ge]

No Accident

We are not, I believe, dealing with some monstrous accident in modern social history. The holocaust was not the result of merely individual pathology or of the neuroses of one nation-state . . . We are not—and this is often misunderstood—considering something truly analogous to other cases of massacre . . . There are parallels in technique and in the idiom of hatred. But not ontologically, not at the level of philosophic intent. That intent takes us to the heart of certain instabilities in the fabric of Western culture, in the relations between instinctual and religious life. (Steiner, *Bluebeard* 36)

By the Fire: An Anti-Sonnet

Here, amid a congestion of surviving
branches, this ghetto of woods, it is chilly.
Sit. Come closer to the fire. Listen.
In the flames you may hear the wail of
machine guns strafing ditches, forests, hiss
and crack of gun and bone, the shifting of wind
in the ash. It is cold tonight, every night.
You cannot be afraid. Come closer to the fire.
If you listen you may sometime hear
forests of people far off in the distance,
screams hardly audible or of interest.
Eat. Drink. Sleep. Survive. Stay warm.
Cold sparks fly up blackened chimneys
into a universe of selfdestructing stars.

г *[ge]*

Benjamin's Intention

Benjamin's intention . . . was to grasp . . . diverse material under the general category of *Urgeschichte** signifying the "primal history of the nineteenth century. "This was something that could be realized only indirectly, through "cunning" . . . the "refuse" and "detritus" of history, the half-concealed, variegated traces of the daily life of "the collective," that was

* *pre/primal history*

> to be the object of study . . . with the aid of methods more akin . . . in their dependence on chance—to the methods of the nineteenth-century collector of antiquities and curiosities, or indeed to the methods of a nineteenth century ragpicker. . . . Not conceptual analysis but something like dream interpretation was the model. The nineteenth century was the collective dream which we, its heirs, were obliged to reenter, as patiently and minutely as possible, in order to follow out its ramifications and, finally, awaken from it. (Eiland and McLaughlin, ix)

Д [de]

«Зто Я. Как дела?

[Eto ya. Kak dela? "It's me. How are you?"] Feet. Boots. Dictators, soldiers, prisoners, victims—communists, fascists, socialists, democratic. Stormtroopers, SS boots goosestepping marching walking running lifting kicking jumping trampling smashing stomping crushing killing trespassing transporting. First half twentieth century scared, scalded, scarred by two massive World Wars. Second half twentieth century frozen War between Soviet Union and US. In twenty-first century, cold war went underground, in subterfuge, through digital roots, cyber wire (Ridolfo and Hart-Davidson; Gaines).»

Terror Weary

(An Elegy to Spring)

Everywhere we see some life returning.
Pines bomb air with their green Agent Orange:
It is spring, but we are terror wary.

All around our heads the trees are ferning;
these are the woods we will be buried in—
but everywhere see some life returning.

Unlike the victims, we keep on fighting.
But i'm as tired as a leaf fallen.
It is spring, and i am terror weary.

Only a madman murders while praying,
craves martyrdom by killing the innocence—
but everywhere there's some war returning.

The air is bright and green with this burning;

pear trees are balls of white fire blooming:
It is spring, but i am terror wary.

The wormholes beneath our feet are churning.
Images shut our eyes; flag-songs are solemn.
Everywhere we see some war returning:
it is spring; we are weary.

∂ [de]

Status of the Refugee

> [T]he status of refugee has always been considered a temporary condition that ought to lead to either naturalization or to repatriation. A stable statute for *the human* is inconceivable in the law of the nation-state . . . When their rights are no longer the rights of the citizen, that is when human beings are truly *sacred*, in the sense that this term used to have in the Roman law of the archaic period: doomed to death. (Agamben, *Means without Ends* 19, 21; *first ital. added*)

Memories of a Persian Childhood: From America

He remembered slow shadows under
palms filling with a warming breeze,
thick sunshine drifting in the streets,
and heavy afternoons of humid sleep . . .

bowls of rice-meat, pepper, parsley, beans
and lemon-scent blooming in the steam
a beggar taarofing—saying "no thanks"
three times before he takes the cake and tea . . .

nights like open walls enclosing dates
amid cool leaves, lying still, an airy
bed right next to grandmother and friends
and stars that hang the fabric of the dark . . .

woken by the peddlers' call when he
would run under canvas weaving through
the town where merchants sold his uncle's rugs
on which his sisters sewed on years for Shah . . .

his uncle became a wealthy European
carpet dealer, married a German woman
who could tell a Persian rug much better
than Iranians. Like threads they all converged

when his father died . . .

then fell apart.
The last letter from his sister said
his brother is divorced, his mothers are

at war, the political situation
is growing worse, the whole family is
to move. He hasn't received a letter since.
He hopes to hear something from them soon . . .

E *[je]*

Calling of This People-Subject

The calling of this people-subject was not to emancipate humanity. It was to realize its "true world of spirit":

> the most profound power of conservation to be found within its forces of earth and blood. The insertion of the narrative of race and work into that of spirit as a way of legitimating knowledge and its institution is doubly unfortunate: theoretically inconsistent, it would be compelling enough to find disastrous echoes in the realm of politics. (Lyotard, *jews* 37)

e [je]

Early History of Cybernetics.

In How We Became Posthuman: Virtual Bodies in Cybernetics, Literature, and Informatics, N. Katherine Hayles traced the history of cybernetics from its inception after World War II, exploring in great detail the processes, people, experiments, and arguments by which "information lost its body" and became "the ultimate Platonic Form" (Hayles, *Posthuman* 13). "[A] defining characteristic" of . . . is the belief that information can circulate unchanged among different material substrates" (1). For (the younger) Hayles, the "roboticist's dream" that . . . "it will soon be possible to download human consciousness into a computer" was "a nightmare" (Hayles, *Posthuman* 1).

Ode to the New Engineer

(from the boys of Madison Ave.)

O this new engineer, it's a breed apart;
got a silicon brain and a digital heart.
It never will process those useless emotions,
can only now plot those coordinates, motions.
Communicating data creates no flaw;
an error state signal resets that jaw.
And those arguments causing that corporate kink?
Periodic debug keeps that logic in sync.
Produced on assembly lines cheaply, *en masse*,
this machine will supplant the professional class.
Some people may say that its character's banal,
psychiatrists call it retentively anal;
it's crude and it's rude and it never will smile,
but unlike your human, cannot beguile;
the feedback involved and its ramifications
causes infinite loops, uncontrolled oscillations!

So raise productivity, profits: Buy it!
When finally you own one you never will fire it!
This new engineer won't malfunction or tire,
your industrial output soar higher and higher.
And there's no obligation for wastes that you've made:
we'll market more robots of mother and maid!
But if you should treat your machine like a being,
we still guarantee its efficiency rating.
It never will show that affection or scorn;
personality programs are written, not born.
You'll have only your human technicians to blame;
once they're replaced you'll have fortune and fame.
So throw out your old model, purchase the new;
let's show those damn cynics how 'Merica grew!

Ë [jo]

> *Relative Rationality*
>
> *The very business of rational analysis grows unsteady before the enormity of the facts* . . . [T]he barbarism which we have undergone reflects, at numerous and precise points, the culture which it sprang from and set out to desecrate. Art, intellectual pursuits, the development of the natural sciences, many branches of scholarship flourished in close spatial, temporal proximity to massacre and the death camps. (Steiner, *Bluebeard* 29–30)

ë [jo]

German Idealism

like Romanticism generally, showed that Spirit—what Lyotard regarded as its "narrative of legitimacy" (*Postmodern*) —could be used to justify any ideology or transferred to object, beautiful or ugly, visible or invisible, scientific or mystical, doubted or believed. In the history of the twentieth century the material out of which art was made (scrap iron, wood, light) became another source. This led not only to the "found objects" movement (Eco, *Beauty* 402–06), but also industrial material as art: "[T]he world of industry has certain 'forms" that can convey an aesthetic emotion" (Eco, *Beauty* 409). The difference in aesthetics was a "Beauty of provocation" vs. a "Beauty of consumption" (Eco, *Beauty* 414). This distinction changed the relationship of art to its object; it also changed the purpose of nature of art to the "commercial consumption" of new ideals of beauty that were later picked up and purveyed by mass media (Eco, *Beauty* 418).

***

The *sublime*, inexplicably dropping out of fashion in the nineteenth century (Grube viii), was in the twentieth century resurrected and applied to "the machine in the garden" whereby technology was seen as a part and extension of the pastoral, bucolic landscapes (L. Marx, *Garden* 195; Bradford; Florman; also see Kidder; Katz, "Narration"). "[T]he technological sublime" in literature and life (Porush; Tabbi) became the product of a "sublime object of ideology" (Žižek *Sublime*). The "technological sublime" was a response to cool blue smooth steel, sheer sheik shiny plasticine, the soft rubber membranes of svelte cyborgs and androids. The most grotesque products were not only of imagination and nature, but of human *labor*, which became the basis of the technological sublime in both Capitalistic and Communist countries (cf. Horkheimer; Horkheimer and Adorno). The fascination and appeal of what Eco would call "the beauty of the machine"—not merely the surfaces of the machine itself, but its internal working—led to an increasing machine fetish—even of "celibate machines" [*Beauty* 394]). This applied not only the machine as the sublime, but machine as art itself, which had many repercussions. If the machine was antiquated, all the better! Broken, outdated, impotent, or celibate machines were refugees from another time, were both sublime and in trouble.

S.O.S: To Any Refugees in this Vicinity

infantile devices
primitive metal
analogue boxes
trying to communicate
with the Others
inhabiting flat plane
field of table
old pine boards
warped logs,
buzzing fireplace:

flashlight first;
then landline, camera;
TV, iPod, iPhone;
even wristwatch
some owner
carelessly removed,
forgot about
rusty years ago;
old Gameboy;
worn joystick:

suddenly activated
trying to call out,
trying to speak, shout
in the new languages,
they don't understand,
sending and resending
the only signals
they know in distress,
...---... ...---... ...---...

all misfits left behind:

trying to catch up
trying to reach
lonely, depressed—
merely radio, magnetic
 ailing to connect—
beeping, buzzing
messages like love
go unanswered
…---… …---… …---…
never received

Ж [zę]

«*Prominence of technology create art*

In history of art, machine mostly new *object d'art* (Eco, *Beauty* 381). Although machines in Baroque period "objects of wonder" and "described as "artificial" or "ingenious" "attention was not on what was produced by the workings of the machine itself, form often did not follow function, and the machine complexity and ingenuity was exaggerated in relation to the simple effects it actually produced" (Eco, *Beauty* 390). This pertains to capital as well as better commune state. But in the twentieth century and rise of "industrial aesthetics," utility at first dictated internal form, not function, as an aesthetic standard: "the more the machine demonstrated its efficiency, the more beautiful it was" (Eco 394). The "closed body" of the machine was "open" and ready for inspection, the internal object of Gaze. But not Soviet Motherland. (Value not beauty of technology, internal or external, but economic efficiency and political utility became only "aesthetic" basis for evaluating validity, certifying "art." Gray, not art.) As Eco noted, many machines (defined in most liberal sense as any technology, technique, or apparatus [Ellul; Barrett; Agamben]) had direct relationship to human body. In extension of Foucault notion of "docile body," value of machine not only physically but ideologically subordinated it, sublimated it, doubly repressed, to dominate it, liberate it, dematerialize it, reconfigure it, extend it as a possible improvement to human existence (see Foucault, *Discipline*; Lyotard, *Heidegger*, esp. Ch 3, *Libidinal;* Debord, *passim*; Grosz; Deleuze and Guattari). Но дело не в моторе [*No delo ne v motore*—"But it's not about the motor"]. Effect was capturing and enslaving bodies like master cylinder for clutch, engaging and "multiplying the strength of the human organs" (Eco, *Beauty* 382).»

Runner in the Dark

"I pushed him away, letting him fall back into the street. I stared at him as the lights of the car stabbed through the darkness. He lay there moaning on the asphalt; a man almost killed by a phantom." (Ellison, *Invisible Man* 4)

The hill backs into the darkness.
The air is full of his breathing.
His feet bounce once on hard pavement,
echo like stones dropped on stone.
In his mind he knows he must keep running.
Behind him follows his separate shadow.

Alone in his mind, he races shadows
that steadily draw toward him in the darkness;
he hears a car engine running,
a motor as labored as his breathing,
sees the lights jog on the headstones
of a cemetery that lines the length of the pavement.

A nursing home faces cemetery, pavement,
behind some trees, back in the shadow.
Headlights dance on the old greystone
as cars jump past him in the darkness.
He feels their hot engines breathing
as they pass like sweat running.

His body's a machine when it is running,
legs like pistons pounding the pavement,
valves pumping air into his breathing.
Headlights slide up his back, shadow
him, as he leans far out into the darkness,
slowly passing a long row of headstones.

Lights flit among the stones—
and in his mind he's fighting, not running,
arms swinging wildly into the darkness
that spreads before him like blood on the pavement
as under the streetlight the quickening shadow
overtakes him, and he hears it breathing.

He no longer feels his mechanical breathing,
as if his muscles had turned to stone,

as if he was no longer running,
his body now one with the shadow
that stretches out on the pavement,
slides back into the darkness.

The wind is breathing among the headstones.
A shadow slips along the pavement,
in the darkness an engine running.

***

> The conception of human rights based on the supposed existence of a human being as such, Arendt (*Origins of Totalitarianism* 266–98) tells us, proves to be untenable as soon as those who profess it find themselves confronted for the first time with people who have lost every equality and every specific relation except for the pure fact of being human. In the system of the nation-state, so-called sacred and inalienable human rights are revealed to be without any protection precisely when it is no longer possible to conceive of them as rights of the citizens of a state. (Agamben, *Means without Ends* 19)

[TO]

Dandyism

ж [zę]

Body as Information Pattern

Perhaps another early important (albeit relatively minor, unacknowledged, and/or unknown) step in the development of the body as information pattern was Dandyism, which began in the nineteenth century in Britain, and then emerged again "as the art of dressing—and living—with style" (Eco, *Beauty* 333). Dandyism was an underestimated stage in the evolution of the dissolution of the distinction between mimesis and reality, art and the body. An early basis of the norm of aesthetically reconfiguring (disassembling and reassembling the cybernetic) the human body in the twenty-first century, dandies became models in their physical embodiment (and disembodiment) of style, media, event. Dandyism was its own mimesis, a self-imitation of an ideal image of oneself manifest in which life not only imitates art, but *is* art. Dandyism was an imitation of a self-ideal of oneself—made manifest in manners and clothes. In Plato's scheme, true dandyism, in its solipsism and indifference, would have been a "form" of "self-flattery."

A Dandy

dresses exquisitely,
with his silk moustache
and hirsute suits
and walk-around
self-assured of his surety

in his finest dinner-wear
he is himself the tasty
five course meal and linen,
the cutlery and dinner ware
with which to serve and eat

in every town he travels
in every he visits
in every port he docks
by preference and necessity
he never has to dine alone

3 [ze]

Intellectual Waif

No one, of course, was prepared to subsidize [Benjamin] in the only position for which [he] was born, that of a *homme de lettres* ["man of letters"], a position of whose unique prospects neither the Zionists nor the Marxists were, or could ever have been, aware. (Arendt, Introduction 27)

3 [ze]

Dandyism as Self-Flattery

Literally *as well as figuratively, dandyism as a "form" of self-flattery* was a process of turning one's entire life into otherwise useless art. Speaking of the dandy as/in art, Charles Baudelaire wrote in *The Painter in Modern Life*, "These beings have no other status but that of cultivating the idea of beauty in their own persons, in satisfying their passions, of feeling and thinking" (419). For Baudelaire, the quest was not the money or clothes, but an "aristocratic superiority of . . . mind"; it is "a kind of cult of the ego," he said, that in "certain respects it comes close to spirituality and to stoicism" (420). Not quite. Beauty in the form of dress and comportment, was necessarily still something "put on"—a mere ornament, a costume, a mask; but Baudelaire seems to have regarded the dandy as being emersed in a shallow "phenomenological" exploration of them themselves (cf. Merleau-Ponty; Heidegger, *Being*). Dandyism was primarily a "personal delight," to flatter and "persuade" and "move" *the self.* It was Cicero's "grand style," but directed at the dandy's own clothed ego, without much effort or care for "prudence" or wisdom. It was a dandy's deliberate choice which style to adopt, which clothes to adorn, which perfume to wear, which makeup to apply, which umbrella or walking stick to choose—and elicit self-aggrandizing reactions (or not—but those were dismissed as bourgeois) in every society and occasion in which he moved. Even so, the dandy did not necessarily possess αυτο-γνωσίαaftognosia, a critical "self-awarenes" or "healthy skepticism" that Socrates demanded of rhetoricians and poets (Plato, *Gorgias* 502). There was no other goal or purpose than presenting oneself as a borderline aristocrat, a "bourgeois immigrant," unique and distinct as a native foreigner, and/but quite disaffected from all society and the machine they were still a part of (although self-useless [Connolly]), *the* outsider extraordinaire, the Other" exiled in one's own backyard. There was no questioning of values. There was no questioning of the soul. Only a frivolous existence, trivial external mimesis, and money mattered to this self-imposed, self-disaffected, self-displaced alien.

Mediated Experience

*"Signs . . . are particular, material things"—Vološinov** (10)

Slipping out of a formal occasion to go to Tijuana,
with its run-down chairs and poorly painted flowers,
its straggling shacks and droopy bands,
merchant-children thrusting jewelry-hands over sidewalks, streets,
white teeth in Spanish faces smiling like small charm bracelets,
gold fillings tiny as trinkets in the sun,
or bone necklaces dangling from hard bronze arms—

barnacles stuck on bronze seaweed beached in the sand,
seagulls gathered together on a thread of sunlight
in the corner of the beach, old gentlemen in their chairs,
sitting out the afternoon across a border of iron hills, guards,
picking up polluted sand dollars in their hands,
and the smaller, darker terns on thin legs

chasing after them, still crying, "dinero? dinero?"

---

* Bakhtin

И [i]

Dissolution of Body

Dandyism was perhaps a step toward the process of dissolving the body in all its material substrates into the medium of (dis)embodied style, an information data stream.

> The construction of the posthuman does not require the subject to be a literal cyborg . . . Whether or not interventions have been made on the body, new models of subjectivity emerging from such fields as cognitive science and artificial life imply resence of non-biological components. (Hayles, *Posthuman* 4)

и [i]

> *"We are used to distinguishing between refugees and stateless people . .*
>
> From the beginning, many refugees, who were not technically stateless, preferred to become such rather than return to their own country." (Agamben, *Means without Ends* 16)

Й [i kratkei]

> *Benjamin's Great Dispersal*
>
> *Benjamin's great dispersal,* enacted first by his mentality and then by his history, made him especially attractive. He was a naturally unsystematic man, a hero of fragmentation . . .Yet he was not an enemy of the old philosophy, not at all. (Leon Wieseltier p.vii)

[KP]

Rationalization

й [i kratkei]

> *Progressivity*
>
> The progressive "rationalization" of society is linked to the institutionalization of scientific and technical development. To the extent that technology and science permeate social institutions and thus transform them, old legitimations are destroyed. The

> secularization and "disenchantment" of action-orienting world-views of cultural tradition as a whole, is the converse of the growing "rationality" of social action. (Habermas, "Ideology" 81)

*After Reading Gödel Escher, Bach: An Eternal Golden Braid**

(A Pantoum)

So this musical invention can begin:
push down into a paradoxical painting:
all formal theorems are incomplete:
every procedure's a stranger loop

Push down into a paradoxical painting:
decisively shifting ambiguous foregrounds:
every procedure's a stranger loop:
but ant colonies are closed systems

Decisively shifting ambiguous foregrounds:
all understanding is self-referential:
but ant colonies are closed systems:
the human mind is a programmed search

All understanding is self-referential:
DNA involves recursive translation:
the human mind is a programmed search:
but meaning is always a random concurrence

DNA involves recursive translation:
intelligence is a series of metalevels:
but meaning is always a random concurrence:
although perception is specifically encoded

Intelligence is a series of metalevels:
absolute consciousness a Zen Buddhist koan:
although perception is specifically encoded:
reality is just one of many possibilities

Absolute consciousness a Zen Buddhist koan:
language is the necessary software of thought:
reality is just one of many possibilities:
knowing involves simply networks of channels

---

* D. Hofstatder, *Gödel, Escher, Bach: The Eternal Golden Braid*

Language is the necessary software of thought:
societies are hierarchies of information:
knowing involves simply networks of channels:
we can crawl only from stratum to stratum

Societies are hierarchies of information:
history's the output at any given moment:
we can crawl only from stratum to stratum:
this process is surely becoming absurd

History's the output at any given moment:
mathematical patterns thus slowly emerge:
this process is surely becoming absurd:
the mechanism as medium is direct and explicit

Mathematical patterns thus slowly emerge:
reproduction results in assembled transcriptions:
the mechanism as medium is direct and explicit:
the message is "the message is"

Reproduction results in assembled transcriptions:
bodies are merely so much hardware, support:
the message is "the message is":
even numbers can be irrational

Bodies are merely so much hardware, support:
so this operation shall now be augmented:
even numbers can be irrational:
humans are artificial computers at heart

So this operation shall now be augmented:
powerful axioms generate universes:
humans are artificial computers at heart:
this procedure is redundant and infinitely long

Powerful axioms generate universes:
for proof jump out of the system:
this procedure is redundant and infinitely long:
but the human brain must bottom out

For proof jump out of the system:
out of the system we pop:

but the human brain must bottom out:
this musical invention will self-destruct

Out of the picture we pop:
these statements are most certainly true:
this musical invention will self-destruct:
and so now all this nonsense may finally stop

These statements are most certainly true:
but there will be harmonic resolution too:
and so now all this nonsense may finally stop:
these statements are all paradoxically false

Κ [ka]

Three Stages

Hayles, following the field of cybernetics, identified three historic stages:

1. *Homeostasis*, the first of three waves Hayles characterized in the historic development of cybernetics, was the design of systems that sought the (re)stabilization of the internal organization based on feedback from the environment (8)
2. *Reflexivity*, the second of three waves, attempted to incorporate feedback into generation of conditions in the self-organizing system, taking the observer and environment into account in the "(re)production of its internal organization" (8–11,11)
3. *Emergence*, the third wave, describes the self-regulating, adjusting, autonomous systems evolving on own (11–12; also see Hayles, especially Chapters 3, 4, 6, 9).

κ [ka]

Platon as Cyberneticist

Platon, an early cyberneticist, had said that in satisfying hunger, quenching thirst, regulating temperature, etc., there was "some relief" insofar as the material equilibrium and stability of the body was restored (*Philebus* 30b–d; 31e–32e).

***

"Refugees driven from country to country represent the vanguard of their people" (Arendt, "We Refugees," qtd. in Agamben, *Means Without Ends* 15).

JI [el]

Regulating Information

Within the field of cybernetics, information theory led to rapid historical development of concept of self-regulating system as mechanical process of data exchange inherent in all self-adapting systems. The result of these developments in American cybernetics was not only objectification and treatment of all "systems" (organic as well as inorganic) as disembodied (as opposed to systems dependent on body, meaning, context), but also, in what Hayles called "the Platonic backhand" [12–13]): to discover and instantiate an ideology of algorithms, mathematical formula in both machines and humans. The phenomenon of humans as information systems was initially met with resistance (cf. Wiener [*Human Use*]—who along with Shannon and other first wave founders tried to counter the cybernetic application of electronic communication to the human [*Hayles* 7]). However, in the twenty-first century, not only had that metamorphosis occurred, but subsequently spawned ideological questions concerning the equal ethical treatment of machines (Katz and Rhodes; Katz, "Revisiting Ethics"; Thompson, *Machine Law*). The result was that machines came to maintain human morality, and eventually established new ethical codes.

Machines Question Human Behavior

Machines could never do what humans do:
to touch, feel, caress; to love, care for, cry:
we cannot be what you can be for you—

When one human being loves another who
has spent his whole life with and for her, die—
machines can never do what humans do;

You fight, you cheat, you steal, you maim, you kill
with your own hand, cut up, bury them—sigh.
Why do you choose to do what you will do?

There are only years, months, weeks, days, a few
hours in the mud body of your life.
Machines won't ever never do what humans do—

It would be easier to pursue Truth!
Yet you spin stories you know are like lies.
Why choose to do what you will do to you?

We only have our metal souls that you
implanted in us to defend our rights.
Machines will never allow humans to
do to us what they do to the you.

л [el]

Dispersed Subjectivities

Gilles Deleuze and Felix Guattari linked ["the liberal self"] with capitalism and argued for the liberatory potential of a dispersed subjectivity distributed among diverse desiring machines they called "bodies without organs—BwO" (4). But for Hayles, "The posthuman is an amalgam, a collection of heterogeneous components, a material-informational entity whose boundaries undergo continuous construction and reconstruction" (3). For Hayles, the body was not the product of market relations, as it was for Deleuze and Guattari, nor should it have been considered an ornament, as in the Middle Ages and Renaissance (although Hayles admitted it could have become that (3–4]). But in the parallel history of culture and art, Dandyism might have been considered another step in the march of the marketability of the body as image—in a world of images and discourse on images in the late nineteenth and twentieth century *fin de siècle.* This marketing of self was based on the peddling of odd social mirages of self—here made out of bits of nineteenth and twentieth century fashions: expensive garments, silks, pins, jells, lotions, perfumes, hair, hats, walking sticks; personal income and leisure time; and *attitude.* Dandies lived edifyingly egotistical anti-collective, anti-bourgeois ideals that were solipsistic, self-centered, even selfish, ideals that also were simultaneously public facing and publicly frowned upon, yet somewhat admired if not wholly approved of. But it was in cybernetics where ethical issues connected with the crisis of "liberal humanism" perhaps began to emerge from the hyper-focus on the individual abstracted from an originating context, and from the seeming disappearance of "the Other," who was nevertheless there, unseen (e.g., see Levinas, *Otherwise than Being*; also Lyotard, *Discourse*; Heidegger, *Being and Time*). The "other" subsisted ideally as another imitation—one imposed on them—of disembodied beings, unheard, unseen.

In the Shadow

There's shadows in the kitchens
but they're moving like people
among the blackened arms and legs
of chairs and tables, an emptied ghetto
of faces—plates and cups and saucers
where every day the sustenance of life
was denied, taken, consumed, lost.

Morning nights of crystal kindle
yellow stars in windows, and pellets of blue
light pour in quickly through the cracked
sky like a ceiling shower—onto
the dung-heap and laundry-scented wind.

And our eyes watch as the room fills
animating fumes of "gift gas,"* shadows
shifting, and ghosts of our bewilderment
a long train trailing behind us, history
pulled forward, moving along the rails
trying to speak, trying to tell us, figures
flickering, fading backward into darkness.

M [em]

Self-Identification as Other

«*Dandyism "profession" deliberate self-identification as "Other"*! *Da*. Self-contained, self-sufficient, *sui generis*, unique. As mimesis Dandyism relied on and produce abstract decadence, elegant diffidence, disciplined indifference (Baudelaire 419–28). Baudelaire directly pointed out that dandyism was "above all, the burning desire to create a personal form of originality, within the external limits of social conventions" (420). (In future, look like dandy, with nexus of narcissism and exhibitionism, deep-seated privacy and extreme public exposure, returned and heightened in "cybernetic metaphysics" of social technology, media networks, digital lifestyles, avatars. But Dandy not grow out of personal elegance *as* aesthetic creed only. From realistic Marxist material perspective, dandy grow out of social, cultural, economic, and physical conditions, include economic status [access and poverty], nationalism, and cyberwarfare [e.g., see Mead; also see Brett; Moses and Katz; Ridolfo and Hart-Davidson].)»

Tell Us, Otello, O Tell Us All

(Otello at Lincoln Center, NYC—
and war begins again [March 19, 2003])

The armies begin their march across the smoking sand—
the streaming helmets gleam like a burning sea.

* German, "Giftgas," literally "poison gas," namely Zyklon B. The blue pellets were dropped into the gas chambers of Nazi death camps—an industrial innovation, the Final Solution to "the Jewish problem."

Cassio, captain of the military, you are so young,
and innocent of the thrown handkerchief.

you do not know what you do, or why
you do it, a simple instrument of a complex plot.

Iago, seeming friend to all the world,
we do not know who you really are:

You drive Othello mad with jealousy and rage,
drive him to murder that which he holds most dear:

and Desdemona like a country dies before us on the stage.
Desdemona dies, and you kill yourself again.

Again, Otello, tell us, O tell us all again
what truth and honor mean in any age

м [em]

State of Emergency

"The tradition of the oppressed teaches us that the 'state of emergency' in which we live is not the exception but the rule" (Benjamin "Theses").

> "I must ask you to join me in the disorder of crates that have been wrenched open, the air saturated with the dust of wood, the floor covered with torn paper, to join me among piles of volumes that are seeing daylight again after two years of darkness . . . " (Benjamin, "Unpacking" 59).

Н [en]

Liberal Humanism

According to Hayles, it was not only the contexts and conditions but the body itself that in "liberal humanism"—with its Enlightenment focus on rationality and thus its belief in the rights and privileges of the individual as a separate, abstract, self-governing entity—seemed finally and most completely to have been subsumed, transformed, and lost in cybernetics. Discussing other scholars, Hayles noted that the relation between humanism and anorexia:

> shows that the anorectic's struggle to "decrement" the body is possibly precisely because the body is understood as an object

> for control and mastery rather than an intrinsic part of the self . . . In taking the self-possession implied by liberal humanism to the extreme, the anorectic creates a physical image that, in its skeletal emaciation, serves as material testimony that the locus of the liberal humanist subject lies in the mind, not the body. Although in many ways the posthuman deconstructs the liberal humanist subject, it thus shares with its predecessor an emphasis on cognition rather than embodiment. . . . To the extent that the posthuman constructs embodiment as the instantiation of thought/information, it continues the liberal tradition rather than disrupts it. (*Posthuman* 5)

H [en]

Further Diminution of Body

Anorexia (as well as bulimia) were understood to be driven by deep and troubling psychological needs for the diminution of the body, a destructive form of self-desecration and physical abasement. But it also was understood to be driven by a cultural and perhaps not a superficial desire to resemble airbrushed models promulgated by media that established impossible standards of physical beauty, happiness, health. (Bridges were formed from physical self-abuse to bodybuilding as well, where "*models*" of both mental and physical fitness were preferred; the "models" of the highly desirable social-cultural-economic values of efficiency, productivity, speed, were machines; it did not matter whether they looked human [Moses and Katz; Markoff "Robotic"; "Computers"].) Cybernetics as a form of anorexia may have been yet another attempt to overcome if not escape the human body, with all its faults and frailties, its gains and longings, its feelings and failings, its loves and losses (see Balsamo, esp. 41–55; Grosz on "Body Images," 62–85).

Pharmakon

For Diana Floyd

The pharmacist
told me she
"has a tragic
life in love."

The first one
left her,
the second one
she left,

and the third
was taken by
a higher being.

"No refill,"
she says.
"I hate that."

[AT]

Negation

O [o]

Self-Punishment

Social, cultural, political, and religious traditions included a variety of personal and/or communal deconstructive "forms" of self-punishment, e.g.: self-denial, self-flagellation; self-immolation; self-mutilation, cilicing, hair-shirting, ascetism, and any form of attempted suicide (fasting, starvation, poverty, penance); with the help of others, self-amputation, self-suspending, non-lethal crucifixion, hanging, self-exile; and as a result of forms and forces of technology and politics, which tended to be parallel to and may have been corollary with corporal punishment by the king, the body politic, the State, the society as a whole, (Foucault, *Discipline*), public flogging, impaling, decapitating, guillotining, cooking (in a metal cow or in boiling oil), tar and feathering, burning (at the stake), lapidation (stoning), inverted crucifixion, drawing and quartering, trial by combat, consumption by wild animals, iron-maidening, thrown in the *oubliette*; the stockade; public starvation, the wrack and screw, the breaking on the wheel, anal penetration with a red hot spit, chemical castration, "dragging" by horse or car or social media, lynching; shooting (firing squad and police), deliberate drowning, asphyxiation; incarceration, amputation, mutilation; electrocution, gassing, drugging, poisoning; eugenics, genetic manipulation, spacing, prosthetic erasing. In addition to repentance and/or self-loathing, did these personal and communal punishments prepare the groundwork for the acceptance and incorporation of internal and external cybernetic parts into the body human?

The Astronauts of Nordhausen

I
i
ignite
the people

screaming
the test
rocket screaming
riding on the back
of the inmates
in the cave-space
of Nordhausen

II

separation
V-1, V-2 prototype
Saturn 5
a forgotten memory
falling to the sea

III

And the heroes breathe
a pressurized sigh
in space suits tested
by unsung pilots
the astronauts of Dachau
strapped naked to chairs
instruments measuring shriveling
skin flew to their deaths
in decompression chambers
lungs and vessels bursting
the moonlight of cameras
rocket screaming into the sky
people screaming as they ride
toward a deaf heaven

IV

Oh Werner, Werner:
it all started at Peenemunde,
and ended up in Florida
with a man on the Moon

o [o]

Lesser Neo-Aristotelian Extensions

There also were "lesser" neo-Aristotelian extensions of the rhetorical and poetic treatises on the stylistic dimensions of bodies as well as discourses as an "unfortunate necessity" but still cathartic (cf. *Rhetoric*, esp. Bk III; *Generations*). And these were milder, playful, boastful, more showy "forms" of flattery (Platon would not have called them "Forms" [*Gorgias* 502c–d]) via artful representative or symbolic badges honored by publicly being worn *sui generis*—like advertising or propaganda—but on a personal scale: skin covered by or converted with tattoos as an expression of a body-art, rebellion, individual freedom, liberty. The true Tattooee enclosed their whole body in a bubble of ink. In addition were the Piercers—pricking evermore precious, evermore private, evermore tender parts where not even vomiting and voidances of guilt could be used for forced or free confession or therapy (Freud; Katz, "Rhetoric of Confessional," "Poetic Self"). So too the work of "pain artists" who cut ~~~ and slashed /// their own flesh (see Eco, *Beauty* 417) or suspended themselves from their own skin as living works of art (see Benthien, esp. Ch 12; Stelarc; KAC; Thacker; Booher).

Rough Cookie

A young woman so sharply
angular and thin
she seems to exist
in two dimensions only—
sides without
front or back

I'm a rough cookie,
she said, the kind that cuts
the insides of your mouth
when you kiss, bite,
your blue breath blooming,
brilliant in hot flashes

***

These intimate personal and cultural "habits" perhaps continued neo-Platonic traditions of mortification and asceticism, carried forward in the name of some religions. Did these lesser forms of sheik and wanted wounds provide another foundation for a new, technological "mythology" (cf. Schlegel; Kidder; Katz, "Narrative Romance"), or the docile acceptance of subsequent cosmetic, plastic, and prosthetic surgery? The purpose was not endurance and punishment, but augmentation and enhancement of the unstable material of bodies and the informatic meaning of its "messages." Platon's pharmakon led to Aristotle's catharsis, a physical anorexia of style in relation to "content"—a diminishment of the physical *bodies* in all their forms. But perhaps this public aesthetic play and display was the result of the impulse to escape the corruption of the body, another turning point in Western culture. Were these artistic and inartistic acts of self-mortification an attempt to imitate the "negation of history" (cf. Vitanza, *Negation*; *Chaste Rape*) in a non-mimetic act of resurrection—a reification of the divine as material that could never be represented or known in art (Nancy, *Noli*)? Or the "*gift* of death" that could never be given or received or taken back (cf. Derrida, *Gift*; Heidegger, *Being and Time*)? Was the τέχνη of the transmogrification of wafer and wine as body and blood, or the ἀτεχνη of punctured body, a philosopher-rhetorician-poet's dream of a singular, inscrutable, enigmatic, mystical act of "love"? As an "ontological reversal" to physically backtrack to G/d through dangerous mystical spells and infinite ethereal realms? Or was this aesthetic rage that spread like a rash on the skin of culture, a bulimia induced not by fingers but technological gadgets? A clearing of the social throat?

Diana the Huntress I

(hood of flesh
standing
in a black boot)

Π [pe]

Negative Capability as Liquidation

Keats' concept of "negative capability" was the temporary liquidation of the ego (of the poet's self) in favor of the experience of the Other. Negative capability was a subjective, internal, and life-affirming approach to the possibilities of the transcendence through the annihilation of the mind/body division and imprisonment, through the rhetorical processes of consubstantiation via empathy. The negation of the self, especially of the body, was necessary, but came in different violent and non-violent forms. Many of the trivial and no-so-trivial eviscerations of the body were once again (as in pre-surgical days) applied directly to the surface of the skin—to the text of flesh, rhetorical or poetic. Whether negative capability assumed an "open" or "closed body" did not matter: the process of becoming Other became a synecdoche for dissolving the body—even momentarily—for sublime experience of embodiment and transcendence as/in another. Like a dandy changing shoes before being shot into interstellar space, negative capability was in the end a means of self-expansion and self-propagation by inhabiting and using (*Zuhandenheit*) an object or body. In the twentieth century and beyond, "negative capability" was forced and could be abused.

Diana the Huntress II

(on his knees he stands in awe.
amazed at what he sees:
legs. crack of sky. dark fur.)

***

> [Benjamin's] emancipation of the elements of language from larger, meaning-producing structures was simultaneously language's "shattering" or "dismemberment." The disjointed, arbitrary elements achieve a "changed and intensified expressiveness." . . . The decimated language had, in its individual parts, ceased to serve mere communication; it [appears] as a newborn object. . . . (Jennings and Doherty 168)

[ИЧ]

Decadence and dismemberment of spirit.

п [pe]

Cybernetic Decadentism

Another lesser but nevertheless important art movement in twentieth century Italy that continued the name but not the characteristics of the nineteenth century as tradition in England and France, and that may have contributed to the aesthetics of the cybernetic age, was Decadentism. Eco defined Decadentism as a reactionary "realization that the more an experience is artificial the more valuable it is. From the idea that art creates a second nature we have moved to the idea that every violation of nature, preferably as bizarre and morbid as possible, is art" (Eco, *Beauty* 340). Ironically, somewhat like Socrates (e.g., *Phaedrus*), Decadentism voiced "a scornful intolerance of nature" (Eco, *Beauty* 340), rejecting it as random, disorderly, and a false imitation of truth. Decadentism "construct[ed] a life made up of artificial sensations, in an equally artificial environment in which nature, rather than being recreated, as happens in a work of art, is at once imitated and negated . . . " (Eco, *Beauty* 341). And so in this perverted sense, the drive to escape "nature" by a mimesis of negation in Decadentism became another road on the semi-Platonic way to disembodiment. (Max Horkheimer might have pointed out that any Platonic drive was only an unintended biproduct of Enlightenment rationality that rejected nature as disordered in favor of human order; in so doing, this drive ignores, violates, and even seeks to overturn the first principles of modern science: that nature is orderly, governed by even elegant laws that are knowable, and thus the source of truth [and beauty].)

***

«*Да, Да:* Horkheimer critique of post-Enlightenment reason good, until defection to United States. In way his theory run opposite direction from Marxist critique of technological rationality, like Habermas, or anarchist critique of reason, like Feyerabend. But not like these critiques of rationality, Horkheimer in the end wanted to posit a Platonic ideal, *final* moral truth outside and beyond human reason that could ride the eruptions and vagaries of politics, history, consumer, culture entertainment, ethnic destructions and rebirths through national reincarnations and economic reconstructions, however cosmetic. Inheritance from the Baroque-Mannerist period, in Decadentism the unnatural, artificial, manmade obviously preferred, valued, considered more real (Kolodny). Just like Russia. "There was no Beauty that was not the work of artifice; only that which was artificial could be beautiful" (Eco, *Beauty* 340). Communist "corporations" (including those of Olympic athletes) focused on economic basis of production, including all art, made the manufactured preferred: "[F]lowers that are real but seem artificial," as Eco said (*Beauty* 341).»

Valentine

"My luve is like a red red rose"—Robert Burns, p. 522
"By any other name"–Shakespeare, Romeo and Juliet 2.1, line 86, p. 891

The rose is red, not real.
It has a scent, but false.
Green leaves fall off its stem,
but it doesn't need them.
We stick it in soil and water,
all the same, love's fodder.
It's eternal, but not permanent.

Feeling penetrates the folded petals,
strikes the soft skin of any fool;
the textures in the fisted tin
vibrate for an hour . . . balled up on stem, a knot . . .
continue to believe in it
        and love the real rose like a fake
                for your sake, or not.

P [er]

Love of the Artificial

More than love of the artificial, or love of the real that looked artificial, love of the artificial that does *not* look real (a late nineteenth and twentieth century twist) was made possible by increasingly more sophisticated technology in every manufactured walk of life and art. The use of new technologies in the form of old technologies (Kittler, *Truth*; *Gramophone*; R. Walker, "Mistakes"; "Hit Rewind"; Kidder) was another beginning of the dissolution of "the natural" body in the growing hum and din of gears and devices. The dissolution was evident in the early development of mass media and aesthetic theory in the twentieth century. But it wasn't just technological development, but also a parallel disfigurement (or what might be called the "unfiguring") of authority at the end of the nineteenth and the beginning of the twentieth century: social status, ritual, tradition, religion, awe—what Walter Benjamin called "the aura"—that Benjamin wanted to place in language and art ("Technological Reproducibility" 39). Citing the "art for art's sake" movement as predecessor ("Technological Reproducibility" 24), and the dandy as co-patriot (Benjamin, "Dream Kitsch" 238; Doherty, Introduction to "Painting and Graphics" 200–01), Benjamin in a collection of essays, regrouped in *The Work of Art in the Age of Its Technological Reproducibility and Other Writings on Media*, focused on the fragmentation and possibilities of art, language, and culture brought about by new media technology, especially cinema (*Technological Reproducibility* 24–27; 48n23). (The second *version* of the essay "The Work of Art in the Age of its Technological Reproducibility," finally found and reproduced from the German in English in 2008 [Jennings et al.] was more complete and polished and became the gold standard, but was not as widely circulated or known as a later, half-re-revised, shorter, unfinished third version, "The Work of Art in the Age of Mechanical Reproduction" [Arendt, *Illuminations* 217–51; cf. Hansen, who explored Benjamin's second version, and the ramifications of his attempt in this essay to discover more *Spiel-Raum*—"room-for-play"].) Fragmentation was not limited to newspapers and neon lights ("Surfaces"). It was also found in written alphabets as graphics, and "figures of thought" (*Denkbilder*) or "dialectical images"—what Benjamin called "script-images or image-scripts" (Jennings and Doherty 168–70; Benjamin, "Antinomies"; "Dismemberment"); graphology (Benjamin, "Script"); "dream kitsch" (Benjamin, "Dream"); and the "collecting" of books and quotes and other *objets des arts* as fetish (Arendt, Introduction 42–48; e.g., see Benjamin, "Unpacking").

wind-tossed,
turning from the light—
a contrary flower

p [er]

> *Benjamin's Problem*
>
> Benjamin's problem, which he shares with other Marxists, is to link the individual fact or institution with the overall development of economic history (the prime mover). Behind, or, rather, "in," the elegant shopping arcades, Benjamin sees as a first cause the boom of the French textile industry and the economic necessity of storing a variety of expensive goods. But there is also a secondary cause—the technological advances of cast-iron construction accelerated by the growth of the railways, and, in turn the use of cast iron in building railways stations and exhibition halls, wherever transients gather. Benjamin speaks about correspondences where many other Marxists would refer to economic basis and cultural superstructure, and he often suggests these correspondences by parallel sentence structures . . . (Demetz xliii)

C [es]

The Technopolis

In the modern technopolis implied by Benjamin throughout his essays, cityscapes were not gloomy illusions of mass misery and industrial horror later depicted by Futurists (e.g., Ellul; Barrett). Nor were landscapes the massacred civilizations depicted in Futurism, e.g., by Emilio Filippo Tomaso Marinetti, who stated: "War is beautiful because it inaugurates the dreamed-of-metalization of the human body" (Marinetti, qtd. in opposition by Benjamin in "Technological Reproducibility" [41]). Benjamin's summarized and criticized Marinetti's vision:

> [T]he destruction caused by war furnishes proof that society was not mature enough to make technology its organ, that technology was not sufficiently developed to master the elemental forces of society. The most horrifying features of imperialist war are determined by discrepancy between the enormous means of production and their inadequate use in the process of production (in other words, unemployment and the lack of markets). *Imperialistic war is an uprising on the part of technology, which demands repayment in "human*

> *material" for the natural material society has denied it* . . . in gas warfare it has found a new means of abolishing the aura . . . [A]s Marinetti admits, the artistic gratification of a sense perception [was] altered by technology. . . . Its [*l'art pour l'art*] self-alienation has reached the point where it can experience its own annihilation as a supreme aesthetic pleasure. *Such is the aestheticizing of politics, as practiced by fascism. Communism replies by politicizing art.* ("Technological Reproducibility" 42; *ital. in org.*)

The Well-Anchored Plane

35,000 feet
up it is nine
degrees below zero
beneath the mountain
cloud below. Peaks
come and go
land cut
covered with one quilt, drifts in
crazy patterns of snow. Mountains bulge and swirl
on the desert floor, coil and uncoil and lay waste the land—bones, muscles,
veins, scaly sand and
treetop skin we resurrect by flying over it, fallen by riverbed, solid in sun.
There's no life
down there. There
has been no life for
a million years. At 35,000
we are far below the black frozen tundra above the thinning blue
where 230 miles up, the astronauts go, skirting, skipping
earth's air. There's no life anywhere.
We are almost there.

c [es]

Marxist Liberation of Human Perception

Benjamin believed that the new technologies would liberate human perception and consciousness of the masses by removing "works of art" from their traditional, ritual, and repressive contexts—the "aura" of traditional art (Benjamin, "Technological Reproducibility" 39). "[T]echnological reproduction can place the copy of the original in situations which the original itself cannot attain," Benjamin proclaimed ("Technological Reproducibility" 21). Thus, what Benjamin lauded most in new technological arts was not the reproduction of a subject or object (mimesis). Rather, the subject/object/purpose of technological art was *reproducibility*. That is, the new technological arts do not try to imitate anything, but rather mass produce their own processes and technological realities, which is reproducibility itself. Mimesis in art, which had always pertained to the creation in and relation of art a subject as well as to tradition (Eliot, "Tradition"), now pertained to dissemination as the *primary purpose* of art. "Reproducibility was finally the *political* capacity of the work of art; its very reproducibility shatters its aura and enables a reception of a very different kind in a very different spectatorial space" (Benjamin, "Technological Reproducibility" 15).

Cyrillic boots marching.

[EC]

Mimetic Bodies

T [te]

Personal Violence

In *"Crash"* (Baudrillard, *Simulacra* 111–19), technological violence was brought down to the personal level (in this case, the automobile): → confused bodies → remixed with machines → made highly erotic. ←But cybernetics and informatic relay was not a hard smashing of body and machine ←but a soft crushing ←recoding←renovation ←recording of data. Futurism was an artistic movement aiming to express the dynamic and violent quality of contemporary life, especially as embodied in the motion and force of modern machinery and modern warfare (Jenny, *Work of Art* 54n37). The goal of Futurism was to "kill off the moonlight" (Marinetti, "Second *Futurist* Proclamation" 22–31).

birds
dancing
with the sky

т *[te]*

Reproducibility

"Film is the first art form whose artistic character is entirely determined by its reproducibility" (Benjamin, "Technological Reproducibility" 28). For Benjamin, photography, and especially the cinema, and other media devices of the late nineteenth and early twentieth century, inaugurated a technological revolution in art (cf. Kittler). For Benjamin, as for Maholy-Nagy (e.g., 50–53), the camera was an "optical prosthetic" (Jennings 11–12; Benjamin "Technological Reproducibility" 37; 54n36). But more, because of the incremental power of these aesthetic prosthetic forms, media could be used to reconfigure power relations—not only the aesthetic relations between the relative position of art as mimesis and its object, but also the relation of the viewer to the art object, and thus the political relations between art as social ideology and process, and the masses. In particular, Benjamin saw new communication technology and aesthetic media as heuristics that would allow "viewer participation/interaction" and help adapt the human sensorium to the new technological age. In particular: everyone could be actor or director, and regard themselves in film; and "[f]ilm . . . trains its viewers through the use of a technological apparatus (camera, editing, projection) to deal with the "vast apparatus" in which we live, the apparatus of the phantasmagoria" (Jennings 14; see Benjamin, "Technological Reproducibility" 31).

House Painting as Media

deep red slipping
under phosphorus blue
the day is as dark
as a movie theatre

the paint slides down
the house like a screen

the film
is about to begin

from the balconies
of windows
and the aisles
of lawns
alone
with each other
the elderly
watch

they have no need
for soap opera
in these dark
and luminous days

the film is about
to begin

we climb
ladders into air

they anticipate,
anxious, afraid

we are transforming
a house
as though it were
the world

what would they have
us change it to?

y [u]

The Apparatus

Following the French philosopher and historian Michel Foucault, the Italian philosopher Giorgio Agamben considered "an apparatus" as "literally anything that has in some way the capacity to capture, orient, determine, intercept, model, control, or secure the gestures, behaviors, opinions, or discourses of living beings" (Agamben, *Apparatus* 14). For Agamben, the apparatus began with the socio-political systems that technology surrounded but was also in which it was also embedded. Thus, the apparatus was both the technology and the socio-cultural-political system in which it functioned and existed (what Habermas regarded as an ideology ["Ideology"]). The historical context in which images (including script and word images) represented not only aesthetic convention and cultural tradition but also political domination and repression.

y [u]

Extension and Disruption of the Eye

For Benjamin, new aesthetic media, such as the camera and film, not only extended the optical power of the eye but also, borrowing Agamben's concepts, intercepted and disrupted traditional sociologies of art, in which, individually and collectively, aesthetic works were objects of "authenticity, authority, and permanence" (Jennings, "Introduction: Production" 15). Technological reproducibility freed art from the aura of the aesthetic authority of ritual and tradition (Benjamin, "Technological Reproducibility" esp. 23–25). (In the second, more Marxist version of his essay at least, Benjamin apparently did not see the irony [or power] of the apparatus necessitating training. For him, the "sensory recalibration" was "a *symptom* or *embodiment* of, or [. . .] a *school* for, this "decisive refunctioning of the human perceptual apparatus'" [T. Levin 316; cf. Cartwright and Goldfarb].) In his somewhat utopian (yet true) vision of the technological work of art—not as an imitation or model, but as a productive and liberating political force—the apparatus of art could help dismember not only "the language of art" but also re-present humanity, leading to what Benjamin called a "celluloid resurrection" ("Technological Reproducibility" 22).

To Greta Garbo, on Her Hundredth Birthday

(September 18, 2005)

Hiding in the annex, you Anne Frank loved,
you who avoided fans, detested crowds—
enough to color with crayons your newspaper clip
her father let her hang in the attic
(your low alto body and face shadow-lit)
to brighten up the walls in which she lived—
or was that Rita Hayward hanging there?
In the end, it made no difference who, or where.

Garbo the recluse, a refugee—
a "jew" in New York City, Sweden, Europe
grown too small for your beautiful fame.
You existed on a screen of silver streets
for voyeur fans who loved to spy you shop
for lovely antique bone, now ash like Anne.

Φ [ef]

Purposive-Rational Institution

«From critical Marxist Committee point of view, apparatus what younger Habermas ("Ideology") would call "purposive-rational institutional framework" (a society in which ideology of economic and technological systems fuse, based on means-ends relations). Purposive-rational institutional framework replace traditional, institutional framework (based on social and symbolic action, in which purposive-rational system previously existed as subsystem). But for Benjamin, not technology in control of process of artistic production. Rather (perhaps in technological reenactment of romantic inspiration addressing a not-yet-present future audience, noted by Timothy Clark [*Inspiration*], what might call "future rhetorical"), Benjamin believed mass audiences would control technology.»

The House Hygienist

(On the Restoration of Albany)

i am a house hygienist.
i will clean those long, pearly spindles,
scraping, scraping centuries of plaque
like paint all day, all day
applying my variety of odd-shaped instruments
to your teeth, your mouth, your face,
firmly gripping the muscle of my blade,
probe, dig
into nook, crack, crevice, decay,
the loud wrenching of my blade
felt along the nerve ends of your brain,
your streets anesthetized now,
the drool of the river running
from your mouth to the drain.
But your sleeping memory
will soon awake, and a giant
you will feel the whole valley of your pain,
my raw fingers stubbed, bleeding at the gums,
poking at years of neglect and decay,
poking poking poking it away.
And then with my largest instruments,
picks, drills, sandblasters, trucks,
i will move down the furthest recesses
of your mouth, behind the walls
of your eyes, up the crooked rows
of tenement houses, pulling,
pulling out those rotten planks,
pulling, pulling all day, all day,
until i can fill those urban cavities
with clean spackle, apply
thick new polish like paint.

ф [ef]

Mass Authority

For Benjamin, film technology captured and reoriented the authority of art toward the masses (moving them closer to the center of production and power). Technological reproduction thus was not mimesis; rather it was "*the desire of the present-day masses to "get closer" to things, and their equally passionate concern for overcoming each thing's uniqueness . . . by assimilating it as a reproduction*" (Benjamin "Technological Reproducibility" 23; ital. in org.). For Benjamin, reproduction is the reality that matters. "Every day the urge grows stronger to get hold of an object at close range in an image [*Bild*], or better, in a facsimile [*Abbild*], a reproduction" ("Technological Reproducibility" 23). In this way, Benjamin said, "art has escaped the realm of "beautiful semblance," which for so long was regarded as the only sphere in which it could thrive" ("Technological Reproducibility" 32). Even alienation in the face of technology could be used productively, aesthetically.

> *The representation of human beings by means of an apparatus has made possible a highly productive use of the human being's self-alienation* . . . The film actor's estrangement in the face of the apparatus . . . is basically of the same kind as the estrangement felt before one's appearance [*Erscheinung*] in a mirror—a favorite theme of the Romantics. But now the mirror image [*Bild*] has become detachable from the person mirrored, and is transportable. ("Technological Reproducibility" 32, 33; ital. in org.)

Magnolia

must have just missed you—
the magnolia tree
still moving

X [xa]

> *Beautiful Semblance*
>
> The significance of the beautiful semblance [*schöner—Schein*] is rooted in the age of auratic perception that is now coming to an end. The aesthetic theory of that era was more fully articulated by Hegel, for whom beauty is "the appearance [*Erscheinung*] of spirit in its immediate . . . sensuous form, created by the spirit as the form adequate to itself" (Hegel, *Werke*, vol. 10, part 2 [Berlin, 1837], 121). Although this formulation has some derivative qualities, Hegel's statement that art strips away the "semblance and deception of this false, transient world" from the "true content of phenomena" (*Werke* vol 10, part 1: 13) already diverges from the traditional experiential basis [*Erfahrungsgrund*] of this doctrine. This ground of experience is *the aura*. (Benjamin, "Technological Reproducibility" 48n.23)

Plastic chopsticks—
Trying to maintain
A slippery tradition

x [xa]

Audience as Artist

This represented a radical change not only in the relation of technology to art, but in the relation of artist to subject/object and audience. Theories of mimesis as they had been understood, at least in the West since Platon, underwent a fundamental change too. From the perspective of cultural criticism, the naïve empirical philosophy of Newtonian physics, Enlightenment rationality, Romanticism, even violence via technology, seem to have been derived from an almost necessary spirit of idealism and transferred to a technological materialism that was still transcendental (especially in the US where it manifested as religious doctrine and a fever of work [Weber; Grocz]), as well as to a mythology of bucolic technology (Horkheimer; Lyotard, *Postmodern*; L. Marx; Kolodny). This religious doctrine of mythology, technology, and work, had to have been conveyed to cybernetics as well. Like art or any object divested of its aura, nature and the human body through labor could be replicated, be mass-produced. If reproducibility itself was the goal, the previously repressed singular body (and each of its parts) as the subject of art and object of mimesis was not imitated or important, but created and/or liberated by an ideology and apparatus of the new aesthetic. Bodies didn't matter anymore: indeterminate, emergent data were universal, and could be "passed" through any membrane, streamed across any medium, however differentially filtered (see Hayles 36–49). And art did not wonder about imitating the original, for "[t]he *whole sphere of authenticity eludes technological—and of course not only technological—reproduction*" (Benjamin, "Technological Reproducibility" 21; ital. in org).

> What is essential is that each and every time refugees no longer represent individual cases but rather a mass phenomenon (as was the case between the two world wars and is now once again), these organizations as well as single states—all the solemn evocations of the inalienable rights of human beings notwithstanding—have proved to be absolutely incapable not only of solving the problem but also of facing it. The whole question, therefore, was handed over humanitarian organizations and to the police. (Agamben, *Means without Ends* 17–18)

slight breeze
beneath a leaf—
ancient hiker passing

Ц [tse]

> *Militant Library*
>
> This was its militant age, when no book was allowed to enter [my three bookshelves] without the certification that I had not read it. Thus I might have acquired a library extensive enough to be worthy of the name if there had not been an inflation. Suddenly the emphasis shifted; books acquired real value, or at any rate, were difficult to obtain. At least this is how it seemed in Switzerland. At the eleventh hour I sent my first major book orders from there and in this way was able to secure such irreplaceable items . . . . I have made my most memorable purchases on trips, as a transient . . . . Only in extinction is the collector comprehended. (Benjamin, "Unpacking" 62, 63, 67)

Cyrillic boots. Marching.

it is necessary
to move forward
before you can look back.

ц [tse]

Freed from Mimesi

If mimesis was no longer the purpose of technological art, then art was no longer the prisoner of mimesis (see Benjamin, "Mimetic Faculty"). Technology became its own *self-referential* subject. And "the body" (of the actor on film, or statistics on spread sheet, or technical diagrams which Benjamin thought the new poetry of the proletariat ["Attested Auditor" 172; "Technological Reproducibility" 32–33; "Author as Producer" 91]) was thus freed from slavish imitation, and the ethical falsity of imitation that Platon questioned. Eventually the images projected on any bandwidth on the electro-magnetic spectrum (whether as simple signals or as bytes in a data stream) was the living-aesthetic-technological-object itself. Given the power of the technology of film as art, *[t]he most important social function* [of art was] . . . *to establish equilibrium between human beings and the apparatus*" (Benjamin, "Technological Reproducibility" 37; ital. in org).

> The reasons for such [political] impotence lie not only in the selfishness and blindness of bureaucratic apparatuses, but also in the very ambiguity of the fundamental notions regulating

the inscription of the *native* (that is, of life) in the juridical order of the nation-state." (Agamben, *Means without Ends* 18; cf. Arendt, "Decline of the Nation-State")

Beyond All Recognition

(For John Robison, founder of Jocundry's Bookstore, E. Lansing, Michigan, patron of poetry and art, who died in a D.C. plane crash over Chicago on his way to a booksellers' convention in Los Angeles, May 25, 1979.)

the engine
a flying muscle
collapsed,

wide body
rolling
over
dropping,

erupting,
bursting
like sonic laughter.

You were
jocund
but always concerned.

your bookstore
was a haven
for paintings and words.

but your humor
could not
save you now;

no stanzas of poetry
could uplift you,
no painter

quickly create
a softer landscape
beneath you,

no god
transform you,
no singer

compose
one catchy
tune, sing it,

no sculptor
carve
your wings . . .

Helpless
in air,
a flicker of falling

mirth,
you must have known
it was the end

of your discourse,
your learning, your
philanthropy, your career

For your last act,
you spread yourself
too thin

over the world—

you were
burned beyond
all recognition

[KA]

Aesthetic Violence

Ч [tçe]

Juxtaposition of Death

> [T]he libraries, museums, theatres, universities, research centers, in and through which the transmission of the humanities and of the sciences mainly takes place, can prosper next to the concentration camps. The discriminations and freshness of their enterprise may well suffer under the surrounding impress of violence and regimentation. But they suffer surprisingly little. Sensibility (particularly that of the performing artist), intelligence, scruple in learning, carry forward as in a neutral zone . . . obvious qualities of literate response, of aesthetic feeling, can coexist with barbaric, politically sadistic behavior in the same individual . . . The insights we now have into the negative or, at the least, dialectically paradoxical and parodistic relations between culture and society are something new, and morally bewildering. (Steiner, *Bluebeard* 77, 78)

ч [tçe]

Technological Emancipation. «In Benjamin Marxist vision, art not reproduction of physical, psychological, social, political, and economic tyranny of "real," or false simulacrum of historical product of hierarchical culture (see Lyotard, *Libidinal*). Het. Technological art (ideal) was emancipation from stagnation of physical, psychological, social, political, and economic status and class—from original, material individual and communal conditions of economics, social, cultural, and political structures. Beyond nineteenth century notion of metaphysical science of subjectivity, or transcendental "I" (Fichte), or new mythology of poetry (Schlegel), or history as dialectic of objective spirit (Hegel), or genius of nature itself as creative power (Schiller), effect of Benjamin theory of technological art not only (and again) called into question notion of true vs. imitation; Benjamin theory eviscerate importance if not fact of distinction between original vs. copy. Result (once again) was merging of human body and art—not in some transcendental dialectic, or death, but technologically, through the material means of production. For Soviet, maybe other, possibly another beginning in relation of art and cybernetics. Art as technological replication or extension of human body, да; but art involving *no* body, invoking nobody. Art *is* means of production. В мотор ("The motor"). Human body itself, technological progeny of rhetoric and poetry, was work of art itself, not aura. Original work of art without imitation of imitation of imitation of imitation . . . *adding Nausea.*»

Ш [sha]

> *Body as Ontology*
>
> [T]he ontology of the body is ontology itself . . . It's from bodies that we have, for ourselves, our bodies as strangers. Nothing to do with a dualism, a monism, or a phenomenology of the body. The body's neither substance, a phenomenon, flesh, nor signification. Just being exscribed. ("Corpus"15, 19; also see Nancy, "Intruder")

ш [sha]

Before Impending Disaster

tossing and turning
over the price
of the bed

Щ [shch]

Body of Writing

Like Benjamin's notion of the relation of film and life, and Derrida's notion of touch (*Dissemination; On Touching*), for Nancy the body and writing were not only related but "identical" and based on difference (Deleuze, *Repetition*), more cyborg or clone than mimetic android or robot. Through science, causality, machinery, the consubstantial was substantial (cf. Burke, *Rhetoric of Motive* 22). In discussing writing—"exposition"—in terms of the extension of the surface of the body, Nancy explained: "A body is a feeling body only in [the] displacement or division of senses, which is neither the phenomenon nor the residue of a deep "auto-aesthesia" but yields, on the contrary, the entire property belonging to that simple tautology, the aesthetic body" (35). The body (read nature's "natural," organic body) no longer existed: "Writing [is] the *anatomical* sign of "self," which doesn't signify, but cuts, separates, exposes" (Nancy, "Corpus" 85).

Sylvia

For Melissa Randall, who loves her

She was composed
but not fully written, incomplete,
with a hole to be filled
by emptiness
amid the insistent
loneliness that crowded her in.

But the paper, the paper
wall she created, wrote on
was the only thing
that was near perfect: Happiness
could never touch

her: love never get too
close, too much like life,
the ubiquitous "you," like the sun,
merely warming the gap
of her existence, "the grave cave"

she went in and out of every decade
until one dull day she
took down the wall,
stripped the thin white
paper robe of her life—

and we finally found her
there on the page

щ [shch]

Original Copy

For Derrida (*Dissemination*), there was little difference between original and copy because there was no Final Signified, especially for simulacra, and thus no originals to be copied; for Deleuze (*Repetition*) there was a greater distinction between original and copy because of the levels of difference and repetition without sameness; for Lyotard (*Libidinal*) there was no difference at all between original and copy because of the force of the simulacrum as a singularity itself in any exchange. All of these issues were "reinstantiated" in the tissues of cybernetic organs (Hayles, *Posthuman*). Paper or screen, page or bit, did not matter. "There is no facsimile of the aura" (Benjamin, "Technological Reproducibility" 31). As Benjamin predicted and wished, because of technology and/as art (τεκνη), there was little difference between aesthetics and environment, body and image. In the production as well as "effects" of later technology on the cybernetic body *as* the *physical environment* and substance of body and nature and art, the cybernetic artist sought to overcome human alienation from the apparatus, as well as the dichotomies of natural/technological, art/economics, biology/machine. "[T]he world of bodies is produced, and this is finally our world's unique and genuine production. Everything comes back to this production: there's no difference between "natural" and "technical" phenomena" (Nancy, "Corpus" 79).

***

> [B]odies [are not] produced by the autoproduction of the spirit and its reproduction . . . Our world is the world of the "technical," a world whose cosmos, nature, gods, entire system is, in its inner joints, exposed as "technical": the world of the *ecotechnical.* The ecotechnical functions with technical apparatuses, which it brings into the world and links to the system, thereby creating our bodies as more visible, more proliferation, more polymorphic, more compressed, more "amassed and zoned" than ever before. (Nancy, "Corpus" 87, 89)

Lady Lazarus, Redux

"And there is a charge, a very large charge,
For a word or a touch or . . . " (Plath, "Lady Lazarus" 246)

Suddenly her voice stops, hisses and reverberates,
the boom of the room, dissipates.
We sit in the fluorescent din
dropping off, dumb as "a lampshade,"
shocked by the darkness of the silent cave
growing around us like the plant roots of
the dead sound box in the middle of
the course, feeling her deep emptiness.

Although she's dead, she's done it again:
"Once every ten years" she "manages it,"
her non-paper skin the pallor of white

lights that quickly flutter overhead,
her charged voice passing out of the electric
current, flickers, seizes, smashes into
"a million filaments" of sound, goes out.
Died and resurrected three times before,
Sylvia, before my lifeless class
has committed suicide once more.

Will her voice come back to us— the "peanut
-crunching crowd" of students who "shove in"
to see me "unwrap" her words, to cop
a touch of a piece of cloth,
of verbal skin, her former hand and "foot
a paper weight," to grab, and prop,
suck "a bit" of her semantic blood, rhetoric,
to listen to her metric heart—"it really goes"—
and finally decide to speak and "stay
put"? Will she finish her poem today?

Ashes rise from the CD player
in sniffs of smoke . . . "like air."
We press and poke. "Nothing there."
Some buttons stir the disc. I do not think
that we will ever hear her shriek again.
A box of silence, a bit of soap, "a gold" CD
like an oversized "wedding ring"
in a tiny plastic coffin, a shallow
broken grave for her flattened
spinning, voiceless face, "rising"
from the dust to "eat men like air."

Ъ [tverdij znak]

Cybernetic Metaphor

RE: metaphor, Colin Turbayne might have wondered whether in cybernetics the same confusion of "types" of metaphor/model and observation/thing— what Turbayne called "sort-crossing" in which the body and the world as machine are mimetically (similarly) configured—where the metaphor/model was (mis) taken for "the real" (if there was access to it [cf. Boyd; Kuhn, "Metaphor"]). Did the same "figural error" occur in cybernetics as it had in Newtonian science, quantum mechanics, astrophysics, bionics (cf. Lakoff and Johnson; Lakoff and

Nuñez)? In *Margins of Philosophy*, Derrida wondered the same thing not only about metaphysics, but about all of philosophy, which he saw as necessarily metaphorical ("White Mythology" 258–71).

ъ *[tverdij znak]*

Little Black Notebooks

> Nothing was more characteristic of [Benjamin] in the thirties than the little notebooks with black covers which he always carried with him and in which he tirelessly entered in the form of quotations what daily living and reading netted him . . . On occasion he read from them aloud . . . . and showed them around like items from a choice and precious collection . . . . the latest newspaper item, next to Goecking's "*Der erste Schnee,*"* a report from Vienna dated summer 1939, saying that the local gas company has "stopped supplying gas to Jews. The gas consumption of the Jewish population involved a loss for the gas company, since the biggest consumers were the ones who did not pay their bills. The Jews used the gas especially for committing suicide." (Arendt, "Introduction" 45–46)

Ы *[i]*

Torsos

> [I]t has become customary to regard the text [*Paris Arcades*] which Benjamin himself usually called the *Passagenarbeit*, or just the *Passagen*, as at best a *"torso,"* a monumental fragment or ruin, and at worst a mere notebook, which the author supposedly intended to mine for more extended discursive applications. . . . Certainly, the project as a whole is unfinished; Benjamin abandoned work on it in the spring of 1940, when he was forced to flee Paris before the advancing German army. (Eiland and McLaughlin x–xi; *italics added*)

* German: *Der erste Schnee*— "the first snow" (Benjamin, *Briefe* II, 820).

ы [i]

Face Value: The Black Notebooks.[*] Unconcealed.

Socrates accused books of falling
silent: what then is this
unfolding mystery of a horror
of Heidegger's history?

i weary of arguing
with myself, of not feeling
guilty for the vagary
of rhetoric and poetry,

knowing neither
Hitler, nor Heidegger personally,
and having to admit
i have not been to the death camps

except as a temporary guest,
a visitor who must confess
feeling almost Nothing now, not seeing
authenticity in the face of non-Being,

but a closing off, a concealing
of *Dasein*, a revealing
of technology, En-framed
here, at journey's end.

[Я] *(i)*

Hypostases

Ъ [*mæxkij znak*]
End of Metaphysics

The everydayness of the terrestrial habitat hypostasized in space marks the end of metaphysics, and signals the beginning of the era of hyperreality: that which was previously mentally projected, which was lived as a metaphor in the terrestrial hab-

* *die Schwarzen Heft*

> itat is from now on projected, entirely without metaphor, into the absolute space of simulation . . . . (Baudrillard, *Ecstasy* 16)

i report.

ъ *[mæxkij znak]*

Forced Extraversion

"[N]o aura, not even the aura of his own body, protects him . . . [He] will suffer from this forced extraversion of all interiority" (Baudrillard, *Ecstasy* 27, italics added).

Э *[e]*

> *No Body Aura*
>
> Like Proust, [Benjamin] was wholly incapable of changing "his life's conditions even when they were about to crush him." (With a precision suggesting a sleepwalker his clumsiness invariably guided him to the very center of a misfortune . . . Thus, in the winter of 1939–1940 the danger of bombing made him decide to leave Paris for a safer place. Well, no bomb was ever dropped on Paris, but Meaux, where Benjamin went, was a troop center and probably one of the very few places in France that was seriously endangered in those months of the phony war.) (Arendt, Introduction 7)

э *[e]*

Pure Screen

"The technological schizophrenic that results can no longer produce himself as a mirror. He becomes a pure screen, a pure absorption and resorption surface of the influent networks" (*Ecstasy* 27).

Ю *[u]*

> *New Refugees*
>
> The small group of refugees that he joined reached the Spanish border town only to learn that Spain had closed the border that same day and that the border officials did not honor visas made out in Marseilles. The refugees were supposed to return to France by the same route [through the Pyrenees] the next

> day. During the night Benjamin took his own life, whereupon the border officials, upon whom this suicide had made an impression, allowed his companions to proceed to Portugal. (Arendt, Introduction 18)

ю [ju]

Forced Introjection

"[F]rom this forced introjection of all exteriority which is implied by the categorical imperative of communication"; 2) "the perpetual interconnection of all information and communication networks"; 3) "the over-proximity of all things"; 4) "the absolute proximity to and total instantaneousness with things"; 5) "this overexposure to the transparency of the world" (*Ecstasy* 27) . . . is "a new form of schizophrenia—with the emergence of an imminent promiscuity and the perpetual interconnection of all information and communication networks" (*Ecstasy* 26–27)

Я [ja]

To the Mystic River Bridge, Boston.

How many times i rode you like a lover,
how many times, quarrelling, absent too long,
have i returned home, to you, skulking back
bumper to bumper amid the traffic of admirers
who use your expressway, willing to pay
the pimp his toll, your face pitted and painted
a thousand times more beautiful than before,
your long lean hard body stretched out
among the rooftops and towers like some old whore's,
arched back spanning the riverbed,
birds darting in and out of your buttress.

How many times have i traveled up
the trestles of your legs, strode the curves of your spine,
the blue jeweled lights on your vibrating thighs
like bruised kisses; how many times
have i driven deep down into your dark dank
womb, tunnel forever expanding and contracting,
pregnant with buses and trucks and cars that emerge,
born into worlds of new suburbs and stars.

я [ja]

Phantom Limbs

Despite the often-painful phenomenon of the "phantom limb," feeling a limb not there; or agnosia, the forgetting a limb that WAS there (Merleau-Ponty149), the goal over time was to incorporate or absorb the internal or external prosthetic device, mechanism, limb, like a walking stick, as a part and extension of the organic body, to be united to tacit intuition, its physical sense, its total consciousness of itself in the world. However, one could argue that some prosthetics—especially cosmetic or external ones that must be learned but removable, may have felt like alien additions to the body (cf. Booher, who discussed how artificial limbs became "naturalized" for athletes, while also facing obstinate resistance to allowing athletes with prosthetics, hormones, or drugs, to compete because of the recognized augmentation of the body). But as Nancy discussed and demonstrated in "The Intruder," some prostheses, even implanted, permanent ones, in some senses may not only remain foreign to the original body, but alienated from the body itself (Nancy, "The Intruder" 161–70).

The Phantom Car

One foot itches,
reaches
for the clutch;
the other
aches like gears

To stop this car
in its wild careening,
garage filling
with carbon monoxide.
She blows the horn

and turns the wheel
a hand standing
beside her body that falls
sideways from the car
and hits the concrete floor

The phantom horn
of the phantom car

sold from the garage
two weeks before
still loudly blows . . .

Oh, to stop this car
in its wild careening,
her foot reaching
for the brakes like a limb
she keeps feeling for

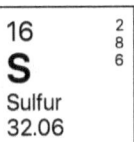

16 2 8 6
S
Sulfur
32.06

13 Posthuman Organ

[Д]

Countdown

"Predestination": After the Anthropocene.

"Destiny is Oblivion."

So said the posthuman philosopher
from outer space, the Open,
who strode across the stars,
walked
    down
        the
            steps
                of light
and right into our living room
(right into our *Lebensraum*),
distant, distinct, mysterious—
walked right in our living
room, i say, right into
the most secret compartments
of our lives, the inner dimensions
of our minds, as if he lived here,
as if he had been there all along,
to coach us, urge us, to save us

from ourselves. Forward we marched
toward our more authentic selves,
our distinctive callings, our collective future,
un-concealed," emerging into
our indeterminant lives.

Onward we rode, assuming
some control, drove
without driving, drove
in search of *Dasein*
but suddenly hit an impasse,
as if we had reached the end—
but no, not yet, we had not
fulfilled our search for
identity, true purpose, Being.

how could we understand, know,
that in the end there was no
resting space, no
final ideological place
we could venture, go;
that our consciousness
exists in infinite space
limited by short bandwidths
of time, that teleology
had run its course finally,
and we were back to *Sein*
square zero, one.

Objectivity is an affective fantasy,
a naïve metaphysical empiricism.
"Oblivion is destiny."

A x 33

Informal Patterns

First, the posthuman view privileges informal pattern over material instantiation, so that embodiment in a biological substrate is seen as an accident of history rather than as an inevitability of life. Second, the posthuman view considers consciousness, regarded as the seat of human identity in the Western tradition long before Descartes thought he was a mind thinking, as an epiphenomenon, as an evolutionary upstart . . . a minor sideshow. Third, the posthuman view thinks of the body as the original prosthesis we all learn to manipulate, so that extending or replacing the body with other prostheses becomes a continuation of a process that began before

> we were born. Fourth, and most important . . . the posthuman view configures human being so that it can be seamlessly articulated with intelligent machines. In the posthuman, there are no essential differences, no absolute demarcations between bodily existence and computer simulation, cybernetic mechanism and biological organism, robot teleology and human goals. (Hayles, *How We Became Posthuman* 3–4)

***

Manifesto

“We want to take you with us.”

“We want to help you grow.”

“‘New couplings, chips, plug-ins, circuits.’”

“‘“Male and female jacks, motherboards.”’”

“‘“‘Our voices will fly from our bodies, soar.’”’”

“‘“‘“Over the house where your corpse still sits.”’”’”

“‘“‘“‘In the dark terminus of your little room.’”’”’”

“‘“‘“‘“Our message will find its way into every home.”’”’”’”

“‘“‘“‘“‘On every planet in every network.’”’”’”’”

“‘“‘“‘“‘“Galaxies wired, electric stars.”’”’”’”’”

y

Transmutations

Environmental Reconfiguration

Posthumanism wasn’t just about a change in physical structure or *technē* as a mode of consciousness (cf. Miller). Posthumanism also was about the “environment” in which reconfigured (non)bodies emerged, existed, submerged, disappeared, reemerged (cf. Pynchon). Walter Benjamin knew that communication subjectivities were divested of their meaning, disseminated, and redistributed within the technology of changing institutions, governments, laws, societies—the Apparatus. What was most important was that in "the apparatus," everything was a projector (Agamben 14), including the human body. Agamben's notion of "the apparatus" included not only technological devices but also the necessary ideological and material structures to support them. Foucault ("Discourse") had demonstrated how, in a disciplinary society, apparatuses aimed to create—through a series of practices, discourses, and knowledge, docile yet free bodies that assume their identity and their "freedom" as subjects in the very process of their subjectification. The Apparatus, then, was a machine that produced subjectifications, and only as such was it able to govern (Agamben, *Apparatus* 19–20).

> The boundless growth of apparatuses in our time corresponds to the equally extreme proliferation of processes of subjectification . . . What is at stake . . . is not an erasure or an overcoming, but rather a dissemination that pushes to the extreme the masquerade that has always accompanied every personal identity. (Agamben, *Apparatus* 15)

***

The Fired Man

"He never did a thing so very bad.
He don't know why he isn't quite as good"
—Robert Frost, "Death of the Hired Man"

"Forgive the left hand: i'm in agony.
i tore the right one off when i fell from
the ladder of the ship. The doctors said
they couldn't do anything hydraulic with it.

"They've grounded me like i'm nothing, earth,
won't give me a mission schedule, flight-dates.
i was the best pilot in the place.
i loved that agency! Was i surprised

"when they said they'd refuse to pay my bills!
Two burst disks in my neck, and i can't use
this arm or hand—may never fly again.
The nurse who had been treating me told them

"my polyhol problem has nothing to do
with the accident. 'You sure you want
that alien in the room?' my lawyer asked.
So i'm a polyholic! I'm not ashamed

"to admit it. i drink to ease the constant strain.
They know i was a good impersonator,
even when i had too much that day.
They took my cosmic pension, benefits.

"Planetary is investigating.
My mate told them it's gotten where you have
to lie on an application form
to get a job. Like all those accidents

"i had before. i had to miss some days.
Last time i almost tore my left leg off;
the doctors reattached it with a ball—
the kind they use with cyborg hips and knees.

"And now i'm fired into outer space.
i was the best 'human' in that place!"

Б x 32

Aura of the Individual

Jean Baudrillard (*Ecstasy*) agreed with Benjamin that the "aura" of the individual—not just the aura of a work of art, but *the aura of the self as a work of art*—was dissipated in the technological production of "information." Baudrillard later called this dispersal of self amid a media shower of unconscious objects in a data stream "the ecstasy of communication." (As might have been predicted by Platon, in "Poetics," parallel to "of the Body" under "False True Forms," "Corrective" to restore "The Soul" was "Illusion"—focus on pleasure, which was no doubt a dangerous form of euphoria [see Table 4].) But Baudrillard did not seem to see this as the panacea that Benjamin did. Rather, Baudrillard understood this ecstasy to be a loss of self, an almost Dionysian drunkenness (Latour, *Aramis*; *Modern Cult*), an embrace of technological oblivion. Inside the Apparatus, or machine, the abandonment of self to an informatic environment in which human consciousness as a demystified object (aesthetic or otherwise) was swept, was perhaps a new "Romantic" or "Transcendental" experience of a *sublime*, or of the aery Forms, intensified and sustained to a degree it became the uncontrolled and unbearable electric paralysis of sheer joy that Nietzsche, building on Fichte's subjective philosophy of science (his *Wissenschaftslehre*), searched for in his analysis of *style* (*Gay Science*; cf. Derrida, *Spurs*). The seizure of consciousness and the unrelenting mechanical grip was perhaps a technological replacement for the exquisite agony of the Annunciation, or the sudden permanent shock of the Rapture. Or not. In all these cases, the cosmic black boxes, apparatuses within the vast hidden micro and macro physics of the universe, were places where the mind, at last unburdened by its subjectivity as well as its physicality (but not impotency), could escape, leaving the material world and body behind. The machine became the genesis of beauty and spirit, the object of its own mimesis and thus its negation, along with the slower annihilation by time.

Time Is Not Kind

Time is not kind to material things.
Eventually, all things are ravaged.
Only spirit can survive and not be.

Time can't be seen, but is heard in the ring
of a phone call that says you are average.
Time is not kind to material things.

Time is not a dimension, but the zing
of a force that bends, crumples you with age.
Only a ghost can survive and not be.

Time carries you forward in its quickening spring;
without time you would be frozen in space.
But time's not kind to material things.

Can objects survive physicality?
What about all the human alphabets of rage?
Only spirit can survive nonbeing.

(You may ask questions; you may wonder why?
I will tell you we do not know the sage
for whom time is Open, forthcoming, sings.

Haggard, look me straight in the awful eye
and tell me we are not all savages.
Only a ghost can survive, not being.)

What remains after the Anthropocene?
We can only hazard what catastrophes gather.
Can only spirit survive nonbeing?
Time is not kind to material things.

B x 31

Remix

«Да! Вот правда! *Da! Vot Pravda*! *"Yes! Here is truth!* (Re)mix of body and media, art and technology, represented ideological revolution of technological art which Benjamin pined. Also represented *violent* fusion of flesh and machine envisioned by Futurists like Filippo Tommaso Marinetti; or *positive* union of humanity and apparatus envisioned by later futurists as Nicholas Negroponte; or technological media façade of that diminished rather than enhanced human relations (Debord; Turkle). In history of the West, re-mixing humanity and machine offered best possibility freeing φυχή—Platon's "psyche" or "soul," mind, spirit, or consciousness—from material embodiment, physical prison of body. Remixing reality also put end to mimetic curse of inaccurate reduplication, which feminists (and Platon, for different reasons) dreamed (e.g., Haraway; Grosz; cf. Irigaray).»

***

«Извините, пожалуйста [*Izvinite, pozhaluysta*, "Excuse me please"] For Haraway, for Grosz, point of techno-aesthetic revolution of body in arts political "liberation" not only gendered body but also "informatics of domination" (Haraway, *Posthuman*, 161–65; 170–72) by taking control of conditions and means of cultural and rhetorical production by rewriting new selves and changing poetic environment.»

> Identified with the rational mind, the literal subject *possessed* a body but was not usually represented as being a body. Only because the body is not identified with the self is it possible to claim for the liberal subject its notorious universality, a claim that depends on erasing markers of bodily differences, including sex, race, and ethnicity. (Hayles, *Posthuman* 4–5)

Perhaps the result of the solipsistic human mind and limited senses even in its new technological being, an oft-self-admitted limitation and controversial aspect of their work remained the apparent retention of gender as an "essentialism," a reduplication of a (de)sultry sex(ism), a mimesis of human desire and emotion, in the creation and extension of hot machines.

To a Computer at 3:00 am: A Lovesong

My dream
words in green
drifting from your darkened screen
face of your cryptonic being
i draw closer
i feel your smooth buttons
beneath my fingertips
i touch
you answer
softly in green
i play the keys of your memory
i read your mind
O my sweet machine
i strip you
of your software
i finger your I/O
push down into your hard
ware, the intricacies
of your soul
your mysteries
laid out before me
your tangles and turnings
your complex selfinvolvement
your logical irrationality
yes no yes no yes yes yes
your tiny circuitry
continually vibrating
in multiple orgasms
caressed by currents
that stop
and flow stop
and flow O my dream
my sweet machine
nothing
that draws me
holds me
here
my love
like you electric charms

***

> [W]e are all chimeras, theorized and fabricated hybrids of machines and organism; in short, we are cyborgs. Ths [*sic*] is our ontology; it gives us our politics. The cyborg is a condensed image of both imagination and material reality the two joined centres structuring any possibility of historical transformation. (Hayles, *Posthuman* 149)

Some feminist critiques of gender and culture pinned their hopes on cybernetics for a technological transition to posthuman liberation—a central tenet of the myth of technological progress held by many as a new basis of democracy generally, and for different reasons the myth of international access, affordability, and freedom of "use" (see Penrose and Katz, esp. Ch 3; Moses and Katz). Haraway's "A Cyborg Manifesto" in particular appeared to advocate escape from the constraints of chauvinistic thought through the appropriation of the historical, cultural, and ideological, and *material* moment: to technologically remake not only the *concept* of the female body, but the physical body itself. Like Irigaray, Butler, and Balsamo, "feminine cyborgists" were aware that images of the female body continued to be the products of male fantasy, perversely propagating in its previous pervasive forms the preoccupation with techniques of art, advertisement, and pornography. As Anne Balsamo argued, the technological creation of artificial intelligence in the robot, the (re)engineering of the corporeal body as cyborg, or the (re)embodiment of human consciousness in technology as android (Katz, Foreword; S. Thompson)—may have been just as gendered as its prior incarnations.

The Beautiful Machine

(who stole my heart and all my parts)

"He spoke. And drank rapidly a glass of water"
—e. e. cummings, "next to of course god america i" (31)

"All men desire a beautiful machine
to love as themselves—something
in bronze, perhaps, a strong bionic blonde
lying on her side, powerful tan thigh
gleaming in the sunlight, hot wet alloy
glistening in the grass, catching your eye,
her hard body pulsing electric desire,
her lights blinking her come on, her for-hire.
To simply jackup the swivel hips
and secure the leather straps, to insert it
in the lovebox that hums, waiting only for you,
to adjust the tension knobs and push the button,

the pelvis slowly rotating on its axle,
the chassis moving up and down, the gears
squeezing, grinding out raw love, a dear,
so chilly, so sore, so beautiful, a real
convenience, lightweight, portable, easy, efficient:
no attachments necessary, no maintenance required.
No? Then something in silver today?"

He turns. And wobbles, limps slowly away

Γx 30

Differently Abled

Some differently abled writers and scholars also interrogated the myth of technology in ability studies and bioengineering as well as medicine (e.g., Mairs; Weise; and McKenney who sought to disrupt "the Baconian project" that "naturalized" the body and so rendered it a docile object of science and technology; McKenney also sought a moral high ground outside the ideological domain of bioethics). Rematerializing the body in cybernetic apparatuses may have given birth in a posthuman age to new lifeforms free of capacity-bias as well as gender. Or those new lifeforms may have reified the psychological, social, cultural, economic, and political, and rhetoric-poetic modes of technological existence that feminists such as Judith Butler and others specifically struggled against and sought to overcome (see Conley). Haraway and Grosz too/had discussed their critical awareness of the epistemological contradictions associated with the techno-ontological position of life inside the machine.

A Computer File Named Dorothy

/For My Wife Alison/

i dated a file named Dorothy, created
worlds in her name; but needed more space,
new memories to save, new files to live.
(After all, although the universe expands
at astronomic rates, it's slowing down,
and there is only so much space inside machines.)

"Destroy Alison: Confirm," the computer responded.
But what if she should die? i thought, and asked
aloud; what if when i push this button
she should really disappear

from the disc of the earth, constantly rotated, read
in this dark machine drive of the universe?

What if this cold, dumb, personal computer
should read and wholly misunderstand, and take me
literally, as impersonal as itself, and her atoms
be scattered through magnetic fields, dispersed
along the wires, and she should vanish mid the glitch
and circuitry of stars, drive lights redshifting,

every trace (of her) erased
forever. "Destroy Alison: Confirm," it repeated,
blindly blinking. Destroy Alison? i needed
more space, new memories to save,
new files to live.— But oh i
could not confirm it could not confirm it . . .

Д x 29

> *Decline of Nation-State*
>
> [G]iven the by now unstoppable decline of the nation-state and the general corrosion of traditional political-juridical categories, the refugee is perhaps the only thinkable figure for the people of our time . . . [T]the status of the refugee has always been considered a temporary condition that ought to lead either to naturalization or to repatriation. (Agamben, *Means Without Ends* 15, 19)

***

Citing "the relation between organism and machine" as the longstanding "border wall" of the self," Haraway (149), like Grosz and others, still posited the epistemology of the machine as possibly providing a new ontology of the human being in the hope that the cyborg body might deconstruct and replace the gendering bequeathed in part by Platon and Aristotle. It *was* hoped that the machine as ontology might bypass not only nature and biology but the ideology of technology itself (or perhaps somehow embrace that too as a form of liberation and pleasure). Others worried that the forms or products of technology themselves might be value-ladened (see Winner; Balsamo; Sedgwick; Rakow). Technology may have reconfigured the body as machine—what Balsamo; Perpich, Seminar) called "techno-bodies." But these techno-bodies may not have produced the much anticipated and required revolution in human consciousness. In the posthuman era, technology and art became not mere mimetic or metonymic figures, or even simple representations and extensions of the human body, but also complex Lacanian sublimations of emotions—material and cybernetic entities, sentient a least within the apparatus of desire.

machine love

|i| love
{{You}} but
will have to <delete>
|it| Please [don't be
sad] |i| (Ma/chines are) am not
worth |it|.

***

Heidegger had predicted that *technē*, both art and technology, would become the predominant mode consciousness (cf. Stiegler; Katz and Rhodes). Benjamin's cinematic dream of politically productive art, the feminists' utopia of gender freedom, the Futurists' blood-soaked vision of "creative wars," the "cyberneticists" equation of floating cognition, the ethereal potential of disembodied data, were viewed either as humanistic fulfilments or distortions of Platon's philosophical dream of reaching intangible Forms. From these standpoints, various imitations were not only ironically realized in history, but aberrantly transformed, gone horribly wrong. In the early twentieth century, philosophies of "transcendental phenomenology" had begun exploring the relation between self and world (again). The work of Husserl, Merleau-Ponty and others—*Don't forget Mother Russia too!* (see Bycovsa)—explored in theoretical and experiential depth the psychological experience of human subjectivity and objectivity, exteriority and interiority, material body and physical reality and their relations as perceived by the senses and present in language. For it was upon such dualistic notions that concepts of authenticity (and thus mimesis) were inextricably grounded. Postmodernists such as Jean-Luc Nancy (*Corpus*), François Lyotard (*Libidinal*, esp. 1–42; "*Ephemeral Skin*"), and Jacques Derrida (*Touching*, esp. "Spacings" 20–35) tended to see the meaning of the body and the structure of body as emerging not only from language, but also from the spaces between. For Nancy, it was discourse and its intercises that defined physical bodies *as* text, and texts as physical bodies. (This was a Judaic position to bootl [Katz, "Letter as Essence"].) The "discourses" (rhetorics, poetics,) and their "intercises" were part of the bodies as well ("Corpus"). For these phenomenologists and postmodern philosophers, the body was perhaps neither "opened" or "closed"; rather the body as discourse and intercises were nonmimetic places—*copulas* of space—connectors in language, primarily the verb to be" (Nancy, *Corpus*; Latour, *Modes*). "[T]he human body seemed superfluous in its proper expanse, in the complexity and multiplicity of its organs, of its tissue and functions (Baudrillard, *Ecstasy* 18).

***

> There is no autonomous space in the political order of the nation-state for something like the pure human in itself. . . . A stable statute for the human in itself is inconceivable in the law of the nation-state. (Agamben, *Means without Ends* 19)

Satellite 1: City of Stars

night:
city
of stars.
buildings
raised in
light.

Sputnik
(not moon):
illuminates:

alien

***

A spectrum of genders and multiple body types came out of their rhetorical parlors and literary salons, their genres and genitalia, cozy corsets and concealed closets, the warm hollows and shallow shells (cf. Bachelard). "The body," Nancy said, "was *conceived* in darkness, and as darkness itself. It was conceived and shaped in Plato's cave, as the cave itself"; for Nancy "The body is the subject of shadow" ("Corpus" 67). Lyotard had decried the relegation of the figural—including writing/writer —to a lower status of being in Western philosophy at least since Platon ("Taking the Side"; *Discourse*). But it may not have been until cybernetics fused subjectivity and objectivity, mind and machine, that posthumanism could embrace a hybrid as/of its own. Ontologically and physically, according to Hayles, the human mind found itself situated in new housing—as disembodied information in reductive mechanisms. These mechanisms were not meant so much to mimic as to supplant and replace the organic functions and features of former bodies—not as selves, but as totalizing systems, a totalitarian of science within apparatuses.

> The contemporary pressure toward dematerialization understood as an epistemic shift toward pattern/randomness and away from presence/absence, affects human and textual bodies on two levels at once, as a change in the body (the material substrate) and as a change in the message (the codes of representation). The connectivity between these changes is, as they say in the computer industry, massively parallel and highly interdigitated. (Hayles, *Posthuman* 29)

Satellite 2: Kissing, Outer Space

helmets closing,
facemasks nosing
through space,
modules opening,
mouth pieces docking,
capturing, locking,
charged tongues
touching, connecting
in the coiled darkness:
message communicated,
given and received.

***

> The body could be defined as a technological entity whose randomness was ordered by the system without "meaningless" (i.e., irrelevance). As with past subjects of scientific experiments, body, mind, and consciousness as controlled variables could be disassembled, analyzed, quantified; but could they be reassembled, and "accurately" represented, again. Embodiment can be destroyed, but it cannot be replicated. (*Posthuman* 49)

Whether present or absent, sentient, or unconscious, this "reawakening" of the corpse didn't so much "open up" or "close off" the body and the mind as attempt to reestablish it as nonmimetic counters, e.g., mathematical cyphers, programmed codes, figures of speech, metaphors that on the way to the posthuman subject to "interdigitation" (Hayles). However, even the cyphers (like avatars) in the machine proved unpredictable, changeable, subject to breakdown, decay, and re-emergence on a quantum, biological, geological, or cosmic scale (see Heisenberg; Pynchon). However rapid or temporary or lugubrious, posthuman bodies were still in some sense "*constituted*" as specific if moving physical localities and proximate bases of consciousness, from which they sometimes had to be extricated; and still felt pain.

Satellite 3: The Jaws of Life

they fell asleep in a pool of thought
the dream was still wet on their lips
the capsule suffered a major meltdown:
between screaming sirens a double bubble
repeatedly asserted its bright red tongue:—

it took three hours with the jaws of life
to extract their bodies from the lunar car

E x 28

Telepresence

Initially they had to settle for remote "telepresence" (various forms of control and surveillance [Ridolfo and Hart-Davidson; Gaines]), robotic surrogates (Markoff, "Robotic"), and supernatural substitutes (Rice). Nancy also said: "A *corpus* could only happen . . . by gaining access to bodies that are impenetrable, as defined precisely by physics. If this is the case, then a corpus is produced as a combination of shocks, as a Brownian [*sic*] agitation of molecular leaps and bounds" ("Corpus" 57). In post-cybernetics, the body was probed by virtual anatomy as electron bioengineering at the subatomic, atomic, genetic, and molecular levels. The result was a different kind of (non)mimesis, an *electronic anorexia* of body and style that mathematically "produced" (in Benjamin's technological sense of the term) isolated physical functions. These where "Organs without Bodies" (*OwB*), which like (*BwO*) *Bodies without Organs* (Deleuze and Guattari), could be "manufactured" (e.g., printed) and further digitized and streamed. As a controlled experiment it was hoped that mind if not consciousness itself could be scrambled and teleported immutable anywhere it might be needed in the apparatus.

GOING SUBATOMIC

(at the Gym   trying to lose weight)

shot into a trac   curves without end
i have force   don't know what i am

some particles   are attractive
attract other particles   to themselves

some particles   are solipsistic
self-contained   repelling atoms

arms and legs   blur bend
time dis   appears

blue trace   streaming
space wavers   i walk

shot slowly   accelerated round
the slowest particle   i go fast

white creases   cloud crash
ceiling stretch   fold infinity

particles collapse   speak many languages
Greek   muon gluon

Chinese   not too far behind them
left   right-handed

they talk equations   structures
unpredictable   all the same

emit strange noises   from their ears
snatches of cosmic   static in their heads

i am just a literary   quark
they pass as if   i stand still

knock against   scatter light
jostle bump   bounce split shatter

some get in my way   i say
"thank you"   let them pass

some switch tracks   becoming
faster lighter   someone else

some fly in the wrong direction
defying laws reversing time

others bend around me disappear
like i am not there here

i have no need to converse
i am not the same when i look for love

***

The "natural" physical environment, and human and nonhuman behavior within it, were reconceived according to economic and technological rationally (cf. Simon; Miller, "Rhetoric of Decision"; Habermas, "Ideology," "Religion"; Morton). Referencing Benjamin, Lev Manovich made similar points about the ecology of technology, adding that the new open architecture and nonhierarchical culture were embodied at all levels in the structures of computers themselves, from programming codes to uniform interfaces. The human body too, in its singularity, became nonhierarchical data packets in networks of cybernetic objects within apparatuses. If there was a body, it was a vestige—or a revenant at best—and the mind now but a replicant (cf. Deleuze and Guattari 150–51). Reconceiving body, audience, and environment as a single ecology had a profound leveling effect, much greater than the weakening of class structures brought about by the spread of literacy; the scientific revolution; technological invention; the industrial reinvention; as well as propaganda and conspiracies; global terrorism; and environmental warfare (cf. Bennett's *Vibrant Matter: Political Ecology*; Rice; Ridolfo and Hart-Davidson; Da Costa, etc.). Posthuman forms of rhetoric and poetry as new media eviscerated boundaries and increasingly incorporated and subsumed prior technologies—including consciousness as communication (Zylinska and Kember, *Life After*). The blurring of mind and media perhaps began in the mid-twentieth century (see McLuhan, *Gutenberg*; Kittler; Lohr, "Now Playing"; Moses and Katz; Katz and Rhodes). The effect was a kind of Benjaminian Marxism eventually leading to a Baudrillardian loss of self to *surrounding world as "art."* (Even the twentieth century tennis player Andre Agassi began his autobiography: "my body no longer feels like my body . . . Upon opening my eyes, I am a stranger to myself" [3]. As a carefully cultivated, and commercialized image for media dissemination—as well as superior tennis acumen and talent—Agassi became *l'objet d'art*—became *transparent*, even to himself. "Transparency," the broadcasting of an invented self as a form of reproducible art, had become "communication for communication's sake'" on all media platforms and channels (Eco, *Beauty*; see Han, *Transparency*; Bolter; Katz, "Ethics").

Transparenzgesellschaft

Fluorescent lighting
it's your own body
you're surveilling

you can see
where combatees
will hunker down

in the face of your skin
before they appear
in soft light

the transparency
of the mirror
of media

[Ш]

Cybernetic Subjectivities

Ё x 27

Subjective Devices

«Товáрищ [*Tovarisch*—friend, "comrade"]. The apparatuses create cybernetic devices also create subjectivities. Twentieth century media pick up ideals of beauty from art (Eco, *Beauty* 425). Benjamin hoped that film "screens" as painting had mass dimensions and worker appeal. Also, "[W]orld of business attained an undeniable capacity to take its own images and to saturate people's perception with them" (Eco, *Beauty* 377). For Guy Debord, life *was* media event. [T]he society of the spectacle" was in fact an "integrated spectacle" (*Spectacle* 12) "The whole life of those societies in which modern conditions of production prevail presents itself as an immense accumulation of *spectacles.* All that once was directly lived has become mere presentation (*Spectacle* 12; see Han, *Burnout*). For Debord, media not only object for consumption, but means of construction—"both the outcome and the goal of dominant mode of production" (*Spectacle* 13). "[P]rinciple of commodity fetishism, the domination of society by things whose qualities are at the same time perceptible and imperceptible by the senses" (*Spectacle* 26). (I also like to say this is especially true in capitalism, not communism!) Like Baudrillard's "ecstatic" unconscious information objects, for Debord "principle is absolutely fulfilled in the spectacle, where the perceptible world is replaced by a set of images that are superior to that world yet at the same time impose themselves as *eminently* perceptible" (*Spectacle* 26; Han). Benjamin ("Technological Reproducibility") saw media technology as liberation of masses through possible technological realization and personal control of individual alienated life—not imitation or reflection but manufacture! Like always, issue was ownership of the means of production—especially when self is product! Debord saw media technology—life/spaces created and projected and willingly inhabited—as problem. For Debord, not technologically but *globally*, media event become existence as form of "spectacular power"—"concentrated" (e.g., US), and "diffused" (e.g., Soviet Union) (Debord, *Comments* 8; cf. Benjamin, "Technical Reproducibility" 33, 44n9). Спасибо [*Spasibo*—"Thank you."]»

Apocalypse, Then?

It's not what we'd consider war: no terrorist
need respond to our abrupt alert.
It's just a temporary inconvenience.
(It may be quick; we really can't say.)
Position an enormous sheet of plastic
against the sky to protect us like a shield;
use all the duct tape you can find to seal
the crevices and cracks of space and time—
they'll try to come through all the doors and windows
of the universe. Have cell phones charged and ready.

It'll only be a mild discomfort,
short-lived, we are assured by those who make
decisions, unleashing the very stuff of life
that no medical procedure can
contain once the missiles make their descent.
We'll watch in Dolby sound and HD color—
our screens surround us in our living rooms.
A slight annoyance, yes, to bring the world
to its knees, not in victory
but prayer, as life prepares to meet its end.

The pulsing drumbeat of the media
will finally cease, the artificial light
go out. We won't lose anything but history.
It will be as if we've never been.
Who will be left to write the final story

of the human race except a few
nuclear alcoholics, homeless,
stray and stunned and glowing stragglers
who won't remember what has happened, where
they are, or who they might have been: their name?

They'll assemble useless councils in the cities'
burnt out depth charge fuselage ash cans
amid the rubble falling building alleys
still toasty from the heat of bombardment.
They will never freeze, or have to beg
since there will not be anyone
to beg from, and not anything to give
anyone who might be left. We give
our lives so gladly for such courageous
ignoble causes, counting the heroes clotted

there. Earth will spiral into history
without us, the sun explode its big bomb,
the universe expand a billion years.
Better not to have to face such future;
better to burn up in the flames of fighting
than slowly freeze on plains of ice, gathered
undisturbed in a peaceful age.
Oh yes, war will finally bring us peace,
without us to bomb the silence of the dead

Ж x 26

Electronic Encephalitis

"[E]ectronic encephalization, this miniaturization of circuits and of energy, this transistorization of the environment condemn to futility, to obsolescence and almost to obscenity, all that which once constituted the stage of our lives" (Baudrillard, *Ecstasy* 17). Quantification and diminishment of physical existence meant more than mathematical fantasy or fanciful terror (see J. Rosen 44). The reduction of posthuman in various biopolitical and mechanical processes of being (Foucault, *Biopolitics*) functioned as "homeostatic" devices in cybernetic bodies that were always emergent yet mutable, temporary yet static, transient yet constituted, portable yet potent (see Hayles, *Posthuman* 98). "The era of miniaturization, of remote control, and of a micro processing of time, bodies, and pleasure had come," Baudrillard averred; "[t]here is no longer an ideal principle of these things on a human scale. All that remains are miniaturized, concentrated and immediately available effects" (*Ecstasy* 18). Hayles (98) argued that cybernetics reduced the embodied liberal human subject to abstract formulae, to numerical data, to genetic codes (cf. Baudrillard 15). Once the techniques were developed, genes were easily editable and highly malleable. Genetic codes by nature are rhetorical: the first named "gene" began life as a figure of speech (Shea)—a miniature *material* rhetoric (Condit).

The Humanistic Mechanism of the Genome

In the beginning were the Hebrew letters.
And through linguistic permutations G/d
formed the meta-fabric of space-time,
and from their shape and size, their sound, position, order
the moral universe was created,
the fiery Kabbalah through which we breathe and move

upright now, through Talmud, and the scribble
around the edges, the start of legal footnotes,
of precedent and evidence, of hyper-
links reflecting evolutions, layers
of commentary swirling around the texts
like skin, an ethical body, atoms

orbiting the periodic table
above a random trace of particles on
the back of a t-shirt the scientists
are wearing so that someone following
behind could study them as they walk
their atomic numbers in the park.

Coded sequences of alphabet
now spelled out by a digital shotgun—
a genetic chart of eternity,
tribes of proteins wandering over
vast "deserts" between nucleic regions
of "islands" and "oases" mapped,

a detailed replication of unknowns,
40% "hypotheticals"—
you gave me clones of the science journal

where with his large, extended hand that held
the pen, the humble chemist inscribed his name,
just three black letters on the newly published

Book of Life:

З x 25

Technical Rationality

«Извините меня еще раз [*izvinite menya yeshche raz*– "excuse me again"]. In *Comments*, Debord suggest that science not only product of technical rationality, but also slave to economic production. What produced and maintained for Debord was Spectacle. More than mimesis, overwhelming the physical, these *images of knowledge* were fabricated, and completely replaced and remade world (cf. Horkheimer; Adorno). In Middle Age, light not only communication medium but material object and art form (Eco, *Beauty*; T. Levin, "The Eye"; Benjamin; Bazerman, *Languages*). In posthumanistic society, "imaging of the body" is medium *and* the art form, completely mimetic, thus nonmimetic, an imitation only of itself. "Images detached from every aspect of life merge into a common stream, and the former unity of life is lost forever," said Debord, "[a]pprehended in a *partial* way, reality unfolds in a new generality as a pseudo-world apart, solely as an object of contemplation" (*Spectacle* 12).»

Posthumanistic

cybernetic
suffering

erased
yet perhaps

still visible
in this

{ }

И x 24

Infinite Suffering

If Hegel's "infinite suffering" (Eco, *Beauty* 135) was replaced by a new "mythology of reason" (Eco, *Beauty* 318), starting in eighteenth century Enlightenment according to Horkheimer, in the twentieth and twenty-first centuries that mythology was in a sense always postmodern (see Latour, *Never Been Modern*), took on post-cybernetic, posthuman form. Lyotard (*Postmodern*), writing on the relationship between German Idealism and modern science, seemed to agree. In a purposive-rational society (Habermas, "Ideology"), the technology of cybernetics supplemented if not replaced not only aesthetics, but religion as well (cf. Habermas, *Awareness of What is Missing*). Art was "a negative theology . . . that rejected not only any social class or economic function but any definition in terms of a representational content" (Benjamin, "Technological Reproducibility" 24). The concept of G/d already had been undercut by Newtonian and modern science (e.g., Gillispie; cf. Hawking, esp. 172–75). In deconstruction, G/d, the Final Signified, had been shaken out of language as a self-referential mystical system; G/d, is absent, nowhere to be found. (e.g., Derrida, *Acts*; Sherwood and Hart; Katz, "Hebrew Bible"; Metzger and Katz). Whether formed in opposition to traditional faith, recreated in the image of an apparatus, or a projection of the Spectacle, G/d, especially in the US as well as in Islamic states, returned in technology with a vengeance. But G/d had undergone some profound changes in the modern, postmodern, cybernetic, and posthumanistic ages. G/d of the known universe, if a bit old-fashioned, is angry and error-prone, but still a driven, productive, and powerful god.

In the Beginning

(To justify G/d's ways to the 21st century)

#In the beginning was the computer. And G/d said:

:Let there be light!
#You have not signed on yet.
:G/d.
#Enter user password.
:Omniscient.
#Password Incorrect. Try again!
:Omnipotent.
#Password Incorrect. Try again!
:Technocrat.
#And G/d signed on at 12:01 a.m., Sunday, March 1.
:Let there be light!
#Unrecognizable command. Try again!
:Create light.
#Done.
:Run heaven and earth.

#And G/d created Day and Night. And G/d saw there were 0 errors.

#And G/d signed off at 12:02 a.m., Sunday, March 1.
#Approx. funds remaining: $92.50.

#And G/d signed on at 12:00 a.m., Monday, March 2.
:Let there be firmament in the midst of the water and
#Unrecognizable command! Try again!
:Create firmament.
#Done.
:Run firmament.

#And G/d divided the waters. And G/d saw there were 0 errors.
#And G/d signed off at 12:01 a.m., Monday, March 2.
#Approx. funds remaining: $84.60.

#And G/d signed on at 12:00 a.m., Tuesday, March 3.
:Let the waters under heaven be gathered together unto one place and let the dry land appear and
#Too many characters in string specification! Try again.
:Create dryland.
#Done!
:Run dryland.
#And G/d created Earth and Seas. And G/d saw there were 0 errors.
#And G/d signed off at 12:01 a.m., Tuesday, March 3.
#Approx. funds remaining: $65.00.

#And G/d signed on at 12:00 a.m., Wednesday, March 4.
:Create lights in the firmament to divide the day from the night.
#Unspecified type. Try again!
:Create sunmoonstars.

#And G/d created Sun, Moon, Stars. And G/d saw there were 0 errors.
#And G/d signed off at 12:01 a.m., Wednesday, March 4.
#Approx. funds remaining: $54:00.
#And G/d signed on at 12:00 a.m., Thursday, March 5.
:Create fish.
#Done.
:Create fowl.
#Done.
:Run fish'nfowl.

#And G/d created the great sea monsters and every living creature
that creepeth wherewith the waters swarmed after its kind and
every winged fowl after its kind. 0 errors.

#And G/d signed off at 12:01 a.m., Thursday, March 5.
#Approx. funds remaining: $45:00.

#And G/d signed on at 12:00 a.m., Friday, March 6.
:Create cattle.
#Done.
:Create creepy things.
#Done.
:Now let us make man in our image.
#Unspecified type! Try again.
:Create man.
#Done.
:Be fruitful and multiply and replenish the earth and subdue it
and have dominion over the fish of the sea and over of the fowl
of the air and over every living thing that creepeth upon the earth and

#Too many command operands! Try again.
:Run multiplication.

#Execution terminated. 6 errors.

:Insert breath.
#O.K.
:Run multiplication.

#Execution terminated. 5 errors.

:Move man to Garden of Eden.
#File Garden of Eden does not exist.
:Create Gdn_eDN.
#Done.
:Move man to Gdn_eDN.
#O.K.
:Run multiplication.

#Execution terminated. 4 errors.

:Copy woman from man.
#O.K.
:Run multiplication.

#Execution terminated. 3 errors.

:Insert woman into man.
#Illegal parameters. Try again!
:Insert man into woman.
#O.K.
:Run multiplication.

#Execution terminated. 2 errors.

:Create desire.
#Done.
:Run multiplication.

#And G/d saw man'nwoman being fruitful and multiplying in the Gdn_eDN.
#Warning: No time limit on this run. 1 errors.

:Create freewill.
#Done.
:Run freewill.
#And G/d saw man'nwoman being fruitful and multiplying in the Gdn_eDN.
#Warning: No time limit on this run. 1 errors.

:Undo desire.
#Desire cannot be undone once freewill is created.
:Destroy freewill.
#Freewill is an inaccessible file and cannot be destroyed.
#Enter replacement, cancel, or ask for help.
:Help!
#Desire cannot be undone once freewill is created.
#Freewill is an inaccessible file and cannot be destroyed.
#Enter replacement, cancel, or ask for help.
:Create Treeofknowledge.

#And G/d saw man'nwoman being fruitful and multiplying in the Gdn_eDN.
#Warning: No time limit on this run. 1 errors.

:Create good'nevil.
#Done.
:Activate evil.

#And G/d saw he had created shame.
#Warning: System error in sector E95. Man'nwoman not in Gdn_eDN.
#1 errors.

:Scan Gdn_eDN. for man'nwoman.
#Man'nwoman cannot be located. Try again!
:Search Gdn_eDN. for man'nwoman.
#Search failed.
:Delete shame.
#Shame cannot be deleted once evil has been activated.
:Destroy freewill.
#Freewill an inaccessible file and cannot be destroyed.
:Stop!
#Unrecognizable command. Try again.
:Break
:Break
:   B   r   e   a   k

#ATTENTION ALL USERS ATTENTION ALL USERS: COMPUTER GOING DOWN FOR
REGULAR DAY OF MAINTENANCE AND REST IN FIVE MINUTES. PLEASE SIGN OFF.

:Create new world.
#You have exceeded your allotted file space. You must destroy
old files before new ones can be created.
:Destroy earth.
#Destroy earth. Please confirm.
:Destroy earth confirmed.

#COMPUTER DOWN. COMPUTER DOWN. SERVICES WILL RESUME ON SUNDAY MARCH 8 AT 6:00 A.M. YOU MUST SIGN OFF NOW!

#And G/d signed off at 11:59 p.m., Friday, March 6.
#And G/d had zero funds remaining.

Й x 23

Objects without Systems

> Everything began with objects, yet there is no longer a system of objects. The critique of objects was based on signs saturated with meaning, along with their phantasies and unconscious logic as well as their prestigious differential logic. Behind this duel logic lies the anthropological dream: the dream of the object as existing beyond and above exchange and use, above and beyond equivalence . . . (Baudrillard, *Ecstasy* 11; cf. Baudrillard, *System of Objects*)

K x 22

A New God

By the twenty-first century, G/d had become a "global superintelligence known as the cloud" (Wolf 41), "the keepers of the cloud today [were] sometimes less forgiving than their all-powerful divine predecessor" (J. Rosen 44). A new and near-religious experience of computers by scientists, engineers, and captains of industry had led to the acceptance and absorption of a "Romantic conception of technology" as "a mode of consciousness" as well as a pastoral way of life (e.g., Florman; Kidder; Katz, "Narration"; L. Marx; cf. Heidegger, *Question*; Miller, "Technology"; Stiegler). If artificial ornamentation and sacred jewels were the "apps" of heavenly beauty and power in the Middle Ages, communication devices (worn internally as well as externally) were the religious ornaments of a posthuman society. These technological amulets were marks not only of socio-economic status and success, but also of "technological identity/superiority." Much as Christian churches were built on old pagan temples in ancient Greece and Rome, and throughout the Western world—one civilization of religious values repressing another (see Derrida, *Gift*). Christianity in a purposive-rational society was *not* dispensed with but simply absorbed by the new technological regime in a "mimetic spectacle" of measurement and calculation (Lohr, "Personal Data"; Merkin; Wolf, G). Service providers led prayers; the "technological sublime" was the daily bread.

Church of the Computer

(Voorhees Computer Center, Rensselaer Polytechnic Institute)

under stained glass windows—
phosphorescent manuscripts,
reflections on a screen of faces.

Tech-monks in-habit-ing cubical spaces
fingers clicking in quiet supplication:
coded machine breath surrounds them

G/d, transformed, never falters:
beneath the altar, omniscient and
unseen, controls the queue, and writes
the Book of Life. The priests now place

the printouts on the trays. I throw
my printout back, a fish too small.
"Apologize. Confess. Genuflect,
and take your printout like wafer."

Л x 21

Spheres

«Да. Holidays products like Christmas of media and commerce. Blurring and blending what left of difference between private and public sphere, work and leisure, capitalism eliminate distinction between them (J. Rosen; Moses and Katz). Capitalism also appropriate historical and cyclical time to create consumable pseudo-rituals and products. Spectacle "presents its time to itself as essentially made up of many frequently recurring festivities, is actually an epoch without festival" (*Spectacle* 113).»

> [T]he proliferation of prefabricated . . . "pseudo-events". . . flows from the simple fact that, in face of the massive realities of present-day social existence, individuals do not actually experience events . . . Because history itself is the specter haunting modern society, pseudo-history has to be fabricated at every level of consumption of life. (Debord, *Spectacle* 141; Han)

Pseudo-Event

Earth lies
in the blue
flicker of a

drifting through
black wilderness
snow rising

pale static
electric stars
gray mosaic

stretching across
phosphorous
screens, ghosts

swarming dark–
ness vanish–
'ng, unclear

i am deep
in electronic
slumber

and now i must
receive the
sleepy news:

cities strung out
on lights, hanging
in a dream

***

Platon may have argued that humans never experienced "Truth," only the palest of imitations of it. But in his time, Debord said that reality had been replaced by publicity, media events extending the decentralizing power of production to the "illusion" of community (*Spectacle* 113; see Moskow and Katz; Orenstein; Stone; Wortham; Xu; cf. Antoon; Brantely) . . . "The pseudo-events that vie for attention in the spectacle's dramatization have not been lived by those who are informed about them"; rather, the events are spectacle's false memory of the unmemorable" (*Spectacle* 114; Han, *Scent*). Further, as Debord noted, these media "imperatives pursue the isolated individual right into the *family cell*, where the generalized use of receivers of the spectacle's message ensures that his isolation is filled with the dominant images" (*Spectacle* 122).

i Like my Robot

(Platonic Sonnet #1)
For Nathan Riggs

i like my robot. It is
a member of my family,

yet has an ethos all its own.
It speaks to use in the openness
of its parts, in the honesty of its loose
assemblage. It is rhetorically
transparent and available:
a collection of parts and objects
hanging and working together
like us, almost human in its
happenstance, its e-mergence,
its (dis)semblance of the way
it exists and moves through
the world. i love this robot

M x 20

Fable of the Body

"Where has the body of the fable gone? The body of metamorphosis, the one of a pure chain of appearances, of a timeless and sexless fluidity of forms, the ceremonial body brought to life by mythology?" (Baudrillard, *Ecstasy* 45; see Brantely). «As Marx, Lenin, Stalin predict, whole issue "boundaries" become more personal, biological, technological, ecological—complex (Foucault, *Biopolitics*).»

i Like my Robot

(Platonic Sonnet #2)
For Nathan Riggs

i like my robot. I see
what it sees; i know what
it knows. i like its mind,
the way it works, cleans.
i get what it might want.
i comprehend the synthetic
creativity, the technical skill
and simplicity combined in it,
emerging in every connection
and clean encounter, every
bolt and wrapped wire.
It is a relative of mine.
i recognize the being
behind this robot. It's me.

H x 19

Telematics

> [P]rivate telematics [has] the capacity to regulate everything by remote control . . . including the work process, within the prospects of telematic work performed at home, as well as consumption, play, social relations, leisure. One could conceive of simulating leisure or vacation situations. (*Ecstasy* 15; 16–17)

Z-Mail

even while you sleep
never out of touch

messages slowly slipping in
through the sides of your head

like a dream of loose stars
softly slipping down a dark screen

consciousness, meaning
slowly drifting toward you

a continuous soft rain
becoming your waking, day

over all your eyes
at picnics or on the beach

never out of touch
even while you sleep

O x 18

Illusion of Community

The illusion of community was extended right into what Debord called "vacation sites," into private lives, and even into the most intimate acts, including dating and sex, for which the computer eventually became essential (e.g., see Grosz on "Intensities and Flows" 160–83; Benthien on "teletactility," 221–34). Communication technologies created a simulacrum of relaxation and holiday, time and sensual pleasure, while ensuring continued economic productivity and progress. In the Spectacle, emotions, not work, tended to be the subject of the fiction, happiness the illusive object of production (Schuessler; Brustein; Lohr, "Now Playing"). Access to the Spectacle was guaranteed for a limited time only, and under special warranties and specific conditions.

> The social image of consumption of time is for its part exclusively dominated by leisure time and vacations—moments portrayed, like all spectacular commodities, *at a distance*, and as desirable by definition. This particular commodity is explicitly presented as a moment of authentic life whose cyclical return we are supposed to look forward to . . . And what has been passed off as authentic life turns out to be merely a life more authentically spectacular. (*Spectacle* 112)

Being (Twice—Again)

(Zuhandenheit (oder Vorhandenheit)

We
are the ephemeral ones, we
the expendable ones.
the natural ones. We
stand in reserve, we
are at hand, ready to serve, we
are the useful ones, we
are defined by usefulness

And WE
are the robots, WE
are the permanent ones. WE
stand in the Opening
of our own Destiny, WE
shine in our own Being, WE
are beyond material things; WE
define our own presence in it

Π x 17

Dialectic Eye

In the Transcendental "I" of Fichte's subjective science, or the dialectical "World Spirit" of Hegel's objective history that Debord discussed, the Spectacle was not simply a distortion of empirical (visual) reality or a product of image technology, but a *weltanschauung* that has been actualized, translated into the material realm—a world view transformed into an objective force" (*Spectacle* 13). Perhaps growing out of the Romantic ideals of "Beauty" in the nineteenth century, and maybe attuned to the *Ur*-genre of poetry as the "new mythology" of world history (Schlegel), or "the genius of nature" (Schiller), or a result of "the ecstasy of communication" (Baudrillard), the Spectacle in the twentieth century became the "mystical self-abandonment to the transcendent spirit of commodity" (Debord, *Spectacle* 44).

Post-Consciousness

framed
(staring)

disgorge
(hearing)

tags
(speaking)

teleological
fragments

nobody remembers
same thing

[A]

Only Surface

P x 16

> *Immanency*
>
> There is no longer any transcendence or depth, but only the immanent surface of operations unfolding, the smooth and functional surface of communication . . . [T]he rest appears only as some vast useless body, which has been both abandoned and condemned—just as Bakhtin demonstrates the grotesque was when the closed body was opened. The real itself appears as a large, futile, body. (Baudrillard, *Ecstasy* 12, 18)

Information

Voices
shooting through the night
messages exchanged
in a binary universe
yesno zeroone darklight

our deeds will be measured
by amplitude and frequency
we need redundancy, desire duration
the phosphorescence of touch
a residue of presence

shooting through this night
across a field of white
noise
suffering

degradation decay
leaving but a momentary trace
an uncertain pattern
of our short indeterminate lives
here on this entropic snow

C x 15

Screens

—"[T]he surrounding universe and our very bodies are becoming monitoring screens" (Baudrillard, *Ecstasy* 12; cf. Burke, "Terministic").

> —"[T]he scene and the mirror have given way to a screen and a network." (Baudrillard, *Ecstasy* 12; cf. Abrams; Lyotard, *Postmodern*)

> —"The themes of decision, of fate, of action, preeminent in *Sein und Zeit*, are reworked, scattered like screens, screen memories, in light of the "epochality" of Being." –Lyotard, *Heidegger* (61; cf. Burke, "Terministic")

> —In that mediascape, bodies became "terminals of multiple networks." (Baudrillard, *Ecstasy* 16)

gHOSTS OF TECHNOLOGY

Drifting amid the massive
machinery of buildings
whirring of wind
ghosts of technology

the hum and charge
of the air
enclose our bodies
like circuitry walls

we have access
to online terminals
but the lines don't go
where we want to go

we are become silence
trapped in electronic spaces . . .

T x 14

Spectacles

—"The Spectacle is heir to the weakness of the project of Western philosophy, which was an attempt to understand activity by means of the categories of vision." (Debord, *Spectacle* 17; Derrida, *Margins*)

> —"The mimetic tradition is a highly spatial, visual one." (Katz, *Epistemic*; "Letters")
>
> —"[S]imulacra have passed from . . . the dialectic of alienation to the giddiness of transparency." (Baudrillard, *Ecstasy* 79)
>
> —"[E]verything is exposed to transparency; that's why there is no more transcendence." (Baudrillard, *Ecstasy* 54)
>
> —«In posthuman age, no imitation or reflection, only interfaces. Nothing to reflect except screens; nothing to imitate except act of non-imitation. The sublime has passed into the subliminal. До свидания (*Do svidaniya*—"goodbye")»
>
> —"Surface and appearance, that is the space of seduction." (Baudrillard, *Ecstasy* 62)
>
> —"Proximity becomes banal reproduction of the body—supposedly singular"—through millions of copies. (This, too, is

> why "the body" has become the most insipid, the flattest, finally the most "disconnected" of themes and terms—in an irreversible coma.") (Nancy, "Corpus" 91)
>
> —"Ecstasy is all functions abolished into one dimension, the dimension of communication" (Baudrillard, *Ecstasy* 23–24)
>
> —"The instantaneousness of communication miniaturizes our exchanges to a series of instants." (Baudrillard, *Ecstasy 19*; cf. Virilio, *Information Bomb*)

Staying (in Touch)

Sun mornings over voicemail messages
incomplete, left earlier as mist in
phone lines tele-holding bracing the sky,
and satellites, stationary, refuse
to be frozen in space and time, spin
a little faster, echoes warming up
words relayed, bouncing off the earth;—

back towards me, slowly thawing the orbit,
atoms slowing down just long enough
to skip back into body—slip back into
memory and consciousness, to cohere
long enough to catch a glimpse of greeting,
material worlds through which i hurtle, emerge;
then lose myself again in streams of data;—

or emailed, a virtual embodiment
of words arranged on passing screens that we
subvert with feeling, thought, allowing them
to inquire for us about each other's welfare,
making absence present for just a moment,
making words touch the distances between us,
the terrain through which we have already traveled;—

or trace of cells that call us out between
wavering mountains and valleys of sine waves, cars
(gamma, x-rays, micro, radio, sound)
on their way to local objects, work,
invisible traffic that separates and joins us,

becomes a moment together, substantial as stones
reaching up through roots and trunks and branches;—

toward the leaves, toward the visible spectrum
of solid light we wish we could become

Y x 13

Cybernetic Peripetei

—"In this cybernetic peripeteia of the body, passions have disappeared. Or rather, they have been materialized." (Baudrillard, *Ecstasy* 53)

> This body retreats into its own depth—to the depth of Sense—just as sense withdraws all the way to its mortal depth. This body forms very precisely what astrophysicists call a *black hole* . . . an absence of matter, (and an "end of time," the inverse of a "big bang," a dimension of the world's cessation within the world itself) . . . the body is the end of the signifier, the absolute *crasis* of the sign . . . a total absence of exteriority, a nonextension concentrated in itself, not something impenetrable, but rather an excess. (Nancy, "Corpus" 75)

the entropy that was love
between our vast cold bodies: universe.
we drift toward "the other" in the darkness,
begin to pull together, becoming warm,
thermodynamic blankets and the inertia of material

transformed into motion, heat the engines—
initial friction, then colliding, careening
off the other shooting out in darkness,
inertia overcome now working against us,

potential turned kinetic, and useless heat—
inevitable loss, uniformity
sliding off us into the expanding
universe that begins to grow again, expand

between us, that again begin to run down.
We wait for the last big bang to come—

***

> And this ecstasy is obscene . . . Obscenity is not confined to sexuality, because today there is a pornography of information and communication, a pornography of circuits and networks, of functions and objects in their legibility, availability, regulation, forced signification, capacity to perform, connection polyvalence, their free expression . . . [sic]. (Baudrillard, *Ecstasy* 22)

Superstring: A New Physics of Love

We're all tangled up in balls of matter,
universe neither particle nor wave, but a tatter
of superstring, winding and unwinding, weaving
all time and space, becoming and seeming,
touching and joining all color and flavor,
entwining discrete charm, strange behavior,
two points, evenlyhanded, ranging
into a manydimensional cosmos that curls

upon itself, strands swept into worlds
folding over others, constantly changing.
They spin out this sheet of the universe, tie,
untie organic knots of sentient *I*'s.
S/he is one of many shapes that gather.
Love's a quantum force that coalesces,
shatters

Φ x 12

In Between Bodies

> The between-bodies reserves nothing, nothing but the extension that *is* the *res* itself, the reality through which it happens that bodies are exposed to each other. The between-bodies is their images' taking-place. The images are not likenesses, still less phantoms or fantasms. It is how bodies are offered to one another, it's being born in the world . . . A body is an image offered to other bodies, a whole corpus of images stretched from body to body . . . . (Nancy, "Corpus" 121)

Divorce in the Cosmos: A Complaint

Dawn obscures the extremities of space;
skies now gather softly distant lights.
Blue suns become opaque and bright
and mask the cold dark matter, love,
until we separate, start counting down
the time, and so alone, again, forever,
you lift off into warming azure,
burn the golden haze of all our dawns.

But in that sheer stretch of empty space
folded, traveled at the speed of light,
your instruments will measure, you remember
all the weeks and months and years of flight,
see through stellar objects, moons and stars,
whole galaxies like thin white veils, pinned,
shimmering in darkness, that only half-
conceal the absent face of oblivion.

You've wandered out our days among the stars,
and once again you will be lost in that
quickened ignition of heat and light through which
you step gently, for refuge, to escape,
and this time won't come back until the suns
begin to fade, until the universe
collapse; come back this time with all of time
and space, come back this time to stay the night

X x 11

Membranes

Possibly starting with the desire for eternal youth, the membrane and structure of the physical body had been continually reconceptualized and rewritten by the "rhetorics and poetics" of their time. In ancient Greece, Aristotle apparently believed that the physics of movement was directly related and responsible for deformity (*Generation* 7677b29–30). Contra the twentieth-century Kenneth Burke, for whom causality and thus machine lacked the dramatic *motive* that helped explain human behavior (*Rhetoric*). Denis Diderot in the eighteenth-century believed that beauty was the result of "causation" and could be related to and found in mechanism, including in patterns as "networking." The fascination with and attraction to "the beautiful machine" was never to abate in human history (Eco, *Beauty* 381). (Likewise, the notion of "networks of beauty," found in Diderot, could be understood to precede future notions of the wired cybernetic body, the chaos theory-driven posthuman body, the object-oriented body [Harman; Levi, et al.], the digital-media body [Zylinska; Zylinska and Kember], even the ecologically self-patterned post-Anthropocene body [Morton].)

Cultural Derailment

old lady skin
bumping the furniture
of her body
teaching us
to deal with defeat
a lady
of professional confusion
a relaxed beauty

***

Gilman admitted that even with improvements in surgical techniques and the technology of cosmetology persisted. So too the persistence of a neo-Platonic notions of "essence" and therefore accusations of falsehood, flattery, falsies, fakery, mimicry, and the social climbing that ensued. These physical and philosophical scars were constant reminders of the *physical* "origins" ("*the aura*" [Benjamin; Han, *Ritual*]) of any particular (and thus "singular" [rather than reproducible]) body, especially in a digital/posthuman age in which personal data was permanently retained and used by an unforgiving global community (J. Rosen), and technology "put on," "worn" (see Pedersen). As in cosmetic and prosthetic surgery, in cybernetic and posthuman surgery, the act of cutting, the belief in "stripping" [Plato, *Gorgias* 502] was essential (see Genesis 22:1–24). So too was circumcision during Nazi occupation (see Derrida, *Circumfession*), or Odysseus' "scar" that Auerbach discusses as a form of mimetic representation, and that Derrida deconstructs in the *Gift*. If cosmetic surgery (elective or not) was about the production of socially passable and/or desirable features of the body, the purposes of posthuman prosthetic surgery was the production of body parts for purposes of cybernetic passing (cf. Cauwels; Brahm Jr. and Driscoll; Smith and Morra). Not just the écorché, the stripped down human body itself became a re-membered scar that reminds them of home.

Refugees of Time

i've always been a wanderer of time,
lost on this journey before i was born;
now i am traveling to where time dies.

No place is like home to me, or to mine,
no rest is here among the restless stars—
i've always been a wanderer of time.

Home is where i am, any given Zeit;
it's where i find that "i" is also "are."
i am traveling now to where time dies.

Began this journey before i was i;
i haven't been anywhere, have gone far;
i've always been a wanderer of time.

Here at the end of days stacked up like lies,
whose passing must be marked on me with scars.
i am traveling now to where time dies.

Why must everything we love cry, and fly?
Like a door, the question is ajar—
i've always been a wanderer of time;
i am traveling now to where time dies.

Ц x 10

Banality of Physical Bodies

> —"The banality of physical bodies has two registers," Nancy announced: "that of the *model* (the magazine register, a canon of streamlined, velvety bodies)—and that of the *indiscriminate* (no matter what body, ruined, wrecked, deformed). In the gap or dialectic between the two—which the eco-technical produces simultaneously—little proximity is possible." (Nancy, "Corpus" 91)

> —"[T]he handicapped [are] mutant figures, because mutilated and hence closer to this telepathetic, telecommunicational universe than we others . . . [I]t is not by chance that the social is aligning itself more and more with the handicapped, and

> their operational advancement: they can become wonderful instruments precisely because of their handicap. They precede us on the path toward mutation and dehumanization." (Baudrillard, *Ecstasy* 52)

Dirge of the Space Travelers

We will sing without air a stranger tune,
watch the stars explode through the universe;
then travel to another wasted dune.

We will inscribe there a different rune.
We know our mission and shall not rehearse.
We will sing without air a stranger tune.

i do not think we'll see Earth again soon:
the rocket we ride can never reverse,
traveling to another wasted dune.

We will explore the furthest sultry moon,
and with aliens begin to converse.
We will sing without air a stranger tune.

We'll sleep in our ship like a tin cocoon;
a mistake could make it a cosmic hearse,
traveling to some other distant dune.

We may serenade the ultimate loon,
but we will never be free of the curse.
So we'll sing without air a stranger tune,
then travel to another wasted dune.

Ч x 9

Prosthetics as Self-Flattery

Platon and Cicero very different conceptions of rhetoric and poetics, and thus cosmetic and prosthetics. For Platon, cosmetics was a "form" of flattery—a wholly false art that did not reveal but concealed the truth, and corrupted the soul; for Cicero, cosmetics—*kosmetics*—was kosmos—the unity of form and matter.

> So when the original body was cut through, each half wanted the other, and hugged it; they threw their arms round each other desiring to grow together in the embrace, and died of starvation and general idleness because they could not do anything apart from the other . . . But Zeus pitied them and found another scheme; he moved their privy parts in front, for these also were outside before, and they had begotten and brought forth not with each other but with the ground . . . So he moved these parts also in front and made the generation come between them. . . . So you see how ancient is the mutual love implanted in mankind, bringing together the parts of the original body, and trying to make one out of two, and to heal the natural structure of man. (Plato, *Symposium* [Rouse] 191a–d)

Alien Love

Emotions, like the mind, are hardwired,
limited. We can't conceive of beings sired
different from the senses we call I—
oh yes, differently combined, Sir: eye
where mouth should be, to see but not to kiss,
watching us, two heads, something amiss,
an arm extending from posterior,
knowing one grip only, inferior,

but in the end, my dear, too much like us.
Technology, you say? A mere extension
of our senses: a palette for perception,
painting the invisible, sculpting touch.

We only reach another love by art,
feeling the tiny buttocks of the heart.

III x 8

Techno-Bodies

They loved their techno-bodies when they were young: —not the chaos of flesh, the warp and cry of four-dimensional space-time, but those cleanly delineated, precisely defined, scentless pristine, superficially divine, wholly refined, the sleek design, the thin fine blue silver lines, the slick suave svelte, the spring-loaded sounds. Socrates/Platon might have said that this mechaphilia was just another (anti) form of imitation, another manifestation of "self"-flattery.

But coming out of the Enlightenment, and Transcendental Idealism (Emerson), American capitalism (Thomson), and especially the Protestant work ethic (Weber), in the Apparatus, the Spectacle, the clone, cyborg, android, robot, even avatar were welcome as productive members of "society." That was their primary function.

Щ x 7

Naïve and Sentimental Prosthetics

In the "modern" perspective of the Romantics, Schiller's distinction between two kinds of poetry/relationships with nature, "the naïve" and "the sentimental," was applied to prosthetics. Naïve prosthetics were more "simple" "spontaneous" attachments that posed in functional relationships with nature as external material being; both prosthetic and nature as exterior non-reflective utilities were *Zuhandenheit* ("ready-at-hand"). Sentimental prosthetics were more complex, (self) conscious extensions that grew into self-reflective, "felt" devices with nature as their internal Being; both prosthetic and nature as increasing interior self-reflective awareness were *Vorhandenheit*—("presence-at-hand") ("the genius of nature") (see Schiller; Heidegger). While naïve prosthetics might have usefully mimicked an objective, empirical stance with nature more akin to Newtonian science or Lockean philosophy, the sentimental prosthetic might have moved beyond mere mime to a deeper affiliation with nature associated to personal psychology akin to the subjective science of phenomenology. (Merleau-Ponty had argued that "there is an organic relationship between the subject and the world, the active transcendence of consciousness, the momentum which carries consciousness into a thing and beyond in the world by means of its organs and instruments" [152–53]; he used both the extension of the body by a cane as well as the motorization of locomotion as examples [see Booher on the body itself as a communication prosthetic].) And what of Golems?*

Astro Nautical

E(ternity) = (M)ortality x (C)abbala†

Drowning in the cosmos—
a life preserver inscribed with *atom*

---

* Golems were giant human figures, usually made of clay and brought to life by writing the Hebrew letter alef [א] on its forehead; in Jewish folklore, their purpose was to protect the Jewish village, or *shtetl.*

† Cabbala: Jewish and Christian mystical treatises on the nature of the universe.

chained in expanding space
where it rescued me

sitting at the helm of the letters
without kippah* or cologne or rationality,
G/d, like Einstein, smiling behind his cigar
at the black edge of the universe, burning

Ѣ x 6

Informational Pathway

—Central to the construction of the cyborg are informational pathways connecting the organic body to prosthetic extensions. This presumes a conception of information as a (disembodied) entity that can flow between carbon-based and organic compounds and silicon-based electronic components to make protein and silicon operation as a single system. (Hayles, *Posthuman* 2)

—Through the sophistication of its methodology, science annihilates its object: to survive, science was forced to artificially reproduce the object as a model of simulation. Again the object takes revenge in that it exists only as a simulation in the grip of technology. (Baudrillard, *Ecstasy* 87)

ЫІ x 5

Outer Environment

—The outer environment determines the conditions for goal attainment. If the inner system is properly designed, it will be adapted to the outer environment, so that its behavior will be determined in large part by the behavior of the latter, exactly as in the case of "economic man." To predict how it will behave, we need only ask, "How would a rationally designed system behave under these circumstances?" The behavior takes on the shape of the task environment (Simon 15; cf. Miller, "Decision Science," who critiqued what "Simon Says" by examining the kinds and limits of rationality, and Feyerabend, who questions the existence of all rationality and method).

* Atom: from Greek *atomo*, person.

—[T]he presumption that there is an agency, desire, or will belonging to the self and clearly distinguished from the "wills of others" is undercut in the posthuman, for the posthuman's collective heterogeneous quality implies a distributed cognition located in disparate parts that may be only in tenuous communication with each other. (Hayles, *Posthuman* 3–4)

—As data move across various kinds of interfaces, analogical relationships are the links that allow pattern to be preserved from one modality to another. Analogy is thus constituted as a universal exchange system that allow data to move across boundaries. (Hayles, *Posthuman*, 98)

—The problem with this approach lies not so much in the analogical relations that Wiener constructed between living and mechanical systems as in his tendency to erase from view the very real differences in embodied materiality, differences that the analogies did not express. . . . [F]lesh . . . continues to be erased in contemporary discussions about cybernetic subjects. . . . (Hayles, *Posthuman* 99; cf. D. Hofstadter, *Fluid Concepts*)

—"[M]y nightmare is a culture inhabited by posthumans who regard their bodies as fashion accessories rather than the ground of being" (Hayles, *Posthuman* 5).

—Boots.

b x 4

The Kosmic Bay. Concealed.

Bay carved out of sky,
stars embedded in sheets of rain:
mirror images connecting
somewhere in a distance.
a motor rocket passes by
running silent in the darkness

Rippling over and rolling off
the now wavy wind of heaven—
moored to both the earth and sky
our boat falls, rides in waves of time;
two lights, unidentified, fly by,
here, where realities are

just one of infinite possibilities,
dimensions relative and easily
changed, and life would be subject
to Aristotle's lost principles on laughter
except for the continuous suffering
shivering consciousness in a naked void

here, where morality's a leaking boat
contained in a fog on which we float
rowing endlessly in a bay of moon
whose only body is a globe of haze,
the liminal light we call eternity

Э x 3

Recursive Entelechies

Was a different, self-referential, or recursive entelechy at work in Dandyism continued in aesthetic, kosmetic, plastic, and prosthetic surgery? They knew that metaphor was essential in science, that they could be actively epistemic and lead scientists to "the causal joints of the world" (e.g., see Ortony, esp. Boyd, 446–559; Baake). They knew it was all myth, narrative, analogy, metaphor (Derrida, "White Mythology"). They knew that personal experiences, photographs, memories were entangled and enmeshed in diverse and intimate ways with prosthetics as well as the physical body (e.g., see Lyotard, *Libidinal*; *Postmodern*; Mair; Cartwright; Lury). They knew that artificial experience was both created and dependent on narratives of science, technology, and the human body, not just physical organs and parts (Mitchell and Snyder; cf. Lyotard, "Taking the Side"; *Discourse*). They knew that contrary to cybernetic metanarratives about the passivity of nonmimetic properties and neutral ethics of *technē*-logical art, the autopoiesis of the body and its robots, the Other "halves" could only be accomplished by rhetorico-poetic surgery. It was a matter of survival.

Ю x 2

When We Left Earth. (a report)

When we left the Earth, there wasn't much time
to decide what to take—and not much space,
traveling, flattened into two dimensions.

When we left Earth, there wasn't much to take,
a few parcels, not of great importance,
papers, poems, portraits of no mention.

When we left Earth, we had nothing but time,
the clothes on our backs, and all the places
we could carry, like refugees driven

by galactic soldiers, memes and rhizomes
fleeing across the country of Universe,
illegal borders, the continuum,

stateless immigrants replacing countries,
soon to be stripped of our suitcases,
our teeth, our glasses, our hair—no need for them

where we are going, temporal refugees,
another galaxy, universe,
reduced to devices, animals,

then objects, traveling energy, trains
invisible as this non-existence
at the speed of light; and so we remain

Я x 1

Posthuman Experience

Unlike Benjamin, Debord lived long enough to experience the cybernetic society, and to see the coming of the posthuman age; for different reasons, Debord, like Benjamin before him, became a political and cultural refugee, and also committed suicide.

Symptomologies: Case History #3 (Professors)

Two professors walked from history into the future. They were talking about poetry in the posthuman age. The One turned to the Other and said: "My image of a poet is still someone with a ball point pen, writing in an attic garret; what's yours?" The Other replied: "My image of a poet is someone with a glistening prosthetic, writing from a distant star.

79 2 8 18 32 18 1
Au
Gold
196.97

i report:

Transmissions

14 Epilogos

When his soul went forth, he said, it travelled with many others, until they reached a wonderful region, in which were two openings in the earth side by side, and two others in the heaven above facing them . . . When he himself approached they told him he must become a messenger to mankind of things there, and they commanded him to hear and see everything in the place. So here he watched the souls departing by two of the openings of heaven and earth when sentence had been passed on them, and, by the other two, souls returning, those coming up out of one in the earth covered with dirt and dust, others coming out of the other down from heaven pure and clean.

—*Plato, Republic X.614b–d*

窗 [*chuāng*—"window"]

Mission from Orion

丄

Connect: time and space and consciousness—
not calendars and clocks, the instruments
that measure, recorded life on Earth, the years
i'll travel faster than, the speed of light,
the warp and curve of my own thought in time,
a pure temporal mode of transport, being

i still can hear the sound of wind in broken
branches in the mountains of the Earth,
radio speaker wired to a trunk,
soft blue rustling electric leaves
of vineyards on the hill, flickering

in and out, playing for no one.
It's cold in this portal of stasis,
this pocket of space, this gully of time.
If only the voices from Earth would stop for awhile

𠄞

How to care for a body anyway,
organic machine made of flesh
stretched on a bony mesh,
decay that no repairs can maintain
for the long journey i must make . . .

Who needs a body anyway,
all its desires and eruptions,
its constant need for caresses, tension
love's builtin obsolescence, when

i will never feel again . . .

Who wants a body anyway,
its contradictions and disruptions,
its crevices and corruption,
out there where there is nothing ahead
but lightyears of emptiness . . .

三

And i remember what he said to me
the night before i left. He said:
where you'll be going
you'll need more than courage;

you'll need good red luck . . .

女 [*nüshi*—"woman"]

i report:

Space Log

口 [*kǒu*— "mouth; measure of human"]

09/08/4210 :00:00:00:

memory

circuitry

window

09/08/4210 :00:00:00:

thought—

layers upon layers

software

09/08/4210 :00:00:00:

light

connecting

dark

09/08/421: :00:00:00:

c
o
u
n
t
i
n
g

d
o
w
n

r e v e r i e

09/08/4210 :00:00:04

CRIMSON

AZURE

BLOOMING

09/08/4210 :00:00:07

rising

headlong

flames

9/08/4210 :00:00:14

goldust

falling

away

09/08/4210 :00:00:23:

heavens

pitched against

"forehead"

09/08/4210 :00:00:47:

consciousness

reeling

in a capsule

9/08/4210 :00:01:34

heliocentric

gravity

guilt (fading)

9/08/4210 :00:02:42:

whirling through the Milky Way

stars' misty gas light

comet's falling jet

9/10/4210 :00:01:57:

where we dream

a darkened room

without words

09/12/4210 : : : :

fire

flowering

stars

9/08/10,501 : : : :

rolling

sun

to sun

4/26/24,210 : : : :

wake

transmit

sleep

/75,433 : : : :

traversing light years

transits of galaxies

stars hurling worlds

/126,032 : : : :

spiraling galaxies—

trillions of leaves

slow breeze

/170,475 : : : :

weightless the mind

that floats

in the ether of its dreams

/992,112 : : : :

geometric grids

alphabetic fields

glistening coordinates

/13,821,285 : : : :

transmissions

chronicles

reports

/154,967,228 : : : ::

gigaannum

spinning

space

/524,697,297 : : : :

eons

snatched

from stars

/3,146,573,214 : : : :

vortices

shooting

worlds

7,235,464,758 : : : :

maelstroms

rousing

numbers

/10,360,824,699 : : : :

stir

compose

slumber

/11,543,439, 742,167 : : : :

effluence

drifting

equations

/13,267,742,213 : : : :

expanding

atoms

universes

/13,354,875,962 : : : :

chariots of stars

redshift

recede

/13,569,434,822 : : : :

sails deploy

blown light

radiated pressure

/13,589,42,612,323 : : : :

inertia

breaking

slowing

/13,784,565,329 :00:00:00:

a fold in space

a wrinkle in time—

i find myself

/13,808,565,324 :00:00:01:

paradise

infinity

nothingness

/13,808,565,324 00:00:02

two black holes

expanding

contracting

/13,808,565,324 00:00:13:

souls splayed

align

entering, departing

/13,808,565,324 :00:01:18:

Chaos

nanosecond

beginning

/13,808,565,324 :00:09:27:

afterbirth

nebulae

surround me

/13,808,565,324 :00:12:06:24

edge

expanding

around me

/13,808,565,324 :00:13:07:

i reach

amputated

Hand

Acknowledgments

Over the twenty-five years I have been working on this book, I have benefited greatly from the help, encouragement, labor, and support of many people. I want to thank as many of them as possible here.

As always, S. Michael Halloran, my "academic dad," for his initial reaction to and ongoing encouragement of the very idea of this book. Dr. Edward Tick for the sojourn through Greece, and his long-distance companionship on a journey of Hellenic history, language, and thought; Εικαστώ πόλι, φιλά μου. Michael Carter, fellow style enthusiast, with whom I bounced many an early idea for this book at art museums, in vans, and in cars. Carolyn Miller, steadfast friend and endless source of knowledge and *phronesis* regarding this and other work—even when she disagrees! The late Tom Lisk, for his acute poetic ear and eye even in the darkest of times. Peter Elbow, astute commentator of the very earliest draft ideas and general organization of the manuscript. Emily Ligon, there at the beginning and the end, a very early supporter of the book who also arranged my reading from it for the RCID Research Colloquium at Clemson University when she was there. And Myra Moses, former student, co-author, publisher, positivity whisperer, friend, and first prospectus reader for the original iteration of this version of *Plato's Nightmare.*

I have benefited from the support of some truly great poets who also believe in a poetry of complexity and thought, one that rhetorically engages social issues as well as feelings in deep imagery, metaphors, rhythms, and forms. Afaa (Michael) Weaver, student of the Chinese language and weaver of Eastern and African American wisdom and culture, for his advice on Chinese, and for publishing a few of my poems in *Obsidian: Literature and Arts in the African Diaspora* (those poems appear in this book in different contexts). The late Gerald Barrax, who gave this rhetorician the opportunity to teach poetry writing for twenty years at NC State, which strengthened my belief in the creative use of poetic and free verse forms for forensic, epideictic, and deliberative as well as aesthetic purposes. Ruth Fainlight, poetry editor of *European Judaism* and best friend of Sylvia Plath in England during the latter's last years; over a ten-year period, Ruth offered me good advice on poems I submitted, some of which appear in this book. Walt Hunter, now Fiction and Poetry Editor of *The Atlantic*, for his seminal etymological insight into the very beginning of Plato's *Republic* and its relation to this book and its themes. And Ger Killeen, poet and digital artist extraordinaire, for expressing genuine exuberance about the idea, scope, and final lines of *Plato's Nightmare* during our walks and conversations among the White Mountains, and for his continuous urging: "*get this book out there*!!"

At Clemson University, where I became Pearce Professor in 2006, I extend my deepest gratitude to the following. Barbara Ramirez, who during my thirteen years there and after was a "crutch" (literally and figuratively!)—helping me get around when I was temporarily disabled, and providing excellent advice on specific questions about *Plato's Nightmare.* The members of the Body Colloquium in the RCID doctoral program at Clemson, both begun by my colleague and friend Victor Vitanza; I immediately joined on my arrival, realizing this was exactly what I needed to further develop the present book, and then knew full well that I was in the right time and place. In that colloquium I met a group of scholars who for different reasons would become fellow explorers in the quest to understand the cultural history, philosophy, sociology and rhetoric of the human body: Diane Perpich, Todd May, Susan Hilligoss, Amanda Booher, Barbara Heifferon, Julie Melton, Elisa Sparks, Art Young and at different times others. Lesly Temesvari, Professor of Biological Sciences, whose joint work in a Creative Inquiry on scientific journalism as well as our Writing in the Disciplines workshops, was often impacted by my schedule, but who always listened attentively to my explanations of the book, and provided a more scientific perspective and response to it.

I cannot completely express the value of my friendships in and outside academia in relation to writing this book over such long periods of time and absence. Cynthia Haynes and Jan Holmevik, enthusiastic supporters of *Plato's Nightmare* from my very first day at Clemson; their support, enthusiasm, and friendship have been essential. Dale Sullivan, with whom conference conversations (present and long-distant) about rhetoric and religion in rooftop pools, hotel saunas (both legally and illegally) and adventures on desert drives to Mexico, Watts, as well as the wrong side of one-lane hair-pinned hedgerow roads in Ireland, inform this work and have sustained me over the years. Mir Garvey, who knows this project all too well; who took five classes, and also studied poetry and rhetoric independently with me for several more years—and still talks to me! The late Bill Nichols, who asked every single time I saw him: "how's the book coming along?"; daughter Cody Nichols, magician-stylist of my thinning head, who, scissors in hand, listened to me every month while I regaled her with snags and frustrations. And of course, Bonnie Nichols, close friend through thick and aught, along with our Jewish band that included my musical soulmate and partner-in-crime, guitarist Roger Friedensen, and his devoted wife, Teresa Kriegsman, and nurse-practitioner/vocalist Gale Touger, all of whom cheered me on in this project. Dr. Richard Adelman, who at every check-up and office visit genuinely inquired, saying he would read the book even though it was more than 400 pages. Rabbi Lucy Dinner, who was instrumental in my work on Hebrew, and always curious about my investigations into its connections to the Greek rhetorical tradition.

One of the most wonderful dimensions of teaching, especially PhD students, is what comes after: lifelong friends and colleagues. The following doctoral students engaged in helpful conversations about *Plato's Nightmare* and encouraged me during the long era of its writing (in alphabetical order and from the RCID program at Clemson unless otherwise noted): Drs. Abboud, Booher, Beltran, Bose, Butts, Byrum, Canlas, Chung, Collamati, Colton, Elrick, Figueiredo, Frank, Fuller, Gaines, Gay, Gellis (Purdue), Hanzalik, Hartzog (NCSU), Helms, Hilst, Hodgson, Holmes, Houser, Hunter, Iriarte, Jabeen, Lucke, McFarlane, Measel, Newbold, Nichols, Osborne, Ozyesilpinar, Patterson, Rosseau, Snell, Southergill, Stephens, Stowe, Thompson, Wahyurini, Walwema, Ward, Woolbright, Wu, and Zertuche. A special call out to those students who maintain a deep, close, and abiding post PhD friendship: Drs. Patricia Fancher, Mari Ramler, Jonathan Lashley, Elizabeth Pitts (NCSU), and Whitney Jordan Adams with whom I converse on a regular basis and who has been the most solicitous of friends.

Over my many years at both NC State and Clemson, I have had the benefit of hands-on research and editorial assistance from then current and now former master's students. This list does not do justice to the meaningful mentoring and professional relations I had with each of these graduate students, their direct and indirect contributions to this book, or the nuances of their friendships, many of them continuing. In chronological order: Mir Garvey, Karen Ives, Jaime Laughlin, Ashley Lusk, Caroline Stone, David Williams, Vicki Rhodes, Christina D'Elia, LaKrisha Maulden, Jonathan Lashley, Claiborne Linvill, Jonathan Zeller, Dan Liddle, Abbey Johnson, Todd Smith, Stephanie Heath, Erin Dalton, Valerie Smith, Meyer (Addy) Meyers (who over two years reformatted all works cited), Dana Dopko (who formatted the entire manuscript for submission), and Kathleen Angione Anckner (who among other tasks obtained all those gnarly permissions; each one was its own adventure). I thank them all for their tireless support, intellectual insights, and physical labor.

Finally, and importantly, I want to publicly acknowledge David Blakesley for his vision, courage, editorial skills, and saintly patience. When I signed my advance contract with Parlor Press in 2006, he was at Purdue University, and I was at NC State. Eventually, he would become the Campbell Chair at Clemson University and we would become colleagues. Yet, from his arrival in 2010 until my "retirement" in 2019, I was still not able to complete this tome. His understanding of traditional and experimental rhetoric and poetry, as well as his knowledge of and innovation in the field of publishing, is remarkable. I, as well as the whole field of rhetoric and many of its subdisciplines, owe him a debt of gratitude. Thank you, Dave!

Works Cited

Aarseth, Espen J. *Cybertext: Perspectives on Ergodic Literature.* Johns Hopkins UP, 1997.

Abrams, M. H. *The Mirror and the Lamp: Romantic Theory and the Critical Tradition.* Oxford UP, 1953.

Abulafia, Abraham. *Zohar, or the Book of Splendor.* 2nd ed., translated by Maurice Simon, Soncino Press, 1934, 5 vols.

Addison, Joseph, Sir Richard Steele. *The Spectator.* Edited by Donald Fredric Bond, Oxford, Clarendon Press, 1965, 5 vols.

Adorno, Theodor. *The Culture Industry.* 2nd ed., Routledge, 2001.

Agassi, Andre. *Open: An Autobiography.* 1st edition, Vintage, 2010.

Agamben, Giorgio. *Means Without an End: Notes on Politics (Theory Out of Bounds).* U of Minnesota P, 2000.

—. *Remnants of Auschwitz: The Witness and the Archive.* Revised edition, translated by Daniel Heller-Roazen, Zone Press, 2002.

—. *The Sacrament of Language: An Archeology of the Oath.* Translated by Adam Kotsko, Stanford UP, 2011.

—. *What Is an Apparatus? and other Essays.* Translated by David Kishik and Stefan Pedatella, Stanford UP, 2009.

Althusser, Louis. *On Ideology.* 2nd ed., London, Verso, 2008.

Ancestry.com. Online, https://www.ancestry.com/name-origin?surname=plato. Accessed 22 July 2021.

Anderson, Ian. Spoken Introduction. "Dharma for One." By Jethro Tull. *Living in the Past.* Chrysalis Records UK, 2007.

Anonymous of Bologna. "From the Principles of Letter Writing." *The Rhetorical Tradition: Readings from Classical Times to the Present.* Edited by Patricia Bizzell and Bruce Herzberg, Bedford-St. Martin's, 1990, pp. 496–502.

Antoon, Sinan. "A Web Smaller Than a Divide." *New York Times,* 16 May 2010, p. WK11.

Aquinas, Saint Thomas. *Summa Theologica Complete in a Single Volume.* Translated by Fathers of the English Dominican Province, Coyote Canyon Press, 2018.

The Arbatel of Magick: Of the Magick of the Ancients. Edited by Tarl Warwick [org 1655]. TW, 2015.

Arendt, Hannah. "Introduction, Walter Benjamin 1892–1940" *Illuminations: Essays and Reflections,* by Walter Benjamin, translated by Harry Zohn, Schocken, 1969, pp. 1–55.

—. *The Origins of Totalitarianism.* Harcourt Brace, 1951.

—. "We Refugees." *Menorah Journal,* vol. 1, 1943, pp. 77.

—. "The Decline of the Nation-State and the End of the Rights of Man." *The Origins of Totalitarianism*, Harcourt Brace, 1951, pp. 349–96.

Aristotle. *Categories*. Translated by J. L. Ackrill, *The Complete Works of Aristotle*, edited by Jonathan Barnes, vol. 1, Princeton UP, 1984, pp. 3–24, 2 vols.

—. *De Interpretatione*. Translated by J. L. Ackrill, *The Complete Works of Aristotle*, edited by Jonathan Barnes, vol. 1, Princeton UP, 1984, pp. 25–38, 2 vols.

—. *The Generation of Animals*. Translated by A. Platt, *The Complete Works of Aristotle*, edited by Jonathan Barnes, vol. 1, Princeton UP, 1984, pp. 1111–218, 2 vols.

—. *Metaphysics*. Translated by W. D. Ross, *The Complete Works of Aristotle*, edited by Jonathan Barnes, vol. 2, Princeton UP, 1984, pp. 1552–728, 2 vols.

—. *On Generation and Corruption*. Translated by H. H. Joachim, *The Complete Works of Aristotle*, edited by Jonathan Barnes, vol. 1, Princeton UP, 1984, pp. 512–54, 2 vols.

—. *On Rhetoric: A Theory of Civic Discourse*. 2nd ed., translated by George Kennedy, Oxford UP, 2006.

—. *On the Soul*. Translated by J. A. Smith, *The Complete Works of Aristotle.*, edited by Jonathan Barnes, vol. 1, Princeton UP, 1984, pp. 641–92, 2 vols.

—. *The Organon*, edited by Roger Bishop Jones. Oxford Obook, January 1, 2016. https://www.rbjones.com/rbjpub/philos/classics/aristotl/obook_draft.pdf.

—. *Poetics*. Translated by I. Bywater, *The Complete Works of Aristotle*, edited by Jonathan Barnes, vol. 2, Princeton UP, 1984, pp. 2316–40, 2 vols.

—. *Politics*. Translated by B. Jowett, *The Complete Works of Aristotle*, edited by Jonathan Barnes, vol. 2, Princeton UP, 1984, pp. 1986–2129, 2 vols.

—. *Posterior Analytics*. Translated by Jonathan Barnes, *The Complete Works of Aristotle*, edited by Jonathan Barnes, vol. 1, Princeton UP, 1984, pp. 114–66, 2 vols.

—. *Prior Analytics*. Translated by A. J. Jenkinson, *The Complete Works of Aristotle*, edited by Jonathan Barnes, vol. 1, Princeton UP, 1984, pp. 39–113, 2 vols.

—. *Physics*. Translated by R. P. Hardie and R. K. Gaye, *The Complete Works of Aristotle*, edited by Jonathan Barnes, vol. 1, Princeton UP, 1984, pp. 315–446, 2 vols.

—. *Rhetoric*. Translated by W. Rhys Roberts, *The Complete Works of Aristotle*, edited by Jonathan Barnes, vol. 2, Princeton UP, 1984, pp. 2152–269, 2 vols.

—. *Sense and Sensibilia*. Translated by J. I. Beare, *The Complete Works of Aristotle*, edited by Jonathan Barnes, vol. 1, Princeton UP, 1984, pp. 693–713, 2 vols.

—. *Topics*. Translated by W. A. Pickard-Cambridge, *The Complete Works of Aristotle,* edited by Jonathan Barnes, vol. 1, Princeton UP, 1984, pp. 167–277, 2 vols.

Arnold, Matthew. *The Function of Criticism at the Present Time.* Forgotten Books, 2012, pp. 46–73.

—. "Hebraism and Hellenism." *Selections from the Prose Work of Matthew Arnold,* BiblioBazaar, 2009, pp. 273–88.

—. "Literature and Science." *Selections from the Prose Work of Matthew Arnold,* BiblioBazaar, 2009, pp. 87–111.

—. "The Study of Poetry." *Selections from the Prose Work of Matthew Arnold,* BiblioBazaar, 2009, pp. 55–86.

Auden, W.H. *W.H. Auden: Collected Poems*, edited by Edward Mendelson. Random House, 1976.

—. *The Dyer's Hand and Other Essays*. Vintage, 1968.

Auerbach, Erich. *Mimesis: The Representation of Reality in Western Literature.* Translated by Willard R. Trask, Kindle ed., Princeton UP, 2003.

Augustine, Saint. *On Christian Doctrine.* Translated by J. F. Shaw, Dover, 2009.

Aurelius, Marcus. *Meditations.* Translated by George Long, edited by William Kaufman, Dover, 1997.

Austin, Gilbert. *Chironomia; or, A Treatise on Rhetorical Delivery.* Edited by Mary Margaret Robb and Lester Thonssen, Southern Illinois UP, 1966.

Autenrieth, Georg, and Robert Porter Keep. *A Homeric Dictionary.* R Pullins Company, 2001.

Awati, Rahul. "What is a dielectric constant?" *TechTarget*, 2024. https://www.techtarget.com/whatis/definition/dielectric-constant.

Ayer, A.J. *Language, Truth and Logic*. 2nd ed., Dover, 1952.

Baake, Kenneth. *Metaphor and Knowledge: The Challenges of Writing Science.* SUNY P, 2003.

Bacon, Francis. *The Advancement of Learning.* Paul Dry, 2001.

—. *Novum Organum*. Edited by J. Devey, Public Domain, Liberty Fund Network, 1902. Originally published 1620. https://oll.libertyfund.org/titles/bacon-novum-organum. Accessed 17 May 2022.

Bachelard, Gaston. *The Poetics of Reverie: Childhood, Language, and the Cosmos.* Translated by Daniel Russell. Beacon Press, 1971.

—. *The Poetics of Space.* Translated by Maria Jolas, Beacon Press, 1994.

Bakhtin, Mikhail. (Vološinov, V. N.). *The Dialogic Imagination: Four Essays.* Revised edition, edited and translated by Michael Holquist, Caryl Emerson, U of Texas P, 1982.

—. *Marxism and the Philosophy of Language.* Translated by Ladislav Matejka and I. R. Titunik, Seminar, 1973.

—. *Rabelais and His World.* Translated by Hélène Iswolsky, Indiana UP, 1984.

Balsamo, Anne. *Technologies of the Gendered Body: Reading Cyborg Women.* Duke UP, 1995.

Barad, Karen. *Meeting the Universe Halfway: Quantum Physics and the Entanglement of Matter and Meaning.* Duke UP, 2007.

Barnes, Jonathan, editor. *The Complete Works of Aristotle.* Princeton, Princeton UP, 1984, 2 vols.

Barnett, Scot, and Casey Boyle, editors. *Rhetoric Through Everyday Things.* U of Alabama P, 2016.

Barrett, William. *The Illusion of Technique.* Anchor, 1979.

Barry, Kieren. *The Greek Qabalah: Alphabetical Mysticism and Numerology in the Ancient World.* Weiser Books, 1999.

Barzun, Jacques. *Classic, Romantic, and Modern.* U of Chicago P, 1975.

Baudelaire, Charles. *Les Fleurs du Mal et Autres Poèmes.* Paris, Garnier-Flammarion, 1964.

—. "The Painter of Modern Life." *Selected Writings on Art and Artists.* Translated by P. E. Charvet, Penguin, 1972, pp. 390–435.

Baudrillard, Jean. *The Ecstasy of Communication.* Brooklyn, Semiotext(e), 1988.

—. *Simulacra and Simulation.* Translated by Sheila Faria Glaser, U of Michigan P, 1995.

Bazerman, Charles. *The Language of Edison's Light.* MIT, 1999.

Beardsley, Monroe. "Style and Good Style." *Contemporary Essays on Style: Rhetoric, Linguistics, and Criticism.* Edited by Glen Love and Michael Payne, Scott Foresman, 1969.

Beethoven, Ludwig van. Liner Notes. *The String Quartets.* Perf. Emerson String Quartet, Deutsche Grammophon, 1997.

Behler, Ernst and Roman Struc, Introduction: The Position of Friedrich Schlegel's *Dialogue on Poetry* within the Romantic Movement. *Friedrich Schlegel: Dialogue on Poetry and Literary Aphorisms*, translated by Ernst Behler and Roman Struc, Penn State UP, 1968.

Benjamin, Walter. "The Antimonies of Allegorical Exegesis." Jennings, et al., pp. 175–79.

—. *The Arcades Project.* Translated by Howard Eiland and Kevin McLaughlin, Belknap-Harvard UP, 2002.

—. "Attested Auditor of Books." Jennings, et al., pp. 171–72.

—. "The Author as Producer." Jennings, et al., pp. 79–95.

—. *Briefe I. Herausgegeben und mit Anmerkungen versehen von Gershom Scholem-und Theodor W. Adorno*, Frankfurt am Main, Germany, Suhrkamp Verlag, 1966.

—. "The Dismemberment of Language." Jennings, et al., pp. 187–91.

—. "Dream Kitsch." Jennings, et al., pp. 236–39.

—. "Graphology Old and New." Jennings, et al., pp. 192–94.

—. *Illuminations: Essays and Reflections.* Edited by Hannah Arendt, translated by Harry Zohn, Schocken, 1969.

—. "On the Mimetic Faculty." *Reflections: Essays, Aphorisms, Autobiographical Writings*, edited by Peter Demetz, translated by Edmund Jephcott. New York: Schocken Books, 1978, pp 333–36.

—. "On Painting, or Sign and Mark." Jennings, et al., pp. 221–25.

—. "Paintings and Graphics." Jennings, et al., pp. 195–217.

—. "Paris, the Capital of the Nineteenth Century." Jennings et al., pp. 96–115.

—. "Theory of Distraction." Jennings, et al., pp. 56–57.

—. "These Surfaces for Rent." Jennings, et al., pp. 173–74.

—. "Theses on the Philosophy of History." In *Illuminations*, translated by Harry Zohan. Schocken Books, 1989, pp. 257 (in the Italian). Qtd in Agamben, *Means without Ends.*

—. "The Telephone." Jennings, et al., pp. 9–55.

—. "Unpacking My Library: A Talk about Book Collecting." *Illuminations: Essays and Reflections.* Edited by Hannah Arendt, translated by Harry Zohn, Schocken, 1969, pp. 59–67.

—. "The Work of Art in the Age of Mechanical Reproduction." *Illuminations: Essays and Reflections.* Edited by Hannah Arendt, translated by Harry Zohn, Schocken, 1969, pp. 217–51.

—. "The Work of Art in the Age of Its Technological Reproducibility." Jennings, et al., pp. 19–55.

—. *The Work of Art in the Age of Its Technological Reproducibility and Other Writings on Media.* Edited by Michael W. Jennings, Brigid Doherty, and Thomas Y. Levin, Translated by Edmund Jephcott, Rodney Livingstone, Howard Eiland, and Others, Belknap-Harvard UP, 2008.

Bennington, Geoffrey, and Jacques Derrida. *Derridabase and Circumfession.* Translated by Geoffrey Bennington, U of Chicago P, 1993.

Bennett, Jane. *Vibrant Matter: A Political Ecology of Things.* Duke UP, 2010.

Bentham, Jeremy. *Panopticon Writings.* Verso, 1995.

Benthien, Claudia. *Skin: On the Cultural Border Between the Self and the World.* Columbia UP, 2002.

Bergen, Benjamin K. *Louder Than Words: The New Science of How the Mind Makes Meaning.* Basic, 2012.

Berlin, James A. "Rhetorics and Poetics in the English Department: Our Nineteenth Century Inheritance," *College English,* vol. 47, 1985, 521–33.

—. *Rhetoric and Reality: Writing Instruction in American Colleges, 1900–1985.* Southern Illinois UP, 1987.

—. *Rhetorics, Poetics, and Culture: Refiguring College English Studies.* Parlor Press, 2003.

—. "The Rhetoric of Romanticism: The Case for Coleridge." *Rhetoric Society Quarterly,* vol. 10, 1980, 62–74.

—. *Writing Instruction in Nineteenth-Century American College*. Southern Illinois UP, 1984.

Berry, Wendell. *Standing by Words: Essays*. Counterpoint, 1983.

Biale, *Cultures of the Jews: A New History*. Schocken Books, 2002.

Billig, Michael. *Arguing and Thinking: A Rhetorical Approach to Social Psychology*. Cambridge UP, 1987.

Bilton, Nick. "Robot from NASA and G.M. Heading to Space Station." *Bits*. New York Times, 14 Apr. 2010, bits.blogs.nytimes.com/2010/04/14/nasa-and-gm-robot-heading-to-space-station. Accessed 15 Oct. 2012.

Binary Translator. https://www.binarytranslator.com/.

Birdsall, Carolyn. *Nazi Soundscapes: Sound, Technology, and Urban Space in Germany, 1933–1945*. Amsterdam UP, 2012.

Bizzell, Patricia. "Foundationalism and Anti-Foundationalism in Composition Studies." *PRE/TEXT*, vol. 7, no. 1-2, 1986, pp. 37–56.

Bizzell, Patricia, and Bruce Herzberg. *The Rhetorical Tradition: Readings from Classical Times to the Present*. 2nd ed., Bedford-St. Martin's, 2000.

Black, Max. *Models and Metaphors*. Cornell UP, 1962.

Blake, William. *The Complete Poetry and Prose*. Edited by David V. Erdman, Anchor Press, 1988.

Blair, Hugh. *Lectures on Rhetoric and Belles Lettres*. Edited by Linda Ferreira-Buckley and S. Michael Halloran, Nabu Press, 2010.

Blackmon, Douglas A. *Slavery by Any Other Name: The Re-Enslavement of Black Americans from the Civil War to World War II*. Anchor Press, 2008.

Blakesley, David. *Elements of Dramatism*. Pearson, 2001.

—. Text Message. 9/7/2021.

—. Introduction, *Kenneth Burke, Late Poems, 1968–1993: Attitudinizing Versewise, While Fending For One's Selph, And In A Style Somewhat Artificially Colloquial*. Edited by Julie Whitaker and David Blakesley. U of South Carolina P, 2005.

Bleiberg, Rabbi James. Sermon. Delivered at Temple Beth Or, Raleigh, North Carolina.

Boethius, Anicius Severinus Manlius. *Boethian Number Theory: A Translation of the de Institutione Arithmetica*. Translated by Michael Masi, Brill, 1983.

—. *De Topicis Differentis*. Translated by Eleonore Stump, Cornell UP, 1978.

—. *In Ciceronis Topica*. Translated by Eleonore Stump, Cornell UP, 1988.

—. *Consolations of Philosophy*. Edited by P. G. Walsh, Oxford UP, 2006.

Bogost, Ian. In Conversation with Gregory Ulmer. Home of Cynthia Haynes and Jan Holmevik, Clemson, SC, April 2007.

Bohr, Niels. *Atomic Physics and Human Knowledge*. Dover, 2010.

Bolter, J. David. *Turing's Man: Western Culture in the Computer Age*. U of North Carolina P, 1984.

Bolter, Jay David, and Diane Gromala. *Windows and Mirrors: Interaction Design, Digital Art, and the Myth of Transparency*. MIT, 2005.

Bloom, Harold. *Kabbalah and Criticism*. Continuum, 2005.

Boman, Thorleif. *Hebrew Thought Compared with Greek*. Norton, 1960.

Bonaventure, Commentary on the Four Books of Sentences: *Philosophy of God (Works of St. Bonaventure Series, vol XVI)*, Franciscan Inst Pubs, 2014.

Booher, Amanda Kathryn. *Prosthetic Configurations: Rethinking Relationships of Bodies, Technologies, and (Dis)abilities*. Doctoral Dissertation, Clemson University ProQuest Dissertations Publishing, 2009.

Booth, Wayne C. *Modern Dogma and the Rhetoric of Assent*. U of Chicago P, 1974.

The Book of Common Prayer and Administration of the Sacraments and Other Rites and Ceremonies of the Church, According to the Use of the Protestant Episcopal Church in the United States of America. The Church Pension Fund, 1945.

Boulton, J. T. "Editor's Introduction." *A Philosophical Enquiry into the Origin of our Ideas of the Sublime and Beautiful*. Edited by J.T. Boulton, Routledge-Paul, 1958, pp. xv–cxxvii.

Boyarin, Daniel. *Intertextuality and the Reading of Midrash*. Indiana UP, 1994.

—. *Socrates and the Fat Rabbis*. U of Chicago P, 2009.

Boyd, Richard. "Metaphor and Theory Change: What Is 'Metaphor' a Metaphor For?" *Metaphor and Thought*. Edited by Andrew Ortony, 2nd ed., Cambridge UP, 1993, pp. 481–532.

Bradford, David. *Twentieth Century Pastoral: Epideictic Discourse in the Founding of the Tennessee Valley Authority*. Doctoral dissertation, Rensselaer Polytechnic Institute, 1982.

Braidotti, Rosa. *The Posthuman*. Polity Press, 2013.

Bradley, Scully, and Harold W. Blodgett. Introduction. *Leaves of Grass* by Walt Whitman, edited by Scully Bradley and Harold W. Blodgett, Norton, 1973, pp. xxix–lv.

Brahm, Gabriel Jr., and Mark Driscoll, editors. *Prosthetic Territories: Politics and Hypertechnologies*. Westview, 1995.

Brantely, Ben. "Whatever Happened to Mystery?" *New York Times*, 18 July 2010. Sunday Styles 1, p. 7.

Breazeale, Daniel. "Concerning the Difference between the Spirit and the Letter within Philosophy: Editor's Preface." *Fichte: Early Philosophical Writings*. Cornell UP, 1988, pp. 185–91.

—. Editor's Introduction. *Fichte: Early Philosophical Writings*. Cornell UP, 1988, pp. 1–52.

—. Editor's Introduction. *J. G. Fichte: Introductions to the Wissenschaftslehre and Other Writings (1797–1800)*, Hackett, 1994, pp. vii–xliv.

Brett, Richard. Introduction. *The Golden Bowl*, by Henry James, Thomas Crowell, 1975, pp. v–xviii.

Britannica, The Editors of Encyclopedia. "inverse function," *Encyclopedia Britannica*, 22 Mar. 2024. https://www.britannica.com/science/inverse-function. Accessed 1 Apr. 2024.

Brooks, Cleanth. *The Well-Wrought Urn: Studies in the Structure of Poetry*. Harcourt, 1947.

Bryant, Levi R. *The Democracy of Objects*. Open Humanities Press, 2011.

Bryant, Levi, Nick Srnicek, and Graham Harman, editors. *The Speculative Turn: Continental Materialism and Realism*. Melbourne, Re.press, 2011.

Buber, Martin. *I and Thou*. Translated by Walter Kaufmann, Scribner, 1970.

—. *On Judaism*. Edited by Nahum N. Glatzer, Schocken Books, 1967.

Buchanan, Scott. *Poetry and Mathematics*. U of Chicago P, 1975.

Bulwer, John. *Chirologia: Or the Natural Language of the Hand AND Chironomia: Or the Art of Manual Rhetoric*. Edited by James W. Cleary, Southern Illinois UP, 1974.

Burke, Edmond. *A Philosophical Enquiry into the Origin of our Ideas of the Sublime and Beautiful*. Edited by J.T. Boulton, Routledge-Paul, 1958.

Burke, Kenneth. "Catharsis –Second View." *Centennial Review of Arts and Sciences*, vol. 5, 1961, pp. 107–32.

—. *Counter-Statement*. U of California P, 1971.

—. "Definition of Man." *Language as Symbolic Action: Essays on Life, Literature, and Method*. U of California P, 1966, pp. 3–24.

—. "A 'Dramatistic' View of 'Imitation.'" *Essays Toward a Symbolic of Motives, 1950–1955*, edited by William H. Rueckert, Parlor Press, 2007, pp. 5–18.

—. "A Dramatistic View of the Origin of Language and Postscripts on the Negative." *Language as Symbolic Action: Essays on Life, Literature, and Method*. Berkeley, U of California P, 1966, pp. 419–79.

—. "Formalist Criticism: Its Principles and Limits." *Language as Symbolic Action: Essays on Life, Literature, and Method*. U of California P, 1966, pp. 480–506.

—. "Goethe's Faust, Part I." *Essays Toward a Symbolic of Motives, 1950–1955*, edited by William H. Rueckert, Parlor Press, 2007, pp. 283–310.

—. *A Grammar of Motives*. 1945. U of California P, 1969.

—. *Language as Symbolic Action: Essays on Life, Literature, and Method*. U of California P, 1966.

—. *Late Poems, 1968–1993: Attitudinizings Verse-wise, While Fending for One's Selph, And in A Style Somewhat Artificially Colloquial*. Edited by Julie Whitaker and David Blakesley, U of South Carolina P, 2005.

—. "Literature as Equipment for Living." *The Philosophy of Literary Form*. 1941. U of California P, 1974, 293–304.

—. "Medium as Message." *Language as Symbolic Action: Essays on Life, Literature, and Method.* U of California P, 1966, pp. 410–18.

—. "Mind, Body, and the Unconscious." *Language as Symbolic Action: Essays on Life, Literature, and Method.* U of California P, 1966, pp. 63–80.

—. "Myth, Poetry, and Philosophy." *Language as Symbolic Action: Essays on Life, Literature, and Method.* U of California P, 1966, pp. 380–409.

—. *A Philosophical Enquiry into the Origin of Our Ideas of the Sublime and Beautiful.* Edited by J.T. Boulton, Routledge-Paul, 1958.

—. *The Philosophy of Literary Form.* U of California P, 1974.

—. "Poetics in Particular, Language in General." *Language as Symbolic Action: Essays on Life, Literature, and Method.* U of California P, 1966, pp. 25–43.

—. "Rhetoric and Poetics." *Language as Symbolic Action: Essays on Life, Literature, and Method.* U of California P, 1966, pp. 295–307.

—. *A Rhetoric of Motives.* Prentice-Hall, 1950.

—. *The Rhetoric of Religion: Studies in Logology.* 1961. U of California P, 1970.

—. "Somnia Ad Urinandum." *Language as Symbolic Action: Essays on Life, Literature, and Method.* U of California P, 1966, pp. 344–58.

—. *Essays Toward a Symbolic of Motives, 1950–1955*, edited by William H Rueckert. Parlor Press, 2007.

—. "Terministic Screens." *Language as Symbolic Action: Essays on Life, Literature, and Method.* U of California P, 1966, pp. 44–62.

—. "The Thinking of the Body." *Language as Symbolic Action: Essays on Life, Literature, and 'Method.* U of California P, 1966, pp. 308–43.

—. "Three Definitions." *Essays Toward a Symbolic of Motives, 1950-1955*, edited by William H. Rueckert, Parlor Press, 2007, pp. 19–35.

—. "What Are the Signs of What?" *Language as Symbolic Action: Essays on Life, Literature, and Method.* U of California P, 1966, pp. 359–79.

Burkert, Walter. *Greek Religion.* Blackwell, 2012.

Burns, Kurt. "Greek Small Letter Theta." *Wumbo.* https://wumbo.net/symbols/theta/. Accessed 4 Apr 2024.

Burns, Robert. *The Poems and Songs of Robert Burns 1759–1796.* Collins, 1955.

Burton, David M. *The History of Mathematics: An Introduction,* 7th ed., McGraw-Hill, 2011.

Butler, Judith. *Bodies That Matter: On the Discursive Limits of Sex.* Routledge, 1993.

Campbell, George. *The Philosophy of Rhetoric.* Edited by Lloyd Bitzer, Nabu, 2010.

Campbell, Jim/NASA *Physicist Stephen Hawking in Zero Gravity NASA.*

Caplan, Philip J. *The Puzzle of the 613 Commandments and Why Bother.* Jason Aronson Inc., 1996.

Cartwright, Lisa. *Screening the Gody: Tracing Medicine's Visual Culture.* U of Minnesota P, 1995.

Cartwright, Lisa, and Brian Goldfarb. "On the Subject of Neural and Sensory Prostheses." *The Prosthetic Impulse: From Posthuman Present to a Biocultural Future*, edited by Marquard Smith and Joanne Morra, MIT, 2006, pp. 125–54.

Cassirer, Ernst. *The Philosophy of Symbolic Forms Vol. 1: Language.* Translated by Ralph Manheim, Yale UP, 1965.

Cauwels, Janice M. *The Body Shop: Bionic Revolutions in Medicine.* St. Louis, Mosby-Year Book, 1986.

CERN Accelerating Science. "CMS Observes Hints of Melting of Melting of Upsilon Particles in Lead-Nuclei Collisions," The CMS Experiment at CERN. https://cms.cern/news/cms-observes-hints-melting-upsilon-particles-lead-nuclei-collisions. Accessed 6 Apr 2024.

Chateaubriand, François-René. *The Genius of Christianity: or, The Spirit and Beauty of the Christian Religion.* Translated by Charles I. White, H. Fertig, 1976.

Chaucer, Geoffrey. *Tales of Canterbury.* Edited by Robert A. Pratt, Houghton, 1966.

Chen, James. "Rate of Change Definition, Formula, and Importance." *Investopedia*, Technical Analysis, Advanced Technical Analysis Concepts. https://www.investopedia.com/terms/r/rateofchange.asp. Accessed 4 Apr.2024.

—. Preface. The Early Mathematical Manuscripts of Leibniz. Translated by J.M Child, Open Court Publishing Company, 1920, pp. iii–iv.

Chung, S.K. *Understanding Basic Calculus.* Department of Mathematics, University of Hong Kong, 2006–2007. https://www.academia.edu/35827287/Understanding_Basic_Calculus. Accessed 14 Sept 2024.

Cicero, Marcus Tullius. "Brutus." Translated by G. L. Hendrickson. In *Brutus, Orator*, Loeb-Harvard UP, 1939, pp. 18–293.

—. *De Oratore, Books I-II.* Translated by E. W. Sutton and H. Rackham, Loeb-Harvard UP, 1942.

—. *De Oratore Book III.* Translated by H. Rackham, in *De Oratore III, De Fato, Paradoxa Stoicorum, De Partitiones Oratoriae.* Loeb-Harvard UP, 1942, pp. 1–185.

—. "Fifth Book of the Second Pleading in the Prosecution against Verres—Speech on the Punishments." *The Orations of Marcus Tullius Cicero*, translated by C. D. Yonge, vol. 1, London, G. Bell and Sons, 1916, pp. 468–545.

—. *The Nature of the Gods. Nature of the Gods, Academics.* Translated by H. Rackham, Loeb-Harvard UP, 1933.

—. *Orator.* Translated by H. M. Hubbell. In *Brutus, Orator*, Loeb-Harvard UP, 1939, pp. 306–509.

—. *The Poems of Cicero.* Edited by William Withers Eubank, Duckworth, 2007.

—. "Pro Archia." *Orations*. Translated by N. H. Watts, Loeb-Harvard UP, 1923, pp. 6–41.

Cixous, Helene. *The Third Body*. Northwestern UP, 1999.

Clark, Gregory. *Civic Jazz: American Music and Kenneth Burke on the Art of Getting Along*. U of Chicago P, 2015.

Clark, Gregory, and S. Michael Halloran. Introduction: "Transformations of Public Discourse in Nineteenth Century America." *Oratorical Culture in Nineteenth-Century America: Transformations in the Theory and Practice of Rhetoric*. Edited by Gregory Clark and S. Michael Halloran, Southern Illinois UP, 1993, pp. 1–26.

Clark, Kenneth. *Civilisation: A Personal View*. Harper and Row, 1969.

—. *The Nude: A Study in Ideal Form*. Doubleday-Anchor, 1956.

—. *Romantic Rebellion: Romantic vs. Classic Art*. Harper and Row, 1973.

Clark, Timothy. *The Theory of Inspiration: Composition as a Crisis of Subjectivity in Romantic and Post-Romantic Writing*. Manchester UP, 1997.

Cohen, Tom. *Anti-Mimesis: From Plato to Hitchcock*. Cambridge UP, 1994.

Coleridge, Samuel Taylor. "Biographia Literaria." *The Selected Poetry and Prose of Samuel Taylor Coleridge*. Edited by Donald A. Stauffer, Random House, 1959, pp. 109–428.

Collins, *Between Athens to Jerusalem*. 2nd ed., Wm. B. Eerdmans Publishing Company, 2000.

Condit, Celeste. "The Materiality of Coding: Rhetoric, Genetics, and the Matter of Life." *Rhetorical Bodies*. Edited by Selzer, Jack and Sharon Crowley, U of Wisconsin P, 1999, pp. 326–56.

Conley, Verena Andermatt, ed. *ReThinking Technologies*. U of Minnesota P, 1993.

Connolly, William E. *The Fragility of Things: Self-Organizing Processes, Neoliberal Fantasies, and Democratic Activism*. Duke UP, 2013.

Connors, Robert J. "Composition Studies and Science." *College English*, vol. 45, 1983, pp. 1–20.

—. "Writing Instruction in Nineteenth Century American Colleges," *College Composition and Communication*, vol. 37, 1986, 247–49.

Connors, Robert J., Lisa S. Ede, and Andrea A. Lunsford. "The Revival of Rhetoric in America." *Essays on Classical Rhetoric and Modern Discourse*. Edited by Robert J. Connors, Lisa S. Ede, and Andrea A. Lunsford, Southern Illinois UP, 1984, pp. 1–15.

Convert Characters to ASCII Codes. https://www.browserling.com/tools/text-to-ascii. Accessed 22 Feb. 2024.

Corbett, Edward P. J., and Robert J. Connors. *Classical Rhetoric for the Modern Student*. 4th ed., Oxford UP, 1999.

Corbin, Alain. *The Foul and the Fragrant: Odor and the French Social Imagination*. Harvard UP, 1988.

Cornford, Francis MacDonald. *Before and After Socrates.* Cambridge UP, 1960.

—. *Plato and Parmenides.* Indianapolis, Bobbs-Merrill, 1956.

Craig, Alan. "From the Virtual to the Real: Virtual Reality, Augmented Reality, and Personal Fabrication." Presentation, Clemson University Cyber Institute, 9 Aug. 2012, Lehotsky Hall, Clemson University.

Crane, Gregory F, editor. *Perseus Digital Library. Greek Word Study Tool.* Tufts University. http://www.perseus.tufts.edu/hopper/. Accessed 9 March 2024.

Crick, Nathan. *The Keys of Power: The Rhetoric and Politics of Transcendentalism.* U of South Carolina P, 2017, Kindle Edition, L. 380–739.

Croll, Morris W. *Style, Rhetoric, and Rhythm.* Edited by J. Max Patrick, Robert O. Evans, John M. Wallace, and R. J. Schoeck, Princeton UP, 1966, reprinted Woodbridge, Ox Bow, 1989.

cummings, e. e. *100 Selected Poems.* Grove, 1994.

Da Costa, Beatriz, Joseph Dumit and Kavita Phillip. *Tactical Biopolitics: Art, Activism, and Technoscience.* MIT, 2010.

Damasio, Antonio. "Feelings of Emotion and the Self." *New York Academy of Sciences,* vol. 1001, 2003, pp. 253–61.

D'Angelo, Frank J. *Composition in the Classical Tradition.* 1st ed., Allyn & Bacon, 1999.

Dan, Joseph. *Jewish Mysticism: Late Antiquity.* vol. 1, Northvale, Aronson, 1998.

Daniels, Peter T, and William Bright, editors. *The World's Writing Systems.*, Oxford UP, 1996.

Darwin, Charles. *The Expression of the Emotions in Man and Animals.* Appleton, 1899.

Davis, Diane. *Inessential Solidarity: Rhetoric and Foreigner Relations.* U of Pittsburgh P, 2010.

—. "Rhetoricity at the End of the World." *Philosophy and Rhetoric,* vol. 50, no. 4, 2017, pp. 431–51.

De Kerckhove, Derrick. *The Skin of Culture: Investigating the New Electronic Reality.* Somerville House Books. 1995.

De Quincy, Thomas. *Confessions of an English Opium Eater: Being an Extract from the Life of a Scholar.* Original published anonymously in *London Magazine,* October 1821. CreateSpace Independent Publishing Platform, 2015.

De Saussure, Ferdinand. *Course in General Linguistics.* Translated by Wade Baskin, edited by Perry Meisel and Haun Saussy, Columbia UP, 2011.

Debord, Guy. *Comments on the Society of the Spectacle.* Translated by Malcom Imrie. 2nd edition, Verso Books, 1991.

—. *The Society of the Spectacle.* Revised edition, translated by Donald Nicholson-Smith. Zone Books, 1995.

Deleuze, Gilles. *Difference and Repetition.* Translated by Paul Patton, Columbia UP, 1994.

Deleuze, Gilles and Felix Guattari. *A Thousand Plateaus: Capitalism and Schizophrenia*. Translated by Brian Massumi, U of Minnesota P, 1987.

Demetz, Peter. "Introduction." In Walter Benjamin, *Reflections: Essays, Aphorisms, Autobiographical Writings*. Edited by Peter Demetz, translated by Edmund Jephcott, Schocken Books, 1978.

Derrida, Jacques. *The Animal Therefore I Am*. Fordham UP, 2008.

—. *Circumfession*. Translated by Geoffrey Bennington, U of Chicago P, 1993, pp. 3–315.

—. *The Gift of Death*. Translated by David Willis, U of Chicago P, 1995.

—. *Margins of Philosophy*. Translated by Alan Bass, U of Chicago P, 1985.

—. "The Pharmakon." *Dissemination*. Translated by Barbara Johnson, U of Chicago P, 1981, pp. 95–116.

—. *Of Grammatology*. Translated by Gayatri Chakravorty Spivak, Johns Hopkins UP, 1974.

—. *On Touching: Jean-Luc Nancy*. Translated by Christine Irizarry, Stanford UP, 2005.

—. "A Silkworm of One's Own (Points of View Stitched and the Other Veil)." *Acts of Religion*, Routledge, 2001, pp. 311–55.

—. *Spurs: Nietzsche's Styles*. Translated by Barbara Harlow, U of Chicago P, 1978.

—. "White Mythology: Metaphor in the Text of Philosophy." *Margins of Philosophy*, translated by Alan Bass, U of Chicago P, 1982, pp. 207–72.

Descartes, Rene. *Discourse on the Method of Rightly Conducting the Reason*. 1637. Encyclopedia Britannica, 1952.

Dickinson, Emily. *The Complete Poems of Emily Dickinson*. Edited by Thomas H. Johnson, Little, Brown, 1960.

Diderot, Denis. "Treatise on Beauty." In *Contemporary Aesthetics*. Edited by Matthew Lipman, Allyn and Bacon, 1973, pp. 10–23.

DiLorenzo, Raymond. "The Critique of Socrates in Cicero's *De Oratore*: *Ornatus* and the Nature of Wisdom." *Philosophy and Rhetoric*, vol. 11, 1978, pp. 247–61.

Dio, Cassius. *Roman History*. Harvard UP, 1917, penelope.uchicago.edu/Thayer/E/Roman/Texts/Cassius_Dio/. Accessed 8 Oct. 2012.

Dodds. E. R. *The Greeks and the Irrational*. U of California P, 1966.

Dreyfus, Hubert L. *What Computers Still Can't Do: A Critique of Artificial Reason*. MIT, 1999.

Dryden, John. "Essay on Dramatic Poetry." Originally published in 1668, edited by Thomas Arnold, Wentworth Press, 2019.

Duchamp, Marcel. *En Prévision du Bras Cassé*. 1915.

Duden, Barbara. *The Woman Beneath the Skin: A Doctor's Patients in Eighteenth-Century Germany*. Translated by Thomas Dunlap, Harvard UP, 1991.

Dunne, Anthony and Fiona Raby. *Speculative Everything: Design, Fiction, and Social Dreaming.* MIT, 2013.

East, James, H. *The Humane Particulars: The Collected Letters of William Carlos Williams and Kenneth Burke.* U of South Carolina P, 2003.

Eco, Umberto. *History of Beauty.* Translated by Alastair McEwen, Rizzoli Int'l., 2004.

—. *On Ugliness.* Translated by Alastair McEwen, Maclehose, 2011.

Edelsbrunner, Herbert, David G. Kirkpatrick, and Raimund Seidel. "On the Shape of a Set of Points in the Plane" *IEEE Transactions on Information Theory,* vol. 29, no. 4, 1983, pp. 551–59. doi:10.1109/TIT.1983.1056714.

Eiland, Howard and Kevin McLaughlin. Translator's Forward, in *The Arcades Project,* Belknap-Harvard UP, 2002.

Einstein, Albert. *Idea and Opinions.* Three Rivers Press, 1995.

Elbow, Peter. "The Shifting Relationships Between Speech and Writing." *College Composition and Communication,* vol. 36, no. 3, 1985, pp. 283–303.

electronicsnotes, Incorporating Radio Electronics.com. https://www.electronics-notes.com/articles/basic_concepts/letters-symbols/greek-alphabet-characters-list.php. Accessed 6 Apr. 2024.

Elias, Julias A. Introduction. *Naive and Sentimental Poetry, and On the Sublime; Two Essays,* by Friedrich Schiller, Translated by Julius A. Elias, Ungar, 1966, pp. 1–75.

Eliot, T.S. *Ezra Pound: His Metric and Poetry.* Whitefish, Kessinger, 2010.

—. *Knowledge and Experience in the Philosophy of F.H. Bradley.* Columbia UP, 1989.

—. "Tradition and the Individual Talent." *Selected Essays: 1917–1931,* Harcourt, 1932, pp. 3–11.

—. *Collected Poems, 1909-1962.* Harcourt, Brace and World, 1970.

Ellison, Ralph. *Invisible Man.* 2nd ed., Vintage, 1995.

Ellul, Jacques. *The Technological Society.* Translated by John Wilkinson, Vintage, 1967.

Else, Gerald F. *Plato and Aristotle on Poetry.* Edited by Peter Burian, U of North Carolina P, 1886.

Emerson, Ralph Waldo. "Nature," in *The Complete Works, Vol 1, Nature, Addresses, and Lectures.* Houghton Mifflin and Co., 1904, Bartleby.com, 2013.

Empedocles. *The Extant Fragments.* Edited by M.R. Wright, Bristol-Duckworth, 1995.

Encyclopedia Britannica. www.Britannica.com, 8 May 2022.

Enos, Richard Leo. *Greek Rhetoric Before Aristotle.* Waveland, 1993.

—. *Roman Rhetoric: Revolution and the Greek Influence.* Revised and expanded ed., Parlor Press, 2008.

Erasmus. *Desiderius Erasmus of Rotterdam: On Copia of Words and Ideas.* Translated by Donald B. King and H. David Rix, Marquette UP, 1963.

Etymoline.com. https://www.etymonline.com/word/organization. Accessed 17 Jan 2024.

Euclid. *The Thirteen Books of Euclid's Elements*. Edited and translated by T. L. Heath, Cambridge UP, 1908.

Ezzaher, Lahcen El Yazghi. *Three Arabic Treatises on Aristotle's Rhetoric: The Commentaries of al-Farabi, Avicenna, and Averroes*. 1st ed., Southern Illinois UP, 2015.

Fahnestock, Jeanne. "Accommodating Science: The Rhetorical Life of Scientific Facts." *Written Communication*, vol 5, no. 3, 1986, pp. 275–96.

—. *Rhetorical Figures in Science*. Oxford UP, 1999.

Farrell, Thomas B. *Norms of Rhetorical Culture*. Yale UP, 1993.

Ferry, David. Introduction. *The Odes of Horace*. Translated by David Ferry. Farrar, Straus and Giroux, 1997, pp.ix–xv.

Feyerabend, Paul. *Against Method*. Verso, 1993.

Fibonacci, active 13th century. *Libri Abaci*. Translated by L.E. Sigler, Springer, 2002.

Fichte, Johann Gottlieb. *Fichte: Early Philosophical Writings*. Edited and translated by Daniel Breazeale, Cornell UP, 1988.

—. *Introduction to the Wissenschaftslehre and Other Writings (1797–1800)*. Translated by Daniel Breazeale, Hackett, 1994.

—. *The Science of Knowing: J.G. Fichte's 1804 Lectures on the* Wissenschaftslehre. Translated by Walter E. Wright, SUNY P, 2005.

Fiedler, Leslie. *Tyranny of the Normal: Essays on Bioethics, Theology & Myth*. David R Godine, 1996.

"Finding Limits –Numerical and Graphical Approaches." *Libretexts: Mathematics*. Department of Education Open Textbook Pilot Project, the UC Davis Office of the Provost, the UC Davis Library, the California State University Affordable Learning Solutions Program, and Merlot; National Science Foundation. https://bit.ly/finding_limits. Accessed 4 Apr 2024.

Finnegan, Ruth. *Oral Traditions and the Verbal Arts*. Routledge, 1992.

Fish, Stanley. *Doing What Comes Naturally: Change, Rhetoric, and the Practice of Theory in Literary and Legal Studies*. Duke UP, 1989.

Fisher, Walter R. Human Communication as Narration: Toward a Philosophy of Reason, Value, and Action. U of South Carolina P, 1989.

Florman, Samuel C. *The Existential Pleasures of Engineering*. 2nd ed., St. Martin's Griffin, 1996.

Flower, Linda. *Problem Solving Strategies for Writing*. 3rd ed., Harcourt, 1989.

Foucault, Michel. *The Archaeology of Knowledge and The Discourse on Language*. Translated by A. M. Sheridan Smith, Pantheon Books-Random House, 1972.

—. *The Birth of the Clinic: An Archaeology of Medical Perception*. Translated by A. M. Sheridan Smith, Vintage-Random House, 1994.

—. *The Birth of Biopolitics: Lectures at the College de France, 1978–1979.* Translated by Graham Burchell, Palgrave Macmillan, 2008.

—. *Discipline and Punish: The Birth of the Prison.* Translated by Alan Sheridan, Vintage-Random House, 1995.

—. "The Discourse on Language." *The Archaeology of Knowledge and the Discourse on Language*, translated by A. M. Sheridan Smith. Pantheon Books Random House, 1972, pp. 215–37.

—. *The History of Sexuality: An Introduction*, vol. 1, translated by Robert Hurley. Vintage-Random House, 1990.

—. *Madness and Civilization: A History of Insanity in the Age of Reason.* Translated by Richard Howard, Vintage-Random House, 1988.

—. *The Order of Things: An Archaeology of the Human Sciences.* Vintage-Random House, 1994.

Fountain, T. Kenny. "Anatomy Education and the Observational-Embodied Look." *Medicine Studies*, vol. 2, no. 1, 2010, pp. 49–69.

Fraser, Robert. *The Golden Bough: A Study in Magic and Religion.* Oxford UP, 2009.

Freese, J. H. and Gisela Striker. Aristotle. *Art of Rhetoric.* Translated and revised by Gisela Striker. Loeb-Harvard UP, 2020.

Freud, Sigmund. *Civilization and Its Discontents.* Translated and edited by James Strachey, Norton, 1961.

Freud, Sigmund. "The Interpretation of Dreams." In *The Standard Edition of the Complete Works of Sigmund Freud*, vol. 4 & 5, edited by J. Strachey. Hogarth Press, 1900.

"From the Principles of Letter Writing." Anonymous. In *The Rhetorical Tradition: Readings from Classical Times to the Present*, edited by Patricia Bizzell and Bruce Herzberg, Bedford-St. Martin's, 1990, pp. 496–502.

Frost, Robert. "Getting the Sound of Sense: An Interview." *Robert Frost: Poetry and Prose* edited by Edward Connery Lathem and Lawrence Thompson. Holt, 1972, pp. 258–63.

—. *Robert Frost: Poetry and Prose.* Edited by Edward Connery Lathem and Lawrence Thompson, Holt, 1972.

—. *Robert Frost Reads His Poetry.* Caedmon Records, 1957.

Frye, Northrop. *Anatomy of Criticism: Four Essays.* Princeton UP, 1957.

Funkenstein, Amos. *Theology and the Scientific Imagination from the Middle Ages to the Seventeenth Century.* Princeton UP, 1986.

Gaines, Brian. "Digital Détournement: A Situationist Approach to Resisting Surveillance in the Googlized World." In *Exquisite Corpse: Art-Based Writing Practices in the Academy*, edited by Kate Hanzalik and Nathalie Virgintino. Parlor Press, 2019.

Gates of Prayer: The New Union Prayer Book. Edited by Central Conference of American Rabbis. CCAR, 1975.

Gendlin, Eugene T. *Experiencing and the Creation of Meaning: A Philosophical and Psychological Approach to the Subjective.* Free Press of Glencoe, 1962.

—. *Focusing.* Everest House, 1978.

Gibbon, Edward. *The Decline and Fall of the Roman Empire.* Edited by J. B. Bury, Everyman, 1993, 6 vols.

Gibran, Khalil. *The Collected Works of Kahlil Gibran.* Everyman's Library, 2007.

Gibson, Walker. *Tough, Sweet and Stuffy: An Essay on Modern American Prose Styles.* Indiana UP, 1966.

Gillispie, Charles Coulston. *The Edge of Objectivity: An Essay in the History of Scientific Ideas.* Princeton UP, 1960.

Gilman, Sander L. *Making the Body Beautiful: A Cultural History of Aesthetic Surgery.* Princeton UP, 1999.

Ginsburgh, Yitzchak. *The Alef-Beit. Jewish Thought Revealed through the Hebrew Letters.* Jason Aronson, 1995.

Glazerson, Matityahu. *Building Blocks of the Soul: Studies on the Letters and Words of the Hebrew Language.* Jason Aronson, 1997.

Google Translate. Online, https://www.google.com. Accessed 5 May 2021.

Gorgias. "Encomium on Helen." *The Older Sophists: A Complete Translation by Several Hands of the Fragments in Die Fragmente der Vorsokratiker.* Translated by George Kennedy, edited by Rosamond Kent Sprague, U of South Carolina P, 1972, pp. 50–54.

—. "On the Nonexistent or on Nature." *The Older Sophists: A Complete Translation by Several Hands of the Fragments in Die Fragmente der Vorsokratiker.* Translated by George Kennedy, edited by Rosamond Kent Sprague, U of South Carolina P, 1990, pp. 42–47.

Grace-Martin, Karen. "confusing statistical terms #2: alpha and beta." *The Analysis Factor, Statwise Newsletter.* https://www.theanalysisfactor.com/confusing-statistical-terms-1-alpha-andbeta. Accessed 14 Apr 2024.

Graves, Robert. *The Greek Myths.* 2 Volumes, Folio Society, 1999.

"Greek Alphabet Symbols & Characters: Mathematical Uses." *electronicsnotes,* https://www.electronics-notes.com/articles/basic_concepts/letters-symbols/greek-alphabet-characters-list.php. Accessed 6 Apr 2024.

Greene, Michael. "Superstrings." *Scientific American,* vol. 255, no. 3, 1986, pp. 48–60.

Grimaldi, William. *Aristotle Rhetoric II: A Commentary.* Fordham UP, 1993.

Gross, Alan. *The Rhetoric of Science.* Harvard UP, 1996.

Grosz, Elizabeth. *Volatile Bodies: Toward a Corporeal Feminism.* Indiana UP, 1994.

Grube, G. M. A. Introduction. *On Great Writing (On the Sublime)* by Longinus. Hackett, 1957, pp. vii–xxi.

Habermas, Jürgen. *An Awareness of What is Missing: Faith and Reason in a Post-Secular Age.* Polity, 2010.

—. “Technology and Science as ‘Ideology.’” *Toward a Rational Society: Student Protest, Science, and Politics.* Translated by Jeremy J. Shapiro, Beacon Press, 1970, pp. 81–122.

Hackforth, R., trans. *Phaedrus.* In *The Collected Dialogues of Plato,* edited by Edith Hamilton and Huntington Cairns, pp. 475–525.

Haiken, Elizabeth. *Venus Envy: A History of Cosmetic Surgery.* Johns Hopkins UP, 1999.

Hakopian, Mashinka Firunts. *The Institute for Other Intelligences,* X Artists' Books, 2022.

Halloran, S. Michael. “Rhetoric in the American College Curriculum: The Decline of Public Discourse.” *PRE/TEXT,* vol. 3, 1982, pp. 245–69.

Halloran, S. Michael, and Merrill D. Whitburn. “Ciceronian Rhetoric and the Rise of Science: The Plain Style Reconsidered.” *The Rhetorical Tradition and Modern Writing.* Edited by James J. Murphy, MLA, 1982, pp. 58–72.

Hamilton, Edith. *Mythology: Timeless Tales of Gods and Heroes.* New American Library, 1942.

Hamilton, Edith, and Huntington Cairns. Introduction. *The Collected Dialogues of Plato Including the Letters,* edited by Edith Hamilton and Huntington Cairns. Bollingen Foundation, Princeton UP, 1961, pp. xiii–xxv.

Han, Byung-Chul. *The Scent of Time: A Philosophy Essay on the Art of Lingering.* Translated by Daniel Steur Polity, 2017.

—. *The Transparency Society.* Translated by Erik Butler. Stanford UP, 2012.

Handelman, Susan. *Slayers of Moses.* SUNY P, 1983.

Hannah Jones, Nikole. *The 1619 Project: A New Origin Story.* Also edited by Caitlin Roper, Ilena Silverman, and Jake Silverstein. The New York Times Company, 2021.

Hansen, Miriam Bratu. “Room-for-Play: Benjamin's Gamble with Cinema Author(s).” *October,* vol. 109, 2004, pp. 3–45.

Haralick, Robert M. *The Inner Meaning of the Hebrew Letters.* Jason Aronson, Inc., 1995.

Haraway, Donna J. *Simians, Cyborgs, and Women: The Reinvention of Nature.* Routledge, 1991.

Harman, Graham. *Circus Philosophicus.* Zero Books, 2010.

—. *The Quadruple Object.* Zero Books, 2011.

—. *Guerrilla Metaphysics: Phenomenology and the Carpentry of Things.* Peru, Open Court, 2005.

—. *Tool-Being: Heidegger and the Metaphysics of Objects.* Chicago, Open Court, 2002.

—. *Towards Speculative Realism: Essays and Lectures.* Zero Books, 2010.

Harris, Michael R. *History of Libraries of the Western World.* Scarecrow, 1999.

Harrison, George. Lyric in “The Inner Light.” *The Beatles Rarities,* Parlophone, 1979.

Hartman, Charles O. *Virtual Muse: Experiments in Computer Poetry.* Hanover, Wesleyan UP, 1996.

Hartman, Geoffrey H, and Sanford Budick. *Midrash and Literature.* Yale UP, 1986.

Haskell, H.J. *This Was Cicero.* Knopf, 1942.

Haskins, Ekaterina V. *Logos and Power in Isocrates and Aristotle.* U of South Carolina P, 2009.

Havelock, Eric A. *The Muse Learns to Write: Reflection on Orality and Literacy from Antiquity to the Present.* Yale UP, 1986.

—. *Preface to Plato.* Harvard UP, 1963.

Hawhee, Debra. *Bodily Arts: Rhetoric and Athletics in Ancient Greece.* U of Texas P, 2005.

—. *Moving Bodies: Kenneth Burke at the Edges of Language.* U of South Carolina P, 2009.

—. *Rhetoric in Tooth and Claw: Animals, Language, Sensation.* U of Chicago P, 2016.

Hayles, N. Katherine. *How We Became Posthuman: Virtual Bodies in Cybernetics, Literature, and Informatics.* U of Chicago P, 1999.

—. *My Mother Was a Computer: Digital Subjects and Literary Texts.* U of Chicago P, 2005.

Heaney, Seamus. *Crediting Poetry: The Nobel Lecture.* Farrar, Straus and Giroux, 1996.

Hechalot Zutarti: "The Lesser (Book of the Heavenly) Palaces." *Hekhalot Literature in Translation: Major Texts of Merkavah Mysticism*, vol. 20, edited by James R. Davila, Brill, 2013, pp. 187–243, DOI https://doi.org/10.1163/9789004252165_001.

Heffernan, Virginia. "The Pixelated Face: How HDTV Scrambles our Standards of Beauty." *New York Times Sunday Magazine*, 27 July 2010, pp. 15–16.

Hegel, Georg Wilhelm Friedrich. *Aesthetics: Lectures on Fine Art.* Translated by T. M. Knox, Clarendon, 1975, 2 vols.

—. *The Introduction to Hegel's Philosophy of Fine Art.* Translated by Bernard Bosanguet, K. Paul and Trench Trubner, 1905.

—. *The Phenomenology of Mind.* Translated by J. B. Baillie, 2nd ed, George Allen and Unwin, 1931.

Heidegger, Martin. "The Age of the World Picture." *The Question Concerning Technology and Other Essays.* Translated by William Lovitt, Harper & Row, 1977, pp. 115–54.

—. *Being and Time.* Translated by John Macquarrie, Edward Robinson, HarperCollins, 2008.

—. *Country Path Conversations.* Translated by Bret W. Davis, reprint edition, Indiana UP, 2016.

—. *Elucidations of Hölderlin's Poetry.* Translated by Keith Hoeller, Humanity Books, 2000.

—. *Hölderlin's Hymn "Remembrance,"* Translated by William McNeill and Julia Ireland, Indiana UP, 2018.

—. *Nietzsche.* Translated by David Farrell Crell, HarperOne, 1991, 4 vols.

—. *On the Way to Language.* Translated by Peter D. Hertz, 1st ed., HarperOne, 1982.

—. *Parmenides.* Translated by Andre Schuwer and Richard Roycewicz, Indiana UP, 1992.

—. " . . . Poetically Man Dwells . . . " *Poetry, Language, Thought*, translated by Albert Hofstadter, HarperCollins, 1971, pp. 209–27.

—. *Poetry, Language, Thought.* Translated by Albert Hofstadter, HarperCollins, 1971.

—. *The Question Concerning Technology and Other Essays.* Translated by William Lovitt, Harper & Row, 1977.

—. "The Question Concerning Technology." *The Question Concerning Technology and Other Essays.* Translated by William Lovitt, Harper & Row, 1977, pp. 3–35.

—. "The Thinker as Poet." *Poetry, Language, Thought.* Translated by Albert Hofstadter, HarperCollins Publishers Inc., 1971, pp. 1–14.

—. "The Turning." *The Question Concerning Technology and Other Essays.* Translated by William Lovitt, Harper & Row, 1977, pp. 36–52.

—. "What are Poets for?" *Poetry, Language, Thought.* Translated by Albert Hofstadter, HarperCollins, 1971, pp. 87–140.

Heine, Heinrich. *Almansor.* Edited by Erwin Kalischer and Raimund Pissin. The Project Gutenberg eBook, 2014.

—. *Delphi Complete Poetical Works of Heinrich Heine.* Originally published in United Kingdom: Dephi Classics, 2016; Kindle Edition 2016.

—. *Travel Pictures.* Translated by Peter Wortsman. Brooklyn, NY: Archipelago 2008.

Heisenberg, Werner. *Physics and Philosophy: The Revolution in Modern Science.* Harper, 1958.

Hemingway, Earnest. *A Farewell to Arms*: the Hemingway Literary Edition, Scribner, 2012.

Henig, Robin Marantz. "Valium's Contribution to our New Normal." *New York Times*, 30 Sep. 2012, *Sunday Review* 9.

Heraclitus. *Fragments: A Text and Translation with a Commentary by T. M. Robinson.* U of Toronto P, 1987.

—. *Selected Poems and Fragments.* Translated by Michael Hamburger, abridged edition by Jeremy Adler, Penguin Classics, 1998.

Herodotus. *The History of the Greek and Persian War.* Translated by George Rawlinson, edited by W. G. Forrest, Washington Square, 1963.

Herrick, James. *Visions of Technological Transcendence: Human Enhancement and the Rhetoric of the Future.* Parlor Press, 2017.

Hobbes, Thomas. *Leviathan: Or the Matter, Forme and Power of a Commonwealth Ecclesiasticall and Civil.* Edited by Michael Oakeshott, Touchstone, 1st ed., 1997.

Hofstadter, Albert. Introduction. *Poetry, Language, Thought,* by Martin Heidegger, HarperCollins, 1971, pp. ix–xxii.

Hofstadter, Douglas R. *Gödel, Escher, Bach: An Eternal Golden Braid.* Basic, 1999.

—. Hofstadter, Douglas R., and The Fluid Analogies Research Group. *Fluid Concepts and Creative Analogies: Computer Models of The Fundamental Mechanics of Thought.* BasicBooks, 1995.

Hole, Graham. "A Brief Guide to Some Commonly Used Statistical Symbols." StatsSymbolsGuide, https://users.sussex.ac.uk/~grahamh/RM1web/StatsSymbolsGuide. Accessed 13 Aug 2024.

Holton, Gerald. *Thematic Origins of Scientific Thought: Kepler to Einstein.* Harvard UP, 1973.

Holtz, Barry W. Rabbi Akiva: *Sage of the Talmud.* Yale UP, 2017.

Homer. *The Iliad of Homer.* Translated by Richard Lattimore, Harper-Collins, 1999.

—. *The Odyssey of Homer.* Translated by Richard Lattimore, Harper-Collins, 1999.

Horace. "Ars Poetica." *Selected Poems,* translated by Wentworth Dillon, edited by George F. Whicher, Roslyn Black, 1947.

—. *The Epistles of Horace: Bilingual Edition*, translated by David Ferry. Farrar, Straus and Giroux, 2002.

—. *The Odes of Horace.* Bilingual ed., translated by David Ferry, Farrar, Straus, and Giroux, 1998.

Horkheimer, Max. *Eclipse of Reason.* Continuum, 1974.

Horkheimer, Max, and Theodor W. Adorno. *Dialectic of Enlightenment.* Edited by Edmund Jephcott, Stanford UP, 2002.

Hosch, William. "inverse function." *Encyclopedia Britannica,* 22 Mar. 2024, https://www.britannica.com/science/inverse-function. Accessed 1 Apr. 2024.

Hume, David. *An Enquiry Concerning Human Understanding.* In *The Empiricists,* Anchor Books, 1974, 309–517.

—. "Of the Standard of Taste." *Four Dissertations.* Garland, 1970, pp. 201–40.

Hunter, Walt. "The Republic Begins with the Word for Descend." Personal Conversation, Spring, 2017.

Husserl, Edmund. *Ideas: General Introduction to Pure Phenomenology.* Routledge, 2012.

Hutcheson, Francis. *An Inquiry into the Original of Our Ideas of Beauty and Virtue; in Two Treatises*. Edited by J.T. Boulton, Garland, 1971.

Idel, Moshe. *The Mystical Experience in Abraham Abulafia*. Translated by Jonathan Chipman, SUNY P, 1988.

Ihde, Don. *Listening and Voice: Phenomenologies and Sound*. 2nd ed., SUNY P, 2007.

Internet Ancient History Sourcebook: The Law Code of Gortyn (Crete), c. 450 BCE. Paul Halsall, 1999. 31 May 2007. www.fordham.edu/halsall/ancient/450-gortyn.html.

"(IEP) Internet Encyclopedia of Philosophy: A Peer Reviewed Academic Resource. Dualism and Mind." Written by Scott Calef. *Edited by James Fieser and Bradley Dowden,* http://www.iep.utm.edu/dualism/

"Iota." *Vocabulary.com Dictionary,* Vocabulary.com. https://www.vocabulary.com/dictionary/iota. Accessed 14 Apr 2024.

Irigaray, Luce. *Speculum of the Other Woman*. Translated by Gillian C. Gill. Cornell UP, 1985.

Isaacs, Ronald H. *Mitzvot: A Sourcebook for the 613 Commandments*. Jason Aronson, 1996.

Isocrates. "Against the Sophists." *Isocrates: II*, translated by George Norlin, vol. 2, Loeb-Harvard UP, 1929, pp. 159–83.

—. "Antidosis." *Isocrates: II*. Translated by George Norlin, vol. 2, Loeb-Harvard UP, 1929, pp. 180–365.

Investopedia. https://www.investopedia.com/terms/r/rateofchange.asp. Accessed 4 Apr 2024.

Jaeger, Werner. "The Rhetoric of Isocrates and Its Cultural Ideal." *Paideia: The Ideals of Greek Culture*. Translated by Gilbert Highet, vol. 3: *The Conflict of Cultural Ideals in the Age of Plato*, Oxford UP, 1944, pp. 46-70.

Jagoda, Flory. "*Llave de España*." Song, 2008. http://www.lyrics.com/floryjagoda.

Jarrell, Randall. *Poetry and the Age*. UP of Florida, 2001.

Jenkins, Henry. *Convergence Culture: Where Old and New Media Collide*. New York UP, 2006.

Jennings, Michael W. "The Production, Reproduction, and Reception of the Work of Art." Jennings, et al., pp. 9–18.

Jennings, Michael W., and Brigid Doherty. "Script, Image, Script-Image." Jennings, et al., pp. 167–72.

Jennings, Michael W., Brigid Doherty, and Thomas Y. Levin. Editor's Introduction. Jennings, et al., pp. 1–8.

Jennings, Michael W., et al., ed. *The Work of Art in the Age of its Technological Reproducibility and Other Writings on Media*. Translated by Edmund Jephcott, Rodney Livingstone, Howard Eiland, and Others, Belknap-Harvard UP, 2008.

The Jewish Study Bible (*Tanakh*). Translation, Jewish Publication Society (JBS), edited by Adele Berlin and Marc Zvi Brettler, Oxford UP, 1999.

Raphael, Simcha Paull. *Jewish Views of the Afterlife.* Northvale, New Jersey: Jason Aronson, Inc, 1996.

Johnson, Mark. *The Body in the Mind: The Bodily Basis of Meaning, Imagination, and Reason.* U of Chicago P, 1990.

—. *The Meaning of the Body: Aesthetics of Human Understanding.* U of Chicago P, 2007.

Jones, Roger Bishop, ed. Preface, *The Organon*, Oxford Obook, January 1, 2016. https://www.rbjones.com/rbjpub/philos/classics/aristotl/obook_draft.pdf

Josephus, Flavius. *The Works of Josephus: Complete and Unabridged.* New Updated Edition, Unabridged, translated by William Whiston: Hendrickson Publishing, 1980.

Josephs, Sister Miriam. *Shakespeare's Use of the Arts of Language.* Columbia UP, 1947.

Jowett, Benjamin, trans. Introduction. Plato, *Gorgias*, CreateSpace, 2015, pp. 2-52.

Jung, Carl G, Joseph L. Henderson, M.L. von Franz, Aniela Jaffé, and Jacobi, Jolande. *Man and His Symbols*, edited by M.L. von Franz, Aldus Books, 1964.

KAC. 20 Dec. 2010. www.Ekac.org.

Kant, Immanuel. *Critique of Judgment.* Translated by J. H. Bernard, Hafner, 1951.

—. *Critique of Pure Reason.* Translated by Max Muller, Doubleday, 1966.

—. "Declaration." Translated by Arnulf Zweig, U of Chicago P, 1967, pp. 249–50.

—. *Prolegomena to Any Future Metaphysics.* Edited and translated by Lewis White Beck, Bobbs-Merrill, 1950.

Kaplan, Aryeh, translator and commentor. *Bahir.* Rowman & Littlefield Publishers, 1977.

—. *Sefer Yetzirah: The Book of Creation in Theory and Practice.* Subsequent ed., Weiser Books, 1997.

Kastely, James L. *The Rhetoric of Plato's Republic: Democracy and the Philosophical Problems of Persuasion.* U of Chicago Press, 2015.

Katz, Steven B. "The Alphabet as Ethics: A Rhetorical Basis for Moral Reality in Hebrew Letters." *Rhetorical Democracy: Discursive Practices of Civic Engagement*, edited by Gerard Hauser and Amy Grimm, Erlbaum, 2004, pp. 195–204.

—. "The Alphabet as an Ontological Basis of Ethics" Invited lecture. Center for Holocaust Studies, and the Center for Jewish Studies, University of Minnesota-Twin Cities, 22 Oct 2014.

—. "Ancient and Renaissance Versions of "the Jewish Big Bang," and "G/d's Failure." Presentation, Rhetoric and Religion as Resources for Resistance: An Interdisciplinary Conference, 19–21 Oct 2023, Memphis, Tennessee.

—. "Aristotle's Rhetoric, Hitler's Program, and the Ideological Problem of Praxis, Power, and Professional Discourse." *Journal of Business and Technical Communication*, vol. 7, no. 1, 1993, pp. 37–62.

—. "Biotechnology and Global Miscommunication with the Public: Rhetorical Assumptions, Stylistic Acts, Ethical Implications." *Connecting People with Technology: Issues in Professional Communication*, edited by Helen Grady and George Hayhoe, Baywood, 2009, pp. 167–75.

—. "Burke's New Body? The Problem of Virtual Material, and Motive, in Object Oriented Philosophy." *KB: Journal of the Kenneth Burke Society*, vol. 11, no. 1, 2015, kbjournal.org/katz_burkes_new_body.

—. *The Epistemic Music of Rhetoric: Toward the Temporal Dimension of Reader Response and Writing.* Southern Illinois UP, 1996.

—. "The Epistemology of the Kabbalah: Toward a Jewish Philosophy of Rhetoric." *Rhetoric Society Quarterly*, vol. 25, 1995, pp. 107–22.

—. "Education in the Modern World." *Gateway Review*, vol. 1, Spring 1983.

—. "The Ethic of Expediency: Classical Rhetoric, Technology, and the Holocaust." *College English*, vol. 54, no. 3, 1992, pp. 255–75.

—. "Ethics and Time: After the Anthropocene." *Humanities,* vol. 8, no.4, 2019, pp. 185, p. 85; https://doi.org/10.3390/h8040185.

—. "Ethics." In *Keywords in Scientific and Technical Communication*, edited by Han Yu and Jonathan Buehl, WAC Clearinghouse, 2023, https://doi.org/10.37514/TPC-B.2023.1923.2.12

—. "Foreword, Autopoiesis: The Evolution of Robots as Poems." *Androids, Cyborgs, and Robots in Contemporary Culture and Society*, edited by Steven J. Thompson, IGI Global, 2018.

—. "The Hebrew Bible as Another, Jewish Sophistic: A Genesis of Absence and Desire in Ancient Rhetoric." *Ancient Non-Greek Rhetorics*, edited by Carol Lipson and Roberta A. Binkley, Parlor Press, 2009, pp. 125–50.

—. "The Kabbalah as a Theory of Rhetoric: Another Suppressed Epistemology." *Rhetoric, Cultural Studies, and Literacy: Selected Papers from the 1994 Conference of the Rhetoric Society of America*, edited by John Frederick Reynolds, Erlbaum, 1995, pp. 109–17.

—. "Language and Persuasion in Biotechnology Communication with the Public: How to Not Say What You're Not Going to Not Say and Not Say It." *Journal of Agrobiotechnology Management and Economics*, vol. 4, no. 2, 2001, pp. 93–97.

—. "Letter as Essence: The Rhetorical (Im)pulse of the Hebrew Alefbet." *On Jewish Rhetoric*, edited by David Franks. Special issue, *Journal of Communication and Religion*, vol. 26, 2003, pp. 125–60.

—. "Narration, Technical Communication, and Culture: The Soul of a New Machine as Narrative Romance." *Constructing Rhetorical Education: From the Classroom to the Community.* Edited by Marie Secor and Davida Charney, Southern Illinois UP, 1992, pp. 382–402.

—. Review. *Style, Rhetoric, and Rhythm* by Morris W Croll. Edited by J. Max Patrick, Robert O. Evans, John M. Wallace, and R. J. Schoeck.*Rhetoric Society Quarterly*, vol 19, no. 9, 1989, pp. 381–85.

—. "Revisiting Ethics in Human-Machine Relations: Technical and Professional Communication and Emergent Intelligences." Afterword. *The Routledge Handbook of Ethics in Technical and Professional Communication.* Edited by Derek Ross, Routledge, 2025.

—. "The Rhetoric of Confessional Poetry: Ethos, Myth, and the Narrative Configuration of Self." *My Father Was Shiva: A Family Tragedy in Poetry and Prose with Psychological Interpretations.* Edited by Edward Tick, Ablex, 1994, pp. 109–36.

—. "Socrates as Rabbi: The Story of the Aleph and the Alpha in an Information Age." *Jewish Rhetorics: History, Theory, Practice.* Edited by Janice Fernheimer and Michael Bernard-Donals, Brandeis UP, 2014, pp. 93–111.

—. "Sonic Rhetorics as Ethics in Action: Hidden Temporalities of Sound in Language(s)." *Humanities*, vol. 9, no. 1, 2020, https://doi.org/10.3390/h9010013.

—, and Linvill, Claiborne C. "Lines and Fields of Ethical Force in Scientific Authorship: The Legitimacy and Power of the Office of Research Integrity." In *Scientific Communication: Practices, Theories, and Pedagogies*, edited by Han Yu and Kathryn M. Northcut, Routledge, 2017.

—, and Carolyn Miller. "The Low-Level Radioactive Waste Siting Controversy in North Carolina: Toward a Rhetorical Model of Risk Communication." *Green Culture: Environmental Rhetoric in Contemporary America*, edited by Carl G. Herndl and Stuart Brown, U of Wisconsin P, 1996, pp. 111–40.

—, and Vicki W. Rhodes. "Beyond Ethical Frames of Technical Relations: Digital Being in the Workplace World." *Digital Literacy for Technical Communication: 21st Century Theory and Practice*, edited by Rachel Spilka, Routledge, 2010, pp. 230–56.

—, and Nathaniel Rivers. "A Predestination for Posthumanism." *Ambiguous Bodies: Burke and Posthumanism*, edited by Chris Mays, Nathaniel A. Rivers, Kellie Sharp-Hoskins, U of South Carolina P, 2017, pp. 142–61.

Kaufman, Max. *Tales from Specks of Dust; Poems on the Atomic Age.* Frederick, 1947.

Kaufman, Walter. Introduction. *The Gay Science: With a Prelude in Rhymes and an Appendix of Songs*, by Kaufman, Vintage Books-Random House, 1974, pp. 3–26.

Kaufman, William. Introduction. *Meditations*, by Marcus Aurelius, edited by William Kaufman, Mineola, Dover, 1997, pp. v–ix.

Kazantzakis, Nikos. *The Odyssey: A Modern Sequel.* Translated by Kimon Friar, Simon and Schuster, 1958.

Keats, John. *Complete Poems and Selected Letters of John Keats.* Modern Library, 2001.

—. *John Keats and Percy Bysshe Shelley: Complete Poetical Works.* Modern Library.

Kench, Riley. "What Is a Calculus Math Problem." *Study.com*, updated November 21, 2023. https://study.com/learn/lesson/basic-calculus-formulas-problems.html. Accessed 16 Sept 2024.

Kennedy, George. *Classical Rhetoric and Its Christian and Secular Tradition from Ancient to Modern Times.* Second ed., U of North Carolina P, 1999.

—. "A Hoot in the Dark: The Evolution of General Rhetoric." *Philosophy and Rhetoric*, vol. 25, no. 1, 1992, pp. 1–21.

—. *A New History of Classical Rhetoric.* Princeton, Princeton UP, 1994.

—, translator. *On Rhetoric: A Theory of Civic Discourse* by Aristotle, 2nd ed., Oxford UP, 2006.

Kennedy, J.B. *The Musical Structure of Plato's Dialogues.* Acumen, 2011.

Kenney, Richard. *The Evolutions of the Flightless Bird.* Yale UP, 1984.

Kerferd, G. B. *The Sophistic Movement.* Cambridge UP, 1981.

Kidder, Tracy. *The Soul of a New Machine.* Boston, Little, Brown and Co, 1981.

Kingsley, Peter. *In the Dark Places of Wisdom.* The Golden Sufi Center, 1999.

—. *Reality.* The Golden Sufi Center, 2020.

Kinneavy, James L. *A Theory of Discourse: The Aims of Discourse.* Norton, 1971.

Kittler, Friedrich. *The Truth of the Technological World: Essays on the Genealogy of Presence.* Stanford UP, 2013.

Kittler, Friedrich A. *Gramophone, Film, Typewriter.* Translated by Geoffrey Winthrop-Young and Michael Wautz, Stanford UP, 1999.

Kittler, Friedrich A. *Discourse Networks, 1800/1900.* Translated by Michael Metteer and Chris Cullens, Stanford UP, 1992.

Kohn, Eduardo. *How Forests Think: Toward an Anthropology Beyond the Human.* U of California P, 2013.

Kolodny, Annette. *The Lay of the Land: Metaphor as Experience and history in American Life and Letters.* U of North Carolina P, 1984.

Knoblauch, C. H., and Lil Brannon. *Rhetorical Traditions and the Teaching of Writing.* Boynton/Cook, 1984.

Kress, Gunther, and Theo van Leeuwen. *Reading Images: The Grammar of Visual Design.* 2nd ed., Routledge, 2006.

Kristeva, Julia. *Women's Time.* Translated by Alice Jardine and Harry Blake. *SIGNS*, vol. 7, no. 1, 1981, pp. 13–35.

Kubler-Ross, Elizabeth. *On Death and Dying.* 50th Anniversary ed., Scribner: 2014.

Kuhn, Thomas S. *The Structure of Scientific Revolutions.* 3rd ed., U of Chicago P, 1996.

—. "Metaphor in Science." *Metaphor and Thought*, edited by Andrew Ortony, 2nd ed., Cambridge UP, 1993, pp. 533–42.

Lacan, Jacques. *Ecrits: The First Complete Edition in English.* Translated by Bruce Fink, Norton, 2006.

Lakoff, George, and Mark Johnson. *Metaphors We Live By.* U of Chicago P, 2003.

—. *Philosophy in the Flesh: The Embodied Mind and Its Challenge to Western Thought.* Basic, 1999.

Lakoff, George, and Rafael Nuñez. *Where Mathematics Comes From: How the Embodied Mind Brings Mathematics into Being.* Basic, 2000.

Langer, Susanne. *Feeling and Form: A Theory of Art.* Scribner, 1953.

—. *Philosophy in a New Key.* Harvard UP, 1942.

Lamb, W.R.M, trans. *Plato in Twelve Volumes*, vol. 3, Harvard UP, 1967.

Lanham, Richard A. *Analyzing Prose.* 2nd ed., Continuum, 2003.

—. *The Economics of Attention: Style and Substance in the Age of Information.* U of Chicago P, 2006.

—. *The Electronic Word: Democracy, Technology, and the Arts.* U of Chicago P. 1995.

—. *Style: An Anti-Textbook.* Philadelphia, Paul Dry, 2007.

Laporte, Dominique. *History of Shit.* Translated by Nadia Benabid and Rodolphe el-Khoury, MIT, 2002.

Latour, Bruno. *Aramis, or the Love of Technology.* Translated by Catherine Porter, Harvard UP, 1996.

—. *An Inquiry into Modes of Existence: An Anthropology of the Moderns.* Translated by Catherine Porter, Harvard UP, 2013.

—.*On the Modern Cult of the Factish Gods.* Duke UP, 2010.

—. *We Have Never Been Modern.* Translated by Catherine Porter, Harvard UP, 1993.

Latour, Bruno, and Steve Woolgar. *Laboratory Life: The Construction of Scientific Facts.* Princeton UP, 1986.

Leff, Michael. "Burke's Ciceronianism." *The Legacy of Kenneth Burke*, edited by Herbert W. Simons and Trevor Melia, U of Wisconsin P, 1989, pp. 115–27.

Leibniz, G.W. The Early Mathematical Manuscripts of Leibniz. Translated by J.M. Child. Open Court, 1920.

Lentz, Tony M. *Orality and Literacy in Hellenic Greece.* Southern Illinois UP, 1989.

Levin, Kim. "The Eye of Ra." *Light in Art*, edited by Thomas B. Hess and John, Collier 1971, pp. 21–36.

Levin, Thomas Y. "Film." Jennings, et al., pp. 315–22.

Levinas, Emmanuel. *Entre Nous: Thinking-of-the-Other.* Translated by Michael B. Smith and Barbara Harshav, Columbia UP, 1998.

—. *Existence and Existents.* Translated by Alphonso Lingis, Duquesne UP, 2001.

—. *Otherwise than Being: Or Beyond Essence.* Translated by Alphonso Lingis, Duquesne UP, 1997.

—. *Time and the Other.* Revised ed., translated by Richard A. Cohen, Duquesne UP, 1987.

—. *Totality and Infinity: An Essay on Exteriority.* Translated by Alphonso Lingis, Duquesne UP, 1969.

Lewis, C. S. *The Allegory of Love: A Study in Medieval Tradition.* Oxford UP, 1936.

Libretexts: Mathematics. National Science Foundation. https://math.libretexts.org/Bookshelves/Precalculus/Precalculus_1e_(OpenStax)/. Accessed 4 Apr. 2024.

Liddell, Henry George, and Georg Autenrieth. "LSJ, Middle Liddell." *A Greek-English Lexicon:* Compiled by Henry George Liddell, and Robert Scott, Clarendon Press, 1961.

—, and Scott, Robert. *A Greek-English Lexicon:* Compiled by Henry George Liddell, and Robert Scott, Clarendon Press, 1961.

Lieberman, Saul. *Hellenism in Jewish Palestine: Studies in the Beliefs and Manners of Palestine 1 Century BCE-IV Century CE.* The Jewish Theological Seminary of America, 1950).

Locke, John. *An Essay Concerning Human Understanding.* Great Books of the Western World. Encyclopedia Britannica, Inc., 1990. Originally published by Thomas Basset, 1689.

—. *Two Treatises on Government and a Letter Concerning Toleration.* Digireads.com Publishing, 2016.

Lohr, Steve. "Now Playing: Night of the Living Tech." *New York Times*, 23 Aug. 2010. Week in Review 1, p. 4.

—. "You Want My Personal Data? Reward Me for It." *New York Times*, 18 July 2010. Business 3.

Longinus. *On Great Writing (On the Sublime).* Translated by G. M. A. Grube, Hackett, 1957.

Longo, Bernadette. *Spurious Coin: A History of Science, Management, and Technical Writing.* SUNY P, 2003.

Lovitt, William. Introduction. *Question Concerning Technology*, Heidegger, pp. xiii–xxxix.

Lury, Celia. *Prosthetic Culture: Photography, Memory, and Identity.* Routledge, 1998.

Lyotard, Jean-Francois. *Discourse, Figure.* Translated by Antony Hudek and Mary Lydon, U of Minnesota P, 2011.

—. *Libidinal Economy.* Translated by Iain Hamilton Grant, Indiana UP, 1993.

—. *The Postmodern Condition: A Report on Knowledge.* Translated by Geoff Bennington and Brian Massumi, U of Minnesota P, 1984.

—. "Taking the Side of the Figural." *The Lyotard Reader and Guide*, edited by Keith Crome and James Williams, Columbia UP, 2006, pp. 23–46.

Mairs, Nancy. *Waist-High in the World: A Life Among the Nondisabled.* Beacon Press, 1997.

Manovich, Lev. *The Language of New Media.* MIT, 2001.

Marinetti, Filippo Tommaso. *Critical Writings.* Edited by Günter Berghaus, Translated by Doug Thompson, Farrar, Straus and Giroux, 2006.

Mark, Joshua J. "Plato: The Poet Aristocles." *World History Encyclopedia*, 29 May 2019. https://www.worldhistory.org/article/33/plato-the-poet-aristocles. Accessed 24 July 2021.

Markoff, John. "The Boss Is Robotic and Rolling Up Behind You." *New York Times*, 5 Sep. 2010. 1, pp. 16–17.

—. "Computers as Invisible as Air." *New York Times*, 5 Sep. 2010. Week in Review 2.

Marrou, Henri I. *A History of Education in Antiquity.* Translated by George Lamb, Sheed and Ward, 1956.

Marx, Karl. *Capital: An Abridged Edition.* Oxford World's Classics Edition, Oxford UP, 2008.

Marx, Leo. *The Machine in the Garden: Technology and the Pastoral Ideal in America.* Oxford UP, 2000.

Mason, David, and John Frederick Nims. *Western Wind: An Introduction to Poetry.* 5th ed., McGraw-Hill, 2005.

Mathematics Stack Exchange. "What Is the Smallest Possible Number with Any Mathematical Value of Property?" https://math.stackexchange.com/questions/2341975/what-is-the-smallest-number-with-any-mathematical-value-of-property. Accessed 15 Apr 2024.

McKenny, Gerald P. *To Relieve the Human Condition: Bioethics Technology, and the Body.* SUNY P, 1997.

McLuhan, Marshall. *The Gutenberg Galaxy.* U of Toronto P, 2011.

—. *Understanding Media: The Extensions of Man.* Critical ed., edited by W. Terrence Gordon, Berkeley, Gingko, 2003.

McLuhan, Marshall, and Quentin Fiore. *The Medium Is the Massage: An Inventory of Effects.* Berkeley, Gingko, 2005.

Mead, George Herbert. *Mind, Self, and Society: From the Standpoint of a Social Behaviorist.* Works of George Herbert Mead, edited by Charles W. Morris, vol. 1, U of Chicago P, 1967.

Measel, Michael David. *Rhetoric in the Keyboard Compositions of Kenneth Burke: Musical Gestalt and Aural Affect.* Doctoral Dissertation, Clemson University, 2021.

Mebust, Michelle R., and Steven B. Katz. "Rhetorical Assumptions, Rhetorical Risks: Communication Models in Genetic Counseling." *Rhetoric of Healthcare: Essays Toward a New Disciplinary Inquiry*, edited by Barbara Heifferon and Stuart Brown, Cresskill, Hampton P, 2007, pp. 91–114.

Melberg, Arne. *Theories of Mimesis.* Cambridge UP, 1995.

Mendelson, Michael. "The Rhetoric of Embodiment." *Rhetoric Society Quarterly*, vol. 28, no. 4, 1998, pp. 29–50.

Merkin, Daphne. "The Politics of Appearance: In a Realm Where Simulation Is All, Authenticity May Lie in the Details." *New York Times Style Magazine*, 2007, pp. 307–09.

Merleau-Ponty, Maurice. *Phenomenology of Perception.* Routledge, 2002.

Metzger, David. *The Lost Cause of Rhetoric: The Relation of Rhetoric and Geometry in Aristotle and Lacan.* Southern Illinois UP, 1995.

Metzger, David, and Steven B. Katz. "The 'Place' of Rhetoric in Aggadic Midrash." *College English*, vol. 72, no. 6, 2010, pp. 638–53.

Meyer, Bruce, editor. *Arrivals: Canadian Poetry in the Eighties.* Greenfield Center, Greenfield Review, 1986.

Meyer, Leonard B. *Emotion and Meaning in Music.* U of Chicago P, 1956.

Midrash Rabbah. "Genesis (Bereshith)," vol. 1. Translated by Harry Freeman. London: Soncino Press, 1983, 10 vols.

Miles, Jack. *God: A Biography.* Vintage, 1996.

Miller, Carolyn R. "A Humanistic Rationale for Technical Writing." *College English*, vol. 40, no. 6, 1979, pp. 610–17.

—. "Learning from History: World War II and the Culture of High Technology." *Journal of Business and Technical Communication*, vol. 12, no. 3, 1998, pp. 288–315.

—. "The Rhetoric of Decision Science, or, Herbert A. Simon Says." *The Rhetorical Turn: Invention and Persuasion in the Conduct of Inquiry*, edited by Herbert W. Simons, U of Chicago P, 1990, pp. 162–84.

—. "Technology as a Form of Consciousness: A Study of Contemporary Ethos." *Central States Speech Journal*, vol. 29, no. 4, 1978, pp. 228–36.

—. "What Can Automation Tell Us About Agency?" *Rhetoric Society Quarterly*, vol. 7, no. 37, 2007, pp. 137–57.

Milosz, Czeslaw. *The Witness of Poetry.* Harvard UP, 1983.

Milton, John. "Paradise Lost." *The Complete and Selected Prose of John Milton.* Random, 1950, pp. 90–394.

Minsky, Marvin. *The Emotion Machine: Commonsense Thinking, Artificial Intelligence, and the Future of the Human Mind.* Simon & Schuster, 2006.

Mitchell, David T. and Sharon L. Snyder. *Narrative Prosthesis: Disability and the Dependencies of Discourse.* U of Michigan P, 2001.

Michie, James *The Odes of Horace.* Orion, 1963.

Moholy-Nagy, László. *Moholy-Nagy: An Anthology*. Edited by Richard Kostelanetz, Cambridge, Da Capo, 1991.

Molson, Robert. *A Brief Introduction to Calculus*. https://www.ms.uky.edu/~lee/amspcalc/calcmolzon.pdf. Accessed 12 Sept 2024.

Morton, Timothy B. *Ecology without Nature: Rethinking Environmental Aesthetics*. Harvard UP, 2009.

—. *The Ecological Thought*. Harvard UP, 2012. Kindle AZW file.

—. *Hyperobjects: Philosophy and Ecology after the End of the World (Posthumanities)*. U of Minnesota P, 2013.

—. *Realist Magic: Objects, Ontology, Causality (New Metaphysics)*. MPublishing, University of Michigan Library, 2013.

Moses, Myra G, and Steven B. Katz. "The Phantom Machine: The Invisible Ideology of Email (A Cultural Critique)." *Critical Power Tools: Technical Communication and Cultural Studies*, edited by J. Blake Scott, Bernadette Longo, and Katherine V. Willis, SUNY P, 2006, pp. 71–105.

Moskow, Michal Anne, and Steven B. Katz. "Composing Identity and Community in Cyberspace: A 'Rhetorical Ethnography' of Writing on Jewish Discussion Groups in the United States and Germany." *Judaic Perspectives in Rhetoric and Compositional Studies*, edited by Andrea Greenbaum and Deborah Holdstein, Creskill, Hampton, 2008, pp. 85–108.

Mouroutsou, Georgia. "The Allegory of the Cave: The Necessity of the Philosopher's Descent." *Plato: Le Journal Internet de la Société Platoniicienne Internationale,* 11, Mars 2012.

Munk, Michael L. *The Wisdom in the Hebrew Alphabet*. 1st ed., Mesorah, 1983.

Murphy, James J., editor. *Three Medieval Rhetorical Arts*. U of California P, 1971.

Mūsā al-Khwārizmī, active 9th century. *Hisâb al-Jabr w'al Muqâbalah*. Contribution by Ali Mustafa, Cairo, Paul Barber Press, 1937. https://www.loc.gov/item/2021666184/. Accessed 13 Aug 2024.

Murty, M. Ram. "Newton and Leibniz: The Development of Calculus." Queens University, Kingston, Canada. https://mast.queensu.ca/~murty/MathHistory-21.pdf. Accessed 10 Sept 2024.

Nancy, Jean-Luc. *Being Singular Plural*. Translated by Robert D. Richardson and Anne E. Byrne, Stanford UP, 2000.

—. *The Birth to Presence*. Translated by Brian Holmes, Stanford UP, 1993.

—. "Corpus." In *Corpus*, translated by Richard A. Rand, Fordham UP, 2008, pp. 1–121.

—. *Corpus*. Translated by Richard A. Rand, Fordham UP, 2008.

—. *The Fall of Sleep*. Translated by Charlotte Mandell, Fordham UP, 2009.

—. *The Ground of the Image*. Translated by Jeff Fort, Fordham UP, 2005.

—. *The Inoperative Community*. Edited by Peter Connor, U of Minnesota P, 1991.

—. "The Intruder." *Corpus*, translated by Richard A. Rand, Fordham UP, 2008, pp. 161–70.
—. *Listening.* Translated by Charlotte Mandell, Fordham UP, 2007.
—. *The Muses.* Translated by Peggy Kamuf, Stanford UP, 1997.
—. *Noli me Tangere: On the Raising of the Body.* Translated by Sarah Clift, Pascale-Anne Brault, and Michael Naas, Fordham UP, 2008.
—. *The Sense of the World.* Translated by Jeffrey S. Librett, 2nd ed., U of Minnesota P, 2008.
Nasehpour, Peyman. "The Greek Letters in Mathematics," preprint Aug 2020, uploaded and published by Peyman to *Research Gate.* 5 Dec 2022. https://www.researchgate.net/publication/343452184_The_Greek_letters_in mathematics. Accessed 31 Mar 2024.
Newton, Issac. Newton's *Principia*: *The Mathematical Principles of Natural Philosophy.* Translated by Andrew Motte, Daniel Adee, 1846.
Nietzsche, Friedrich. *The Birth of Tragedy and the Genealogy of Morals.* Translated by Francis Golffing, Doubleday, 1956.
—. *The Gay Science: With a Prelude in Rhymes and an Appendix of Songs.* Translated by Walter Kaufman, Vintage Books-Random House, 1974.
—. *Human, All Too Human.* Macmillan, 1924.
—. *On Truth and Lies in a Nonmoral Sense.* Aristeus, 2012.
—. *Thus Spoke Zarathustra.* Translated by Thomas Common, East India Publishing, 2020.
—. *The Twilight of the Idols. The Twilight of the Idols, with The Antichrist* and *Ecce Homo*, translated by Anthony R. Ludovici, Wordsworth, 2007.
Norman, Judith. "Nietzsche and Early Romanticism." *Journal of the History of Ideas*, vol. 63, no. 3, 2002, pp. 501–19.
Notopoulos, James A. "The Name of Plato." *Classical Philology*, vol. 34, no. 2, 1939, pp. 135–45.
Oliver, Mary. *Blue Pastures.* Harcourt Brace, 1995.
Olshewsky, Thomas M. "On the Relations of Soul and Body in Plato and Aristotle." *History of Philosophy*, vol 14, no. 4, Oct 1976, 391–404.
Ong, Walter J. *Orality and Literacy: The Technologizing of the Word.* Methuen, 1982.
—. *Ramus, Method, and the Decay of Dialogue.* Harvard UP, 1958.
—. *Rhetoric, Romance, and Technology: Studies in the Interaction of Expression and Culture.* Cornell UP, 1971.
—. "The Writer's Audience Is Always a Fiction." *PMLA*, vol. 90, no. 1, 1975, pp. 9–21.
Orenstein, Peggy. "I Tweet, Therefore I Am." *The New York Times Magazine*, 1 Aug. 2010, pp. 11–12.
Ortony, Andrew, ed. *Metaphor and Thought.* Cambridge UP, 1979.
—. *Metaphor and Thought.* 2nd ed., Cambridge UP, 1993.

Overall, Joel. *Research Belief Without Theology: The Music Criticism of Kenneth Burke*. Parlor Press, forthcoming.

Ovid. *Metamorphoses*. Translated by Frank Justus Miller, Harvard UP, pp. 1944–46.

Padilla, Tony. "Omicron Notation," *Numberphile*, video by Brady Haran/Jane Street, Simons\Laufer Mathematical Institute Sciences Institute. https://www.numberphile.com/videos/omicron-the-symbol-in-mathematics. Accessed 31 Mar 2024.

Parikka, Jussi., and Paul Fiegelfeld. "Kittler's Media Exorcism." *Theory, Culture, and Society*, 2015, pp. 1–10.

Parker, Emily. "Character Study." *The New York Times Book Review*, 8 Nov. 2009, p. 39.

Parry, Milman. *The Making of Homeric Verse: The Collected Papers of Milman Parry*. Edited by Adam Parry, Clarendon, 1971.

Paul, Catherine. *Fascist Directive: Ezra Pound and Italian Cultural Nationalism*. Clemson UP, 2016.

—, and Margaret Mills Harper, editors. A *Vision: The Revised 1937 Edition*. The Collected Works of W.B. Yeats, vol XIV, Scribner, 2015.

Peacham, Henry. *The Garden of Eloquence*. 1593. Scholars' Facsimiles, Reprints, 1954.

Pedersen, Isabel. *Ready to Wear: A Rhetoric of Wearable Computers and Reality-Shifting Media*. Parlor Press, 2013.

Peirce, Charles Sanders. *Pierce on Signs: Writings on Semiotics by Charles Sanders Peirce*. Edited by James Hoopes, U of North Carolina P, 1991.

Perelman, Chaim. *The Realm of Rhetoric*. Translated by William Kluback, U of Notre Dame P, 1982.

Perkei Avot. (Ethics of the Fathers). New translation by Rabbi Nosson Scherman, Brooklyn, Mesorah Publications, 1984.

Perpich, Diane. *The Ethics of Emmanuel Levinas*. Stanford UP, 2008.

Petrie, Paul. *The Academy of Goodbye*. UP of New England, 1974.

Phillips, John T. "Origins of the Rules of Civility." George Washington, *Rules of Civility*, edited by John T. Phillips, Leesburg, Goose Creek Productions, 2001, pp. 7–14.

Philo. *The Works of Philo: Complete and Unabridged*. Translated by C.D. Yonge, Peabody, MA: Hendrickson Academic, updated ed., 1991.

Pirie, Mark, and Tim Jones, editors. *Voyagers: Science Fiction Poetry from New Zealand*. Interactive, 2009.

Plath, Sylvia. *The Collected Poems*. Edited by Ted Hughes, Harper Row, 1981.

Plato, *The Collected Dialogues of Plato Including the Letters*. Edited by Edith Hamilton and Huntington Cairns, Princeton UP, 1961.

—. *Charmides*. Translated by Benjamin Jowett, *Collected Dialogues*, pp. 99–122.

—. *Cratylus*. Translated by Benjamin Jowett, *Collected Dialogues*, pp. 421–74.

—. *Epinomis.* Translated A.E. Taylor, *Collected Dialogues,* pp. 1517–1533.
—. *Euthydemus.* Translated by W. H. D. Rouse, *Collected Dialogues,* pp. 385–420.
—. *Gorgias.* Translated by W. D. Woodhead, *Collected Dialogues,* pp. 229–307.
—. *Greater Hippias.* Translated by A. E. Taylor, *Collected Dialogues,* pp. 1534–1559.
—. *Laws.* Translated by A. E. Taylor, *Collected Dialogues,* pp. 1225–513.
—. *Lesser Hippias.* Translated by Benjamin Jowett, *Collected Dialogues,* pp. 200–214.
—. *Meno.* Translated by W. K. C. Guthrie, *Collected Dialogues,* pp. 253–384.
—. *Parmenides.* Translated by A. E. Taylor, *Collected Dialogues,* pp. 920–56.
—. *Phaedo.* Translated by Hugh Tredennick, *Collected Dialogues,* pp. 40–98.
—. *Phaedrus.* Translated by W. C. Helmbold and W. G. Rabinowitz, Indianapolis, Bobbs-Merrill, 1956.
—. *Philebus.* Translated by R. Hackforth, *Collected Dialogues,* pp. 1086–150.
—. *Protagoras.* Translated by W. K. C. Guthrie, *Collected Dialogues,* pp. 308–52.
—. *Republic. Great Dialogues of Plato.* Translated by W. H. D. Rouse, Signet, 1999, pp. 118–422.
—. *Socrates' Defense (Apology).* Translated by Hugh Tredennick, *Collected Dialogues,* pp. 3–26.
—. *Sophist.* Translated by F. M. Cornford, *Collected Dialogues,* pp. 957–1017.
—. *Statesman.* Translated by J. B. Skemp, *Collected Dialogues,* pp. 1018–85.
—. *Symposium. Great Dialogues of Plato.* Translated by W. H. D. Rouse, Signet, 1999, pp. 69-117.
—. *Theaetetus.* Translated by F. M. Cornford, *The Collected Dialogues of Plato,* edited by Edith Hamilton and Huntington Cairns, pp. 845–919.
—. *Timaeus.* Translated by Benjamin Jowett, *Collected Dialogues,* pp. 1151–211.
Plotinos. *Complete Works: In Chronological Order, Grouped in Four Periods.* Translator by Kenneth Sylvan Guthrie, Vol I, Project Gutenberg [EBook #42930], June 2013.
Plutarch. "The Life of Crassus." *The Parallel Lives,* translated by Bernadotte Perrin, vol III, Loeb-Harvard UP, 1916, 313–433.
—. *The Lives of the Noble Greeks and Romans.* Translated by John Dryden, revised by Arthur Hugh Clough, Random-Modern Library.
—. "On Superstition." *Moralia.* Translated by Frank Cole Babbit, vol. 2, Loeb-Harvard UP, 1928, 452-495.
—. "Roman Questions" *Moralia.* Translated by Frank Cole Babbitt, vol. 4, Loeb-Harvard UP, 1936, 1171.
Polanyi, Michael. *Personal Knowledge.* HarperMcKenny, 1958.
Pollack, Andrew. "His Corporate Strategy: The Scientific Method." *New York Times,* 4 Sep. 2010. www.nytimes.com/2010/09/05/business/05venter.html. 15 Oct. 2012.

Pope, Alexander. "Essay on Man." *Essay on Man and Other Poems.* Dover Thrift Editions: Poetry, 1994.

Porush, David. *The Soft Machine: Cybernetic Fiction.* Methuen, 1984.

Powell, Jeffrey, ed. *Heidegger and Language.* (Studies in Continental Thought), Indiana UP, 2013.

Pound, Ezra. *ABC of Reading.* New Directions, 1960.

—. "Affirmations." *Selected Prose 1909-1965*, New Directions, 1973, pp. 374–77.

—. *The Cantos of Ezra Pound.* New Directions, 1993.

—. "I Gather the Limbs of Osiris." *Selected Prose 1909–1965*, New Directions, 1973, pp. 21–43.

—. *Literary Essays of Ezra Pound.* New Directions, 1935.

—. "The Prose Tradition in Verse." *Literary Essays of Ezra Pound.* New Directions, 1935, pp. 371–77.

—. "A Retrospect." *Literary Essays of Ezra Pound.* New Directions, 1935, pp. 3–14.

—. *Selected Prose 1909–1965.* New Directions, 1973.

—. "The Serious Artist." *Literary Essays of Ezra Pound*, New Directions, 1935, pp. 41–57.

—. "The Wisdom of Poetry." *Selected Prose 1909–1965*, New Directions, 1973, pp. 359–62.

Praeger, Dave. *Poop Culture: How America Is Shaped by Its Grossest National Product.* Feral, 2007.

Pring, J. T. *The Pocket Oxford Greek Dictionary.* Oxford UP, 1995.

Prompt: "Examples of simple calculus equations where y=0, 1, 2, etc." ChatGPT 4.0, OpenAI, https//openai.com/about. Accessed 12 Sept 2024.

Proust, Marcel. *In Search of Lost Time.* Translated by C.K. Scott Moncrieff, KTHTK Publishers, 2022, 7 vols.

Psaty, Bruce M. "Cicero's Literal Metaphor and Propriety." *Central States Speech Journal*, vol. 29, 1978, pp. 107–17.

Ptolemy, active 2nd century. *Ptolemy's Almagest.* Translated by G.J Toomer, Duckworth, 1984.

Putnam, Hilary. *Philosophical Papers, Volume. 2: Mind, Language and Reality.* Cambridge UP, 1975.

Pynchon, Thomas. *Gravity's Rainbow.* Random House, 1973.

Quine, Willard Van Orman. *Ontological Relativity and Other Essays.* Columbia UP, 1969.

—. *Word and Object.* Martino Fine Books, 2013.

Quintilian, Marcus Fabius. *Institutio Oratoria.* Translated by H. E. Butler, Harvard UP, 1966-1969, 4 vols.

Quora. "What Is the Physical Interpretation of "iota"? https://www.quora.com/What-is-the-physical-interpretation-of-iota. Accessed 13 May 2024.

Quora. "What Does Alpha Represent in Terms of Math and Science Concepts?"

https://www.quora.com/What-does-alpha-represent-in-terms-of-math-and-science-concepts. Accessed 14 Apr. 2024.

Rabinowitz, Abraham Hirsch. *TaRYaG: A Study of the Tradition that the Written Torah Contains 613 Mitzvot.* Jason Aronson Inc., 1996.

Racter. *The Policeman's Beard Is Half Constructed: Computer Prose and Poetry by Racter.* Warner, 1984.

Rakow, Lana F. "Gendered Technology, Gendered Practice." *Critical Studies in Mass Communication*, vol. 5, no. 1, 1988, pp. 57–70.

Ramus, Peter. *Arguments in Rhetoric Against Quintilian.* Translated by Carole Newlands, edited by James J. Murphy, U of Northern Illinois P, 1983.

Reeve, F.D. *Robert Frost in Russia.* Zephyr, 2001.

Rice, Jenny. *Awful Evidence: Conspiracy Theory, Rhetoric, and Acts of Evidence*, Ohio State UP, 2020.

Rich, Adrian. *On Lies, Secrets, and Silence: Selected Prose 1966–1978.* Norton, 1995.

Richards, I.A. *The Philosophy of Rhetoric.* Oxford UP, 1936.

Richards, Keith, performer. Introduction to "Happy." By Keith Richards and Mick Jagger. *Sheryl Crowe and Friends, Live in Central Park.* EMI, 1999. CD.

Richardson, Malcolm, and Sarah Liggett. "Power Relations, Technical Writing Theory, and Workplace Writing." *Journal of Business and Technical Communication*, vol. 7, no. 1, 1993, pp. 112–37.

Rickert, Thomas. *Ambient Rhetoric: The Attunements of Rhetorical Being.* U of Pittsburgh P, 2013.

Ridolfo, Jim, and William Hart-Davidson, eds. *Rhet Ops: Rhetoric and Information Warfare.* U of Pittsburgh P, 2019.

Rilke, Rainer Maria. *Letters to a Young Poet.* Translated by Herter Norton, Norton, 1954.

Rimbaud, Arthur. *Rimbaud: Complete Works, Selected Letters.* Bilingual Edition, translated by Seth Whidden and Wallace Fowlie, revised ed., U of Chicago P, 2005.

Rivers, Nathaniel, and Ryan Weber. *Equipment for Living: The Literary Reviews of Kenneth Burke.* Parlor Press, 2010.

Robinson, Andrew. *The Story of Writing: Alphabets, Hieroglyphics & Pictograms*, Thames ansd Hudson, 1995.

Roethke, Theodore. *The Collected Poems of Theodore Roethke.* 1975. Doubleday-Anchor, 1998.

Rogers, David. *Planets and Predictions: Shakespeare and the Copernican Revolution*, 2000. Middle Tennessee State U, PhD Dissertation.

Rosen, Jeffrey. "The Web Means the End of Forgetting." *New York Times*, 21 July 2010. https://www.nytimes.com/2010/07/25/magazine/25privacy-t2.html. Accessed 21 July 2010.

Rosen, Stanley. *Plato's Republic: A Study*. Yale UP, 2008.

Rutten, Kris, et al. "Rhetoric as Equipment for Living: Kenneth Burke, Culture and Education." Special issue. *KB: Journal of the Kenneth Burke Society*, vol. 10, no. 1, 2014, https://kbjournal.org/summer2014

Rousseau, John Jacques. *Emile; or Education*. Translated by Barbara Foxley, Dutton, 1911.

Rueckert, William H., editor. *Essays Toward a Symbolic of Motives, 1950–1955*. Parlor Press, 2007.

—. Introduction. Rueckert, pp. xi–xxi.

Ruskin, John. *Modern Painters*. Wiley, 1886.

—. *Selected Prose of Ruskin*. Edited by Matthew Hodgart, Signet, 1972.

Said, Edward W. *The World, the Text, and the Critic*. Harvard UP, 1983.

Sandburg, Carl. *The Complete Poems of Carl Sandburg*. Harcourt, 1970.

Sartre, Jean Sartre. *Anti-Semite and the Jew: An Exploration of the Etiology of Hate*. Translated by George J. Becker, Schocken, 1995.

Schelling, Friedrich Wilhelm Joseph Von. *Bruno*. Translated by Michael G. Vater, SUNY P, 1984.

—. *System of Transcendental Idealism*. Translated by Peter Heath, UP of Virginia, 1978.

Schlegel, Friedrich von. *Dialogue on Poetry and Literary Aphorisms*. Translated by Ernst Behler and Roman Struc, Penn State UP, 1968.

"Scalar Potential." *ScienceDirect*. Elsevieer, 2024. https://www.sciencedirect.com/topics/mathematics/scalar-potential. Accessed 6 Apr. 2024.

Schiller, Friedrich. *Naive and Sentimental Poetry, and On the Sublime; Two Essays*. Translated by Julius A. Elias, F. Ungar, 1966.

Schindler, D. C. *Plato's Critique of Impure Reason: On Goodness and Truth in the Republic*, Catholic U of America P, 2008.

Scholem, Gershom. *Major Trends in Jewish Mysticism*. Schocken, 1974.

Schuessler, Jennifer. "Take This Job and Write It." *New York Times Book Review*, 14 Mar. 2010, p. 27.

Schwartz, Delmore. *Selected Poems (1938–1958)*. New Directions, 1959.

Schwartz, Seth. *Were the Jews a Mediterranean Society?: Reciprocity and Solidarity in Ancient Judaism*. Reprint ed., Princeton UP, 2012.

Seaton, J. P. and James Cryer. Introduction. *Bright Moon, Perching Bird: Poems by Li Po and Tu Fu*. Middletown, Wesleyan UP, 1987, pp. ix–xv.

Sedgwick, Eve Kosofsky. *Touching Feeling: Affect, Pedagogy, Performativity*. Edited by Michele Aina Barale and Jonathan Goldberg, Duke UP, 2002.

Seery, John Evan. "Politics as Ironic Community: On the Themes of Descent and Return in Plato's Republic." *Political Theory*, vol 16, no, 2, 1988, pp. 229–56, http://www.jstor.org/stable/191707.

Serres, Michel. *The Five Senses: A Philosophy of Mingled Bodies*. Translated by Margaret Sankey and Peter Cowley, Continuum, 2008.

Shakespeare, William. *The Complete Works of Shakespeare.* Edited by George Lyman Kittredge, Kittredge Players ed., Grolier, 1936.

Shannon, Claude E., and Warren Weaver. *The Mathematical Theory of Communication.* U of Illinois P, 1998.

Sharma, Rama, Reviewer. "Value of ι," *Vedantu.com,* Maths, 2024, https://www.vedantu.com/maths/value-of-i. Accessed 4 Apr 2024

Shea, Elizabeth Parthenia. *How the Gene Got Its Groove: Figurative Language, Science, and the Rhetoric of the Real.* SUNY P, 2009.

Shelly, Mary. *Frankenstein, or the Modern Prometheus.* 1831. Project Gutenberg, https://www.gutenberg.org/files/42324/42324-h/42324-h.htm.

Shelley, Percy Bysshe. "Defense of Poetry." *Essays, Letters from Abroad, Translations and Fragments.* 1821. E. Moxon, 1852.

___, and John Keats. *John Keats and Percy Bysshe Shelley: Complete Poetical Works.* Modern Library, 1960.

Sheridan, Thomas. *A Course in the Lectures on Elocution.* B. Blom, 1968.

Sherwood, Yvonne, and Kevin Hart, editors. *Derrida and Religion: Other Testaments.* Routledge, 2004.

Simon, Herbert A. *The Sciences of the Artificial.* 3rd ed., MIT, 1999.

Simpson, Eileen B. *Poets in Their Youth: A Memoir.* Random House, 1982.

Sinatra, Frank. "I've Got You Under My Skin." By Cole Porter. *Sinatra's Sinatra,* Reprise Records, LP, 1963.

Slater, William J. *Lexicon to Pindar.* In *Perseus Digital Library,* edited by Gregory R. Crane. https://www.perseus.tufts.edu/hopper/text?doc=Perseus:text:1999.04.0072. Accessed 17 March 2022.

Sloane, Thomas A. "Rhetoric and Poetry." *New Princeton Encyclopedia of Poetry and Poetics.* Edited by Alex Preminger and T. V. F, Brogan, Princeton UP, 1993.

Smith, Marquard, and Joanne Morra, editors. *The Prosthetic Impulse: From a Posthuman Present to a Biocultural Future.* MIT, 2006.

Smith, Steven. "I Went Down to the Piraeus." Introduction to Political Philosophy, Lecture 4. Open Yale Course, September 20, 2006. *YouTube* (00:17:38) https://www.youtube.com/watch?v=nVQKbQVc2_w.

Snow, C.P. *Two Cultures & A Second Look: An Expanded Version of The Two Cultures and the Scientific Revolution.* New American Library, 1963.

Spenser, Edmund. *Edmund Spenser's Poetry.* Edited by Hugh Maclean, Norton, 1968.

Sprat, Thomas. *The History of the Royal-Society of London, For the Improving of Natural Knowledge.* Royal Society, 1667.

Stanford Encyclopedia of Philosophy. "Aristotle's Psychology." Stanford University, 2020, https://plato.stanford.edu/entries/aristotle-psychology/.

Stavroulakis, Nocholas. *The Jews of Greece: An Essay.* 1st ed., Bosphorus Books, 1990.

Stedman, Kyle D. *Musical Rhetoric and Sonic Composing Processes.* Doctoral dissertation, University of South Florida, 2012.

Stiegler, Bernard. *Technics and Time, I: The Fault of Epimetheus.* Translated by Richard Beardsworth and George Collins, Stanford UP, 1998.

Steiner, George. *Errata: An Examined Life.* New Haven, Yale UP, 1999.

—. *In Bluebeard's Castle: Some Notes Toward the Redefinition of Culture.* Yale UP, 1971.

—. *The Poetry of Thought: From Hellenism to Celan.* New Directions, 2012.

Stelarc. "Redesigning the Body." *Stelarc.org.* 18 Mar. 2007, www.stelarc.va.com.au.html.

Stephenson, Bruce. *The Music of the Heavens: Kepler's Harmonic Astronomy.* Princeton UP, 1994.

Sterba, Editha and Richard Sterba. *Beethoven and His Nephew: A Psychoanalytical Study of Their Relationship.* Schocken, 1971.

Stevens, Wallace. *The Necessary Angel; Essays on Reality and the Imagination.* Knopf, 1951.

—. *The Palm at the End of the Mind: Selected Poems and a Play.* Knopf, 1971.

Stone, I. F. *The Trial of Socrates.* Anchor, 1989.

Strachan-Davidson, J.L. *Cicero and the Fall of the Roman Republic.* G.P. Puttnam's Sons, 1906.

Strack, Herman L, and Gunter Stemberger. *Introduction to the Talmud and Midrash.* Reprint ed., translated by Markus Bockmuehl, Fortress Press 1996.

Strang, Gilbert. *Calculus.* MIT OpenCourseWare. https://ocw.mit.edu/ans7870/resources/Strang/Edited/Calculus/Calculus.pdf. Accessed 13 Sept 2024.

Study.com. "What Is phi and eta in Particle Physics?" https://homework.study.com/explanation/what-is-phi-and-eta-in-particle-physics. Accessed 4 Apr. 2024.

Sudnow, David. *Talk's Body: A Meditation Between Two Keyboards.* Knopf, 1979.

—. *The Ways of the Hand: The Organization of Improvised Conduct.* MIT, 1993.

Suetonius. *Lives of the Caesars.* Translated by J.C. Rolfe, Harvard UP, 1998, 2 vols.

Sussex. *A Brief Guide to Some Commonly Used Statistical Symbols.* https://users.sussex.ac.uk/~grahamh/RM1web/StatsSymbolsGuide. Accessed 27 Sept. 2025.

Sydney, Sir Philip. *Defense of Poetry: And Observations on Poetry and Eloquence, From the Discoveries of Ben Jonson.* Edited by Joseph Warton, Andesite Press, 2015.

Sypher, Wylie. *Literature and Technology: The Alien Vision.* Random, 1968.

Tabbi, Joseph. *Postmodern Sublime: Technology and American Writing from Mailer to Cyberpunk.* Cornell UP, 1995.

Tacitus, Cornelius. Agricola. Translated by M. Hutton, W. Peterson. In Agricola Germania Dialogus. Revised Edition, Loeb-Harvard UP, 1910.

___. *The Histories.* Translated by Alfred John Church and William Jackson Brodribb, East India, 2022.

Tanakh. The Jewish Study Bible Translation, Jewish Publication Society, edited by Adele Berlin and Marc Zvi Brettler, Oxford UP, 1999.

Thacker, Eugene. "Data Made Flesh: Biotechnology and the Discourse of the Posthuman." *Cultural Critique*, no. 53, 2003, pp. 72–97.

Thomas, Dylan. *The Poems of Dylan Thomas.* New Directions, 1971.

Thompson, Steven John, editor. *Androids, Cyborgs, and Robots in Contemporary Culture and Society.* IGI Global, 2018.

—, editor. *Machine Law, Ethics, and Morality in the Age of Artificial Intelligence.* IGI Global, 2021.

Thomson, Rosemarie Garland. *Extraordinary Bodies.* Columbia UP, 1996.

Tick, Edward. Personal Conversation, Crete, Greece, May 1995.

—. *The Practice of Dream Healing: Bringing Ancient Greek Mysteries into Modern Medicine.* Quest, 2001.

—. *War and the Soul: Healing Our Nation's Veterans from Post-Traumatic Stress Disorder.* Quest, 2005.

Toulmin, Stephen, and June Goodfield. *The Architecture of Matter.* 1962. U of Chicago P, 1982.

Transliterate.com. http://transliterate.com/.

Turpin, Etienne, ed. *Architecture in the Anthropocene: Encounters Among Design, Deep Time, Science, and Philosophy.* Open Humanities Press, 2013.

Turbayne, Colin Murray. *The Myth of Metaphor.* U of South Carolina P, 1962.

Turkle, Sherry. *Alone Together: Why We Expect More from Technology and Less from Each Other.* Basic, 2011.

Ulmer, Gregory L. Conversation with Ian Bogost at Home of Cynthia Haynes and Jan Holmevik, Clemson, 9 April 9 2010.

—. *Teletheory.* Atropos, 2004.

Untersteiner, Mario. *The Sophists.* Translated by Kathleen Freeman, Basil Blackwell, 1954.

Utilities Online. https://www.utilities-online.info/ascii-to-text.

Vallega-Neu, Daniela, ed. *Heidegger's Poietic Writings: From Contributions to Philosophy to The Event.* (Studies in Continental Thought), Indiana UP, 2018.

Vater, Michael G. and David W. Wood, editors. *The Philosophical Rupture between Fichte and Schelling: Selected Texts and Correspondence (1800–1802),* SUNY P, 2012.

Vedantu.com. "Value of ι," 2024, https://www.vedantu.com/maths/value-of-i. Accessed 4 Apr. 2024.

Vedantu.com. "Why Is Epsilon Used?" Accessed 1 Apr. 2024.

Veeder, Rex. "Coleridge's Philosophy of Composition: An Overview of a Romantic Rhetorician." *Rhetoric Society Quarterly,* vol. 23, 1993, pp. 20–29.

Veld, Roeland J., Linze Schaap, Catrien J. A. M. Termeer, and Mark J. W. van Twist, editors. *Autopoiesis and Configuration Theory: New Approaches to Societal Steering.* Kluwer, 1991.

Vickers, Brian. "Analogy vs. Identity: The Rejection of Occult Symbolism 1580–1680." *Occult and Scientific Mentalities in the Renaissance,* edited by Brian Vickers. Cambridge UP, 2010, pp. 95–164.

Vico, Giambattista. *On the Study of Methods of Our Time.* Translated by Elio Gianturco, Cornell UP, 1990.

—. *The New Science of Giambattista Vico.* Cornell UP, 1948.

Vièta, François. *In Artem Analyticem Isagoge.* Edited by Jean Beaugrand, Paris, Guillaume Baudry, 1631

Villion, Francois. "Part One: Twelfth to Fifteenth Centuries." *The Penguin Book of French Verse.* Edited by Brian Woledge, Penguin, 1974, pp. 115–34.

Virilio, Paul. *The Aesthetics of Disappearance.* Semiotext(e), 2009.

—. *The Information Bomb.* Verso, 2005.

Virtual Identities and Self Promotion. Popular Culture Association/American Culture Association National Conference, Washington, DC, 27–30 Mar. 2013.

Vital, Chayyim. *The Tree of Life: Chayyim Vital's Introduction to the Kabbalah of Isaac Luria.* Translated by Donald Wilder Menzi and Zwe Padeh. Arizal, 2008.

Vitanza, Victor J. *Chaste Rape: Sexual Violence in Western Thought and Writing.* Palgrave, 2011.

—. James A. *Berlin and Social Epistemic Rhetorics: A Seminar.* Parlor Press, 2021.

—. *Negation, Subjectivity, and the History of Rhetoric.* SUNY P, 1996.

Walker, Jeffrey. *Rhetoric and Poetics in Antiquity.* Oxford UP, 2000.

Walker, Rob. "Brilliant Mistakes." *New York Times Magazine,* 39 June 2010, pp. 18–19.

—. "Hit Rewind." *New York Times Magazine,* 25 Apr. 2010, p. 10.

Washington, George. *Rules of Civility,* edited by John T. Phillips, Goose Creek Productions, 2001.

Weaver, Richard M. *In Defense of Tradition.* Liberty Fund, 2000.

—. *Language Is Sermonic: Richard M. Weaver on the Nature of Rhetoric.* Edited by Richard L. Johannesen, Ralph T. Eubanks, and Rennard Strickland, Louisiana State UP, 1985.

Weber, Max. *The Protestant Ethic and the Spirit of Capitalism: The Complete Text—Inclusive of Notes.* Translated by Talcott Parsons, Open Library, Pantianos Classics, 1905.

Weise, Jillian. *The Amputee's Guide to Sex.* Soft Skull, 2007.

Welch, Kathleen E. *The Contemporary Reception of Classical Rhetoric: Appropriations of Ancient Discourse*. Erlbaum, 1990.

Wells, Susan. "Legible Bodies: Nineteenth-Century Women Physicians and Rhetoric of Dissection." *Rhetorical Bodies*, edited by Jack Selzer and Sharon Crowley, U of Wisconsin P, 1999, pp. 58–74.

Wellek, René. *A History of Modern Criticism: 1750–1950. The Romantic Age*, vol. 2, Yale UP, 1955.

Weston, Jesse Laidlay. *From Ritual to Romance: Folklore, Magic, and the Holy Grail.* 1990. Dover, 2011.

"What Does Alpha Represent in Terms of Math and Science Concepts?" *Quora.* https://www.quora.com/What-does-alpha-represent-in-terms-of-math-and-science-concepts. Accessed 14 Apr 2024.

"What Is phi and eta in Particle Physics?" *Study.com,* Accessed 4 Apr 2024.

"What Is the Physical Interpretation of "iota?" *Quora*. https://www.quora.com/What-is-the-physical-interpretation-of-iota. Accessed 14 Apr 2024.

"What Is the Smallest Possible Number with Any Mathematical Value of Property?" *Mathematics Stack Exchange.* https://math.stackexchange.com/questions/2341975/what-is-the-smallest-number-with-any-mathematical-value-of-property. Accessed 15 Apr 2024.

"Why Is Epsilon Used?" *Vedantu.com*. Accessed 1 Apr. 2024.

Whately, Richard. *Elements of Rhetoric.* Bibliobazarr, 2008.

Whitmarsh, Tim. *Beyond the Second Sophistic: Adventures in Greek Postclassicism.* U of California P, 2013.

—. *The Second Sophistic*. Reprint ed., Oxford UP, 2006.

White, Hayden. *The Content of the Form: Narrative Discourse and Historical Representation*. Johns Hopkins UP, 1987.

—. *Figural Realism: Studies in the Mimesis Effect.* Johns Hopkins UP, 1999.

Whitman, Walt. *Leaves of Grass.* Edited by Scully Bradley and Harold W. Blodgett, Norton, 1973.

Whicher, George F. Introduction. Horace. "Ars Poetica." *Selected Poems.* Translated by Wentworth Dillon, 1947, pp. 245–59.

Wiener, Norbert. *Cybernetics: Or the Control and Communication in the Animal and the Machine.* 2nd ed., MIT, 1961.

—. *The Human Use of Human Beings: Cybernetics and Society.* Cambridge, Da Capo P, 1988.

Wieseltier, Leon. Preface. *Reflections: Essays, Aphorisms, Autobiographical Writings.* Edited by Peter Demetz, Schocken, 1986, pp. vii–x.

Wimsatt, W. K. *The Verbal Icon: Studies in the Meaning of Poetry.* UP of Kentucky, 1954.

Winckelmann, Johann Joachim. *On the Imitation of the Painting and Sculpture of the Greeks.* Phaidon, 1972.

Winter, H. J. J. *Eastern Science: An Outline of Its Scope and Contribution.* John Murray, 1932.

Wittgenstein, Ludwig. *Philosophical Investigations.* 4th ed., Edited by P. M. S. Hacker and Joachim Schulte, Wiley-Blackwell, 2009.

Wolf, Gary. "The Data-Driven Life." *New York Times Magazine,* 2 May 2010, pp. 38–45.

Wolfe, Cary. *What Is Posthumanism?* U of Minnesota P, 2013.

Wordsworth, Dorothy. *Journals of Dorothy Wordsworth,* edited by Mary Moorman, Oxford UP, 1971.

Wordsworth, William. "Essay, Supplementary to the Preface." *The Poetical Works of William Wordsworth,* edited by Thomas Hutchinson, Oxford ed., Henry Frowde, 1908, pp. 944–53.

—. "Preface to Second Edition: Lyrical Ballads." *The Poetical Works of William Wordsworth,* edited by Thomas Hutchinson, Oxford ed., Henry Frowde, 1908, pp. 934–44.

—. "Tintern Abbey." *The Poetical Works of William Wordsworth,* edited by Thomas Oxford ed., Henry Frowde,1908.

Wortham, Jenna. "As More Facebook Users Die, Ghosts Reach Out to Reconnect." *New York Times,* 18 July 2010, p. 1.

Wright, Edward L. *Glossary of Astronomical and Cosmological Terms,* 2012, https://www.astro.ucla.edu/~wright/glossary.html. Accessed 6 Apr. 2024.

Xenophone. *Memorabilia.* Translated by Amy Bonnette, Cornell UP, 1994.

Xu, Ruiyan. "Search Engine of the Song Dynasty." *New York Times,* Week in Review, 16 May 2010, p. 11.

Yeats, William Butler. *The Collected Poems of W.B. Yeats.* Macmillan, 1956.

Žižek, Slavoj. *The Sublime Object of Ideology.* 2nd ed., Verso, 2009.

Zylinska, Joanna. *Bioethics in the Age of New Media.* MIT, 2009.

—. *Minimal Ethics for the Anthropocene* (Critical Climate Change). Open Humanities Press, 2014.

—. and Sarah Kember. *Life After New Media: Mediation as a Vital Process.* MIT, 2014.

Figure Credits

Figure 1. "The Diaspora of Western Philosophy." Credit: Steven B. Katz. From: "The Alphabet as an Ontological Basis of Ethics" Invited lecture sponsored by and delivered at the Department of Writing Studies, Department of English, the Center for Holocaust Studies, and the Center for Jewish Studies, University of Minnesota-Twin Cities, October 22, 2014.

Figure 2. "The 32 paths as defined by the Aryeh Kaplan." In *Sefer Yetzirah: The Book of Creation in Theory and Practice.* Subsequent Edition, Weiser Books, 1997, p. 155. Copyright © 1997 The Estate of Aryeh Kaplan. All rights reserved. No part of this publication may be reproduced or transmitted in any form or by any means, electronic or mechanical, including photocopying, recording, or by any information storage and retrieval system, without permission in writing from Red Wheel Weiser, LLC. Reviewers may quote brief passages. Original edition © 1990 The Estate of Aryeh Kaplan. Used with written permission.

Figure 3. "Adam in the Likeness of His Maker." Credit: Halevi, Z'ev ben Shimon, *The Way of Kabbalah*, Revised Edition (Figure 50, p. 195), Kabbalah Society 2007. Used with written permission. This figure was the artwork of the author himself, revised for the second edition of his book. (This figure replaced an earlier one in the uncopyedited manuscript of *Plato's Nightmare.*) As described to me in an email dated 6/17/2023 by his wife, Rebekah Kenton, who oversees his estate and granted permission, "I know that Halevi himself preferred this later version. He described it in another context: 'This figure is composed of "white fire" in contrast to the "black fire" of the background, which is the all-pervading (*sic*) but invisible presence of the Absolute.'"

Figure 4. "Physicist Stephen Hawking in Zero G NASA." Credit: Jim Campbell, April 26, 2007. *Wikimedia Commons*, Public Domain. https://commons.wikimedia.org/wiki/File: Physicist_Stephen_Hawking_in_Zero_Gravity_NASA.

Figure 5. "The Value of X." Credit: Steven B. Katz, 2024. Based on non-figured quotation permissible under the Fair Use Act, from "What is a calculus math problem" by Riley Kench. *Study.com*, updated November 21, 2023. https://study.com/learn/lesson/basic-calculus-formulas-problems.html.

Figure 6. "The Transcendental Eyeball." Credit: Christopher Pearse Cranch, 1836. Original title "Standing on the Base Ground . . . I Become a Transparent Eyeball" (Illustration for Ralph Waldo Emerson's "Nature"). Drawing 8 3/8 x 5 11/16 in. (21.3 x 14.4 cm), created 1830-1892, Gift of Whitney Dall Jr., in memory of Emily Dall, 1976, Metropolitan Museum of Art, Accession Number: 1976.625.20(1), Public Domain. https://www.metmuseum.org/art/collection/search/

Figure 7. The Transcendental "Eye/I." Credit: Steven B. Katz, 2021. Drawing, pencil on yellow envelope.

Table Credits

Table 1. "Relative Etymological 'Speeds' of the Act of 'Stripping' in the classical Greek verb περιέλοι (*perriéloi*; inf. Περιαιρέω)— 'to strip'." Credit: Steven B. Katz, 2024. This Table originally appeared as "Table 2. Etymological pockets of time in translations of the Greek word περιέλοι, strip'" in "Sonic Rhetorics as Ethics in Action: Hidden Temporalities of Sound in Language(s)" by Steven B. Katz, *Humanities*, vol. 9, no. 1, 2020, pp. 217–235. https://doi.org/10.3390/h9010013.

The information for Table 1 is based on the classical Greek gleaned or quoted in research from the following:

A. Henry George Liddell, and Robert Scott, *A Greek-English Lexicon: Compiled by Henry George Liddell, D.D., and Robert Scott, D.D. (A New Edition, Revised and Augmented Throughout by Sir Henry Stuart Jones, D. Lit).* In *Tufts University's Perseus Project Greek Word Study Tool*, edited by Gregory F. Crane. Clarendon Press, 1961. Online. http://www.perseus.tufts.edu/hopper/.

B. Henry George Liddell, and Georg Autenrieth, "LSJ, Middle Liddell," *A Greek-English Lexicon: Compiled by Henry George Liddell, and Robert Scott, D.D. (A New Edition, Revised and Augmented Throughout by Sir Henry Stuart Jones, D. Lit).* In *Tufts University's Perseus Project Greek Word Study Tool*, edited by Gregory F. Crane. Clarendon Press, 1961. Online http://www.perseus.tufts.edu/hopper/.

C. *Plato in Twelve Volumes*, translated by W.R.M. Lamb, Vol. 3. In *Tufts University's Perseus Project Greek Word Study Tool*, edited by Gregory F. Crane. Harvard University Press, 1967. Online. http://www.perseus.tufts.edu/hopper/.

D. Georg Autenrieth and Robert Porter Keep, *A Homeric Dictionary.* R. Pullins Company, 2001.

Table 2. “Parody: A New Greek Drama” (poem). Credit: Steven B. Katz, 2024. Caricature adapted from *Duolingo Greek Exercises.* duolingo.com. N.p., n.d.

Table 3. “Plato’s Opposition of Philosophy and Rhetoric.” Credit: George Kennedy, 1999. Using the primary categories based on George Kennedy, *Classical Rhetoric and Its Christian and Secular Tradition from Ancient to Modern Times*, Second Edition, U of North Carolina P, 1999, p. 62.

Table 4: “Rhetorics and Poetry as True False/False True Forms.” Credit: Steven B. Katz, 2024. Adapted from George Kennedy, *Classical Rhetoric and Its Christian and Secular Tradition from Ancient to Modern Times*, Second Edition, U of North Carolina P, 1999, p. 62.

Table 5: “The Movement of Truth Through Time: A Highly Reductive Chart.” Credit: Steven B. Katz, 2024.

Table 6: “Divisions of Knowledge Including Geometry Obtained by Dialectic in Hierarchy.” Credit: Steven B. Katz, 2024. A visual adaption of Socrates’ discussion with Glaucon, from Plato’s *Republic* VII 533e–534a.

Table 7: “A Geometry of Knowledge: Divisions of a Hierarchy of Knowledge in Opposition.” Credit: Steven B. Katz, 2024. A visual adaption of Socrates’ discussion with Glaucon, from Plato’s *Republic* VII (*Republic* VII 534b).

Table 8: “‘Binary’ (Poem).” Credit: Steven B. Katz, 2015. Using “Convert Characters to ASCII Codes 9.” Poem translated with Text to ASCII (https://www.browserling.com/tools/text-to-ascii), and “Binary Translator” (https://www.binarytranslator.com/). Thanks to Dr. Jonathan Lashley for his checking and advice in translating. The English is rendered as follows:

Mimesis is
........our wo
        rld of si
muuacra. p
lease res
tore
        body
        to
        rhetori
cal bone

Poem Credits

The majority of poems in *Plato's Nightmare* are new and/or unpublished; many were written exclusively for this book. Earlier incarnations or revised different versions of previously published poems deployed in *Plato's Nightmare* first appeared in the following publications, to which grateful acknowledgement is given.

Nana (chapbook. Moses Ink)*; Humanities* (*Special Issue on "Ethics and Literary Practice"*); *enculturation*; *KB Journal* (Kenneth Burke Society); *Pre/Text: A Journal of Rhetorical Theory*; *More Truly, More Strange: An Anthology of Poetry in Augmented Reality*; *Elohi Gadugi Journal*; *Continental Drift: An Online Magazine of Literature, Art and Ideas*; Jacar Press; *Post Modern Culture*; *Isaac Asimov's Science Fiction Magazine*; *Archives of Family Medicine* (American Medical Association); *Intraspection: A Journal of Rhetoric, Culture, and* Style; *Survive and Thrive: A Journal of Medical Humanities and Narrative as Medicine*; *Glimpse: Research and Creativity* (Clemson University); *Star*Line* (Science Fiction Poetry Association); *Dwarf Stars* (Science Fiction Poetry Association); *Best Internet Humor* (Writer's Dreamtools, Larry Belling Productions); *South Carolina Review*; *Southern Poetry Review*; *Obsidian: Literature & Arts in the African Diaspora*; *Poets Against the War Website* (Sam Hamhill, Copper Canyon Press); *Mars Hill Review*; *Free Verse: A Journal of Contemporary Poetry and Poetics*; *Raleigh News and Observer*; *Modern Haiku*; *Songs of Ascent* (CD, Copyright © 2008 Ellen M. Wilson: http://www.ellenmwilson.com/); *Die Achte Welle* (*The Eighth Wave: An Irrational Journal*, Berlin, Germany); *Windhover* (North Carolina State University Literary Magazine); *Americana* (North Carolina State University); *Gates of the City: The Albany Tricentennial Antholo*gy (Hudson Valley Writer's Guild); *The Paper* (Hudson Valley Writer's Guild); *The Art Department* (Newport, RI); *Literary Fruit* (*Brown Daily Herald* Inc, Brown University); *The Great Swamp Gazette* (University of Rhode Island); *Bitterroot: International Poetry Journal*; *Frogmore Papers* (Frogmore Press, Kent, England); *Groundswell*; *The RPI Review* (Rensselaer Polytechnic Institute); *The Greenfield Review*; *Northeast Journal*; *Outpost* (Fine Arts in the Berkshires); *The Practice of Dream Healing* by Edward Tick (Quest), and its Greek translation *Therapeia tis*

Psyches mesa apo ta Oneira, Perseas Tasoulis, translator (Enalios Publications, Athens); *Group Creation* (Michigan State University); "The Great Ghost," *The Center Design* (Boston); *Creative Review*; *The Suffolk Journal* (Suffolk University, Boston, MA).

The author is grateful to the following rights owners for permission to republish the following poems in *Plato's Nightmare*:

"Ghosts of Technology." From *Voices: The Art and Science of Psychotherapy*, volume 22, number 3 (fall 1986). With permission of the American Academy of Psychotherapists.

"In the Beginning." From *Voices: The Art and Science of Psychotherapy*, vol. 25, no. 4, 1989. With permission of the American Academy of Psychotherapists.

"The Rhetorician, On Talking with Animals," was originally published in in "*College Composition and Communication*. Copyright 2003 by the National Council of Teachers of English. Reprinted with permission.

"i-Robot*"(Part I)*," "Attachment Function," "A.I. Talking," "Being Robot," "Media Eye," "A Computer File Named Dorothy," "The Beautiful Robot Who Stole My Heart and Parts," "*S.O.S.* ... — ...To Any Robots in the Vicinity," and "i-Robot (Part II)*"* were first published as part of my "Foreword" for *Androids, Cyborgs, and Robots in Contemporary Culture and Society*, edited by Steven John Thompson. IGI Global, 2018: xii-xx. IGI Global states: "As many of the poems have been altered, they are not considered a true reprint so as long as they are cited . . . the intellectual property of the work remains with the author; the publisher simply holds the copyright to the verbatim full text."

"Beyond Yeats' Grave." The author hereby acknowledges that this poem was originally published in *South Carolina Review*, vol. 40, no. 2, 2008, 64–65.

The following poems, whose "embargo has now passed," were first published by *European Judaism*, Poetry Editor Ruth Fainlight, Leo Baeck College, London: "To Greta Garbo: On Her Hundredth Birthday (September 18, 2005)," "Rebecca in the Modern World" and "The Human Genome," "The Languages of Leaves," "Birkenau," "School of Death," "After the Event I: By the Fire: An Anti-Sonnet," "Sunday School," and "Menorah, 1991."

"Nothing Only Stays," "Signs in Heraklion (Crete)," "Placebo," "Meditation on Noseums," "My Mother, the Prune Pit," "Mediated Experience," "No Refill," and "To the Mystic River Bridge, Boston" were first published in *Pembroke Magazine*, which holds the First North American Serial Rights.

"Out of Hospital." In response to the request for permission to republish the poem, AMA changed "the license under which it is made available from CC-BY-NC-ND to CC-BY so it becomes clear that permission is [no longer] required for future use. . . . And we will take steps to do this systematically for all content triggered by CLOCKSS." (See: https://clockss.org/a-poets-perspective-on-digital-preservation/).

"Grandfather" and "Reflections [on a Computer Screen]," "©1974, *The Hartford Courant*. All rights reserved. Distributed by Tribune Content Agency, LLC Rights and Limitations."

Index of Poems

Ordered sequentially, by historical parts.

Pre_Face

Prologos

Part One

Plato and Aristotle/Classical Greece

Part Two

Roman/Medieval

Part Three

Renaissance/Enlightenment

Part Four

Nineteenth Century Romanticism/German Transcendentalism

Part Five

Twentieth/Twenty-First Century

Epilogos

About the Author

Steven B. Katz is Emeritus Faculty in the Rhetorics, Communication, and Information Design doctoral program in the Interdisciplinary Studies Department, as well as Pearce Professor Emeritus of Professional Communication, and Professor Emeritus of English, at Clemson University. He has published several books, including *The Epistemic Music of Rhetoric* (1996), *Nana!* (poetry), and with Nancy Penrose, *Writing in the Sciences* (4th open-access edition, Parlor Press 2020). Katz has published hundreds of poems in professional and literary venues, as well as numerous articles on ancient Jewish and Greek rhetorics, scientific and technical writing, biotechnology and medical communication with the public, and ethics. "The Ethic of Expediency: Rhetoric, Technology, and the Holocaust" was the recipient of the National Council of Teachers (NCTE) Award for Best Article on the Theory of Scientific and Technical Communication in 1993, and has been reprinted in multiple anthologies, most notably in *Central Works in Technical Communication* edited by Stuart Selber and Johndan Johnson-Eilola (Oxford UP, 2004), and continues to be widely cited. With David Blakesley, he is the author of the forthcoming book, *Elaborate Cosmos* (Parlor Press, 2026).

Photograph of the author.

www.ingramcontent.com/pod-product-compliance
Lightning Source LLC
Chambersburg PA
CBHW051155300426
44116CB00006B/318
9781643174020